DA 90 CRO

THE SOCIETY FOR
POST-MEDIEVAL ARCHAEOLOGY
MONOGRAPH 5

CROSSING PATHS
OR
SHARING TRACKS?

CROSSING PATHS
OR
SHARING TRACKS?

Future directions in the archaeological study of
post-1550 Britain and Ireland

Edited by

AUDREY HORNING *and* MARILYN PALMER

Boydell & Brewer Ltd
2009

First published 2009
The Boydell Press, Woodbridge

Disclaimer: Statements in the volume reflect the views of the authors
and not necessarily those of the Society, editors or publisher

ISBN 978 1 84383 434 2

The Boydell Press is an imprint of Boydell & Brewer Ltd
PO Box 9, Woodbridge, Suffolk IP12 3DF, UK
and of Boydell & Brewer Inc.
668 Mt Hope Avenue, Rochester, NY 14620, USA
website: www.boydellandbrewer.com

The publisher has no responsibility for the continued existence or accuracy of URLs for
external or third-party internet websites referred to in this book, and does not guarantee
that any content on such websites is, or will remain, accurate or appropriate.

A CIP record for this book is available
from the British Library

This publication is printed on acid-free paper

Printed in Great Britain by
CPI Antony Rowe, Chippenham, Wiltshire

CONTENTS

SECTION TWO: ANALYTICAL APPROACHES

SECTION THREE: OF PEOPLE AND THINGS

ACKNOWLEDGEMENTS

The editors wish to thank all of the authors for agreeing to work to a very tight timetable following the April 2008 Crossing Paths or Sharing Tracks? conference, and especially for contributing their valuable experience and insights to the ongoing discourse over the future of the study of post-1550 Britain and Ireland. We are also most grateful to Matthew Johnson for writing the Foreword to this volume, and for his active participation in the conference itself. Matthew Champion of Boydell & Brewer, and Sarah May, Monographs Editor for the Society for Post-Medieval Archaeology, have both been very helpful in facilitating the publication of this volume. The following individuals also provided invaluable assistance and guidance during the course of the conference and volume preparation: Nick Brannon, Tracy Collins, David Crossley, James Gardiner, Mark Gillings, David Gwyn, Lesley McFadyen, Michael Nevell, Sharon North, Deirdre O'Sullivan, Jim Symonds, Claire Strachan, Ian West and Ruth Young, while several of our colleagues in the Centre for Historical Archaeology at the University of Leicester deserve special mention for their support of both ventures: Chris King, Sarah Tarlow and Richard Thomas. We are grateful for the interest shown by the Vice-Chancellor of the University of Leicester, Professor Robert Burgess, and the Head of the School of Archaeology and Ancient History at Leicester, Professor Colin Haselgrove, and for financial sponsorship from the School. Finally, we very much appreciate the support and involvement of the Association for Industrial Archaeology (AIA), the Irish Post-Medieval Archaeology Group (IPMAG), and the Society for Post-Medieval Archaeology (SPMA).

ABBREVIATIONS

AHRC	Arts and Humanities Research Council
AIA	Association for Industrial Archaeology
ALGAO	Association of Local Government Archaeology Offices
AMS	accelerator mass spectrometry
AONB	Area of Outstanding Natural Beauty
ARCUS	Archaeology Research Consultancy at the University of Sheffield
CAD	computer-aided design
CAU	Cambridge Archaeology Unit
CBA	Council for British Archaeology
CHAT	Contemporary Historical Archaeology and Theory
CRM	cultural resource management
DGLA	Department of Greater London Archaeology
DUA	Department of Urban Archaeology
EAMC	Examining the Archaeology of Early Modern City
EDX	energy dispersive X-ray fluorescence
EH	English Heritage
ELC	European Landscape Convention
EPSRC	Engineering and Physical Sciences Research Committee
GBIAS	Greater Belfast Industrial Archaeology Survey
GIS	geographic information system
HEFCE	Higher Education Funding Council for England
HER	Heritage Environment Fund
HLC	historic landscape characterisation
HLF	Heritage Lottery Fund
HLLA	high-lime low-alkali
HMSO	Her Majesty's Stationery Office
IHAI	Industrial Heritage Association of Ireland
IM&T	industrial, maritime and transport
IPMAG	Irish Post-Medieval Archaeology Group
ISIA	Irish Society for Industrial Archaeology
LAARC	London Archaeological Archive and Research Centre
LLHAC	Lewisham Local History and Archives Centre
MoLAS	Museum of London Archaeology Service
MoRPHE	Management of Research Projects in the Historic Environment
MPP	Monument Protection Programme
NMI	National Museum of Ireland
NUI	National University of Ireland (Cork, Dublin, Galway)
OASIS	Online Access to the Index of Archaeological Investigations
OSA	Office for Subversive Architecture
PAS	Portable Antiquities Scheme
PPG	Planning Policy Guidance

QUB	Queen's University Belfast
RAE	Research Assessment Exercise
RCAHMS	Royal Commission on the Ancient and Historical Monuments of Scotland
RCHME	Royal Commission on the Historical Monuments of England
RMLEC	Roman and Medieval London Excavation Committee
SEM	scanning electron microscope
SHA	Society for Historical Archaeology
SHIERS	Strategy for the Historic Industrial Environment Reports
SIAS	Scottish Industrial Archaeology Society
SPMA	Society for Post-Medieval Archaeology
TAG	Theoretical Archaeology Group
UCC	University College Cork
UCD	University College Dublin
UU	University of Ulster

GENERAL INTRODUCTION

By AUDREY HORNING & MARILYN PALMER

The chapters in this volume represent revised versions of papers presented at the April 2008 conference entitled *Crossing Paths or Sharing Tracks? Future Directions in the Study of Post-1550 Britain and Ireland* held at the University of Leicester. The idea for the conference was sparked by a series of conversations between the Editors reflecting on the proliferation of organisations catering to people interested in studying aspects of the archaeology of the last five hundred or so years. Our concern in these conversations was that the discipline was fragmenting, and that people who should be working together and learning from one another were eschewing those conversations in favour of gathering together with more 'like-minded' individuals. We were disturbed by seemingly harmful characterisations, such as the view that 'post-medieval archaeology' meant 'old-fashioned' artefact research whereas 'historical archaeology' meant theory-driven archaeology. The emergence of the Contemporary Historical Archaeology and Theory conference in 2003 seemed to support the notion that theory was indeed outside the remit of the Society for Post-Medieval Archaeology (SPMA), a perception of considerable concern to the Society, which had been working in earnest to broaden its base and its appeal.

Trouble was also brewing within the Association for Industrial Archaeology (AIA), as the 2005 publication of two volumes promoting the incorporation of social approaches to industrial sites sparked a fierce debate between proponents of 'technocentric' versus 'sociocentric' approaches, as discussed in depth in several papers in this volume. Perennial debates over 'when' post-medieval archaeology 'begins' and 'ends', and when industrial archaeology 'takes over' flared up again. In our view, such wrestling over ownership was hardly likely to further the discipline as a whole. Meanwhile, a series of conversations (held primarily in a number of Belfast pubs) led to the 1999 emergence of a new organisation focused upon promoting the study of the archaeology of post-1550 Ireland, the Irish Post-Medieval Archaeology Group (IPMAG). No sooner had the ink begun to dry on the Group's constitution than rumblings of discontent were heard elsewhere on the island. Why had IPMAG chosen the term 'post-medieval' rather than 'historical'? Didn't the 'colonial' history of Ireland make the approach of North American historical archaeology far more appropriate? And wasn't 'post-medieval' a synonym for atheoretical anyway?

Of further concern to us was recognition of some serious schisms between professional sectors (academic, commercial and government) and between professional and amateur. Changes in university provision in both Britain and Ireland has led to a situation in which archaeology graduates receive only a minimum of field and laboratory instruction, leading many in the commercial and government sector to view the work of their academic colleagues as largely irrelevant to 'real life'. At the same time, the boilerplate and largely non-integrated character of much grey literature frustrated attempts, from many quarters, to address and evaluate the vast quantities of data arising from developer-funded projects on an array of post-1550 assemblages, sites and monuments. While the increasing professionalisation of the study of post-medieval and industrial archaeology, precipitated by the growth of developer-funded archaeology and the creation of a number of dedicated university posts, is certainly a welcome development, it has carried with it the potential to devalue the significant contributions of amateur, or avocational, practitioners – particularly in the recording and preservation of industrial heritage.

We did not (and do not) claim to have a solution to these problems. However, we felt that one obvious step towards defining a 'way forward' was to try to bring together representatives of the various organisations and proponents of the seemingly oppositional points of view. Getting everyone in the same room at the same time, hopefully to not only hear what each other had to say, but to talk with one another, seemed a logical way to kick-start discourse. We hoped that conference delegates would find some common ground, and ultimately share with one another the enthusiasm as well as frustration that we all experience in our diverse ways of seeking to understand the archaeology of the early modern and modern worlds.

So, we drafted a call for papers, and hoped to get enough responses to fill out a one-day programme. To our delight, that one-day event turned into two days, and then ultimately into three nearly full days. Over eighty people attended the conference, with presentations from thirty-two speakers, starting with a keynote address from Charles Orser and ending with a closing address by Stephen Mrozowski. While the programme was packed, there was no shortage of conversation and even heated discussion. As will be clear from the papers that follow, no single future direction for the discipline emerged from the conference. What did emerge was, first, a recognition that each of the societies fulfils different yet complementary aims, pursued by largely overlapping groups of members, and second and most importantly, a mutual willingness to continue the dialogue between societies, across sectors, and on either side of the Irish Sea (and ultimately, globally). It must be acknowledged that many topics of central importance to the international discipline of historical archaeology were not formally addressed at the conference, and thus are underrepresented in this publication. This volume does not claim to be a comprehensive synthesis of the entirety of the field. It is first and foremost a reflection of the concerns, debates and contributions of post-medieval, historical and industrial archaeological practice within Britain and Ireland in 2009. In the pages that follow can be found a distillation of the *Crossing Paths or Sharing Tracks?* conference discussions, in all their variety and vibrancy.

FOREWORD

By MATTHEW JOHNSON

First let me thank the Editors, Audrey Horning and Marilyn Palmer, for asking me to write this Foreword. This set of papers, in all its diversity, forms a snapshot of the field at a critical moment. I see this book as a key milestone where the field has achieved a point of critical maturity in what it thinks and in what it does.

Of course, such an observation on 'the field' already takes a position on one of the issues that is up for debate in the papers that follow. I believe passionately that all the contributors to this volume, as varied in perspective as they are, are part of one discipline, Archaeology, whose singular and common purpose is the understanding of humans in the past through the study of the material traces that humans left behind. It is the systematic combination of materiality and humanity that makes archaeology distinctive. What makes us archaeologists, as opposed to mindless collectors of old junk, is a sense of rigour and consistency about how we gather our material and marshal it into arguments about past processes, and how we then judge our own and others' arguments as strong or weak according to a set of shared rules.

The central question facing archaeology in the 21st century is: what should those rules be? The authors of the papers take very different positions on how this one discipline, as it is applied to the later historical period, could or should be done in theory and practice. They also take very different if more implicit positions on a second, more subtle question, of whether there is more than one legitimate way to do archaeology. Do we favour an eclecticism and tolerance of different approaches, which carries the danger of lapsing into a disabling relativism in which all approaches are considered of equal merit and critical dialogue is attenuated? Or do we want a rigorous core to the discipline, with the attendant danger that it leads to a dogmatic sectarianism in which the views of others are dismissed as valueless? There is a spectrum of possible positions between these two extremes. However, most of these disagreements have to me a feeling of family disagreements – often powerfully expressed because they arise within a common, assumed frame of reference and mutual respect if not affection for the views of one's peers.

The conference arose from the organisers' ongoing and conflicting feelings over the proliferation of organisations – industrial, 'post-medieval', later historical –that study the archaeology of Britain and Ireland after 1500. I share their ambiguity. The different organisations and conferences that have sprung up in the last thirty years are a measure of growth and intellectual vitality. Archaeologies of later historic Britain and Ireland, of whatever kind, are here to stay; the bad old days when archaeology was considered by some to be coterminous with prehistory and Classical studies will never return. However, the proliferation of organisations also carries a danger of Balkanisation of the discipline. I see this problem particularly acutely through my writing on theory. All too frequently, theoretical positions are asserted, not in refutation of thinking in another area of Archaeology as a discipline, but as if that thinking had never happened.

Many of the papers in this volume openly conflict over the right way forward for the discipline, taking very different positions over what the shared rules of archaeology could or should be, and indeed over the extent to which they should be shared at all. I take this conflict as a sign of intellectual health. Too often in the past, and too often in other contexts, scholars have been held back from intellectual progress by a culture of deference to established authority. The diversity of views expressed here represents anything but such an authority.

The plea for 'diversity' in such a context is seductive, since it carries a sense of tolerance, and also an acknowledgement that there are very different motivations and desires in personal make-up of different individuals and groups (for example, between the University professor, the heritage manager, the amateur industrial archaeologist and the freelance ceramics specialist). Respect for and tolerance of intellectual diversity must be a first principle in scholarship, as it should be in cultural life. However, it also carries concerns.

Many papers point to divisions in the field that are actually and potentially disabling. The most obvious of these is the gap between the perspectives and aspirations of the world of the universities, the 'professional'/CRM world, and the world of museums. Again, I see difficulty and tension here, but a tension that is ultimately progressive and enabling rather than a source of unmitigated woe. Other disciplines – English, History, most obviously – are largely or exclusively 'academic' in their scope. There are few possible 'vocational' routes for the graduate of English or History other than into academe. In my view, these disciplines are intellectually the poorer for this lack of engagement. In the main uninterrupted by questions of management, conservation and the public realm, the literary scholar and the historian is free to pursue pure research, unfettered by such mundane realities. The result is scholarship that often seems rather unchained from the world around us. I oversimplify, and have been unduly provocative; but the point remains that for all its tensions, the great diversity of perspectives given by professional versus academic archaeology is as much as source of strength as of weakness.

These 'problems' of heritage and conservation, which nag so insistently at archaeological scholarship, arise from the materiality of archaeology. One of the most powerful and distinguishing features, and strengths, of our discipline is that it deals with physical things. Kick a steam turbine and it hurts. That materiality gives many of us headaches around planning and conservation issues, but it also gives what we study an immediacy and appeal denied to other disciplines.

If we remember this materiality, the debate within industrial archaeology over the proper subject of study is thrown into proper perspective. A mature discipline rejects the either/or of 'social life' versus 'machines'. Social life is nothing if not materially expressed and embedded; machines can never be properly understood outside the context of the social relations of production. Sir Neil Cossons has recently asked us to deal with the 'veracity' of industrial archaeology. Karl Marx's profound insight, in its own way as foundational to modern life as that of Darwin, was to see that tools and machines were part of humanity, and that to make a division between 'technology' and 'society' was to fail to perceive the world as it really is. The implication for archaeologists of industry, and for all post-1500 archaeologists, is clear: we cannot study social life without a deep understanding of technical processes, and we cannot understand technical processes without a deep understanding of social context.

Such an observation makes archaeology very difficult. It challenges the scholar to master theory, to read around the cultural context of the period, and to grasp an ever-increasing range of other data sources alongside those of traditional archaeology. Such a project is difficult enough for the Neolithic, but for the later historical period...? But it is a truism to say that it also makes archaeology very exciting and challenging.

The challenge of a mature archaeology of the period after 1500 is to address the very difficult, but very rewarding, issues that concern modern archaeology as a whole. Where prehistorians engage in abstract debates over archaeology as a product of modernity, we grapple empirically with understanding the processes of modernity, and the artefacts those processes left behind – factories, prisons, plantations, tea-sets, window glass. Where theorists fret about whether objects have agency, we study a period when objects and agency come together as never before, human beings and machines articulated in new and challenging ways. Where postcoloniality is the topic of the day at theoretical conferences, we engage with the archaeological record of colonies and of responses to colonisation.

It is no coincidence, I think, that the last fifty years have seen archaeology become a much more theoretically rigorous and explicit discipline, and have also seen the archaeology of historic and recent periods flourish. In this brief Foreword, I have tried to indicate that this florescence is much more than growth in the scope and a widening of disciplinary margins. What the papers in this volume show is that historic, post-medieval or industrial archaeology, call it what you will, leads the discipline of archaeology as a whole in intellectual urgency and rigour. It serves to redefine in the most fundamental way what we do as archaeologists and as scholars of humanity.

Part One

Of Practice & Paradigm

Of Practice & Paradigm

INTRODUCTION

By AUDREY HORNING and MARILYN PALMER

The nine chapters in this section set out individual views on the contemporary practice of archaeology of the past five hundred years. Chapter 1, by Charles Orser, situates the practice of historical archaeology into a global context, considering the dialectic between scales of analysis. How do we acknowledge those global forces resultant from early modern European expansion such as capitalism and class formation without losing sight of understandings of individual human action rooted in the material evidence of archaeological sites? Orser grounds his discussion with a consideration of the archaeology of 19th-century rural Ireland, and argues strongly that 'now is the time that archaeologists must think even more determinedly about linking theory and practice'.

Following Orser's overview of the multi-scalar character of historical archaeology and its theoretical underpinnings are three chapters that focus very specifically upon the debates within contemporary British industrial archaeology, which were themselves a spark for the original *Crossing Paths or Sharing Tracks?* conference. In chapter 2, David Gwyn provides an eloquent and measured overview of the debate between industrial archaeologists over the centrality and relative merits of approaches prioritising technology and approaches that prioritise the human experience. Gwyn situates his discussion in the context of the overall development of industrial archaeology, born in the aftermath of the Second World War, and long characterised by two interest groups: a sizable corps of avocational industrial archaeologists 'who found for themselves an interesting and challenging hobby to follow', and a much smaller, if at times more vocal, academic cohort.

While Gwyn ultimately sees no fundamental rupture in contemporary industrial archaeology, in the next chapter Michael Nevell acknowledges that there are 'extreme elitist' voices in industrial archaeology that reject contemporary research agendas and 'do not wish to engage with the wider archaeological community'. Not shying from self-reflexivity, Nevell then admits his own greater interest in the social, rather than technological, elements of industrial production. Using the distribution of mills in the Greater Manchester region, Nevell then illustrates how the two approaches, technological and social, invariably provide contrasting explanations for similar data sets. In the final analysis, he suggests that 'the current debate should not be about whether we should do these things and whether this is truly industrial archaeology, but how well we understand the interconnection between machine and landscape, society and technological change'.

Shane Gould follows Nevell's discussion, in chapter 4, with another thoughtful discussion on the 'technocentric' versus 'sociocentric' divide, suggesting that the debate between those industrial archaeologists who prioritise technological explanations versus those who prioritise social interpretations is rather 'anodyne', given the fundamental importance and validity of both aspects to the future development of industrial archaeology. Gould sets out in detail the work of English Heritage in sponsoring such integrated research into industrial sites. In particular, Gould provides an overview of the contributions made by regional research frameworks documents, themselves part-sponsored by English Heritage, and each addressing social and technological concerns.

The next two chapters, 5 and 6, take us back to a consideration of practice in Ireland as first introduced by Charles Orser. Colin Breen and Tadhg O'Keeffe present contrasting interpretations of the character, accomplishments, and potential of Irish historical archaeology, a topic that similarly inspired a heated debate at the *Crossing Paths or Sharing Tracks?* conference itself. Breen outlines the recent development of interest in Irish post-medieval or historical archaeology (both he and O'Keeffe prefer the term historical archaeology), turning a critical eye on the island's lack of university provision versus the expansion of postgraduate and general public interest in the topic. In an Irish context, understandings of the material heritage of the post-1550 period are inevitably entwined with politics, a factor that clearly contributed to the late development of the discipline. Breen sees the late 1990s as a crucial turning point for the emerging discipline, as the 1999 establishment of the Irish Post-Medieval Archaeology Group (IPMAG) made the practice of historical archaeology somewhat more respectable. The creation of IPMAG clearly built upon the foundations laid by pioneers in Irish post-medieval archaeology, most notably individuals like Nick Brannon and American scholars including Eric Klingelhöfer and Charles Orser.

Despite the growing interest and respectability of the discipline of Irish post-medieval or historical archaeology, Breen provides a wealth of evidence that indicates a continuing lack of attention to the period in academic and commercial sectors, exacerbated by a lack of basic understanding of history and material culture. O'Keeffe, however, discerns the opposite. In his estimation, there is too much material culture from the period being excavated and retained without sufficient efforts at interpretation, and 'the overwhelming volume of the data is, I think, proving to be an impediment to progress in Historical Archaeology in Ireland'. O'Keeffe also strongly chastises IPMAG for what he sees as a lack of engagement with interpretative issues such as capitalism, class, colonialism, and Improvement, and urges Irish archaeologists to turn away from the basic historical and material culture research advocated by Breen and to instead engage more with the theoretical emphasis of North American-inspired global historical archaeology.

From the wranglings over the character of Irish historical archaeology, which has evolved to be inclusive of industrial sites and issues (as discussed further in Section Two by Colin Rynne), we turn, in chapter 7, to a specific consideration by Tony Crosby of English industrial heritage and the role of the Heritage Lottery Fund in promoting site conservation and public engagement. Unlike David Gwyn, who questions what he sees as 'a sense of Little England, or at best of Little Britain, [lurking] behind some writing on industrialisation', Crosby proclaims the value of encouraging a positive, personal connection for British people to what he terms 'our industrial heritage'. This personal connection to the past is a perspective recognised and encouraged through the work of the Heritage Lottery Fund (HLF), as described by Crosby, 'Interpreting the heritage asset by drawing out its value, significance and meanings can promote wider appreciation and ultimately encourage greater participation.' Crosby cites a series of case studies in which the HLF supported the conservation and reuse of industrial buildings by local communities as evidence for the significant and positive social impact of the funding body.

Crosby's presentation of the viewpoint of an organisation critical to the practice and preservation of industrial sites within the United Kingdom segues into the far more personal perspective on post-medieval archaeology presented by Paul Courtney in chapter 8. Courtney takes the reader on a fascinating, if at times sobering, journey through the development of post-medieval archaeology from his first teenage experience of an SPMA conference through to the present. Courtney raises the issue of semantics, comments on the expansion of commercial archaeology, and laments what he sees as a devaluing of material culture expertise of independent consultants, as well as an increasing gulf between the aims and subject matter of academic versus developer-funded archaeology. Unlike O'Keeffe, Courtney finds little value in imposing the approaches of North American anthropological historical archaeology onto European post-medieval archaeology, arguing that 'what Pierre Bourdieu has termed *habitus* influences different trans-Atlantic outlooks', contrasting the small, bounded and often-defended polities of Europe with the American notion of an open frontier. As for the term historical archaeology itself, it is 'simply confusing in a European setting where it is often taken to start in the late Iron Ages'. The ninth and final chapter in this first section, written by Jim Dixon, is a meditation upon the character of contemporary archaeology. Dixon's piece provides a valuable, personal insight into the inspiration behind the 2003 establishment of the Contemporary Historical Archaeology and Theory (CHAT) conference and discussion list. Far from debating semantics and period divisions, contemporary archaeology, in Dixon's estimation, is focused upon inclusivity and is actively an 'anti-discipline'. Dixon is upbeat about the future and unconcerned with any seeming rifts between industrial, post-medieval, historical and contemporary archaeologies. As he puts it, 'archaeology is not a finite resource and it will stand up to being looked at in a multitude of different ways'.

The nine chapters in this first section clearly demonstrate that the entwined disciplines of industrial archaeology, historical archaeology, post-medieval archaeology, and contemporary archaeology are nothing if not vibrant. That the individual authors seldom agree completely with one another, and in many cases argue their positions passionately, should be seen as indicative of the success of the original aim of the *Crossing Paths or Sharing Tracks?* conference: to encourage debate and discourse between and among all those engaged in the study of the material heritage of post-1550 Britain and Ireland.

The Dialectics of Scale in the Historical Archaeology of the Modern World

By CHARLES ORSER

This chapter continues the ongoing exploration of scale as it pertains to the practice of historical archaeology. Ideas from non-archaeologists are used to present a way to create dialectical multiscalar analyses of archaeological sites from the second millennium CE. An example from early 19th-century rural Ireland illustrates the way such an interpretive framework may be framed.

INTRODUCTION

Questions about archaeological scale have been inherent in the discipline for many years. Archaeologists began to think about issues of scale as soon as they began to look beyond the boundaries of their sites and into the world beyond. As a result, considerations of scale will always be pertinent in archaeological thinking. Historical archaeologists, particularly those investigating the second millennium CE, may be especially interested in issues of scale because of the rise of a true worldwide globalisation during the period of their expertise. For these archaeologists, the linkage between 'the local' (the site) and 'the global' (the world outside the site) is a subject of profound interest.

The purpose of this chapter is to explore issues of scale in the archaeology of the most recent centuries, or what I have elsewhere termed 'global historical archaeology'[1] and 'modern-world archaeology'.[2] I believe that archaeologists will only be able to address important topics like globalisation after they have created useful models that will help them to link individual, sociohistorically unique sites with other sites and regions. In post-Columbian history, the connections are trans- and multinational as well as multicultural. This discussion offers one way for archaeologists to begin fashioning multiscalar analyses that hopefully will contribute to understanding further the broad historical processes that affect our daily lives.

ISSUES OF SCALE

In their recently edited collection entitled *Historical Archaeology*, Martin Hall and Stephen Silliman list the six themes they perceive as centrally important to today's historical archaeology. Presenting scale first, they succinctly state the central question of concern:

'How does a historical archaeology of the modern world hold in the same frame attention to the "small things forgotten" of everyday life and particular individuals and the global system of distribution characteristic of modernity?'[3] Using the common white clay smoking pipe as an example, they note that these ubiquitous archaeological finds may have been manufactured in Amsterdam in the 17th century, but that archaeologists discover them in New York, Brazil, South Africa, South-east Asia and everywhere else around the world that traders from the Dutch Empire plied their wares. The similarity of finds across widely diverse environments is difficult to ignore. Later in the same volume, Matthew Johnson notes that 'the major task' facing historical archaeologists today is 'not to shift focus on an exclusively larger scale, but to grasp the relationship between the small-scale' and the 'wider processes of transformation, and the colonial experience'.[4]

Observations such as these clearly indicate that the issue of scale remains at the heart of much archaeological analysis and that it presents a challenge worth confronting. As in many cases, archaeologists can take their lead from scholars in related fields because the linkage between the local and the global has long been a topic of considerable interest throughout the social sciences and humanities. The works of Andre Gunder Frank and Immanuel Wallerstein perhaps have been the most prominent in the scholarship, but many others have also been engaged in local–global research.[5] Archaeologists, too, have formulated research designs that have looked beyond their site's limits and into the wider world. In fact, some element of extra-site concern has been embedded within archaeology since the development of settlement archaeology. Settlement archaeology as a specialisation is now fifty years old, but even before this development, archaeologists working at remote sites had essentially crossed the threshold of their sites' boundaries when they began to wonder about the wider world in which their sites' former residents lived. And, when they made the semantic shift from 'settlement studies' to 'landscape studies', they had resolutely moved into the realm of multiscalar analysis. Nonetheless, it remains true that 'there has yet to be a full appreciation of the inherent possibilities of scale in historical archaeology'.[6] Perhaps the clearest problem involves inventing ways of situating the local in the global and vice versa. Only through understanding this connection will historical archaeologists make a serious contribution to the examination of globalisation and its local impacts.

We should not expect that finding concrete, unambiguous linkages between scales will be easy or straightforward. No simple mechanism exists to connect the things archaeologists find buried in the earth with the wider sociocultural processes at work in the world. Unlike scholars in related fields like history and geography, archaeologists tend to be uniquely associated with specific places on the earth's surface. Archaeology is uniquely site-specific in necessary ways, and few archaeologists would ever wish to abandon that focus. Most professional archaeologists were probably drawn to archaeology originally because of the thrill of discovery and the joy of excavation at a particular place. As a result, the archaeologists' connection with specific places has always been a strong, practical aspect of archaeological practice. The archaeologists' connection to 'the local' has often worked against what they might accomplish on a broader scale. It has been the practice of archaeology – the very practical consideration of moving earth – that has constituted the main criticism of any archaeology that seeks to look beyond a site's physical boundaries. Critics of an explicit global perspective contend that archaeologists cannot adopt a wider view without engaging in speculative over-reaching.

On one level, the critics are absolutely correct. No one can excavate an entire world system or even significant parts of one. Regardless, despite both the criticisms and the many directions that archaeology will take in the future, historical archaeologists are perfectly situated to provide tangible links between the often-small sites they investigate and the larger world around them. Twenty-first-century archaeologists need not revert to speculative antiquarianism to prove the unique interpretive power of historical archaeology as a way to examine the broad-scale sociohistoric process of the second millennium CE.

Much of the thinking about local–global connections is necessarily theoretical, but the subject is also uniquely practical. The connection between theory building –whether or not globally focused – and the excavation of individual sites has been made especially immediate because of the explosion of cultural resource management archaeology around the world. As archaeologists working in the private sector face increasing challenges to explain the value of archaeology – and here we can consider 'value' in both economic and intellectual senses – it becomes imperative for archaeologists to be able to defend their research as an important tool for conceptualising the world around them. In other words, archaeologists need not surrender their theory-building goals as they seek to respond to the developer's probing questions regarding the need for archaeological research and analysis. When the idea of site interconnectedness is made explicit, no one site can be summarily written off as 'not significant'. Ultimate significance may appear obvious only in relation to other sites.

Recent research in historical archaeology continues to show that many archaeologists are thinking about issues of scale. Even so, the need for thoughtful, sustained programmes of multiscalar research requires reiterating. Archaeologists can stay true to their commitments as privileged scholars at the same time that they can work on a practical level to save archaeological remains from destruction. As such, it is important to continue the discussion of 'digging locally and thinking globally'.[7] At this point in the history of historical archaeology, it is no longer a case of whether its practitioners should think in multiscalar terms, but rather how they might seek to accomplish this difficult task.

DRAWING TOGETHER SEVERAL THREADS

This exploration draws together ideas from three scholars, none of whom are archaeologists. The diversity of their ideas, and the way in which they entwine, is attractive because their union provides the foundation for a multiscalar archaeological analysis of the modern world. An excellent starting point has been suggested by cultural anthropologist William Kelleher. Kelleher has been engaged in analysing the construction of identity in the social spaces of the borderlands area of Northern Ireland for many years. Anthropologists generally find the subject of identity formation inherently interesting wherever they choose to study it, but it appears especially fascinating in contested landscapes like that of Northern Ireland during the Troubles. Kelleher's analysis is insightful and theoretically graceful, and his observations on identity formation and its relation to the production of material space are especially compelling and conceptually useful for historical archaeologists.

Kelleher conducted his original research in the 1980s in a town he called Ballybogoin.[8] His research presents several insights that are worthy of archaeological attention, even by people never intending to work in Ireland but who have an interest in identity formation and its relation to the creation of space. Kelleher begins with the simplistic dualism prominent in the media: that the people of Northern Ireland can be divided into binary opposites, Protestant and Catholic, that can be historically contextualised as 'coloniser' and 'colonised'. In this essentialised reading of history, the Troubles, being wholly sectarian, are relatively easy to understand. People with only a passing knowledge of Northern Ireland would be able to recite this version with little difficulty. Many Irish Americans – who may know little about the realities of Irish cultural history – have adopted this facile perspective as part of the mythology that encapsulates their view of the Emerald Isle. Anthropologists, however, know that no social situation can ever be so straightforward, and so Kelleher's examination reveals some of the complexities of the town's social networks.

In his effort to map identities, Kelleher sought to untangle the town's many levels of social interaction. Even expressions of class – which one might initially imagine as relatively uncomplicated – were enacted within diverse and overlapping networks of social relations. These relations included vectors of physical location, religion, demography, economy, politics and family that through their articulation created the town's socio-environment.

Kelleher also mapped the ways in which various power relations were overlain on the landscape, in effect providing a perfect ethnographic example of two of Henri Lefebvre's constructed social spaces: 'spatial practice' (which includes the physical spaces themselves and the knowledge and experiences of moving through them) and 'representational space' (the space that is lived through associated images, symbols and mythic narratives).[9] Kelleher discovered that the town had been culturally coded as 'Protestant space' because it had been designed and administered by a centralised religious/political authority that was identified as British. Thus, 'British' was a code word for 'Protestant' in the same way that 'American' is used as a code word for white, Anglo and middle class.

All archaeologists know that the physicality involved in the production of social space leaves powerful imprints. Even short-term visitors to Northern Ireland know that one way spatial practice is encoded on physical space is through the imposition of representational space. Emotionally charged murals, flags and painted kerbstones demarcate physical space and employ deeply rooted, contextually significant mythic images meant to define territory and to create identity as a conflation of space and time.[10]

In a return visit to the town in the 1990s, Kelleher re-examined the process of identity formation and focused explicitly on a concept he called 'making home'.[11] This part of his analysis has particular relevance for archaeologists interested in the local–global nexus because his notion of 'making home' is not at all 'hearth-centric'. In Kelleher's analysis, the makers of a home adopt a conceptual vision that looks both inside and outside the home. One of his explicit concerns is with how the process of making home is impacted by and reacts to various globalising forces outside the homemakers' control or even influence. This idea has important implications for archaeology, especially because so much archaeology is focused on individual households. In fact, many archaeologists maintain that their ability to examine households in minute detail is one of their discipline's greatest strengths. They even sometimes use the term 'household archaeology' to describe the field because the household – both as a unit of archaeological analysis and as a past social space – can be an unavoidable archaeological subject.[12] Kelleher's definition of 'home' is consistent with this idea because he defines it as 'both a material and social fact, an entity with objective and subjective dimensions'.[13]

One of the key elements in Kelleher's concept of 'making home' centres on the way in which the processes of place making and identity formation are linked. In a place like Northern Ireland during the Troubles, one might easily accept that the created social spaces encompass various relations of power that help to define the process of homemaking. In fact, situational power relations may determine when an individual perceives him or herself to be either 'at home' or 'not at home'. Are we 'at home' when we are actually in our house or are we at home when we are within the spatial boundaries of our 'hometown'? Of course, these are old questions and the answer largely depends on what representational space we wish to conceptualise as we ponder them. Equally important is realising that the definition adopted references the scale on which the issue is conceptualised.

To help address this point, Kelleher provides an interesting encounter between a British soldier and a local informant with whom Kelleher was walking down the street. No words were exchanged by either party as the British soldier raised his rifle and pointed it at them. The soldier slowly backed away and the encounter was over. This brief experience encouraged Kelleher to think about the notion of home, and it forced him to conclude that an important element of making home may not lie in understanding when we are 'at home' but rather in realising when we are 'not at home'. In other words, the sense of 'not being at home' may provide a way to realise that 'home' may be an illusion of coherence and safety 'based on the exclusion of specific histories of oppression and resistance and even the repression of differences within oneself'.[14]

As is true everywhere, relations of power constitute a major piece of the equation in Northern Ireland. Whether its residents could feel secure in their homes during the Troubles is an interesting question that reverberates today in places like Iraq, Afghanistan and the inner cities of the United States, where innocent people can get shot in their bedrooms by bullets passing through the walls. That the illusion of safety 'at home' can be shattered by the imposition of the outside world foregrounds the inside/outside dialectic when 'making home'.

Kelleher's interpretation of homemaking allows us to understand better an anthropological definition of globalisation. As stated by anthropologist Michael Kearney, globalisation 'refers to social, economic, cultural, and demographic processes that take place within nations but also transcends them, such that attention limited to local processes, identities, and units of analysis yields incomplete understanding of the local'.[15] Kearney further notes that globalisation involves 'the intensification of world-wide social relations which link distant localities in such a way that local happenings are shaped by events occurring many miles away and vice versa'.[16] In this view, then, globalisation, which is often incorrectly labelled as wholly Eurocentric, is a multidirectional process.

If archaeologists begin to conceptualise their sites as homes in Kelleher's sense, then they can begin to think outside the home as another way of 'thinking outside the box'. Further, if archaeologists can begin to appreciate 'not being at home' as an archaeological subject, then they immediately find themselves inexorably moving beyond the site's boundaries and into the wider world.

Kelleher's notion of 'making home' can be extended by adding Lefebvre's formulation of rhythmanalysis.[17] Lefebvre's concept, like Kelleher's, is poetically human while also intensely analytic. At its very heart, Lefebvre intends rhythmanalysis to constitute a way to perceive time, space and everyday life dialectically. It offers a way to observe unity in opposition.

Lefebvre argues that every human being is engaged in a series of simultaneously acting, intertwined rhythms that extend from the intensely personal –the beating of one's heart – to the broadly natural – the changing of the seasons. The diversity of the rhythms, however, operates dialectically in a manner that is only perceived when one or several of the rhythms are disturbed:

> And yet each of us is this unity of diverse relations whose aspects are subordinated to action towards the external world, oriented towards the outside, towards the Other and to the World, to such a degree that they escape us. We are only conscious of most of our rhythms when we begin to suffer from some irregularity.[18]

The concept of rhythm as used by Lefebvre neatly reunites the quantitative elements that one would equate with daily living – all those things both material and non-material that demarcate space and time – with its more qualitative elements – all those things that link space and time together. The rhythms are conceptualised as webs, and, as Lefebvre writes: 'Our rhythms insert us into a vast and infinitely complex world.'[19] This world operates simultaneously on various micro and macro levels and, given the immensity of the many scales that can exist in the living world – and here Lefebrve means 'scale' as a unified spatio-temporal dimension – he argues that each individual only grasps and perceives that which corresponds to his or her own rhythms. This conclusion leads to the need for multiscalar analysis because what is perceived at one level may be invisible at another.[20]

Lefebvre's concept of rhythm, when used cautiously and contextually, appears to provide a useful concept for archaeologists interested in the local–global nexus. The combination of Kelleher's idea of home building and Lefebvre's concept of rhythmanalysis is further extended by adding another concept that further permits archaeologists to advance the goal of creating powerful multiscalar, dialectical analyses. Such an advancement in archaeological interpretation will help to propel the discipline into the foreground of interpreting modernity, however one may wish to define it.

The final useful concept is 'time–space compression'. As defined by David Harvey, time-space compression represents 'processes that so revolutionize the objective qualities of space and time that we are forced to alter, sometimes in quite radical ways, how we represent the world to ourselves'.[21] Harvey qualifies this concept in a way that directly pertains to the historical archaeology of the modern world because he uses the word 'compression' in conjunction with the history of capitalism. For him, capitalism has created an increased pace of life and a shrinking of spatial barriers that provides the very definition of time–space compression.

What appears significant in time–space compression for historical archaeologists is the way in which the process may affect the rhythms of homemaking. For archaeologists, the most obvious place to observe the effects of time–space compression is probably in transformations of material culture assemblages through time, but its effects can undoubtedly also be seen in landscapes, as well as in mapmaking, land reclamation projects, industrial designs and work schedules, and in many of the other subjects historical archaeologists typically study. But no matter what the subject, time–space compression is clearly multiscalar; it operates dialectically across space and through time. In a world experiencing capitalist-based time–space compression, traditional rhythms can be sped up and perhaps even disrupted to the point of arrhythmia.[22]

A MULTISCALAR OUTLINE OF EARLY 19TH-CENTURY RURAL IRELAND

Every sociohistorical situation is amenable to dialectical multiscalar analysis. However, the interpretive depth of the analysis will of course depend upon the sources of information available. A thorough contextualisation is imperative to complete such an examination. Historical archaeologists of the modern era are fortunate to typically have access to a rich number of diverse sources upon which they can draw. In the brief outline that follows, I use fifteen years of historical archaeological research in rural Ireland, in counties Roscommon, Sligo and Donegal, as a background to illustrate the early stages of a multiscalar dialectical analysis. Readers will note that this presentation is merely heuristic. The research design for the overall project, however, was always explicitly concerned with formulating the basis of the global–local nexus as a viable element of archaeological analysis and historical interpretation.[23]

Rural life in pre-Famine Ireland, or rural life anywhere for that matter, was a world of many complex webs of interaction and rhythm. The inhabitants of the thousands of tenant farms that dotted the countryside were engaged in complex networks that were intertwined and embedded within one another. Numerous intersecting rhythms can be easily identified in historic rural Ireland.[24] Rhythm One is agricultural. As subsistence farmers, many Irish families were participants in a rhythm of planting and reaping that was universal for all farming cultures. Cyclical rhythm constitutes the essence of the agrarian life. For many places around the world, including much of rural Ireland, the agricultural cycle of production also included periodic scarcity, or what in Ireland were often called the 'the meal months', when the supply of potatoes was depleted in the summer, forcing families to eat meal, which they had to purchase on credit.[25] Rhythm Two was a cycle of land ownership. As renters, Irish tenant farmers were part of a biannual cycle wherein they were required to pay one-half of their rent in May and one-half in November. The operation of this rhythm was infrangibly linked to Rhythm One because the ability to pay rent was directly related to agricultural production. This rhythm was unquestionably based on power. Failure to submit the proper amount of rent on time could create additional elements of the rhythm as tenants in arrears might be required to appear in court or be otherwise summoned to account for their lapse in payment. Thus, Rhythm Two conflated agricultural production with relations of power based on land tenure and ownership.

Rhythm Three was an organised religious rhythm that depended on religious affiliation and degree of observance. This rhythm would involve annual feast days, holidays, and other celebrations and festivals designated by the church of one's attendance. A related rhythm, Rhythm Four, was experienced by cultural traditionalists who still observed some measure of the pre-Christian rites, such as visiting a holy well to receive relief from pain. Rhythms Three and Four could be observed by the same families, and these religious rhythms were never entirely divorced from the other rhythms. Rhythm Five, which we might term a socioeconomic rhythm, was organised around the occurrence of long-established fairs and market days. This rhythm also never stood in isolation because in many cases the rent-paying rhythm and this rhythm coincided perfectly when some tenants were required to pay rent on fair days. A sixth, legal, rhythm might be based on the assizes, when law-breaking tenants were required to appear before the magistrate.

Other rhythms can be identified, but the point is that each of these rhythms neatly coexisted and in fact were entwined in the course of daily life.[26] Each of them operated on a different spatio-temporal scale. One rhythm might involve family members only, whereas others might be wholly personal. Another rhythm might involve total strangers, but others were kin-based. Some rhythms may have taken months to play out, while others might have taken moments. The central idea, however, is that these rhythms – each with its own cultural logic and contextual meaning – dialectically functioned together to create unity from diversity; in effect, the rhythms worked as part of the homemaking process in early 19th-century rural Ireland.

The dual concepts of rhythmanalysis and homemaking allow us to create interpretations that may add significantly to our understandings of specific places at specific times, or in Lefebvre's terms, to begin to conceptualise how the analytically contextualised social spaces interacted. But, as archaeologists thinking in multiscalar terms, it is especially interesting to think about the rhythms of homemaking when the affects of time–space compression are factored in. Examined diachronically, the affects of time-space compression might be linked to what have been termed 'moments of danger'.[27]

Archaeologist Christopher Matthews has explicitly used the concept of 'moments of danger' to explore the nature of history making in Annapolis, Maryland.[28] Matthews's analysis resembles Kelleher's interpretation of homemaking, and as part of his analysis he identifies six chronological moments of danger in the history of Annapolis. He labels these moments: class formation, revolution, marginalisation, the arrival of the United States Naval Academy, the failure of industry, and commodification. The first process began with the earliest founding of the city in the 17th century, and the final process, commodification, began when elite residents consciously conceived Annapolis as 'The Ancient City'. This purposeful action created a dedicated representational space constructed around a mythic image of the past that could help to protect the homes of the wealthy and at the same time attract tourists wishing to spend the night where George Washington slept. But each of the moments, even though they are chronological, has an intersecting rhythm that is constantly being reconceived in the process of creating the cultural history of the city. Each is involved, on various scales and in diverse ways, with the process of homemaking in 'The Ancient City'.

In rural Ireland, it is possible to consider changes in the rhythms of homemaking in the light of moments of danger because individual farm families unquestionably confronted such moments on a regular basis. The appearance of the meal months, the biannual requirement to pay rent, and the constant possibility of eviction for non-payment would all constitute moments of explicit danger.

Again thinking in multiscalar terms, it is important to recognise that moments of danger can come from global directions. The enactment of the Corn Laws, the Act of Union and the Gregory Act all had the potential to affect rural Irish homemaking in significant ways. Some of these effects might be quite localised and would have clear archaeological manifestations. For example, various embargoes and problems with commercial transportation may have occasioned an intense, periodic reliance on locally produced coarse earthenware ceramics in rural Irish homes. The construction of new roads may have brought new kinds of refined earthenware to the farmers, thus altering their rhythm of food consumption. The patterns on transfer-printed fine earthenware vessels may have contributed to the development of new rhythms as people began to think about the wider world around them. And of course, the most profound moments of danger would be the periodic famines that swept through the countryside, causing disease, mass eviction and emigration.[29]

Once evicted and on the road, rural travellers faced new moments of danger and new rhythms of homemaking. Without question, the arrival of these immigrants in their new homeland – whether it was the United States, Canada, Australia or wherever – occasioned the construction of new rhythms in an unfamiliar network of social relations. To some extent, the idea of a complex web of interwoven rhythms is similar to the concept of epochal structures.[30] The concept of the epochal structure remains useful, but the addition of Lefebrve's concept of rhythmanalysis assists in interpreting the internal workings of the structures. Epochal structures need not be viewed as rigid frameworks of sociocultural behaviour or as essentialisations of history. Like epochal structures, Lefebrve's rhythm concept is amorphous enough to require sociohistorical contextualisation, but it lacks the appearance of what some might construe as conceptual rigidity.

The connection between old and new rhythms also helps us to conceptualise transnational linkages, or in the Irish case specifically, a trans-Atlantic connection. In diasporic terms and when thinking dialectically, any examination of daily life in rural Ireland must be cognisant of Irish life elsewhere to be truly whole. This conclusion initially seems counterintuitive. Irish farm life in County Roscommon, for example, appears to be worlds away from the rough and tumble life of the Five Points in New York City. Analytically, we may wish to keep the two localities apart, but the resultant analysis has the potential to be one-dimensional.[31]

CONCLUSION

In many ways, there may be nothing particularly new in the above. Perhaps this is merely of equivalent of when the new archaeology was described as 'old wine and new skins'.[32] Even so, historical archaeologists have important contributions to make by keeping the dialectics of the local and the global always in mind, and to struggle to find new ways of thinking and new ways of interpreting what geographers now call 'glocalization'.[33]

Can historical archaeology sustain an interest in the global–local nexus long enough to make the contributions promised at the dawn of the profession's academic development in the late 1960s? The answer to this question is currently unknown.

Historical archaeologists often appear to be poor consumers of theory. When they find something new and interesting – sometimes its source may be anthropology, sometimes history, and sometimes even philosophy – they tend to consume it with the fervour of a fad. They become intensely intrigued for a while, get extremely active and then discard the idea for the next new thing. They seldom seem to give adequate time to interrogate a complex concept fully to determine its true utility in the archaeological world. This approach is bad practice. Archaeologists, like all serious scholars, should think broadly and openly, and indeed should investigate all seemingly pertinent perspectives. But in the search for innovative methods and intriguing concepts, archaeologists need not jettison the old before fully investigating them. Some ideas, of course, should be jettisoned, and for good reason, but other concepts, perspectives and views should be given more time for experimentation and trial. The close examination of the local through the perspective of the global and vice versa provides a perfect example.

Archaeologists have much to learn about the creation of the modern world, and an infinite number of vectors of inquiry remain unexplored. Calls for an archaeological praxis are certainly nothing new, but perhaps now is the time that archaeologists must think even more determinedly about linking theory and practice as never before. As the practice of historical archaeology expands across the globe – becoming a truly global pursuit for the first time – its practitioners have greater opportunities to have their ideas enter the lexicon of everyday thinking. Historical archaeologists of the modern world, however identified, have a tremendous amount to contribute to understanding the day-to-day elements of the process of globalisation – beginning with how and when it began and how it links us to a past that is both far away and forever close. The large issues that confront us in our daily lives and that confronted our ancestors in innumerable ways must not be forgotten in our struggle to understand local life and to retrieve the often tiny artefacts from the past.

NOTES

1. Orser 1994, 1996.
2. Orser 1999, 2004.
3. Hall & Silliman 2006b, 8.
4. Johnson 2006, 318.
5. Frank 1978; Wallerstein 1974, 1979.
6. Hall & Silliman 2006b, 8.
7. Orser 1996, 183–204.
8. Kelleher 2003.
9. Lefebvre 1991, 38–9.
10. See, for example, Rolston 1992, 1998.
11. Kelleher 2000.
12. For a brief history of this interest, see, for example, Allison 1999; Deetz 1982; King 2006.
13. Kelleher 2000, 142.
14. Here Kelleher is citing Martin & Mohanty 1986, 196.
15. Kearney 1995, 548.
16. Kearney 1995, 548.
17. Lefebvre 2004.
18. Lefebvre & Régulier 2004, 77.
19. Lefebvre & Régulier 2004, 82.
20. For an in-depth discussion, see Marquardt 1985, 1992.
21. Harvey 1990, 240.
22. Lefebvre 2004, 51–6.
23. For information about the overall research project, see Orser 2006.
24. More detail on these rhythms appears in Orser 2007, 79–88.
25. Woodham-Smith 1991, 36.
26. See, for example, Danaher 1972.
27. Benjamin 2006, 391.
28. Matthews 2002.
29. The concept of moments of danger has been explicitly applied to Ireland: see Kirkland 1996.
30. Donham 1999.
31. Thankfully, the archaeologists who analysed the Five Points materials did not choose this path.
32. Taylor 1972.
33. Murray 2006, 54–6.

BIBLIOGRAPHY

Allison, P.M. (ed.), 1999, *Archaeology of Household Activities*. London: Routledge.

Benjamin, W. 2006, *Selected Writings, volume 4, 1938–1940*, ed. H. Eiland & M. Jennings. Cambridge, MA: Belknap Press of Harvard University Press.

Bintliff, J. (ed.), 2004, *A Companion to Archaeology*. Malden, MA: Blackwell.

Danaher, K. 1972, *The Year in Ireland*. Cork: Mercier.

Deetz, J.F. 1982, 'Households: a structural key to archaeological interpretation', *American Behavioral Scientist* **25**: 717–24.

Donham, D.L. 1999, *History, Power, and Ideology: Central Issues in Marxism and Anthropology*. Berkeley: University of California Press.

Elden, S. & Moore, G. (trans.) 2004, *Rhythmanalysis: Space, Time and Everyday Life*. London: Continuum.

Frank, A.G. 1978, *World Accumulation, 1492–1789*. New York: Monthly Review Press.

Hall, M. & Silliman, S.W. (eds) 2006a, *Historical Archaeology*, Malden, MA: Blackwell.

Hall, M. & Silliman, S.W. 2006b, 'Introduction: archaeology of the modern world', in Hall & Silliman (eds), 2006, 1–19.

Harvey, D. 1990, *The Condition of Postmodernity: An Enquiry into the Origins of Cultural Change*. Cambridge, MA: Blackwell.

Hicks, D. & Beaudry, M.C. (eds) 2006, *The Cambridge Companion to Historical Archaeology*. Cambridge: Cambridge University Press.

Johnson, M. 2006, 'The tide reversed: prospects and potentials for a postcolonial archaeology of Europe', in Hall & Silliman (eds), 2006, 313–31.

Kearney, M. 1995, 'The local and the global: the anthropology of globalization and transnationalism', *Annual Review of Anthropology* **24**: 547–65.

Kelleher, W.F. Jr 2000, 'Making home in the Irish/British borderlands: the global and the local in a conflicted social space', *Identities* **7**: 139–72.

Kelleher, W.F. Jr 2003, *The Troubles in Ballybogoin: Memory and Identity in Northern Ireland*. Ann Arbor: University of Michigan Press.

King, J.A. 2006, 'Household archaeology, identities, and biographies', in Hicks & Beaudry (eds), 2006, 293–313.

Kirkland, R. 1996, *Literature and Culture in Northern Ireland since 1965: Moments of Danger*. London: Longman.

Lauretis, T. de (ed.), 1986, *Feminist Studies, Critical Studies*. Bloomington: Indiana University Press.

Lefebvre, H. 1991, *The Production of Space*, trans. D. Nicholson-Smith. Oxford: Blackwell.

Lefebvre, H. 2004, 'Elements of rhythmalanysis: an introduction to the understanding of rhythms', in Elden & Moore, 2004, 1–69.

Lefebvre, H. & Régulier, C. 2004, 'The rhythmanalysis project', in Elden & Moore, 2004, 71–83.

Leone, M.P. (ed.) 1972, *Contemporary Archaeology: A Guide to Theory and Contributions*. Carbondale: Southern Illinois University Press.

Marquardt, W.H. 1985, 'Complexity and scale in the study of fisher-gatherer-hunters: an example from the eastern United States', in Price & Brown (eds), 1985, 59–98.

Marquardt, W.H. 1992, 'Dialectical archaeology', in Schiffer (ed.), 1992, 101–40.

Martin, B. & Mohanty, C.T. 1986, 'Feminist politics: what's home got to do with it?', in Lauretis (ed.), 1986, 191–212.

Matthews, C.N. 2002, *An Archaeology of History and Tradition: Moments of Danger in the Annapolis Landscape*. New York: Kluwer Academic/Plenum.

Murray, W.E. 2006, *Geographies of Globalization*. London: Routledge.

Orser, C.E. Jr 1994, 'Toward a global historical archaeology: an example from Brazil', *Historical Archaeology* **28**(1): 1–18.

Orser, C.E. Jr 1996, *A Historical Archaeology of the Modern World*. New York: Plenum.

Orser, C.E. Jr 1999, 'Negotiating our "familiar" past', in Tarlow & West (eds), 1999, 273–85.

Orser, C.E. Jr 2004, 'The archaeology of recent history: historical, post-medieval, and modern-world', in Bintliff (ed.), 2004, 272–90.

Orser, C.E. Jr (ed.), 2006. *Unearthing Hidden Ireland: Historical Archaeology at Ballykilcline, County Roscommon*. Bray: Wordwell.

Orser, C.E. Jr 2007, *The Archaeology of Race and Racialization in Historic America*. Gainesville: University Press of Florida.

Price, T.D. & Brown, J.A. (eds) 1985, *Prehistoric Hunter-Gatherers: The Emergence of Cultural Complexity*. Orlando, FL: Academic Press.

Rolston, B. 1992, *Drawing Support: Murals in the North of Ireland*. Belfast: Beyond the Pale.

Rolston, B. 1998, *Drawing Support 2: Murals of War and Peace*. Belfast: Beyond the Pale.

Schiffer, M.B. (ed.) 1992, *Archaeological Method and Theory*, vol. 4. Tucson: University of Arizona Press.

Tarlow, S. & West, S. (eds) 1999, *The Familiar Past? Archaeologies of Later Historical Britain*. London: Routledge.

Taylor, W.W. 1972, 'Old wine and new skins: a contemporary parable', in Leone (ed.), 1972, 28–33.

Wallerstein, I. 1974, *The Modern World-System: Capitalist Agriculture and the Origins of the European World-Economy in the Sixteenth Century*. New York: Academic Press.

Wallerstein, I. 1979, *The Capitalist World-Economy*. Cambridge: Cambridge University Press.

Woodham-Smith, C. 1991, *The Great Hunger: Ireland, 1845–1849*. London: Penguin.

An Amorphous Farrago? The Contribution of Industrial Archaeology

By DAVID GWYN

This discussion is offered as a contribution to the debate within industrial archaeology specifically as to the appropriate focus of the discipline. There has been much discussion in recent years as to the rival claims of an archaeology that emphasises the social context of industrialisation on the one hand, and the importance of the direct study of engineering technology on the other. It will be argued here that there is no necessary and inevitable conflict between these approaches, that common ground is possible and that they can inform each other to their mutual benefit and to the benefit of archaeological study of the period from 1550 onwards.

INTRODUCTION

This volume, as the proceedings of a conference arranged jointly by the Association for Industrial Archaeology, the Society for Post-Medieval Archaeology and the Irish Post-Medieval Archaeology Group, is, as might be anticipated, theoretically diverse. But then, an archaeological conference that took as its period the years 1550 to the present day, and that took as its locale the restless lands of England, Ireland, Scotland and Wales, set itself an ambitious task. It was made even more so by encompassing not only academic or intellectual understanding of the dynamics of this period but also the questions of management and interpretation. A readiness to consider different approaches is a precondition of coming to terms with so broad a scope. Our 16th-century starting-point was a period of profound paradigmatic change, which experienced radically altered ways of thought, altered political and tenurial relationships, and, perhaps above all else, the European recognition of the human 'other' in the populations of the New World. The period as a whole witnessed the Enlightenment, and – eventually – growing plebeian and female participation in the political process. It witnessed shifts, sometimes violent, in the power-relationship between centre and periphery, both within the constituent communities of the Atlantic isles and in their relationship with the rest of the world. Many of us consider that its defining experience was the scientific and industrial revolution. So much of the built and landscape fabric with which we are familiar was bequeathed to us in the last five hundred years or so. We are contemplating a vast subject, one that has generated no shortage of approaches.

This chapter has to begin by looking at the second half of this time-span. There has been much discussion in recent years as to the rival claims of an archaeology of the period from 1750 that emphasises the social context of industrialisation on the one hand, and the importance of the direct study of engineering technology on the other. This has aroused controversy and fundamental disagreement as to the nature and scope of industrial archaeology, which has led the author of one recent paper to describe it as an 'amorphous farrago' – shapeless and confused intellectual fodder.[1] 'Farrago', be it noted, is in Latin a mixed animal feed, and not the least challenge of preparing this discussion has been to sustain this alimentary metaphor usefully. Another author who has addressed this issue recently has preferred to speak of archaeological 'sects', 'liturgies' and 'churches', and has observed that 'Ecumenism is in short supply' in industrial archaeology.[2] What follows cannot be any more than a personal 'take' on the issue, but I will suggest both that the mixture offers considerable advantages to industrial archaeology and that it also has the capacity to confer strength on the study of the archaeology of Britain and Ireland more generally. This disagreement is not only of concern to industrial archaeologists; if there is to be common ground between all those who interest themselves in the archaeology of the recent past, then we need all to understand how we all see ourselves.

BACKGROUND: INDUSTRIAL ARCHAEOLOGY

Industrial archaeology was born from the dislocations of the Second World War; its parents were on the one hand the university system, through its sponsorship of extra-mural classes, and on the other a voluntary sector of men and women who found for themselves an interesting and challenging hobby to follow. At Bath University, Professor Angus Buchanan established the Centre for Study of the History of Technology in 1964. Here the card-index National Record of Industrial Monuments was housed. The Centre was also host to the meetings that led to the establishment in 1973 of the Association for Industrial Archaeology, whose house-journal, *Industrial Archaeology Review* (1976 to date), superseded *The Journal of Industrial Archaeology* (1964 to 1980). A few other academic appointments were made but on the whole the discipline failed to gain any critical mass in the university system. Even so, in the United States, a master's programme was established by Professor Pat Martin at Michigan Technological University, and in England Dr Marilyn Palmer was awarded a chair in industrial archaeology at the University of Leicester in 2000. In Ireland, Dr Colin Rynne introduced classes in industrial as well as in post-medieval archaeology at University College Cork.

In both the United Kingdom and in the Republic of Ireland it was changes in statutory requirements that forced industrial archaeology on practitioners. The adoption of Planning Policy Guidance (PPG) notes 15 and 16 expanded the opportunities for developer-funded recording, while English Heritage's Monument Protection Programme (MPP) was initiated in 1991. Scotland was quicker off the mark, with the work of John Hume and the Scottish Industrial Archaeology Survey (SIAS) at the University of Strathclyde in carrying out extensive thematic surveys before the SIAS was formally transferred to the Scottish Royal Commission in 1985. The Welsh Royal Commission began recording the more important industrial sites in the 1960s; its staff have gone on to publish a series of important works on canals, early railways and collieries in south Wales, as well as a major survey of Swansea's copper-smelting landscapes. Cadw appointed a full-time industrial archaeology specialist in 1990, and the four Welsh archaeological trusts also began to take an interest in industrial archaeology. In Northern Ireland, Professor Rodney Green's *The Lagan Valley* (1949) marked the beginnings of industrial archaeology in the six counties, and in the 1980s the Historic Monuments Branch of the Department of the Environment established the Greater Belfast Industrial Archaeology Survey (GBIAS). In the Republic, the Irish Society for Industrial Archaeology (ISIA) was formed in the early 1970s. The long-standing 1700 cut-off for archaeology in the National Monuments legislation suggests that for Dublin officials, archaeology ended with the final collapse of the Catholic order at the Battle of the Boyne. It was amended in 1987 to the extent that the Office of Works can use its discretion where later sites are concerned (but see Rynne and Breen this volume for further consideration). In 1996, the Industrial Heritage Association of Ireland was formed, covering the thirty-two counties.

Other archaeologies of the recent past had grown since the 1950s. Post-medieval archaeology founded its own society in 1966 and later published its own journal and research agenda. On the whole, from the start post-medieval archaeology formed a more cohesive professional discipline, led by university and museum archaeologists who tended to focus more on excavation and artefact analysis than on cataloguing what survived in the way of sites. As such, it also initially emphasised the archaeology of consumption rather than that of production. Historians and archaeologists, including William Hoskins and Maurice Beresford, followed more recently by Trevor Rowley and Mick Aston, also redefined the study of landscape as the perspective and context that gave monuments their meaning.[3] In 1982, Barrie Trinder published *The Making of the Industrial Landscape*, which focused on 'mines and manufactures and their immediate surroundings'[4] but which also argued that agriculture and landscapes of recreation need to be regarded as products of industry. Dr Trinder took as his starting point the England and Wales of Celia Fiennes and Daniel Defoe at the turn of the 17th and 18th centuries, and traced the process of industrialisation within this 'landscape of busy-ness'. The *longue durée* also informed an extensive landscape survey of the Ironbridge Gorge by Judith Alfrey and Catherine Clark, published in 1993 as *The Landscape of Industry*. The landscape context of industrialisation was developed by Marilyn Palmer and Peter Neaverson, in *Industry in the Landscape 1700–1900*.[5]

In 1998, Palmer and Neaverson went on to publish *Industrial Archaeology: Principles and Practice*, in which they argued strongly that industrial archaeology needed to define its relationship with these other forms of archaeological inquiry that looked at the more recent past.[6] Neaverson and Palmer, as 'second generation' industrial archaeologists, noted the failure to build an adequate theoretical base on the foundations laid by pioneers, just as folk life studies had proved to be a one-generation discipline. The failure lay, they suggested, in the limited number of academic posts and a consequent absence of theoretical models. Industrial archaeology had remained largely untouched by the 'new archaeology' of the 1960s and 1970s and its emphasis on culture process, with the result that too many practitioners adhered strictly to the functional interpretation of 'industrial remains'. Social landscape and cultural interaction were still largely ignored.

CURRENT DEBATES IN INDUSTRIAL ARCHAEOLOGY

Of late, several attempts have been made to evolve an archaeology of the 18th to 21st centuries that draws on the varied approaches that are available and are theoretically informed. In published form, they have met with a varied reception. *The Archaeology of Industrialization*, edited by David Barker and David Cranstone and published by Maney in 2004, lost much of its impact in that it had taken five years from the initial joint AIA/ SPMA conference to come out in book form, and in including papers that had not been delivered at the conference and that were barely relevant – they had in fact been offered at another conference four years earlier. Reviewers described the contributions as ranging 'from dull or incoherent to inspirational' and suggested that because of the lack of strong editorial direction 'it is not the strong and coherent case for integrated, inter-disciplinary studies of the past 500 years that it really should be'.[7]

By contrast, academic reviewers of *Industrial Archaeology: Future Directions* (Plenum Press, New York, 2004), edited by Eleanor Casella and Jim Symonds, were more enthusiastic.[8] Audrey Horning described this volume, which arose out of the Theoretical Archaeology Group conference held at Manchester University in 2002, as 'a critical turning point in the expansion of industrial archaeology to include theoretically-informed social as well as technological analyses'.[9] It is noticeable how around this time an increasing number of industrial archaeological articles were appearing with the word 'social' in the title. *Future Directions* was followed by *Understanding the Workplace: A Research Framework for Industrial Archaeology in Britain* (2005), a special edition of *Industrial Archaeology Review* funded by English Heritage and edited by the present author and by Professor Marilyn Palmer.[10]

If the academic community by and large welcomed these two volumes, others were less convinced. This dissatisfaction broke surface with a letter entitled 'Our fascination with machines' published in *Industrial Archaeology News* 136 (Spring 2006). The letter was written by Roger Holden, an authority on the textile industry of the north-west of England and author of several papers in *Industrial Archaeology Review* as well as *Manchester Region History Review*, the *Journal of Industrial History* and *Textile History*. While accepting the importance both of theoretically informed work and of the social context of industrialisation, he found himself particularly unconvinced by the papers published in *Understanding the Workplace*, and even more so by those in *Industrial Archaeology: Future Directions*, which he felt took industrial archaeology out of its proper sphere and into areas that were prescriptive, obscure and that were predominantly 'social archaeology'. What proved to be a typographical error vitiated the meaning of Mary Beaudry's paper in *Future Directions*, but Mr Holden quite reasonably could not see why the industrial archaeology community was being asked to write 'antriumphalist histories' (it should have been 'anti-triumphalist histories'), and complained about the impenetrable 'theory-heavy' prose of some of the contributions.

Roger Holden made the sensible point that instead of vapid and technically weak analysis:

> … we should have a wide outlook that enables us to relate to other contexts, not only social but also economic, financial, business, political, scientific, architectural etc. But it is impossible for one person to have interest and expertise in all these areas…. We need to learn from those who do have expertise in

these areas, but the converse is also true. I quite frequently come across cases where other historians and archaeologists could have benefited from a better technological understanding.[11]

Holden's letter prompted further correspondence expressing various views on the debate, most of which was characterised by a sense that this was a nuanced discussion. These letters appeared in issues 137–40 of *Industrial Archaeology News* (2006–7). The divide, such as it was, reflected a duality that is more marked in industrial archaeology than in any other archaeological sub-discipline. This duality exists between practitioners who teach in universities or work in contracting units, who have degrees in archaeology but very often no particular background in technology; and the voluntary sector, in which engineers are very well represented. What has made the situation more complicated is that separate forums have evolved. Those whose primary focus is technology see little need to attend or contribute to conferences that are heavy on theory, and still less to buy the published proceedings, which are very expensive – *The Archaeology of Industrialization* retailed at £58 and *Future Directions* at $89.95. Academic archaeologists, on the other hand, under pressure to produce the meta-narratives of archaeology, and contractors who have to show a grasp of multi-period sites, rarely choose to acquire a detailed understanding of technology, but do develop the facility to contextualise.

The case against a social archaeology of industrialisation was set out subsequently in *Industrial Archaeology Review* by Dr Ron Fitzgerald, and here I must hold up my hand and say that I encouraged Dr Fitzgerald, in my role as editor of the *Review*, to publish these two papers in successive volumes in order to confront a perceived bias in the way in which industrial archaeology has come to be approached. We had long been known to each other, and I was aware both that he was very unconvinced by much of what was being published in the name of industrial archaeology and also that he and Roger Holden were not alone in their views.

I had been reluctant to become involved in the debate, for several reasons. As it broke, I was coming to terms with these issues in my own study of the industrial-era archaeology of Gwynedd[12] and felt little inclined to reiterate my arguments elsewhere without being able to draw on the evidence at some length. However, I had had the sense that some recent published attempts to analyse industrial sites, while having a worthwhile point to make, had indeed been soggy in their attempts to discuss technology – effectively the point made by Roger Holden in his first letter. A belief that the machine does indeed deserve a central place in our understanding of industrial society was strengthened by work as an archaeological practitioner, by involvement in several conservation and replication initiatives, and by working as a hands-on railwayman, on historic locomotives and as a director. On the other hand, I also firmly believed that industrial archaeology needed to be opened up to other approaches to the recent past, and to learn from them as well as contributing to them. As editor of the *Review*, I felt it was my role to open debate rather than push (or appear to be pushing) a party line; if a 'social' archaeology was perceived to be becoming an orthodoxy rather than a point of view, it deserved to be challenged. It was clear that Dr Fitzgerald would make the point strongly and cogently. Furthermore, I had begun to feel that the requirements of *Industrial Archaeology Review* led to a 'social' bias; the *Review* very properly, as befits an international peer-reviewed period archaeology journal, requires that all papers that are accepted for publication should contextualise their subject-matter within the broader patterns of meaning or theory. In practice, although there are many exceptions, this tends to favour the work produced by contracting units and academic departments rather than that of individuals or small groups. Of course, a point not always appreciated by members of the Association for Industrial Archaeology is that their house-journal can only print articles that are submitted to it in the first place.

Dr Fitzgerald's criticisms were taken up by Sir Neil Cossons in his lectures to the Society of Antiquaries of London in October 2006 and January 2007, published as 'Industrial Archaeology: the Challenge of the Evidence' in *The Antiquaries Journal* in 2007.[13] Cossons' eloquent and detailed analysis argues *inter alia* that 'Fitzgerald's recent and trenchant criticisms' have brought 'veracity to the debate' and suggests that 'industrial archaeology will benefit hugely from re-engaging with reality'.[14]

DISCUSSION: THE AMORPHOUS FARRAGO

The purpose of the present chapter is not primarily to take issue with any of the above points of view but to examine the implications of the debate and specifically to explore some of the issues they raise within the context of a meeting such as the Leicester conference and this volume. Effectively, Dr Fitzgerald makes two points in one; in restating the centrality of technology to understanding modern society, he argues both that archaeological analysis of sites and artefacts from this period require a deeper understanding of technology than most archaeologists can now muster, and that public interpretation of industrial society also requires more technically informed understanding than it now receives. The first of his papers is entitled 'Historic Building Record and the Halifax Borough Market Doors', an exercise in building technology, in which Dr Fitzgerald states, with entirely characteristic vigour, that:

> Periodically, Industrial Archaeology experiences a conclave of the tribal elders who retreat into cabal, spread the entrails of chickens and goats and ultimately produce the 10n+1 version of Whither Industrial Archaeology? The content of this document remains substantively the same but is variously coloured by the prevailing orthodoxies of the social sciences, humanities and most recently, the archaeological establishment. It is largely impervious to reality and does nothing to alter the prevailing course of events.[15]

The gravamen is therefore firstly that successive re-examinations of what constitutes industrial archaeology are self-defeating and in the hands of a clique. As it is:

> Industrial Archaeology emerges as an amorphous farrago of oral history, social history, labour history, urban history, family history, ethnography, historical geography or archaeology. Effectively the subject matter of Industrial Archaeology is anything that anyone wants it to be. That Industrial Archaeology continues to be a vehicle for such a heterogeneous rag-bag of interests points to a continuing vacuum at the heart of the subject.[16]

Instead, Dr Fitzgerald argues, 'the central characteristic of Industrial Archaeology is the generation of original knowledge by the exploitation of a resource that is not primary to other disciplines', namely, the physical evidence for science, technology, the techniques of manufacture, civil and mechanical engineering, for which the accurate measured drawing should be the primary means of analysis. Documentation should be at most a supporting element.

The second paper by Dr Fitzgerald, 'The Stone Dam Mill Engine', addresses the same issue through a close study of an engine house in a Halifax textile mill. Here we read:

> It is, of course, inarguable that there exists a social and economic context within which technology operates but equally in western societies since the 17th century, the dominant attribute of economic development has been science and technology. Attempting to study a changing technological society without a detailed knowledge of the science and technology itself is simply perverse.[17]

Distinctive industrial-era technologies do indeed become more prevalent in Western societies from the 17th century onwards – though, interestingly, there was often nothing new about many of them even then. The force-pump, the industrial mill and the railway all have pre-modern, indeed pre-medieval, origins. It is also worth recalling that the social and economic context of this period simultaneously called for very different, non-technically based, answers to their challenges, which operated alongside the sort of distinctive 'industrial revolution' environments that Neil Cossons takes as his theme. Indeed, even the assertion that science and technology become the dominant attribute is open to question. For instance, slavery – the exploitation of low-tech human 'machines' – was vastly increased in this period; initially in the colonies that Western societies established beyond the Atlantic, then in the 20th century on a massive scale under the Soviets and the Nazis, two dictatorships with a strange relationship with modernity. The whole question of the relationship between bond workers, free labour and technology still awaits a significant contribution from archaeologists, although a number of interesting possibilities have been outlined by very different scholars working in different areas.

A few examples will have to suffice. Professor Veront Satchell's and Shani Roper's recent paper in *Industrial Archaeology Review* has challenged the notion that slavery was inimical either to economic progress or to technical innovation in a West Indian context.[18] Conversely, the 16th-century diffusion of technology in the central European mining areas, with their long traditions of the independent miner, reflects competition from the slave-worked low-technology mines of South America.[19] Dr Andrew Dawson's study of Philadelphia engineers from 1830 to 1890 as a class and of their milieu has highlighted white mechanics' concerns about a free market in labour and conversely the support for emancipation voiced by workshop owners. Workshop practice, machine tools, heavy engineering items and, to a great extent, patronage of the city's civic architecture were bound up with the question of the rights of African-Americans.[20]

By the same token, much of western Europe, still less the rest of the world, did not industrialise at all in the strict sense, yet it is important to note that archaeologists have argued that in different ways they were adapting to, or creating the conditions for, a modern, commercial, society.[21] This is surely another area in which industrial archaeologists very much need to connect with post-medievalists and with historical archaeologists, and where we need to at least be aware of the means of analysis open to us. To regard technology as a complete, self-justifying system is an even less cogent position than is ignorance of its undeniable role in the modern world, although one correspondent to *Industrial Archaeology News* felt certain enough to state that 'our job is to put before those who do not share our passion our knowledge of how human society is, and always will be, dictated by technology'.[22] Technology does sometimes convince us that it can acquire a life of its own, like Zola's runaway troop train on its way to the front in *La Bête Humaine* or like the production line that drives Chaplin to a mental breakdown in *Modern Times*, but it is itself purely a social construct.

It is also interesting that the most impressive of the detailed analyses of individual machines and devices published recently have been those that are not only technically informed but are also sensitive to their social dimension. Neil Cossons singles out for praise the archaeological study of Stephenson's *Rocket* by Bailey and Glithero, yet what makes this a truly remarkable investigation is that it fully acknowledges not only the engineering of the locomotive but also its status as a cultural artefact – in terms of the society that built it and used it, and in terms of the society that preserved and celebrated it.[23] To the list of such publications I nominate a perhaps improbable candidate. Fitzgerald's 'Historic Building Record and the Halifax Borough Market Doors' is an excellent example of a study that contextualises its subject within the history not only of technical capacity but also of retailing, in an overview that extends from Yorkshire to Paris to Milan. Furthermore, although the doors are analysed as building technology, this paper so elegantly straddles the production/consumption divide and draws so capably on documentary evidence that one cannot help but regret that it did not appear in *The Archaeology of Industrialisation*. Work of this standard in fact dispels the notion that 'social' and 'technical' are opposites in an archaeological dichotomy, and suggests that if we wish to stick with the notion of industrial archaeology at all, we should recognise that the distinguishing characteristic of archaeology is that it is an investigation into human society. The machine is social archaeology; there is no archaeology that is not social archaeology. Recognition of this may open the way to a more holistic understanding of the ways in which industrial archaeologists can contribute to understanding the world as it has evolved from the 16th century.

Both Fitzgerald and Cossons address the 'curatorial shortfall', the prevailing technical ignorance of those who present, or attempt to present, the industrial revolution within museums, Fitzgerald making explicit the link between industrial archaeology's neglect of technology and the failure of museums to appoint staff with a knowledge of the subject:

> Subsequently, such museums have proved to be a major casualty of the change of identity that has overtaken Industrial Archaeology generally. Technologically informed staffs have been dispensed with in favour of the proponents of the *social agenda* whose contribution to the gallery consists of the facile storyboard or trite voiceovers that descend into the toe-curlingly patronising.[24]

Indeed so; but on the other hand, 'dumbing down' or simply 'being dumb' can take several forms. A technically well-informed museum curator of a nationally important collection recently took what was surely the wise step of removing from a collection of stationary engines a set of interpretative panels that dwelt on such arcana as steam chest pressures and valve gear (while keeping the information on file for those with a serious interest) and substituting for them information that might intrigue the non-specialists who make up the vast majority of the museum's visitors, contrasting (for instance) a compound mill engine of 1907 with a simple of 1864. The following might be a model of non-technical but informative and accurate interpretation:

> This engine, made in 1907 by McNaught's of Rochdale, drove a factory making flannelette sheets. It was delivered to the mill from its makers to the factory by barge, as both were on the Rochdale Canal. It was in use until 1970. By 1907, powerful mill engines like this were widespread throughout Northern industries. Weavers' wages depended on how much cloth they made. If the engine broke down it would halt production. Therefore it was important that engines were well cared for and ran smoothly. Technical innovations on this engine made it more efficient than the beam engine it replaced.[25]

Compare this approach with that of a major coal-mining museum in a former colliery that stresses the importance of coal in steel-making, in warfare, in transport and in domestic life yet neglects to mention what it is, or to illustrate the fact – elementary to most people over forty, almost entirely unappreciated to anyone below the age of twenty – that this black stuff burns and thereby gives off heat. It is an interesting coincidence that Roger Holden's initial letter was published alongside another, which complained about the National Railway Museum's use of 'gimmicks' such as a Thomas the Tank Engine face on a locomotive at the expense of *Mallard*, the locomotive that achieved the world steam record of 126mph but which was being ignored in the main hall. The correspondent remarks that 'we ought to be proud of our Industrial Heritage, and not resort to gimmicks to increase its popularity amongst the general public'.[26] But firstly there is nothing so dumb as failing to engage the very young in the industrial past (and *Thomas the Tank Engine* is a far more eloquent story than Mallard's record-breaking run), and secondly to state that we should be proud of our industrial heritage is an assertion, and not a given. Who in any case are 'we'? Not the general public, evidently, yet not all industrial archaeologists will feel happy at being conscripted into this potentially elitist enterprise, and we might in any case have different affiliations. A four-square cotton mill by a northern stream is an impressive sight, no doubt, and is readily identifiable as part of 'industrial heritage' but its cultural meaning will be very different for an English member of the Association for Industrial Archaeology than it will be for the descendant of a Gujarat weaver or of a Carolina plantation slave. Mary Beaudry's point about anti-triumphalist archaeology may not have been clearly expressed but remains valid.

This is important because just occasionally a sense of Little England, or at best of Little Britain, lurks behind some writing on industrialisation. Without a doubt, Britain industrialised early, and perhaps it was 'The First Industrial Nation', although it would be interesting and worthwhile to compare its 18th-century industrial archaeology with what survives of Peter the Great's and Frederick the Great's attempts to industrialise their dominions. Clearly, it also makes sense to study the industrial archaeology of parts of the world that decided to emulate Britain, often with British capital and often with British machinery, in terms of technology transfer and of learning from 'the workshop of the world'. Yet somehow other cultures only figure when they decide to do something like the British, and there must also be a powerful argument for examining the archaeology of cultures that adapted in different ways to the global reach of Western industrialisation, either by perpetuating and adapting existing indigenous systems or by undergoing radical but non-technical changes. These also form part of the archaeology of a world that experienced fundamental changes that in some places, but not others, were expressed as industrialisation.

CONCLUSION

I suspect that industrial archaeology is currently going through a period of self-reassessment that is somehow necessary once a particular discipline reaches a particular stage in its development. For instance, the hegemony once enjoyed (in Britain at least) by political and constitutional history was challenged in the middle of the 20th century by social history, perhaps as a consequence of the pressures of the war years, and then by labour history, which itself came to be questioned by feminist and gender history. Similarly the 'new archaeology' of the 1960s and 1970s was soon challenged by approaches that stress historical context and change, social and physical environments, active material culture and the active archaeologist. A closer parallel might be the debates over structuralism that engulfed one university department of English literature in particular in the late 1970s and early 1980s, when an old guard suspicious of theory advocated a return to content-based studies. The point was made then that those who profess to distrust theory are probably themselves in the grip of an earlier theory, but it is also hard to deny that academic publications, grant-bids and seminar papers can sometimes be written in tiresomely 'theory-heavy' manner, in which the names of Michel Foucault and Merleau-Ponty are invoked in much the same way that a medieval schoolman constantly returns to the authority of Aristotle and Isidore. What should nourish sometimes chokes. Sadly, the requirements of the Research Assessment Exercise are not always suited to archaeology, a discipline where the devil is in the detail.

All credit, then, to Roger Holden, Ron Fitzgerald and Neil Cossons for challenging a potential bias, but for myself the value of their contribution is in stimulating debate rather than in recalling industrial archaeology to its ancient virtues. If industrial archaeology is an amorphous farrago, then it is at least intellectual fodder of a sort. If it is confused, then so be it; confusion is preferable to a rigid intellectual certainty. If its academic proponents endlessly re-examine the mix, then all to the good – that is what academics do, and should do. If it leaves the non-specialist unnurtured in technical matters, then let us at least go on asking ourselves how, and on whose terms, people might want to be fed information about the industrial past. A conference that includes as well as members of the Association for Industrial Archaeology, the Society for Post-Medieval Archaeology and the Irish Post-Medieval Archaeology Group will only add to the mix, and there is much nourishment in the pages that follow.

NOTES

1. Holden 2007a, 51.
2. Cossons 2007, 13–14.
3. Rowley 2006; Hoskins 1973; Beresford 1957; Aston 1985.
4. Trinder 1982, 5.
5. Palmer & Neaverson 1994.
6. Palmer & Neaverson 1998.
7. Barker & Cranstone 2004; Wakelin 2005; Tarlow 2005.
8. Casella & Symonds 2004.
9. Horning 2006.
10. Gwyn & Palmer 2005.
11. Holden 2006.
12. Gwyn 2007.
13. Cossons 2007.
14. Cossons 2007, 40.
15. Fitzgerald 2007a.
16. Fitgerald 2007a, 51.
17. Fitzgerald 2007b, 115.
18. Satchell & Roper 2007.
19. Lewis 1970 9, 16
20. Dawson 2004.
21. Dalglish, this volume; Rynne 1999; Gwyn 2007.
22. Irwin. 2006.
23. Cossons 2007, 16; Bailey & Glitheroe 2000.
24. Fitzgerald 2007b, 116.
25. http://emu.msim.org.uk/htmlmn/collections/online [accessed 3 April 2008].
26. Mickleburgh 2006.

BIBLIOGRAPHY

Aston, M. 1985, *Interpreting the Landscape: Landscape Archaeology and Local History.* London: Batsford.

Bailey, M. & Glithero, J. 2000, *The Engineering and History of Rocket.* London and York: National Railway Museum.

Barker D. & Cranstone, D. (eds) 2004, *The Archaeology of Industrialization.* Maney: Leeds.

Beresford, M. 1957, *History on the Ground: Six Studies in Maps and Landscapes.* London: Methuen.

Casella, E. & Symonds, J. (eds) 2004, *Industrial Archaeology: Future Directions.* New York: Plenum.

Cossons, N. 2007, 'Industrial archaeology: the challenge of the evidence', *Antiquaries Journal* **87**, 1–52.

Dawson, A. 2004, *Lives of the Philadelphia Engineers: Capital, Class and Revolution, 1830–1890.* Aldershot: Ashgate.

Fitzgerald, R. 2007a, 'Historic building record and the Halifax Borough Market Doors', *Industrial Archaeology Review* **29**:1, 51–74.

Fitzgerald, R. 2007b, 'The Stone Dam Mill engine house', *Industrial Archaeology Review* **29**:2, 115–31.

Gwyn, D. 2007, *Gwynedd: Inheriting a Revolution: The Archaeology of Industrialisation in North-west Wales.* Chichester: Phillimore.

Gwyn, D & Palmer, M. 2005 (eds), *Understanding the Workplace: A Research Framework for Industrial Archaeology in Britain* (special issue), *Industrial Archaeology Review* **27**:1.

Holden R. 2006, 'Our fascination with machines', *Industrial Archaeology News* **136**, 11.

Horning, A. 2006, review of Casella & Symonds 2005, *Industrial Archaeology Review* **28**:2, 123.

Hoskins, W.G. 1973, *English Landscapes.* London: British Broadcasting Corporation.

Irwin, C. 2006, 'A breath of realism', *Industrial Archaeology News* **137**, 8.

Lewis, M.J.T. 1970, *Early Wooden Railways.* London: Routledge & Kegan Paul.

Mickleburgh, Tim 2006 'Dumbed down steam engines?', *Industrial Archaeology News* **136**, 11.

Palmer, M, & Neaverson, P.A. 1994, *Industry in the Landscape 1700–1900.* London: Routledge.

Palmer, M & Neaverson, P.A. 1998, *Industrial Archaeology: Principles and Practice.* London & New York: Routledge.

Rowley, T. 2006, *The English Landscape in the Twentieth Century.* London: Hambledon Continuum.

Rynne, C. 1999, *The Industrial Archaeology of Cork City and its Environs.* Dublin: Stationery Office.

Satchell, V. & Roper, S. 2007, 'The William James Foundry 1817–1843: an exposé of local metallurgical enterprise', *Industrial Archaeology Review* **29**:2, 105–13.

Tarlow, S. 2005, review of Barker & Cranstone 2004, *Industrial Archaeology Review* **28**:2, 123.

Wakelin, P. 2008, review of Barker & Cranstone 2004, *Landscape History* **27**, 128–9.

People Versus Machines or People and Machines? Current Research Directions within British Post-medieval and Industrial Archaeology

By MICHAEL NEVELL

This chapter reviews the continuing debate about the scope and role of industrial archaeology that was sparked by the publication of Understanding the Workplace, a research framework published by the Association for Industrial Archaeology in 2005. Since this volume focuses upon the landscape and social impacts of industrialisation, a number of industrial archaeologists have felt that the traditional interests of the discipline, the survey and recording of manufacturing processes and power systems, were being ignored or even marginalised. This discussion argues that such is not the case; that rather this research framework is complementary to these traditional research activities. Furthermore, it argues that there is now a range of approaches that provide a research toolkit, a set of archaeological methodologies and theoretical approaches that can be applied to the archaeology of industrialisation. Some of these approaches concentrate wholly upon the recording of technology, others upon the landscape changes and social context. None is exclusive of the other; indeed, they work best when these issues are considered together. Together, they provide a shared research agenda allowing industrial archaeologists to explore our understanding of the interconnection between machine and landscape and society and technological change during the era of industrialisation

INTRODUCTION

Since the publication of the Association for Industrial Archaeology's first overarching research agenda in 1991 and the publication of David Crossley's book on *Post-Medieval Archaeology in Britain* in 1990[1] there has been a huge upsurge in the excavation and survey of 16th-, 17th-, 18th- and 19th-century sites. Most of this new work has been done through the medium of developer-funded rescue archaeology, which in turn has led to an increasingly large body of data and a consequent need to both order and interpret this information. Understandably this new work has led to new theories and debates about the material culture of these centuries, and indeed the development of several distinctive archaeological approaches based around the physical remains recovered. A brief summary of these developments can be found in my Rolt Memorial Lecture of 2005.[2] I don't see the need, and it is not my intention, to repeat the overview of the development of industrial archaeology presented in that lecture, but I do see the need to review the continuing debate about the scope and role of post-medieval, industrial, and historical archaeology, particularly in respect to industrial archaeology.

THE CURRENT DEBATE WITHIN INDUSTRIAL ARCHAEOLOGY

Between the spring of 2006 and the winter of 2007 there was a vigorous debate on the nature of industrial archaeology in the pages of *Industrial Archaeology News*,[3] which was picked up in several articles in *Industrial Archaeology Review* and was also mentioned in the pages of the *Newsletter* of the Society for Post-Medieval Archaeology. As also discussed by Gwyn and Holden in this volume, this debate was sparked by the publication of the research agenda volume *Understanding the Workplace: A Research Framework for Industrial Archaeology in Britain* by the Association for Industrial Archaeology (AIA) in 2005.[4] The focus of this volume was the landscape and social impacts of industrial archaeology during the latter part of the post-1550 period.

The comments sparked by this 2005 research volume fall into three categories. Some correspondents argued that industrial archaeology is completely separate from so-called 'mainstream' or 'conventional' archaeology. To these writers, the absence of detailed studies of industrial manufacturing processes within the 2005 agenda volume was an attempt to marginalise traditional approaches to industrial archaeology. These writers suggest that not only is industrial archaeology just about the archaeology of technology, an ancient debate that goes back to the 1950s, but that it can only be practised by those with science and business backgrounds. This extreme elitist view found its fullest expression in the preamble to two otherwise scholarly papers in *Industrial Archaeology Review*[5] in which the writer concluded that 'the image industrial archaeology extends to the outside world remains one of a lack of definition, absence of coherent methodology and falling short of academic credibility'.[6] Such comments appear to be founded upon, firstly, a complete lack of understanding of archaeology as a discipline based upon the examination of physical evidence and secondly, on a misreading of the aims of the 2005 Research Agenda, which quite explicitly stated that the volume was designed to be a complement to, not a replacement of, the study of technological processes and their development.[7] There is also, in the above-cited criticism of the 2005 volume, a complete rejection of the intellectual framework that both industrial archaeology and post-medieval archaeology have developed since Crossley's and Palmer's works in the early 1990s, and a dismissal of the early 21st-century industrial archaeology field-recording techniques pioneered within the professional units as 'inadequate' and 'uncritical'. In the end, one has to accept that critics such as these do not wish to engage with the wider archaeological community and that the best we can do in an early 21st-century context is to respect their point of view.

Of more relevance and academic coherence are a set of opinions best exemplified by the well-informed and thoughtful comments of Roger Holden, whose initial letter in the spring edition of *Industrial Archaeology News* sparked the debate.[8] His intellectual strand puts the understanding of technology within an economic/business history point of view at the heart of industrial archaeology studies during the period of industrialisation. It accepts the need for a wider context but rejects theorisation that fails to engage with technology by hiding behind social-science jargon. From this point of view, the lack of discussion of technology within the *Understanding the Workplace* volume risks separating two sides of the same debate; technology from society. Further, it was argued by some of those who contributed to either *Industrial Archaeology Review* or *Industrial Archaeology News* that the

Workplace volume gave the impression that the industrialisation period could be studied without any understanding of the role of technology in reshaping society.

Finally, there are the well-documented views of researchers such as myself and Marilyn Palmer who have been arguing since the late 1990s for the widening of industrial archaeology to include landscape and social issues.[9] The conference upon which the *Understanding the Workplace* volume is based 'was intended to stress the role of human agency in the creation of the artefacts, buildings and landscapes that survive from our period'.[10] The role of this conference and the subsequent *Understanding the Workplace* volume was neither to advocate the supplanting of the study of technology, nor to minimise its role, but to provide a complementary line of discussion based around its social impact.

At this point, it is worth noting that the latter view has much in common with that of British historical archaeologists such as Sarah Tarlow. For instance, Tarlow has recently suggested that 'in re-assessing our approach to the archaeology of the eighteenth and nineteenth centuries we must consider the central issues of power, in equality, capitalism and class'.[11] While many industrial archaeologists would probably question whether these were the central issues during this period in Britain, rather than being the consequences of industrialisation, her assertion does open new avenues for debate between historical archaeology and industrial archaeology. We need to be aware of the historical archaeology tradition in our discussions,[12] if only to say that we have considered them and regard some or all of these issues as more suited to historical archaeology approaches than industrial archaeology methodologies.

TECHNOLOGY, INDUSTRIALISATION AND SOCIAL CHANGE

Central to all three strands of opinion that have been debated since the publication of the *Understanding the Workplace* volume is the role of technology in the transformation of British society during the 18th and 19th centuries. I have argued elsewhere[13] that the part played by technological change during this period might best be understood through looking at the wider role of industrialisation and that industrial archaeologists, with their interest in the development of technology, landscape and society, are best placed to do this within a British context.

At this point it is useful to remind ourselves what we mean by industrialisation. In the context of Britain during the 18th and 19th centuries, industrialisation refers to rapid technological change leading to extensive urbanisation, the development of large-scale factory-based industries, and social changes such as the growth of an urban working class, the development of a surplus-producing agricultural sector, and the growth of an extensive middle class. The culmination of the industrialisation process is a society that moves from being an agrarian, rural-based community to an urban, manufacturing-based, one.

As Matthew Johnson has reminded us on several occasions, these changes have deep roots that take us back in to the late medieval period and the emergence of a fully monetary, capitalist economy in Britain on the back of transformations in landholding and use in the countryside and the emergence of the idea of the individual.[14] Whether industrialisation is a consequence of the emergence of a capitalist system as outlined by Johnson, or whether industrialisation is a separate but related process, is a discussion well worth having but not appropriate for the present purposes. This debate will, however, have implications for the way archaeologists view the development of a world economy in the later 19th and 20th centuries based around mass-production and urbanisation. Taking a long view on these processes does allow broad trends and linkages to be studied at a local, regional and national level.

The thrust of the Manchester Methodology,[15] for instance, was to attempt to bring order to the mass of new archaeological data for the period 1600–1900 by studying the link between contemporary social structures and the emergence of new types of archaeological sites, particularly industrial ones, during these centuries; in other words, to link local people with manufacturing industries. As both David Gwyn and Colin Rynne have noted, the social categories used in the original study area of Tameside, North-West England, are not directly applicable in areas such as the Vale of Ffestiniog in North Wales, and County Offaly in the Republic of Ireland, both areas where the Manchester Methodology has been applied.[16] However, the principle of linking archaeological sites to social groupings over time does appear to be transferable between the three countries, allowing comparisons to be made between these three areas during the era of industrialisation, and emphasising, if nothing else, how localised this phenomenon could be.

Individual studies using this methodology do not provide an explanation of the causes of the industrial transition, but they do provide a way of describing the changes that took place during the period. Furthermore, one might suggest that an archaeological explanation of the industrialisation phenomenon in the islands of Britain might be sought in the differences visible between these individual regional studies. However, we are a long way from having a critical mass of studies that would allow comparisons with the industrial and non-industrial areas of England, Ireland, Scotland and Wales. To achieve this critical mass would require summarising much of the regional grey literature database and targeted local and regional fieldwork, alongside a detailed knowledge of local industries and their social context. It would have to be a multi-disciplinary project requiring an understanding of both the industrial and social context at local and regional levels.

One way of beginning to bring together the local and regional social context of industries might be to look at the growing number of published regional research frameworks within England. The English regional research initiatives sponsored by English Heritage have taken a variety of approaches but follow a standard format of assessment, agenda and strategy.[17] Within the assessment volumes, each chapter deals also with a standard set of broad issues from rural settlement and land-use, urban settlement, ritual, religion and ceremony to technology and production, trade, exchange and interaction and defence, warfare and military activity. Of those assessment volumes so far published (East Midlands, East of England, London, the North West, the South West, West Midlands, and Yorkshire) various approaches to the archaeology of the post-1550 centuries have been taken. Both the South West and London volumes incorporate a single chapter covering the post-medieval, industrial and modern eras. In contrast, other regions have adopted a two-chapter approach. In the West Midlands volume, the era is divided into the earlier post-medieval period and later post-medieval period, while the East Midlands had post-medieval and modern chapters, and the North West post-medieval and industrial chapters. Yet this diversity of approach and nomenclature hides many common themes from region to region, which would help in identifying suitable areas for the Manchester Methodology approach. The fact that we can even begin to contemplate such a research project is a testament to the way in which the recording of industries and the development of a variety of theoretical approaches to the era of industrialisation have grown in the last decade.

RECONCILING PEOPLE AND MACHINES: INTERPRETIVE ARCHAEOLOGIES

With such a range of approaches to the era of industrialisation is there really a need for the continued tensions between those more interested in technology than landscape, and those more interested in social context than in industry? After all, different data sets can be analysed in different ways. Take, for instance, the example of textile mill distribution and their potential meanings around Manchester. Between the mid-18th century and 1926, 1,617 textile mill sites (spinning, weaving and finishing), spanning the cotton, silk and wool branches of the industry, were built within the Manchester region (Greater Manchester).

In 1999 and 2002, Roger Holden published two articles that studied the distribution of later steam-powered textile mills in the Manchester area.[18] Holden noted that many post-1890, steam-powered mills were located beside water-courses, both canals and rivers, and most notably in mill towns such as Ashton-under-Lyne, Dukinfield and Stalybridge in Tameside, where the river Tame and the Ashton and Huddersfield canals ran side-by-side. His 1999 paper set out to examine why this was the case. That steam engines needed water for their boilers was well understood. Less well-known was the need for water for condensing. Most late-period mill engines condensed exhaust steam through the use of a jet of cold water; this produced a vacuum on the exhaust side of the piston, thus increasing the working pressure range and increasing the efficiency of the engine. Condensing water thus needed to be cold water and could not be recycled until it had been allowed to cool. In these late-period mills, the use of condenser water was roughly twenty-five times that required to feed the boilers. Thus, a 2,000hp engine, a size frequently found in mills built after 1900, would need roughly 1,300 gallons of condenser water per minute as opposed to around 52 gallons of boiler water per minute. Therefore, the best location for a later-period mill was by a large, fast-flowing, river where the condenser water could be taken from the river and returned without the worry of cooling it (Fig. 3.1).

Holden was able to demonstrate that late-period mills clustered along water-courses because of the need for a cold water supply for the engine condensers. If a river-side or canal-side location was not possible, then a reservoir or lodge would have to be built as some expense. At least one day's supply of water was needed, which in the later period could have amounted to a capacity of more than one million gallons, the water being left to cool overnight. One of the consequences of this requirement was that many late-period mills had more than one reservoir to allow for continuous production. It was not until the arrival of electric power that mills could be truly free of the topographical and technological constraints of the need for a water supply. In this case, a basic understanding of steam engineering and thermodynamic theory proved to be the key to understanding this late-period, water-side, mill distribution pattern in the Manchester region.

Figure 3.1 Cavendish Mill on the Ashton Canal in Ashton-under-Lyne, Tameside. A mill of 1884–5 built
beside a canal in order to provide water for its condensing steam engines

Using data from the other end of the date-range for mill-building in the Manchester area, I have spent the last few years studying the distribution of 18th-century textile mills. Of the 1,617 textile mills sites known to have been established within the Manchester region between the mid-18th century and 1926, 387, or 24 per cent, were built during the 18th century. Furthermore, the majority of these mills, 228, were cotton-spinning sites, followed by 53 wool-scribbling sites, 37 fulling mills, 58 finishing sites and 11 silk mills (Fig. 3.2).

A striking feature of this textile mill distribution pattern was its upland character; most of these mills could be found above 100m AOD in minor river valleys. Out of 387 mill sites, 288 or 74 per cent were concentrated in five areas: the modern boroughs of Bury, Rochdale, Oldham, Tameside, and Stockport which lie along the Pennine fringes to the north and east of the city of Manchester.[19] This area included nine minor upland river valleys: the Carrbrook, Castleshaw Brook, Cheesden Brook, Kirklees Brook, Mellor Brook, Micklehurst Brook, Naden Brook, the River Spadden and Strine Dale at the head of the Medlock, which supported six or more water-powered textile mills from the 18th century. Why should this distribution pattern be skewed towards the uplands in this way?

It is possible that the sources studied are at fault, and there is some evidence to suggest that the two county maps of the period, Burdett's map of Cheshire published in 1777 and Yates's map of Lancashire published in 1785, under-represented the number of 18th-century water-powered textile mills because of the dates when they were surveyed, namely, the

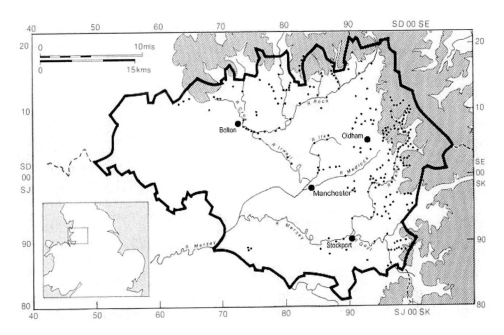

Figure 3.2 The distribution of 18th-century textile mills around Manchester

1770s and early 1780s. However, the other major sources for early textile mills, principally land-tax returns, insurance records, estate maps and newspaper advertisements, have been extensively searched across the whole region. It is unlikely that more than a handful of sites have been overlooked.

The answer to this puzzle is unlikely to be one of technology, since 18th-century water-wheel technology differed little between the cornmill, which could be found all over the North-West during this period, and the textile mill, which was not. Indeed, the gearing and line-shafting systems of the first mills drew heavily upon the technology employed in contemporary cornmills, which in North-West England were most common in the lowlands.[20] The two most likely conditioning factors are topographic and social constraints. A mill's water supply needed to be controlled before it reached the water-wheel, and this was done through a series of weirs, leats and reservoirs. Those parts of the landscape where it was easiest to build such features in the later 18th century were where there were no existing water-mills (such as cornmills) controlling the water-rights; in other words, in the more marginal upland areas around Manchester where grain growing was uncommon.

Furthermore, these areas of Bury, Rochdale, Oldham, Tameside and Stockport were where probate and estate records demonstrate that many upland farmers were acquiring surplus income from home-based textile manufacture earlier in the 18th century. This was in part reflected in the building of three-storey weaver's cottages in these areas during this period. There were thus many upland farmers both experienced in textile production and with money to invest. The fact that 387 textile mills were built in and around Manchester during the 18th century is a testament to the willingness of many of these individuals to invest in the new textile mill technology.

Thus, we might argue that the distribution of textile mills around Manchester during this period was defined by the equation MD = C + T over SC, where MD equals mill distribution, C equals capital, T equals technology and SC equals the social context. Or, to put it another way, mill distribution was conditioned by the availability of capital and access to appropriate technology, within in a social context that encouraged or at the very least did not penalise this kind of investment (Fig. 3.3).

Using this analogy, one wonders what the technological and social constraints restricting the distribution of Irish textile mills were during the same period. As Colin Rynne has noted, by the mid-19th century the linen textile mills of Ireland were confined mostly to the Ulster region of the island, but in the late 18th century had been more widespread with significant centres of mill production in Cork and Drogheda in the south and south-east.[21] A study of the distribution and investment patterns of these early mills might provide useful comparative data with the Manchester evidence, perhaps revealing whether similar constraints were at work.

What these two Manchester case studies demonstrate is that different interpretative frameworks will provide different answers from the same or similar sets of data. Neither answer will be wholly wrong, neither will be wholly right, but by acknowledging the role of technology, landscape and society our interpretations of the archaeological data will be more rounded in their conclusions. What this brief study of Manchester mill-distribution patterns demonstrates, therefore, is the application of interpretive archaeologies that might help us recover the motivations behind the industrialisation process at a local and regional level.

CONCLUSION: A SHARED RESEARCH AGENDA

Seventeen years on from the AIA's first wide-ranging research agenda and ten years on from the publication of Palmer & Neaverson's landmark field handbook *Industrial Archaeology: Principles and Practice*,[22] industrial archaeologists have developed a wide range of approaches

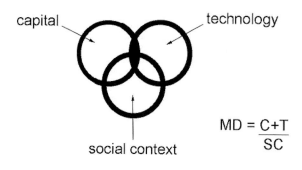

Figure 3.3 A diagram expressing the theoretical relationship between mill distribution, technology and social context

to the era of industrialisation. What these approaches provide is a research toolkit, a set of archaeological methodologies and theoretical approaches that can be applied to the archaeology of industrialisation across four broad areas of study, including (a) technological and economic; (b) social and landscape approaches; (c) industry-specific studies; and (d) site-specific surveys.

Some of these approaches concentrate wholly upon the recording of technology, others upon the landscape changes and social context. None is exclusive of the other; indeed, they work best when these issues are considered together. The *Understanding the Workplace* volume refined these areas further, suggesting nine broad topics where the archaeological study of the overlap between industry and people could be fruitfully pursued. These were: continuity and change; production and consumption; understanding the workplace; industrial settlement patterns; class, status and identity; social control, paternalism and philanthropy; the scientific analysis of artefacts and industrial residues; historic landscape characterisation; and the international context of industrialisation.

It should be clear from the above discussion and from these approaches that industrial archaeology in the early 21st century has not turned its back on the understanding and recording of technology. This practice remains central to the discipline. Rather, industrial archaeology has evolved to include a wider discussion of the impact of technological change on the landscape and on contemporary social structures. The publication of the *Understanding the Workplace* volume should not be seen as a strait-jacket within which industrial archaeologists are required to work, but rather as suggested research themes that complement the continuing study and recording of the manufacturing processes and power systems that lead the industrialisation process. Such research agendas are meant to be part of a continuing discussion within the discipline; sharing ideas, aims and interests, while acknowledging that individual researchers have always had and will continue to have their own areas of interest.

Therefore, for some industrial archaeologists to advocate concentrating wholly on the study of technology is to limit the debate and our research of the period by ignoring the individuals who built and ran the machines, those who used the technology, and the landscape and social impact of technological change that is one of the key features of the Industrial Revolution. Equally, we need to understand the technological changes of this period so that we can understand the wider context of the industrialisation process. Therefore, the current debate should not be about whether we should do these things and whether this is truly industrial archaeology, but how well we understand the interconnection between machine and landscape, society and technological change; an understanding that Tom Rolt, the founding father of Industrial Archaeology, first began.

NOTES

1. Palmer 1991; Crossley 1990. The current chapter has developed from conversations with most of the parties involved in the debate in the pages of *Industrial Archaeology News*.
2. Nevell 2006.
3. *Industrial Archaeology News* 136 (Spring 2006) to 143 (Winter 2007).
4. Gwyn & Palmer 2005.
5. Fitzgerald 2007a & b.
6. Fitzgerald 2007a, 51.
7. Palmer 2005, 11.
8. *Industrial Archaeology News* 136, 18.
9. Nevell 2005 & 2006; Palmer & Neaverson 1998; Palmer 2005.
10. Gwyn & Palmer 2005, 13.
11. Tarlow 2007.
12. Gwyn & Palmer 2005, 11–13.
13. Nevell 2005.
14. Johnson 1996 & 1999.
15. Nevell & Walker 2004.
16. Gwyn & Palmer 2005.
17. Details of these publications can be found on English Heritage's website.
18. Holden 1999 & 2003.
19. Nevell 2008.
20. Rynne 2006, 222–8.
21. Rynne 2006, 206; Rynne 2007, 250–8.
22. Palmer & Neaverson 1998.

BIBLIOGRAPHY

Crossley, D.W. 1990, *Post-Medieval Archaeology in Britain*. Leicester: University of Leicester Press.

Fitzgerald, R. 2007a, 'Historic building record and the Halifax Borough Market Doors', *Industrial Archaeology Review* **29**:1, 51–74.

Fitzgerald, R. 2007b, 'The Stone Dam Mill engine house', *Industrial Archaeology Review* **29**:2, 115–31.

Gwyn, D. & Palmer, M. 2005 (eds), *Understanding the Workplace. A Research Framework for Industrial Archaeology in Britain* (special issue), *Industrial Archaeology Review* **27**:1.

Holden, R. 1999, 'Water supplies for steam-powered textile mills', *Industrial Archaeology Review* **21**:1, 41–51.

Holden, R. 2003, 'Some cotton mills and their water supplies', *Industrial Archaeology North West* **3**, 20–2.

Johnson, M. 1996, *An Archaeology of Capitalism*. Oxford: Blackwell.

Johnson, M. 1999, 'The new post-medieval archaeology', in Egan, G. & Michael, R.L. (eds), *Old and New Worlds*. Oxford: Oxbow Books.

Nevell, M. 2005, 'Industrialisation, ownership, and the Manchester Methodology: the role of the contemporary social structure during industrialisation, 1600–1900', in Gwyn & Palmer (eds), 2005, 87–96.

Nevell, M. 2006, 'The 2005 Rolt Memorial Lecture: Industrial archaeology or the archaeology of the industrial period? Models, methodology and the future of industrial archaeology', *Industrial Archaeology Review* **28**:1, 3–16.

Nevell, M. 2008, 'The archaeology of industrialisation and the textile industry: the example of Manchester and the south-western Pennine uplands during the 18th century (Part 1)', *Industrial Archaeology Review* **30**:1, 33–48.

Nevell, M. & Walker, J. 2004, 'Industrialisation in the countryside: the roles of the lord, freeholder and tenant in the Manchester area 1600–1900', in Barker, D. & Cranstone, D. (eds), *The Archaeology of Industrialisation*. Leeds: Maney, 53–78.

Palmer, M. 1991, *Industrial Archaeology: Working for the Future*. Ironbridge: Association for Industrial Archaeology.

Palmer, M. & Neaverson P. 1998, *Industrial Archaeology: Principles and Practice*. London: Routledge.

Rynne, C. 2006, *Industrial Ireland 1750–1930: An Archaeology*. Cork: Collins Press.

Rynne, C. 2007, 'The archaeology of power and industry', in Horning, A., Ó Baoill, R., Donnelly, C. & Logue, P. (eds), *The Post-Medieval Archaeology of Ireland, 1550–1850*. Bray: Wordwell, 241–62.

Tarlow, S. 2007, *The Archaeology of Improvement in Britain, 1750–1850*. Cambridge: Cambridge University Press.

A Review of the Archaeological Contribution to the Understanding of the Industrial Past

By SHANE GOULD

This chapter considers how advances in archaeological method and theory over the past twenty years have enhanced the academic understanding of the remains from the industrial past. It examines the period 1750 to date, with an emphasis very much on what is traditionally termed 'industrial archaeology', while taking into account the broader social landscape that emerged during the so-called industrial revolution period. The emphasis is very much on heritage management and, in particular, the way in which planning related work is contributing to current research agendas. The focus is centred on England, but many of the themes discussed will be of wider relevance throughout the United Kingdom and further afield.

NATIONAL AGENCIES AND THE PRACTICE OF INDUSTRIAL ARCHAEOLOGY

Having emerged from the voluntary sector in the 1960s, the international importance of Britain's industrial heritage was increasingly recognised by national bodies during the 1990s. Through the work of national agencies, including the former Royal Commission on the Historical Monuments of England, extensive research volumes have been produced for important categories of building that became widespread during the 18th, 19th and 20th century, including textile mills, potteries, farmsteads, workhouses, hospitals and prisons.[1] In some cases, the research has moved beyond the specific site-type to consider the broader social landscape of settlement by describing housing provision, religious institutions, schools and the supporting infrastructure. This is best exemplified in a publication on the Swindon Railway Works and, in Wales, by the research on the copper refineries of the Swansea area.[2] In England, the findings from these surveys were often used by English Heritage to enhance the statutory list of buildings of special architectural or historic interest where the list was under-represented. This can be seen in the thematic listing programme for Manchester textile mills undertaken in the mid-1990s.[3]

English Heritage also initiated the Monuments Protection Programme (MPP), which from 1992 dramatically increased the number of industrial sites that were afforded statutory protection primarily through scheduling.[4] Using its 'Step' approach, the MPP began with a research report (Step 1), which considered the existing state of knowledge, the research gaps and put forward priorities for management, designation and research. Not only did the MPP result in a significant increase in the number of protected monuments, in many cases it provided for the first time a national statement for the industry in terms of physical remains and enhanced the evidence base for the management of the resource at a local level. Step 1 Reports have been completed for twenty-three industries and the national site assessments are set out in eighteen Step 3 Reports (Table 4.1), but this work was curtailed when resources were diverted to the delivery of the government's reform of the heritage protection system.[5] English Heritage is now piloting the use of SHIERS (Strategy for the Historic Industrial Environment Reports) as an alternative. These aim to inform English Heritage and others in the management of industrial sites by providing a framework for the stewardship of the surviving resource. SHIERS have been completed for maltings and are currently being prepared for engineering works, breweries, cranes and nuclear installations.[6]

More recently, English Heritage initiated a series of publications under the general title of 'Informed Conservation', which consider a particular area, its buildings, landscapes and their future conservation. Often prepared in partnership with a local planning authority, nine volumes have been produced on distinctive industrial districts or building types within a town or region. They include Northamptonshire's boot and shoe industry, the buildings of the Sheffield metal trades, and the flax and hemp industry of Bridport, while others are in preparation.[7]

A number of local authorities have also been enhancing their information base, the Historic Environment Record, by carrying out local surveys of poorly understood site-types or those that are thought to be particularly at risk. Such surveys include an examination of glassworks in Dudley, of Cornish engine houses, and of maltings and workhouses in Essex.[8] By understanding the surviving resource and establishing future priorities, these surveys help in the conservation and management of sites through the planning framework.

Table 4.1

MONUMENTS PROTECTION PROGRAMME INDUSTRY REPORTS

The Step 1 Reports provide overviews of each industry, whilst Step 3 Reports contain the list of sites that were assessed with recommendations for management and possible statutory protection. The completed Step 1 and 3 Reports are available for consultation at the National Monuments Record (Swindon), the Council for British Archaeology (York), Leicester University and the Institute for Industrial Archaeology (Ironbridge).

Completed Step 1 Reports:

Alum, arsenic, brass, chemicals, clay, coal & coke works, copper, dovecotes, electricity production, gas, glass, gunpowder, icehouses, iron & steel, lead, lime-burning, minor metals, oil, salt, stone, tin, water supply, zinc.

Completed Step 3 Reports:

Alum, arsenic, brass, coal, copper, dovecotes, electricity production, glass, gunpowder, icehouses, iron & steel, lead, lime-burning, minor metals, stone, tin, water supply, zinc.

The 1995 University of Leicester monograph, *Managing the Industrial Heritage* provides a useful overview of this significant body of work with contributions from the key statutory agencies.[9] The publication marked an important threshold in the development and growing maturity of industrial heritage management, but a number of authors raised questions over the direction of industrial archaeology, with its emphasis on sites of production and an apparent absence of any corresponding analysis of the social dimensions of industrialisation and its material manifestations.[10] A key criticism was that the subject, unlike other archaeological sub-disciplines, lacked an academic research framework; a framework that was not only rooted in the functionalist tradition, but moved beyond the factory gates to consider the social and political dimension of the physical remains and what they can tell us about the past.

INDUSTRIAL ARCHAEOLOGY AND THE ENGLISH PLANNING SYSTEM

During the 1990s, there was also a significant change in the way the historic environment was managed within the English planning process, following the introduction of *Planning Policy Guidance Note 16: Archaeology and Planning* (PPG16), and *Planning Policy Guidance Note 15: Planning and the Historic Environment* (PPG15).[11] Local planning authorities were now able to request that developers provide sufficient information to understand the possible impact of their proposals on the significance of a heritage asset and, where necessary, implement a mitigation strategy to offset any damaging affects arising from that development. This has created a multi-million-pound industry of historic environment consultants and contractors who offer their services to developers to address these planning requirements.

The introduction of PPG15 and 16 took place at a time when there was a growing interest among local authority archaeology and historic buildings conservation officers in the management of the industrial past, leading to a marked increase in the number of industrial sites that have been assessed and recorded through the development control process. The techniques involve historic building and area assessment, conservation plans and statements, historic building records, and archaeological evaluations, excavations and watching briefs. When programmed at the right time and when the resulting information is of an appropriate standard, this process will lead to better conservation outcomes, while enhancing the existing body of knowledge for a particular building, site or area.

For example, the residential conversion of the redundant Grade II-listed Coggeshall Brewery in Essex was shaped and informed by an independent assessment of its significance.[12] This assessment resulted in revisions to the original proposals to incorporate many of the surviving fixtures and fittings and the creation of a detailed record of a small 19th-century brewery. A copy of the assessment report was deposited in the Historic Environment Record and is publicly available. Similarly, discussions on the reuse of Perran Foundry in Cornwall were guided by the preparation of a conservation plan that was submitted as part of the application.[13] Having gained planning and listed building consent, a detailed programme of historic building investigation and recording, together with carefully targeted archaeological excavation, will be implemented to fine-tune the designs, with the programme based on an explicit research design. In both cases, it was necessary to understand the technology of these industries, particularly the supply of power, and how this technology was reflected in the surviving fabric. The analysis also benefited from the preparation of process flow diagrams, which spatially demonstrated the movement of materials around the site and illuminated the functional relationships between the buildings and individual rooms.

Traditional techniques of below-ground archaeological investigation are also helping to understand industrial sites and processes. Although much of this work is still in its infancy, the potential contribution of archaeological recording is becoming readily apparent as shown by recent evaluations and excavations on iron and steel works in Sheffield, glass works in Manchester and the Black Country, and waggonways in the North-East. In the case of the latter, there had been no archaeological information on their construction until the work in 1995 at Lampton D Pit, which was followed by a number of further excavations improving the understanding of waggonway form and function.[14]

In order to encourage good practice English Heritage has published a range of specific and generic advice and guidance including *Science for Historic Industries* (see Bayley, Dungworth, and Paynter, this volume), which describes the methods and techniques for evaluating and

Table 4.2

REGIONAL RESEARCH FRAMEWORKS
North West
Completed and published
North East
Completed and published
Yorkshire
Resource Assessment and Agenda in progress
West Midlands
Resource Assessment and Agenda publication in progress
East Midlands
Resource Assessment and Agenda published. Strategy in progress
Eastern England
Completed and published. Updated Strategy in progress
London
Resource Assessment and Agenda published. Strategy in progress
Greater Thames Estuary
Completed and published. Updated Strategy in progress
South East (Thames-Solent)
Resource Assessment and Agenda in progress
South East (Kent)
Resource Assessment and Agenda in progress
South West
Research Framework at publication stage

excavating 17th- to 19th-century industrial sites together with the role of archaeological science.[15] Industrial summaries are provided for five industries that are often encountered on archaeological sites to help shape future work and sampling strategies; namely, the glass, iron, pottery, tanning and textile industries. Another key publication is *Understanding Historic Buildings: A Guide to Good Recording Practice*, which gives detailed advice on the approaches and techniques for the recording, analysis and interpretation of historic buildings, including those from the industrial period. This publication is accompanied by a companion document, *Understanding Historic Buildings: Policy and Guidance for Local Planning Authorities*, which promotes the importance of historic building investigation and recording within the English planning framework.[16]

THE ROLE OF RESEARCH FRAMEWORKS

Much of the above-described advice and guidance was produced to raise standards in response to growing concerns within the historic environment sector over the variability and quality of the work resulting from the development control process through the application of PPG15 and 16. Given the substantial growth in the number of unpublished reports, or grey literature, being produced by consultants and contractors, it is extremely difficult to gain an overview of its quality, academic rigour and contribution to the existing research base. In 1996, English Heritage published *Frameworks for Our Past: A Review of Research Frameworks, Strategies and Perceptions*, which subsequently developed into a national programme where research frameworks are produced, at a regional level and for particular periods or themes, to help guide and focus the work undertaken through PPG15 and 16.[17] Local authority historic environment advisers, consultants and contractors, and the voluntary sector have been closely involved in preparing regional research frameworks. Although these framework documents all include sections on the historic industrial environment, there has yet to be a national synthesis of their content or a critical assessment of how the research agendas and strategies are actually helping to shape the work undertaken within the planning system (Table 4.2).

As part of this process, the Association for Industrial Archaeology updated its 1991 statement, *Industrial Archaeology: Working for the Future*, by the publication in 2005 of *Understanding the Workplace: A Research Framework for Industrial Archaeology in Britain*.[18] With its emphasis on the wider context of industrialisation this has been criticised in some quarters for moving away from what was seen as the traditional focus of industrial archaeology, as discussed by David Gwyn in chapter 2 of this volume. To reiterate, since the late 1990s there has been a growing debate over the definition, scope and the very term 'industrial archaeology' between those who feel its roots lie in the history of technology and engineering, and those who advocate a broader social approach.

In a sense, such a debate is rather anodyne as both aspects are needed if the discipline is to move forward. The investigation and analysis of former industrial sites requires skills over and beyond those normally acquired through traditional archaeological practice, which includes an understanding of the history of technology, engineering and metallurgy. When faced with the empty shell of an industrial building, the excavated remains of machine bases or process residues, these specialist skills are essential. However, industrial sites did not operate in a social vacuum, and equal weight should be given to the people who once worked there and whose lives are reflected in the material remains. The manufactory was only one element of much wider landscape and technological changes during the 18th and 19th centuries that not only transformed industry, but also the society within it. Of course, this recognition is nothing new. A number of the publications cited above also consider the broader relationship between industry and settlement, or describe important building types that became widespread during this period, but are not 'industrial' in their character.[19]

THE APPLICATION OF ARCHAEOLOGICAL THEORY TO THE INDUSTRIAL PAST

The publications noted above overcame some of the criticisms put forward by contributors to *Managing the Industrial Heritage* who felt that the focus of industrial archaeology needed to consider the wider aspects of industrialisation as well as sites of manufacture.[20] However, in their consideration of the buildings, settlements and landscapes, the authors of these volumes often describe the remains as passive and the analysis rarely moves beyond a functionalist interpretation. There is no consideration of the wider social processes that were at play and how this is manifested in the material record – changing class relationships and the emergence of a capitalist society, power, politics and ideology, the growth of urbanism, religion, and the role of the family and gender. Such theoretical perspectives that acknowledge the dynamic property of the physical remains are common in archaeological interpretations of the more distant past and in the work on 18th- and 19th- century sites in the New World.

The progress of the subject at the turn of the millennium was recently described, albeit from a functionalist position, in *Perspectives on Industrial Archaeology*,[21] whereas a number of other publications and articles have started to show a growing interest in the application of archaeological theory to the interpretation of industrial period sites in England. They include *The Familiar Past? Archaeologies of Later Historical Britain*; *The Archaeology of Industrialization*; *Industrial Archaeology: Future Directions*; and, most recently, *The Cambridge Companion to Historical Archaeology*.[22] This is very much an emerging field, but it demonstrates how the academic basis of the subject is developing with the adoption of an explicit body of theoretical inquiry. However, very often the models presented cannot be easily translated into raising standards or determining future priorities for the work undertaken through the planning process. It also represents a worrying disconnection between the theory and practice within industrial archaeology.

The following example demonstrates how social theory can be employed to enhance the practice of industrial archaeology and improve standards in the recording of sites through the planning process. The Industrial and Agricultural School at Brentwood, Essex, was erected in 1854 for pauper children, and when a planning application was submitted for its demolition, a recording condition was attached to the permission. It would have been a simple exercise to undertake a basic architectural survey, but the historic environment contractor was also asked to consider the spatial configuration within the school and how its design and layout reflected the thinking behind the 1834 New Poor Law. The building was located away from the main settlement in an elevated position and would have appeared imposing to all those who approached it (Fig. 4.1). This was a new building type that appeared in the landscape

Figure 4.1 Brentwood Industrial and Agricultural School, Essex. Most of the administrative functions were located within the front range; the masters' accommodation lay within the central gabled block, while the committee room stands to the left (AOC Archaeology)

and whose very presence was meant to act as a deterrent. The school adopted a strict spatial division between those areas occupied by staff and children, which was further reinforced in the position of staircases and the interior decoration. The presence of a ceramic frieze of Psalm 23, The Lord is My Shepherd, uncovered within the dining room, and iron risers on the staircase balustrade to prevent children using them as slides set the moral tone for the establishment. In the longer term, barrack schools were regarded as a failure by producing children who were poorly adjusted to cope with the outside world, and later alterations to the site thus reflect changing attitudes to the provision of child care. The analysis and interpretation of the Brentwood School greatly benefited from the preparation of spatial maps and permeability diagrams showing the movement and deliberate segregation of staff and children within the building (Fig. 4.2). Such an analysis would not have been possible from the fragmentary documentary record alone.[23]

This approach was continued and further developed in the investigation and analysis of a large number of former hospitals and schools in Essex, which became redundant from the late 1990s onwards. They included workhouses, psychiatric institutions, and general, specialist and cottage hospitals. Through this substantial body of work, it is now possible to examine in considerable detail the implications of the introduction of the New Poor Law and general health provision in terms of the surviving built fabric. Drawing on the national publications by the former Royal Commission on the Historical Monuments of England and English Heritage,[24] whose emphasis was very much on architectural form and function, these surveys also considered how ideas of status, display, movement, segregation and control were reflected in the physical fabric. All this recording was undertaken through the planning process, funded by developers, with the reports made publicly available.

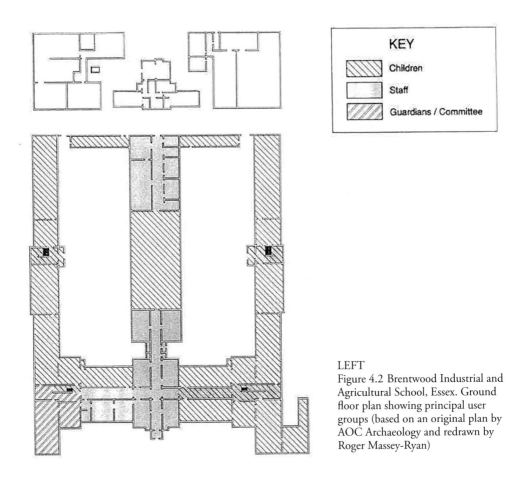

KEY

Children

Staff

Guardians / Committee

LEFT
Figure 4.2 Brentwood Industrial and
Agricultural School, Essex. Ground
floor plan showing principal user
groups (based on an original plan by
AOC Archaeology and redrawn by
Roger Massey-Ryan)

FUTURE PRIORITIES

Having undertaken this brief review, it can be seen that considerable progress has been made in the method and theory relating to the practice of industrial archaeology over the past twenty years. Improved techniques, together with a better understanding of the built and archaeological record, have enhanced the interpretation of sites of manufacture. Through the application of methods that draw on the history of technology, engineering and metallurgy, industrial archaeology is contributing to the existing state of knowledge on the functional understanding of these sites and how they developed through time. This may sometimes complement or even challenge established documentary narratives, while in some instances the data is being used to examine the adoption, spread or resistance to new technology, the concept of 'proto-industrialisation' and the ongoing debate over whether an 'industrial revolution' took place during the 18th and 19th centuries.

Progress is also being made in the understanding of the wider industrial landscape through the examination of non-industrial site-types and in the development, layout and social structure of settlement and landscape. Recent work on dwellings, for example, is providing valuable insights into the housing provision for different social classes, living conditions and the associated material culture. This is illustrated at Hungate in York where archaeological excavations are revealing important social information on the people who inhabited a large area of poor-quality 19th- and 20th-century working-class housing.[25]

Perhaps it is in the application of archaeological theory to the industrial past that more work needs to be done. The subject now has a developing body of theoretical inquiry, which is moving the discipline beyond the traditional focus on production and functionalist interpretation to acknowledge the dynamic property of the physical remains and what they can tell us about past human relationships. However, the archaeological contribution to the social transformations that took place during the industrial revolution period is only just beginning.

CONCLUSION

The following five priorities are suggested for the management and conservation of the industrial heritage within the English planning framework.

The first priority must be training and capacity building. This needs to be improved at all levels from those who are taking decisions on planning applications, to the consultants and contractors undertaking the work, and to the graduates and postgraduates entering the profession.

Second, there is a need for continuing improvements in methodology. Techniques for the evaluation of industrial sites are steadily improving, but this is a developing field. Similar improvements are needed in historic building investigation and recording, especially in the understanding of technology and process flows. The information will help in establishing the significance of these sites and in producing better conservation outcomes.

Third, research must remain an important priority. There has been a significant expansion of developer-funded work, but it is extremely difficult to access the resulting grey literature, to assess its quality and contribution to the existing research base. A review of regional research frameworks together with a meaningful sample of the grey literature would help to address this, while more should be done to encourage the synthesis and wider dissemination of the information. The results from a number of planning related investigations have recently been examined in the publication on Murray's Mill, Ancoats, which considers the proto-history of the steam-driven textile mill, and further examples that draw together the results from grey literature reports into a meaningful analysis are needed.[26]

Fourth, there needs to be a greater awareness of and attention to the 20th century. Only fleeting references have been made to the remains from the 20th century, which tend to be poorly studied and are at major risk from redevelopment. Techniques need to be established for the understanding and recording of these sites in order to establish future priorities. The Contemporary and Historical Archaeology in Theory Conference Group (CHAT) has begun to address some of these issues,[27] while the English Heritage contribution to this debate is described in its Change and Creation programme, the *Images of Change* publication, and a recent issue of the *Conservation Bulletin*.[28]

Fifth, and finally, there needs to be a greater connection between the theory and practice of industrial archaeology. Most of the work is now undertaken through the planning process, with considerable sums being spent each year on the investigation and recording of sites. Priorities need to be established at all levels within the discipline to focus this work, and although research frameworks have been established for particular industries and themes they are by no means complete. However, perhaps the greatest challenge is to consider how archaeological method and theory can make a meaningful contribution in understanding the technological, economic and social transformations that took place during the industrial revolution period and to ensure that the work undertaken within the planning framework is focused with these research questions in mind. Such a development would involve all sectors – the academics, the local authority curators, and the consultants and contractors – working in partnership to ensure that the investigation and recording of sites undertaken in response to the planning process has a clear research focus. Without such a focus, there is a real risk that when sites become threatened with imminent destruction, the research questions are academically inadequate or at worst, are not posed at all.

ACKNOWLEDGEMENTS

The following friends and colleagues provided information and comment during the preparation of this chapter: Peter Boland, Graham Fairclough, Keith Falconer, Nick Johnson and Steve Trow.

NOTES

1. Barker 1991; Barnwell & Giles 1997; Brodie, Croom & Davies 2002; Calladine & Fricker 1993; Giles & Goodall 1992; Morrison 1999; Richardson 1998; Williams & Farnie 1992.
2. Cattell & Falconer 1995; Hughes 2000.
3. English Heritage 1995.
4. English Heritage 2000; Dungworth & Paynter 2006; Stocker 1995.
5. Department for Culture, Media and Sport & Welsh Assembly Government 2007; Department for Culture, Media and Sport 2008.
6. SHIERS (Strategy for the Historic Industrial Environment Reports) are to be made publicly available on the English Heritage website: <http://www.english-heritage.org.uk.html>.
7. Morrison & Bond 2004; Wray, Hawkins & Giles 2001; Williams 2006.
8. Boland 1995; Gould 2001; Sharpe, Lewis, Massie & Johnson 1991.
9. Palmer & Neaverson 1995.
10. Clark 1995; Gould 1995.
11. Department of the Environment 1990; Department of the Environment & Department of National Heritage 1994.
12. Cooper-Reade 1996.
13. Boyd-Brent & Filmer-Sankey 2005.
14. Ayris, Nolan & Durkin 1998.
15. Dungworth & Paynter 2006.
16. English Heritage 2006; 2008.
17. Olivier 1996.
18. Palmer 1991; Gwyn & Palmer 2005.
19. Barnwell & Giles 1997; Brodie, Croom & Davies 2002; Cattell & Falconer 1995; Hughes 2000; Morrison 1999; Morrison & Bond 2004; Richardson 1998; Williams 2006.
20. Clark 1995; Gould 1995.
21. Cossons 2000.
22. Barker & Cranstone 2004; Casella & Symonds 2005; Tarlow & West 1999; Hicks & Beaudry 2006.
23. Upson 1998.

24. Morrison 1999; Richardson 1998.
25. *Yorkshire Archaeology Today.*
26. Miller & Wild 2008.

27. http://www.bris.ac.uk/archanth/events/chat.html
28. Bradley, Buchli, Fairclough, Hicks, Miller & Schofield 2004; Penrose 2007; *Conservation Bulletin* 2007.

BIBLIOGRAPHY

Ayris, I.M., Nolan, J. & Durkin, A. 1998, 'The archaeological excavation of wooden waggonway remains at Lampton D Pit, Sunderland', *Industrial Archaeology Review.* **20**, 5–22.

Barker, D. 1991, *Potworks: The Industrial Architecture of the Staffordshire Potteries.* London: Royal Commission on the Historical Monuments of England.

Barker, D. & Cranstone, D. (eds) 2004, *The Archaeology of Industrialization.* Leeds: Maney.

Barnwell, P.S. & Giles, C. 1997, *English Farmsteads, 1750–1914.* Swindon: Royal Commission on the Historical Monuments of England.

Boland, P. 1995, 'Case study: the identification and preservation of the industrial archaeology of the Black Country', in Palmer & Neaverson (eds), 1995, 91–5.

Bradley, A., Buchli, V., Fairclough, G., Hicks, D., Miller, J. & Schofield, J. 2004, *Change and Creation: Historic Landscape Character 1950–2000.* London: English Heritage.

Brodie, A., Croom, J. & Davies, J.O. 2002, *English Prisons: An Architectural History.* Swindon: English Heritage.

Calladine, A. & Fricker, J. 1993, *East Cheshire Textile Mills.* London: Royal Commission on the Historical Monuments of England.

Casella, E.C. & Symonds, S. (eds) 2005, *Industrial Archaeology: Future Directions.* New York: Springer.

Cattell, J. & Falconer, K. 1995, *Swindon: The Legacy of a Railway Town.* London: Royal Commission on the Historical Monuments of England.

Clark, C. 1995, 'Ticking boxes or telling stories? The archaeology of industrial landscapes', in Palmer & Neaverson (eds), 1995, 45–8.

Conservation Bulletin – Modern Times 2007, **56**.

Cossons, N. (ed.) 2000, *Perspectives on Industrial Archaeology.* London: Science Museum.

Department for Culture, Media and Sport & Welsh Assembly Government 2007, *Heritage Protection for the 21st Century.* London: Department for Culture, Media and Sport.

Department for Culture, Media and Sport 2008, *Draft Heritage Protection Bill.* London: TSO.

Department of the Environment 1990, *Planning Policy Guidance 16: Archaeology and Planning.* London: HMSO.

Department of the Environment & Department of National Heritage 1994, *Planning Policy Guidance 15: Planning and the Historic Environment,* London: HMSO.

Dungworth, D. & Paynter, S. 2006, *Science for Historic Industries: Guidelines for the Investigation of 17th- to 19th-Century Industries.* Swindon: English Heritage. http://www.helm.org.uk/upload/pdf/Science-Historic-Industries.pdf

English Heritage 1995, *Manchester Mills: Understanding Listing.* London: English Heritage.

English Heritage 2000, *MPP 2000: A review of the Monuments Protection Programme, 1986–2000.* London: English Heritage.

English Heritage 2006, *Understanding Historic Buildings: A Guide to Good Recording Practice.* London: English Heritage.

English Heritage 2008, *Understanding Historic Buildings: Policy and Guidance for Local Planning Authorities.* London: English Heritage.

Giles, C. & Goodall, I.H. 1992, *Yorkshire Textile Mills 1770–1930.* London: Royal Commission on the Historical Monuments of England and West Yorkshire Archaeology Service.

Gould, S. 1995, 'Industrial archaeology and the neglect of humanity', in Palmer & Neaverson (eds), 1995, 49–53.

Gould, S. 2001, 'The identification, recording and management of the more recent archaeological and architectural heritage of Essex', *Industrial Archaeology Review* **23**(1), 11–24.

Gwyn, D. & Palmer, M. 2005 (eds), *Understanding the Workplace: A Research Framework for Industrial Archaeology in Britain* (special issue), *Industrial Archaeology Review* **27**:1.

Hicks, D. & Beaudry, M.C. (eds) 2006, *The Cambridge Companion to Historical Archaeology*. Cambridge: Cambridge University Press.

Hughes, S. 2000, *Copperopolis: Landscapes of the Early Industrial Period in Swansea*. Aberystwyth: Royal Commission on the Ancient and Historical Monuments of Wales.

Miller, I. & Wild, C. with contributions from Little, S., McNeil, R. & Moth, K. 2008, *A & G Murray and the Cotton Mills of Ancoats*. Oxford: Oxford Archaeology.

Morrison, K. 1999, *The Workhouse: A Study of Poor-Law Buildings in England*. Swindon: English Heritage.

Morrison, K. & Bond, A. 2004, *Built to Last? The Buildings of the Northamptonshire Boot and Shoe Industry*. Swindon: English Heritage.

Olivier, A. 1996, *Frameworks for Our Past: A Review of Research Frameworks, Strategies and Perceptions*. London: English Heritage.

Palmer, M. 1991, *Industrial Archaeology: Working for the Future*. Ironbridge: Association for Industrial Archaeology.

Palmer, M. & Neaverson, P. (eds) 1995, *Managing the Industrial Heritage*, Leicester Archaeology Monograph **2**. Leicester: University of Leicester Press.

Penrose, S. 2007, *Images of Change: An Archaeology of England's Contemporary Landscape*. Swindon: English Heritage.

Richardson, H. (ed.) 1998, *English Hospitals 1660–1948*. Swindon: Royal Commission on the Historical Monuments of England.

Sharpe, S., Lewis, R., Massie, C. & Johnson, N. 1991, *Engine House Assessment: Mineral Tramways Project*. Truro: Cornwall Archaeological Unit, Cornwall County Council.

Stocker, D. 1995, 'Industrial archaeology and the Monuments Protection Programme in England', in Palmer & Neaverson (eds), 1995, 105–13.

Tarlow, S. & West, S. (eds) 1999, *The Familiar Past? Archaeologies of Later Historical Britain*. London: Routledge.

Williams, M. 2006, *Bridport and West Bay: The Buildings of the Flax and Hemp Industry*. Swindon: English Heritage.

Williams, M. & Farnie, D.A. 1992, *Cotton Mills in Greater Manchester*. Preston: The Greater Manchester Archaeological Unit in association with the Royal Commission on the Historical Monuments of England.

Wray, N., Hawkins, B. & Giles, C. 2001, *'One Great Workshop': The Buildings of the Sheffield Metal Trades*. Swindon: English Heritage.

Yorkshire Archaeology Today. 2007, **12**.

UNPUBLISHED SOURCES

Boyd-Brent, J. & Filmer-Sankey, W. 2005, *Perran Foundry Conservation Plan*, Alan Baxter & Associates.

Cooper-Reade, H. 1996, *Report on the Recording and Survey of Gardners' Brewery, Bridge Street, Coggeshall, Essex*, Essex County Council Field Archaeology Group.

Upson, A. 1998, *St Faiths Hospital, London Road, Brentwood, Essex: Historic Building Record*, AOC Archaeology.

REGIONAL RESEARCH FRAMEWORKS

NORTH WEST

<http://www.liverpoolmuseums.org.uk/mol/archaeology/arf/html>

NORTH EAST

<http://www.durham.gov.uk/durhamcc/usp.nsf/pws/A4A17A5B36B6B9D58025724
2003F61D0?opendocument.html>

WEST MIDLANDS

<http//www.arch-ant.bham.ac.uk/research/fieldwork_research_themes/projects/
wmrrfa/intro.html>

EAST MIDLANDS

<http://www.le.ac.uk/ar/research/projects/eastmidsfw/index.html>

EASTERN ENGLAND

<http://www.eaareports.demon.co.uk.html>

LONDON

<http://www.museumoflondonarchaeology.org.uk/English/ArchiveResearch/
Researchstrat.html>

GREATER THAMES ESTUARY

<http://www.thamesweb.com/page.php?page_id=63&topic_id=10.html>

SOUTH EAST (THAMES–SOLENT)

<http://www.buckscc.gov.uk/bcc/content/index.jsp?contentid=-222423834.html>

SOUTH EAST (KENT)

<http://www.kent.gov.uk/environment/our-environment/kents-heritage/south-east-
research-framework.html>

SOUTH WEST

<http://www.somerset.gov.uk/somerset/cultureheritage/heritage/swarf.html>

The Research Framework page on the Association of Local Government Archaeological Officers (ALGAO UK) website also contains useful information:

<http://www.algao.org.uk/Association/England/Regions/ResFwks.html>

Twenty Years A'growing: University-based Teaching and Research of Historical Archaeology on the Island of Ireland

By COLIN BREEN

From relatively humble beginnings the subject area of historical archaeology has become established within a number of university archaeology departments on the island of Ireland. This has been largely facilitated by the work of a number of individuals and more recently by the establishment of the Irish Post-Medieval Archaeology Group (IPMAG). This chapter examines the current situation with regard to teaching provision and aspects of research, and addresses a number of issues effecting the future sustainable development of the subject.

INTRODUCTION

The title of this chapter borrows from Muiris Ó Súilleabháin's 1933 *Twenty Years A-Growing*,[1] which details life on the Blasket Islands off the south-west coast of Ireland. It was a reflection and personal memoir of the growth of community and a commentary on then-contemporary island lifeways. This short piece is a similar personal reflection on the emergence and subsequent development of post-medieval or historical archaeology on the island of Ireland and an overview from a university perspective of where the subject stands today. It must be stressed that this piece represents a snapshot in time of the state of the subject and is likely to be dated within a year or two. Nevertheless, it is valuable to begin develop a retrospective view at this important juncture, given that historical archaeology will develop further in new and exciting ways over the coming years. One quick comment is also probably required here about terminology. The descriptor historical archaeology is preferred over that of post-medieval archaeology. The latter has been used more prevalently in Ireland, following British practice, but it is clear that archaeologists in Ireland do not confine either their practice or research in random chronologies or date frameworks that pre- or post-date arbitrary dates; for example, after 1550 or 1600. The term historical archaeology appears therefore to be more inclusive and representative of the profession and archaeological record in Ireland.

SUBJECT DEVELOPMENT

The emergence of research in historical archaeology on the island of Ireland can be traced back to the early Spanish Armada shipwreck excavations undertaken by Colin Martin and others in the late 1960s and 1970s.[2] During the same period, Tom Delaney began a series of important rescue excavations at Carrickfergus in 1970s,[3] while Nick Brannon initiated a number of innovative investigations on a series of post-medieval sites across Northern Ireland.[4] The universities took little note of this work and were far slower to participate. It is interesting to compare the current situation with that of medieval archaeology in the 1970s and early 1980s. It was only during those years that research and teaching of and about medieval remains and material culture became accepted practice, following the 1987 publication of Terry Barry's *Medieval Ireland*. Most archaeology of post-1600, with the possible exception of analysis of structures such as 'fortified houses' and some ceramic material, was excluded from university curricula. This situation remained unchanged until the late 1990s after a period of gradual enlightenment when a number of initiatives and individuals began to effect change.[5]

Somewhat subjectively, the 1999 establishment of the Centre for Maritime Archaeology at the University of Ulster is seen here as a pivotal moment, as was the subsequent appointment of a number of key individuals to posts at University College Cork (UCC), University College Dublin (UCD) and in a more short-lived post at the Queen's University of Belfast (QUB). Both UCC and UCD now have dedicated historical archaeology posts, two staff members at QUB have broad historical archaeology interests while two staff members at NUI,G have interests which extend well into the post-medieval period, although both would probably see themselves as medievalists. Three academic staff members at the Centre for Maritime Archaeology at the University of Ulster (UU) have strong historical archaeology profiles.

However, the key impetus for change came with the establishment of the Irish Post-Medieval Archaeology Group (IPMAG) in 1999, a cross-representative and all-island group of academics, government and museum archaeologists, professional archaeologists and the general public. A subsequent conference held at QUB in February 2001, entitled *The Archaeology of Post-Medieval Ireland 1550–1850*, was a formative event and the ensuing publication constitutes a landmark volume.[6] A series of important conferences have subsequently taken place, the publication of which will further advance the available reference material in this subject area.

UNIVERSITY COURSE PROVISION: HISTORICAL ARCHAEOLOGY

There are currently five full undergraduate degree programmes offered on the island of Ireland. Three BA programmes are offered at the National University of Ireland constituent colleges at Cork, Dublin and Galway. A further BSc in Applied Archaeology is offered at the Sligo Institute of Technology, while a BA in Heritage Studies is offered at the Galway/Mayo Institute of Technology. A combined history with archaeology degree is available at the University of Dublin, Trinity College. In Northern Ireland, QUB offers both a BA in Archaeology and a BSc in Archaeology and Palaeoecology. The themes of these degrees are, for the most part, broadly similar: firmly rooted in developing a strong practical and theoretical understanding of the archaeological record in Ireland within the broader context of Britain and North West Europe, while at the same time developing the core skills an archaeologist will require in a professional environment.

In terms of module or unit provision, historical archaeology is variously served in the different institutions. The Department of Archaeology at UCC offers four dedicated modules at an undergraduate level, placing particular emphasis on the development of settlement forms, economy, society and material culture in this period while also addressing urbanisation, industry and colonial theory at final-year level. The School of Archaeology at UCD offers two modules with a strong historical archaeological content as part of its undergraduate degree. In their first year students are introduced to European expansion and later use the archaeological record to examine identity in Ireland in the second millennium AD. Elsewhere, students at the archaeology department at NUI,G undertake a final year module examining Gaelic and colonial society in Ireland to AD 1650 through landscape, architectural and material cultural evidence within a defined theoretical framework. Year-two archaeology students at QUB undertake a module on Historic Ireland, studying the material remains of Ireland's inhabitants between the 5th and 17th centuries. Each of the above institutions also has a set of strong modules focused on the medieval period.

At a postgraduate level, there are currently two degree programmes on offer that offer specialisms in historical archaeology: an MA in Historical and Contemporary Archaeology at UCD and an MA in Architectural Heritage at UCC. At UCD, students take two specialised modules in post-medieval material culture and post-medieval buildings archaeology, while at UCC students are offered a module on the archaeology of buildings and a second on historic buildings evaluation, in which they examine conservation practice and the regulatory environment surrounding protection and investigation. Queen's students are briefly introduced to post-medieval landscapes and process in the School of Geography, Archaeology and Palaeoecology's landscape master's programme. It is unfortunate that the same school abandoned its plans to develop a full master's programme in historical archaeology. Two modules in maritime archaeology are taught at the University of Ulster in its MSc Maritime Archaeology (distance learning), which include maritime aspects of the historical period. They attempt to integrate both material culture, landscape approaches and theory but cover a very broad chronological period and do not necessarily belong in the above list. There remains a long-running aspiration to develop a master's programme in Historical Archaeology but as of yet the university has not formally moved on this.

GRADUATE RESEARCH

While the provision of historical archaeology teaching across the university spectrum is limited, there does appear to be far more engagement with the subject at a postgraduate research level. Table 5.1 is of note as it documents the number of what could be broadly termed historical archaeology master's dissertations submitted in the Department of Archaeology at UCC during the period 1995–2005. In this ten year period, just under 30 per cent of all dissertations could be included in this category. This is a significant number, and it would be interesting at a future date to see how this compares with other university departments across the country. There are a number of reasons that could be put forward for this postgraduate interest in the subject. The particular interest of staff members leading postgraduate programmes is one crucial factor, but to this could be added the readily 'accessible' nature of historical archaeological material culture, physical remains and landscapes. Many students undertaking short taught master's programmes may not have the finance and logistics to undertake extensive periods of fieldwork or data collection in remote rural landscapes. It is clear from an analysis of the projects that have been undertaken that most are of an urban or industrial character, often focused on sites in relatively close proximity to the respective universities. Other factors are also clearly at play including the heavily under-researched nature of the subject area, the relative ease of access to supporting historical information and the specific interest of the students themselves, including their political and social interests. Regardless of these factors, it is clear that historical archaeology is a popular area of research, more so than many staff at the various departments will care to admit.

Table 5.1 UCC MA dissertations 1995–2005

UCC (Department of Archaeology)	
Period	1995–2005
Total no. of MA dissertations	113
No. of Hist. Arch dissertations	33 (29.2%)

In terms of doctoral-level research we see a greater degree of engagement with the subject area. Table 5.2 provides a representation of students undertaking either MPhil or PhD research at five universities as of March 2008. It is a clear indicator of the potential future health of the subject of Irish historical archaeology that fourteen (or nearly 15 per cent of all archaeology research students) individuals are currently undertaking advanced study within the realms of the broader subject area. If we take into account students from other countries (especially the United States) who are undertaking Irish-based research, this figure becomes significantly enhanced. The extent of in-depth doctoral-level engagement with Irish historical archaeology bodes well for the future of professional involvement with the subject area and for the expansion of research and knowledge.

Table 5.2 Currently registered research students from select third-level institutions

Institution	No. of current MPhil/ PhDs	No. of Historical Archaeology PhDs	Percentage
UCD	20	4	20
UCC	21	3	14
NUIG	19	2	11
QUB	27	2/3	11
UU	6	2	33

This information was gleaned from publicly available data on the various institutions' web pages in March 2008.

RESEARCH OUTPUT

One of the strongest indicators of the strength of university-based research is the extent and form of published output. Fortunately, the universities in the Republic of Ireland have been spared the stresses of the current United Kingdom Research Assessment Exercise (RAE), but publication is still recognised as a key indicator of strength. Trying, however, to assign a value to particular publications is fraught with difficulties. Suffice to say here that publication of any sort coming from Irish archaeology departments is to be welcomed and will continue to contribute in the most positive sense to the further development of the subject.

It is appropriate to highlight a number of key developments in terms of publications. First and foremost is the recent appearance of the published volume of IPMAG's first conference in 2000.[7] This publication is a milestone in Irish archaeology, and provides for the first time a comprehensive reference volume for students, professionals and the general public alike. Its scope reflects not only the incredible wealth of material in Ireland, but also the growing extent and engagement of archaeologists with this resource. Other key indicators include a series of international articles that have appeared both in the *International Journal of Historical Archaeology*[8] and the journal *Historical Archaeology*.[9] Significant articles have also appeared in the *International Journal of Nautical Archaeology*,[10] *Archaeological Dialogues*,[11] *Post-Medieval Archaeology* and other journals of repute. Mention should of course be made to two major North American professors, Charles Orser[12] and Eric Klingelhöfer,[13] who continue to research and publish on Irish material and who have made a major external contribution to the development of the subject. A cursory perusal of articles in Ireland's popular quarterly magazine, *Archaeology Ireland* under the editorship of Tom Condit, reflects also the increasing popularity of the subject on a national basis.

Table 5.3 presents an overview of articles that have appeared in the journal in the period from 1998 to 2006, which clearly reflects the increasing appearance of articles on subject matter related to historical archaeology over this time period.

Table 5.3 Historical Archaeology articles in *Archaeology Ireland*, 1998–2006

Year	No. of articles	No. of historical articles
2006	33	8
2005	38	10
2004	38	7
2003	36	2
2002	35	2
2001	28	2
2000	36	4
1999	30	4
1998	14	1

A final word on output should relate to a series of books that have appeared over the last five years. The output of Colin Rynne, and specifically his publications in the area of post-medieval industry, is worth particular mention.[14] A cautionary note is warranted as well. With the increasing professionalism of Irish historical archaeology, many of the publications are appearing in journals that may not be readily available to the general public. There remains the possibility that we are in effect alienating a large portion of the public from our work and findings by publishing less in local journals and other more populist formats. In Ireland, as elsewhere, practitioners need to be aware of this issue and need to examine new and more innovative ways of engaging the public and ensuring the dissemination of information.

TEACHING DEVELOPMENT

In a timely development in 2007, the United Kingdom Higher Education Academy held a seminar on teaching historical archaeology in the British university environment.[15] This seminar was arranged in order to generate discussion of the opportunities and challenges in teaching historical archaeology and to present a series of case studies exploring how the subject is taught in archaeology departments in the United Kingdom. A number of key issues emerged, which were viewed as having negative impacts for the future development of historical archaeology curricula in particular. The decline of the teaching of medieval history at secondary school level has left many students who subsequently take up historical archaeology options with limited experience of necessary research skills as well as basic knowledge. Students also appear to have difficulty in coming to grips with varying and rigorous methodologies and with applying critical analysis to various data types, with the associated limited appearance of aspects of scientific archaeology having a related effect. Suggestions put forward at the seminar included the development of sessions devoted to research skills, the greater integration of scientific themes into the curricula and the development of more innovative assessment and variation of the sources of evidence undergoing analysis.

No seminar of a similar kind has taken place in Ireland, and there has been a distinct paucity of pedagogic discussion about the development of the subject area of historical archaeology in our universities. It is clear immediately from the preceding discussion that there are a number of key issues facing the subject within the university environment. Critically, a number of university and third-level institutes have no provision for the teaching of landscape and material culture remains from the post-1600 period. Among the limited departments and schools that do have some provision, there are a range of differing approaches and emphases in teaching material. Such differences are to be welcomed. A single undergraduate curriculum is not to be advocated here, although an element of the inclusion of the 'basics' is important across all subject providers. Differences in teaching can have a subsequent impact in professional practice and approaches, highlighting the need for some degree of commonality in teaching provision. Two immediate comments spring to mind here. As with the situation in the United Kingdom, it could be argued that students in Ireland do not have enough engagement with scientific analysis. Limited use of statistical analysis is common and an awareness of various scientific methodologies is lacking within the discipline. Secondly, it is apparent that material culture still remains very much a secondary player behind architectural and landscape studies. Greater consideration of these elements is required.

Ultimately, one of the primary questions that needs to be asked is whether or not current historical archaeology teaching and provision in Ireland is adequately responding to contemporary needs and challenges. A straightforward answer would be to say no, simply on the basis of teaching provision and distribution. On a more detailed level, the answer may also be 'no' given the prevailing level of ignorance of and outright dismissal accorded to the more recent archaeological levels and material culture on development sites. This is also a broader institutional issue, given the paucity of published data and the antipathy displayed by the state bodies, commercial units and survey mechanisms for sites post-dating 1600.

Another critical question is whether or not theoretical considerations are given precedence over data and fieldwork studies. There certainly seems to be an emerging paradigm in which historical archaeology emerges as a heavily theoretically driven subject area. Theoretical engagement is of course both important and necessary, but do we have a sufficient base level of data to substantiate the often overly ambitious theories we are prone to construct? It would appear that the often inflated and theory-laden publications that have emerged in the broader context of global historical archaeology can serve to alienate more than attract, as considered elsewhere in this volume. Are we also sacrificing the local for the global? Can we continue to postulate about global interactions and systems when we have yet to come to terms with the local environment and context? These are important questions, which need to be addressed when we are at such a formative stage in the development of Irish historical archaeology.

EXTERNAL ISSUES

Outside of the universities, a number of other key issues impacting upon the practice of Irish historical archaeology are apparent that directly impact upon university practice. Levels of understanding and appreciation of post-medieval and early modern material remain problematic. The situation has improved in recent years, but many commercial practices still serve to sideline the historical archaeological resource. Primary among these practices are the disregard for constituent parts of the post-medieval landscape including field systems, urban and rural settlement forms, and a multitude of other structures and remains. Existing machine-testing and excavation techniques still disregard the upper levels and material on sites in an attempt to access earlier material. Both government bodies and commercial companies need to pay greater attention to post-medieval resources and implement coherent strategies for both dealing with and curating these resources. The continuing virtual absence and non-integration of these sites, monuments and landscapes into statutory sites and monuments records is a key factor hampering appreciation of the value of post-medieval archaeology. Likewise, the museum services need to move away from categorising the material culture of the past four hundred years as 'folklife' and instead afford it greater archaeological attention. All parties must come together and begin to develop agreed approaches to tackling post-medieval sites in both commercial and research contexts and to examine ways in which the large body of grey literature can be integrated into research frameworks.

CONCLUSION

The past twenty years have been both an exciting and at times frustrating period, witnessing the emergence and firm establishment of historical archaeology across Ireland.

While the universities have played a part in these developments, it has largely been the work of external individuals and more recently the work of IPMAG that has been at the forefront. The universities now have a crucial pedagogic and research role in order to further develop and facilitate the future expansion of study of historical archaeology. IPMAG laid a foundation for this development with its 2007 useful text and reference book, but an expansion and widespread adoption of teaching in this area is urgently required. Similarly, the implementation of sustainable long-term research programmes and the continued encouragement of postgraduate research is needed to ensure the future vitality of the subject.

There is a case to be made that teaching partnerships should develop to further develop and aid teaching strategies. IPMAG, for example, may consider organising pedagogic programmes that could be offered and shared between all the archaeology subject providers. Professional Development courses could also be developed and offered through the Institute of Archaeologists of Ireland (IAI). It may be that these courses could be offered through distance learning and the generation of online or a digital material culture teaching resource packs.

Much has been achieved in a short space of time but there remains much to do.

ACKNOWLEDGEMENTS

The author would like to thank Dr Audrey Horning for her invitation to contribute to this volume and for her continued unending enthusiasm for the development of Historical Archaeology in Ireland, north and south.

NOTES

1. Ó Súilleabháin 1933.
2. Breen & O'Sullivan 2007; Martin & Parker 1988.
3. Simpson & Dickson 1981.
4. Brannon & Blades 1980; Robinson & Brannon 1981– 2.
5. Breen 2007; Donnelly & Brannon 1998; Donnelly & Horning 2002.
6. Horning, Ó Baoill, Donnelly & Logue 2007.
7. Ibid.
8. Breen 2006; Donnelly 2004; 2005; Forsythe 2007; Horning 2007b; 2004.
9. Breen & Forsythe 2007; Callaghan & Breen 2007; Horning 2007a; 2002.
10. Forsythe 2006.
11. Horning 2006; O'Keeffe 2006.
12. Orser 1996; 2006.
13. Klingelhofer 1992; 1999a; 1999b; 2000; 2005.
14. Rynne 1991; 1993; 1998; 1999; 2000; 2001; 2006.
15. HEA 2007.

BIBLIOGRAPHY

Barry, T. 1987, *Medieval Ireland*. Dublin: Routledge.

Brannon, N.F. & Blades, B.S. 1980, 'Dungiven bawn re-edified', *Ulster Journal of Archaeology* **43**, 91–6.

Breen, C. 2006, 'Social archaeologies of Utopian settlements in Ireland', *International Journal of Historical Archaeology* **10**:1, 64–80.

Breen, C. 2007, *An Archaeology of South-west Ireland, 1570–1670*. Dublin: Four Courts Press.

Breen, C. & Forsythe, W. 2007, 'The French shipwreck *La Surveillante*, lost in Bantry Bay, Ireland, in 1797', *Historical Archaeology* **41**:3, 39–50.

Breen, C. & O'Sullivan, A. 2007, *Maritime Ireland: A Coastal Archaeology of Island Communities*. Stroud: Tempus Press.

Callaghan, C. & Breen, C. 2007, 'Investigations of the *Taymouth Castle*, a 19th century composite ship lost off the coast of Northern Ireland', *Historical Archaeology* **41**:3, 25–38.

Donnelly, C. 2004, 'Masshouses and meetinghouses: the archaeology of the penal laws in early modern Ireland', *International Journal of Historical Archaeology* **8**:2, 119–32.

Donnelly, C. 2005, 'The I.H.S. monogram as a symbol of Catholic resistance in 17th- century Ireland', *International Journal of Historical Archaeology* **9**:1, 37–42.

Donnelly, C. & Brannon, N. 1998, 'Trowelling through history: historical archaeology and the study of early modern Ireland', *History Ireland* **6**:3, 22–5.

Donnelly, C. & Horning, A. 2002, 'Post-medieval and industrial archaeology in Ireland: an overview', *Antiquity* **76**, 557–61.

Forsythe, W. 2006, 'The archaeology of the kelp industry in northern Irish islands', *International Journal of Nautical Archaeology* **35**:2, 218–29.

Forsythe, W. 2007, 'On the edge of improvement: Rathlin Island and the modern world', *International Journal of Historical Archaeology* **11**:3, 221–40.

Funari, P.P.A., Hall, M. & Jones, S. (eds) 1999, *Historical Archaeology: Back from the Edge*. London: Routledge.

HEA 2007, 'Teaching Historical Archaeology' <http://www.hca.heacademy.ac.uk/resources/reviews/TAF/TAF-TeachingHistoricalArchaeology.php>.

Horning, A. 2002, 'Myth, migration, and material culture: archaeology and the Ulster influence on Appalachia', *Historical Archaeology* **36**:4, 129–49.

Horning, A. 2004, 'Archaeological explorations of cultural identity and rural economy in the north of Ireland: Goodland, Co. Antrim', *International Journal of Historical Archaeology* **8**:3, 199–216.

Horning, A. 2006, 'Archaeology, conflict, and contemporary identity in the north of Ireland: implications for theory and practice in Irish historical archaeology', *Archaeological Dialogues* **13**:2, 183–99.

Horning, A. 2007a, 'On the banks of the Bann: the riverine economy of an Ulster Plantation village', *Historical Archaeology* **41**:3, 94–114.

Horning, A. 2007b, 'Materiality and mutable landscapes: re-thinking seasonality in the north and west of Ireland', *International Journal of Historical Archaeology* **11**:4, 358–78.

Horning, A., Ó Baoill, R., Donnelly, C.J. & Logue, P. (eds) 2007, *The Archaeology of Post-Medieval Ireland, 1550–1850*. Bray: Wordwell.

Klingelhöfer, E. 1992, 'Renaissance fortifications at Dunboy Castle, 1602: a report on the 1989 excavations', *Journal of the Cork Historical and Archaeological Society,* **97**: 85–96.

Klingelhöfer, E. 1999a, 'Elizabethan settlements: Mogeely Castle, Curraglass and Carrigeen, Co. Cork (Part 1)', *Journal of the Cork Historical and Archaeological Society* **104**, 97–110.

Klingelhöfer, E. 1999b, 'Proto-colonial archaeology: the case of Elizabethan Ireland', in Funari *et al.* (eds), 1999, 165–79.

Klingelhöfer, E. 2000, 'Elizabethan settlements: Mogeely Castle, Curraglass and Carrigeen, Co. Cork (Part II)', *Journal of the Cork Historical and   Archaeological Society* **105**, 155–74.

Klingelhöfer, E. 2005, 'Edmund Spenser at Kilcolman Castle: the archaeological evidence', *Post-Medieval Archaeology* **39**:1, 133–54.

Martin, C. & Parker, G. 1988, *The Spanish Armada.* London: Penguin.

O'Keeffe, T. 2006, 'Starting as we mean to go on. Why we need a theoretically-informed historical archaeology', *Archaeological Dialogues* **16**, 208–11.

Ó Súilleabháin, M. 1933, *Twenty Years A-Growing.* Dublin: Clólucht an Talbóidigh.

Orser, C.E. 1996, *A Historical Archaeology of the Modern World.* New York: Plenum.

Orser, C. (ed.) 2006, *Unearthing Hidden Ireland: Historical Archaeology and Anthropology at Ballykilcline, County Roscommon.* Bray: Wordwell.

Robinson, P.S. & Brannon, N.F., 1981–2, 'A seventeenth-century house in New Row, Coleraine', *Ulster Journal of Archaeology* **44**&**45**, 173–8.

Rynne, C. 1991, *The Industrial Archaeology of Cork City and its Environs: A Sites and Monuments Record.* Dublin: The Royal Irish Academy.

Rynne, C. 1993, *The Archaeology of Cork City and Harbour.* Cork: Collins Press.

Rynne, C. 1998, *At the Sign of the Cow: The Cork Butter Market 1770–1924.* Cork: Collins Press.

Rynne, C. 1999, *The Industrial Archaeology of Cork City and its Environs.* Dublin, Stationery Office.

Rynne, C. 2006, *Industrial Ireland 1750–1930: An Archaeology.* Cork: Collins Press.

Rynne, C. & Wigham, B. 2001, *A Life of Usefulness: Abraham Beale and the Monard Ironworks.* Cork: Sitka Press.

Simpson, M.L. & Dickson, A. 1981, 'Excavations in Carrickfergus, County Antrim', *Medieval Archaeology* **25**, 78–89.

Irish 'Post-medieval' Archaeology: Time to Lose our Innocence?

By TADHG O'KEEFFE

Those of us on this side of the Atlantic who choose to describe our field as historical archaeology rather than post-medieval archaeology generally buy into two ideas. One is that 'historical archaeology' connotes a complex, ideologically rationalised, praxis; it is not simply the archaeological study of the historically recorded past. The second is that historical archaeology's study area is the entire world; no matter how local our focus, global patterns will still be visible and critical. I subscribe happily to these views, but I also argue that in Ireland, where the field is relatively new, we use this consensus as a platform on which to develop a more nuanced, place-specific, dimension to historical-archaeological philosophy and practice.

INTRODUCTION

This chapter is essentially an opinion piece. The first part of its title signals, through the use of inverted commas, a scepticism that is shared by an increasing number of British archaeologists but by fewer Irish archaeologists than some of us would like. The phrase 'post-medieval' carries the imprimaturs of two of the general-archaeological organisations – the long-established Society for Post-Medieval Archaeology and the more youthful Irish Post-Medieval Archaeology Group – represented at the conference of which these are the proceedings. But, such support notwithstanding, it is a phrase that deserves to be surrounded by the flashing lights of inverted commas, lest it remain naturalised, with its implications for how we approach the modern and contemporary pasts loitering unnoticed under the radar of critical thinking about archaeology and its conceptualisation of historic time. Some may argue that a discussion of the appropriateness of the term 'post-medieval' is no more than an exercise in semantic hair-splitting, and maybe even that it is a waste of time when so much remains to be done. However, as long as there is a possibility that our subject is weakened conceptually, or has its vision limited, by the retention of a term that was coined at its birth, the critique of 'post-medieval' as a construct is valid. Moreover, a conference (and book) subtitled *Future directions in the archaeological study of post-1550 Britain and Ireland* is precisely the context in which we should look around our house and see what needs to be put in order.

The second part of my title borrows its phraseology from a New Archaeologist.[1] Forty years ago David Clarke and like-minded colleagues identified problems in the normative explanations of the past that were offered by the cultural historians who preceded them, and they proceeded to offer a manifesto for a new critical archaeology in which the process of interpretation was sharpened by ethnographic parallels on the one hand and by the generation of scientific paradigms one the other.[2] The fate of the so-called New Archaeology will be familiar to most readers of this volume: the postmodern turn exposed the shortcomings of a predictive archaeology. In this discussion I suggest that the archaeological study of post-1550 Ireland – Britain is not my concern here – requires a transformation as dramatic as that which Clarke and others effected for prehistorians a couple of generations ago. The problem, as I see it, is that the archaeological practice that we have developed in Ireland around the remains of the 'post-medieval' period is, *on the whole*, concerned with documentation rather than explanation, and is too heavily dependent on conventional historical models to ever challenge historians' narrative reconstructions of the recent past. So, the innocence to be lost is an innocence about History, the discipline. But it is also an innocence about science or, more accurately, about what is assumed to be the scientific method: I question here the efficacy of collecting data outside the context of research questions; I question the presumption, implicit in much of the relevant literature ('grey' and published), that data constitutes the neutral, objective, baseline without which we cannot formulate questions about the past.

The chapter that follows is a call-to-arms to colleagues in the community of Irish archaeologists who describe themselves as 'post-medieval archaeologists' or, as I prefer, Historical Archaeologists (note the use of upper-case letters). Its starting point is my contention that we, as a collective constituted of practitioners ('professionals') and educationalists (academics), punch *below* our weight. This is not because our sub-discipline is so new that it has yet to bed down – it may be 'in its infancy', as one contributor to the debate at Leicester put it, but we're not! – but because our ambitions are often too modest, our targets too easily met. So, identifying 'fortified houses', dating sgraffito and accurately recording floor surfaces in abandoned buildings and connecting them to documented historic phases, is bread-and-butter stuff, and much of it is done very well, but are we happy that we are saying all that there is to say?

I further contend that we contribute much less to public comprehensions of the present, and to public awareness of the embeddedness of the modern past within the present, than we are individually capable of, or that the praxis of our discipline permits. Let me cite Audrey Horning's paper on archaeology, conflict and contemporary identity in Northern Ireland as an example of what we can offer.[3] Readers of periodicals such as *Irish Historical Studies* and *History Ireland* should find Horning's reflections to be far more radically revisionist and critically reflexive than most of the reflections published by historians following in the wake of Roy Foster's revisionist tome, *Modern Ireland 1600–1972*.[4] Her reflections suggest grounds on which we, as archaeologists, might challenge that widely held view of Ireland as a post-colony that one finds articulated by some critics.[5] What Horning provides, then, is more than simply an argument for a nuanced reading of colonial matter for an audience of fellow professionals: she provides a demonstration of what our particular branch of archaeology, through its 'professional' and academy-based archaeologists, can inject into public discourse about the abstract notions of colonialism and post-colonialism (Fig. 6.1),

TOP
Figure 6.1 The Twelfth of July: Ulster unionists celebrate their history and tradition in Belfast

LEFT
Figure 6.2 Moore Street, Dublin: the contemporary fabric of Ireland's African community in decay

and about the much less abstract politics and social values of heritage (Fig. 6.2) and the heritage industry.

It should be our ambition to use our subject's critical apparatus to wedge ourselves into the public consciousness and make ourselves relevant on issues other than those conservation- or preservation-related ones for which we, or at least some among us, are routinely wheeled out. The explanation for this shortfall between what we can do and what we actually do is, I suggest, that we are too archaeological in a traditional sense and not archaeological enough in a non-traditional sense. We possess both the tools and the licence to make informed, non-rhetorical, intercessions in public debate about identity and ideology, and to contribute meaningfully to policy formation with respect to any issue in which there is a demonstrably 'modern' spatio-material dimension. That goal of meaningful and informing participation in public discourse requires us to engage first with our discipline's epistemology. Ignoring Theory/theory is simply not an option for us.

Many British archaeologists reading this will be astonished that the importance of theory *still* needs to be asserted in an Irish context, especially if they are familiar with Irish writers in the *International Journal of Historical Archaeology*, or have heard Irish contributions to Theoretical Archaeology Group (TAG) and Contemporary Historical Archaeology and Theory (CHAT) conferences. But I suggest that the proceedings of the first IPMAG conference from 2001 offer the clearest evidence that we in Ireland have some ground to make up.[6] This multi-author volume merits the highest praise for securing the place of the 'post-medieval' in the Irish archaeological consciousness, and for being a resource that will be returned to again and again. I hope that my praise for it is recognised in the foreground of my more critical comments.

The volume's content illuminates, I think, the gap between where we are and where we should surely be. Without highlighting individual papers, the normative interpretations on display in a significant number of the contributions either fit comfortably within conventional historical readings of the past, or at least give no impression of a discipline that sees itself challenging those readings. Many colleagues are content with this. My view, however, is that a critical engagement with the discipline of history is necessary, and must be near the top of the agenda of our own, still-youthful, discipline.

In dealing with materials surviving from the recent past historians have had a long head-start on us, so it is somewhat inevitable that their narratives form a lens through which we think about our own material. Given that archaeologists of all periods have expended so much energy over the past forty years and more debating archaeology's philosophies and methodologies, we should be very careful about engaging with the product of a cognate discipline without satisfying ourselves first that the product in question is the result of careful consideration by that discipline of its own philosophies and methodologies. There is no point in us generating very sophisticated, theoretically adroit readings of our archaeological material, and then anchoring those readings to a narrative of historical process that is based very largely on historians' research on a narrow range of documentary material. This is not a criticism of history – historians do what they do – but rather a warning to us to recognise that what they do is not necessarily central to what we do.

Given the bewilderingly large scale of the modern historical archaeological record, the role of a Post-Medieval Archaeology or a Historical Archaeology of Ireland must be to transcend, not replace, the historians' narrative history of the past five centuries. We can transcend History, both discipline and narrative, by presenting a menu of imbricated, contingent, historical–sociological readings of the materialities and spatialities of which society, inequalities and all, is constructed. But my sense is that the potential of archaeological inquiry to do that is rarely acknowledged, much less exploited, in many of the papers in the volume under discussion.

Bearing witness to this is the absence from most of those papers of those very words and concepts – capitalism, modernity, Georgian Order, improvement, power/resistance, technicity, class, globalism – that have proved useful prisms in the literature on Global Historical Archaeology, especially that coming out of Britain, the Americas and the English-speaking southern hemisphere. Yes, these concepts are present in places, but one would have to dig deep in the book to locate any explicit discussion of them. Let us take, for example, the issue of improvement.[7] This is a theme around which we can comprehend so much of what happened in Ireland in the 18th and 19th centuries.[8] Improving activists and activators of all types – industrial, agricultural, administrative, social/moral – are known to have traversed urban and rural Ireland right into the twentieth century; some of them were guided by an ideology of improvement and others were simply *de facto* improvers. The greatest single project of improvement was the restructuring of the rural Irish landscape after the mid-19th-century famine (Fig 6.3). I now want to dwell here briefly on just two

LEFT
Figure 6.3 A straight-lined stone wall in eastern Connemara from the post-Famine period

of the themes that demand to be addressed explicitly by Irish 'post-medieval' archaeologists: colonialism/post-colonialism, and modernity and capitalism.

COLONIALISM/POSTCOLONIALISM

Colonialism is the only one of the four haunts of Global Historical Archaeology identified by Chuck Orser[9] that makes an appearance in a good number of the contributions to the IPMAG volume. But, as seems to be typical of Irish scholars in many fields (among them History and, especially, Historical Geography), it is not interrogated as a construct in its own right. It is assumed to be the agency of, and therefore to be indivisible from, colonisation. The word conjures, therefore, a sense of Ireland as a place of contestation between polarised communities, their ethnic and religious differences issuing from colonising events of the periods around 1600 (the Plantations) and, before that, 1200 (the 'Anglo-Norman' 'invasion'). Colonialism thus informs much of the debate about power and resistance in Historical Archaeology in Ireland,[10] although some writers have identified that power-and-resistance relationships in modern-historical Ireland can actually be decoupled from the matter of colonialism.[11]

We must accept that Ireland was subject to colonisation processes, but the matter of Ireland's status as an actual *colony* of England, later Britain, from the end of the middle ages to the early 20th century is very problematic. Without entering into that debate here, suffice it to say that England's, and later Britain's, relationship with Ireland from the early 1600s to the start of the 1900s was simply not comparable with her relationship with other parts of the world in which she developed interests and planted people during that same period. Her close ties with England from the 17th century, and its union with Britain from the start of the nineteenth, suggest that the word colony is singularly inappropriate in this context,[12] whatever its appropriateness for eastern America or the Indian subcontinent over the same long period. By the time it achieved its political independence just after the First World War, Ireland looked nothing like an overseas colony: for example, its people were largely English-speaking, often by choice rather than coercion, the 'new' national flag with its orange-coloured acknowledgement of Protestant tradition (a talking point for archaeologists in itself) was already more than half-a-century old, having been unfurled first in 1848, and Dublin's cityscape was already populated with monuments to dead Nationalist heroes.

'Native' and 'coloniser' are politically essentialist dichotomised constructs and they carry much less cultural value in a 'post-medieval' Irish context than many historians seem to think. At ground level, as it were, people generally got on with the job of living not fighting, whether in the 17th century or the 19th, and social relations were often conditioned more by class than by any other factor. Landowners of Plantation-era Munster, for example, built their houses according to a set of templates, regardless of their religion or ancestry. Catholic farmers in late 18th- and early 19th-century south-east Ireland, for example, had far more in common with their Protestant neighbours than they had with the Catholic peasants of Connemara. The prostitutes who worked in Dublin's famous 'Monto' red-light district were not differentiated, either by themselves or their 'clients', according to religion or place of origin.

But the common assumption that Ireland was indeed a colony in both cultural and political terms is especially manifest in the ease with which Irish scholars, following the lead of Declan Kiberd,[13] have adopted a post-colonial perspective on the island's history. The historiography is vast, with a good deal of it generated by responses to Stephen Howe's particular colono-scepticism.[14] Nowhere is the belief that Ireland passed from colony to post-colony more evident than in the historiography of Dublin, and nowhere is that belief more obviously wrong-headed. For example, Andrew Kincaid, like Kiberd a professor in the field of literature, presents Dublin as a post-colonial space.[15] His book (according to the blurb on the back cover) purports to show 'how perpetrators of colonialism have made use of urban planning and architecture to underscore and legitimate [sic] ideologies'. Kincaid's book is an excellent survey of Dublin's 20th-century growth, but it is not at all clear how the city's post-independence spaces and buildings – a mish-mash of Catholic sentimentalism (housing estates laid out in Celtic-cross design), tentative internationalism (Fig. 6.4), and other things besides – can be heard to possess subaltern or counter-colonial voices. The emphasis in A.J. Christopher's conclusion that 'by 1911, Dublin, *despite its colonial status*, bore more resemblance to the contemporary North American city than the colonial model, mainly based on tropical and sub-tropical research'[16] is similarly misplaced. The comparison with North American cities of the era is fascinating in and of itself, and raises questions about the colonial status of those cities. At very least, the words 'despite its colonial status' should be replaced with 'as befitting its status as a city in Great Britain'.

LEFT
Figure 6.4 Liberty Hall, Dublin: a 1960s skyscraper

What all this means is that we should be wary of interpreting archaeological material in post-1500 Ireland according to the model of colonialism/post-colonialism. This is another way of saying that labels like 'Irish', 'English', 'British', 'Anglo-Irish' and so on, should be understood as inherently problematic and should only be used with the appropriate battery of qualifications. There is far greater value for historical archaeologists in the counter-model, first articulated with clarity by Seán Connolly,[17] of a post-Restoration Ireland in which divisions of class and social order mattered much more than perceived divisions of native and colonial culture. Connolly's vision of an early modern Ireland that is to some degree under the influence of contemporary metropolitan Europe is more enticing than the alternative: a vision of Ireland as an island battleground between the Irish and the British, between landlords and peasants, between Catholics and Protestants, and so on.

MODERNITY AND CAPITALISM

I have indicated here and elsewhere[18] that 'post-medieval archaeology', with or without the 'Irish' in front of it, raises troublesome issues. Briefly, there is the presupposition in the Irish context that we understand the middle ages sufficiently well to know when it finishes, culturally and temporally. There is the added assumption that the medieval and post-medieval periods are sequential anyway, the upshot of this being that the phenomenon known as '*the* Renaissance' (as distinct from the many other renaissances assumed to have taken place in history[19]) is somewhat stranded in the time–space between medieval and post-medieval. There is a second problem that is even more germane to this chapter: 'post-medieval' is a term with no global meaning that is applied to an archaeology that has global meaning.

The case for conceiving of the archaeology of the period after *c.* 1500 as a global archaeology is absolutely compelling, even if the global spaces traversed by its constituent actants, both animate and inanimate (see Latour 2005 for explication), were largely Atlantic spaces in the 1500s and 1600s, and remained dominated by Atlantic geopolitics until the emergence of 'the Pacific rim' in the last century. So, to describe the archaeology of the post-1500 period in these islands as 'post-medieval' is to miss a critical point: the material in question must be understood primarily not by reference to the materiality of preceding insular contexts but by reference to the new spatial environment in which it was produced and consumed. I think Donald Meinig was corrected in describing that new spatial environment as 'the New World' in its own right: both Europe and the Americas were old worlds, and the 'sudden and harsh encounter' between them in the later 15th and 16th centuries transformed both of them and 'integrated them into a single New World'.[20]

Many colleagues, especially North American, describe the archaeology of the post-1500 world in terms of capitalism,[21] but we should really add the prefix 'global'. Capitalism is a system of organising wealth in which assets (money, most obviously, but also land, technical equipment, and so on) are used to generate payment for labourers who, because of what we would describe today as wage-fixing, create a profit for those who possess the assets to begin with. Understood in this way, capitalism certainly manifested itself in certain socioeconomic sectors at local and regional levels in Europe before the 'end' of the middle ages: we see it in, for example, the first stirrings of open-field enclosure and the concomitant rise in commercial farming in lowland Britain, in the new, product-specialising, industrial zones of 15th-century Continental Europe, and in the Baltic and North Sea ports of the Hanseatic League. But there is an argument that capitalism only replaced feudalism across Europe, and thus brought Europe into a new era, *after* the overseas colonies created by European expansion in the 1500s and 1600s began to feed surplus wealth back to Europe itself.[22] It should also be noted that colonial spaces overseas served the European capitalist project by accepting population surpluses *from* Europe as well as delivering capital surpluses *to* Europe. In Ireland, for example, where rising population numbers among the peasants and the proletariat of the 18th and 19th centuries narrowed profit margins, control of capital by the state and by private interests was partly effected through migration schemes, mainly to the Americas.[23]

Whether the discovery of the Americas explains the rise of capitalism or not, it was certainly in the context of that discovery that capitalism achieved what Derek Gregory describes as its 'time–space colonisation'.[24] The (now-expanded) known world was reconceptualised in the 16th and early 17th centuries according to Cartesian geometry. Its spaces, 'cartographised' through the imposition of imaginary grids, were bureaucratised through the state regulation of public administrative systems. Ideas of temporality were similarly transformed, not least because the discovery of people in the Americas and elsewhere who were not a part of European history altered the European sense of historicity itself.[25]

The world of global capitalism *is*, then, the modern world, and therefore the archaeology of the period between the 16th and early 20th centuries is nothing less than the archaeology of modernity. Now, that term is difficult and confusing. Michel-Rolph Trouillot, for one, has admitted to 'being ambivalent about the extent to which [it] can be conceptualised'.[26] Susan Friedman has mapped how *modern* (-*ity*, -*ism*) can mean not just different things but precisely opposite things.[27] She has done a service to all of us who have found it difficult to divine a consistent, non-contradictory view of its defining features, even by trying to work backwards from our understanding of post-modernity. The root of the problem is, obviously, the contexts in which 'modern' is used as an adjective (or, more precisely, the job that it is expected to do as an adjective in those contexts). Particular confusion arises from the fact that 'modern' has been applied to 17th-century phenomena in some quarters but has also been used to describe what were *de facto* avant-garde movements in individual artistic endeavours (art, literature) in the early twentieth century. Given that 'modern' stands alongside 'medieval' and 'ancient' as the colloquial expression for a great slab of historic time, it seems right to use it to describe the time-period from *c.* 1500 into the 20th century, and to describe a world which, four or five centuries after it first formed, is still recognisably ours (in a way that, say, the medieval world isn't).

If we wish to refine it further, we could consider dividing the modern period into three stages. There is conceivably an Early Modern stage, starting around 1500 when the 'zero-degree of existence' of non-Western peoples prior to *c.* 1500 'provide[d] both a justification for the colonizing enterprise and an imaginary empty space for the projection of a modernist angst'.[28] There is conceivably a High Modern stage, starting in the later 1700s with the Industrial Revolution and running through, arguably, to the first great war of the

20th century; such a stage is characterised by tensions between industry ('manufacturing') and craft on the one hand, and between medievalism (constructed as the antithesis of modernity) and the avant-garde on the other. And there is conceivably a Late Modern stage, the duration of which is the interwar period, not because that two-decade period has an internal cohesion but because 'the multinational corporate flows of late capitalism' and the 'new forms of imperialism' that Jameson takes to be characteristic of post-modernism[29] begin after the Second World War.

But whether or not we divide it into phases, the bottom line is that the archaeology of Ireland after *c.* 1500 is both the archaeology of modernity in Ireland and – there is a subtle difference here – the archaeology in Ireland of modernity. The former fixes our gaze on Ireland while acknowledging the wider context of modernity, but the latter is preferable because it foregrounds modernity and acknowledges that Ireland is a place in which modernity's multiple configurations and meanings can be explored.

If we accept that the discipline of Archaeology in the broadest sense is both a formative ingredient and an end-product of modernity, as Julian Thomas has explored,[30] then we must see that Historical Archaeology occupies the extraordinary position of studying modernity reflexively from the inside and empirically from the outside. Engaging with the concept of modernity, therefore, has two benefits for us as Historical Archaeologists: it provides a context other than the normatively historical in which we can explain our material, and it is a means by which our discipline makes itself heard properly in the wider search for human self-comprehension.

DATA AND RESEARCH QUESTIONS

The National Museum of Ireland's ability to present a balanced representation of Ireland s prehistoric and *historic* evolution in material form is critically bound up with the positioning, or repositioning, of archaeology within its overall remit. That repositioning, however, is unlikely to happen unless there is a wider debate about the theoretical framework governing the practice of archaeology in Ireland. This would have to include a realistic assessment of the manageability of incremental data collection through unprecedented levels of excavation, and information gathering in the form of exhaustive or more likely inexhaustible survey work.[31]

My final comment is that connections between our data and such themes as capitalism and modernity depend on the formulation of specific research questions. These questions need to be thought about and phrased carefully, but it is actually the database that presents the biggest challenge. It is a ready-made resource, and the problem is its vastness. It is underfoot (Fig. 6. 5), it is in the corner of the eye (Fig. 6.6), it is perpetually under threat (Fig. 6.7), it is on sale (Fig. 6.8). Because we have no philosophical perspectives on the efficacy of data collection, the overwhelming volume of the data is, I think, proving to be an impediment to progress in Historical Archaeology in Ireland.

Let us think about the body of data that is conventionally described under the heading of material culture. A recently published (2008) governmental evaluation of the National Museum of Ireland's (NMI) management of the national archaeological collection of all periods[32] drew public attention to 'significant shortcomings' in that institution's management

LEFT
Figure 6.5 Nineteenth-century cobbles lining the footpath in Kilworth, Co. Cork

BELOW
Figure 6.6 A vestige of Jacobs Biscuits factory, Dublin

of the material in its custody. The report noted poor storage conditions, identified a lack of adequate temperature and humidity control, and observed that conservation activities were aimed primarily at preparing material for exhibition. The NMI's estimate that it has almost four million objects in its collections makes me, for one, sympathise with it in its plight: how can a country of about one million taxpayers sustain flawless curatorial practises in an ideal curatorial environment for that volume of material? The aspirations expressed in the report are lofty indeed, but the resource for which our museum colleagues have responsibility is unmanageably large, and is getting larger.

The most interesting revelation in the report is that 911,000 objects 'lend themselves to being recorded in detail'. What, then, are the other 3,000,000-plus objects? Is it the case that they are of a nature that does not allow detailed recording, or are they adjudged not to be worth the effort? Whichever the case, why are they being kept? Are these among the objects for which proper temperature and humidity control is regarded as a necessity? Many of those 3,000,000-plus archaeological objects in question are either old acquisitions, made at a time when storage was not a pressing issue, or acquisitions linked to archaeological excavations, the numbers of which have increased by a staggering amount over the past fifteen years. The value of *physically* (as distinct from *electronically*) saving material from the excavation of 'post-medieval' sites deserves particular discussion, because the quantity of material produced since the middle ages is incomprehensively vast and has none of the rarity value associated with prehistoric objects.

If excavators follow rigorously the letter of the law, clay pipe fragments recovered from, say, urban rescue excavations will find their way into the national collection. We all know that excavators make judgement calls on what objects from their excavations get bagged separately and what objects do not get bagged at all, but every small fragment of clay pipe, to choose a ubiquitous object type, does have a legal right to make the journey from the excavation trench to the museum, and then to find its final home in the museum environment. But the clay pipe fragment that is brought to the National Museum by the suburban gardener who found it in the sweet pea bed will not end up in the national collection, not because it is intrinsically less valuable but because the context of its discovery underscores its ordinariness and so devalues it. Equally, an excavated 19th-century glass bottle sherd belongs by law in the national collection and will (probably) be delivered dutifully, but archaeologists happily allow complete examples of the same bottle type languish on the high shelves of mock-traditional Irish pubs, alongside old typewriters, stoneware jars, spinning wheels and unread books. What defines 'archaeological material' of the recent historic past seems, in reality, to be context of discovery: certain objects have supremacy in our curation of the recent material past not by virtue of what they in particular tell us about the past but by virtue of the methodology – excavation mainly – by which they have been retrieved. The counter-argument – that it is the *context* of their discovery rather than the *methodology* by which they are discovered that imparts value to these (usually broken) objects – is a bogus one: contexts are preserved by record, because excavation is acknowledged to be a destructive process, so unless the clay pipe fragment is going to be stored in the soil matrix in which it is found, there is really no argument to be made for retaining the excavated clay pipe fragment and not retaining the one found by happenstance.

TOP
Figure 6.7 The façade of the former Presbyterian church, Sean Mac Dermott Street Lower, Dublin

RIGHT
Figure 6.8 Antiques on sale near Lisburn, Co. Down

To summarise, then, the argument that we should retain everything that we adjudge to be archaeological clearly makes little sense, not least with respect to the modern past. I am sure I will not be misrepresented on this point: I am not suggesting the large-scale destruction of our resource, but rather a careful consideration of policies of accessioning, recording and retention/non-retention. First, it is a matter of economics. The cost of processing every object or fragment before storage, the cost of storage itself, and the cost of retrieving such material for an intrepid researcher some day in the distant future, might be prohibitive when weighed against the type of knowledge that might eventually accrue from re-examination. Second, it is a matter of archaeological philosophy (or theory, if one prefers that word). Whether in material form or in the form of feature plans and Harris matrices, data has neither ontological reality nor intrinsic value. Data is what we chose it to be, no more, no less.

The archaeologist's 'scientific' method of collecting data offers a comforting illusion of objectivity. That illusion is not a subterfuge of science but an example of how easily non-scientists misunderstand the nature of science. Contrary to what is commonly believed (even among many scientists), scientific truth does not transcend cultural truth. The realisation that science is itself a cultural production demystifies science for those of us who prefer the near-relativism of post-processualism to the alleged certainties of empiricism. But one thing that scientists do with data is put it at the service of specific problems. They collect data to answer questions, on the presumption that the data is already 'out there' waiting to be collected. We, on the other hand, *often* collect and store data quite blindly, waiting for the data collections to disgorge answers to unasked questions. Rescue excavations, almost by their nature, are driven by a desire to catch as much data as possible, the assumption being that the data will eventually say something to somebody.

I want to finish this chapter by suggesting a route by which Irish Historical Archaeology might lose this innocence with respect to data. The first step involves facing up to the surfeit of material data (of objects, in other words). Let us, as a community of professional archaeologists and academic archaeologists, agree with that point made above about data having no intrinsic value, no ontological reality. Let us agree that its value is always conditional on the needs that we have for it, and, on that basis, let us agree *in principle* that it must *merit* recording or retention. The second step involves establishing criteria, specific to individual cases, by which the merits of specific data are evaluated. Put less abstractly, let us ask questions about the past, rather than about the data, and let us collect and interrogate the data accordingly. I suggest that those questions are formulated to address major themes such as those listed above, precisely because such themes illuminate the human condition. And finally, let us agree that mistakes will be made and let us agree not to worry about that. If a research-oriented Historical Archaeology is possible in rescue archaeology contexts, as I believe it is, it is almost certain that we will have regrets later about things that we did or that we left undone. Yes, we will someday wish that we dug certain surfaces more carefully (because 19th-century floors will have suddenly become interesting), or that we kept those tiny fragments of cream ware (because we may now have found more of the same vessel). But it is worth remembering that field-walkers in the ploughzone long ago realised the futility of worrying on a Saturday what they might have found if they had walked on the

Friday. We need to adopt the same mindset. The more data we accumulate the less we are likely to be able to say.

ACKNOWLEDGEMENTS

My thanks to Audrey Horning and Marilyn Palmer for inviting me to speak at the Leicester conference, to Liam Downey, former director of Teagasc and now of UCD School of Archaeology, for providing many insights into the scientific mind, and to Pat Cooke, UCD School of Art History and Cultural Policy, for valuable comments on this chapter.

NOTES

1. Clarke 1973.
2. Clarke 1968; Binford & Binford 1968.
3. Horning 2006.
4. Foster 1988.
5. See Said 1989, for example.
6. Horning et al. 2007.
7. See Tarlow 2007 for England.
8. See Barnard 2008.
9. Orser 1996.
10. Delle 1999.
11. Frazier 1999; Smith & O'Keeffe forthcoming.
12. O'Keeffe 2006.
13. Kiberd 1995.
14. Howe 2000; see Kennedy 1993 for a valuable critique of Irish post-colonialism.
15. Kincaid 2006.
16. Christopher 1997, 151; emphasis added.
17. Connolly 1992.
18. O'Keeffe 2006; O'Keeffe & Quirke 2009.
19. See Panofsky 1962.
20. Bailyn 2005, 56, quoting Meinig.
21. Leone & Potter 1996.
22. Wallerstein 1974.
23. See Duffy 2004.
24. Gregory 1994.
25. See Koselleck 1985.
26. Trouillot 2003, 36.
27. Friedman 2001, 494.
28. Spurr 1993, 96.
29. Jameson 1990.
30. Thomas 2004.
31. Cooke 2004, 78; emphasis added.
32. <http://audgen.gov.ie/viewdoc.asp?DocID=1094>

BIBLIOGRAPHY

Bailyn, B. 2005, *Atlantic History: Concept and Contours*. Cambridge, MA: Harvard University Press.

Barnard, T. 2008, *Improving Ireland? Projectors, Prophets and Profiteers, 1641–1786*. Dublin: Four Courts Press.

Binford, S.R. & Binford, L. 1968, *New Perspectives in Archaeology*. Chicago: Aldine Press.

Christopher, A.J. 1997, '"The second city of the Empire": colonial Dublin, 1911', *Journal of Historical Geography* **23**(2): 151–63.

Clarke, D. 1968, *Analytical Archaeology*. London: Methuen.

Clarke, D. 1973, 'Archaeology: the loss of innocence', *Antiquity* **47**(185): 6–18.

Connolly, S.J. 1992, *Religion, Law and Power: The Making of Protestant Ireland*. Oxford: Oxford University Press.

Cooke, P. 2004, *The Containment of Heritage: Setting Limits to the Growth of Heritage in Ireland*. Dublin: Policy Institute, TCD.

Delle, J.A. 1999, '"A good and easy speculation": spatial conflict, collusion and resistance in late sixteenth-century Ireland', *International Journal of Historical Archaeology* **3**(1): 11–35.

Duffy, P. (ed.) 2004, *To and From Ireland: Planned Migration Schemes c.1600–2000*. Dublin: Geography Publications.

Eagleton, T. *et al.* 1990, *Nationalism, Colonialism and Literature*. Minneapolis: University of Minnesota Press.

Foster, R. 1988, *Modern Ireland 1600–1972*, London: Penguin.

Frazier, B. 1999, 'Reconceptualising resistance in the historical archaeology of the British isles: an editorial', *International Journal of Historical Archaeology* **3**(1): 1–10.

Friedman, S.S. 2001, 'Definitional excursions: the meanings of modern/modernity/modernism', *Modernism/Modernity* **8**(3): 493–513.

Gregory, D. 1994, *Geographical Imaginations*. Oxford: Blackwell.

Horning, A. 2006, 'Archaeology, conflict, and contemporary identity in the north of Ireland: implications for theory and practice in Irish historical archaeology', *Archaeological Dialogues* **13**(2): 183–199.

Horning, A., Ó Baoill, R., Donnelly, C. & Logue, P. 2007, *The Archaeology of Post-Medieval Ireland, 1550–1850*. Bray: Wordwell.

Howe, S. 2000, *Ireland and Empire*. Oxford: Oxford University Press.

Jameson, F. 1990, 'Modernism and imperialism', in Eagleton *et al.* 1990, 43–6.

Kennedy, L. 1993, 'Modern Ireland: post-colonial society or post-colonial pretensions?', *The Irish Review* **13**: 107–21.

Kiberd, D. 1995, *Inventing Ireland: The Literature of the Modern Nation*. London: Vintage.

Kincaid, A. 2006, *Postcolonial Dublin: Imperial Legacies and the Built Environment*. Minneapolis: University of Minnesota Press.

Koselleck, R. 1985, *Futures Past. On the Semantics of Historical Time*. Cambridge, MA: Harvard University Press.

Kruger, B. & Mariani, P. 1989, *Remaking History*. Seattle: Bay Press.

Latour, B. 2005, *Reassembling the Social: An Introduction to Actor–Network Theory*. Oxford: Berg.

Leone, M. & Potter, P.B. (eds) 1996, *An Archaeology of Capitalism*. New York: Kluwer.

Lyttleton, J. & Rynne, C. 2009, *Plantation Ireland*. Dublin: Four Courts Press.

O'Keeffe, T. 2001, 'Concepts of "castle" and the construction of identity in medieval and post-medieval Ireland', *Irish Geography* **34**(1): 69–88.

O'Keeffe, T. 2006, 'Starting as we mean to go on. Why we need a theoretically-informed historical archaeology', *Archaeological Dialogues* **13**(2): 208–11.

O'Keeffe, T. & Quirke, S. 2009 'Ightermurragh castle in context', in Lyttleton & Rynne 2008.

Orser, C.E. 1996, *An Historical Archaeology of the Modern World*. New York: Kluwer.

Panofsky, E. 1962, *Renaissance and Renascences in Western Art*. New York: Harper & Row.

Said, E.W. 1989, 'Yeats and decolonization', in Kruger & Mariani 1989, 3–30.

Smith, S.V. & O'Keeffe, T. forthcoming, *Archaeologies of Power and Dissention: Rural Communities of the Middle Ages and Beyond*. New York: Springer.

Spurr, D. 1993, *The Rhetoric of Empire: Colonial Discourse in Journalism, Travel Writing, and Imperial Administration*. Durham, NC: Duke University Press.

Tarlow, S. 2007, *The Archaeology of Improvement*. Cambridge: Cambridge University Press.

Thomas, J. 2004, *Archaeology and Modernity*. London: Routledge.

Trouillot, M.-R. 2003, *Global Transformations: Anthropology and the Modern World*. Basingstoke: Palgrave.

Wallerstein, I. 1974, *The Modern World-System I. Capitalist Agriculture and the Origins of the European World-Economy in the Sixteenth Century*. New York: Academic Press.

Encouraging Interest in the Recent Past

By TONY CROSBY

The Heritage Lottery Fund (HLF) was set up in 1994 to distribute money raised by the National Lottery to heritage projects throughout the United Kingdom. HLF is therefore a comparatively recent participant in the conservation, management and interpretation of the industrial heritage of the United Kingdom. However, HLF's contribution to the conservation of and public involvement with industrial heritage has already been considerable. This chapter outlines HLF's definition of industrial heritage and its funding for projects within this heritage sector. It considers how this investment can be made sustainable in the long term by encouraging the adaptive reuse of former industrial buildings and interest among local communities in their recent past. In order to demonstrate the positive impact that this investment has had on the historic character of the areas involved and their communities, evaluative case studies from a wide range of industrial heritage projects are referenced throughout.

INTRODUCTION

The following prophetic extract from a 1925 article by a local historian writing in a history journal about early railway stations in Essex forms a fascinating introduction to a discussion of popular interest in the recent past:

> The study of railway stations from an archaeological point of view has not yet become popular. Probably, indeed, this is the first article ever written upon the subject. Some might even ask whether such a study exists, or could exist, seeing that archaeology is the study of things ancient, and the world does not yet possess even one single railway station as much as one hundred years old: for the first railway was not opened until 1825, and the centenary is being celebrated this month.
>
> In time, perhaps, we may hear of the formation of a Society for the Study and Preservation of Ancient Railway Stations. This will be able to prevent destruction being indulged in too freely and to raise funds, by public subscription, either to restore in appropriate style specially choice examples or to excavate among and trace the foundations of others which, like our ancient abbeys, have long lain in ruins. But this is not yet.[1]

Unfortunately, Christy's hopes did not 'prevent destruction being indulged in too freely' in the case of the demolition of the Euston Arch but, even before that event in 1962, the 1950s saw the genesis of industrial archaeology and a growth in interest in the recent, post-1750, industrial past.[2] This period saw the start of the railway preservation[3] and canal restoration movements and of the preservation of a number of small industrial sites such as wind and water mills, engine houses and pumping stations, all with technology, structures and buildings of the previous two hundred years – our industrial heritage. Many of these industrial sites have from the start been run by volunteers, people with a passionate interest in the technology, processes and places of the industrial revolution, but it would appear that some are beginning to struggle with an ageing and declining volunteer base, a loss of traditional skills and a declining number of visitors as competition grows from other heritage and visitor attractions.[4]

As discussed throughout this volume, there has been much debate recently in the pages of both Industrial Archaeology News and Industrial Archaeology Review about the relative emphasis given to the technology of industrialisation and the social context in which industrialisation took place. This author's view is that industrial archaeology should encompass the three overlapping themes of 'Technology' (machines, mechanical engineering and processes), 'Places' (landscapes, sites, structures, buildings and architecture) and 'People' (engineers, inventors, entrepreneurs and workers). An industrial archaeological site has no single meaning, but a number of overlapping meanings such as technical, scientific, architectural, social and economic. The study of the social context of industrialisation is as important as the study of the technology and the places where it all took place (after all archaeology is the study of past human activity), and probably no one of us has the knowledge, expertise or interest to be able to do all three. Likewise, it is The Heritage Lottery Fund's view that people are important to the conservation of industrial heritage, as important as they were in creating it. One way of helping people to understand and develop an interest in the past and their heritage is to draw out the stories of those who lived and worked in the past and with whom we can all identify in some way or other. When people have developed an understanding of and interest in their (and others') history and heritage they are more likely to value certain aspects of it. They can then be encouraged to help to assess the significance and value of heritage assets, and to care for them in the ways described below for the education and enjoyment of a wider public.

THE HERITAGE LOTTERY FUND

The Heritage Lottery Fund (HLF) was set up in 1994 to distribute the money raised by the National Lottery to heritage projects throughout the United Kingdom. It is, therefore, only comparatively recently that HLF has had an impact on the conservation, management and interpretation of the built heritage. However, over the first fourteen years of its existence, HLF made a considerable contribution to the conservation of and public involvement with industrial heritage. Up to the end of March 2008, HLF had awarded over £743 million to 1,990 industrial, maritime and transport heritage projects across the whole of the United Kingdom. These awards range from major grants to national industrial and transport museums (including the three national mining museums (see Fig. 7.1); major canal restorations such as of the Kennet and Avon; the restoration of historic ships (such as the Cutty Sark and SS Great Britain); conservation work on gunpowder, salt, gas and pottery manufacturing sites; as well as pumping stations, lead mining sites, seaside piers,

LEFT
Figure 7.1 The former
Caphouse Colliery, now
the National Mining
Museum for England

signal boxes and wind and watermills. HLF has also funded projects at all of the United Kingdom's eight industrial World Heritage Sites (Fig. 7.2)

HLF has identified five broad categories of heritage. These include: (1) historic buildings, such as places of worship, castles and historic houses; (2) natural and designed landscapes, such as public parks, and habitats and species; (3) records and collections held in museums, libraries and archives; (4) intangible heritage such as cultural traditions and oral history; and (5) sites and objects linked to industrial, maritime and transport heritage (IM&T). However, industrial heritage is not identified by a particular era such as the traditionally defined industrial revolution era or post-1750, but rather by the type and function of the building, structure or collection of artefacts. Thus, some of the earlier industrial buildings that HLF has funded are malthouses from the 16th and 17th centuries. The oldest parts of Great Dunmow Maltings in Essex are 16th century, with refurbishment

RIGHT
Figure 7.2 New
Lanark cotton mill
village, now a World
Heritage Site offering
visitor attractions,
educational visits and
accommodation (photo:
Glyn Satterley)

in 1780 and modification in the 19th century. Elsey's Yard malthouse in Bury St Edmunds, Suffolk, dates from 1620. At the other end of the chronological scale is the investment that has been made in preserving aspects of 20th-century industry, principally in the road transport and aviation industries. Other aspects include the land-based oil industry of the interwar period, with a project at Dukes Wood oil drilling site in Nottinghamshire[5] and of the 20th-century chemical industry.

In April 2008, HLF launched its new strategic plan, 'Valuing our heritage: Investing in our future'. The three strategic aims, little changed, are to: (1) conserve the UK's diverse heritage for present and future generations to experience and enjoy; (2) help more people, and a wider range of people, to take an active part in and make decisions about heritage; and (3) help people to learn about their own and other people's heritage. Conservation has been one of HLF's core aims since it was established; however, conservation is not viewed as a one-off, once-and-for-all event. It is the process of caring for heritage in a way that makes sure it remains relevant, accessible and in good condition. Conservation involves managing change in a way that is sensitive to what is considered important. When HLF invests in the protection of a building or site, it is done because of its perceived value to the public, and it expects to see that investment protected in the long term.

Although many HLF grants are awarded to sites and buildings that are recognised as being of national importance, such as listed buildings, HLF's view of heritage is broad and is grounded in what people value. Therefore, the people who apply for a grant will explain why the heritage asset is important to the local community, as well as the region or the nation. If it is not officially protected in some way, they will explain its heritage value and explain what public consultation has been carried out to find out why the heritage asset is important and to whom. In this way people are encouraged to take an interest in their heritage, assessing its value and significance, and helping to ensure that a broad range of heritage is conserved for the future, not just that which is officially protected.

ADAPTIVE REUSE

If a heritage building is to be conserved and passed on to future generations, a sustainable future use must be found, otherwise despite preservation and restoration work, it will again eventually fall into a derelict state. To receive HLF funding, an applicant needs to demonstrate that there is a viable and sustainable future use for the building so that it is maintained and the investment has provided value for money. It is unlikely that a derelict industrial site can be returned to its original use, although there are exceptions. The most obvious are those buildings related to the inland waterways and heritage railways. The restoration of the Anderton Boat Lift between the Trent and Mersey Canal and the River Weaver Navigation in Cheshire has brought it back into use again for transferring boats (albeit leisure craft rather than working narrow boats) between the two waterways. Stations and other railway structures have been put back to original use as part of working heritage railways. Many of the preserved wind and water mills are again grinding corn for sale as flour to visitors. However, one of the most innovative projects that has involved an industrial building, machinery and process being returned to its original use is at the Frogmore Mill on the Apsley Paper Trail in Hertfordshire.[6]

Frogmore Mill was in use for making paper using hand-held moulds in 1774. The Fourdrinier brothers commissioned the development of a continuous paper-making machine based on a French concept, and the world's first continuous paper-making machine was installed at Frogmore Mill in 1803, with a second, much improved and larger machine installed there the following year. The steam-powered machine that is currently in use at Frogmore Mill was built in 1895 and installed at the mill in 1907. The Apsley Paper Trail is a social enterprise producing 100 per cent recycled paper on a heritage site where paper has been produced for over 230 years using machinery over 110 years old. In most cases, however, a new use has to be found for redundant industrial buildings, and these are many and varied. Those uses can include conversion into museums, either as a museum of that particular industry such as the London Canal Museum or a more general industrial museum such as the Museum of Science and Industry in the former railway buildings at the Manchester end of the Liverpool & Manchester Railway. Another use is that of an archive, such as Warner Textile Archive in the former silk mill in Braintree, Essex, or as a visitor attraction in and of itself, as with the SS Great Britain in Bristol. Residential, business and mixed uses can be appropriate, as in the regeneration areas in places like Ancoats in Manchester and the Rope Walks area of Liverpool. Other structures can be converted for educational purposes, as with the conversion of the Derby Roundhouse for use as part of Derby College; or for community use, as in the case of the two malthouses mentioned above, as well as the former Richmond Station in Yorkshire and the Red Store at Lerryn in Cornwall.

ENCOURAGING INTEREST

Sustainability of former industrial buildings requires a new use being found, but HLF also wants to see people become involved in projects, given that the other two HLF strategic aims focus on people's participation in and learning about heritage. Encouraging involvement requires stimulating people's interests and providing a range of opportunities. Such opportunities include managing the building and its new use; for example, serving as trustees or specialist advisers; or engaging in general support through membership of a friends' groups, making subscriptions, and raising funds. Other opportunities include operating and maintaining machinery, vehicles and infrastructure; and organising and leading activities for visitors. At a more general level, individuals may go to the site as visitors attending events and activities; as users of the facilities provided, such as members of community groups; as learners taking part in school visits or adult education courses; or as trainees learning heritage conservation skills.

Many of the people involved will be volunteers. However, how is their interest stimulated and encouraged? First, the value and significance of the heritage asset needs to be established, be it national, regional or local. For many of the national heritage assets, 'value' and 'significance' may be established nationally and by experts in the particular field. However, local people must always be involved in the discussions about value and significance so that they understand why a local building has been listed and so that they can help identify heritage assets that may be of more regional or local value to individuals or communities. The various meanings of a site, structure or building need to be drawn out and communicated, and these meanings could be historical, technological, architectural, scientific, social, economic, or spiritual. Interpreting the heritage asset by drawing out its value, significance and meanings can promote wider appreciation and ultimately encourage greater participation.

CASE STUDIES

Through research into a representative sample of projects awarded grants, HLF is able to evaluate whether the projects achieved their original aims, such as finding sustainable new uses for redundant and derelict industrial buildings, and also how far its own aims of conservation, participation and learning have been met. A few case studies will illustrate this process of evaluation; these examples are taken from research and evaluation reports that are available on the HLF website.[7]

STONE RAILWAY STATION, STAFFORDSHIRE

The Stone Railway Station is a Grade II-listed building in a conservation area. Built in 1848 by the North Staffordshire Railway Company, it is deemed to be of local and regional significance as an example of the Company's architecture and the work of its architect, W.S. Hunt. However, the building was deteriorating through rot, damp, water ingress and forced entry and vandalism, having been substantially disused since the 1970s and totally disused since 1999. The project sought to undertake conservation work on this valued building to retain its original character (built in a North Staffordshire Jacobean-style of red brick with stone detailing and three spiked gables to the front elevation) and remove later unsympathetic additions and alterations. In order to support its future maintenance, income revenue from a new use was needed. Following consultation by the Town Council with local community groups and the receipt of letters of support, it was agreed that the building would be used by the local community, including the local Railway Society, for a range of social and cultural activities. Therefore, meeting rooms of various sizes and catering facilities were developed. Evaluation of the project, undertaken by interviewing a sample of local residents, showed that residents felt the restored building helped make the local area a good and attractive place to live and work, the building was safe and easy to use, and it provided an important connection to the area's history and a sense of pride.

RED STORE, LERRYN, CORNWALL

The Red Store is a Grade II-listed warehouse situated in a conservation area and an Area of Outstanding Natural Beauty on the river Fowey. Built in 1870, the three-storey, stone structure was used to store corn and fertiliser that were being transported on the river and hence it has a link to Lerryn's maritime history. The Red Store fell out of use and into disrepair from the late 1950s, so if this locally valued building was to be retained, a new and sustainable use had to be found for it as advocated by the parish council and local residents. Therefore, in 2005/6, two craft spaces were created on the upper floor and let to local artists and crafts people, while the ground floor is used as a community resource space for exhibitions and a community information centre with a heritage and learning focus. There is a high level of volunteer involvement in the running of the building with a volunteer management committee, volunteers acting as stewards when the centre is open and for special events and working on the local history archive.[8]

TOWER CURING WORKS/TIME AND TIDE MUSEUM, GREAT YARMOUTH, NORFOLK

The Tower Curing Works was built in Great Yarmouth in the late 19th century for herring curing and is a Grade II-listed, two-storey, red-brick building (Fig. 7.3). Adaptive reuse of the building resulted in the creation of the Time and Tide Museum, which concentrates on maritime, fishing and other local history and which replaced the previous Maritime Museum. During the development phase of the museum, there was extensive consultation by the Preservation Trust with the local community in a continuing process of involving the local people in the themes and design of new displays. This community participation along with the increases in visitor numbers, educational visits and volunteer opportunities resulted in a sustainable future for the building. Evaluation of the project demonstrated that the new museum has made a small but valuable economic contribution to the local area in terms of additional employment and the impact of additional visitors to the town.[9]

ADAMS BUILDING, LACE MARKET, NOTTINGHAM

This Grade II*-listed mid-19th-century building was a textile factory, lace warehouse and salesroom and is a distinctive building within the lace market area of Nottingham, which is home to a high concentration of listed industrial buildings characterised by such tall Victorian warehouses and factories. By the 1990s it was only in partial use by low-margin clothing companies situated in part of an inner city area in need of regeneration. The conversion of the Adams Building was undertaken in partnership with New College Nottingham and it is now used by the college as the city campus by students aged 16–19

LEFT
Figure 7.3 The former Tower Curing Works, Great Yarmouth, now used to house the Time and Tide Maritime Museum

and for adult education (Fig. 7.4). Economic impact research involving interviews with users and staff of the building, and local stakeholders such as businesses, has shown that this conversion has stimulated the regeneration of the area into a creative and cultural quarter. Associated service industries use many other former industrial buildings, thus creating a sustainable economic future for this former industrial area.[10]

CHATHAM HISTORIC DOCKYARD, KENT

Chatham Historic Dockyard enjoyed four hundred years of maritime activity prior to its closure in 1984, and contains over a hundred buildings and structures, some dating back to 1704, and most of which are protected (Fig. 7.5). A new use for the dockyard area was needed following closure and now the dockyard itself along with its many artefacts and vessels serves as a major visitor attraction with 130,000 visitors a year. However, this is only one part of the story of the regeneration of the dockyard; the visitor attraction is one of a number of complementary uses of this mixed-use site. There are over a hundred small businesses employing over a thousand people within the walls of the historic dockyard. Over four hundred people also live in the dockyard, in properties that range from historic residences, large and small, to modern new homes. Volunteer opportunities are many and there are already over two hundred volunteers associated with the five different volunteer groups helping to conserve various collections at the Chatham dockyard.[11]

ROPEWALKS, LIVERPOOL

The ropewalks area of Liverpool developed from the 18th century between the dock area on the Mersey estuary and the commercial centre of the city, and it currently contains ninety-five listed buildings. It is characterised by long, straight streets that were used as ropewalks and were once lined with warehouses, factories and merchants houses. Like so many similar former industrial areas of English cities, during the late 20th century the ropewalks area became run-down and characterised by derelict buildings and vandalism. Following a Townscape Heritage Initiative project, this part of Liverpool, well-placed between the tourist area of Albert Dock and the city centre, has evolved into a desirable area to live and to work. The improved environment has attracted tourists as well as residents and business, with a thriving night-time culture matched by a day-time economy based on art, music and design studios.[12]

CONCLUSION

Former industrial buildings that have fallen into disuse and dereliction, but which may be of national, regional, or local significance, do not have to be lost, but can be conserved for future generations to learn about, use and enjoy. However, successful and sustainable conservation of our industrial heritage is dependent upon a number of factors. First, there needs to be an understanding of the value and significance of the individual sites, structures, buildings and landscapes, much of which comes from (industrial) archaeological and historical study and research. People, and particularly those from the communities local to the site in question, need to be involved in deciding issues of value and significance in

LEFT
Figure 7.4 The college library within the Adams Building, Nottingham, a former lace factory, warehouse and salesroom (photo: Ray Main)

BELOW
Figure 7.5 Chatham Historic Dockyard, now a mixed-use site consisting of visitor attractions, business community and residential properties

order to encourage interest and gain their commitment to conservation of the site. Second, resources for the capital work of physical restoration and the running costs involved need to be sought. While some of the capital (and revenue for the life of the project) may come from HLF, ongoing revenue needs to be sought from elsewhere, and most sensibly from the new use to which the building is put. In other words, it must be an economically and socially sustainable new use and one that stimulates continued participation from local people. Engaging people and developing a broad constituency of understanding and support will help ensure that the physical remains of our industrial heritage are valued and protected in the future.

NOTES

1. Christy 1925, 146.
2. This rise in the interest in industrial archaeology and heritage has been recently outlined in Cossons 2007.
3. The history of railway and tram preservation has been recorded in detail in Dunstone 2007.
4. Cossons 2007, 39.
5. <http://www.dukeswoodoilmuseum.co.uk/History.htm> [last accessed 7 May 2008].
6. <http://www.thepapertrail.org.uk/default.asp?V_DOC_ID=829>.
7. <http://www.hlf.org.uk/EnglishPublicationsAnd
8. Info/> [last updated 7 April 2008].
9. HLF 2006b.
10. HLF 2006a.
11. HLF 2005.
12. HLF 2005.
13. HLF, New Life: Heritage and Regeneration, 2004, 50–2: <http://www.hlf.org.uk/NR/rdonlyres/C2B421FF-DDB6-41B5-BEB9-3D5D5378948D/0/New_Life_2004.pdf>.

BIBLIOGRAPHY

Christy, M. 1925, 'Some early Essex railway stations', *Essex Review* **34**: 146–55.

Cossons, N. 2007, 'Industrial archaeology: the challenge of the evidence', *Antiquaries Journal* **87**: 1–52.

Dunstone, D. 2007, *For the Love of Trains: The Story of British Tram and Railway Preservation*. Hersham: Ian Allan.

Heritage Lottery Fund (HLF) 2005, *The Economic Impacts of Funding Heritage: Case Studies for 2005*. <http://www.hlf.org.uk/English/PublicationsAndInfo/AccessingPublications/Research+and+Evaluation.htm>.

Heritage Lottery Fund (HLF) 2006a, *The Economic Impacts of Funding Heritage: Year 2 Summary Report, 2006 Case Studies*. <http://www.hlf.org.uk/English/PublicationsAndInfo/AccessingPublications/Research+and+Evaluation.htm>.

Heritage Lottery Fund (HLF) 2006b, *Social Impact of Heritage Lottery Funded Projects: Year 2 Summary Report, 2006 Case Studies*. <http://www.hlf.org.uk/English/PublicationsAndInfo/AccessingPublications/Research+and+Evaluation.htm>.

Post-Medieval Archaeology: A Personal Perspective

By PAUL COURTNEY

Subject definition within any discipline cannot escape the everyday structures and operation of power that exist within that profession. I have therefore set out to express my personal, and undoubtedly biased thoughts, on post-medieval archaeology with no expectation they will be shared. This chapter discusses the definition of the subject and some central issues for the present and future. The ill-defined and fragmented discipline that exists in Britain can at times be exasperating. However, it also reflects a long historical tradition of forming clubs and societies that serves as an important safeguard of intellectual freedom, providing niches for the idiosyncratic and sheer bloody-minded.

INTRODUCTION

Defining one's subject or discipline is itself an act of power. Archaeologists are very good at dispassionately examining power relations in the past, but rarely so detached when it comes to their own professional structures. I have therefore decided to give a personal (and undoubtedly biased) but hopefully honest outpouring of my thoughts on post-medieval archaeology. If it has any virtue it is because I have a deep-seated passion for the subject, hold no formal position and I am not part of the archaeological establishment. My intent, at least, is one of transparency rather than egotism.

DISCOVERING A WIDER WORLD

I was only 11 when SPMA was formed in 1966, though I attended my first lecture on the subject a couple of years later: the late Adrian Oswald talking on clay pipes to the Nene Valley Archaeological Society in a Northamptonshire village hall. However, my schoolboy enthusiasm was really sparked by working on urban digs in Leicester. I joined the society in 1972 at the age of 17 on the proceeds of a summer's digging wages, and I attended my first conference a few months later at King's Manor in York. There were probably few there who were familiar with Bourdieu or Foucault: but in contrast to some current mythology, the subject was actually quite exciting in those early days. Many of the early papers in *Post-Medieval Archaeology*, and indeed its American equivalents, are intuitively perceptive and were often far better written than later contributions. My memories of that first conference are a bit hazy, not least a result of an effort to get in some serious under-age drinking.

However, I met such luminaries as Peter Brears, John Ashdown and Kenneth Barton, and learned of the fur trade from Karlis Karklins of Parks Canada – cross-Atlantic contact has long roots. Perhaps a major difference was that the conference was dominated by that dying breed, the specialist museum curator with a few local government conservation officers and freelance diggers thrown in.

One of the major changes has been the increasing internationalisation of the subject. I don't mean, by this, the long tradition of British archaeologists going off to do archaeology in sunny climes, but the increasing international everyday transfer of information. Hardly a week goes by when I don't receive or send a request for information from American or continental colleagues. This has been enabled by cheap flights, visa waivers and, above all, the internet. After my early meeting with Karlis my next real encounter with historical archaeology was finding Stanley South's *Method and Theory* book in my university library as a research student.[1] Like most Europeans I was simply baffled by its desire to make archaeology scientific.

My epiphany didn't come until the mid-1980s (after I had gained my doctorate) when I attended a theoretical discussion group in Cardiff University organised by Mary Braithwaite, one of Ian Hodder's research students. I was galvanised by the set text in one session, a Dethlefsen and Deetz paper on gravestones.[2] I subsequently read Deetz's *In Small Things Forgotten* and a small heap of books by Ivor Noël Hume.[3] Most significantly, I joined the Society for Historical Archaeology and subsequently the Council for North-Eastern Historical Archaeology. At a time when post-medievalists were an exotic rarity in provincial Britain, I looked forward excitedly to the regular arrival of their journals and newsletters.

I have been a member of SHA for over two decades and have made a serious study of the methodology, theory and historiography of American historical archaeology.[4] Yet, despite its life-changing impact upon me, I still don't consider myself a historical archaeologist in the American sense. I may have outgrown Kerouac (another epiphany), but I still love barbecue, bourbon and Star Trek. However, I don't primarily work in America; I am not American and have no wish to be. My own intellectual baggage is still rooted in European traditions of stratigraphy, landscape studies, history and increasingly European ethnology or folk studies. Indeed, I consider a major outcome of my undoubtedly enriching encounter with American historical archaeology is that it has made me more acutely aware of the distinctively European aspects of my own cultural and intellectual identity. I must stress here that I am not seeking to impose walls between Americans and Europeans but the opposite; understanding difference is an important key to mutual comprehension and dialogue.

A major difference of American archaeology is its roots in cultural anthropology. This is responsible for both some of its great advances and originality as well as some of its traditional weaknesses. It has been *historically* very strong on ethnicity, for instance, and weaker on regional and class analysis, though the latter at least is changing.[5] Certainly, no one school has any monopoly on understanding the past. As Ian Hodder has noted, American archaeology's embeddedness in cultural anthropology still forms one of the major intellectual fissure lines in world archaeology.[6] At a more superficial level, there has been a degree of convergence as post-structural theory, for instance, has influenced both sides of the Atlantic. Even history and anthropology have absorbed much from each other in recent decades.

However, differences also reflect the different physicality of America, its politics and culture. A knowledge of American campus politics (re *race*) is pretty useful if you want to understand the arguments in plantation archaeology over the years. The deep-seated conservatism of American workers has surely influenced the Annapolis school espousal of Althusser, notably the concept that workers are kept in their place through ideological brainwashing.[7] I am also becoming increasing convinced that what Pierre Bourdieu has termed *habitus* influences different trans-Atlantic outlooks.[8] The patchwork of distinctive European *pays* a few miles across contrasts with the vast distances of many American regions. I certainly developed acute paranoia driving through the endless woods of Nova Scotia a few years back. However, my distrust of global archaeology is not one of parochialism, just a different perception of how one can link local and international perspectives.[9] Again I have been brought up researching a Europe full of barriers from the petty marcher lordships of medieval Wales to myriad local toll regimes and the military lines of Vauban in early modern Europe, not on an 'open' frontier.

I would argue that Europeans need to approach American historical archaeology with a critical eye. However, equally they ignore it at their peril. As has been said of scientists, 90-something per cent of all the historical archaeologists who have ever lived are alive today and working in the United States. Despite, to British eyes, a somewhat oppressive professionalism with the insistence on anthropology training and the sanctity of the PhD, it is also incredibly varied. This reflects the size and wealth of America, its regional variation and the sheer number of institutions available to provide niches for both the brilliant and cantankerous. I should also mention Canadian archaeology, which has strong anthropology connections, but its eclectic mix of British, French and American influences makes it more intellectually accessible to many Europeans. The Parks Canada material culture unit publications were a revelation to many of us. Unfortunately, Parks Canada's wonderfully hierarchical and prolific publication programme is a thing of the past after heavy government cutbacks.[10] Quebec continues to produce important publications on excavations and material culture in the French language.[11] Peter Pope's book on Newfoundland, *From Fish to Wine*, is in my opinion one of the best regional studies of recent decades, not least because of its sophisticated integration of the economic and cultural spheres.[12]

DEFINING THE DISCIPLINE

The very lack of definition of post-medieval/historical archaeology has always appealed to me, particularly its fuzzy overlap with cognate disciplines: history, geography and the social sciences. As Chris King elegantly argued in a recent SPMA newsletter editorial, it is best defined simply as a period discipline.[13] As he pointed out, it is reductionist to define it merely as the archaeology of capitalism or colonialism, although these are undoubtedly important paradigms. As my great intellectual hero, the late Marc Bloch (historian of France and martyr of the French Resistance), proclaimed:

Capitalism with a capital 'C', what date shall we assign to its appearance? The twelfth century in Italy? The thirteenth in Flanders? At the time of the Fuggers and the Exchange at Antwerp? The eighteenth century, or even the nineteenth? There are as many birth certificates as there are historians.[14]

Nothing much has changed there seventy years on and several million post-doctoral words later, though one might add the 15th-century farmers and fishermen of the Low Countries to Bloch's list.[15] The main point is that there is no simple consensus as we look upon the world differently, and the subject should be as inclusive as possible. I am also suspicious of philosophies that echo the Whig interpretation of history: that is, history seen as inevitably progressing towards the present, whether in the 'stages of history' of classical Marxism or Francis Fukuyama's 'end of history' thesis.[16]

Unlike Chris King, and many younger practitioners in the United Kingdom, I find the term historical archaeology overly trendy, and simply confusing in a European setting where it is often taken to start in the late Iron Ages.[17] This is despite the fact my training and interests cross both the medieval and post-medieval periods and the disciplines of history and archaeology. However, life is short, and I feel the content rather than the title of the discipline is ultimately more significant. I can therefore live with being an 'historical archaeologist' – but not if it implies an intellectually nonsensical divorce from the subject's origins, long-term evolution and the pioneering work of the first generation. I am both grateful to my predecessors and have an inkling of what it cost them to pursue the subject in one's own time, with little access to grants and little glory to which to look forward.

Chronological division seems inevitable, though we should remember how arbitrary any divisions are.[18] Our current divisions largely reflect 19th-century assessments of the importance of the Reformation and Renaissance that are no longer held – at least in the disciplines that created these concepts. The term early modern is even more loaded than post-medieval in that it reflects the antiquated idea that the Renaissance was the birthplace of modernity.[19] However, as long as we don't take it too seriously, 1500 is as good as anything else. The end-date of 1750 is one I have never accepted. Indeed, *Post-Medieval Archaeology* has published many papers on the later period but at its inception bowed to the industrial archaeologists as the lead advocates for the later period. It is doubtful that this reflected any ideological divergence from America, merely a gentlemanly acceptance of the fact that industrial archaeology was more developed and regional than in the United States. I would argue that it was a mistake at a time when few if any industrial archaeologists aspired towards being total archaeologists of town and countryside. Whether it would have made a real difference, given the marginality of all later archaeology, is another matter.

AT THE COALFACE: ARCHAEOLOGY IN 2008

Archaeology has expanded in the United Kingdom in both the academic and commercial sectors. I chose to study archaeology at Cardiff in 1974 as the university was about to appoint a medievalist, Stuart Wrathmell. The department also aimed to appoint the United Kingdom's first post-medievalist at the first funding opportunity. Unfortunately, in a climate of stagnation and then cutbacks in university spending it was never to happen. We now have some very truly talented, even brilliant, scholars in our universities who are changing the perception of the subject among their colleagues and students. Leicester in 2008 seems awash with them (Marilyn Palmer, Sarah Tarlow, Audrey Horning and Chris King). We still need yet more posts in British academia, but the situation has hugely improved. Above all, their students are also filtering out into the commercial and heritage worlds and will gradually rise into more influential positions. On the downside, I hope the hegemony of the Research Assessment Exercise (RAE) doesn't produce a dull if fashionable conformity of approach. The RAE can also probably be blamed for the rash of £80-plus collections of essays produced by the so-called prestige publishers.

The introduction of developer funding in 1991 brought large sums of money into commercial archaeology. It created a small mountain of sheer word-processed garbage (aimed solely at ticking boxes in the planning process); but it also produced some very fine archaeological studies and much in between. Manchester, Sheffield, Birmingham, Ironbridge, Stoke and London have produced, or will shortly produce, some major post-medieval studies of fine quality using varied funding sources.[20] There has also been a huge growth in above-ground recording of buildings and total landscapes. The volumes being produced by the recent and ongoing regional research frameworks exercise partially funded by English Heritage, as already discussed by Shane Gould in this volume, mostly contain not one but two chapters on the post-1500 period.[21] At first glance, then, the last seventeen years may look like the golden age of post-medieval archaeology. However, a closer look would show a more unsettling picture. Over much of the country you would struggle to find an excavation brief that extends beyond 1500 even on large urban excavations. The implication is that where post-medieval archaeology competes with Roman and medieval strata it can be bulldozed if inconvenient or, if dug, has a low post-excavation and publication priority (for exceptions, see Cessford, chapter 22 and Jeffries et al. chapter 23). I could cite endless horror stories but I earn little enough these days in commercial archaeology as it is.

There are also some fundamental structural problems in commercial archaeology that will come to haunt us in decades ahead. Despite the existence of a few university-based commercial units as at Leicester and Manchester, I am worried by a growing gulf between the nature, aims and indeed subject matter of university and PPG16 archaeology. One other major issue in PPG16 work is dissemination of information. There is no point in recording if it is not made easily accessible. The creation of OASIS, based at the Archaeological Data Service at York, as a repository of digital reports has been a major step forward, but to date only a minority of reports end up there. It should be compulsory for all recording projects to be logged there and the project's continued funding should be given our highest national priority.

Commercial archaeology in the UK has generally done well in promoting technical and managerial skills, but in the writer's opinion has also experienced a decline in 'academic' or 'period' skills. Such a decline is difficult to quantify, but I have seen numerous technically proficient reports, even at monograph level, which fall down on basic academic interpretation. The complex reasons for this decline really merit a book, although most relate to an increasingly accountancy culture and the way we classify and value knowledge. It reflects not only increasing pressures in the commercial world but changes in the United Kingdom's education system. Owing to an obsession with league tables, schools are sending even their ablest students to university with little sense of long-term history, having repeatedly studied the Tudors and Nazis at different levels.[22] Academic research in general outside of the academy is also becoming increasing difficult as the literature both expands and becomes more expensive. The digital revolution also has had a downside in that knowledge is increasingly becoming a commodity. Universities are dropping hard copies of journals or sending them to distant external stores in favour of electronic journals. Non-university researchers are in effect excluded from free or cheap access to digital libraries like JSTOR even if they pay for university library cards.

Certainly, units no longer employ specialist historians. Freelance documentary research is becoming rarer because units involved in competitive tendering will not add to their costings if briefs from curators don't ask for it. This is leading to resurgence in the 'prehistoric' approach to the archaeology of historic periods with sites divorced from their historical and landscape contexts. It is time the 'handmaiden' debate was laid to rest. The cutting edge of combining historical and archaeological sources is at a very high level both in the academic and commercial worlds.[23] Nevertheless, it requires a high degree of expertise and either a polymathic researcher or good communication within a multidisciplinary team. Documentary research takes skill (knowledge of Latin, palaeography, history of law etc.) and experience. Sending the most inexperienced and cheapest member of the unit down to the record office is only likely to result in pages of gobbledygook as repeated in thousands of desktop studies of the last two decades.

Finds specialists are increasingly working freelance and are an ageing breed. The fees units are prepared to pay are mostly ludicrous when you need to be putting large sums into a stakeholder pension to get any return, plus buying your own books and et cetera. However, I suspect the impact will be delayed somewhat by people with inadequate pensions living in caravans working into their dotage to support themselves. At the moment, a more pressing concern is probably the growth of 'do it yourself' finds reporting in the viciously competitive small contract end of the market. Field archaeologists who seem capable of engaging in discussion with their specialists on the stratigraphical and taphonomical aspects of their finds assemblages are also depressingly rare.[24]

Archaeology units often tend to favour self-proclaimed generalists and are likely to fund training in CAD, GIS or management and costing skills rather than, say, attendance at a period conference. I believe this is based on a fallacy. Actually, it is those employees who develop a speciality who are likely to be better generalists as their in-depth knowledge of one field spills over into their general work. The increase in university-based research in post-medieval/historical archaeology is wonderful, but inevitably has its own fashionable agendas focused by the needs of the RAE and grant-giving bodies. It thus only partially overlaps with and is no substitute for research in the wider archaeological world. Nevertheless, we need to work on building communications between both spheres.

TOWARDS THE FUTURE

In addition to the eastern seaboard of North America, I have also developed a passion for the medieval/post-medieval archaeology of Continental Europe, especially France and the

Low Countries.[25] As in the United Kingdom, its intellectual roots are closer to history than anthropology, though European ethnology (the academic version of folk studies) has been widely influential. However, national traditions continue to play an important role in the marked distinctiveness of archaeology across the Continent. The spread of commercial and heritage-orientated archaeology has increased the amount of excavation and recording work undertaken but has also exacerbated problems of non-publication. International communication is especially difficult for those outside academia who are often on low salaries and enjoy little access to grants and subsidies. A small but noticeable growth in the number of specialist post-medieval posts in universities can also be seen. The leading American and British journals have also responded by publishing an increasing number of papers by their European colleagues. SPMA held a small but successful conference in Livorno (Italy) in 2006 and as I write, is planning future conferences in Denmark and the Netherlands. We need to build on these efforts by improving networking both between nations and between the academic and commercial/heritage sectors.

I don't know or want to know in advance the intellectual future of historical/post-medieval archaeology. It will appear without the dead hand of the present prescribing it in advance. However, I will suggest a couple of areas of great potential, but there are innumerable others. The first is the below-ground archaeology of everyday agrarian life and society, which has been hardly tackled in the United Kingdom and most European countries, especially for the lowlands.[26] The other topic is the archaeology of the European nation state. The late Stephan Epstein, for instance, has pointed to its role in the development of capitalism, while American sociologist Chandra Mukerji has given us some useful pointers with her work on the material culture of the 17th century French absolutist state.[27]

Is the subject as fragmented in the United Kingdom as the *Crossing Paths or Sharing Tracks?* conference programme suggested? Undoubtedly. I can see why people are irritated by yet another sub-group competing for conference attendees or producing yet another journal you can't afford. However, I would suggest the urge to form interest groups is deeply rooted in British culture, from the learned societies of the 17th century, to the friendly societies of the 18th century and the chums' battalions obliterated on the Somme. If one desires a theoretical rationale one can point to E.P. Thompson's classic, *The Making of the English Working Class* or Jürgen Habermas's writings on the 'public sphere', as epitomised by the 18th-century bourgeois café.[28] However, the plethora of archaeological and related groups and societies gives people an opportunity to find similarly minded people and to publish. They are an important defence of academic and personal freedom in an increasingly state-ist society that should be cherished. It really doesn't a matter a hoot if people really just want to write monographs on the typology of nuts in steam engines – good luck to them. Those of us who want to be holistic theoretical *international* archaeologists can equally well just get on with it. It clearly does matter in terms of national advocacy, but societies like SPMA and AIA have special roles and responsibilities here. In particular, we need to encourage continued dialogue and joint initiatives, especially on the advocacy front. However specialist our personal interests, we should no longer be questioning the need for a more total approach to post-medieval and industrial Britain that doesn't ignore lowland farms and 19th-century urban cesspits.

CONCLUSION

The road ahead is going to be as hard as ever, and we have not ended the marginalisation of the subject. We have made important and I hope lasting advances in academia. It may be rheumatism and age that are wearing me down, but my own experience tells me it is getting harder to transcend the bean-counting agendas of the commercial and heritage sector. However, I don't believe you can keep real talent and enthusiasm totally down. Unfortunately, I don't think we will see any revolution soon, but I am sure we will see a steady trickle of good and occasionally great papers and books on post-medieval archaeology over the following decades from both within and without academia.

I have a special affection for SPMA despite having once been membership secretary for ten years, a job guaranteed to give you a warped view of fellow members. It has always been a members' society, welcoming to everyone; and whilst small it has both kept the journal going and always had a strong and varied conference programme. After thirty-six years of paying my dues, I will be most disappointed if it ever becomes a talking shop for an elitist group of whatever origin. The strength of post-medieval archaeology is that it has been a broad church uniting academics, field archaeologists, amateurs, specialists and generalists. This is something we should fight to retain. In what I think are going to be trying times ahead, SPMA, AIA, IPMAG and other societies will have a crucial role both as advocates for the subject but also as a point of connection/networking and friendship for those archaeologists who wish to learn about and make a real contribution to our understanding of the past.

NOTES

1. South 1977.
2. Dethlefsen & Deetz 1966.
3. Deetz 1977; Noël Hume 1975 and 1982.
4. Courtney 1999.
5. Mrozowski, this volume.
6. Hodder 2003.
7. See Leone 1984 for a classic Annapolis school study.
8. Bourdieu 1977.
9. Orser, this volume.
10. Sussman 1979; Jones & Sullivan 1985; Miville-Deschenes 1987.
11. Moussette 1994; Brassard & Leclerc 2001
12. Pope 2004.
13. King 2007.
14. Bloch 1953, 174–5.
15. Hoppenbrouwers & Van Zanden 2001.
16. Fukuyama 1992. See Hay 2005 on the Whig thesis.
17. Andrén 1998.
18. Courtney 1997.
19. Sluhovsky 2006, 169–78.
20. Nevell & Walker 1999; Egan 2005; Ratkai 2008.
21. Brennard 2006; Cooper 2006.
22. Compare Horning 2007, 8–9.
23. Courtney 2006.
24. Blinkhorn & Cumberpatch 1999; Chadwick 2000.
25. Courtney, in press.
26. Lucas 2003; Newman 2005; Casella 2005.
27. Epstein 2000; Mukerji 1997; 2003 and 2007.
28. Thompson 1968; Habermas 1962.

BIBLIOGRAPHY

Andrén, A. 1998, *Historical Archaeology in Global Perspective*. New York: Plenum/Springer.

Blinkhorn, P.W. & Cumberpatch, C.G. 1997, 'The interpretation of artefacts and the tyranny of the field archaeologist', in *Assemblage* **4**: <http://www.assemblage.group.shef.ac.uk/4/>.

Bloch, M. 1953, *The Historian's Craft*. New York: Knopf (originally published posthumously as *Apologie pour l'histoire*. Paris: Armand Colin, 1949).

Bourdieu, P. 1977, *Outline of a Theory of Practice*. Cambridge: Cambridge University Press.

Brassard, M. and Leclerc, M. 2001, *Identifier la céramique et le verre anciens au Québec*. Québec City: Centre Universitaire des' Études sur les Lettres, les Arts et les Traditions.

Brennand, M. (ed.) 2006, *The Archaeology of North West England. An Archaeological Framework for the North West Region, vol. 1*. Resource Assessment. *Archaeology North West* **8** (special issue).

Casella, E.C. 2005, '"Social workers": new directions in industrial archaeology', in Casella & Symonds (eds), 2005, 3–32.

Casella, C. & Symonds, J. (eds) 2005, *Industrial Archaeology: Future Directions*. New York: Springer.

Chadwick, A. 2000, 'Taking English archaeology into the next millennium – a personal review of the state of the art'. *Assemblage* **5**: <http://www.assemblage.group.shef.ac.uk/5/chad.html>.

Cooper, N.D. (ed.), 2006, *The Archaeology of the East Midlands: An Archaeological Resource Assessment and Research Agenda*. Leicester: School of Archaeology and Ancient History, University of Leicester.

Courtney, P. 1997, 'The tyranny of constructs: some thoughts on periodisation and culture change', in Gaimster & Stamper (eds), 1997, 9–24.

Courtney, P. 1999, 'Different strokes for different folks: the transatlantic development of historical and post-medieval archaeology', in Egan & Michael (eds), 1999, 1–9.

Courtney, P. 2006, 'Historians and archaeologists: an English perspective', *Historical Archaeology* **41**(2): 34–45.

Courtney, P. (in press), 'The current state and future prospects for theory in European post-medieval archaeology', in Majewski. & Gaimster (eds).

Deetz, J. 1977, *In Small Things Forgotten: The Archaeology of Early American Life*. New York: Anchor Books.

Dethlefsen, E. & Deetz, J. 1966, 'Death's heads, cherubs, and willow trees: experimental archaeology in Colonial cemeteries', *American Antiquity* **31**(4): 502–10.

Egan, G. 2005, *Material Culture in London in an Age of Transition*. London: MoLAS.

Egan, G. & Michael, R.L. (eds) 1999, *Old and New Worlds*. Oxford: Oxbow.

Epstein, S.E. 2000, *Freedom and Growth: The Rise of States and Markets in Europe, 1300–1750*. London: Routledge.

Fukuyama, F. 1992, *The End of History and the Last Man*. New York: Free Press.

Gaimster, D. & Stamper, P. (eds) 1997, *The Age of Transition; The Archaeology of English Culture 1400–1600*. Oxford: Oxbow.

Habermas, J. 1962, *Strukturwandel der Öffentlichkeit. Untersuchungen zu einer Kategorie der bürgerlichen Gesellschaft*. Neuwied: Luchterhand. English translation: *The Structural Transformation of the Public Sphere: An Inquiry into a Category of Bourgeios Society*. Cambridge: Polity.

Hay, W.A. 2005, 'Reconsidering Herbert Butterfield', *Historically Speaking: The Bulletin of the Historical Society* **6**(3) (Jan/Feb): <http://www.bu.edu/historic/hs/januaryfebruary05.html>.

Hodder, I. 2003, 'Archaeology as a discontinuous domain', in Van Pool & Van Pool, (eds), 2003, 5–8.

Hoppenbrouwers, P. & van Zanden, J. Ll (eds) 2001, *From Peasants to Farmers? The Transformation of the Rural Economy and Society in the Low Countries (Middle Ages–19th century) in the Light of the Brenner Debate*, Comparative Rural History of the North Sea Area (CORN) Publication Series 4. Turnhout: Brepols.

Horning, A. 2007, 'Cultures of contact, cultures in conflict?: Identity construction, colonialist discourse, and the ethics of archaeological practice in Northern Ireland', *Stanford Journal of Archaeology* **5**, 107–33.

Jones, O.R. & Sullivan, C. 1985, *The Parks Canada Glass Glossary for the Description of Containers, Tableware,*

Flat Glass, and Closures. Ottawa: Parks Canada.

King, C. 2007, 'Editorial. How do we define post-medieval archaeology?', *Post-Medieval Archaeology Newsletter* **65**(2): 1–2.

Leone, M. 1984, 'Interpreting ideology in historical archaeology: using the rules of perspective in the William Paca Garden in Annapolis, Maryland', in Miller & Tilley (eds), 1984, 25–35.

Lucas, G. 2003, 'Reading pottery: literature and transfer-printed pottery in the early nineteenth century', *International Journal of Historical Archaeology* 7(2): 127–43.

Majewski, T. & Gaimster, D. (eds) in press *The International Handbook of Historical Archaeology.* New York: Springer.

Miller, D. & Tilley, C. (eds) 1984, *Ideology, Power and Prehistory.* Cambridge: Cambridge University Press.

Miville-Deschenes, F. 1987, *The Soldier Off Duty. Domestic Aspects of Military Life at Fort Chambly under the French Regime as Revealed by Archaeological Objects.* Ottawa: Parks Canada.

Moussette, M. 1994, *Le site du palais de l'intendant à Québec: genèse et structuration d'un lieu urbain.* Québec City: Septentrion.

Mukerji, C. 1997, *Territorial Ambitions and the Gardens of Versailles.* Cambridge: Cambridge University Press.

Mukerji, C. 2003, 'Intelligent uses of engineering and the legitimacy of state power', *Technology and Culture* **44**: 655–76.

Mukerji, C. 2007, 'The great forest survey of 1669–1671: the use of archives for political reform', *Social Studies of Science* 37(2): 227–53.

Nevell, M.D. & Walker J.S.F. 1999, *Tameside in Transition: The Archaeology of the Industrial Revolution in Two North-West Lordships 1642–1870.* Ashton-under-Lyne: Tameside Metropolitan Borough Council.

Newman, R. 2005, 'Farmers and fields: developing a research agenda for post-medieval agrarian society and landscape', *Post-Medieval Archaeology* **39(2): 205–14.**

Noël Hume, I. 1975, *Historical Archaeology.* New York: Norton.

Noël Hume, I. 1982, *Martin's Hundred.* New York: Knopf.

Pope, P.E. 2004, *From Fish into Wine: The Newfoundland Plantation in the Seventeenth Century.* Chapel Hill: University of North Carolina Press.

Ratkai, S. (ed.) 2008, *The Bull Ring Uncovered: Excavations at Edgbaston Street, Moor Street, Park Street and The Row, Birmingham City Centre, 1997–2001.* Oxford: Oxbow.

Sluhovsky, M. 2006, 'Discernment of difference, the introspective subject and the birth of modernity', *Journal of Medieval and Early Modern Studies* **36**(1): 169–95.

South, S. 1977, *Method and Theory in Historical Archeology.* New York: Academic Press.

Sussman, S. 1979, *Spode/Copeland Transfer-Printed Patterns Found at 20 Hudson's Bay Company Sites.* Ottawa: Parks Canada.

Thompson, E. P. 1968, *The Making of the English Working Class,* 2nd edn. London: Victor Gollancz (first edn, 1963).

Van Pool, T.L. & Van Pool, C.S. (eds) 2003, *Essential Tensions in Archaeological Method and Theory.* Salt Lake City: University of Utah Press.

An Archaeological Avant-Garde

By JAMES R. DIXON

In recent years, vague attempts have been made to characterise Contemporary Archaeology as an archaeology of modern material culture; of post-war archaeology; as archaeology 1950–2000; or more widely as a reflexive, interdisciplinary historical archaeology. I would argue, in opposition to some of these attempts, that Contemporary Archaeology is inspired by, rather than shackled to, any temporal period or subject of study. Rather, Contemporary Archaeology has the potential to be defined through its mode of engagement with the world, an engagement in which 'traditional' archaeology, interdisciplinary work, materiality, politics, and more are inextricably linked. With reference to recent projects originating in a number of different arenas, this chapter attempts to describe the Contemporary Archaeologist and their place within the subject discussion of this publication. Through this effort, I hope to stake a claim for Contemporary Archaeology as a truly avant-garde movement with the potential to profoundly influence the future of the discipline.

INTRODUCTION

For at least ten years, there has been much discussion within the field, referred to by this volume, of the relationship between 'Industrial Archaeology', 'Post-Medieval Archaeology' and 'Historical Archaeology'. The discussion incorporates different types of material, different dates, and different research agendas, and it doesn't appear to be near to resolution. Perhaps, rather than trying to find some unifying thread between these different fields, it is of more use to archaeology, certainly in terms of strengthening archaeological theory and practice, to work to establish them as different, or even opposed, ways of seeing.[1] By this I mean that each of the above disciplines can assuredly bring a different focus, different body of theory and historical development and different ways of working to the wider field without any need to integrate them. The creation of all-encompassing research agendas, something that would be an inevitable result of any attempt to answer the question of what the above sub-fields actually are and how they relate to each other, should be seen as secondary in importance to the need to be comfortable and confident with the way we work; comfortable with people working in different ways to ourselves; and confident that other ways of working primarily serve to challenge and strengthen Archaeology rather than posing a threat. Archaeology is not a finite resource, and it will stand up to being looked at in a multitude of different ways.

Fundamentally, archaeology is about the relationship between people and things. How we, as archaeologists in the 21st century, approach this relationship in a knowing, thoughtful, holistic manner is of the utmost importance both to our understanding of historical material and to the great potential for archaeology to make a meaningful contribution to everyday life. In this discussion, I present a particular way of seeing derived from the newly emerging field of contemporary archaeology. It is necessarily personal, such is the need I perceive for archaeologists to consider in depth their own stances within the wider field of archaeology before (or at least alongside) any attempt to understand others, whether past or present.

CONTEMPORARY ARCHAEOLOGY

In the 21st century, particularly since the founding of the Contemporary and Historical Archaeology and Theory (CHAT) conference group, the phrase 'contemporary archaeology' has begun to appear on the archaeological 'horizon'. There certainly does appear to be such a thing as contemporary archaeology, but it has seemed thus far to defy description. In my experience of working with the CHAT group, there are many people who would tentatively describe themselves as contemporary archaeologists, but each of them likely has a different idea of what they mean by 'contemporary'. Any quick look through the available literature[2] will reveal contemporary archaeology to be the archaeology of the 20th century. Or perhaps it is the archaeology of AD 1950–2000. Or the study of modern-day material culture. Or archaeology with added modern media techniques and perspectives.

Which is it? Well, of course, it's all of them. However, like with the sub-fields mentioned at the beginning of this chapter, we can go further than getting 'bogged down' attempting a definition. To tie contemporary archaeology down as a period division is surely unhelpful, unimaginative and somewhat predictable? The SPMA has dropped its 'cut-off' date of AD 1750 and it would be a shame if another group were to impose a new date upon the SPMA by declaring that contemporary archaeology begins in a certain year. There is much to be gained from fuzzy boundaries and overlapping interests. That being so, the first thing to be done here is to draw a distinction between two different concerns. In practice they are not so easily divisible nor should they be. They are intertwined, both in origins and in practice, but there is an important distinction to be made nonetheless.

The distinction I draw is between contemporary archaeology, the subject of this chapter, and archaeology of the contemporary past. The latter first really came to the fore with the book by Gavin Lucas and Victor Buchli, *Archaeologies of the Contemporary Past*[3] and perhaps reached its zenith thus far with media coverage of 'The Van Project' led by Cassie Newland and John Schofield, which saw the 'excavation' and post-ex analysis of a Ford Transit Van.[4] I don't want to take anything away from this important work, but I wish to go a step further. While The Van Project made the useful point that we can apply traditional archaeological methods to modern and unconventional sites and artefacts, my personal wish is to move away from such a focus towards developing contemporary archaeology as a distinct approach inspired by the contemporary world, but with applications across whatever periods of history we choose to engage with.

Despite the use of the phrase 'avant-garde' in the title, this discussion is most certainly not a manifesto. It is not my intention that everyone take up the ideas I will suggest here;

indeed, it would be disappointing if that happened. I do not see a need for a unified contemporary archaeology 'movement', as I believe the ultimate conclusion of undertaking a contemporary archaeology to be a strongly held personal conviction of whatever position one finds through this undertaking. In a sense, and although I will not elaborate too much on this idea here, contemporary archaeological work and thought has the potential to develop archaeology as a philosophy that is, at one and the same time, highly relevant to how we approach the past, the present, and the future.

Avant-garde has a lot of different implications depending on your background.[5] Daniel Miller, for instance, in the introductory essay of *Acknowledging Consumption*, makes use of the term 'vanguard', asserting that studies of consumption are leading the way in establishing a new way of interpreting history.[6] This sense of the vanguard as 'the leaders of the way' is a typically Anglophone interpretation of the avant-garde concept,[7] which implies somehow that the vanguard are the first discoverers of a 'truth'. Here, I will use a more continental, artistic sense of the phrase. I see my avant-garde as those sent out to explore 'no-man's land', with more predisposition to antagonism than to leadership. The no-man's land in question is, in part, today, the early 21st century. But this no-man's land is also the space between people and things, between past and present, and between myself and others. I wish to investigate new ways of working that have been inspired by modern, changing conceptions of what can be considered archaeological and make a case for the relevance of these contemporary archaeological approaches to all time periods. I will discuss three main points: Territory, Process and Reflection. The examples I give will be of where I have encountered, dealt with or used these ideas in my own work. As befits the personal nature of the field that I outlined above, my intention is try to give an overview of contemporary archaeology as I see it.

TERRITORY

Recently, and partly as a response to the wording of funding body directives,[8] there has been a rise in the number of projects describing themselves as inter-, cross- or multi-disciplinary. There is a case for saying that archaeology is multidisciplinary as a matter of course. This can take us two ways. It is often said that archaeology is the only department you need in a university because you can do anything else within it, but I'm aware that logically the opposite must be equally possible: that perhaps archaeology is the only department you don't need because you can do it within almost any other subject. This brings me to my first point about contemporary archaeology: it is none of the above; rather, my contemporary archaeology is an anti-discipline.

As stated earlier, most archaeology crosses boundaries. One of the very reasons that this chapter exists is because of contemporary archaeologists looking at non-traditional things that gives rise to a whole new series of questions for us to ask. With archaeologists looking at iPods, mobile telephones or computer games, economic systems, or sustainable housing, the subject is moving into a whole new realm. One such non-traditional thing is engineered crash-testing. As an archaeologist, I find the world of accident simulation fascinating. The journals are full of descriptions of micro-seconds of violent physical contact between objects told holistically in terms of justifications, parameters, results and conclusions.[9] There is unlikely to be anything that comes as close to placing material culture at the centre of a continuity between past, present, and future as the literature surrounding accident simulation. The material culture itself is fascinating; one laboratory uses a 1kg steel cube as the best physical representation of, very specifically, 'the aggressiveness' of a medium-sized mountain rock, dropped rather than thrown, from an overhead bridge onto a train cabin window by disaffected youths.[10] And they are very strict about each of these points.

The implications of the material properties, materiality or physicality of things are also an interesting aspect of accident simulations. The ability of a steel tube to withstand certain collision conditions may have direct consequences for the autonomy of wheelchair users the world over.[11] It is, of course, very human too, and a degree of angling here or there, a millimetre's difference in the thickness of some steel may be the difference between life and death or disablement.[12] It is worth pointing out that the primary objective of crash-testing is to recreate exactly past 'real-world' accidents (which has some resonance with experimental archaeology) rather than to test new designs, which is a much later part of the process.

Things that I have learned from my archaeological study of engineered crash testing include both an increased appreciation of the physicality of objects and a more holistic approach to events and things and what they do. Crash-testing is bound up in science, politics, materiality, ethics and so on, but then if we're honest about it, so is everything else, now and historically. What my encounter with the world of accident simulation has given me is a whole new set of questions to ask of material culture. Whereas The Van Project sought to ask traditionally archaeological questions of unconventional material, I don't see anything wrong with allowing material to dictate its own interrogation (although I mean less that data 'speaks' to us and more that we should be aware of the existing fields of inquiry, academic or otherwise, surrounding things we come to anew as contemporary archaeologists), something that has to be borne in mind as we begin to consider the material of our own time. The wider implication is that perhaps looking at modern material we can learn how to approach the chaotic complexity of worlds past and present. Ideas reached through reading around crash testing, for instance, can be applied to material culture related to revolutionary France or to the 1381 Peasants' Revolt.

A good example of this approach can be seen in the work of existential historian and philosopher Jacques Rancière. In his work on France in the 1830s and 1840s,[13] he looks specifically to contemporary workers' journals as a means of capturing the 'non-working moments of dreaming',[14] of what he calls 'worker-intellectuals'. One metal worker, Jérôme-Pierre Gilland, writes extensively discussing his own social, economic, and political situation through a lens of the manufacturing processes he is involved in and, more importantly for us, the objects he comes into contact with in his daily practice. Rancière finds in his writings 'the depicted virtues of forged metal'.[15] Here, as with crash-testing, we can see the explanation of a situation (political dissatisfaction / social implications of car crashes) through the materials present. Following the workers' journals and the experimental data of the crash laboratory, we see speculations on the future based on material histories evolve into new material presents, where both objects and their sociopolitical implications are intentionally changed through direct action. I would certainly argue that people writing about objects is as much a concern of the contemporary archaeologist as anything else.

Being actively anti-disciplinary allows us to come at things from non-traditional directions, and is a case of establishing 'places for thinking' that suit each of us. Where contemporary archaeology can lead, and is leading in this area, is in purposefully 'trespassing' in other disciplines and, on behalf of everybody else, asserting the archaeologist's right to ramble. Simply put, you can be archaeological anywhere and we should actively try our best to be archaeological everywhere regardless of any perceived restrictions. Of course, if this is to be the case we have to be tolerant of those from other disciplines who choose to trespass in archaeology!

PROCESS

My first point on process follows on from this. To archaeologically paraphrase Doreen Massey,[16] 'In place of an archaeology which searches for material culture to employ in the production of historical narratives, contemporary archaeology looks to the act of searching as the essential space of the archaeological.' Recently, I reviewed an exhibition by artist Johan Grimonprez at the Whitechapel Gallery in London called 'Looking for Alfred'.[17] The centrepiece was a film of a number of Alfred Hitchcock look-alikes in variously Hitchcockian scenarios in the Palais des Beaux Arts in Brussels. We look for Alfred but he's always just disappearing around a corner, up stairs or through a door. The film starts with a nonsense story based on one of Hitchcock's own. Two men are travelling on a train. In the luggage rack above them is an unusually shaped package. One man asks the other, 'What's that you have in the luggage rack?' The other replies, 'That's a MacGuffin.' 'What's a MacGuffin?' asks the man. 'It's an apparatus for capturing lions in the Adirondack mountains of New York.' 'But there are no lions in the Adirondack mountain of New York.' 'Well then,' says the man, 'that's no MacGuffin. You see a MacGuffin is nothing at all!' In filmic terms, a MacGuffin is a plot device that drives a story on while being of little or no relevance of itself.

Cornelius Holtorf has told us that all archaeology is contemporary archaeology in the sense that it 'offers a perspective from which the past and its remains can be understood in the light of our present'.[18] Perhaps, then, the idea of 'the past' is more a prompt than an objective, and maybe there is some mileage in looking to the past not as what we find, but as the reason that we seek. To focus on the hunt rather than the treasure is, I believe, to realign archaeology with its origins, to rejuvenate the joy of the unexpected discovery.

In 2003, I undertook a desk-based assessment looking at a late-19th-century estate landscape in south Cheshire.[19] Between around 1860 and 1910, successive Dukes of Westminster made large-scale changes to their lands, including the planning and rebuilding of several entire villages and the re-landscaping of the estate house at the centre of it all. This made an interesting enough landscape assessment, and I thought no more of it until the next time I was in Chester, a year or so later. Wandering around the town, I noticed a large number of buildings bearing the Grosvenor insignia, the family name of the Dukes of Westminster. Investigating Grosvenor Park, I found constructed ruins, a statue of one of the Dukes, and buildings built in the same style and by John Douglas, the same architect as in the villages I had been looking at for my desktop assessment. Carrying on to the riverside, I found yet more: a row of trees planted by Grosvenor, architect-designed, and now listed, ice-cream stalls and an impressive iron bridge, all looked over by Chester's Roman walls and medieval south gate and bridge. Most importantly, walking along the riverside, I noticed a small sign advertising boat trips on the river Dee as far as the very villages at the centre of my study.

The trip, south through the two villages I had focused upon and along the eastern border of the estate house and garden between them, was essential to my understanding of this historic landscape. As we drifted along, I saw that there were farmhouses dotted along the way, alternately on the left and right banks and always on top of a ridge. There were repeated but fleeting glimpses of the Alfred Waterhouse clock-tower at the centre of the estate, and when you couldn't see it, you could hear its bells chime. At the end of the journey, another iron bridge. At the first of the villages, you walk from the river up a gentle slope towards the centre. On your right as you walk is a high stone wall that, if you try, you can see over into a series of neat, walled fields, each with an architect-designed barn. Further on, the church. Behind the church, the end of the hunt. The treasure. Behind the late-19th-century church was another. Smaller. Ruined. And the resting place of the very men who had designed the landscape I had just travelled through. Wonderful things indeed.

The landscape as designed by the Dukes of Westminster is one that ties together the history of Cheshire, and of the Grosvenor family in particular, with a number of other phenomena, not least agricultural improvement in a time of national decline, income from the family's lands in Belgravia, London and the very idea of local tourism. The boat trip too is historic: it is listed in 19th-century copies of the Chester Chronicle.[20] So this landscape is meant to be experienced and, in the present day, can be. Without the temporal experience of two hours on that little boat, without the visual, the aural and the haptic experience of that tour, the estate is simply data. The eventual unexpected discovery of the graves of the dukes surrounded as they were by birdsong-punctured silence is, to an extent, the reason the whole of this part of Cheshire exists. There is a tangential point to be made here about the limitations of certain forms of archaeological work, and the fact that by staying in the library you can easily miss the point of a site entirely. More importantly, after some time of having imposed myself and archaeological inquiry upon the site, to follow this historic route, both geographically and temporally different from my previous work, gave me an entirely new kind of engagement with the site that was dictated by the landscape itself. My later visits to the estate house were certainly helped by my ability to put the formal garden with its sightlines and architectural references within a wider 'landscape of experience'.

This might sound a lot like phenomenology, but it isn't quite, at least not as phenomenology has been used in archaeology.[21] I don't seek to make guesses about what people thought when they where here before, but I know, with hindsight, that I would not have the understanding of that landscape that I do now if I had not experienced it in this way and very consciously as a 21st-century archaeologist. More than providing answers about what the landscape may mean, I find that such an experience conditions the way I write about it and the way I am able to explain what the landscape is. To me, this kind of micro-study, of my experiences on a given day, is of equal if not greater importance than an attempt to shoehorn the landscape into any master narrative, whatever the basis of this might be, and it is only allowing conclusions to be drawn from process that allows this to happen. There are two areas where this way of working is much practised: firstly, in contemporary art where artists often set themselves tasks, not as an end in themselves, but to facilitate a primary engagement with a place or landscape; the second is an idea being developed in geography called non-representational theory, which looks to establish the immediacy of sensual experience as an object of study.[22] In both of these areas, and in this facet of contemporary archaeology, experience is brought to the fore as a preferred starting point for work. It may not provide any new facts, but perhaps facts are given undue authority anyway. I like to think that in contemporary archaeology we judge people first on the questions they ask and only secondly on any answers they may give.

In her 1967 work, *On Interpretation*, Susan Sontag talks about the incessant habit of interpreters looking for the latent content behind things. Certainly this resonates in archaeology, whether we see it in Marxist interpretations of individual objects or grand narratives like Capitalism, Improvement or Industrialisation. What I've always loved about archaeology is that it works from stuff out, but I think that importance has to be given to the sensual and very real relationship between the archaeologist and the thing, whether it is a landscape, document or potsherd. So, a focus on process is central to contemporary archaeology as we use new ways of seeing and encountering things to think about what we do, which brings me on to Reflection.

REFLECTION

Earlier, I talked about territory and how we should ignore boundaries and push out as far as possible. Well, if we do that, we have to accept it happening in the other direction. We, as archaeologists, have no intrinsic right to past material culture. Historical geographers and environmental historians, for instance, do things that look pretty much identical to what we do. The only thing that truly distinguishes us from anyone else is that we are archaeological. Something that has run through this whole discussion is the idea that you can do whatever you like as an archaeologist so long as it is done archaeologically. I will avoid the potential pitfall in attempting an 'across-the-board' definition of that term by saying that the archaeological will be differently defined by each individual and that it is only by having different ideas playing out alongside or in opposition to each other that we can come close to reflecting the complexity of the world.

The ability to approach this mass of shifting ideas comes about through an ingrained reflexivity, and it is perhaps this aspect of my contemporary archaeology that is the most personal. It is important to be constantly aware of what has influenced you in the way you think, whether this is empirical experience, aspirations, television shows, or anything else. By being so aware, it may be possible to begin to consider concepts of irrationality, spontaneity and imagination, all important things in any attempt to lessen a reliance on preconceived frameworks. Again, this is certainly inspired by modern material. When we are literally doing the archaeology of ourselves it is hard not to ask some quite personal questions. This can certainly be carried over into any other period of study. If you ever cease asking why you're doing what you're doing, there becomes little point in doing it.

CONCLUSION

Through this chapter I have spoken about three, admittedly from among many, characteristics of contemporary archaeology, and what these do in practice and what they mean for the wider field. They are all interconnected. We have territory and the idea of contemporary archaeology as an active 'anti-discipline', purposefully situating itself outside the mainstream in order to ask new questions and to accept new questions being asked. Of course, the study of post-medieval archaeology was once right there on the edge, striving for credibility within the wider discipline (there is still reluctance among some to begin to consider the last two centuries when the archaeology of earlier post-medieval periods is still not fully understood, a position I reject as I don't think that the archaeology of any period is or will ever be 'done'), and the study of 20th- and 21st- century archaeologies will, in time, become part of the established archaeological canon. We have the focus on process and on direct experience rather than on interpretation. Professional and academic guidelines dictate that we must, however, provide answers of some sort, but the aspiration towards process-led modes of engagement is, I think, a worthy one. Finally, we have reflection and the constant questioning of what we do and why. Clearly, this is not limited to contemporary archaeology, but it is and should be something that is explicit in contemporary archaeological work.

Although I started with a literal definition of avant-garde, perhaps we contemporary archaeologists, as defined by me of course, are not too far from an artistic avant-garde after all. Any artistic avant-garde is asking the question 'what is art?' in one form or another, and it is there that we converge. My three points have all come down to personal questioning of what it is to be archaeological and to working within that question itself more so than attempting to answer it. In that way we are an avant-garde in the artistic sense, thriving on antagonism and intoxicated by the sheer exhilaration of movement beyond the bounds of regularity.

A formalisation of some of these ideas may be seen in John Law's recent work on the concept of 'messy research'[23] in which he writes that formal academic inquiry may miss out on a lot and that research frameworks assume that the world is to be understood as 'a set of fairly specific, determinate, and more or less identifiable processes'.[24] Rather, he advocates, as I do here, 'messier' ways of working that take nothing for granted and seek to unmake methodological habits. The idea that research is creative rather than an objective discovery of truth is central to my contemporary archaeology, and while I see that period distinctions, meta-narratives and all-encompassing research frameworks may be of use to some archaeologists in formulating their ideas, my personal thought is that archaeology has the potential to do much more than try to understand the past, namely, to understand ourselves and use our perspective on the relationship between people and things to consider how we think and act in the present. I will close by saying that it doesn't really matter what you think of contemporary archaeology, but it does matter that you think of it at all. Question what we do and how because therein lies the future.

ACKNOWLEDGEMENTS

I would like to thank Audrey Horning, Laura McAtackney, Angela Piccini and Sarah May for commenting on this paper at various stages and the organisers of the *Crossing Paths or Sharing Tracks?* conference for allowing me to take part.

NOTES

1. Berger 1972.
2. See Buchli & Lucas 2001; Penrose 2007.
3. Buchli & Lucas, 2001.
4. Myers et al. 2008; Myers 2007.
5. Poggioli 1968.
6. Miller 1995, 1–57.
7. Poggioli 1968, 28.
8. For instance, the AHRC Landscape and Environment networks and the EPSRC Heritage Science programme <http://www.ahrc.ac.uk/apply/research/sfi/ahrcsi/landscape_environment.asp< [accessed 24/05/2008]; <http://www.heritagescience.ac.uk/index.php?section=1> [accessed 24/05/2008].
9. Mukherjee et al. 2006; Simms & Wood 2006: Simic et al. 2006

10. Simic *et al.* 2006, 357–9.
11. Rodríguez Senín et al. 2006, 425.
12. Yao et al. 2006.
13. Rancière 1989.
14. Rancière 1989, viii.
15. Rancière 1989, 4.
16. Massey 2005, 10.
17. Dixon 2004.
18. Holtorf 2005, 15.
19. Dixon 2008 unpublished.
20. Chester Chronicle, 1 May 1897.
21. Tilley 1994.
22. For instance, Wylie 2006.
23. Law 2004.
24. Law 2004, 5.

BIBLIOGRAPHY

Berger, J. 1972. *Ways of Seeing*. London: Penguin Books

Buchli, V. & Lucas, G. 2001, *Archaeologies of the Contemporary Past*. London: Routledge.

Chester Chronicle, 1 May 1897, CRO: MF 204/21 (Chester Record Office).

Dixon, J. 2004, 'The Photographers' Gallery looks for Alfred and listens to Alina'. <http://www.24hourmuseum.org.uk> [accessed 14/12/2004].

Holtorf, C. 2005, *From Stonehenge to Las Vegas: Archaeology as Popular Culture*. Lanham, MD: AltaMira Press.

Law, J. 2004, *After Method: Mess in Social Science Research*. Routledge: London.

Massey, D. 2005, *For Space*. London: Sage Publications.

Miller, D. 1995. *Acknowledging Consumption*. London: Routledge.

Mukherjee, S., Chaula, A. & Iyer, S.K. 2006, 'Positioning of motorcyclist dummies in crash simulations', *International Journal of Crashworthiness* **11**(4): 337–44.

Myers, A. 2007, 'The Van: screws and Christmas crackers', *The Archaeologist* **64** (spring), 18–19.

Penrose, S. 2007, *Images of Change: An Archaeology of England's Contemporary Landscape*. Swindon: English Heritage.

Poggioli, R. 1968, *The Theory of the Avant-Garde*. London: Belknap Press.

Rancière, J. 1989. *The Nights of Labour: The Workers' Dream in Nineteenth Century France*. Philadelphia: Temple University Press.

Rodríguez Senín, A., Martínez Sáez, L. & Vicente Corral, T. 2006, 'Experimental evaluation of the wheelchair occupant protection under different impact conditions using commercial wheelchairs', *International Journal of Crashworthiness* **11**(5): 425–41.

Simic, G., Lucanin, V. & Milkovic, D. 2006 'Elements of passive safety of railway vehicles in collision', *International Journal of Crashworthiness* **11**(4): 357–9.

Simms, C.K. & Wood, D.P. 2006, 'Effects of pre-impact pedestrian position and motion on kinematics and injuries from vehicle and ground contact', *International Journal of Crashworthiness* **11**(4): 345–55.

Tilley, C. 1994. *The Phenomenology of Landscape*. Oxford: Berg.

Wylie, J. 2006, 'Depths and folds: on landscape and the gazing subject', Environment and Planning D: *Society and Space* **24**: 519–35.

Yao, J.F., Yang, J.K. & Fredriksson, R. 2006, 'Reconstruction of head-to-hood impact in an automobile-to-child-pedestrian collision', *International Journal of Crashworthiness* **11**(4): 387–95.

UNPUBLISHED SOURCES

Dixon, J. 2008, '*Performing Heritage in Two Cheshire Villages*'. Manuscript in possession of the author.

Myers, A., Schofield, J., Newland, C. & Nilsson, A. 2008, '*Contemporary archaeology in practice: excavating Transit Van J641 VUJ*', paper presented at the 2008 Society for American Archaeology conference, Vancouver.

Part Two

Analytical Approaches

Analytical Approaches
INTRODUCTION

By AUDREY HORNING and MARILYN PALMER

The nine papers in this section turn from general consideration of practice and paradigms to specific considerations of analytical approaches, expressed through a number of case studies. All the papers are concerned in one way or another with the materiality of post-medieval and industrial archaeology, whether demonstrated in artefacts, structures or landscapes, and the way in which that materiality articulates with human agency.

English Heritage-based archaeological scientists Justine Bayley, David Dungworth and Sarah Paynter open this section, in chapter 10, with a plea that archaeologists working on post-medieval and industrial sites should make more use of materials science in trying to reconstruct historic industries through the examination of process residues. Focusing upon evidence from the historic glass industry, and using English and Irish case studies, the authors convincingly demonstrate the interpretive potential of scientific analysis, not just by providing technical details of industries but also information about the people who owned them or worked in them. For example, analysis of the residues from the remains of the Silkstone glasshouse in Yorkshire indicates that the glassworkers were quickly aware of and adopted the latest technology in the form of flint glass, thereby indicating the potential for further research on the reasons for such innovation in a comparatively isolated area. Bayley, Dungworth and Paynter therefore contribute further to the debate regarding the relative merits of technocentric and social interpretative frameworks that was discussed in Section One, stressing that industrial sites did not operate in a social vacuum.

This theme is continued by Richard Thomas, in chapter 11, in his consideration of the potential of zooarchaeological analysis in post-medieval and industrial archaeology, demonstrating its value not just for a better understanding of farming practices and diet but also for appreciating the profound changes to the way in which humans thought about and treated animals. Thomas opens with a sobering statistical account of the dearth of faunal analysis on British and Irish post-medieval assemblages, and proceeds to demonstrate the kinds of questions that could be asked and insights gained through highlighting his own work on assemblages that were deemed worthless by the excavators. Thomas's paper pulls no punches, and demands a reply from practitioners. How can we adequately investigate the impact of Improvement (a topic to which O'Keeffe urged us to pay greater attention in Section One and Daglish also advocates in this section) if we ignore and discard the principal source of evidence for the improvement of livestock?

The third contribution in this section, chapter 12, continues this theme of a more insightful treatment of excavated material. Michael Berry argues that recent controlled excavations of sites from post-1550 Britain and Ireland, in both research and rescue contexts, have often failed to integrate different parts of the record, leading to a breakdown between theory and practice. His aim is to achieve a more sophisticated understanding of the relationship between deposit and assemblage, and between different assemblage types. Making use of a case study of data from the excavation of the Mount Vernon House for Families, a structure in which the first American president George Washington housed part of his enslaved African-American workforce, he suggests that an approach beginning with a close analysis of the finds data in relation to stratigraphic positioning enables a more complete story of the site to be constructed based upon the identified status groups and deposit signatures.

We turn now from considerations of the potential value of scientific approaches in post-medieval and industrial archaeology to the broader themes hinted at in the first section of this book, specifically here those of colonialism, post-colonialism, landscape and settlement. In chapter 13, Colin Rynne returns the reader to Ireland, arguing forcibly that the essentially European nature of Ireland, in terms of race, culture and religion, and its physical proximity to England, renders colonial and post-colonial labels inappropriate as a means of characterising the island's subjugation to Britain. He illustrates this by means of a case study of the British-built naval victualling dockyard of Haulbowline Island in Cork harbour, where storehouses were built in the first half of the 19th century to take advantage of Cork's key position in the Atlantic trade in essential foodstuffs such as butter, pork and beef. Britain's colonial trade network, and the armed conflicts that were undertaken both to expand and maintain it, provided enormous prosperity for the Cork region. With the rise in the demand for Irish agricultural goods, as Rynne says, 'even the smallest Catholic dairy farmer in south Munster could directly profit from the exploitation of the colonial concerns of English and continental imperial powers'. Thus Rynne is able to suggest that the British naval base on Haulbowline Island was in fact a physical expression of Cork's willing participation in Britain's colonial enterprises rather than a symbol of Ireland's colonial subjugation. Additionally, of course, he situates an industrial site within a contemporary debate, thereby giving greater meaning to the physical characteristics the Haulbowline storehouses shared with similar buildings in Bermuda and Jamaica as well as in England.

The remaining chapters in this section are concerned with the analysis and meaning of historic landscapes and settlements, themes of major importance in post-1550 archaeology since we are living within an environment created largely as a result of decisions taken in that period. Here again, there is debate between those to whom landscapes are empirical and functional, the material backdrop to human activity in the past, and those to whom landscape is socially constructed and embodies not just the ways in which people did things in the past but a range of different meanings and values that it had for people in both the past and the present.

In chapter 14, Paul Belford suggests that we should be seeking to explore the motivations of those who created industrial landscapes and used them to express what he describes as a new English identity, one that was increasingly capitalist in nature. Interestingly, from his standpoint as Head of Archaeology and Monuments for the Ironbridge Gorge Museum Trust, Belford argues that industrial landscapes appear to be more highly valued when they are firmly post-industrial and that they are almost uniquely caught between the polarised forces of archaeology and conservation.

This is a theme taken up by Caron Newman, in chapter 15, in her discussion of the potential of Historic Landscape Characterisation (HLC), a tool developed by English Heritage to allow for the categorisation of historic landscapes by means of a GIS-based analysis of historic maps and other documentary sources. Newman stresses that, although HLC was primarily developed for the sustainable management of landscapes, it does have value as a research tool, illustrating this from her own work on the landscapes of Cumbria in north-west England. She responds to detractors of HLC (mainly academic archaeologists) by convincingly demonstrating the utility of the approach for exploring the origins and development of settlements and field systems, and for providing a baseline against which post-medieval processes, such as industrialisation and the expansion of agriculture, can be examined. Her chapter is illustrative of one of the goals of this publication and of the *Crossing Paths or Sharing Tracks?* conference, which was to bring together practitioners from a range of professional backgrounds to encourage greater understanding of the range of approaches employed across the sectors in a bid for enhanced understanding and collaboration.

In chapter 16, David Cranstone presents a fascinating case study of the Whitehaven region, also in Cumbria, in which he systematically and very effectively dismantles the notion that it is possible to separate industrial and historical/ post-medieval archaeology, or to separate technological from social approaches. Cranstone also takes aim at the idea of industrial archaeology being a period discipline starting, as traditionally defined, in 1750. Instead, through his case study of an industrial landscape concerned largely with extractive and metallurgical industries, he proposes alternative models of a 'chemical' followed by 'physical' Industrial Revolution, or an 'extractive' followed by a 'manufacturing' one, both seen as being within a 'long Industrial Revolution' that extended back to the late medieval period. This theme has also been touched on by Paul Belford, equally based on an example from a landscape dominated by extractive and metallurgical industries, but again stressing the importance of early industrial development within a rural landscape. Around Wednesbury in the Black Country of Staffordshire, fractured manorial and monastic control encouraged the development of coal and iron mining by the early 14th century, the establishment of a significant pottery industry during the 15th century, and the development of substantial ironworking enterprises from the 16th century, all well before the classic period of industrialisation.

Next, in chapter 17, Richard Newman broadens the discussion of landscapes of industry with a fascinating dissection of the phenomenon of abandoned settlements in the contemporary landscape. Far from being medieval in origin, as often perceived and even recorded, Newman clearly demonstrates that the establishment and subsequent abandonment of upland villages in his two case study areas of Glamorgan in Wales and part of Lancashire in north-west England are seemingly linked to the fortunes of industrial enterprises, often undertaken on land previously regarded as marginal in terms either of physical location or position within the existing hierarchy of settlement. Like Cranstone's consideration of the Whitehaven cultural landscape, Newman reminds us of the impossibility of separating or segmenting examinations of industrialisation from the archaeological study of post-medieval rural settlement.

In chapter 18, Chris Dalglish ends this section with a similar consideration of post-medieval landscapes and rural settlements in the central Scottish Highlands, taking as an example the pre-Improvement landscape of the Campbells of Glenorchy. His argument respects Charles Orser's emphasis on the dialectic of scales of analysis, suggesting that changes were not only determined at the macro-scale by the estate or by changing economic conditions, but were also brought about by estate tenants acting in accord with their own particular circumstances. He therefore stresses the active role of people at all levels, who shaped their own particular landscapes but at the same time acted, consciously or unconsciously, with reference to the wider world. Daglish also returns us to discussions earlier in this section by adding palaeo-environmental work to materials science and zooarchaeological analysis as often neglected approaches in post-medieval and industrial archaeology, a theme returned to by Steve Mrozowski in the final chapter of this book.

The nine chapters in this second section clearly demonstrate the potential of different approaches towards post-1550 archaeology in Britain and Ireland, with relevance for the practice of historical archaeology elsewhere in the world. The first three chapters are a clarion call for better treatment of finds on excavated sites, stressing that techniques that are standard for excavated material for earlier periods of archaeology also have considerable potential for the interpretation of both post-medieval and industrial sites. The remaining chapters demonstrate how modern approaches to landscape archaeology can enhance our understanding of the period. The section also introduces the question of sustainable management of post-1550 sites and landscapes. This is a theme more generally associated with industrial archaeology but here equally touched on by those concerned with the management of the historic environment, a term that is widely used to define the tangible heritage of historic buildings and townscapes, parks and gardens, designed landscapes, ancient monuments, archaeological sites and landscapes, all of which are particularly relevant to the post-1550 period.

Science for Historic Industries – Glass and Glassworking

By JUSTINE BAYLEY, DAVID DUNGWORTH & SARAH PAYNTER

The systematic application of scientific techniques to questions relating to industries of the post-medieval and industrial periods is a recent phenomenon. The focus of this chapter is on using materials science to answer archaeological questions. Some commonly used analytical techniques are briefly described, and case studies are used to demonstrate the application of these techniques to archaeological glass and glassworking sites. The problems and opportunities of excavating post-medieval industrial sites are summarised. During this period glass furnaces changed from wood to coal as a fuel, and the form of the structure changed and increased in size. Two contrasting 17th-century glasshouses, at Shinrone and Silkstone, are used as examples of the benefits of scientific investigation of excavated finds. Many different compositions of glass were made during this period, and the changes demonstrate alterations (usually improvements) in quality. For some types of glass a sufficiently large database of analyses exists to permit the composition to be used as a dating tool.

INTRODUCTION

Scientific techniques are regularly used in archaeological investigations of medieval and earlier sites, but their systematic application to questions relating to industries of the post-medieval and industrial periods is a recent phenomenon.[1] There are many different techniques that can be used, running from geophysical prospection and scientific dating methods such as dendrochronology and thermoluminescence, to the range of biological and earth sciences collectively known as environmental archaeology. Here the focus is on materials science, which uses many different physico-chemical techniques to answer archaeological questions, largely by analysing inorganic materials such as glass, ceramics, metal alloys, chemical residues and waste slags.

THE PROBLEMS AND OPPORTUNITIES OF INDUSTRIAL SITES

The upsurge in excavations of 'brown-field' sites prior to redevelopment has provided an opportunity to develop existing techniques – both archaeological and scientific – so they are better suited to the large scale of the structures and deposits that are often encountered. There was no history of using scientific investigative techniques in industrial archaeology, although many of the structures and machines that were surveyed and recorded were examples of the application of 18th- and 19th-century science and engineering. In order to help those archaeologists who were trained mainly on sites of earlier date but are now excavating post-medieval industrial sites, English Heritage has recently published a guidance document that contains examples of the application of a wide range of scientific techniques to these types of sites.[2] The problems encountered are different from those at earlier periods for a number of reasons.

The first is the scale of industrial features, as many historic industries operated in very large structures and used huge quantities of raw materials. For example, in the 16th century the furnaces used for making glass typically had a footprint of less than 20m² but in later periods, the furnaces became larger and larger until by the mid-19th century the footprint was over 100m². Conventional trial trenches or test-pits will usually be too small to make any sense of features on this sort of scale. The quantities of raw materials were equally large, and huge quantities of waste materials were generated as well as the desired product. To give an idea of scale, a late 18th-century blast furnace typically produced 2000 tons of cast iron each year, and at least 1000m³ of slag. If this had been dumped in a conical heap beside the furnace, the heap would be taller than the blast furnace in less than a decade, and after two decades or so the blast furnace would be in danger of being engulfed by its own slag heap.

Despite the quantities of waste produced, many industries continue to operate on the same site for extended periods. This was possible because many of the process residues could be sold on as raw material for another industry. In the 18th and 19th centuries, the bottle glass industry increasingly made use of waste from the iron, soap and gas industries as raw materials,[3] and in turn some of its waste was used by the brass casting industry and in the manufacture of alum and saltpetre.[4] This recycling does, however, add a further difficulty to interpreting excavated assemblages as some process residues are under-represented or even missing from the archaeological record.

The waste that could not be recycled was often used to raise ground levels. Many areas of our historic towns are built on flood plains, but the ground levels are often a metre or more higher than they were in the medieval period. The outcome for archaeologists is that many of the waste products will be missing from a production site, but they can instead turn up in made ground on sites where completely different industries were carried out. Before the advent of canals, and especially railways, bulk transport of materials was difficult and expensive so movements were over relatively short distances, but in the 19th century slags, for instance, were used as raw materials in many civil engineering projects and were transported over considerable distances.

A potential argument against the need to use the techniques of archaeological science, or even excavation, for industrial sites is that documentary sources contain all the answers. In rare cases this can be so, but the surviving documentary records were mostly made by the owners of sites and so focus on money, building-plans or specifications of large pieces of equipment rather than the day-to-day details of people and processes. Plant was often modified when the original structure failed to work in the expected way (as with the Hotties[5]), so the surviving plans do not fit the archaeological remains. The terminology used in documents may be obscure, for instance, the 17th-century glassworks at Silkstone (see below) are described in a will as having a green house and a white house – referring to the colour of the glass produced.[6] Industrial espionage was widespread in the early modern period, so some documents may contain deliberately misleading accounts.[7] Sometimes the travel diaries of these 'spies', for example that of the Swede, Angerstein, can be a useful source of information.[8] Even in the few cases where technical details have been recorded, these often focus on the raw materials and the products,[9] which are often absent from the archaeological record, rather than on the process residues. It is certainly true that ancillary activities are very rarely recorded; at Derwentcote, County Durham, the only evidence for processes other than cementation steel-making came from analysis of the slags.[10] There is thus a real role for science in filling in the details of the whole range of processes carried out on a particular site, processes that were often continually modified by those working there.

SCIENTIFIC TECHNIQUES AND THEIR APPLICATION TO HISTORIC GLASSWORKING

Science cannot provide a panacea, but it does give an objective measure of what is present and can demonstrate how materials were produced. It can add to the interpretation of the archaeological deposits, but only if there is good liaison between all the specialists working on a particular project. The major role for materials science is in trying to reconstruct historic industries through the examination of process residues. The techniques used are similar to those employed in modern industrial studies where people want to understand how a production process went wrong. It is desirable to examine the whole range of raw materials and products, but even when these are not all available considerable progress can be made.

A number of different microscopic and analytical techniques are used routinely. Chemical analysis usually determines which elements are present in a sample or object, and in what quantities, though sometimes techniques are used that can identify the compounds present. It is the question that is being posed that determines which technique is used.

Microscopy provides enlarged images. Particularly useful is a scanning electron microscope (SEM) as it can work at high magnifications while still giving a good depth of field for a 3D object, features that cannot be combined in a conventional optical microscope. The SEM can also produce images where the contrast is due to differences in composition (Fig. 10.1a). The SEM becomes a really powerful tool when a method of chemical analysis (energy dispersive X-ray fluorescence (EDX)) is integrated into it. Discrete areas or particles can be analysed, and changes in composition across the sample can be mapped (Fig. 10.1b). The SEM–EDX cannot detect the trace levels of elements that some techniques can achieve but it is nevertheless a very powerful tool for understanding process residues.

The potential of scientific techniques to contribute to integrated historical and archaeological projects investigating post-medieval and later industries can be illustrated by a number of recent projects relating to glassworking. On glass production sites the aims of the scientific investigation are normally to identify the raw materials and fuel used; to determine the composition(s) of the glass being made; to identify the products being manufactured from it; and to say something about the furnace conditions. The data

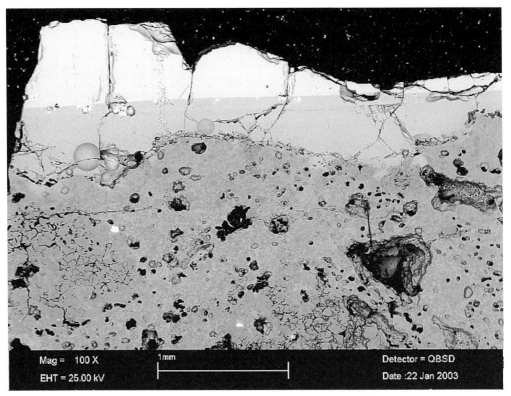

Figure 10.1a Backscattered electron image showing the interface between a crucible and the adhering layer of glass. Note the darker-coloured interaction zone between the glass (light) above and the heterogeneous ceramic below.

obtained can then be compared both with information from any documents that relate to the site, and with scientific data from other glassworking sites as is demonstrated below for Shinrone and Silkstone.

Scientific analyses have also provided information that complements and expands conventional studies of glass artefacts. The aim is usually to identify the type(s) of glass used to make them, and then to relate this compositional data to their chronology or context. The examples below deal with early lead crystal drinking glasses and with the changing technology of window glass production.

Many different types of glass were produced in the late medieval and later periods, and most of these are mentioned in the examples below. All these glasses were based on silica, which was normally in the form of sand but sometimes calcined and crushed flint was used instead. It was important that the sand had a low iron content if the glass was to be colourless, though dark green glass could be made from less pure ingredients. Prior to the introduction of synthetic alkalis (see below), ashes from plants were usually the other major constituent. These contained variable amounts of alkali, that is soda and/or potash,

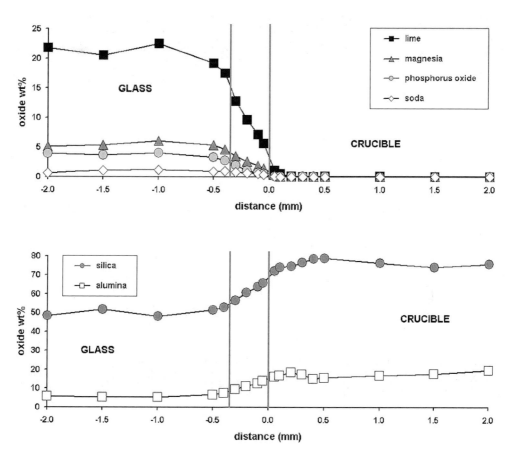

Figure 10.1b Analyses made along a line running from the unaltered glass down into the crucible in Fig. 10.1a, showing how the glass and crucible interact. Care must be taken to avoid the interaction zone when analysing glass adhering to crucibles or the results will not represent its true composition

which act as fluxes, strongly influencing the melting and working temperature of the glass. Sometimes lead oxide was used as a glass flux, for example, to produce lead crystal glasses. The glass of this period can contain a large amount of lime, introduced unrecognised with either the sand or plant ash. When glassmakers purified their raw materials in an attempt to make good colourless glass they often reduced or even eliminated the lime, so the glass they made suffered from crazing and crizzling and was not durable.[11]

GLASSWORKING AT SHINRONE, COUNTY OFFALY

An upstanding 17th-century wood-fired glasshouse survives at Shinrone, County Offaly. Two seasons of excavation were carried out at the glasshouse by Caimin O'Brien and Jean Farelly, and glassworking waste and products were recovered, samples of which were analysed by Sarah Paynter. The findings are described in full elsewhere.[12] Documentary sources provide a context for the scientific investigations. In the later part of the 16th century glassworkers from Lorraine and Normandy came to England, bringing with them a glassworking tradition that differed from that then in use.[13] The glass made by the immigrant glassworkers was harder, brighter and less susceptible to weathering than the glass manufactured previously by English glasshouses. Analyses have shown that the glass made by the French glassworkers contained higher concentrations of lime and lower levels of potash relative to the earlier English-made forest (potash) glass, so the former is often referred to as HLLA (high-lime low-alkali) glass. Some members of these French glass-making families subsequently relocated from England to Ireland, and were in the Shinrone area in the 17th century.

In 1615, Sir Robert Mansell was awarded a monopoly on all types of glassmaking in England, while the use of wood fuel by the industry in England was prohibited.[14] Glass production at Shinrone is likely to have commenced at about this time, encouraged by the monopoly in England, and ceased around 1641 when a bill was introduced to prohibit the felling of trees to fuel glass furnaces in Ireland. The exceptionally preserved Shinrone glasshouse is an invaluable source of information on the glass industry, not only for early 17th-century Ireland but also for England in the previous half century when wood-fired furnaces were still in use, as the archaeological remains in England are sparse in comparison.

Figure 10.2 Bar chart showing composition of glass made at Shinrone and Glaster compared with other bottle, vessel and window glass found at Shinrone

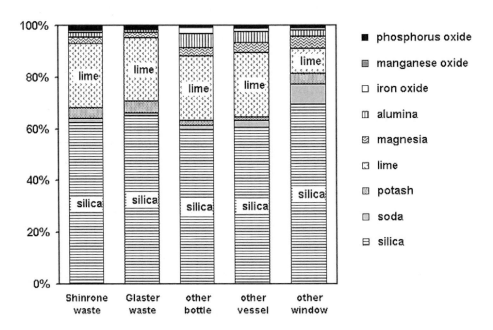

The finds assemblage from Shinrone comprised two visibly distinct types of pale green window glass (one with iridescent weathered surfaces), vessel glass, lumps and dribbles of glass, bottle glass, droplets of transparent blue glass, crucible fragments and furnace fragments. Small samples were removed from examples of all these classes of finds and were analysed using an SEM–EDX. The type of glass being made at the site was characterised by analysing dribbles and lumps of glass, likely to have been discarded during glassworking. The Shinrone glass had an HLLA composition, but it was subtly distinct from the HLLA glass produced at a nearby glasshouse at Glaster and also at glasshouses of various dates in England. It was therefore possible to distinguish the objects that had been made at Shinrone from those that had been brought to the site by comparing their compositions with the Shinrone glassworking waste (Fig. 10. 2). The pale green window glass with iridescence and the majority of the vessel fragments from the site were all made from Shinrone glass, indicating that both windows and vessels were being produced at the site. The pale green window glass (without iridescence), all of the bottle glass and several pale olive fragments of vessel glass were made elsewhere.

The furnace was constructed from sandstone and the internal surface was covered in a transparent blue glaze, which analysis showed was rich in potash. The glaze had been produced by the reaction of potash-rich waste gases from the burning wood fuel with the silica-rich sandstone.[15] Small droplets of blue potash-rich glass that formed when drips of glaze fell from the interior surfaces of the furnace onto the floor below were also recovered from the site. The presence of this potash-rich glaze confirms the use of wood fuel at Shinrone.

Large sherds of used crucibles were found, made from specialised refractory clay and tempered with quartz (sand) and grog. With use, both the internal and external surfaces of the crucibles had become unintentionally glazed by drips of the glass being melted in them as well as by interaction of the crucible ceramic with the potash-rich vapour from the wood fuel. None of the glassy deposits in the crucible fragments analysed had compositions exactly matching the glass originally contained in them, owing to contamination from the crucible ceramic and the fuel vapour.

Previous work has established that HLLA glass was made from plant ashes, but these have a very variable composition, depending on factors such as the species of plant, the geology where the plant is growing, the part of the plant, the time of year and the temperature used for ashing.[16] Species such as oak and beech are known to produce lime-rich ashes[17] and the ratios of elements present in the oak ash are comparable to those in the Shinrone glass. The woodland in the Shinrone area was predominantly oak according to records[18] so oak ash combined with sand are likely to have been the major constituents of the glass made there. The HLLA glass made at Shinrone and Glaster contains much less phosphorus (<1.8% P_2O_5) and manganese (<0.31% MnO) than HLLA glass from English glasshouses. Both of these elements are derived predominantly from the plant ashes used to make the glass, and this difference may be attributable to the geology of the region where the plants were grown.

The temperatures necessary to melt samples of HLLA archaeological glass have been experimentally determined.[19] Similar temperatures of around 1260–1290°C would have been necessary to melt the Shinrone glass, and the temperature attained in the furnace may have exceeded this slightly.

GLASSWORKING AT SILKSTONE, YORKSHIRE

Documentary sources indicate that there was a glasshouse at Silkstone in the second half of the 17th century, but unlike Shinrone no above-ground traces have survived and until recently the exact location of the glasshouse was unknown. Since then, excavation and a programme of scientific research have provided a wealth of information about this glasshouse.[20] It was built in the late 1650s and continued in use until the end of the century; the documentary sources do not provide an exact date for the end of glass production, but the archaeological evidence points to c. 1700. The excavation found no *in situ* remains of the furnaces but did uncover a deep stratigraphic sequence. This consisted of two working floor surfaces composed of tiny fragments of coal and glass waste separated by a layer of demolition rubble. The floor surfaces appear to have accumulated within a glasshouse, and the furnaces can only have been a few metres away from the excavated trench. The first floor surface probably belongs to the 1660s or 1670s, but the second is firmly dated by associated clay pipes to the last two decades of the 17th century.

The excavation recovered substantial quantities of glassworking waste, and the decision to take soil samples from the working floor surfaces allowed the recovery of almost microscopic residues such as tiny threads and droplets of glass. The waste all falls into two broad groups based on colour: a dark green glass, which was used primarily for the manufacture of wine bottles, and colourless (or very pale green) glass, which was used to make drinking glasses and other tablewares. The production of both types of glass is also indicated in one of the written sources, which refers to the green house and white house (white in this context meaning colourless).[21] Chemical analysis has shown that the dark green glass was a HLLA glass of the same type that was made at Shinrone. There are minor differences in the composition of this glass in the different phases of production at Silkstone, but these do not appear to be of great technological importance. Merrett, writing in the 1660s, describes dark green glass as being made from many different plant ashes (in addition to sand) and that there was a trade in these ashes to supply glass manufacturers and other industries.[22] Isotopic analysis of samples of this glass indicate that at least some raw materials came from far beyond Yorkshire – indeed, the closest areas with similar isotopic ratios are Wales, the Lake District and Scotland.[23]

The analysis of the colourless and pale green glasses used to make drinking vessels reveals significant technological change between the two phases of production. In the first phase the glass is a pale green mixed alkali glass, which is characterised by a high strontium content (Fig. 10.3). The strontium content (and its isotopic ratio) indicates that the plant ash used was seaweed or kelp.[24] Seaweed is known to have been widely used in glassmaking in the 18th and early 19th centuries, but Silkstone provides the earliest evidence for its use – perhaps surprising given that Silkstone is 90km from the coast. In the later phase of glassmaking the old recipe for the manufacture of glass used in making tablewares was abandoned in favour of a lead–potash–silicate glass (usually called flint glass in contemporary

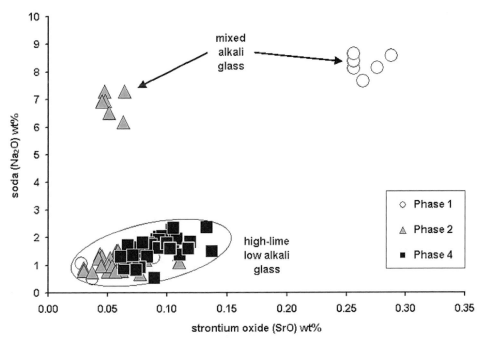

Figure 10.3 Scatter plot of Na_2O vs SrO for Silkstone glass. The raised strontium content of one of the Phase 1 mixed alkali glass shows it had been made using seaweed (kelp) ash.

sources). The research at Silkstone showed that little was known about the composition of early flint glass and the role of George Ravenscroft who was credited with its invention.[25] Subsequent research into flint glass (see below) indicates that Silkstone adopted this new type of glass very quickly. Ravenscroft's patent did not expire until 1681, but the new glass was being produced in Silkstone from *c.* 1680 (possibly even infringing the patent).

LEAD CRYSTAL

The research into the compositions of the Silkstone glassworking debris showed the early introduction of a lead–potash–silicate (flint) glass. Despite the significant economic role of this glass, very little scientific research had been undertaken previously on its origins. Merrett writes in the 1660s that 'Glass of Lead, 'tis a thing unpractised by our Furnaces … And could this be made as tough as that of Chrystalline 'twould far surpass it.'[26] The invention of flint glass is traditionally attributed to Ravenscroft who obtained a patent in 1674. Unfortunately, the patent provides little specific information: it describes the glass as simply 'a particular sort of Cristaline Glasses resembling Rock Cristall'[27] and does not mention any of the ingredients used. A number of contemporary sources suggest that the glass was made using a variety of materials, including quartz pebbles, flint, sand, borax, tartar and saltpetre.[28] A programme of chemical analysis has now investigated samples of vessel glass of this period, in particular several examples of vessels that bear a raven seal,

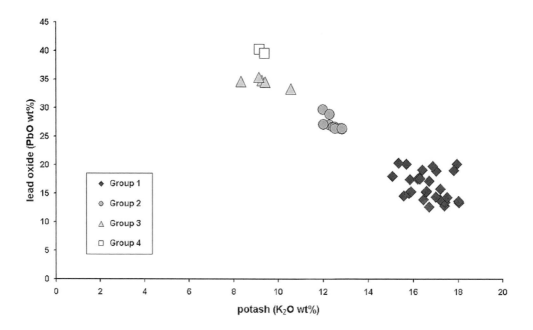

ABOVE: Figure 10.4a PbO vs K$_2$O for early lead crystal glass, showing four compositional groups. BELOW: Figure 10.4b Correlation of composition with date for early lead crystal glass. The groups are the same as in Figure 10.4a.

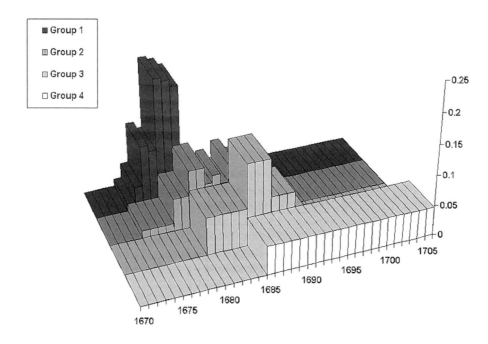

which are believed to have been produced by Ravenscroft's glasshouses. The vessels were made using two different types of glass: some were soda-rich alkali glasses with compositions similar to those produced in Venice at this time, and some were lead–potash–silicate glasses. Glasses of similar compositions to the Ravenscroft lead glass (Group 1 in Fig.10.4a) are also represented by vessels with no seal or with other types of seal, and some of these are likely to have been produced by other glasshouses. Unfortunately the practice of using seals was not introduced until 1676 and it has not been possible to positively identify any of Ravenscroft's early vessels (that is, those from 1674–6). The proportions of lead and potash in the Group I glass did not provide a stable glass (all extant examples have suffered from corrosion or crizzling) and after Ravenscroft's patent expired, flint glassmakers increased the proportion of lead and reduced the proportion of potash to rectify this (Figs 10.4a and 10.4b).

WINDOW GLASS

Window (and other flat) glass was manufactured using a variety of forming techniques and ingredients depending on its intended use. In addition, techniques and ingredients changed over time as new technologies were developed. The composition of window glass reflects the nature of the ingredients used, and it often has little to do with the forming technique. The window glass of the 16th and 17th centuries is usually a HLLA glass, which differs little from that used for the manufacture of bottles and common drinking vessels (Table 10.1, Fig. 10.5a). The analysis of window glass produced after *c.* 1700, however, shows that a significant change had occurred in the ingredients used. For the rest of the 18th century and the first few decades of the 19th century almost all window glass was a mixed alkali glass (Table 10.1). One of the most distinctive aspects of the composition of this mixed alkali glass is the relatively high levels of strontium oxide. This oxide is likely to derive from the use of kelp as the principal flux in window glass manufacture. The widespread use of kelp in the glass industry in the 18th and early 19th centuries is corroborated by documentary evidence.[29] Muspratt also makes it clear that the use of kelp came to a dramatic end in the 1820s owing to the availability of synthetic soda. Nicholas LeBlanc had developed a technique for converting common salt into sodium carbonate at the end of the 18th century but this was not introduced into Britain until the 1820s. Nineteenth-century window glass produced after *c.* 1820 is almost always a soda-lime glass, which unlike the HLLA and mixed alkali glasses contains low levels of impurities (Table 10.1).

Table 10.1 Typical compositions of window glass manufactured in England c. 1600 to c. 1920

Type and period	Na2O	MgO	Al2O3	SiO2	P2O5	K2O	CaO	Fe2O3	SrO
HLLA c. 1570–c. 1700	3.3	3.1	2.7	61.5	2.0	4.0	20.0	1.5	0.10
Mixed-alkali c. 1700–c. 1820	9.4	5.4	3.1	66.2	0.3	4.3	8.8	0.7	0.40
Soda-lime (synthetic) c. 1820–c. 1920	12.0	0.3	1.5	72.3	<0.2	0.6	13.2	0.2	0.05

Data from Mortimer 1993; Dungworth 2006; Turner 1926.

PALACE HOUSE MANSION, NEWMARKET

An unexpected discovery during the course of restoration work at Palace House Mansion, Newmarket in 1996–7, was a late-17th-century sash window, complete with much of its original glass. A long red brick range (including the window) had been added to the property in 1671, just three years after it had been bought by King Charles II as a hunting lodge. Because of subsequent alterations to the building, part of the window had been cut away by the early 18th century; it had only survived because it had been sealed behind new brickwork during further alterations in the 19th century.[30]

The window (2.75 by 1.5m) is made of oak and is divided into four equal quarters. The glazing in the upper part was fixed, but the two lower quarters were rising sashes, only one of which survives. These were counterbalanced on one side only by cylindrical lead weights that were strung, like beads, on a flax sash cord. Three glazed panels were found. The largest is in the sash and is made up of five rows of three rectangular panes (the central ones being 240 by 180mm) set in lead cames. Above this, part of a panel of fixed glazing survives with two rows of three panes. On the other side, above the lost sash, is another fixed panel of leaded diamond-shaped panes. The panel with diamond-shaped panes would have been part of the original glazing scheme, which was blocked off when the sash below it was cut away to make a doorway. The other half of the window appears to have remained in use and was reglazed with panels made of rectangular panes, possibly when the alterations were made in the early 18th century.

Figure 10.5a Chronological range of different compositional types of window glass. The grey zones are known from analyses of dated window glass while the white ones show the pattern that is expected to emerge from future work

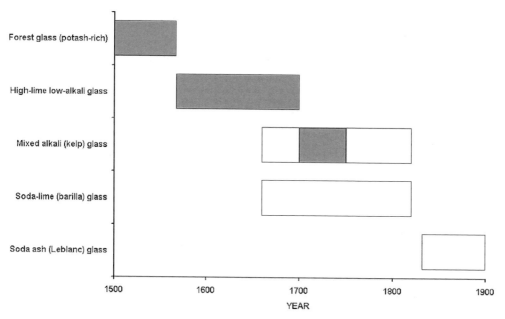

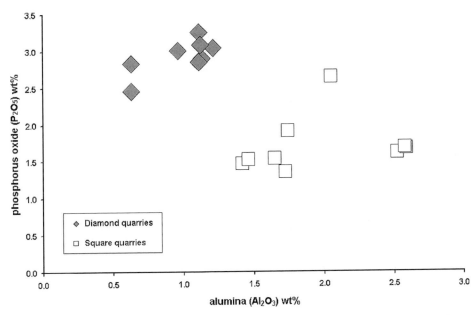

Figure 10.5b The composition of window glass of two phases from Palace House Mansion, Newmarket.

All the panes have a range of pale greenish tints and appear to be cut from slightly bubbly cylinder-blown glass. Analyses were made of samples from nine of the diamond-shaped panes and from nine of the rectangular panes from the smaller of the two panels. All the glass has a HLLA composition, though there are slight differences between the diamond and rectangular panes (Fig.10.5b). These differences may be due to differences in date, or just the use of glass from different production sites.

The building was a royal hunting lodge, and the window was in the king's bedchamber,[31] so the glass might have been expected to be the latest type which, according to data collected in the English Heritage Archaeological Science Laboratory (Fig.10.5a), should have been a mixed-alkali glass. The HLLA composition of the glass is thus somewhat surprising as it would have been less transparent, and somewhat darker in hue than mixed-alkali glass. The window falls right at the end of the period when HLLA glass was regularly used for glazing windows; perhaps better glass was not available in Newmarket at the time the building was erected and then modified, some while later.

CONCLUSIONS

This review of the contribution that materials science can make to the archaeology of the post-medieval and industrial periods has demonstrated that materials science can help to identify wastes and residues, and hence the processes carried out on particular production sites. The scientific investigation can also identify the raw materials and fuel used, the composition of the products made on site, and provide information on process variables that cannot be obtained by conventional archaeological or historical research.

The local raw materials used at the late wood-fired furnace at Shinrone were identified, and the products of the furnace could be differentiated from glass objects brought to the site, and even from glass made at Glaster, a nearby contemporary glasshouse. The slight differences in composition between HLLA glasses produced at different glasshouses also illustrates the potential of glass compositional data as an aid in determining where glass was made. The contamination of glass remaining in the crucibles was demonstrated, and explained. That the glass was all HLLA is not surprising as the individuals who are known to have worked the site were from immigrant families who had brought this technology to England in the previous century. Silkstone, in contrast, emerges as a glasshouse with far-reaching economic and technological links. It produced a range of tablewares and bottles using raw materials from coastal areas and some region in the north or west of the British Isles. Despite its provincial location, the glassworkers were quickly aware of, and adopted, the latest technology in the form of flint glass.

When studying the products of the glass industry, scientific analyses provide information on composition. With growing datasets this information has the potential to feed back into mainstream archaeology by dating finds or associating them with a particular manufacturer or source area. The very short-lived changes in lead crystal composition (Fig.10.4b) are one example of this, and on a longer time-scale the changes in window-glass composition (Fig.10.5a).

This technical information cannot stand on its own but has to be combined with other archaeological and historical research to provide a holistic picture of the past, as the examples above have shown. To be successful, this requires dialogue and interchange of information between the different specialists working on particular projects so they can capitalise on the new information and fully interpret it.

Archaeology must tell stories about the past, providing not only technical details of industries but information about the people who owned them or worked in them; industrial sites did not operate in a social vacuum. Science has the potential to contribute to this wider picture too. When a sufficient body of scientific data has been amassed, it should be able to illuminate the distribution and use networks that led products of industries to their final resting places – after they had been transported, bought, used and discarded by people in the British Isles and beyond.

ACKNOWLEDGMENTS

The authors would like to thank John Vallender for his help with the illustrations.

NOTES

1. Bayley & Crossley 2004; Bayley & Williams 2005.
2. Dungworth & Paynter 2006.
3. Berg & Berg 2001, 129; Pellatt 1849, 33.
4. Muspratt 1860, 206.
5. Krupa & Heawood 2002, 86.
6. Dungworth & Cromwell 2006, 162.
7. Charleston 1984, 111–13.
8. Berg & Berg 2001.
9. e.g. Parkes 1823.
10. McDonnell 1997, 93–100.

11. Cable 2001, 211; Hurst Vose 1980, 113.
12. O'Brien, Farelly & Paynter 2005.
13. Kenyon 1967, 13–14; Godfrey 1975, 33–7; Crossley 1983.
14. Godfrey 1975, 68.
15. Misra, Ragland & Baker 1993.
16. Sanderson & Hunter 1981; Stern & Gerber 2004.
17. Turner 1956, 290T; Sanderson & Hunter 1981, Table 1; Stern & Gerner 2004, Table 1.
18. O'Brien pers comm.
19. Cable & Smedley 1987.
20. Dungworth & Cromwell 2006.

21. Ashurst 1987.
22. Cable 2001, 322–3.
23. Dungworth, Degryse & Schneider (forthcoming).
24. Dungworth, Degryse & Schneider (forthcoming).
25. Charleston 1984, 110.
26. Cable 2001, 373–4.
27. MacLeod 1987, 789.
28. Dungworth & Brain 2005.
29. Buckley 2003, 91; Parkes 1823, 192.
30. Baggs 1997.
31. Baggs 1997.

BIBLIOGRAPHY

Ashurst, D. 1987, 'The Silkstone glasshouses', Old West Riding 12: 15–19.

Baggs, A.P. 1997, 'The earliest sash-window in Britain?', Georgian Group Journal 7: 168–71.

Barker, D. & Cranstone, D. (eds) 2004, The Archaeology of Industrialization, Society for Post-Medieval Archaeology Monograph 2. Leeds: Maney.

Bayley, J. & Crossley, D. 2004, 'Archaeological science as an aid to the study of post-medieval industrialization', in Barker & Cranstone (eds), 2004, 15–23.

Bayley, J. & Williams, J. 2005, 'Archaeological science and industrial archaeology: manufacturing, landscape and social context', Industrial Archaeology Review 27(1): 33–40.

Berg, T. & Berg, P. (trans.) 2001, R R Angerstein's Illustrated Travel Diary 1753–1755. London: Science Museum.

Buckley, F. 2003, Old English Glass Houses. Sheffield: Society of Glass Technology.

Cable, M. (ed.) 2001, The World's Most Famous Book on Glassmaking, The Art of Glass by Antonio Neri, translated into English by Christopher Merrett. Sheffield: Society of Glass Technology.

Cable, M. & Smedley, J. 1987, 'Liquidus temperatures and melting characteristics of some early container glasses', Glass Technology 28: 94–8.

Charleston, R.J. 1984, English Glass and the Glass Used in England, c.400–1940. London: Allen & Unwin.

Cranstone, D. 1997, Derwentcote Steel Furnace: An Industrial Monument in County Durham. Lancaster: Lancaster University Archaeological Unit.

Crossley, D.W. 1983, 'The development of English glass furnaces in the sixteenth and seventeenth centuries', Journal of Glass Studies 25: 147–53.

Degryse, P., Henderson, J. & Hodgins, G. (eds) (forthcoming), Isotopes in Vitreous Materials. Leuven: Leuven University Press.

Dungworth, D. 2006, Silkstone, South Yorkshire. Composition of Early Eighteenth-Century Window Glass, Research Department Report 18/2006. Portsmouth: English Heritage.

Dungworth, D. & Brain, C. 2005, Investigation of Late 17th-Century Crystal Glass, Centre for Archaeology Report 21/2005. Portsmouth: English Heritage.

Dungworth, D. & Cromwell, T. 2006, 'Glass and pottery manufacture at Silkstone, Yorkshire', Post-Medieval Archaeology 40: 160–90.

Dungworth, D. & Paynter, S. 2006, Science for Historic Industries: Guidelines for the Investigation of 17th- to 19th-Century Industries, Swindon: English Heritage. <http://www.helm.org.uk/upload/pdf/Science-Historic-Industries.pdf>.

Dungworth, D., Degryse, P. & Schneider, J. (forthcoming), 'Strontium isotopes and seaweed', in Degryse, Henderson & Hodgins (eds) (forthcoming).

Godfrey, E.S. 1975, The Development of English Glassmaking 1560–1640. Chapel Hill: University of North Carolina Press.

Hurst Vose, R. 1980, Glass. London: Collins.

Kenyon, G.H. 1967, The Glass Industry of the Weald, Leicester: University of Leicester Press.

Krupa, M. & Heawood, R. 2002, 'The Hotties': Excavation and Building Survey at Pilkingtons' No 9 Tank House, St Helens, Merseyside. Lancaster: Oxford Archaeology North.

MacLeod, C. 1987, 'Accident or design? George Ravenscroft's patent and the invention of lead-crystal glass', Technology and Culture 28: 776–803.

McDonnell, G. 1997, 'The slags and residues', in Cranstone 1997, 93–100.

Misra, M.K. Ragland, K.W. & Baker, J.A. 1993, 'Wood ash composition as a function of furnace temperature', Biomass and Bioenergy 4(2): 103–16.

Mortimer, C. 1993, Analysis of Window Glass from Chastleton House, Oxfordshire, Ancient Monuments Laboratory Report 117/1993. London: English Heritage.

Muspratt, S. 1860, Chemistry. Theoretical, Practical and Analytical. Glasgow: Mackenzie.

O'Brien, C., Farelly, J. & Paynter, S. 2005, The 17th Century Glasshouse at Shinrone, Co. Offaly, Ireland, Centre for Archaeology Report 39/2005. Portsmouth: English Heritage.

Parkes, S. 1823, Chemical Essays, 2nd edn. London: Baldwin, Craddock & Joy.

Pellatt, A. 1849, Curiosities of Glass Making. London: Bogue.

Sanderson, D. & Hunter, J. 1981, 'Composition variability in vegetable plant ash', Science and Archaeology 23: 27–30.

Stern, W.B. & Gerber, Y. 2004, 'Potassium–calcium glass: new data and experiments', Archaeometry 46: 137–56.

Turner, W.E.S. 1926, 'The composition of glass suitable for use with automatic glass-forming machines', Journal of the Society of Glass Technology 10: 80–94.

Turner, W.E.S. 1956, 'Studies in ancient glasses and glassmaking processes. Part V. Raw materials and melting processes', Journal of the Society of Glass Technology, 40: 277T–300T.

Bones of Contention: Why Later Post-medieval Faunal Assemblages in Britain Matter

By RICHARD THOMAS

The purpose of this discussion is to call attention to the significance of later post-medieval assemblages of animal bone in Britain. While faunal remains are routinely studied as part of the post-excavation process, it remains the case that detailed analyses of later post-medieval collections are infrequently undertaken and/or published. There are many reasons that might account for this situation, not least a lack of appreciation of the significance of zooarchaeological inquiry in this period. I argue that the centrality of animals to later post-medieval society and the dramatic changes that occurred in the nature of animal exploitation and human–animal relationships from the mid-18th century mean that animal bone evidence is not of peripheral or limited interest and should, therefore, be afforded a higher place on research agendas.

INTRODUCTION

Animal bones are one of the most ubiquitous archaeological finds, and it is well recognised that their detailed study can shed light on a diverse range of past human activities. These include the identification of subsistence strategies; economic regimes; the use of animals and animal parts in craft and industry; attitudes to animals; and the symbolic role of animals in cosmology, ritual/religion and as food items. The importance of these lines of investigation, together with the abundance of faunal remains on many sites, has meant that analyses of animal bone are now routinely undertaken as part of the post-excavation process. Despite their centrality, however, zooarchaeological studies of the later post-medieval period in Britain, defined here as dating from the mid-18th century, are remarkable for their absence.

As a zooarchaeologist with research interests in the later medieval and post-medieval periods I have often been frustrated by the infrequency with which later post-medieval assemblages of animal bones have been subjected to detailed analysis and publication.[1] This chapter thus seeks to explore how this situation has arisen and to highlight to curators, archaeological project managers and historical archaeologists more generally, why later post-medieval animal bone assemblages should be afforded a higher status than is currently the case. The latter aim will be achieved through the presentation of two case studies: one of which can be described as broadly post-processual in perspective (exploring changing attitudes to animals) and the other more economic and processual in nature (dealing with the improvement of domestic animals).

ANIMALS AND THEIR BONES IN LATER BRITISH HISTORICAL ARCHAEOLOGY

If one surveys the entire print run of articles published within the journal *Post-Medieval Archaeology* (the journal of the Society for Post-Medieval Archaeology) between 1998[2] and 2006 that focus on British material, the dearth of research papers and excavation reports that consider animal bones from sites dating from the mid-18th century is striking. Out of the 23 published excavations that included specialist reports, four contained detailed animal bone reports (a further two make reference to the existence of animal bone reports in archives). Not a single one of these contained analysed material from contexts dated after the late 18th century. Moreover, there is not a single British-based research article (out of a total of 31) that deals with the role of animals within this time period. Even if one surveys the major zooarchaeological monographs from multi-period sites with chronology extending into the post-medieval period, they rarely extend beyond a 1750 cut-off.[3]

The low profile of animals, and their remains, is also evident in the recent surfeit of publications that encompass historical archaeology and related fields in Britain. In synthetic overviews of the period, whole chapters are devoted to landscapes, for example, but with little consideration of what actually populated them. Where animals are mentioned it tends to only be those that were of marginal importance to society, and it is historical sources that are relied upon.[4]

Within industrial archaeological literature too, animals and their products have also been sadly neglected.[5] Animal power is occasionally mentioned, but this is usually within the context of its replacement by mechanical alternatives.[6] Even where the industrial processing of animal products is discussed in depth, the most direct form of evidence for their production and supply – animal bones – is ignored.[7] This situation is clearly exemplified in Riley's recent survey of production and consumption research within industrial archaeology: the comment that 'some industrial archaeologists do not accept agriculture as falling within their purview' is particularly telling.[8]

This problem is not just restricted to academic texts, however; in research framework documents for the later post-medieval period, while attention has now begun to be directed towards issues such as consumption habits and the agricultural economy,[9] explicit reference to animal bone evidence as a means of exploring these issues is often absent. In the North-East Regional Review, for example, one identified research theme is changing consumption patterns in the post-medieval period: ceramic and other artefactual evidence are cited as windows through which this issue might be explored, yet the direct remains of food consumption (that is, plants and animals) are wholly ignored.[10] It is interesting to observe that where the same research theme is identified for earlier chronological periods, animal bone evidence is highlighted as an important investigative tool.[11]

This is not to deny that exceptions exist. It is well recognised, for example, that zooarchaeological data has an important role in elucidating aspects of breed improvements.[12]

The potential of using animal bone evidence to explore later post-medieval period industrial activities has also been noted.[13] However, if one considers the centrality of animals to the lives of people in the later post-medieval period, these examples cover only limited aspects of the full range of human interactions with animals.

The neglect of 'biological content' within the traditions of industrial and later historical landscape archaeology is not just restricted to animals,[14] but it is one that requires urgent redress. Of course, the lack of discussion may reflect the absence of animal bone site reports dating to this period; we might thus have a 'chicken and egg' situation. However, historical archaeologists have an important advocacy role, and they need to raise the questions that can be addressed through zooarchaeological inquiry and extol the potential of this type of evidence. This has certainly been the case across the Atlantic, for example, where general texts on historical archaeology have frequently highlighted the virtue of later post-medieval animal bone reports.[15]

There are doubtless important problems with collections of animal bones dating from the 18th century, some of which are outside of the control of the archaeologist. For example, later post-medieval sites are frequently truncated by later development and they can be affected by problems of residuality, particularly when they supersede medieval layers. Waste management and the recycling of by-products too, may have been much more effective in this period, and consequently have resulted in the collection of impoverished samples of animal bones.

However, other factors are controllable. One reason why later post-medieval assemblages of animal bones in Britain have been neglected is because they are often sacrificed at the expense of the 'more interesting' earlier periods.[16] This certainly accords with the situation in Ireland where Eileen Murphy, in an overview of post-medieval zooarchaeology between 1550 and 1850, notes that 'it is still often the case that post-medieval remains are withheld from study because excavators wrongly assume that the analysis of such late material will not provide any meaningful results'.[17] This 'sacrifice' can occur either during excavation, where 'modern' material is stripped to gain access to earlier archaeological deposits, or during post-excavation, as the potential of recovered finds is 'assessed'.[18] The decision to undertake detailed analysis of assessment reports is based entirely on the premise of cost-effectiveness; however, establishing the worthiness of material to be studied requires an understanding of the potential by both specialists and project managers. It is clear that the potential of animal bone assemblages from later post-medieval contexts is not fully appreciated. To take one example, at Stafford Castle only archaeological material from the 11th to the mid-17th century was included in the final publication: later material from the site was not presented because it 'did not complement the medieval castle in any way, but rather denuded what remained'.[19]

Of course, a further problem, and one that has been much lamented,[20] is that even where detailed analyses are undertaken, they are frequently published as 'grey literature', that is, client and archive reports that are not available as publications with ISSN or ISBN registrations. This situation makes it difficult even for specialists to be aware of what other relevant data exist,[21] let alone those seeking to undertake synthetic accounts.

Irrespective of the cause, such problems do not appear to have encumbered faunal analyses further afield, where later post-medieval assemblages are more frequently subjected to detailed study and synthesised within the wider body of historical archaeological literature; North America serves as an excellent example. As early as 1977, Otto demonstrates the significant role of zooarchaeology in understanding status differences at antebellum plantation sites, and this is a theme that has continued to witness much coverage.[22] Indeed, the role of food in identity formation has formed one of the central elements of later post-medieval zooarchaeological inquiry in North America; it has been used to explore relationships between diet and colonial identities, diet and ethnic identities, and the symbolic role of particular food items within society.[23] Consumption habits, as revealed by zooarchaeological analysis, have also been integrated into smaller-scale studies of rural farmsteads.[24] Economic questions have not been neglected either. For example, Landon has charted the expansion and industrialisation of meat production and supply to meet the growing urban demand from the 17th to early 19th centuries.[25] The impact of environmental change, husbandry practice and technological developments have been investigated for domestic animals and fish,[26] and attitudes to animals are also being explored.[27]

The evident disparity in interest in later post-medieval assemblages of animal bones between Britain and North America is striking, and may partly reflect the different development trajectories of post-medieval archaeology within those countries.[28] Regardless of the cause, however, one of the primary, resolvable, problems is the lack of awareness of the potential of faunal remains in exploring key archaeological questions in this period.

The current paucity of published later post-medieval animal bone assemblages makes it difficult to undertake the kind of synthesis already produced for Ireland, and for earlier periods in Britain, at the present time.[29] Consequently, the remainder of this chapter will detail two avenues of zooarchaeological investigation that have the potential to make a meaningful contribution to later post-medieval archaeology.

ANIMALS AND AGRICULTURAL PRODUCTIVITY

As Richard Newman has recently emphasised, despite the acknowledged centrality of agriculture and food production to post-medieval society, this has 'not been reflected in subsequent research into post-medieval agrarian society and landscape'.[30] While it is true that the later post-medieval period is well blessed with documentary sources, long the preserve of economic historians, such evidential strands are not unbiased. Zooarchaeological data have the potential to provide a means of testing traditional historical narratives, by enabling the exploration of changes in agricultural practice across both time and space.

Major technological changes were occurring within the realms of agricultural practice and production in this period, which included the development of new breeds of livestock (see below); the introduction of new forms of agricultural machinery that 'changed the productivity and rhythm of much farm work',[31] and the expanded use of artificial feed and hay, which decoupled the relationship between seasonality and natural cycles of milk production.[32]

Social change also profoundly affected agriculture practice. The urban population boom, for example, facilitated the industrialisation of meat and dairy production, and the drive to increase output resulted in major changes to the conformation and appearance of domestic livestock through breeding programmes. The scale of demand is exemplified by the dramatic rise in the number of cattle that passed each year through Smithfield market in London; the number rose from 76,210 in 1732 to 159,907 in 1830.[33] By the late 19th century, however, Britain was experiencing a major agricultural depression. This resulted not only in a reduction in the total farmed area, but also witnessed a massive decline in agricultural investment as food and land prices declined.[34] Zooarchaeological data are ideally placed to contribute to these debates, yet it is only with respect to animal improvements and the nature and timing of the Agricultural Revolution that this source of evidence has been used to date, and so it is to this topic that I will now turn.

The Agricultural Revolution can be defined as 'a widespread technological change in British farming practice that facilitated a sustainable increase in agricultural productivity'.[35] From the early 20th century until the 1960s there was little doubt among historians that this change occurred between 1760 and 1840 in a movement closely linked to the Industrial Revolution, enabling the farming community to feed the growing population.[36] Some of the traditional features perceived to have led to a productivity increase included parliamentary enclosure of land, the introduction of new farming technology, the introduction of new crops and crop rotations, and improvements in livestock breeding,[37] all brought about by a small number of innovators.

By the 1960s this view was challenged. Eric Kerridge, for example, argued that many of the innovations that were viewed as constituting an 18th/19th-century revolution in agricultural practice, did not occur at all, were insignificant or appeared much earlier. Instead, it was argued that the Agricultural Revolution took place in the 16th and 17th centuries and only received 'finishing touches' from the likes of Robert Bakewell.[38] While Kerridge's argument was not unquestioningly accepted,[39] by the 1970s the period encompassed by the Agricultural Revolution was considered to be a multi- staged event occurring from 1560 to 1880.[40] More recently, historical studies have either contended that: (1) 18th- and 19th-century changes in agricultural practice were part of a long and gradual process, which comprised different stages of significant development varying across space and time;[41] and (2) while earlier improvements in agricultural practice occurred, the 18th and 19th centuries were revolutionary because of the magnitude of change.[42]

Zooarchaeology is well placed to contribute to this debate, because it provides a line of inquiry independent of historical livestock productivity data from which previous interpretations have been developed.[43] By taking measurements of animal bones it is possible to explore long-term changes in the shape and size of domestic livestock. These data can provide a rough proxy for productivity change because a functional relationship exists between skeletal size and body weight.[44]

Over the past ten years, a number of zooarchaeological studies have been published regarding the timing and nature of improvements in animal husbandry in later medieval and post-medieval England.[45] These studies have revealed increases in animal size occurring at different sites from the 14th to the 17th centuries (Table 1); however, the picture is a complex one. There is, for example, a great deal of regional variation, with outlying sites,

Site	Sheep	Cattle	Pig	Domestic fowl	Reference
Baynard's Castle, London	no change	late 14th–early 16th	-	-	Armitage (1977)
Castle Mall, Norwich	late 16th–early18th	late 16th–early18th	late 16th–early18th	mid/late 14th–early 18th	Albarella et al. (1997)
Dudley Castle, West Midlands	mid-14th	mid-14th; mid-16th–mid-18th	mid-14th	mid-14th	Thomas (2005c, forthcoming)
Exeter, Devon	16th	16th	-	16th–17th	Maltby (1979)
Launceston Castle, Cornwall	15th–mid-19th	15th–mid-17th; mid-17th–mid-20th	15th–mid-17th	no change	Albarella and Davis (1996)
Lincoln, Lincolnshire	early 16th	17th–mid-18th	17th–mid-18th	late 15th	Dobney et al. (1996)
Okehampton Castle, Devon	late 16th–17th	no change	no change	-	Maltby (1982)
Pontefract Castle, West Yorkshire	by 17th	by 17th	by 17th	-	Richardson (2002)
Prudhoe Castle, Northumberland	no change	15th–16th	no change	-	Davis (1987)
Stafford Castle, Staffordshire	-	mid-14th–16th	-	16th	Sadler and Jones (2007); Sadler (2007)

Table 1: Summary of the timing of size increases in domestic livestock observed on British sites that span the medieval and post-medieval periods. A hyphen indicates where no data are available.

such as Launceston Castle, Cornwall, generally experiencing later developments than central localities. Moreover, there is considerable variation in the timing of size changes; at some sites the changes occur over a short period of time,[46] while at others it is a much more gradual affair.[47] Taken together, the currently available evidence undermines the idea of a single, widespread revolution in agricultural practice and supports the assertion that improvements in animal husbandry occurred as part of a long-term and gradual process. Moreover, the complexity of the picture suggests that the 'stimulus for improvement at any site would have reflected a combination of local, regional and national environmental and socio-economic conditions'.[48] The triggers and timing of improvements in animal size may have also varied by species. At sites such as Lincoln, there is clear difference in the timing of improvement in sheep and cattle.[49] Elsewhere, the causes of size change have been associated with different factors. At Dudley Castle, for example, the mid-14th-century size increase in pigs has been linked to changes in the local environment (specifically a reduction in woodland), coupled with the emergence of sty-farming, while for sheep and cattle it has been linked to the changed social context in the wake of the Black Death.[50]

While these data support a gradualist interpretation, it is necessary to examine the situation in the 18th and 19th centuries where others have argued for a revolution in

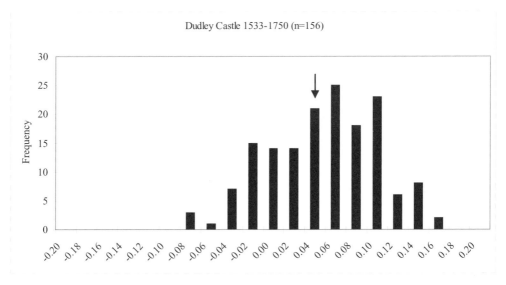

Dudley Castle 1533-1750 (n=156)

Figure 11.1 Histograms comparing the size of domestic fowl post-cranial bones from Stafford Castle (below) and Dudley Castle (above) using the log-ratio scaling technique. The arrows indicate the population mean.

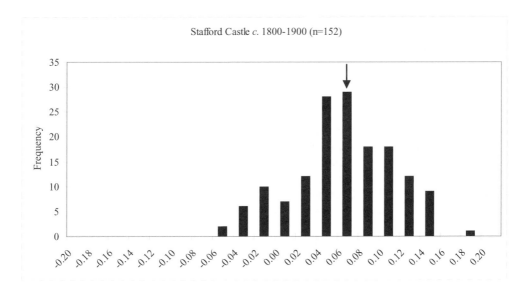

Stafford Castle c. 1800-1900 (n=152)

agricultural practice, and specifically in animal husbandry. Absence of changes in the faunal record in assemblages of this date might lead us to call into question the very concept of an Agricultural Revolution. Alternatively, the existence of significant changes in animal size in this period might support the idea that an Agricultural Revolution did occur in accordance with the documentary record.

In order to test this problem, faunal biometrical evidence from the later 18th and 19th centuries, when historical sources inform us that productivity expanded quickly and in a sustainable manner, require publication. Unfortunately, such datasets are rare. A 19th-century assemblage of animal bones from Stafford Castle revealed evidence for sheep that were somewhat larger on average than those from slightly earlier dating deposits located at Dudley Castle (only 40km away), perhaps indicating that new breeds of sheep were introduced into the region, or that existing sheep were improved, sometime in the later 18th or 19th century.[51] Increases in the size of sheep were also observed into the 19th century at Launceston Castle, while in Bedford the presence of cattle with 'partially improved' horns argues against Kerridge's hypothesis that improvements in animal husbandry had been completed by the 18th century.[52] However, further data from Stafford Castle testifies to the complexity of the situation. If one compares the post-cranial bone measurements of domestic fowl from 19th-century Stafford Castle with those from mid-16th to mid-18th century Dudley Castle, for example, while the average size of the birds appears larger at Stafford Castle, this is not statistically significant (Fig. 11.1).[53] These data further support the idea that different livestock underwent different transformations in size at different places and times. The question of whether the 19th-century size changes identified so far were 'revolutionary' or part of a continuum will remain open, however, until more datasets of later post-medieval animal bone measurements are collected and made available.

CHANGING ATTITUDES TO ANIMALS

While animal bone evidence has long been employed to explore facets of past economy, more recent research has emphasised the extent to which it can also be used to shed light upon other dimensions of human existence.[54] The later post-medieval period provides an excellent context within which to study such issues, since it witnessed profound changes to the way in which humans thought about and treated animals.

If one steps back into the medieval period, it is clear that attitudes towards animals, and nature in general, were strongly influenced by the Church. Only Man was created in God's own image and given dominion over all other living creatures.[55] Medieval sources record little affection for animals; they were mostly viewed in terms of their functional affordances.[56] Even during the early modern period in England, animal pets were seen as 'morally suspect'; one 17th-century observer noted that 'over familiar usage of any brute creation is to be abhorred'.[57] The intellectual movements of the Renaissance appear to have hardened attitudes to animals, with the emergence of the idea that animals were automata, capable of 'complex behaviour' only in a purely mechanistic sense; thus, they could not reason, nor experience pain, and various experiments were undertaken to demonstrate this fact.[58]

By the 17th century, attitudes were beginning to change. The Stuarts in particular were so obsessed with pets that in 1617 James I(VI) was accused of loving his dogs more than his subjects.[59] By 1700 'all the symptoms of obsessive pet-keeping were in evidence' and the early 17th century even witnessed a change in law to class pets as private property in response to the view that they were kept for 'private emotional gratification'.[60] At the same time, increasing concern for domestic animal welfare was expressed in popular husbandry manuals.[61]

From the 18th century, fondness for pets was more regularly expressed in literature,[62] and the death of pet animals was increasingly marked with elaborate tombstones.[63] The foundation of the London Veterinary College in 1791 testifies to increased professionalism among those concerned with animal health.[64] It was not until the 19th century, however, that current attitudes to animal welfare emerged. Sentimental sculptural representations of pet animals, the formation of organisations such as the Liverpool Society for Preventing of Wanton Cruelty to Brute Animals (1809) and the Society for the Prevention of Cruelty to Animals (1824), provide good exemplars of this change in attitude.[65] During the same period, concern was expressed at the condition in which animals were kept, such as Mrs Beeton's critique of veal production in her 1861 *Book of Household Management*, while cruel sports involving animals were increasingly scrutinised and in some cases outlawed.[66]

Although contemporary literary and artistic evidence can provide a glimpse of attitudes towards pet-keeping in the medieval and post-medieval periods, such pieces of evidence should not be considered in isolation since their interpretation is problematic: in particular, they mostly reflect attitudes among the educated elite (both secular and religious). While 'attitudes' to animals are more challenging to interpret from archaeological remains, they do provide us with a counter-balance against which traditional historical narratives can be tested.

A survey of medieval and post-medieval archaeological excavations in Britain showed that the numbers of possible 'pet animals' found was generally low, and there appears to be no unequivocal evidence that these animals were in fact kept as pets.[67] Both cat and dog skeletons tend to be recovered from contexts throughout these periods suggestive of rubbish disposal rather than reverential burial, and the frequent occurrence of butchery marks indicates their exploitation as commodities. This picture is beginning to change, however. Recent excavations of 19th-century backyards of urban households at Hungate, York, for example, have revealed an abundance of buried dog skeletons.[68] At Stafford Castle, the presence of one complete dog skeleton, at least eighteen partial cat skeletons and, intriguingly, a tortoise bone from 19th-century contexts within the centre of the keep, further testify to the growth in pet-keeping and sentimental attitudes towards animals.[69] Recent analysis of palaeopathological lesions in the lower limb bones of cattle from Dudley Castle has also revealed a sharp decline in their frequency from the mid-16th to the mid-18th century.[70] While a declining slaughter age for cattle forms one explanation for this phenomenon, it is not possible to exclude the fact that this reflects better animal care during the period. Certainly, contemporary husbandry books frequently warned that overwork would directly result in 'pestilence' and that animals should be provided with adequate nourishment and a dry place to rest to repair the damage caused by hard labour.[71]

At the present time, however, there are too few reported assemblages to be able to explore this change in attitudes in any quantifiable way. Further zooarchaeological research in this period will hopefully enable us to not only establish the timing of this change in attitudes more closely, but also explore the social context within which it occurred.

CONCLUSION

The two detailed examples presented above clearly demonstrate the significant role of faunal evidence in addressing questions of wider significance within studies of later post-medieval society. These are by no means the only research questions that can be explored using zooarchaeological data in this period, however, as the survey of North American research presented above demonstrates.

Other areas of concern include the identification of changing food consumption habits and the way in which diet was used in the expression of identity. From the mid-18th century, animal products provided a major source of industrial materials, such as wool for the cloth industry and leather for tanning and other forms of hide preparation, not to mention marrow and fats for tallow, soap and other chemical industries. As Philip Armitage has demonstrated, animal bones and horn-cores were used as building materials for a variety of purposes that included: the construction of boundary walls (e.g. ha-has) and roads, decoration, infilling of walls, lining soakaways, and industrial pits and cess pits.[72] Although mechanisation was beginning to revolutionise industry in this period, the power provided by traction animals was still exceptionally important, particularly along the canal network and for pulling agricultural equipment. Palaeopathological evidence may provide a direct means through which the exploitation of animals for this purpose can be identified archaeologically.[73] Such evidence could also be used in conjunction with other forms of zooarchaeological evidence to assess the impact on animal husbandry of the shift to mechanical alternatives. The role of animals within exploration, warfare and sport also deserves further exploration than has currently been the case.[74]

Zooarchaeological analyses could be usefully employed to document the introduction, spread and impact of new species in the later post-medieval period such as the brown rat (*Rattus norvegicus*), grey squirrel (*Sciurus carolinensis*), American mink (*Mustela vison*) and the Chinese Muntjac (*Muntiacus reevesei*).[75] Changing patterns of animal and/or habitat exploitation may also be visible through the analysis of skeletal remains of animals. For example, it is well recognised that modern red deer have undergone a dramatic depreciation in size, possibly as a consequence of the marginalisation of their habitat. Biometrical analyses of animal bone have demonstrated that this was a phenomenon of more recent history;[76] however, the paucity of later post-medieval animal bone assemblages has meant that it has not been possible to establish the timing of this change, and hence the historical social, economic and environmental context in which it occurred.

There are good intellectual reasons for studying faunal assemblages of the later post-medieval period. The wealth of documentary records, photographs, and sometimes oral history and folklore, can potentially provide for a much richer and nuanced understanding of past human–animal relationships.[77] The combination of these sources can also afford zooarchaeologists with the opportunity to test the reliability of their models against known historical events, before those models are applied to earlier periods where such supporting evidence is sparse or missing altogether.

Before all this can be achieved, however, later post-medieval zooarchaeology needs advocates: zooarchaeologists need to be aware of the importance of material from this period when writing assessment reports; historical archaeologists need to consider the central role of animals within society and raise the questions that can be addressed using animal bone evidence; and curators and archaeological project managers need to be advised, particularly through research framework documents, of the importance of animal remains from later post-medieval sites. With greater awareness and publication of faunal datasets from this period, an exciting and diverse range of research possibilities will open up.

ACKNOWLEDGMENTS

I am indebted to Audrey Horning for allowing me to raid her personal library during the preparation of this manuscript.

NOTES

1. e.g. Thomas 2005a, 102; 2005b, 85–6.
2. This date marks the point at which the aims and scope of the journal were changed from 'the post-medieval period before the onset of industrialization' to 'the post-medieval period' more generally.
3. e.g. Albarella *et al.* 1997; Dobney et al. 1996; Maltby 1979; Thomas 2005c; although see Albarella & Davis 1996 for an important exception.
4. e.g. Holtorf & Williams (2006, 250–1) on zoological gardens and Newman (2001, 118–20) on game.
5. e.g. Casella & Symonds 2005; Cranstone 2001.
6. e.g. Palmer & Neaverson 1998, 45.
7. e.g. Palmer & Neaverson 2005.
8. Riley 2005, 45.
9. although see Newman 2005, 207–8 for a useful critique of the extent to which agriculture was previously considered within post-medieval archaeology.
10. Petts & Gerrard 2006, 181.
11. Petts & Gerrard 2006, 151, 169.
12. e.g. Bayley & Williams 2005; Huntley & Stallibrass 1995; Petts & Gerrard 2006; SPMA 1988; Webster 2007. Tarlow's use of zooarchaeological data with respect to animal improvement (Tarlow 2007, 64–6).
13. Bayley & Williams 2005, 36.
14. e.g. Kealhofer 1999, 378; Newman 2005.
15. e.g. Orser 2002.
16. Thomas 1999, 342.
17. Murphy 2007, 371.
18. *sensu* MoRPHE and PPN3; English Heritage 2006,
2008.
19. Soden 2007, 7; fortunately the materials have been retained in the site archive to facilitate future research.
20. e.g. Brennand 2007, 189–91; Thomas & Stallibrass 2008, 3.
21. e.g. Lauwerier & de Vries 2004; Van der Veen *et al.* 2007.
22. e.g. Lev-Tov 2004; Otto 1977; Reitz 1987; Reitz & Zierden 1991; Schulz & Gust 1983.
23. e.g. Cantwall & Wall 2001, 222–3; Cheek 1999; Franklin 2001; Reitz 1995; Scott 2007.
24. e.g. Groover 2003; Price 1985.
25. Landon 1996.
26. Cossette & Horad-Herbin 2003; Reitz 2004; Reitz & Ruff 1994.
27. Warner & Genheimer 2008.
28. e.g. Courtney 1999, 4; Newman 2005, 206.
29. e.g. Albarella 1997, 2006; Grant 1988; Murphy 2007; Sykes 2006.
30. Newman 2005, 205.
31. Barnwell 2005, 114.
32. Barnwell 2005, 115.
33. Perren 1978, 32.
34. Barnwell 2005, 116.
35. Thomas 2005b, 72.
36. e.g. Beckett 1990, 1.
37. Beckett, 1990, ix; Overton 1984, 119.
38. Kerridge 1967.
39. e.g. Mingay 1969.

40. Beckett 1990, 9.
41. Allen 1991; Beckett 1990; Thirsk 1987.
42. Campbell & Overton 1993; Mingay 1989; Overton 1996a, 1996b; Turner *et al.* 2001.
43. Overton 1996a, 12; Williamson 2002, 165.
44. Hildebrand 1982; see Thomas 2005b for a more thorough discussion of this approach.
45. e.g. Albarella 1997; Davis 1997; Davis & Beckett 1999; Thomas 2005b.
46. e.g. Dudley Castle, West Midlands; Thomas 2005b, 2005c.
47. e.g. Castle Mall, Norwich; Albarella *et al.* 1997.
48. Thomas 2005b, 85.
49. Dobney *et al.* 1996.
50. Thomas 2005b, 2005c, 2006.
51. Thomas 2005b.
52. Albarella & Davis 1996; Hutchins & Steadman 1999.
53. Student's two-tail t-test (t-stat = −1.445; P(T < = t) = 0.149).
54. e.g. O'Day *et al.* 2004.
55. Genesis 1:26; 9:3.
56. Salisbury 1994, 14, 16.
57. Cited in Thomas 1983, 40.
58. Thomas 1983, 33–5.
59. Thomas 1983, 107.
60. Thomas 1983, 111–12, 117.
61. Curth 2002.
62. e.g. Rhodes 1988, 58–60; Williams 1980, 87–90.
63. e.g. Feeke 2000a, 12; Toms 2006, 17.
64. Cotchin 1990.
65. Craske 2000; Ritvo 1994, 108; Velten 2007, 169.
66. Maehle 1994, 100; Velten 2007, 166;
67. Thomas 2005a.
68. Connelly *et al.* 2008.
69. Thomas submitted.
70. Thomas forthcoming.
71. Curth 2002, 380.
72. Armitage 1989.
73. e.g. Bartosiewicz *et al.* 1997.
74. e.g. Clutton-Brock 1992, 160–4, 172–7; see Lohan 2008 for a recent interesting Irish example of a zooarchaeological study of a Crimean War horse.
75. Yalden 1999, 183–9.
76. Thomas 2005c, 63.
77. e.g. Price 1985.

BIBLIOGRAPHY

Albarella, U. 1997, 'Size, power and veal: zooarchaeological evidence for late medieval innovations', in de Boe & Verhaeghe (eds), 1997, 19–30.

Albarella, U. 2006, 'Pig husbandry and pork consumption in medieval England', in Woolgar *et al.* (eds), 2006, 72–87.

Albarella, U. & Davis, S. 1996, 'Mammals and birds from Launceston Castle, Cornwall: decline in status and the rise of agriculture', *Circaea* **12**: 1–156.

Albarella, U., Beech, M. & Mulville, J. 1997, *The Saxon, Medieval and Post-Medieval Mammal and Bird Bones Excavated 1989–1991 from Castle Mall, Norwich, Norfolk*, Ancient Monument Laboratory Report 72/97. London: English Heritage.

Allen, R.C. 1991, 'The two English Agricultural Revolutions, 1450–1850', in Campbell & Overton 1991, 236–54.

Armitage, P. 1977, 'The Mammalian Remains from the Tudor Site of Baynard's Castle London. A Biometrical and Historical Analysis', unpublished PhD thesis, Royal Holloway College / British Museum of Natural History.

Armitage, P.L. 1989, 'Gazetteer of sites with animal bones used as building materials', in Serjeantson & Waldron (eds), 1989, 201–23.

Astill, G. & Grant, A. (eds) 1988, *The Countryside of Medieval England*. London: Basil Blackwell.

Baker, A.R.H. & Gregory, D. (eds) 1984, *Explorations in Historical Geography: Interpretative Essays*. Cambridge: Cambridge University Press.

Barnwell, P.S. 2005, 'Farm buildings and the industrial age', in Gwyn & Palmer (eds), 2005, 113–20.

Bartosiewicz, L., Van Neer, W. & Lentacker, A. 1997, *Draught Cattle: Their Osteological Identification and History*, Annalen Zoölogische Wetenschappen **281**. Tervuren: Koninklijk Museum voor Midden-Afrika.

Bayley, J. & Williams, J. 2005, 'Archaeological science and industrial archaeology: manufacturing, landscape and social context', in Gwyn & Palmer (eds), 2005, 33–40.

Beckett. J.V. 1990, *The Agricultural Revolution*. Oxford: Basil Blackwell.

Brennand, M. 2007, *Research and Archaeology in North West England. An Archaeological Research Framework for North West England: Volume 2. Research Agenda and Strategy*, Archaeology North West **9**. Manchester: Council for British Archaeology, North West.

Campbell, B. & Overton, M. 1991, *Land, Labour and Livestock: Historical Studies in European Agricultural Productivity*. Manchester: Manchester University Press.

Campbell, B.M.S. & Overton, M. 1993, 'A new perspective on medieval and early modern agriculture: six centuries of Norfolk farming, c.1250–c.1850', *Past and Present* **141**: 38–105.

Cantwall, A.-M. & Wall, D.Z. 2001, *Unearthing Gotham: The Archaeology of New York City*. New Haven & London: Yale University Press.

Casella, E. & Symonds, J. (eds) 2005, *Industrial Archaeology: Future Directions*. New York: Springer.

Chambers, J.D. & Mingay, G.E. 1966, *The Agricultural Revolution 1750–1880*. London: B.T. Batsford.

Cheek, C.D. 1999, 'An evaluation of regional differences in colonial English foodways', in Egan & Michael (eds), 1999, 349–67.

Clutton-Brock, J. 1992, *Horse Power*. London: Natural History Museum Publications.

Connelly, P., Kendall, T., Hunter-Mann, K. & Mainman, A. 2008, 'The archaeology of modern urban poverty', *Current Archaeology* **215**: 26–33.

Cossette, E. & Horard-Herbin, M.-P. 2003, 'A contribution to the morphometrical study of cattle in colonial North America', *Journal of Archaeological Science* **30**: 263–74.

Cotchin, E. 1990, *The Royal Veterinary College: A Bicentenary History*. Buckingham: Barracuda Books.

Courtney, P. 1999, 'Different strokes for different folks: the transatlantic development of historical and post medieval archaeology', in Egan & Michaels (eds), 1999, 1–19.

Cranstone, D. 2001, 'Industrial archaeology – manufacturing a new society', in Newman 2001, 183–210.

Craske, M. 2000, 'Representations of domestic animals in Britain 1730–1840', in Feeke (ed.), 2000b, 40–54.

Curth, L.H. 2002, 'The care of brute beast: animals and the seventeenth century medical market-place', *Social History of Medicine* **15**: 375–92.

Davis, S.J.M. 1987, *Prudhoe Castle, A Report on the Animal Remains*, Ancient Monument Laboratory Report 162/87. London: English Heritage.

Davis, S.J.M. 1997, 'The Agricultural Revolution in England: some zooarchaeological evidence', *Anthropozoologica* **25, 26**: 413–28.

Davis, S.J.M. & Beckett, J.V. 1999, 'Animal husbandry and agricultural improvement: the archaeological evidence from animal bones and teeth', *Rural History* **10**: 1–17.

de Boe, G. & Verhaeghe, F. (eds) 1997, Environment and Subsistence in Medieval Europe: Papers of the 'Medieval Europe Brugge 1997' Conference, Volume 9. Zellik: Instituut voor het Archeologisch Patrimonium Rapporten 9.

Dobney, K., Jaques, S.D. & Irving, B.G. 1996, *Of Butchers and Breeds: Report on Vertebrate Remains from Various Sites in the City of Lincoln*. Nottingham: Lincoln Archaeological Studies 5.

Egan, G. & Michael, R.L. (eds) 1999, *Old and New Worlds*. Oxford: Oxbow Books.

English Heritage 2006, *Management of Research Projects in the Historic Environment. The MoRPHE Project Managers' Guide*. Swindon: English Heritage.

English Heritage 2008, *Management of Research Projects in the Historic Environment. PPN3: Archaeological Excavation*. Swindon: English Heritage.

Feeke, S. 2000a, 'An introduction to the exhibition', in Feeke 2000b, 5–12.

Feeke, S. (ed.) 2000b, *Hounds in Leash. The Dog in 18th and 19th Century Sculpture*. Leeds: Henry Moore Institute.

Franklin, M. 2001, 'The archaeological dimensions of soul food: interpreting race, culture, and Afro-Virginian identity', in Orser (ed.), 2001, 88–107.

Grant, A. 1988, 'Animal resources', in Astill & Grant (eds), 1988, 149–87.

Groover, M.D. 2003, *An Archaeological Study of Rural Capitalism and Material Life: The Gibbs Farmstead in*

Southern Appalachia, 1790–1920. New York: Kluwer Academic/Plenum.

Gwyn, D. & Palmer, M. (eds) 2005, 'Understanding the workplace: a research framework for industrial archaeology in Britain', *Industrial Archaeology Review* **27** (1), 1–177.

Hicks, D. & Beaudry, M. (eds) 2006, *The Cambridge Companion to Historical Archaeology.* Cambridge: Cambridge University Press.

Higham, R.A., Allan, J.P. & Blaylock, S.R. (eds) 1982, *Excavations at Okehampton Castle, Devon. Part 2 – The Bailey*, Devon Archaeological Society **40**, 19–151.

Hildebrand, M. 1982, *Analysis of Vertebrate Structure.* New York: John Wiley & Sons.

Holtorf, C. & Williams, H. 2006, 'Landscapes and memories', in Hicks & Beaudry (eds), 2006, 235–54.

Horning, A., Ó Baoill, R., Donnelly, C. & Logue, P. (eds) 2007, *The Post-Medieval Archaeology of Ireland 1550–1850.* Bray: Wordwell.

Huntley, J.P. & Stallibrass, S. 1995, *Plant and Vertebrate Remains from Archaeological Sites in Northern England: Data Reviews and New Directions*, Architectural and Archaeological Society of Durham and Northumberland, Research Report **4**.

Hutchins, E. & Steadman, S. 1999, 'Evidence for 17th- and 18th-century cattle improvements in Bedford', *Environmental Archaeology* **4**: 87–92.

Kealhofer, L. 1999, 'Adding content to structure: integrating environment and landscape', in Egan & Michael (eds), 1999, 378–89.

Kerridge, E. 1967, *The Agricultural Revolution.* London: Allen & Unwin.

Landon, D.B. 1996, 'Feeding colonial Boston: a zooarchaeological study', *Historical Archaeology* **30**(1): 1–153.

Lauwerier, R.C.G.M. & de Vries, L.S. 2004, 'Lifting the iceberg – BoneInfo and the battle to save archaeological information', in Lauwerier & Plug (eds), 2004, 167–75.

Lauwerier, R.C.G.M. & Plug, I. (eds) 2004, *The Future from the Past: Archaeozoology in Wildlife Conservation and Heritage Management.* Oxford: Oxbow Books.

Lev-Tov, J.S.E. 2004, 'Implications of risk theory for understanding nineteenth century slave diets in the southern United States', in O'Day *et al.* (eds), 2004, 304–17.

Lohan, K. 2008, 'Dickie Bird: the story of the rediscovery of an honoured Crimean War and cavalry horse', *Archaeology Ireland* 22(2): 13–14.

Maehle, A-H. 1994, 'Cruelty and kindness to the "brute creation": stability and change in ethics of the man-animal relationship 1600–1850', in Manning & Serpell (eds), 1994, 81–105.

Maltby, M. 1979, *The Animal Bones from Exeter 1971–1975.* Sheffield: Exeter Archaeological Reports **2**.

Maltby, M. 1982, 'Animal and bird bones', in Higham *et al.* (eds), 1982, 114–35.

Maltby, M. (ed.) 2006, *Integrating Zooarchaeology.* Oxford: Oxbow.

Manning, A. & Serpell, J. (eds) 1994, *Animals and Human Society: Changing Perspectives.* New York & London: Routledge.

Mingay, G.E. 1969, 'Dr. Kerridge's "Agricultural Revolution": a comment', *Agricultural History* **42**(4): 477–82.

Mingay, G.E. (ed.) 1989, *The Agrarian History of England and Wales Volume VI, 1750–1850.* Cambridge: Cambridge University Press.

Murphy, E. 2007, 'An overview of livestock husbandry and economic practices in the urban environments of post-medieval Ireland', in Horning *et al.* (eds), 2007, 371–91.

Newman, R. 2001, *The Historical Archaeology of Britain, c.1540–1900.* Stroud: Sutton Publishing.

Newman, R. 2005, 'Farmers and fields: developing a research agenda for post-medieval agrarian society and landscape', *Post-Medieval Archaeology* **39**(2): 205–14.

O'Day, S., Van Neer, W. & Ervynck, A. (eds) 2004, *Behaviour Behind Bones: The Zooarchaeology of Ritual, Religion, Status and Identity.* Oxford: Oxbow Books.

Orser, C.E. (ed.) 2001, *Race and the Archaeology of Identity.* Salt Lake City: University of Utah Press.

Orser, C.E. 2002, *Encyclopaedia of Historical Archaeology.* London: Routledge.

Otto, J.S. 1977, 'Artifacts and status differences – a comparison of ceramics from planter, overseer, and slave sites on an antebellum plantation', in South (ed.), 1977, 91–118.

Overton, M. 1984, 'Agricultural revolution? Development of the agrarian economy in early modern England', in Baker & Gregory (eds), 1984, 118–235.

Overton, M. 1996a, 'Re-establishing the English Agricultural Revolution', *Agricultural History Review* **44**: 1–34.

Overton, M. 1996b, *Agricultural Revolution in England: The Transformation of the Agrarian Economy 1500–1850*. Cambridge: Cambridge University Press.

Palmer, M. & Neaverson, P. 1998, *Industrial Archaeology: Principles and Practice*. London: Routledge.

Palmer, M. & Neaverson, P. 2005, *The Textile Industry of South-West England: A Social Archaeology*. Stroud: Tempus.

Perren, R. 1978, *The Meat Trade in Britain, 1840–1914*. London: Routledge & Kegan Paul.

Petts, D. & Gerrard, C. 2006, *Shared Visions: The North-East Regional Research Framework for the Historic Environment*. Durham: Durham County Council.

Pluskowski, A. (ed.) 2005, *Just Skin and Bones? New Perspectives on Human–Animal Relations in the Historic Past*. Oxford: British Archaeological Reports International Series **1410**.

Price, C.R. 1985, 'Patterns of cultural behaviour and intra-site distributions of faunal remains at the Widow Harris site', *Historical Archaeology* **19**(2): 40–56.

Purdue, J.R., Klippel, W.E. & Styles, B.W. 1991, *Beamers, Bobwhites, and Blue-Points: Tributes to the Career of Paul W. Parmalee*. Springfield: Illinois State Museum Scientific Papers **23**.

Reitz, E. 1987, 'Vertebrate fauna and socio-economic status', in Spencer-Wood (ed.), 1987, 101–19.

Reitz, E. 1991, 'Cattle bones and status from Charleston, South Carolina', in Purdue *et al.* 1991, 395–407.

Reitz, E. 1995, 'Pork on the southern coastal plain: nutrition or symbol?', in Ryan & Crabtree 1995, 79–89.

Reitz, E. 2004, '"Fishing down the food web": a case study from St Augustine, Florida, USA', *American Antiquity* **69**(1): 63–83.

Reitz, E. & Ruff, B. 1994, 'Morphometric data for cattle from North America and the Carribbean prior to the 1850s', *Journal of Archaeological Science* **21**: 699–713.

Rhodes, N. 1988, *William Cowper: Selected Poems*. Manchester: Carcanet Press.

Richardson, J. 2002, 'The mammal bones', in Roberts 2002, 363–85.

Riley, R. 2005, 'The notions of production and consumption in industrial archaeology: towards a research agenda', in Gwyn & Palmer (eds), 2005, 41–7.

Ritvo, H. 1994, 'Animals in nineteenth century Britain: complicated attitudes and competing categories', in Manning & Serpell (eds), 1994, 106–26.

Roberts, I. 2002, *Pontefract Castle. Archaeological Excavations 1982–86*, *Yorkshire Archaeology* **8**. Leeds: West Yorkshire Archaeology Service.

Ryan, K. & Crabtree, P.J. 1995, *Symbolic Role of Animals in Archaeology*, MASCA **12**. Philadelphia: University of Pennsylvania Museum of Archaeology and Anthropology,

Sadler, P. 2007, 'The bird bone', in Soden (ed.), 2007, 172–8.

Sadler, P. & Jones, G. 2007, 'The mammal bone', in Soden (ed.), 2007, 161–71.

Salisbury, J.E. 1994, *The Beast Within: Animals in the Middle Ages*. New York & London: Routledge.

Schulz, P.D. & Gust, S.M. 1983, 'Faunal remains and social status in 19th-century Sacramento', *Historical Archaeology* **17**(1): 44–53.

Scott, E.M. 2007, 'Pigeon soup and plover in pyramids: French foodways in New France and the Illinois Country', in Twiss (ed.), 2007, 243–59.

Serjeantson, D. & Waldron, T. (eds) 1989, *Diet and Crafts in Towns*. Oxford: British Archaeological Reports British Series **199**.

Soden, I. (ed.) 2007, *Stafford Castle: Survey, Excavation, Research 1978–1998. Volume II – the Excavations*. Stafford: Stafford Borough Council.

South, S. (ed.) 1977, *Research Strategies in Historical Archaeology*. New York: Academic Press.

Spencer-Wood, S. (ed.) 1987, *Socio-Economic Status and Consumer Choices: Perspectives in Historical Archaeology*. New York: Plenum Press.

SPMA, 1988, *Research Priorities for Post-Medieval Archaeology*. London: Society for Post-Medieval Archaeology.

Stallibrass, S. & Thomas, R. (eds) 2008, *Feeding the Roman Army: The Archaeology of Production and Supply in the NW Provinces*. Oxford: Oxbow Books.

Sykes, N. 2006, '"From *Cu* and *Sceap* to *Beffe* and *Motton*": the management, distribution, and consumption of cattle and sheep in medieval England', in Woolgar *et al.* (eds), 2006, 56–71.

Tarlow, S. 2007, *The Archaeology of Improvement in Britain, 1750–1850*. Cambridge: Cambridge University Press.

Thirsk, J. 1987, *England's Agricultural Regions and Agrarian History in England, 1500–1700*. Basingstoke: Macmillan Education.

Thomas, K. 1983, *Man and the Natural World: Changing Attitudes in England 1500–1800*. London: Penguin Books.

Thomas, R. 1999, 'Feasting at Worcester Cathedral in the 17th century: a zooarchaeological and historical investigation', *Archaeological Journal* **156**, 342–58.

Thomas, R. 2005a, 'Perceptions versus reality: changing attitudes towards pets in medieval and post-medieval England', in Pluskowski (ed.), 2005, 95–105.

Thomas, R. 2005b, 'Zooarchaeology, improvement and the British Agricultural Revolution', *International Journal of Historical Archaeology* **9**(2), 71–88.

Thomas, R. 2005c, *Animals, Economy and Status: The Integration of Zooarchaeological and Historical Evidence in the Study of Dudley Castle, West Midlands (c.1100–1750)*. Oxford: British Archaeological Reports British Series **392**.

Thomas, R. 2006, 'Of books and bones: the integration of historical and zooarchaeological evidence in the study of medieval animal husbandry', in Maltby (ed.), 2006, 17–26.

Thomas, R. forthcoming, 'Diachronic trends in lower limb pathologies in later medieval and post-medieval cattle from Britain', *Documenta Archaeobiologiae* **6**.

Thomas, R. submitted, 'Translocated testunididae: the earliest archaeological evidence for land tortoise in Britain', *Post-Medieval Archaeology*.

Thomas, R. & Stallibrass, S. 2008, 'For starters: producing and supplying food to the army in the Roman north-west provinces', in Stallibrass & Thomas (eds), 2008, 1–17.

Toms, J. 2006, *Animal Graves and Memorials*. Princes Risborough: Shire Publications.

Turner, M.E., Beckett. J.V. & Afton, B. 2001, *Farm Production in England 1700–1914*. Oxford: Oxford University Press.

Twiss, K. (ed.) 2007, *The Archaeology of Food and Identity*. Carbondale: Center for Archaeological Investigations Occasional Paper **34**.

Veen, M. van der, Livarda, A. & Hill, A. 2007, 'The archaeobotany of Roman Britain: current state and identification of research priorities', *Britannia* **38**, 181–210.

Velten, H. 2007, *Cow*. London: Reaktion Books.

Warner, M.S. & Genheimer, R.A. 2008, '"Cats here, cats there, cats and kittens everywhere": an urban extermination of cats in nineteenth-century Cincinnati', *Historical Archaeology* **42**(1): 11–25.

Webster, C.J. 2007, *The Archaeology of South West England. South West Archaeological Research Framework Resource Assessment and Research Agenda*. Taunton: Somerset County Council.

Williams, K. 1980, *The Poetical Verse of Christopher Smart 1: Jubilate Agno*. Oxford: Clarendon Press.

Williamson, T. 2002, *The Transformation of Rural England: Farming and the Landscape 1700–1870*. Exeter: University of Exeter Press.

Woolgar, C.M., Serjeantson, D. & Waldron, T. (eds) 2006, *Food in Medieval England. Diet and Nutrition*. Oxford: Oxford University Press.

Yalden, D. 1999, *The History of the British Mammals*. London: T. & A.D. Poyser.

Finds, Deposits, and Assigned Status:
New Approaches to Defined Relationships

By MICHAEL BERRY

Recent controlled excavation of archaeological sites of post-1550 Britain and Ireland, in both research and rescue contexts, has often failed to integrate different parts of the record systematically, leading to a breakdown between theory and practice. This chapter examines the relationship between deposit and assemblage, and thereby the use of deposit status designation. This research seeks to adopt a more accurate definition of status, overcoming the conceptual inadequacy that links find to deposit. The analysis of status will proceed on the following basic assumptions: firstly, that status is the relationship between the find and the context (or parent deposit); and, secondly, that this relationship is based upon information on the function, chronology and spatial characteristics of the finds and contexts. It will be demonstrated how the integration of finds and site data allows for more fruitful interpretation of excavation data. This approach helps to match site details with research agendas in both academic and commercial contexts, achieving maximum potential for research output.

INTRODUCTION

The role of the finds assemblage in archaeological interpretation has evolved over many decades, with the relationships between assemblages and their parent deposits treated in many different ways during the long development of archaeological field practice. A look at the last forty years of archaeological excavation reveals a steady increase in the number and manner of controlled excavation methods. Methods such as single-context planning and the Harris matrix have placed a focus upon establishing stratigraphic sequences and gaining better control over the recovery of finds. Overall, controlled excavation methods have been based on obtaining finds assemblages from clear contexts, rather than just recovering structural evidence and bits of treasure. This is, in part, a result of the development of contract-driven archaeology. In order to justify the expense of both government and private sector investment, the recovery of cultural heritage was argued to be necessary not just at the individual artefact level but as a collective assemblage.[1]

These developments were all for the good of archaeological practice. However, this chapter examines what is believed to be a failing both in general method, as well as a break between theory and practice. In essence, a breakdown has occurred in archaeology between the practices at the front end and the analysis at the back end. A great amount of energy and time is spent linking finds with site evidence at the contextual level in the field, while at the analysis stage this information is often disregarded and interpretation is based upon finds assemblages from the site-wide or phase level. Despite warnings against the folly of developing a single 'laundry list' approach to a site assemblage,[2] the technique remains the standard practice in archaeology. Thus publication has changed little over the decades, most reports still comprising a description of topographical developments, with separate specialist reports providing dates and perhaps broad ideas of site function.

Richard Bradley[3] addressed this failure in output when he looked closely at the excavation report as its own literary genre. Bradley noted that the common format of a report sees stratigraphic evidence occupying one section and the artefact analysis another (see also similar discussion by Mrozowski, this volume). It is not always clear that any common aim exists among the authors of respective sections. Specialists can focus upon the finds themselves, only using excavation evidence to illuminate areas of their own concerns. Taken to its extreme, this could reduce field archaeology to a service industry, mindlessly catering to the needs of specialists. In any case, it seems clear from Bradley's work that the format of the excavation report has not changed dramatically in seventy years.[4]

More recent trends within the discipline have moved towards recognising and correcting some of the problems resulting from this development. Intensification of archaeological excavation, especially in urban settings, has drawn attention to the problems that forces of cultural and natural formation pose for interpretation of assemblages.[5] The following discussion will consider two of these related problems: firstly, despite the controlled manner of recovery, little is often done to identify the relationships between finds and their deposits; and, secondly, approaches to addressing disturbance have most often been via narrow or insufficient classifications of deposit status. In this chapter 'status' refers to the ascribed condition of a deposit and the finds within. This definition incorporates the most common use of the term 'deposit status', and the opposing use to be suggested below. The following discussion aims to revisit concepts of status in light of the failings of previous approaches, and to offer a way forward towards improved integration of finds and site evidence. This will demonstrate that new ways of constructing the narrative of a site's history are possible, but only if we develop a more sophisticated understanding of the relationship between deposit and assemblage. This approach has the potential to help those who study any period of archaeological interest.

THE PROBLEM: CONCEPTS OF STATUS

Few terms in archaeology are used so often, and given as little consideration, as that of the concept of status. As excavation methods became increasingly standardised ways to use finds and their contexts of recovery for interpretation, status took on a more important role. Some *pro forma* context sheets for deposits, as a standard, require a prompt for the excavator to assign impressions of deposit status. While some context record sheets may provide a simple space to describe impressions, others will include check boxes listing the options: primary, secondary, *de facto*. These determinations are followed up by specific specialist analysis to create further interpretations. Most archaeologists highly value this information on deposit status and would even advocate an increased input of this data in the field as an aspect of standard practice.[6] The theoretical grounding for the use of status terminology, frameworks of analysis and what this means for interpretation in practice are important considerations. However, the basis on which these terms are assigned is of the most immediate concerns.

Some early archaeological approaches to the archaeological record regarded the site as a petrified reflection of the past. Finds were thought directly to reflect past activity with no intermediary factors to blur the lines between find and behaviour. It was working in the face of this situation that prompted Michael Schiffer to pose criticisms of practice at that time. Schiffer[7] advocated a consideration of formation processes as factors in affecting finds locations and behavioural aspects that result in the archaeological record. He asked questions about the nature of the archaeological record, how remains are produced and about what variables determine what is recovered. Schiffer believed that formation processes should be a consideration during interpretation.[8] He offered a model for viewing material finds as moving through various systemic contexts towards the archaeological context and eventual recovery. Systemic context, more widely understood as the 'life' history of an object, is defined as the processes that a durable object participates in during its life: procurement, manufacture, use, maintenance, and discard.[9]

There have been many previous criticisms regarding assumptions of deposit status. In reviewing Whallon's spatial analysis at Guila Naquitz, Schiffer warned that it was not enough to assume that materials on an occupation floor were primary products of processing activities; he pushed for a more convincing argument.[10] In reaction to concerns with spatial patterns and behavioural activity displayed in the archaeological record, Schiffer designed terms with which to define the status of finds in a deposit and assert the value of such finds for interpretation. These terms have become almost standard terminology on archaeological sites: '*de facto* refuse', 'primary refuse', 'secondary refuse'. The first term was proposed in the context of an investigation of abandonment practices as cultural factors for patterns of disposal. Schiffer defined *de facto* refuse finds as those that reach archaeological contexts without the performance of discard activities.[11] Essentially these are finds that are lost or abandoned. In addition to finds that retain some use-value within a society, Schiffer proposed terms that recognised the recovery of finds that are stored; he introduced the term 'provisional refuse' for reference to stored refuse having a perceived value for future reuse.[12] The following terminology defined by Schiffer was constructed with an aim to know some of the determinants of variability in patterns of refuse transport and disposal. Schiffer proposed to distinguish refuse as primary or secondary. Both forms are intentionally discarded cultural material, their difference being in the location of discard: primary material is discarded in its location of use, and secondary material is discarded in a separate area than that of the one of use.[13] The difference is found between finds left on a workshop floor and those that are collected and removed to a midden dump.

The development of cultural resource management (CRM), or rescue excavation, and the subsequent pressures of developer-funded archaeology have led to some concerning practices with the use of definitions of status. Roskams[14] suggested that the modern excavation team, with separate specialists operating exclusive of each other, has led to a breakdown in interpretation and integration between data on find and context. As a result, contexts are assigned a certain status so that specialists can focus upon sections of an assemblage that are 'important' and archive the rest for some unknown future archaeologist's interest, or simply discount it. This follows one tradition in archaeology, whereby the primacy of the assemblage type is established during interpretation.

Worse still, as Roskams points out, is the tendency to define the status of a deposit solely in terms of its physical properties, lumping together all such finds in association. This follows a noted propensity of archaeologists to conceptualise our surroundings around the physical nature of objects and deposits. Terminology is often used in reference to a deposit as a whole, essentially objectifying the deposit by defining its assumed status. Deposits are viewed as containers for finds and not reflective of activity. Despite the fact that stratigraphic contexts have been well accepted as the 'material results of events in time',[15] in the field, contexts are routinely investigated with a focus upon the spatial extent and regarded as a pit, et cetera, thereby treating the deposit as an object.[16] This follows another tradition, whereby the primacy of the deposit type is established during interpretation.

Roskams clarified the problems with assumptions of material status by clearly defining the aim of deposit status. He advocated that status be defined not by the physical properties of a deposit but by the *relationship* between find and stratigraphic context.[17] In each case the basis for determining this relationship is devised by an understanding of the functional, chronological and spatial characteristics of the finds and their associated contexts. Using these three factors Roskams[18] proposed four type categories for a more representational deposit status: Type A, in which finds are contemporary with, and functionally connected to, the stratigraphic unit from which they were derived; Type B, in which finds are broadly contemporary with, yet functionally and perhaps spatially distant from, the context in which they were found; Type C, in which finds are functionally and chronologically unrelated to the context in which they were found, but derived locally; and Type D in which finds are unrelated to the context in which they were found, imported to the place of deposition, and earlier in date than that context. By using the above definitions, assemblages could be investigated in more depth in order to infer past actions. Also, with reference to modern funding and organisational concerns, the use of more refined definitions could help with the organisation and management of assemblages, making it clearer to developers or other funding sources what is the specific aim of investigation.

A WAY FORWARD

The type categories suggested by Roskams were initially presented by the author in the context of a conference paper intended to share ideas and concepts that were admittedly at an initial stage. It was widely acknowledged that greater refinement of such terms and their application could come from further thought and subsequent testing with real-life material. There are two approaches that may be attempted at the outset; the first is by refining or adjusting the terms already presented, and the second by theorising additional terms and definitions to complement the four type categories already proposed.

If one starts by reviewing the four types already presented in order to refine the categories, there are several possible ways forward. To begin, adaptations are possible if the terminology used in the definitions of each concept is refined. Types A and D are accepted in this chapter as already presented by Roskams. These are the two most explicit status types used in this approach. An example of Type A is an assemblage of tableware ceramic forms found within a kitchen area, dating directly to the time and use of the building. An example of Type D finds would be those same tableware fragments, gathered and removed from their site of use at a much later point in time, and deposited within a landscaping fill at a different location. Unlike these two examples, Type B and C definitions can be improved by dealing with their respective terminologies.

Type B refers to items that although chronologically synchronised are functionally and spatially *distant* from their context of recovery. Herein lies a problem: how distant is distant? Are finds considered functionally and spatially connected if found within the same building? What if the archaeologist is not dealing with bounded structures but instead production areas outside an encampment? In that case, should the lithic debitage that remains at the location, material that was created by one individual sitting around a hearth, be considered Type A? How far around the same hearth area do those microliths need be scuffed before they transfer to Type B status? The original use of a somewhat vague spatially based term requires some adjustment to the definition. Schiffer struggled with similar problems around the application of his primary status term on material found adjacent to use areas. He advocated an episodic policy of broadening the primary status concept to include discard at activity-related locations but not at locations of use.[19] While it would be absurd to create hard definitions of 'distant' (10m separation is distant, 9.99m is close?), separate definitions of Type B could be made in the future. Or more reflexively, different definitions could be made depending on the circumstances of their use. We need only to be explicit (to ourselves as much as to others) in the meaning applied in each case. For the present, we can only make informed decisions based on site-specific data to separate finds spatially. Some finds will always fall between 'grey' areas, but decisions must be made. In the future, specific definitions may be made concerning distance as further studies reveal a better understanding of the application of the term.

Turning next to Type C, this incorporates material that is both functionally and chronologically unconnected to the deposit but is derived locally. An example of this type is material that was recovered from a landscaping fill laid outside a house. This material may pre-date the fill layer, and is functionally disconnected from its original use location, but its use did originate from within the house structure. The original definition is slightly problematic owing to the term 'derived'. In certain scenarios it would not be uncommon to encounter material that meets the spirit of the definition of Type C. Yet this material cannot be defined as specifically manufactured locally, during previous periods, as the term may suggest. For example, consider Chinese export porcelain recovered at a historic-period military site. The material was introduced into the site by a travelling regiment as part of the Officers Mess collection. The porcelain was certainly not manufactured locally, nor was it traded, bought or distributed locally. Despite that fact, this material is certainly an aspect of the site's life history, and is due consideration as such, yet it may be seen as not meeting the present definition of Type C status. To avoid confusion the term 'utilised' could be more applicable both for clarity and to allow the status type to be applicable to a wider range of archaeological deposits and sites.

The next step in the refinement of deposit status types is to theorise new terms and definitions to add to the four already accepted. A review of the basis for the current definition of status reveals that there are several deciding factors that dictate the exact relationship between find and context. Each of the three factors (chronology, function and space) leads to additional subdivisions. For considerations of temporal factors there are three variations for the relationship between a find and its derived stratigraphic unit: a find directly linked with a point in time, finds broadly contemporary to that period, and those not contemporary. For considerations of functional factors there are two variations for the relationship between a find and its derived stratigraphic unit: a find functionally related, and a find not related in function. For considerations of spatial factors there are three variations for the relationship between a find and its derived stratigraphic unit: a find having been utilised at that location, a find having been utilised either locally or in the vicinity, and a find that was not utilised at that spatial location. For reasons of completeness these variations and the resulting permutations of each can be tabulated for review (Table 1).

These permutations result in a few useful and interesting types in addition to the types that are not useful for analysis. Most possibilities do not seem to offer useful insights into a find or its stratigraphic unit not encompassed by the types already accepted. However,

Table 1. A List of possible permutations of the relationship between a find and its derived stratigraphic unit.

Permutations	Temporal	Functional	Spatial	Notes
1	Point	Related	Location	Type A
2	Point	Related	Vicinity	Type B
3	Point	Related	Not related	Not useful
4	Point	Not Related	Location	Not useful
5	Point	Not Related	Vicinity	Not useful
6	Point	Not Related	Not related	Not useful
7	Period	Related	Location	Within Type A use
8	Period	Related	Vicinity	Within Type B use
9	Period	Related	Not related	Not useful
10	Period	Not Related	Location	Not useful
11	Period	Not Related	Vicinity	Type E
12	Period	Not Related	Not related	Not useful
13	Not Contemporary	Related	Location	Not useful
14	Not Contemporary	Related	Vicinity	Not useful
15	Not Contemporary	Related	Not related	Type F
16	Not Contemporary	Not Related	Location	Not covered below
17	Not Contemporary	Not Related	Vicinity	Type C
18	Not Contemporary	Not Related	Not related	Type D

two permutations from the table are useful and will be included in the assembled list. The first, below termed Type E (permutation 11), would be for finds that are functionally unrelated, but spatially (broadly so) and more importantly temporally related to the strata from which they were recovered. An example of this would be a cooking pot in a smelting workshop; this is interpreted as functionally unrelated but originating from within the same building complex at the same time period of occupation. Type E finds would have obvious comparisons to Schiffer's *de facto* refuse, the pot forgotten in the corner. In this case the term 'function' may require a closer examination. How we choose to define function could have a great effect upon our interpretations of different status deposits. Is the function of a building always implicit? Can a space only have one function? These issues will have to be faced while testing status definitions against real site data, and may need to be revised at a later date. As before, the most important point is to be explicit about the reasons supporting our assessments.

The second new type, termed Type F (permutation 15), would cover finds that are functionally related, but spatially and temporally unrelated to the deposit from which they were derived. An example of this type would be the reapplication of plaster contents removed from an earlier wall but deposited separate from the wall structure. Later applications of plaster are removed from the wall, mixed with original plaster and deposited away from the wall. This example may at times be difficult to determine, mainly owing to the close relationship between function and space. Both are in many ways connected; functionally, activities exist within a specific space, and therefore to determine a type that separates the two would be rarer that any of the original four types. Based upon the three factors affecting status (functional, chronological and spatial), this is a possible permutation of the three factors. However, it is a highly unlikely form, and would largely represent a coincidental event. From an archaeological standpoint this is most interesting if a large number of such finds existed. In the example of the wall plaster presented above, this would only be interesting if large amounts of redeposited plaster were recovered. Perhaps the redeposition represents a deliberate cultural action by the inhabitants of the site. The repeated nature of a specific form of refuse disposal has a potential to reveal something about the activities of the inhabitants of a site.

The remaining status types are useful for various reasons and are discussed below in the order that they will be recognised and used. Type A includes finds contemporary with, and functionally connected to, the stratigraphic unit from which they were derived. Type B includes finds that are broadly contemporary with, yet functionally and/or spatially disconnected from, the stratigraphic unit in which they were found. Type C refers to finds that are functionally and chronologically unrelated to the stratigraphic unit in which they were found, but utilised locally. Type D includes finds unrelated to the stratigraphic unit in which they were found, imported to the place of deposition, and earlier in date than that unit. Type E refers to finds that are functionally unrelated, but spatially (broadly so) and temporally related to the stratigraphic unit from which they were recovered. Finally, Type F includes finds that are functionally related, but spatially and temporally unrelated to the stratigraphic unit from which they were derived.

The introduction of status designations that focus upon a find and its relation to its context may be a more strenuous and demanding procedure than those before it. Determining the status of precise finds among the thousands that are recovered on site may be difficult. Yet it is important to demand new levels of precision to push practice forward. In the thirty years since the development of primary/secondary status designations the practice of archaeology has advanced greatly, but not in this sphere. Surely the present state of archaeological practice is up to the demands of more exacting status types? The use of status types to create deeper, more integrated interpretive frameworks is a goal that will benefit all who utilise these sorts of archaeological data.

The aim of this approach is to arrive at results that will reflect cultural processes more fully than is presently undertaken, and so serve as a foundation for more wide-ranging interpretations. At present the most common result of excavation is to produce solely chronologically based narratives combined with specialist analysis based upon grouped site-wide assemblages. More insightful ways of grouping archaeological data should allow us to tell a different story of each site, based on a more sophisticated understanding of the relationship between deposit and assemblage. The resulting accounts may move from simple, chronological descriptions to more sophisticated accounts of activity types on the sites in question.

In order to understand the relationships discussed above, and to use them successfully to create new narratives, a broader range of deposit and assemblage data is needed. Better understandings of deposits are necessary. We require a clear idea of what deposits are constituted of and how we interpret their function. Our approach to deposit-related data also needs to be adjusted. Different deposit types need to be better defined by developing our understanding of the relationships between the two analytical levels; that is, the physical deposit type (for example, silt, sand, clay), and higher-order interpreted deposit type (for example, dump, fill, occupation deposit). It may then be possible to analyse the complexity and consistency of moving between these two levels during analysis.

It will also be necessary to integrate and understand a wider range of assemblage data. The research presented here has focused upon the most commonly found artefactual and ecofactual types of material: ceramics and bone. This process begins by integrating quantifiable assemblage information for fragmentation and formation history (summarised in Table 2). The results of each fragmentation measure are then ranked from most disturbed to least disturbed, and examined in respect to the ordered site sequence to determine the evolving character of the site's deposits. The aim is to develop methods to account for the combined ceramic and faunal deposit signature of a site assemblage and to ask the question, does the character of the ceramic assemblage match that of the faunal, or do they diverge? Any similarities or differences in assemblage signatures then need to be compared with the deposit classifications, to see what correlations emerge. Are more 'integrated' signatures reflected by these analytical relationships, allowing us to determine which kinds of deposits and activities produce which types of assemblages?

Towards these ends a methodology has been developed that combines all the elements of the site data and has had success with two different forms of output. These two can be seen, in the first instance, as a sort of half-way step by developing integrated site narratives, related to the site chronology, and secondly, a full step forward, basing the site narrative upon events or 'happenings', free of the chronological groupings. Arriving at these two results required a rather lengthy in-detail methodology, which will not be discussed here. The remainder of this chapter will instead attempt to summarise some results in the context of a case study, with an emphasis on successes with defining deposit signatures and developing new site narratives. This simple example should demonstrate the possibilities of a more integrated approach to site data whatever the chronological period under study.

CASE STUDY

With the theoretical basis established in the previous sections, the following study will test the methodology against data from a post-medieval site, the 18th-century House for Families, Mount Vernon, Virginia, which once housed members of George Washington's enslaved labour force. The data was retrieved from the publicly available Digital Archaeological Archive of Comparative Slavery,[20] and was further supported by archive reports kindly made available by staff of the Mount Vernon Archaeology Department. The excavation of the House for Families took place in two parts, first by the Virginia Research Center for Archaeology in 1984–5, and later by the Mount Vernon onsite archaeological staff in 1989–90. The only surviving portion of the structure is a small brick-lined storage cellar remnant, formed by three walls and approximately 1.2m deep (Fig. 12.1).

Mount Vernon is a large plantation and estate covering nearly 3,240 hectares. The site is most famous as the residence of George Washington from 1754 to 1799. The plantation

Table 2. The list of measures of fragmentation used to estimate the formation history of ceramic and bone assemblages.

Measure of Fragmentation	Explanation
Mean Sherd Weight (gm)	Total sherd weight (gm) divided by sherd count
Avg sherds/vessel	Sherd count divided by minimum vesell count
Completeness	EVE's divided by evreps (See Orton 1985)
Brokenness	Sherd count divided by EVE's (See Orton 1985)
Units Per Volume (gm/m3)	Total sherd weight (gm) divided by estimated deposit volume
%Burnt	Frequency of burnt ceramic sherds in each deposit
Type A Freq	The frequency of Type A ceramics present
Type B Freq	The frequency of Type B ceramics present
Type C Freq	The frequency of Type C ceramics present
Type D Freq	The frequency of Type D ceramics present
Type E Freq	The frequency of Type E ceramics present
Type F Freq	The frequency of Type F ceramics present
NISP:MNI	Ratio of NISP to MNI (See Lyman 1994)
% Whole	The proportion of whole specimens
Teeth:Mandible	Ratio of loose teeth to mandible fragments
%Small	Frequency of carpals, tarsals, sesamoids, and phalanges

LEFT
Figure 12.1 Mount Vernon, House for
Families. Site plan overlaid on rectified
excavation photograph (based upon
images from the Digital Archaeological
Archive of Comparative Slavery)

was divided into a central residence and farm, accompanied by four outlying farms. The
population of enslaved labourers at Mount Vernon lived in the outlying farms, named
Union, Muddy Hole, Dogue Run and River, or at the main residence, the Mansion House
Farm. In 1786, records show that 67 of the 216 enslaved people at Mount Vernon were
housed at the Mansion House Farm.[21] Enslaved individuals tied to outlying farms mainly
worked as field hands, whereas those at the Mansion House Farm primarily served as house
servants or skilled craftsmen.[22]

The House for Families was a slave residence situated close to the Mansion House
Farm and was apparently constructed to house most of the enslaved workforce of the
farm and residence (Fig. 12.2). The quarter appears on a 1787 map of the plantation.
Archival evidence suggests the building was of wood-frame construction, built atop brick
foundations. It was a large structure, two storeys high, six bays in length, with gable-end
chimneys.[23] Based upon archival sources, it is believed that the residence was constructed
around 1760 and was demolished around the fall of 1792 or winter of 1793.[24]

This case study has used a different means of viewing the site data, particularly with
regard to the theme of the interpretation. The excavators followed a specific research agenda

LEFT
Figure 12.2 Detail from
1792 Edward Savage
painting 'A view from the
northeast'. The House for
Families is the two-storey
structure at the centre
of the image (from the
Digital Archaeological
Archive of Comparative
Slavery, House for
Families site images
archive)

during the excavation of the House for Families. Beginning with the historical record and structural knowledge of the house, the investigation focused upon the diet and material wealth of the former inhabitants. Based upon earlier assumptions about the austerity of enslaved lifestyles, the excavators were surprised to find a rich assemblage of faunal remains and ceramic material. It was suggested that the inhabitants of the House for Families were benefiting from their close proximity to the main house. Informed by the entire site assemblage, analysis was focused upon the types of meals consumed, the related domestic items, the extent of day-to-day control of whites over the lives of enslaved Africans and African-Americans, and the overall standard of living.

The examination of the site was based firstly upon historical records and secondly upon the whole site assemblage. This 'outward-in' approach is not uncommon in historical and post-medieval archaeology. The following examination of the House for Families presents an alternative theme or approach. This is 'inward-out'. By beginning with the finds data, viewed at the most basic discrete levels and then together, a different story of the site can be constructed based upon the identified status groups and deposit signatures.

This site was chosen for analysis as a part of the author's PhD research because it addressed a range of needs. The site's historic-period occupation provided a particularly strong temporal resolution, and the site was occupied for a relatively short period of time, which to some degree limits the likelihood of residual material. Additionally, the deposit type was also well suited, as the House for Families deposits are both midden-based and associated with a domestic structure. This allowed for a review of common interpretive labels used by excavators, such as 'fills', et cetera. Finally, the site assemblage at the House for Families was well suited to study. There are sufficient amounts of well-analysed ceramics and faunal material in manageable quantities to make for fruitful analysis. All sixteen of the measures outlined in Table 12.2 were performed upon the House for Families' ceramic and faunal assemblage. The results of this analysis were used to develop the deposit signatures discussed below.

As noted in the previous section, one of the aims of this research is to better to understand deposits, how they are constructed and what activities they reflect. Commonly held assumptions about what constitutes a fill deposit, or how destruction layers are identified, are often upheld without detailed scrutiny. Although not intended as a criticism, the following discussion of the House for Families sequence offers a re-examination of the existing phasing and interpretation. The excavators, based in part on the ceramic seriation, interpreted the cellar as having been filled by three mainly distinct deposition episodes characterised by the earliest infilling of the cellar with primary waste (Phase 1), redeposited industrial waste from a nearby smith's shop (Phase 2), and the latest fills from the destruction of the structure (Phase 3). By building up interpretations based upon distinct deposit signatures, rather than treating the site assemblage as a whole, an addition to the existing narrative is presented.

This story unfolds as follows. Occupation of the structure was represented by a complex series of deposits representing different use and disposal activities. It was difficult to distil distinct signatures for deposits originally interpreted as occupational waste or fill. Despite the initial interpretation as a single functional type of layer, these deposits expressed a mixed nature with their transformation history and to some extent their deposit status. The finds were originally interpreted as a group, as primary waste directly related to the occupation of the structure. The ceramics were entirely of Type A status in the earliest layers, but increasing frequencies of residual Type C material was found in the latest occupational layers. The movement towards greater frequencies of Type C status ceramics suggests either the increasing curation of material by the occupants, or some other new processes resulting in deposition.

On the whole, these were dense deposits of large, relatively well-preserved ceramics with mostly whole or intact cow and sheep bones. However, these types of results were mixed throughout the sequence. At different points a deposit of large intact ceramics is followed by several deposits of very small ceramics. This suggests that the interpretive category fails to account for the different functional activities behind discrete episodes within the occupational fills.[25] It is likely that different kinds of processes within the House for Families are involved in the deposition of occupationally related fills.

At a later point in time the occupational deposits were purposely capped by material containing finds dating to that time and place, but from an unrelated location (Type B status ceramics). This interpretation, offered by the excavators, indicates a distinct effort to cover the material within the structure's cellar, perhaps for hygienic reasons. The ceramic assemblage within the capping layer was composed of generally small but unburnt sherds. The faunal remains are equally as disturbed, comprised primarily of small, complete bones. The clear distinction from the occupational waste signature suggests that the capping fill was imported and not associated with the structure. Following the primary life use of the structure, the cellar was likely used for the disposal of displaced waste imported from other areas. This material included well-broken and burnt ceramics with intact but small bone remains, and was mixed between presently used material and those from earlier periods (Types B and D ceramics). This signature supports the existing interpretation of a deposit of by-products from a nearby smith's shop.

The displaced deposits were later covered by material interpreted as resulting from the destruction of the House for Families. The signature represented by the destruction-related deposits indicates a consistent and specific refuse disposal pattern. The feature was used as a place to dispose of large, intact ceramics both from that period and from earlier periods of use on the site, and whole pieces of bone. This signature indicates dumping from a singular activity centre or source based upon the uniformity of the material. This reveals possible details about the process involved in the destruction of the structure. Later, modern activities left behind a few traces of small, broken mostly residual ceramics (Types C and E).

The above narrative has allowed us to examine and perhaps confirm existing interpretations of deposits and their related activities (capping fill and displaced waste from the blacksmith's shop), as well as suggesting different interpretations (multiple types of occupation waste). If groups of deposits are regarded as reflective of a single type of activity, the possibility exists that nuances and subtle differences in cultural processes will be overlooked. By employing this method of defining deposit signatures linked to interpretations, we are able to test existing assumptions of how deposits are created as well as developing new understandings of the relationship between deposit and process.

An alternative source for constructing a site narrative comes from organising the transformation data in a different fashion. If the faunal assemblage data is used as the main guide for examining the House for Families we can isolate a series of major 'events' based upon a selection of three of the sixteen measures used in the analysis of the site (Fig. 12.3). The line graph presented organises the rank order results of the fragmentation analysis listed from the top, or least fragmented, to the bottom, or most fragmented. As a means

Figure 12.3 A timeline of land-use events at the House for Families. Each fragmentation measure is ranked based upon results from top to bottom, least fragmented to most fragmented. The stratigraphic sequence is organised from left to right, from the latest deposits to the earliest

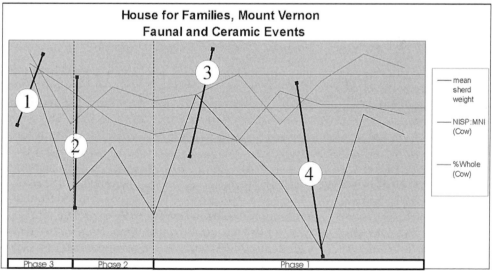

of comparing the results of the varied fragmentation measures each context within the sequence is allotted a rank based upon the relative results of that measure (for example, the lowest mean sherd weight, representing the most fragmented context in the sequence, is given the lowest rank for that measure and therefore appears as the deepest point on the line).

The stratigraphic sequence is organised from left to right, from the latest deposits (Phase 3) to the earliest (Phase 1), depicting a timeline of land use at or around the House for Families. The site's chronological phasing is plotted along the bottom of the graph to enable one to link each event with a phase or period, although it is not the intention of this method to link land-use events to specific temporal periods. With ceramic measures organised in the same line graph as the faunal measures, it can observed that the ceramic material corroborates these events. This method of presenting the contextual data reinforces the agreement between the ceramic and faunal data (although this will not always be the case), and more importantly the value in integrating this information.

The main implication of the line graph is that four major events took place within the House for Families, which can be characterised as follows. The latest deposits laid in the demolished structure included intact and undisturbed ceramic and faunal material (point 1). This event was followed closely by the deposition of a largely disturbed and fragmented assemblage (point 2). Point 3 demonstrates a second event in which less disturbed remains were deposited. The observed peak indicates a distinctive signature of this activity from those that came before or followed after. This event is followed by deposition of fragmented material representing a largely broken assemblage 'happening' (point 4). It is interesting to note that despite the fact that these events are presented synchronically and are not linked by a chronological narrative, that events 3 and 4 all occur within the same interpretive deposit type (occupational waste deposits) and within the same broad phase as defined by the excavators (Phase 1). This clearly shows that as the data within the House for Families is organised in other ways, different interpretations are possible for previously grouped material and that the idea of waste disposal as a catch-all interpretation is insufficient. In any case, I believe that even this simple example demonstrates that the movement from a chronologically based narrative to a land-use-based narrative provides an interesting and useful way to investigate a site, challenging the common practice to cling to rigid chronologies and conceptions of compartmentalised time.

CONCLUSIONS

There are several implications that can be drawn from the above discussion. This work has focused upon several relationships that I believe required investigation. These are the relationship between excavator terminology and practice relating to deposits, the relationship between artefacts and ecofacts and their parent deposits, and the relationship between chronology and the construction of site narrative. The aim is to be able to define more consistent methods of recording, quantifying and analysing deposits and assemblages, both for academic research and for commercial contexts, in order to ensure that existing investment is fully exploited. Particularly in this area, the aim is to define sampling strategies that target site assemblages from specified deposit types for subsequent detailed, and integrated, analysis. Finally, the results will reflect cultural processes more fully than is presently done, and so serve as a foundation for more wide-ranging interpretations. Refined deposit signatures allow for more exact links between deposits and cultural processes.

More insightful ways of grouping archaeological data should allow us to tell a different story of each site, based on a more sophisticated understanding of the relationship between deposit and assemblage, and between different assemblage types, because they enter the archaeological record in different ways. In some cases, the resulting accounts may move from simple, chronological descriptions, to more sophisticated accounts of activity types on the site in question. On occasion, this may mean providing simply different accounts. Either way it should generate 'better', or at least more interesting and incisive, reports that justify the considerable expense and effort that is required for the controlled collection of assemblages and careful description of the stratigraphic record of a site. The need to better utilise investment unites archaeologists of every period and area of specialist interest.

It is important to note that the case study presented here is an early example of the method and its potential. Future work may make it possible to determine which measures of fragmentation are better at revealing the nature of a deposit. Other future possibilities include tracking changes in interpreted deposit types from a specific area in order to understand how processes that result in deposition evolve over time (for example, the nature of waste deposits, fills, construction and destruction deposits). The implications for urban archaeology are very promising as both academic and developer-funded work is increasingly interested in understanding the evolution of urban neighbourhoods. An improved understanding of the ways in which waste, construction and destruction deposits are generated and disposed of in urban settings is central to interpreting urban life.

Finally, if we begin to build integrated interpretations up from discrete levels more effective reports may be possible. Archaeological reports are often characterised as the monotonous listing of finds and stratigraphic units that seldom encourage interest in the material. The method of developing interpretations advocated here may contribute to more interesting and thus useful reports, while still meeting the technical needs of archaeologists and their clients. Additionally, by developing greater interaction between different branches of archaeology (field excavators, finds specialists, zooarchaeologists), we can foster more inclusivity and hence advancement in practice. The isolation of archaeology's practitioners benefits no one with an interest in preserving and understanding the past.

ACKNOWLEDGEMENTS

This chapter and the conference paper it is based upon would not have been possible without the help of several people. Special thanks go to Steve Roskams for his continued advice and support. Thanks to Eleanor Breen, formerly at Historic Mount Vernon, for her help with providing data. Matthew Johnson kindly provided additional advice. Finally, thanks are due to my wife, without whom none of this would be possible.

NOTES

1. Roskams 1992, 27.
2. Miller 1991, 2.
3. Bradley 2006.
4. Bradley 2006, 667.
5. See Beck 2006; Pollard 2001; Sullivan 1989; Villa 1982; Murray 1980; Baker 1978; Bradley & Fulford 1980; and Halstead et al. 1978 to name only a few.
6. Hammer 1993, 362
7. Schiffer 1972.
8. Schiffer 1972, 156.
9. Schiffer 1972, 158.
10. Schiffer 1972.
11. Schiffer 1972, 160.
12. Schiffer 1996.
13. Schiffer 1972, 161.
14. Roskams 1992.
15. Fedele 1984.
16. Lucas 2001, 157.
17. Roskams 1992, 28.
18. Roskams 1992, 28–9.
19. Schiffer 1996, 58.
20. 2004, <http://www.daacs.org>.
21. Pogue 1991, 1.
22. Pogue 2003, Background, 2 June 2007.
23. Pogue 2003, Background, 2 June 2007.
24. Pogue 2003, Background, 2 June 2007.
25. Pogue 1991, 8.

BIBLIOGRAPHY

Baker, C.M. 1978, 'The size effect: an explanation of variability in surface artifact assemblage content', *American Antiquity* **43**(2): 288–93.

Beck, M. 2006, 'Midden ceramic assemblage formation: a case study from Kalinga, Philippines', *American Antiquity* **71**(1): 27–51.

Bradley, R. 2006, 'The excavation report as a literary genre: traditional practice in Britain', *World Archaeology* **38**(4): 664–71.

Bradley, R. & Fulford, M. 1980, 'Sherd size in the analysis of occupation debris', *Bulletin of the Institute of Archaeology* **17**: 85–94.

Digital Archaeological Archive of Comparative Slavery 2004, Thomas Jefferson Foundation, <www.daacs.org>.

Fedele, F.G. 1984, 'Towards an analytical stratigraphy: stratigraphic reasoning and excavation', *Stratigraphica Archaeologica* **1**: 7–15.

Halstead, P., Hodder, I. & Jones, G. 1978, 'Behavioral archaeology and refuse patterns: a case study', *Norwegian Archaeological Review* **11:** 118–31.

Lucas, G. 2001, *Critical Approaches to Fieldwork*. London: Routledge.

Lyman, R.L. 1994, *Vertebrate Taphonomy*. Cambridge: Cambridge University Press.

Miller, G. 1991, 'Thoughts towards a user's guide to ceramic assemblages', *Council for North-eastern Historical Archaeology Newsletter* **18**: 2–5.

Murray, P. 1980, 'Discard location: the ethnographic data', *American Antiquity* **45**(3): 490–502.

Orton, C. 1985, 'Two useful parameters for pottery research', *Computer Applications in Archaeology* **13**: 114–20.

Pogue, D. 2003, 'House for families', *Digital Archaeological Archive of Comparative Slavery* <http://www.daacs.org/ >.

Pollard, R.J. 2001, 'Assemblage formation processes: a case study from Leicester', in Roskams (ed.), 2001, 207–12.

Roskams, S. 1992, 'Finds context and deposit status', in *Interpretation of Stratigraphy: A Review of the Art*, ed. K. Steane. Lincoln: City of Lincoln Archaeology Unit Report **31**, 27–9.

Roskams, S. (ed.) 2001, *Interpreting Stratigraphy: Site Evaluation, Recording Procedures and Stratigraphic Analysis*, BAR International Series **910**. Oxford: Archaeopress.

Schiffer, M.B. 1972, 'Archaeological contexts and systemic context', *American Antiquity* **37**: 156–65.

Schiffer, M.B. 1974, 'On Whallon's use of dimensional analysis of variance at Guila Naquitz', *American Antiquity* **39**(3): 490–2.

Schiffer, M.B. 1996, *Formation Processes of the Archaeological Record*. Salt Lake City: University of Utah Press.

Sullivan, A.P. 1989, 'The technology of ceramic reuse: formation processes and archaeological evidence', *World Archaeology* **21**(1): 101–14.

Villa, P. 1982, 'Conjoinable pieces and site formation processes', *American Antiquity* **47**: 276–90.

UNPUBLISHED SOURCES

Hammer, F.A. 1993, 'Excavation and post-excavation recording methods in British archaeology today: investigation of strategies pursued by 70 archaeological units and projects during the 1980s', unpublished PhD thesis, University of York.

Pogue, D. 1991, *Summary Report on the House for Families Slave Quarter Site (44 Fx 762/40–47)*, Mount Vernon Plantation, Mount Vernon, Virginia: Mount Vernon Ladies' Association.

Haulbowline Island, Cork Harbour, Ireland, c.1816–1832: A New Archaeological Perspective on Ireland's 'Coloniality'

By COLIN RYNNE

Many aspects of Ireland's landscapes and material culture, dating from the early modern period up to Independence and partition in 1922, continue to be viewed as symbols of a 'colonial' past. However, to an overwhelming majority of specialists working directly with the primary source material for Irish history and archaeology the notion, as proposed by nationalist historians and postcolonialists, that the essential relationship between Ireland and the United Kingdom was that of 'colony' and 'metropolitan state', both misrepresents and oversimplifies the nature of that association. By dividing the native and settler populations into colonists and colonised, postcolonial discourse theory, as applied to Ireland, offers a one-dimensional, reductivist view of the experience of immigrant and native populations. Not all colonists were the same, while English rule was experienced in many different ways by settlers and natives alike. Recent work on the archaeology of the former Royal Naval base at Haulbowline, built in 1816–22 to supply the entire British South Atlantic fleet, enables and offers a contrasting view to the traditional, essentially nationalist, interpretation of Ireland's many-sided subjugation to Britain's interest as 'colonial'. It is argued here that Haulbowline was in every way part of a colonial project, but one in which Irish people were very much junior partners rather than victims. Indeed, the very presence of such an installation in Ireland, as in the case of a post office or courthouse, should really be viewed as evidence that the island was a fully functioning part of the United Kingdom rather than a British colony.

INTRODUCTION: POSTCOLONIALITY AND IRELAND

For an overwhelming, almost total, majority of Irish historians and archaeologists, the notion that the essential relationship between Ireland and the United Kingdom was that of 'colony' and 'metropolitan state' bears no relation to the evidence they encounter on a daily basis. Yet postcolonial studies in Ireland has never really been much concerned with the 'evidence'. Of course, no one really expects the literary critics who make up their ranks to be or to become historians. Like everybody else, they are entitled to question modern historiographical methodologies or revisionist views of Irish history, but only so far. Indeed, in their opposition to the views of 'revisionist' historians of Ireland, they have as yet failed to produce a convincing defence of the essentially nationalist idea that Ireland was, up to independence in 1922, simply a British colony. Thus far their essential message to the revisionists has been this: we disagree with your interpretation of primary source materials, which *we are not inclined to consult*. For them the theory is always more important than the facts, the political conviction superior to the historical realities.[1]

During the Plantation period of the 17th century, there can be little doubt most of Ireland was treated as a source of primary exploitation, as a *de facto* colonial entity. But the relationship between the new immigrant communities and the natives soon developed social and political accommodations much more complicated than the binary polarities of 'colonist' and 'colonised' suggested, somewhat naively and ahistorically, by the exponents of postcolonial discourse theory. Sectarian tensions certainly remained among the upper echelons of the immigrant communities – those, of course, who had the most to lose.[2] Yet among the greater part of the immigrant and native populations the notional, idealised and homogenised 'colonial discourse' between 'English' and 'Irish', 'Catholic' and 'Protestant' or 'coloniser' and 'colonised' simply did not exist.[3]

Hitherto postcolonialists have refused to acknowledge the complexities of identity-formation in early modern Ireland. From their historical perspective, Ireland's 17th-century relationship with Britain never really changed until the island, as they would have it, was 'decolonised' in 1922. They have, however, experienced serious difficulties in maintaining this idea with anything near the historical certainty required to theorise Ireland's pre-1922 relationship with Britain as a colonial discourse. Their first real problem is that almost all Irish historians – even those who see manifest colonial elements in Ireland's nineteenth-century administration as part of the United Kingdom – reject the notion that Ireland can be viewed as a postcolonial entity.[4] Furthermore, even though they rely exclusively on secondary historical accounts they have, nonetheless, been known to denounce counterfactual challenges by other historians to their most basic assumptions as 'modernist', 'historicist' or 'empiricist'. Are we to assume that the secondary accounts that they employ to bolster their own arguments are untainted by these traits, or is this merely, as historians might infer, a blatant double standard? As Linda Connolly has recently pointed out '[they] have been noted for vehemently challenging the standpoint and ideology of [Irish] historical revisionism, in particular. However, when it comes to theorizing *its own historical methods*, postcolonial criticism has been uncharacteristically demure.'[5]

Up to very recent times, the assumption that Ireland had simply been a British colony was used to frame, generally in a negative way, the manner in which later historic landscapes were viewed in the Republic of Ireland. Facets of the built environment, in particular, such as demesnes, military installations and even courthouses, were seen as vestiges of Ireland's 'colonial' subjugation to Britain. Their continued existence was, in certain quarters, even viewed as unwelcome reminders of a colonial past that should be best forgotten. From the outset the new state was very clear about the past it believed more appropriate to commemorate or, more properly, those pasts that it chose to ignore. This selective memory was effectively enshrined in the Republic of Ireland's National Monuments legislation, beginning with the Act of 1930, in which the period after AD 1700 was officially considered not to be of archaeological interest. Only with the amending legislation of 1994 were post-1700 landscapes in Ireland formally shorn of their 'colonial' taint.[6] However, a key problem concerning the way in which certain aspects of the built environment, and in particular pre-1922 government buildings and military installations, continue to be viewed, still remains.

In the first, formative phase of the British Empire (1600–1783), Ireland's relationship to Britain was at best anomalous, at worst 'profoundly ambiguous'.[7] It had its own House of Commons and House of Lords, which was sufficient, according to one recent view, to mark it off 'decisively from every colony acquired subsequently by England, all of which retained their colonial status'.[8] As early as 1494, with the introduction of Poyning's Law,[9] the English had severely curbed any independent action by the Irish parliament, a form of legislative subjugation to the Westminster that was further underlined by the Declaratory Act of 1719, under which the Irish House of Lords was denied any appellate jurisdiction. In 1782, Irish protestants managed to have the restrictions Poyning's Law imposed on their parliament removed, and for a short period, up to the passing of the Irish Act of Union in 1800, were able to make law for the kingdom of Ireland relatively unhindered. However, in the aftermath of United Irishmen's rebellion of 1798, the British government decided to iron out any constitutional anomalies posed by Ireland, beginning with the dissolution of the Irish parliament.[10] From 1801 up to 1922, Ireland formed part of, and all of its inhabitants became citizens of, the United Kingdom of Great Britain and Ireland.

Many buildings constructed during the Union, such as Royal Irish Constabulary stations, military installations, post offices, workhouses and courthouses were intended to ensure that Ireland could satisfactorily function within this new political entity. Seldom, however, have they been viewed as such. Since the 18th century, local government within Ireland also encouraged considerable infrastructural development, to the extent that by the 19th century Ireland's road and canal networks had clearly outpaced its general lack of industrialisation. The success of these attempts at equalisation with the rest of the United Kingdom were such that at partition, in 1922, Ireland was not 'decolonised' but effectively seceded from the Union. The incoming nationalist government, as a recent study has shown, took it up and ran it as a going concern, while its subsequent economic failures had nothing to do with a postcolonial condition but with its own disastrous policies.[11] In 1922 Ireland was also, despite its general level of economic development relative to other regions of the United Kingdom (and indeed to the Lagan valley in Ulster) very much a European country and not a Third World region. This latter circumstance, its position within the United Kingdom, and the advantages it enjoyed as a consequence of this, clearly marked it off from colonies controlled by European imperial powers in general. And this, indeed, is where the experience of natives of Britain's colonies and those of Ireland diverge. Ireland was very much part of England's imperial project, but more as active collaborator/junior partner than as victim. As will be argued below, the British naval base on Haulbowline Island in Cork harbour, rather than symbolising Ireland's 'colonial' status, was in fact a physical expression of its willing participation in Britain's colonial subjugation of other regions of the globe. Britain's colonial trade network and, in particular, the armed conflicts it pursued in its expansion and maintenance, provided enormous prosperity for the Cork region. With the rise in the demand for Irish agricultural goods, even the smallest Catholic dairy farmer in south Munster could directly profit from the exploitation of the colonial concerns of English and continental imperial powers.

THE BRITISH NAVAL VICTUALLING YARDS ON HAULBOWLINE ISLAND 1816–1832, AND THE BRITISH IMPERIAL PROJECT IN THE SOUTH ATLANTIC

On one level, the Union had been presented to its detractors as a means of enabling greater Irish involvement in Britain's burgeoning overseas empire. On another level, up to 1793, this had effectively been denied to the majority of the Irish population. Anti-catholic legislation prohibited, among other things, Irish catholics from joining the British army. However, with the acquisition of both Canada and India, as a result of the Seven Years' War (1756–63), any hostility that may have existed towards Irish catholics as a lurking political threat began to wane in London. The increasing English demands for manpower for imperial expansion transformed Ireland's white, male, English-speaking catholic population into an ideal reservoir of recruits for the new colonies.[12] When enabled to do so, catholic Irishmen enlisted in their thousands, so much so that within forty years of the passing of the Act of Union almost forty per cent of the British army's rank and file consisted of Irishmen.[13] This latter statistic does, of course, speak volumes about 'Irishness' and 'Britishness', with regard to the perceived identities of those Irish catholics who joined the British military. The origin and confessional allegiance of these men was clearly no impediment to enlistment (so much for 'othering') and active participation in the British imperial project, one of the much-vaunted fruits of the Union. Yet it was also an opportunity for them, through such participation, to pursue a 'British' identity.[14]

Irishmen were less well represented in the British navy, but the agricultural wealth of their homeland came to provide many of the onboard necessities for this branch of the British armed forces, from the early 18th century onwards. In part, the island's ability to accommodate Britain's needs was directly related to its involvement in the lucrative provisions trade based on the creation of the Atlantic economy and the colonial trade networks of Britain, France, Portugal and Spain. The southern Irish ports of Cork and Waterford were to become important beneficiaries of this trade well before the Union was passed, a position they were to maintain up to the end of the Napoleonic Wars. Of all the 18th-century Irish ports, however, Cork was clearly the most important single supplier of 'wet' provisions (that is, butter, pork and beef) for both the British army and navy. Up to 1782, indeed, it enjoyed a virtual monopoly of the provisioning of British naval and army supply ships, and even after this date it still accounted for two-thirds of wet provisions sourced in Ireland by the British military.[15]

A Cork harbour location became, therefore, the obvious choice when the Admiralty decided to revamp its victualling facilities in Ireland, early in the 19th century, in order that these could accommodate the entire needs of the British South Atlantic fleet (Fig. 13.1). The harbour had long been an important assembly point for Atlantic convoys, and its increasing strategic importance to Admiralty had been underlined with the expansion of its defences. As early as 1795 it had been decided to construct new storehouses on Haulbowline Island to replace those already in existence in Kinsale harbour to the east. In 1806, orders were issued for what was to become an important British naval base on the island, protected by the artillery fort on nearby Spike Island and with unrivalled access to the rich agricultural hinterland of Cork harbour.[16]

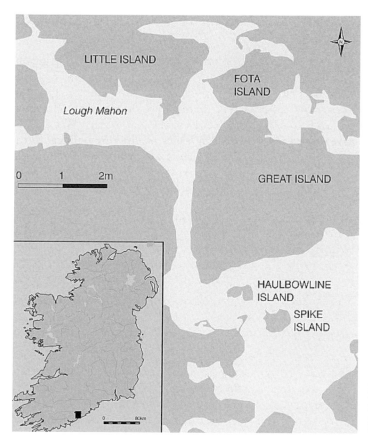

LEFT
Figure 13.1 Location map, Haulbowline Island, Cork Harbour, Ireland.

An Admiralty plan of 1807 shows the original extent of the island, with its slightly modified early 17th-century star-shaped fort, along with the proposed modifications to its shoreline to accommodate the storehouses and wharfage.[17] From the outset the island was physically divided between the Admiralty and the Board of Ordnance, by a substantial boundary wall extending (roughly on a north–south axis) across it. The Board of Ordnance lands comprised around ten acres at the west of the island, and although each jurisdiction was kept distinct and carefully separated by the boundary wall, a large and imposing cut stone gateway arch enabled access to each territory at the northern extremity of the wall. Work appears to have begun first on the Ordnance complex, with the construction of a Martello tower in 1813, upon which some £3,000 had been expended up to its completion in 1814. Earlier, in 1810, two large powder magazines were under construction on the adjacent Rocky Island (but had still not been completed by 1814).[18] However, the progress of works on the Admiralty section of the island remains unclear. According to Wakefield, writing in 1812, over £10,000 had been spent on the Haulbowline complex by 1811.[19] On present evidence, this would appear to have involved the substantial ground works for the quaysides and housing for naval personnel, to be followed, in 1816, with the commencement of the construction of the victualling yards.

Royal dockyards, such as Chatham, Plymouth and Portsmouth, along with their overseas equivalents at, for example, Malta, Gibraltar, Minorca, Antigua and Port Royal, Jamaica, were designed to construct, repair and supply Royal Navy ships.[20] This was also the rationale behind the Haulbowline naval base which, like the others, was equipped with dockyards, victualling and ordnance yards. By the second half of the 19th century, its development can be further paralleled with that of other home and overseas Royal Naval bases with the construction of a zymotic hospital, for the treatment of tropical diseases. There are also close similarities in both the design and the Georgian architectural forms employed in the six Haulbowline naval storehouses, with the other home naval bases, which have hitherto escaped notice. The central storehouse in the north-facing range, for example, has a campanile and clock tower (Fig. 13.2), a relatively common feature of 18th- and 19th-century British naval storehouses.[21] The Haulbowline storehouses also have distinctive mansard-style roofs with stone parapets, which are clearly derived from their southern English counterparts.[22] Given these similarities in design, and with those of certain later dockyard complexes, there can be few reasons for doubting Frederick O'Dwyer's suggestion that the Haulbowline victualling yards were designed by Edward Holl, architect to the Navy Board (1804–24).[23] Holl was also responsible for important buildings at Chatham, Sheerness (with John Rennie), Portsmouth and Bermuda.

Nevertheless, while Holl was very influential in the design of many naval buildings, he was not personally involved in their construction. This was to have interesting and

Figure 13.2 Campanile and clock tower on Haulbowline Island north-facing victualling storehouse, c. 1814. The building is currently used by the Irish navy

in many ways unique consequences for his Cork harbour dockyards. The Haulbowline victualling yards, built between 1816 and 1822, were to become the only home or overseas naval buildings whose construction was to be overseen by a female building contractor. Mrs Elizabeth Deane – mother of Sir Thomas Deane of the famous Victorian Deane and Woodward architectural practice – had taken over her husband's building firm after his premature death, undertaking important construction contracts up to her own death in 1828. Elizabeth was conveyed in a ten-oared galley from her home at Lapp's Quay, Cork to Haulbowline Island on a regular basis to oversee the works, an achievement that was commemorated in a contemporary song:

> But not forgetting Haulbowline Island,
>
> That was constructed by Mrs Deane:
>
> Herself's the lady that has stowed the water,
>
> To supply the vessels upon the main.[24]

The song refers to the water tanks, to the west of the east-facing storehouses, which were designed to hold up to one million gallons of water. The construction technique employed in the storehouses, which were provided with what appears to be an early form of transitional fireproofing, unique in Ireland, may well have influenced Edward Holl's use of cast iron in later naval buildings, such as the Port Royal, Jamaica (c. 1817) and Bermuda yards (1822–31).[25] However, while the cast iron columns and beams supporting the internal floors of the Haulbowline stores have a fish-backed profile similar to those of English fire-proofed buildings of the period, in contemporary British buildings, these beams are used to support a matrix of brick segmental jack arches (Fig. 13.3).[26] But at Haulbowline, the series of flanged sockets set into the upper edges of the girders were used to support wooden joists. Nevertheless, the Haulbowline internal iron framing (apart from being the earliest recorded example of its type in Ireland) appears to have no obvious Royal Naval exemplar elsewhere.[27]

The victualling yard at Haulbowline, in its heyday, was in full operation between 1816 and 1832, during which it was responsible for the provisioning of the entire British South Atlantic fleet.[28] Its virtual abandonment was largely a consequence of the end of the Napoleonic wars and in the 'downsizing' of the British armed forces. As a staging post for Irish agricultural produce, it symbolises the south Munster region's engagement with Britain's colonial trade networks as an important trading partner, rather than as a place of primary colonial exploitation. In this discourse, from the 17th century onwards, we can observe the descendents of English colonists forming a partnership with an increasing number of indigenous catholic stakeholders, to exploit the economic opportunities presented by the expansion of European colonial empires.[29] This collaboration was decidedly 'un-colonial' and is, perhaps, the principal reason why it became possible for all parties concerned to forge an important transformation in the economic development of south Munster.

Arising out of this co-operation was a highly innovative market structure for the Munster butter trade created, on a wholly voluntary basis, by an association of Cork butter exporters in 1769, which was to become known as the Committee of Merchants. Their Cork Butter Market, centred on the Shandon area of Cork city, went on to develop one

Figure 13.3 Cast iron framing of c. 1814 in Haulbowline Island victualling storehouse.

of the most effective marketing structures existing anywhere in Europe. The Committee's diligence in grading, packing and weighing the butter created a series of internationally recognised quality brands for the market's products, while at the same time ensuring that all butter brought to the market was sold on the same day.[30] The success of this entirely local institution led to the creation of a truly international market, underpinned by a 'degree of impartiality and administrative effectiveness that was rare by the public standards of the eighteenth century'.[31] Under this arrangement, all of the market's stakeholders, even the relatively insignificant County Cork, Kerry, Limerick and Waterford farmers, could obtain a fair price for their firkins of butter, from butter factors and merchants servicing the trade networks of Britain, France, Spain and Portugal's overseas colonial empires.

CONCLUSION

This interesting example of social agency could never have arisen in a 'colonial' discourse, predicated by the rigid maintenance of racial and social inequalities. However, the essentially European nature of Ireland, in terms of race, culture and religion, and its physical proximity to England, generally renders colonial labels (and the more recent theoretical brands associated with them) rather inappropriate as a means of characterising the island's subjugation to Britain.[32] Nor can this notionalised 'coloniality' be properly applied to Ireland's later historic landscapes, as a means of understanding their development. Indeed, rather than problematising these as colonial vestiges, they could be more profitably explored, from an archaeological perspective, as marginal regions of the United Kingdom.

NOTES

1. Kennedy's paper (1996) remains the most scathing analysis of attempts to apply postcolonial theory to Ireland. For an excellent and comprehensive account of the colonial debate, see Howe 2000. For more recent criticism of postcolonial views of Irish history, from different perspectives, see Horning 2006; Connolly 2007; Rynne 2008. To date, the response of postcolonialists to the rejection of colonial and postcolonial discourse theory, by historians in general, have been muted: see, for example, Cleary 2003, 2007; David Lloyd 2003. Said's (2003, 179) response to Howe's thesis was to call him an 'England supporter' (whatever that means).

2. Ford 2005.

3. Canny 1988, 53.

4. Whelan 2001, 25, appears to be alone among Irish historians in attempting to employ the postcolonial concept of 'othering' to 18th-century Irish catholics. However, Irish catholics were by no means seen as threatening and inimical to 'Britishness', as is evident by their numbers in the British army, which they were allowed to join from 1793 onwards.

5. Connolly 2007, 191.

6. In May 2008, the opening of the Battle of the Boyne heritage centre in County Meath, by the then Taoiseach, Bertie Ahern and the Rev. Ian Paisley, First Minister of the Northern Ireland Executive, was the first real public acknowledgement by the Irish government of an important symbol of Unionist identity. The ceremony was conducted in the presence of dignitaries from Northern Ireland and the Republic, including senior members of the Orange Order.

7. Bartlett 1998, 2001 and 2003.

8. Bartlett 2001.

9. Kelly 2007.

10. For an excellent account of the rationale behind the passing of the Act of Union, see Kelly 2001.

11. Girvan 2004.

12. Barlett 2003, 51.

13. Bartlett 2001, 257. According to Dickson 2005, as many as one in ten males from the Munster region seem likely to have served in the British forces in the period 1793–1815.

14. Bartlett 2001. Bartlett also lays down an effective challenge to Colley's argument (1992, 8), that the Irish could never be British.

15. Dickson 2005, 367–8.

16. Brunicardi 1982, 18.

17. PRO MPHH 1/11. As this map conclusively demonstrates, there were no naval dockyards on the island in 1805, as suggested in recent accounts, e.g. Bielenberg 1991, 105–6; Dickson 2005, 409.

18. Williams 2003.

19. Wakefield 1812, II, 816.

20. Coad 1983, 17. This otherwise excellent account, which modestly admits to not being an 'exhaustive survey', is curiously remiss in omitting any reference to the Haulbowline base, despite the excellence of the physical survivals of the ordnance magazines, the victualling storehouses and the associated dockyard. An enormous amount of documentation relating to the site is also preserved in the British National actives. See, for example, NA, Navy Board In Letters, 1812–1822, ADM 106/1982, Yards In Letters 1828–1832, ADM 106/1984.

21. See Coad 1983, 86–7, for illustrations of campanile clock towers at Chatham (1774) and Portsmouth (1776) dockyards.

22. Coad 1983, fig. 84, p. 87; fig 87, p. 89, Portsmouth, 1763 (whose end elevations are very similar to those of the Haulbowline storehouses) and fig. 90; Chatham, 1793.

23. O'Dwyer 1997, 5.

24. O'Dwyer 1997, 5, Croften Croker 1839, 272.

25. Coad 1983, 106–7, 151.

26. Rynne 2006, 401.

27. Even in the Melville Square storehouse designed by John Rennie for the Royal William yard, and begun in 1829, the cast iron columns were used to support wooden cross beams: see Coad 1983, fig. 123.

28. In 1837 the facilities were described as follows: 'On Halbowling [sic] Island are the spacious and admirably designed naval storehouses, tank and other requisites now abandoned' (Lewis 1837, I, 415).

29. Dickson 2005, 495.

30. Rynne 1998; Dickson 2005, 375.

31. Dickson 2005, 376–7.

32. Connolly 1992, 111.

BIBLIOGRAPHY

Bartlett, T. 1998, '"This famous island set in a Virginian sea": Ireland in the British Empire, 1690–1800', in Marshall (ed), 1998, 253–75.

Bartlett, T. 2001, 'Britishness, Irishness and the Act of Union', in Whelan & Keogh (eds), 2001, 243–58.

Bartlett, T. 2003, '"An Union for Empire": the Anglo-Irish Union as an imperial project', in Brown et al. (eds), 2003, 50–7.

Bielenberg, A. 1992, *Cork's Industrial Revolution 1780–1880: Development or Decline?* Cork: Cork University Press.

Brown, M., Geoghan, P.M. & Kelly, J. (eds) 2003, *The Irish Act of Union, 1800: Bicentennial Essays.* Dublin: Irish Academic Press.

Brunicardi, N. 1982, *Haulbowline, Spike and Rocky Islands in Cork Harbour.* Fermoy: Éigse Books.

Canny, N. 1988, *Kingdom and Colony: Ireland in the Atlantic World 1560–1800.* Baltimore & London: Johns Hopkins University Press.

Carroll, C. & King, P. (eds) 2003, *Ireland and Postcolonial Theory.* Cork: Cork University Press.

Cleary, J. 2003, 'Misplaced ideas? Colonialism, location and dislocation in Irish studies', in Connolly (ed.), 2003.

Cleary, J. 2007, *Outrageous Fortune.* Dublin: Field Day Publications.

Coad, C. 1983, *Historic Architecture of the Royal Navy. An Introduction.* London: Victor Gollancz.

Colley, L. 1992, *Britons: Forging the Nation 1707–1837.* New Haven: Yale University Press.

Connolly, C. (ed.) 2003, *Theorising Ireland.* Basingstoke: Palgrave.

Connolly, L. 2007, 'The limits of "Irish studies": historicism, culturalism, paternalism', in Flannery & Mitchell (eds), 2007.

Connolly, S.J. 1992, *Religion, Law and Power: The Making of Protestant Ireland 1660–1760.* Oxford: Oxford University Press.

Croften Croker, T. 1839, *The Popular Songs of Ireland.* London: Henry Colburn.

Dickson, D. 2005, *Old World Colony: Cork and South Munster 1630–1830.* Cork: Cork University Press.

Flannery, E. & Mitchell, A. (eds) 2007, *Enemies of Empire: New Perspectives on Imperialism, Literature and Historiography.* Dublin: Four Courts Press.

Ford, A. 2005, 'Living together, living apart: sectarianism in early modern Ireland', in Ford, A. & McAfferty, J. (eds) 2005, *The Origins of Sectarianism in Early Modern Ireland.* Cambridge: Cambridge University Press, 1–23.

Girvan, T. 2004, *Preventing the Future: Why was Ireland Poor for so Long?* Dublin: Gill & Macmillan.

Horning, A. 2006, 'Archaeology, conflict and contemporary identity in the north of Ireland. Implications for theory and practice in comparative archaeologies of colonialism', *Archaeological Dialogues* **13**(2): 183–200.

Howe, S. 2000, *Ireland and Empire: Colonial Legacies in Irish History and Culture.* Oxford: Oxford University Press.

Kelly, J. 2001, 'The Act of Union: its origins and background', in Whelan & Keogh (eds), 2001, 46–66.

Kelly, J. 2007, *Poyning's Law and the Making of Law in Ireland.* Dublin: Four Courts Press.

Kennedy, L. 1996, *Colonialism, Religion and Nationalism in Ireland.* Belfast: Institute for Irish Studies.

Lewis, S. 1837, *A Topographical Dictionary of Ireland.* London: S. Lewis & Co.

Lloyd, D. 2003, 'After history: Historicism and Irish postcolonial studies', in Carroll & King (eds), 2003, 46–62.

Marshall, P. (ed.) 1998, *The Oxford History of the British Empire.* Oxford: Oxford University Press.

O'Dwyer, F. 1997, *The Architecture of Deane and Woodward.* Cork: Cork University Press.

Rynne, C. 1998, *At the Sign of the Cow: The Cork Butter Market 1769–1924.* Cork: Collins Press.

Rynne, C. 2006, *Industrial Ireland 1750–1930: An Archaeology.* Cork: Collins Press.

Rynne, C. 2008, 'The Rolt Memorial lecture 2007: Technological change as a "colonial discourse": The Society of Friends in 19th-century Ireland', *Industrial Archaeology Review* **30**(1): 3–17.

Said, E. 2003, 'Afterword: reflections on Ireland and postcolonialism', in Carroll & King (eds), 2003, 177–85.

Wakefield, E. 1812, *An Account of Ireland, Statistical and Political*, 2 vols. London: Longman.

Whelan, K. 2001, 'The other within: Ireland, Britain and the Act of Union', in Whelan & Keogh (eds), 2001, 13–33.

Whelan, K. & Keogh, D. (eds) 2001, *Acts of Union: The Causes, Contexts and Consequences of the Act of Union*. Dublin: Four Courts Press.

Williams, W.J. 2003, 'Early nineteenth-century gunpowder magazines on Rocky Island, Co. Cork', *Journal of the Cork Historical and Archaeological Society* 7, 83–96.

English Industrial Landscapes – Divergence, Convergence and Perceptions of Identity

By PAUL BELFORD

This chapter examines the way in which industrial landscapes have been perceived throughout the post-medieval period, and explores the effect on current research and conservation of prevailing attitudes to 'landscape archaeology' and 'industrial archaeology'. Using a variety of examples, it is argued that industrial landscapes should be seen as neither urban nor rural but as entirely separate entities incorporating elements of both. Existing ways of looking at rural or urban landscapes are therefore inadequate for the technological, social and cultural complexities represented by industrial landscapes. One key theme that can be drawn out from the study of industrial landscapes is that of identity, and particular emphasis is given to investigating the ways in which industrial landscapes have given rise to specifically English identities.

INTRODUCTION

England is the birthplace of industrialisation. Almost all English landscapes can be said to be industrial landscapes, in that they have been shaped by the forces of industrialisation. Sometimes these forces have been very direct and are highly visible: as in the declining industrial conurbations of the West Midlands, or the former textile towns of West Yorkshire and Lancashire. Elsewhere, temporally more distant industrial activity has been softened by later land use: the gentle undulations of Derbyshire lead mining, the heavily wooded Ironbridge Gorge in Shropshire, or the almost suburban former ironworking landscapes of Surrey. Even in the apparent rural idyll of the post-medieval country estate it is possible to find steam-powered corn-mills and pump houses and electrical power stations. Indeed, the quintessential English farming landscape, with its quilt-like pattern of small fields and woodland, is a resource that was harnessed in a systematic way to provide food and other materials for the growth of English industrialisation in the 18th and 19th centuries.

Three main issues can be examined in relation to the industrial landscapes of England. Firstly, notwithstanding the fact that almost all industrial landscapes owe their underlying structure to topographical and geological factors, it is also the case that the flesh on these natural bones is the result of human agency. The extent and impact of this human agency is often overlooked, particularly, as Marilyn Palmer has recently reminded us, in rural and upland landscapes.[1] Secondly, our understanding of what makes an industrial landscape, and how we value those landscapes, has changed remarkably over the five centuries or so of large-scale industrialisation in this country. Again this has had an effect on how such landscapes have been (and continue to be) designed and managed. Finally, and emerging from both of the previous concerns, there is the question of our existing relationships with industrial landscapes.

DIVERGENCE: STUDIES OF LANDSCAPE AND INDUSTRY

The broad church of global historical archaeology has emerged from a number of different disciplines and endeavours over the years. These are adequately chronicled elsewhere in this volume (see especially the chapters by Charles Orser, Paul Courtney, David Cranstone and Shane Gould). Within this broad church sit a number of smaller congregations who have grappled with industrial landscapes. However, the two most appropriate sub-disciplines within which the archaeological study of such landscapes might come together – landscape archaeology and industrial archaeology – have found each other somewhat on the margins of their own spheres of interest. Consequently, industrial landscapes have rather fallen into the no-man's land between the two.

Industrial archaeology was formerly 'constrained by its origins', developing selective site-specific studies at the expense of broader settings.[2] In fact this approach was criticised early in the discipline's development by those who preferred to consider industrial sites 'in the context of the landscape which they produced'.[3] Nevertheless, a 'landscape archaeology' of industrialisation did not begin to emerge until the 1980s.[4] This was arguably less the consequence of industrial archaeologists dealing with landscape, as with landscape archaeologists investigating industrial remains. Yet, as Mark Bowden has acknowledged, the use of analytical landscape survey in the investigation of industrial landscapes 'is a relatively recent phenomenon', and much of this work is confined to rural and upland situations.[5] Landscape archaeology has been equally constrained by its early development. The powerful legacy of W.G. Hoskins is problematic for the study of industrial landscapes. Despite devoting almost one-third of the page count of *The Making of the English Landscape* to industrial, urban or modern landscapes, Hoskins's disapproval makes itself felt on virtually every one of those pages. In the course of less than a hundred words on page 171 (for example), St Helens is described as 'the most appalling town of all', copper working had resulted in Anglesey 'being poisoned, every green thing blighted, and every stream fouled' and 'in the Potteries and the Black Country especially, the landscape of Hell was foreshadowed'.[6]

Efforts have also been made by economic historians, social historians, environmental historians, historical geographers and buildings archaeologists to describe and understand the processes that shaped English industrial landscapes. Of these, few have tried to develop an overall archaeological synthesis of the multiplicity of changes to the English landscape that took place during the process of industrialisation. The earliest, and one of the most popularly successful, was Barrie Trinder's *The Making of the Industrial Landscape* (1982). This, by the author's own admission, was an 'historical' study rather than an archaeological one.[7] The first distinctively archaeological approach was produced twelve years later by Marilyn Palmer and Peter Neaverson; their *Industry in the Landscape 1700–1900* set out a 'six-point plan' for analysing industrial landscapes.[8] Both of these studies explored the industrial archaeology of Britain as a whole during the later post-medieval period. Significant studies with a more localised focus in England have included Clark and Alfrey's analysis of the Ironbridge Gorge, and, more recently, Mike Nevell's more explicitly theoretically informed study of 'the archaeology of the industrial revolution in the north-west of England'.[9] It is evident that we should not be looking at industrial landscapes solely through filters given to us by the schools of 'landscape' or 'industrial' archaeology. Rather, we should be seeking to explore the motivations of those who created those industrial landscapes and used them to express their identity. As David Gwyn has remarked, industrial landscapes are reflections of social and economic identities – they are a 'discursive space … in which cultural and ideological priorities are expressed'.[10]

DIVERGENT PLACES: RURAL AND URBAN

For most urban-dwelling English people since the industrial revolution[11] the rural countryside has been a symbol of primitive freedom. The most seductive scenes are places where, in D.H. Lawrence's memorable phrase, 'the spirit of aboriginal England still lingers'.[12] As a consequence, the word 'landscape' is usually taken to be synonymous with the word 'countryside'. In this view, the countryside is a place that has evolved organically without reference to the people who live and work there. This rural other is contrasted with the more familiar urban – it is the English equivalent of the North American wilderness (an equally imagined construct) that provided, as Simon Schama has said, 'the antidote for the poisons of industrial society'.[13] Yet that industrial society was not exclusively urban. Indeed, urban places were often specifically non-industrial until the development of steam power. In contrast, analysis of post-medieval urban landscapes has developed along a very different trajectory.[14] Perhaps because urban boundaries are more familiar and more clearly demarcated, labelled and numbered, it has been easier to describe and analyse what Amos Rapoport called 'systems of settings' within them.[15] Industrial processes and activities have taken place in both rural and urban settings; moreover those settings have changed over time – places once rural are now urban and vice versa. For those of us trying to understand industrial landscapes in their various spatial and temporal contexts, this pervasive dichotomy between rural and urban is not helpful.

RURAL INDUSTRIAL LANDSCAPES

One of the most curious juxtapositions of rural setting and urban form occurs at Bliss Mill near Chipping Norton in Oxfordshire (Fig. 14.1). Here a neo-classical textile mill, essentially a high-Victorian country house with a large chimney, lurks in bucolic rural surroundings. The mill was built in 1872–3 for William Bliss II for the manufacture of fine tweeds and fabrics, and was designed by George Woodhouse. Weaving sheds were added in *c.* 1910, and the mill remained in use until 1980.[16] It would be difficult to find a location closer both physically and mentally to the ideal of the heart of rural England, yet the mill itself is redolent of the dark and satanic urban landscape of Bradford. Interestingly, Bliss Mill is less than 10km away from Steeple Barton, where W.G. Hoskins wrote *The Making of the English Landscape*. Hoskins described north Oxfordshire as 'the most satisfying valley scenery in the whole of England', but could not find room for this remarkable building,

LEFT
Figure 14.1 Urban
industry in an
agricultural landscape?
Bliss Mill, Oxfordshire:
built in 1872–3 for the
manufacture of woollen
cloth.

instead only tangentially referring to 'the tweed of Chipping Norton' in connection with
the decline of small market towns.[17] Yet however much the mill might be an unwelcome
'urban' intrusion into a 'rural' landscape, its existence both now and in the past cannot be
ignored. Nor can its impact on the people of Chipping Norton. The dramatic example
provided by Bliss Mill is anomalous by the very nature of its intrusiveness, but the example
serves to highlight the false dichotomy prevailing between perceptions of rural and urban.
This tension of opposition is also present in the notion of a 'designed landscape'. The term
is most frequently adopted for large country estates, although it has also been used to refer
to planned urban settlements.[18] It is not usually applied to the broad spectrum of industrial
landscapes.

     One end of this spectrum is represented by landscapes of early mining. Locations of
the desired minerals were dictated by geology, and in such circumstances there would seem
to be little scope for conscious design. However, the rights to mine were closely regulated
and controlled, albeit by a bewildering variety of often archaic systems, and mining
landscapes developed according to known rules of order, structure and form. These include
the Moormaster system prevalent in County Durham, the Cornish Stannary system and
the free miners of the Forest of Dean.[19] As on the surface of the landscape, so below it
– the 'hidden' subterranean landscape was also closely demarcated and regulated with what
Martin Roe has termed 'hidden boundaries'.[20]

     As well as landscape modifications associated with mining itself, there were also
settlements of the miners and their families. These often took the form of 'squatter'
settlements, usually characterised as 'amorphous … [with] little evidence of planning'.[21]
However, their location, character and extent resulted from deliberate design decisions
made (or not made) by the free miners who built them and by the manorial landholders on

whose land they squatted. As William Court pointed out over seventy years ago, 'Industrial capitalism did not grow … upon the ruins of feudalism, but in the interstices of the older society.'[22] Some of the most remarkable of these landscapes developed on the edges of ordered space in the West Midlands. In north Staffordshire the population of a marginal agricultural landscape enjoyed relative economic freedom; 'shielded by seigneurial negligence from the pressures of improving landlords', they were free to develop the clay and coal beneath their feet in more profitable ways.[23] As a result, different patterns of land ownership resulted in different landscape patterns emerging in the Potteries' six towns.[24]

URBAN INDUSTRIAL LANDSCAPES

Meanwhile at other end of Staffordshire, and extending into Warwickshire and Worcestershire, the same geology created the Black Country. Here the so-called 'Ten Yard Seam' of the South Staffordshire Coalfield lay very close to the surface and frequently outcropped.[25] Here again the combination of geology and land ownership enabled the post-medieval development of industrial landscapes. Existing medieval or earlier urban centres did not shape the patterns of later development. At Wednesbury, for example, fractured manorial and monastic control encouraged the development of coal and iron mining by the early 14th century, the establishment of a significant pottery industry during the 15th century,

Figure 14.2 Development in the interstices of the medieval landscape? Wednesbury Forge, Staffordshire. This view shows some of the 18th- and 19th-century features, including the base of a water-power sluices (left), the base of a windmill (centre), one of six wheelpits (bottom right) with later turbine, and part of a steam engine base (centre right) (photo: Graham Eyre-Morgan)

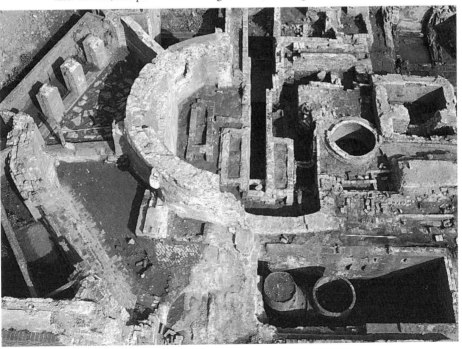

and the development of substantial ironworking enterprises from the 16th century.[26] All of these activities took place away from the original nucleus of settlement.

The most significant industrial complex was Wednesbury Forge. In use from the 16th to the 21st century, this forge produced guns and tools for export around the world – it was also a significant locale in the mindset of local people through which shared identities were constructed.[27] The site represents many of the complexities inherent in extra-urban industrial landscapes. An early post-medieval rural scene: a water-powered site, built with timbers hewn from the intersticial Cannock Chase; the wheelpits and tailraces cut through the coal seams that were being exploited in adjacent fields (Fig. 14.2). Yet over time the growth of the forge encouraged the development of a new urban landscape on the fringes of the old one. By the end of the 19th century there were rows of workers' housing, streets, a church, a school and – that most important piece of infrastructure for urban identity – a football pitch. The development of Wednesbury was echoed in other parts of the Black Country, where, despite appearances of homogeneity to the outsider, each locale maintained its own industrial and cultural identities well into the 20th century.[28]

Comparable developments can be traced elsewhere. Mike Nevell and colleagues have shown how the transition from 'farmer to factory owner' in the Manchester region was a multi-layered process that took place over several generations.[29] The process of industrialisation affected rural and urban places in different ways at different times; manufacture took place both in towns and farms, and the whole was interlinked by a complex system of networks of social and economic exchange.[30] Such landscapes were only embryonic industrial communities from our own Whiggish perspective of progressive history. As Barrie Trinder has reminded us, at the time they were places where people – however they made their living – 'lived lives closely shaped by the seasons and the elements'.[31] Coal miners in Gloucestershire, metal workers in Worcestershire and cloth weavers in Lancashire were also subsistence farmers. Such patterns of life continued well into the 20th century (see, for example, Eleanor Casella and Richard Newman, this volume).

This ambiguity about place at the other end of the spectrum is clearly illustrated in the development of Sheffield. This was a town (by any measure an urban place) famous for its metalwork manufactures, although most of that manufacture took place in semi-rural locations, on the various water-powered sites on the streams that flowed into the Sheffield basin.[32] As in the Black Country, villages in the Sheffield hinterland developed particular specialisms, which in turn fostered social and cultural identities. The subsequent urbanisation of Sheffield took place in locales that were defined by earlier rural experience. The earliest expansion occurred in the 'Crofts', to the west of the medieval town. Here, planned urban development took place with reference to an earlier rural landscape. The 'Crofts' themselves were the enclosed relics of former open strip fields, a liminal – indeed intersticial – place, outside the town boundary and outwith the control of manor, church and embryonic craft gild. The street layout preserved the memory of the former rural landscape both in its form and in the naming of locales within it. The 'Crofts' was the scene of much early industrial innovation; later grid-plan developments attempted to overcome the perceived moral and physical degeneracy that was regarded as pervading earlier 'organic' landscapes such as the 'Crofts', but ultimately failed to do so.[33]

LEFT
Figure 14.3 An urban industrial landscape? The Grand Union Canal at Great Barr Street, Birmingham. This is a complex designed landscape of interlinked systems with global connections. In this view, among other features: Fyffes' banana warehouse (1890); the Gun Barrel Proof House for official testing of guns prior to export (1813); and the former terminus of Curzon Street Railway Station (1839).

LANDSCAPES OF SYSTEMS

The process of industrialisation also created distinctively new landscapes that are simultaneously rural and urban. For linear networks such as canals, railways and roads it is 'not always possible to determine where a site begins or ends',[34] and so a different archaeological approach needs to be taken.[35] In England, the investigation of linear networks has always been one of the strengths of industrial archaeology. Such networks transcend the distinction between rural and urban landscapes; they also provide a physical and conceptual link between industrial production and consumption (Fig.14.3). A canal, for instance, had the power to turn somewhere like Paddington 'from a quiet rural village … into the animated terminus of an efficient transport system'.[36] More recent networks of electricity supply and mobile telephone communications have continued this trend, blurring the distinction between rural and urban. These systems connected places within and between such locales as the Black Country, Lancashire, South Yorkshire and elsewhere, themselves part-urban and part-rural landscapes that transcended older-established boundaries of land ownership and administration.

DIVERGENT VALUES: SCIENCE AND ART

For much of the 16th, 17th and 18th centuries, the gently rolling snowball of industrialisation was generally perceived as a force of progress and enlightenment. The beginning of the post-medieval period saw the rise in Humanism and concomitant philosophical developments that led ultimately to the Enlightenment. The revival of Aristotelian thought during the later middle ages had encouraged the development of empirical observation and reasoned deduction. Nature should be observed, and the works of man should imitate nature.

Although the early empiricism of thinkers such as Francis Bacon owed much to the revival of Aristotle, later developments were strongly influenced by Platonic thought, and in particular Plato's Theory of Forms – in which the myriad observable natural particular forms could be structured into a hierarchy of universal forms. The work of early thinkers such as Bacon, Galileo and Descartes paved the way for later development by scientific pioneers such as Boyle, Hooke and Newton. The work of these early scientists – what would now be called 'pure science' – informed improvements in real-world technologies, particularly metallurgy – in other words, 'applied science'. This enabled what David Cranstone (this volume) has elegantly termed a 'chemical industrial revolution' during the 17th and 18th centuries.

This changing understanding of the world took place amid the not unrelated social and cultural upheaval of the Reformation. In England, the most significant material expression of the Reformation was the dissolution of the monasteries. The Ironbridge Gorge provides a typical example of the positive effect which the process of dissolution had on the development of industrialisation. Here, part of the estates of the Priory of Much Wenlock – already containing coal mines and ironworks – were acquired by Sir Robert Brooke.[37] The two succeeding generations (Sir John Brooke and Sir Basil Brooke) developed a substantial coal, iron and steelmaking enterprise from the 1570s through to the Civil War.[38] The Brookes used their industrial wealth to develop the former monastic grange at nearby Madeley into a substantial Elizabethan country house, emphasising their legitimacy as creators and controllers of the surrounding landscape (Fig. 14.4). Their enthusiasm for the aesthetics of this landscape was demonstrated to their peers by the construction of the Lodge in *c.* 1600. Located above the confluence of Coalbrookdale with the Severn Gorge, the Lodge was the perfect spot to view coal mining, limestone quarrying, the smoke and noise of the furnaces, and the broad sweep of the River Severn carrying manufactured

LEFT
Figure 14.4 Madeley Court, Shropshire. The late-16th-century gatehouse built by the Brooke family with profits from their mines and ironworks in Coalbrookdale.

goods away to profitable markets. At precisely this moment, the actual word and concept of 'landscape' (or 'landskip') was being introduced into the English language from the Dutch 'landschap'.[39]

The marriage of art, science and technology was perpetuated through the 18th century. At Coalbrookdale, the Brooke ironworking complex was further developed by the Darby family, with the substantial involvement of their fellow Quaker capitalists, the Goldneys. The focus of their operations was iron founding. Abraham Darby I had developed a technique for coke smelting and sand casting through a combination of empirical observations and experimentation.[40] The resulting Coalbrookdale Company specialised in lightweight precision castings, which in turn enabled the development of steam technology. Like their Catholic forebears the Brookes, various Quaker families that ran Coalbrookdale were to some extent outside the establishment. And, like the Brookes, they used the landscape as a mechanism for displaying the commercial and aesthetic productivity of their industrial enterprises. This landscape was illustrated in 1758 by the deeply fashionable landscape engraver Francois Vivares (Fig. 14.5). The Coalbrookdale engravings depict the furnaces and chimneys of the ironworks, the burning of coke, the smoke and fumes, and even the export of the finished products – yet they also show an ornamental tower on the hill above, dominating a landscape of substantial gentry houses, with associated polite landscape features such as a geometric walled garden and an avenue.

Figure 14.5 A picturesque landscape of industry. One of two engravings of Coalbrookdale made by Francois Vivares in 1758 (reproduced with the permission of the Ironbridge Gorge Museum Trust).

This designed landscape tapped into the prevailing enthusiasm for an industrial picturesque, part of a broader movement that emphasised antiquity, wilderness and nature in counterpoint to the modern sensibilities of those who passed through such landscapes. Visitors were already coming to admire the sublimity of the scene, marvelling at the 'awful and magnificent' prospect of industry.[41] Coalbrookdale was an essential stop on the late 18th-century 'Grand Tour' of the English landscape. Indeed, English industrial landscapes generally formed an important part of many itineraries. Astonishingly there was also, in the late 18th century, a fashion for mine tourism, in which curious and wealthy persons (including men of the church) were lowered in buckets, dragged in wagons and ferried in boats deep into the earth in order to marvel at the sublime subterranean scenery.[42] Archaeological evidence suggests that some of elements of the Coalbrookdale water power system were modified to establish a picturesque effect akin to the cascades of large country houses.[43] For Coalbrookdale the culmination of this puritan pursuit of the picturesque was an extraordinary project to oust Charon himself from this landscape with the products of Vulcan. The Iron Bridge across the river Severn was completed in 1779 and opened three years later; it became an instant tourist attraction.

Yet the close interconnections between art and science were already beginning to unravel. The construction of the Iron Bridge marked a shift in perception of industrial landscape. The avant-garde lesbian poet Anna Seward was among the first to look critically at the environmental impact of industry on the landscape. Seward was a friend of the Darwin family and of the Wedgwoods, and so occupied the fringes of the social world occupied by Boulton, Watt and other Lunar Society luminaries.[44] She was thus uniquely placed to offer an insightful analysis of the processes of industrialisation. In her poem of *c.* 1785 entitled *Colebrookdale* she equated the industrial development of the eponymous ironworks with sexual violation of the landscape:

… thou venal Genius of these outraged groves, / And thy apostate head with thy soil'd wings / Veil! – who hast thus thy beauteous charge resign'd / To inhabitants ill-suited; hast allow'd / Their rattling forges, and their hammer's din, / And hoarse, rude throats, to fright the gentle train, / Dryads, and fair hair'd Naiedes; – the song, / Once loud and sweet, of the wild woodland choir / To silence; – disenchant the poet's spell, / And to a gloomy Erebus transform / The destined rival of Tempean vales.[45]

Seward is no Wordsworth, but her imagery is powerful. While few would necessarily go as far as Sharon Setzer has done in arguing for Seward's 'nascent ecofeminist consciousness', she was certainly beginning to challenge masculine narratives of progressive history, and to question the rationale of industrialisation.[46]

DIVERGENT ETHICS: ARCHAEOLOGY AND CONSERVATION

The ways in which perceptions of industrial landscapes altered in the 19th century has profoundly affected the manner in which they are treated today. Current approaches to industrial landscapes remain ambivalent. Many of the traditions of landscape studies stem from the antipathy felt in the mid-20th century to the bewildering changes being wrought by the motor car, mass bombing and urban redevelopment. The effect of this thinking was to develop the notion of conservation, both of the so-called natural environment and of what we would now call the historic environment. David Matless has argued that the development of a conservation ethos in the early 20th century was not, in fact, a backward-looking expression of despair; rather it was part of a forward-looking approach that saw planning – both urban and rural – as the cornerstone for the development of a new English society.[47] Such a society required demarcation between different attributes – this was not an egalitarian project but one in which everyone (and everything) knew its place. Industrial activity, therefore, was predominantly urban. However, as Matthew Johnson has more recently elaborated, such voices were as much a continuation of two centuries of Seward-like Romantic angst as they were a product of mid-20th-century hand-wringing over 'that old society falling into ruin'.[48]

This neo-Romantic perception still informs much conservation and management policy and strategy at national and local level. Influence is brought to bear on decision-making in these areas from powerful lobby groups such as the National Trust (founded in 1895) and the Council for the Protection of Rural England (founded in 1926). This thinking has subsequently been enshrined in legislation, from the Town and Country Planning Act (1947) onwards. Of course, the notion of a pre-industrial rural idyll as the natural state of English landscape is clearly nonsense – even the most remote upland has had vegetation controlled by grazing, and has usually been the scene of mining and other industrial activities. Yet industrial activities in the landscape are acknowledged only if well and truly relict. Here, the gradual decay of buildings, the smoothing over of spoil heaps and the silting up of pools, conspire to provide an 'antiquarian aesthetic'[49] that conforms to notions of the modern picturesque and obscures the original motivations behind human interactions with the landscape.

Industrial landscapes are almost uniquely caught between the polarised forces of archaeology and conservation. This is largely related to the origins of the discipline of industrial archaeology, which had as its primary focus the repair and restoration of historic buildings and machinery. The pioneers of industrial archaeology in the 1950s and 1960s were not doing 'archaeology', rather they were engaged in machine- and site-specific conservation. Today – as the papers in this volume so eloquently make clear – the study of the industrial past is firmly part of mainstream archaeology. More work on sites and landscapes associated with industrialisation is being done every year in the real world of commercial archaeology, by people who will record Bronze Age enclosures one week with the same enthusiasm as they will record a 16th-century watermill or 20th-century domestic floor surfaces the following week. Nevertheless, conservation of industrial sites proceeds, and often, in this author's experience, without due regard for archaeological findings. The development of Ironbridge is a case in point. Before the 1990s a great many buildings were demolished, and archaeology destroyed by the insertion of structures intended to protect certain parts of the historic environment. Today, the largely wooded landscape is valued without irony as a 'natural resource' by middle-class property owners who have gentrified the former industrial settlement and imposed their own romantic view on the scene.

In short, industrial landscapes appear to be more highly valued when they are firmly post-industrial. They are no longer (to paraphrase Anna Seward) the thrusting playboys of youth, despoiling the forest glades with their contaminated ejaculations; instead they become tired old men reminiscing about the good old days: sagging and wilting, and objects of affection. We put some of them in care and create heritage landscapes around them instead. The result of this rose-tinted approach to landscape has meant that the post-medieval historic environment has actually lost out – both to the heritage of earlier periods and to other aspects of the environment. In mitigating the impact of new development and other landscape changes today, the so-called natural environment (which does not actually exist and is infinitely renewable) is accorded a much higher priority than the historic environment (which clearly does exist, and is finite and non-renewable). Ironically, it is now easier to prevent destruction of the historic environment by using the natural environment as a shield than it is by arguing for any intrinsic historic environment value of such features.

CONVERGENCE: INDUSTRIAL LANDSCAPES AND ENGLISH IDENTITY

English industrial landscapes appear to have been ill-served by the divergent forces that have attempted to create, study, conserve and develop them. Yet the process of post-medieval industrialisation is one of the most important elements in the make-up of modern English society. In the 16th, 17th and 18th centuries, industrialisation was at the heart of the great changes that took place as a result of the Reformation. Industrialisation provided the instruments by which the (Copernican) universe could be measured, it provided the means for transmitting the knowledge of those measurements throughout Europe, and it provided the opportunity for those outside the traditional spheres of advancement to create wealth and influence for themselves. And, at the same time as the new industrialists such as the Brookes of Coalbrookale were creating a new industrial ideal place, so Raleigh, Frobisher, Grenville, Drake, Somers and others were discovering an entirely different sort of new place somewhere else. The discovery and exploitation of the New World provided a counterpoint to the Old World, which enabled, for the first time, the creation of a conscious English identity. This was a curious, inquisitive and increasingly capitalist identity; an identity focused on industrial production and global exportation. Industrial landscapes, therefore, formed an important part of the iconography of this new English identity. By the end of the 18th century, these English industrial landscapes were famous throughout Europe and North America, and were emulated around the world.

However, it would be wrong to pursue a jingoistic agenda of a united English identity. The creation of industrial landscapes did not result from a universally agreed agenda; moreover many of the individuals harnessed in the manufacture of and within these places were 'not from round here' – being imported from other parts of the country or indeed from overseas. Furthermore, the creation of many of these industrial landscapes would have been impossible without certain contributions from elsewhere – the supply of cotton to Lancashire, sugar to Bristol and tobacco to London, for example. Thus a complex series of industrial landscapes are present beneath the manicured lawns of industrial heritage. In post-industrial England we can choose which aspects of this multifaceted past we decide to display; but elsewhere in the world, 18th-century England is very much alive. The English experience of industrialisation is being replicated in present-day China – massive use of natural resources, environmental degradation, poor working and living conditions, and the export of cheap consumer goods to the wider world.

Unfortunately the English industrial landscape is often either pigeonholed or overlooked entirely. As the chapters in this volume by David Gwyn, David Cranstone, Richard Newman and Chris Dalglish demonstrate, industrial landscapes contain so much more than relic industrial remains. They also provide evidence for the complex processes of creating and displaying identities. Such landscapes are important for the future – however much of a certain type of English identity is to do with rejection of that industrial past. Clearly we have failed to argue a convincing case for the importance of industrial landscapes in helping to shape English identities. To ignore their significance in this regard is to deny the possibilities which a global historical archaeology can offer for changing the world around us. The issues so central to the study of English industrial landscapes – pollution, religious conflict, environmental degradation, population movement, territorial aggression, capitalism and globalisation – are most urgently relevant to the world today. Archaeologists of industrial landscapes – neither 'industrial' nor 'landscape' archaeologists but a hybrid with a foot in both camps – need to explicitly engage with ongoing theoretical debates in global historical archaeology, and move beyond that to a broader engagement with the modern world. Future approaches should develop what David Cranstone has called the archaeology of 'psychology and mindset',[50] analysis of which can take place on many different social, temporal and spatial levels. In modern England we need to do much more than hark back to a non-existent pre-industrial state; rather we need to discover the stories of industrialisation, and celebrate the process that originated in England and ultimately changed the world.

ACKNOWLEDGEMENTS

The author is grateful to the conference organisers and editors for the opportunity to contribute to both the conference and the published volume. A particular debt is owed to Marilyn Palmer for her discussion of an early draft of this chapter and suggestions which have improved the final version. Many thanks are also due to various people for their input over many years to a number of projects, ideas and discussions that have, in one way or another, formed the *corpus* of thinking on which this chapter is based. These include: Mary Beaudry, Mark Bowden, Kate Clark, David Cranstone, David Crossley, Brian Dix, Emma Dwyer, Graham Eyre-Morgan, Jon Finch, Kate Giles, David Gwyn, Mark Horton, Edward Impey, William Mitchell, John Powell, Simon Roper, Paul Stamper, James Symonds, Barrie Trinder, Anna Wallis, Sophie Watson and Tom Williamson. Inaccuracies of fact, interpretation and language are of course entirely the fault of the author, for which indulgence from the reader is sought. Particular thanks must go to Kate Page-Smith, whose natural talent for landscape archaeology is inspirational, and whose love and support has been invaluable.

NOTES

1. Palmer 2007, 3.
2. Palmer & Neaverson 1998, 16.
3. Osborne 1976, 41; Palmer & Neaverson 1987, 459–60.
4. Palmer 1990, 277–9.
5. Bowden 1999, 139.
6. Hoskins 1955, 171. In the heat of the moment Hoskins appears to have overlooked the fact that Anglesey is in Wales and does not therefore constitute part of the English landscape.
7. Trinder 1982, 3. Trinder's title clearly pays homage to Hoskins, who is also the first person named in Trinder's acknowledgements (Trinder 1982, 259).
8. Palmer & Neaverson 1994, 15–17.
9. Alfrey & Clark 1993; Nevell (ed.) 2003.
10. Gwyn 2004, 50.
11. The term 'industrial revolution' is deployed here in its traditional meaning, essentially: the period from about 1700 to about 1850 in which the entire economic and social landscape was transformed by the use of fossil fuels, resulting in rural depopulation, urban expansion and all the rest. For a sophisticated discussion of the meanings of this term, and ways forward for describing these processes of change in the period, see David Cranstone's chapter in this volume.
12. Lawrence 1925, 56–7.
13. Schama 1995, 7.
14. See, for example, Mayne & Murray 2001.
15. Rapoport 1990, 16–19.
16. Derrick, Wade & Waters 1985, 9; Binney *et al.* 1990, 105.
17. Hoskins 1951, 42-43.
18. Mayne & Murray 2001; Belford 2004, 172–3.
19. Blackburn 1994, 71–4; Nicholls 1866, 74–5; Newman 2004, 28; Pennington 1973, 25–40.
20. Roe 2007, 12–14.
21. Newman 2004, 29.
22. Court 1938, 74.
23. Baker 1991, 2–3.
24. Baker 1991, 6–8.
25. Greenslade & Jenkins 1967, 68–9.
26. Ede 1962, 26–7,30; Dilworth 1976, 111; Hodder 1992, 96–8.
27. Belford forthcoming.
28. Hooke 2006, 177.
29. Nevell (ed.) 2003.
30. Nevell 2003, 29–42; Redhead 2003, 70–2.
31. Trinder & Cox 1980, 114.
32. Crossley 1989, vii–ix; Crossley 2004, 79–84.
33. Belford 2006, 136.
34. Clark 1987, 263–5.
35. See, for example, Worth 2005, 135–54.
36. Spencer 1961, 21.
37. Baugh 1985, 35–46; Pevsner 1958, 193–4; Randell 1880, 59–60.
38. Belford 2007, 134–7; Belford & Ross 2004, 215–25; Belford & Ross 2007, 105–21.
39. Schama 1995, 10.
40. Ashton 1924, 249–52; Belford & Ross 2007, 108–9; Raistrick 1953, 22–34; Smiles 1863, 82.
41. Morgan 1992, 264.
42. Moir 1964, 91–6.
43. Belford 2007, 145–6.
44. Coffey 2002, 141–64; Uglow 2002.
45. Scott 1810, 319.
46. Setzer 2007, 69.
47. Matless 1998.
48. Johnson 2007, 57.
49. Cossons 2007, 17–18.
50. Cranstone 2004, 317.

BIBLIOGRAPHY

Alfrey, J. & Clark, C. 1993, *The Landscape of Industry: Patterns of Change in the Ironbridge Gorge*. London: Routledge.

Ashton, T.S. 1924, *Iron and Steel in the Industrial Revolution*. Manchester: Manchester University Press.

Baker, D. 1991, *Potworks: The Industrial Architecture of the Staffordshire Potteries*. London: Royal Commission on the Historical Monuments of England.

Barker, D. & Cranstone, D. (eds), 2004, *The Archaeology of Industrialization*, Society for Post-Medieval Archaeology Monograph **2**. Leeds: Maney.

Barnwell, P.S. & Palmer, M. (eds) 2007, *Post-Medieval Landscapes*, Landscape History after Hoskins **3**. Macclesfield: Windgather Press.

Baugh, G.C. (ed.) 1985, *A History of Shropshire, Volume XI: Telford*, Victoria County History, Institute of Historical Research. Oxford: Oxford University Press.

Belford, P. 2006, 'The world of the workshop: archaeologies of urban industrialisation', in Green & Leech (eds), 2006, 133–49.

Belford, P. 2007, 'Sublime cascades: water and power in Coalbrookdale', *Industrial Archaeology Review* **29**(2): 133–48.

Belford, P. forthcoming, 'Five centuries of iron making: excavations at Wednesbury Forge', *Post-Medieval Archaeology* **42**(2).

Belford, P. & Ross, R.A. 2004, 'Industry and domesticity: historical archaeology in Coalbrookdale', *Post-Medieval Archaeology* **38**(2): 215–25.

Belford, P. & Ross, R.A. 2007, 'English steelmaking in the seventeenth century: the excavation of two cementation furnaces at Coalbrookdale', *Historical Metallurgy* **41**(2): 105–23.

Binney, M., Machin, F. & Powell, K. 1990, *Bright Future: The Re-Use of Industrial Buildings*. London: SAVE Britain's Heritage.

Blackburn, A. 1994, 'Mining without laws: Weardale under the Moormasters', in Ford, T.D. & Willies, L.M. (eds) *Mining before Powder*. Matlock: Peak District Mines Historical Society, *Bulletin* **12**(3), 1994, 69–75.

Bowden, M. (ed.) 1999, *Unravelling the Landscape: An Inquisitive Approach to Archaeology*. Stroud: Tempus Publishing.

Casella, E.C. & Symonds, J. (eds) 2005, *Industrial Archaeology – Future Directions*. New York: Springer.

Clark, C. 1987, 'Trouble at t'mill: industrial archaeology in the 1980s', *Antiquity* **61**: 169–79.

Coffey, D. 2002, 'Protecting the botanic garden: Seward, Darwin and Coalbrookdale', *Women's Studies* **31**(2): 141–64.

Cossons, N. 2007, 'Industrial archaeology: the challenge of the evidence', *The Antiquaries Journal* **87**: 1–52.

Court, W.H.B. 1938, *The Rise of the Midland Industries 1600–1838*. Oxford: Oxford University Press.

Cranstone, D. 2004, 'The archaeology of industrialisation – new directions', in Barker & Cranstone (eds), 2004, 313–20.

Crossley, D. (ed.) 1989, *Water Power on the Sheffield Rivers*. Sheffield: Sheffield Trades Historical Society / University of Sheffield Division of Adult Continuing Education.

Crossley, D. 2004, 'Water power in the landscape: the rivers of the Sheffield area', in Barker & Cranstone (eds), 2004, 79–88.

Derrick, Wade & Waters 1985, *Bliss Tweed Mill, Chipping Norton: A Feasibility Study*, Report for West Oxfordshire District Council and A.C. Nicholas Holdings Ltd.

Dilworth, D. 1976, *The Tame Mills of Staffordshire*. London: Phillimore.

Ede, J. 1962, *History of Wednesbury*. Wednesbury: Simmons Publishing.

Green, A. & Leech, R. (eds), 2006, *Cities in the World 1500–2000*, Society for Post-Medieval Archaeology Monograph **3**. Leeds: Maney.

Greenslade, M.W. & Jenkins, J.G. (eds) 1967, *A History of the County of Stafford, Volume II*, Victoria County History, University of London Institute of Historical Research. Oxford: Oxford University Press.

Gwyn, D. 2004, 'Landscape, economy and identity: a study in the archaeology of industrialisation', in Barker & Cranstone (eds), 2004, 35–52.

Hodder, M.A, 1992, 'Excavations in Wednesbury, 1988 and 1989: the medieval and post-medieval settlement, and the 17th-century pottery industry', *Transactions of the South Staffordshire Archaeological and Historical Society* **32**: 96–115.

Hooke, D. 2006, *England's Landscape: The West Midlands*. London: Collins/English Heritage.

Hoskins, W.G. 1951, *Chilterns to the Black Country*, Festival of Britain 'About Britain' Guide **5**. London: Collins.

Hoskins, W.G. 1955, *The Making of the English Landscape*. London: Hodder & Stoughton (8th impression, 1969).

Johnson, M. 2007, *Ideas of Landscape*. Oxford: Blackwell Publishing.

Kent, S. (ed.) 1990, *Domestic Architecture and the Use of Space*. Cambridge: Cambridge University Press.

Lawrence, D.H. 1925, 'St. Mawr', together with 'The Princess'. London: Martin Secker.

Matless, D. 1998, Landscape and Englishness. London: Redaktion.

Mayne, A. & Murray, T. (eds) 2001, The Archaeology of Urban Landscapes: Explorations in Slumland. Cambridge: Cambridge University Press.

Moir, E. 1964, The Discovery of Britain: The English Tourists. London: Routledge & Kegan Paul.

Morgan, K. (ed.) 1992, An American Quaker in the British Isles: The Travel Diaries of Jabez Maud Fisher, 1775–1779. Oxford: Oxford University Press.

Nevell, M. 2003, 'From linen weaver to cotton manufacturer: Manchester during the 17th and 18th centuries and the social archaeology of industrialisation', in Nevell (ed.), 2003, 27–44.

Nevell, M. (ed.) 2003, From Farmer to Factory Owner: Models, Methodology and Industrialisation, Archaeology North-West 6 (Issue 16 for 2001–3). Manchester: University of Manchester Archaeology Unit.

Newman, R. 2004, 'Industrial rural settlements: genesis, character and context', in Barker & Cranstone (eds), 2004, 25–34.

Nicholls, H.G. 1866, Iron Making in the Forest of Dean (facsimile reproduction 1981). Coleford: Douglas MacLean.

Osborne, B.S. 1976, 'Patching, scouring and commoners: the development of an early industrial landscape', Industrial Archaeology Review 1(1): 37–42.

Palmer, M. 1990, 'Industrial archaeology: a thematic or a period discipline?', Antiquity 64: 275–82.

Palmer, M. 2007, 'Introduction: post-medieval landscapes since Hoskins – theory and practice', in Barnwell & Palmer (eds), 2007, 1–8.

Palmer, M. & Neaverson, P. 1987, 'Industrial archaeology: the reality', Antiquity 61: 459–61.

Palmer, M. & Neaverson, P. 1994, Industry in the Landscape, 1700–1900, London and New York: Routledge.

Palmer, M. & Neaverson, P. 1998, Industrial Archaeology: Principles and Practice. London: Routledge.

Pennington, R.R. 1973, Stannary Law: A History of the Mining Law of Cornwall and Devon. Newton Abbot: David & Charles.

Pevsner, N. 1958, Shropshire. Harmondsworth: Penguin Books.

Raistrick, A. 1953, Dynasty of Ironfounders: The Darbys and Coalbrookdale (revised edn 1989). Sessions Book Trust / Ironbridge Gorge Museum Trust.

Randell, J. 1880, History of Madeley, including Ironbridge, Coalbrookdale and Coalport (facsimile reprint 1975). Shrewsbury: Salop County Library.

Rapoport, A. 1990, 'Systems of activities and systems of settings', in Kent. (ed.), 1990, 9–20.

Redhead, N. 2003, 'The Castleshaw and Piethorne valleys: the industrial exploitation of a Pennine landscape', in Nevell (ed.), 2003, 68–78.

Roe, M. 2007, 'Hidden boundaries/hidden landscapes: lead mining landscapes in the Yorkshire Dales', in Barnwell & Palmer (eds), 2007, 9–22.

Schama, S. 1995, Landscape and Memory. London: HarperCollins.

Scott, W. (ed.) 1810, The Poetical Works of Anna Seward, Vol. 2. Edinburgh: Ballantyne.

Setzer, S. 2007, '"Pond'rous Engines" in "Outraged Groves": the environmental argument of Anna Seward's "Colebrook Dale"', European Romantic Review 18(1): 69–82.

Smiles, S. 1863, Industrial Biography: Iron Workers and Tool Makers. London: John Murray.

Spencer, H. 1961, London's Canal: The History of the Regent's Canal. London: Putnam.

Trinder, B. 1982, The Making of the Industrial Landscape (1997 edn). London: Phoenix.

Trinder, B. & Cox, J. 1980, Yeomen and Colliers in Telford. Chichester: Phillimore.

Uglow, J. 2002, The Lunar Men: The Friends Who Made the Future. London: Faber & Faber.

Worth, D. 2005, 'Gas and grain: the conservation of networked industrial landscapes', in Casella & Symonds (eds), 2005, 135–54.

Historic Landscape Characterisation: More Than a Management Tool?

By CARON NEWMAN

Historic Landscape Characterisation (HLC) has been undertaken in many counties across England, with similar programmes carried out in Wales and Scotland. Designed mainly as a management tool, it provides an historic dimension to landscape character assessment. It is frequently criticised by academic landscape archaeologists and historians and is seen as having no value for research purposes. This discussion addresses some of the criticisms and examines the use of HLC as a research tool in relation to recent work undertaken in Cumbria.

INTRODUCTION: HISTORIC LANDSCAPE ANALYSIS

Historic landscape characterisation (HLC) was devised during the 1990s as a tool to aid land management, by influencing spatial planning policy and informing planners in their decision making on individual applications. It provides an historic dimension to landscape character assessment, a methodology defined by the Countryside Commission in the 1980s to understand the landscape holistically.[1] HLC also takes an holistic approach and recognises that all landscape has an historical character, but unlike landscape character assessment, it concentrates on the cultural nature of landscape and does not accord equal weight to the natural elements. There have been a number of recent reviews[2] of the application and process of HLC, and it is not the intention here to repeat these commentaries in detail. In summary, however, English Heritage's own review of the uses of HLC sees it entirely in terms of its potential for land management.[3] Steve Rippon noted, in his review of historic landscape analysis, that it is both a study of the origin and historical development of an area of landscape, and a description of historic landscape character to inform planners and landscape managers, therefore also seeing HLC largely as a planning tool.[4] More recently, however, Rippon has examined the research potential of historic landscape characterisation in one of a series of papers originally given at a Theoretical Archaeology Group (TAG) conference, which includes papers both supporting and criticising historic landscape characterisation.[5]

A number of university-based landscape archaeologists and historians have criticised the HLC approach as lacking in time depth as well as intellectual rigour and relevance.[6] One of the issues is the late date of the baseline data, usually the First Edition six inch to one mile Ordnance Survey maps.[7] Some of the criticisms are valid, but some are based on a misunderstanding of the nature and purpose of HLC. Now that HLC programmes have been carried out throughout much of Britain, however, the research potential of this approach to historic landscape has begun to emerge. Its value as a research tool has been especially emphasised by Turner,[8] who considers that HLC helps 'to promote an archaeological understanding of landscape'.[9] He also sees it as an aid to appreciating the meanings and values invested in landscapes.[10] Specifically, HLC has proven to be of value in contextualising sites and in improving the appreciation of post-medieval processes of landscape change, especially in relation to settlement pattern, enclosure and industrialisation. This chapter examines the use of HLC as a research tool, especially in relation to recent work undertaken in Cumbria.[11]

Nationally, HLC has been seen as significant for providing overviews of predominantly post-medieval derived landscapes.[12] This is hardly surprising as to date it has been based on the use of the earliest nationwide, county-scale accurate mapping, the First Edition six inch to one mile Ordnance Survey. Dating generally from the 1840s to the 1860s in North West England, this has the advantage of being reasonably accurate with subsequent changes being easily traceable through later editions based on the same survey principles. As Rippon notes, in using historic landscape characterisation to understand the origins and developments of a landscape, the earliest complete cartographic sources should be used,[13] but tithe, corn rent, enclosure and estate maps are not consistent or ubiquitous, and can be awkward to use. Extrapolating back in time from the First Edition maps, however, leads to uncertainty, which increases the further back one goes.

SCOPE OF HISTORIC LANDSCAPE CHARACTERISATION

In parallel with the development of an historic environment response to landscape character assessment, natural environment specialists developed the use of biogeographic zones known as Natural Areas. Although using different criteria, these were developed through a similar approach to landscape character assessment and historic landscape characterisation.[14] The identification of natural areas, and the use of terms such as 'Areas of Outstanding Natural Beauty' (AONB) has long biased public and political debate on landscape towards the valuing of perceived wild and natural places. As early as the 18th century, William Marshall, an agricultural commentator, stated that 'no spot on this island can be said to be in a state of nature'.[15] W.G. Hoskins reiterated in the 1950s[16] that very little of Britain's landscape was untouched by man, yet the appreciation of the full impact of human activity on the landscape throughout history is still not always realised. Land management decisions were usually based on aesthetic or natural environment principles rather than on an understanding of the historical development of the landscape. This is in part because the dataset on the historic environment was site-based rather than landscape-based. HLC enables a wider view of the historic environment and provides an historic dimension to the landscape character assessment process.[17] By using similar approaches to mapping biodiversity, land cover and the historic environment, it is possible to combine datasets and compare them. This enables different aspects of the landscape, including the cultural dimension, to be given appropriate weight within a landscape character assessment.

The historic landscape can be studied at various scales of resolution,[18] and these are usually linked to an existing land unit such as an estate or parish.[19] County-based HLC programmes, however, are designed to work at a county level only, where they provide a relatively rapid overview, with robust but broad-brush conclusions. When the county data is applied at an estate or parish level, it is criticised for lacking detail and differentiation, as it immediately becomes clear that the data is smoothed and local detail lost. This criticism, though frequent, is misguided and misunderstands the intentions behind the county HLC programmes as characterisation needs to be applied at different scales in order to be useful. A further criticism that HLC is mechanistic is related to attempts to ensure that the analyses are clear in process and scientifically repeatable. This approach to HLC is itself open to criticism, however, as so much of the data is subjective rather than objective, and as with other social sciences its appropriateness for scientific treatment can be questioned.[20]

HERITAGE MANAGEMENT AND HISTORIC LANDSCAPE RESEARCH

Modern heritage management and historic landscape research coincide in relation to post-processual historic landscape theory.[21] Both concern themselves with the wider spatial aspect of the historic environment, dealing with context, connectivity and interrelationships, rather than individual sites and findspots. Temporal boundaries and periodisation are abandoned, and contemporary archaeology is embraced.[22] Landscapes are conceived as complex and as matters of perception, rather than collections of artefacts or sets of resources.[23] They are viewed less as physical constructs and more as individual, mental constructs. These are issues that are not only addressed by academic theorists, but are established principles within the European Landscape Convention.[24] The need to frame heritage policy within the context of public inclusion and well-being has led to the primacy of the individual's view of landscape, both contemporary and in the past, over an 'Hoskinian' characterisation of landscape by historical type or district.

HLC developed in a heritage-management context in which it is acknowledged that the cultural landscape is a perception and not a concrete reality. It is mutable through time, across cultures and between individuals and interest groups who may lay claim to all or part of a landscape: 'If we want to discover the meaning of landscapes for people it is best to think of them not as collections of material objects, but as social and cultural constructions of the people who use them.'[25]

This approach to heritage management also rejects value judgements that compartmentalise the landscape into areas of greater or lesser importance or historicity. In practice, however, HLC and its use within spatial planning does not seem to sit comfortably with this philosophy. The key difficulty inherent in the HLC methodology is that it not only greatly simplifies out of necessity, but it also quantifies the landscape as groups of physical features and shared characteristics. Moreover, value judgements of various types will, of necessity, be applied to areas of landscape by policy-makers.[26] Modern heritage philosophy and the HLC approach need not be seen as in conflict, however, because the attribution of contemporary values to a landscape, based upon current political imperatives and concerns, is an aspect of perceiving and attributing meanings to landscapes. Furthermore, landscape perception is, of course, based on materiality:[27] the physical features and shared characteristics. HLC provides a readily understandable, interpreted contemporary view of a landscape based on set criteria. Visitors, inhabitants and those working in the landscape have different perceptions and apply value judgements based on varying criteria. The issues surrounding perception, character and value are especially relevant to the Lake District. This is a highly valued landscape, designated as a national park, for which there are many, often competing, historical and contemporary perceptions of its nature dependent on the social standpoint of the perceiver (Plate 1). It is a landscape that has many cultural associations with important artistic and literary figures, such as Wordsworth, Turner and Ruskin. The current initiative to gain World Heritage Site inscription for the Lake District is based on those cultural associations of the landscape. HLC, while not itself attributing value to specific areas within the Lake District, nevertheless has helped to identify the 'Outstanding Universal Values' that will be used to make the case for inscription.[28]

While HLC programmes in England and Scotland do not attribute relative importance between areas of landscape,[29] they do allow the identification of local distinctiveness. This is of value in itself as it defines those elements of a landscape that make it important to those who live in, or visit, that landscape.[30] It is crucial to a sense of place or identity. In assisting the recognition of local distinctiveness, HLC begins to move away from a mere quantification of physical attributes to embrace concepts of cultural meaning invested in a landscape. As Graham Fairclough has recently pointed out, the public, especially those who may live in a valued landscape area, may place values upon it that are different from those of landscape or heritage experts.[31] They may value the landscape for its associations, memories and links to personal identity. All of these, however, may be wrapped up in a sense of place and local distinctiveness. HLC helps to identify and categorise the elements and connections that contribute towards the distinctiveness to which the public relate.[32]

CONTEXTUALISING SITES

The county-wide focus of HLC programmes provides a clear and simple picture of countryside historic character and aspects of change. This both enables questions to be posed concerning the reasons for noted patterns, and also provides a tool for the initial testing of theories. For example, the noted pattern of fossilised strip fields in Cumbria is related to settlement pattern and morphology. HLC provides a very clear picture of the more intensively exploited areas of the flatter, lower-lying townships of Cumbria, which are dominated historically by nucleated settlement patterns and open fields divided into strips. Until recently, this pattern was seen to be focused on the Eden valley, but HLC clearly shows it to have been more widespread and to be partially obscured in west Cumbria by post-medieval industrial developments as well as moorland and wetland enclosure (Plate 2). HLC also clearly reveals the boundary zones between this type of agrarian and settlement landscape and the more dispersed settlement landscapes and less open agricultural fieldscapes of much of the Lake District. Consequently, county-based HLC is capable of

Plate 1: Rydal Park, Ambleside, in the Lake District National Park. Man-made and natural features within a valued and contested landscape.

Plate 2: Dundraw in north-west Cumbria. Reclaimed wetland enclosure (yellow and green fields) partially obscures the older pattern of former commonfields (blue fields), particularly on modern maps.

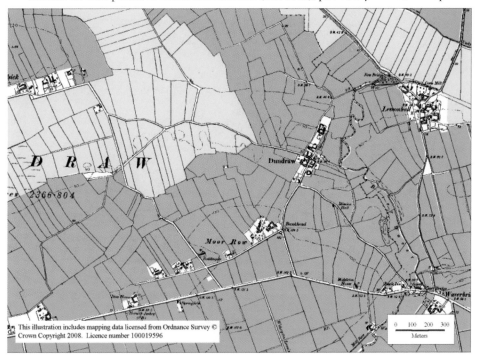

This illustration includes mapping data licensed from Ordnance Survey © Crown Copyright 2008. Licence number 100019596

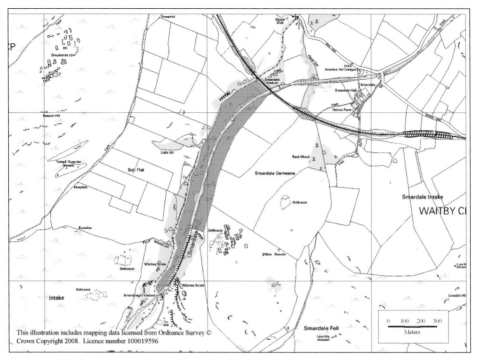

This illustration includes mapping data licensed from Ordnance Survey ©
Crown Copyright 2008. Licence number 100019596

Plate 3: Ancient valley-bottom woodland at Smardale, near Kirkby Stephen in east Cumbria. The woodland coincides with an area of dense remains of charcoal burners' huts and pitsteads.

Plate 4: The Netherby estate, with Netherby Park at the centre shown in pink, with large areas of ornamental plantation shown in dark green. This is a landscape replanned in the late 18th century. Planned enclosures of open common are coloured light orange, while replanned and reorganised older enclosures are shown in blue. The white area is Scotland, where a similar landscape is evident.

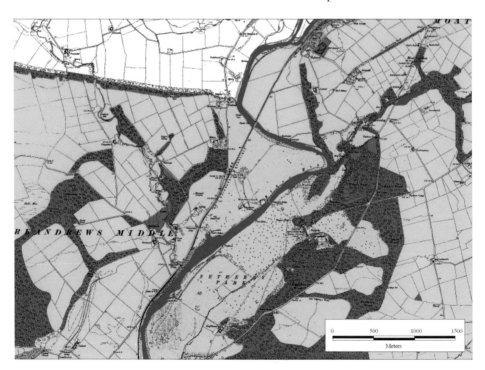

Plate 5: Saltom Pit, 1820 vertical-winder engine-house (photo: Simon Roper).
Plate 6: Bone china christening cup, overglazed enamelled, bearing the name 'William'. © Museum of London Archaeology Service, photographed by Andy Chopping.

Plate 7: Selection of 'Moralising China' (left to right): refined whiteware, transfer-printed children's plate, bearing one of Benjamin Franklin's maxims; refined whiteware, black transfer-printed children's plate, bearing Jane Taylor poem, 'My Grandmother'; refined whiteware, underglazed transfer-printed and overglaze-painted decoration, children's plate, bearing excerpt from 'Isaac's Prayer' (© Museum of London Archaeology Service, photographed by Andy Chopping).

Plate 8: A collage by the American artist Judith Supine, which was fixed to the viaduct in Grimsby Street. At the time of the survey (2007) Supine and several other contemporary and street artists were exhibiting at the Leonard Street Gallery, EC2.

raising questions concerning the patterns of rural settlement defined nationally by Roberts and Wrathmell.[33] It reveals the intricacies of local adaptation and settlement change, which Roberts and Wrathmell's national survey cannot do. By enhancing the data range of a county-based historic landscape characterisation, through the use of 18th-century county maps, the subtleties of post-medieval settlement development can begin to be teased out.

As a map-based tool, HLC is especially useful for identifying and locating patterns, which is the first concern of any landscape archaeologist. Patterns give distinctive character to an area,[34] and they are the strongest indicator of an area's developmental history. In Cumbria, for example, the large areas of rectilinear fields formed through planned enclosure in the late 18th and 19th centuries define areas of former open, common pasture. These areas lacked medieval and post-medieval settlements and, following enclosure, were for a while given over to arable farming. Consequently, today such rectilinear field patterns often coincide with areas lacking in known archaeological sites. Late-enclosed common pasture constitutes one landscape type in Cumbria. Another landscape type, with particular categories of archaeological sites associated with it, is ancient woodlands. Surveys of ancient woodlands, as at Haverthwaite and Troutbeck in the Lake District, and Smardale Gill in east Cumbria (Plate 3), have revealed considerable survival of monuments associated with primarily post-medieval woodland industries.[35] These include charcoal pitsteads, woodland workers' huts and potash kilns. The extent and distribution of coppiced woodland within Cumbria, and particularly in the southern half of the county, is not just the result of woodland craft industry, but is tied to the major local industries of metal processing and bobbin making, which played a significant role in shaping the historic landscape character of the area.[36]

Another opportunity for researching the distribution of, and possible correlation between, monument classes and landscape types, is the interface between anciently enclosed land and the open moorland. It has a particular potential for the analysis of the ebb and flow of settlement and field systems.[37] HLC does not immediately identify relic archaeological landscapes, because it is based on relatively modern mapping. A geographical information system, however, allows HLC to be enhanced through the addition of historic environment record data and field survey data. This allows the complexity of the landscape to be better appreciated, as issues of development through time can be articulated.

PROCESSES OF LANDSCAPE CHANGE

The landscape is forever changing in relation to an array of forces. Social, economic, political and natural pressures all influence the pace of landscape change. County historic landscape characterisations have proven to be especially useful at identifying change from the mid-19th century through to the present day, and this time-depth can be extended with caution, through the use of tithe, enclosure, estate and late-18th-century county maps. Through this means, historic landscape characterisation can provide an overview of the historical diversity that comprises an area of landscape.[38]

Conversely, HLC is also very useful for identifying landscapes that epitomise particular types of formation processes, though not necessarily at the county scale. While processes such as the 18th- and 19th-century enclosure movement are well represented, industrial impacts are under-represented both because of the county scale, and the generally small size of individual industrial enterprises. Even a seemingly widespread industrial landscape such as the copper-mining area of Coniston with its extensive spoil heaps, is hardly visible at a county scale.[39] More widespread processes, such as settlement and agriculture, however, are readily identifiable and interpretable as a county scale. In Cumbria in the 18th and 19th centuries, there are large districts characterised by regular, linear, nucleated settlements surrounded by long strip-like fields with reversed-S shaped boundaries. This landscape type is the result of post-medieval processes that effectively fossilised a medieval landscape layout of commonfield strips and planned settlements. These processes included other characteristics invisible within a county-based HLC, such as the building of durable multi-roomed houses, specialist agricultural buildings and the use of permanent hedges and walls to enclose open field strips. These implicit characteristics can be made explicit through characterisation at a finer resolution, such as at a township scale.

RESEARCH VALUE

If HLC is approached properly with both an understanding of its limitations and its fitness for purpose with regard to scale, it can be a useful research tool. It has been noted, for example, that historic landscape characterisations in north-west England have acted as a stimulus for the archaeological analysis of the post-medieval rural landscape.[40] Overall, as a research tool, HLC is perhaps more useful for the questions it helps to pose and frame rather than for any answers it might provide. It is a trigger for focusing further research and as a starting point to more detailed examination.

At a regional scale, HLC's greatest potential lies in providing a regional overview of landscape types, enabling definitions of inter-regional distinctiveness and intra-regional diversity. It can also break down barriers between neighbouring areas. For example, comparisons of the historic landscape characterisation for the Netherby area of north Cumbria with neighbouring parts of Scotland has demonstrated that the two border areas shared a cultural landscape. The Rev. Robert Graham inherited the Netherby estate in 1757, and he set about improving it in a similar way to southern Scottish landlords. He introduced the use of lime and drained a thousand acres of mossland, made enclosures and plantations and built roads. He reorganised the settlement structure of his estate, some existing settlements disappeared and new hamlets of eight to ten houses were created.[41] Interestingly, the county map of 1774,[42] surveyed while the process was under way, indicates that the pre-improvement landscape was also similar to the other side of the border, consisting of settlements that in Scotland were known as fermtouns (Plate 4). The comparison of the Cumbrian and Scottish historic landscape characterisations clearly confirms that these historical similarities are indeed represented in, and underlie, the modern landscape.

HLC can also be used for examining perceptions of locality through time through comparison with earlier classifications of areas sharing distinctive characteristics, such as was attempted in the late-18th-century Board of Agriculture reports.[43] HLC has the potential to test the accuracy of the perceptions of the agricultural commentators, by linking the reports to 18th-century county maps.

At a county scale, HLC is seen as providing a potential context for defining local distinctiveness, for exploring the origins and development of settlements and field systems, and for providing a baseline against which post-medieval processes, such as industrialisation and the expansion of agriculture, can be examined.[44] The greatest potential for historic landscape characterisation at a county scale, however, probably lies in combining mapped physical data with mapped intangibles, such as perceptions and cultural associations. In summary, historic landscape characterisation can be used as a gateway to a county-scale analysis of pre-19th-century landscapes, which can enhance and deepen the relevance of the characterisation of 19th- and 20th-century landscape development that they already provide.

ACKNOWLEDGEMENTS

Thanks are due to Cumbria County Council for allowing access to their data and reproduction of the maps used in the illustrations. Particular thanks are owed to Jo Mackintosh, Nick Martin and Richard Newman.

NOTES

1. Fairclough 1999b, 6–7.
2. Austin 2007; Clark *et al.* 2004; Rippon 2004; Rippon 2007; Turner 2006; Turner 2007; Williamson 2007.
3. Clark *et al.* 2004.
4. Rippon 2004, 143.
5. Rippon 2007.
6. Austin 2007; Williamson 2007.
7. Williamson 2007, 66.
8. Turner 2006 and 2007.
9. Turner 2007, 46.
10. Turner 2007, 46.
11. Newman & Hardie 2007 for the Lake District National Park; work is ongoing for the rest of the county.
12. Newman 2005, 210.
13. Rippon 2004, 144.
14. Cooke 1999, 125–9.
15. Knowles 1983, 7.
16. Hoskins 1955.
17. Rippon 2004.
18. Rippon 2004, 77; Fairclough 1999b, 13.
19. Newman 1999.
20. Gaddis 2002, 60–2, 91–2.
21. Fairclough 2008, 298–9.
22. Fairclough 2008, 298.
23. Johnson 1999, 103.
24. Fairclough 2008, 298–9.
25. Evans *et al.* 2001, 53.
26. Newman 1998.
27. Turner 2007, 43.
28. Richard Newman pers comm..
29. Fairclough 1999a, 5; Rippon 2004, 74–5.
30. See Allen 1999, 164.
31. Fairclough 2008, 299.
32. Turner & Fairclough 2007.
33. Roberts & Wrathmell 2002.
34. Knowles 1983, 9.
35. Bowden 2000, 29–32; Parsons 1997.
36. Newman & Hardie 2007, 104–5.
37. Hodgson 2007.
38. Clark *et al.* 2003, 91.
39. Newman & Hardie 2007, 152.
40. McNeil & Newman 2006, 147.
41. Routledge 2000, 4.
42. Donald 1774.
43. Newman 2005, 210.
44. Brennand 2007.

BIBLIOGRAPHY

Allen, T. 1999, 'The management of the rural landscape', in Grenville, J. (ed.), *Managing the Historic Rural Landscape. London*: Routledge, 163–72.

Austin, D. 2007, 'Character or caricature? Concluding discussion', *Landscapes* **2**: 92–105.

Bowden, M. (ed.) 2000, *Furness Iron: The Physical Remains of the Iron Industry and Related Woodland Industries of Furness and Southern Lakeland*. Swindon: English Heritage.

Brennand, M. (ed.) 2007, *Research and Archaeology in North West England. An Archaeological Research Framework for the North West Region. Volume 2, Research Agenda and Strategy*. Manchester: CBA North West.

Clark, J., Darlington, J. & Fairclough, G. (eds) 2003, *Pathways to Europe's Landscape. European Pathways to the Cultural Landscape*.

Clark, J., Darlington, J. & Fairclough, G. 2004, *Using Historic Landscape Characterisation*. London: English Heritage.

Cooke, R.J. 1999, 'Nature conservation: taking a wider view', in Grenville, J. (ed.) , *Managing the Historic Rural Landscape*. London: Routledge, 125–36.

Donald, T. 1774, *Map of the County of Cumberland*. London.

Evans, M.J., Roberts, A. & Nelson, P. 2001, 'Ethnographic landscapes', *CRM* **5**, 53–6.

Fairclough, G. 1999a. 'Historic landscape characterisation', paper presented at an English Heritage Seminar, 11 December 1998.

Fairclough, G. 1999b, 'The countryside context', in Fairclough, G., Lambrick, G. & McNab, A. (eds), *Yesterday's World, Tomorrow's Landscape*. London: English Heritage.

Fairclough, G. 2008, 'New heritage, an introductory essay – people, landscape and change', in Fairclough et al. (eds), 2008, 297–312.

Fairclough, G., Harrison, R., Jameson, J.H. Jr. & Schofield, J. (eds) 2008, The Heritage Reader, London: Routledge.

Gaddis, J.L. 2004, *The Landscape of History*. Oxford: Oxford University Press.

Hicks, D., McAtackney, L. & Fairclough, G. (eds) 2007, *Envisioning Landscape: Perspectives and Politics in Archaeology and Heritage*. Walnut Creek, CA: Left Coast Press.

Hodgson, J. 2007, 'Burnt mounds in the Lake District, Cumbria', in Burgess, C., Topping, P. & Lynch, F. (eds), *Beyond Stonehenge: Essays on the Bronze Age in Honour of Colin Burgess*. Oxford: Oxbow Books.

Hoskins, W.G. 1955, *The Making of the English Landscape*. London: Hodder & Stoughton.

Johnson, M. 1999, *Archaeological Theory: An Introduction*. Oxford: Blackwell Publishers.

Jones, M. & Rotherdean, I.D. (eds) 1998, 'Landscapes – perception, recognition and management: reconciling the impossible?', *Landscape Archaeology and Ecology 3,* Sheffield.

Knowles, C. 1983, *Landscape History*. London: The Historical Association.

McNeil, R. & Newman, R. 2006, 'The industrial and modern period resource assessment', in Brennand (ed), 2006, 165–94.

Newman, C. & Hardie, C. 2007, *The Cumbria Historic Landscape Characterisation Project: The Lake District National Park*. Cumbria County Council.

Newman, R. 1998, 'Historic cultural landscapes: recognition, definition and classification within the planning process', in Jones & Rotherdean (eds), 1998.

Newman, R. 1999, 'Iron working and mining enterprises', *Keer to Kent* **38**: 14–15.

Newman, R. 2005, 'Farmers and fields: developing a research agenda for post-medieval agrarian society and landscape', *Post Medieval Archaeology* **39**(2): 205–14.

Parsons, M.A. 1997, 'The woodland of Troutbeck and its exploitation to 1800', *Transactions of the Cumberland and Westmorland Antiquarian and Archaeological Society* **97**: 79–100.

Rippon, S. 2004, *Historic Landscape Analysis: Deciphering the Countryside*, Practical Handbooks in Archaeology **16**, CBA.

Rippon, S. 2007, 'Historic landscape characterisation: its role in contemporary British archaeology and landscape history', *Landscapes* **2**: 1-14.

Roberts, B.K.& Wrathmell, S, 2002, *Region and Place: A Study of English Rural Settlement*. London: English Heritage.

Turner, S. 2006, 'Historic landscape characterisation: a landscape archaeology for research, management and planning', *Landscape Research* **31**(4): 385–98.

Turner, S. 2007, 'Landscape archaeology for the past and future: the place of historic landscape characterisation', *Landscapes* **2**: 40–9.

Turner, S. & Fairclough, G. 2007, 'Common culture: the archaeology of landscape character in Europe', in Hicks et al. (eds), 2007.

Williamson, T. 2007, 'Landscape characterisation: some queries', *Landscapes* **2**: 64–71.

The Whitehaven Coast 1500-2000 – Post-Medieval, Industrial *and* Historical Archaeology?

By DAVID CRANSTONE

A review of current debates on the nature and direction of 'Industrial Archaeology' is presented, emphasising the importance of technology and industry within a holistic archaeology of the later second millennium CE, itself situated within a historical archaeology that in Britain extends back to the Roman period. The debate between 'Industrial' and 'Post-Medieval' archaeology is seen as part of the 'two cultures' of sciences and humanities, and the specific connections of industrial archaeology to engineering and thus to physics are emphasised. The definition and chronology of the Industrial Revolution are re-examined, and alternative models of a 'chemical' followed by a 'physical', or an 'extractive' followed by a 'manufacturing' Industrial Revolution are proposed, both seen as being within a 'long Industrial Revolution' that extended back to the late-medieval period. These themes are then examined in a case study of the Whitehaven coast. A classic 'industrial landscape' of coal mining and associated transport is shown to derive from this 'long Industrial Revolution' which in this case took off in the 1630s; however, the landscape and its industrialisation were framed by its medieval antecedents, and represent a landscape of power, symbolism, identity and colonialism as well as one of practical industry. The Whitehaven survey therefore forms part of the holistic archaeology of the later second millennium CE previously advocated; however, the need for 'unity in diversity', respecting difference and welcoming contributions from the full range of the 'two cultures', is stressed.

INTRODUCTION

The future directions of 'Industrial Archaeology' in Britain, and its relationships to 'Post-Medieval Archaeology', have been the focus of healthy debate over the last few years. Barker & Cranstone 2004, Casella & Symonds 2005 and Gwyn & Palmer 2005 together form a wide-ranging review of archaeological approaches to industry and industrialisation at the start of the third millennium CE; the last of these in particular forms almost a manifesto for a sea-change from technocentric approaches to a 'social archaeology' of industry.[1] As discussed in the previous chapter, the debate has been taken forward by Nevell[2] (reacting in part to the present author's paper[3] in Casella & Symonds 2005), by Holden[4] and others in the Letters section of *Industrial Archaeology News* and most trenchantly by Fitzgerald[5] in *Industrial Archaeology Review*, forming respectively an industrial archaeology grassroots and a 'hard engineer' reaction to the perceived swing to social archaeology represented by Gwyn & Palmer 2005. Most recently Cossons[6] has entered the debate from a heritage management focus, although it is puzzling that this provocative and interesting paper was written with virtually no reference to the debate within archaeology and industrial archaeology of which it forms a part.

There has also been debate, although perhaps not as much as there should be, over the use of the term 'Historical Archaeology', both in its North American (and other New World) sense as effectively a replacement for 'Post-Medieval' and in its broader literal meaning as the archaeology of literate societies (or of societies for which a historical record, internal or external, survives – the difference in definitions is not important in the present context).[7] In England, this gives a historical archaeology starting at or shortly before the Roman conquest, and forming a major sub-discipline matching and succeeding prehistory – it is interesting to see at least one eminent prehistorian (Sir Colin Renfrew) moving in the same direction.[8]

My evolving positions in these debates have been published before and do not need rehearsing in detail.[9] To summarise very briefly, I believe strongly that the narrow definition of historical archaeology as confined chronologically to the period after *c.* 1500 (let alone specifically 1492 as advocated by some American writers) is seriously inappropriate and even colonialist in an Old World context, whereas the broad literal definition has major value in highlighting the commonalities and shared issues of the historic periods from the Roman onwards (effectively the 'archaeology of AD' as opposed to BC in the British context). On the relationship between 'Post-Medieval' and 'Industrial', I remain firmly in favour of a holistic and diverse archaeology of the later second millennium CE that includes technocentric and social approaches (and others) without fundamental period or topic sub-divisions; the term we use for this archaeology is much less important, though I am (reluctantly) coming round to Tarlow & West's usage of 'later historical' as being being the most appropriate, if anodyne and relative, term for a period that includes the 20th century as well as the 16th century, and includes topics such as religion and vernacular architecture that can only tenuously be related to 'Industry'.[10] However, that holistic 'later historical' archaeology (or whatever we call it) must include the study and detailed technical understanding of industry and production along with more humanistic concerns, and in this respect, although certainly not in all others, I am very much in agreement with Fitzgerald and Cossons.

In a holistic archaeology of the later second millennium, the question of whether the 'Industrial Revolution' is a useful concept, and if so what date-range is assigned to it, is not of fundamental importance. The concept certainly has some value – the changes in technology and production were enormous, and affected every area of society. However, the concept of a clear period break between a 'Post-Medieval' period and an 'Industrial Revolution' is not, in my opinion, helpful – the origins of most elements of the 'revolution' can be traced back well into the post-medieval, if not into the medieval period. This applies with particular force to the start-date often given for the Industrial Revolution, of 1750 – probably the conventional date, to the extent that any specific start-date does or should exist. Such a late date has always surprised me – in my own areas of interest (mainly metals and other extractive industries), a date of *c.* 1700 reflects the fundamental changes more closely. This choice of dates may, however, illuminate some interesting elements, both in the nature of the industrial archaeology research community and in the nature of industrialisation.

In previous papers, I have suggested that the difference between the post-medieval and industrial archaeology communities forms part of the 'two cultures' separation between the humanities and the sciences.[11] There is truth in this, but I would like to modify the second half of the equation; I would suggest that the intellectual roots of most industrial archaeology lie very much in engineering and mechanics, and hence ultimately in the pure science of physics, rather than in the full range of sciences. This may explain the otherwise surprising reluctance of industrial archaeology to engage with archaeological science. The study of process residues (surely a key element of any holistic study of industrialisation) is based primarily on chemistry (admittedly this is an area in which chemistry and physics overlap), while environmental science is obviously closely linked to biology. The recent English Heritage publication on *Science for Historic Industries: Guidelines for the Investigation of 17th- to 19th-Century Industries*[12] (see Bayley, Dungworth & Paynter this volume) may help to remedy this reluctance to engage with archaeological science. The link between industrial archaeology and physics may also explain the tendency for 'industrial archaeology' and 'historical metallurgy' to remain rather separate communities,[13] the latter linking more to chemistry (and also to the extractive rather than the manufacturing industries – and of course to both the chemistry and the physics of hot processes, rather than the room-temperature environment of most engineering and mechanics). This separation to an extent reflects contemporary interests – among the leading 18th-century ironmasters, William Reynolds had an active interest in chemistry,[14] while John Wilkinson (a friend and marriage-relative of Joseph Priestley) invited James Watt for a holiday at his experimental ironworks at Wilson House ('The different fluxes – & Cinders – together with the different Metal would I think be a high Treat to you …').[15]

The intellectual roots of the discipline may also explain the tendency to adopt a late start-date, whether explicitly or implicitly; 1750 does broadly mark the inception of a 'mechanical Industrial Revolution' centred on machinery and the machine-based factory. However, this development of mechanics was dependent intellectually on the late-17th-century development of Newtonian mechanics and the 'Enlightenment' of the whole 18th century (the links are elegantly explored by Jacob[16]), and practically on the development of the steam engine from Newcomen onwards; on the reverberatory furnace for non-ferrous metal smelting (and many other metallurgical operations) at the end of the 17th century, and on the linked developments of coke smelting and the foundry sector in the iron industry in the early 18th century.

The massive Crowley ironworks at Winlaton Mill and Swalwell on Tyneside, developed rapidly from the 1680s to the 1710s, also prefigured many of the organisational features of the late-18th-century factory system, with their own 'laws', social control, management structures and social security system.[17] These practical developments in turn depended on coal – both on a substantial and efficient mining industry, developed from the late middle ages onwards[18], and on the development of grates, chimneys, ashpits and other features required for the efficient combustion of coal as opposed to wood and peat.

The first industry to switch from wood and peat to coal was salt, and the links between the salt and coal industries were close, especially in Scotland.[19] The 'panhouse' process of saltmaking, using coal fuel to evaporate unconcentrated seawater in large iron pans, was probably the first coal-fuelled industry (as opposed to adventitious uses of coal in processes that were normally fuelled with wood, charcoal or peat) anywhere. Current research suggests that this process was perfected on the Firth of Forth in the mid-15th century, following a period of development in central Britain more broadly.[20] The panhouse process may also have been the first industrial process in Britain to require consistent 24-hour shift-working,[21] pre-dating the introduction of the (charcoal-fuelled) blast furnace in the 1490s, although the saltpans did not demand the continual 24-hour-a-day-for-several-months 'campaigns' of the blast furnace, and working hours may possibly have been shorter in the 15th century than in the 17th and 18th centuries from which Whatley's documentation dates.

These facts and interpretations suggest some alternative analyses of the 'Industrial Revolution': first, we could view the Industrial Revolution as a two-stage phenomenon, consisting of (broadly) an earlier 'chemical Industrial Revolution' (from perhaps the 1680s to c. 1750), followed by the more conventional 'mechanical Industrial Revolution' of the later 18th century. Or, second, we could again see it as consisting of a two-stage phenomenon, this time consisting of an earlier 'extractive Industrial Revolution' (whose origin could be placed at any one of several points between the mid-15th century and the late 17th centuries), followed by a 'manufacturing Industrial Revolution' from c. 1750. Thirdly and alternatively, we could identify a 'long Industrial Revolution', starting arguably in the 15th century, as opposed to the conventional 'short Industrial Revolution' of the 18th century (itself starting c. 1700 rather than c. 1750). The last model could be extended further, to include Gimpel's controversial concept of a mechanical Industrial Revolution of the 12th and 13th centuries; this model is not explored in the present chapter.[22]

These ideas are not presented as absolute truth – they are models, which may contain useful insights that can be tested out as useful ways of looking at the broad phenomenon of industrialisation. Most importantly, all of these models challenge any idea of a separation between 'Post-Medieval' and 'Industrial' periods, or of an over-separation between technology and industrialisation on the one hand, and social, tenurial, economic and intellectual elements of society on the other.

THE WHITEHAVEN COAST

Some of these above ideas about the industrial revolution can be illustrated and developed through discussion of a recent landscape survey near Whitehaven on the west coast of Cumbria, conducted by myself and assisted by Simon Roper of Ironbridge Archaeology.[23] The survey, commissioned by the National Trust, covered a strip of land about 3km long along the coast and up to 1km wide, which was passing into National Trust management, and was undertaken for management rather than research purposes. The landholding was an entirely modern creation, centred on the coastal cliffs and the open land behind, and specifically drawn to exclude the built-up areas of Whitehaven town centre (immediately east of the north end of the project area, which did include part of the south side of Whitehaven Harbour) and the housing estates to its south. The project area therefore excluded both the historic town of Whitehaven and the inland half of what is a well-defined natural unit and historic landscape (the 'Howgill ridge'), together with an important strip of coal-related historic industry along the Pow Beck valley to the east of this ridge; the biases introduced by this boundary rendered any formal attempt to use the 'Manchester methodology' inappropriate.[24] The Howgill ridge forms part of the Cumberland Coalfield, the main seams dipping west from outcrops along the east slope of the ridge, to below sea-level at the coast (though some thin upper seams do outcrop in the coastal cliffs). To the south, the exposed coalfield is bounded by a scarp of south-dipping Permian red sandstone, with thin limestones and seams of gypsum/alabaster and anhydrite in the shales under the sandstone; the project area included the coastal outcrops of the gypsum/alabaster, and extended onto the crest of the inland sandstone scarp and part of its continuation as the dramatic cliffs of St Bees Head.

At first sight, the archaeology of the study area is that of a classic English 'industrial landscape', dominated by coal mining. However, research soon demonstrated that the industrial phase was superimposed on a landscape with much greater time-depth, and also formed part of a broader 17th- to 20th-century cultural landscape.

The area that is now West Cumberland had a complex cultural history through the first millennium, including British ('Cumbric'), Northumbrian, Scandinavian, Scottish and Gaelic (probably Irish or Manx) influences, before final incorporation into England in the 1150s. What became St Bees Priory, and its estates, was handed over by Coremac [and?] Gille Becoc, the Gaelic formulation for the priests of a saint's shrine, to become an English Benedictine house in c.1130, at which point detailed historical documentation begins.[25] The project area was part of these estates until the Dissolution, forming part of at least two monastic-owned townships and manors (potentially of even earlier origins). One of these, Sandwith, extending into the south end of the survey area, then passed into the lordship of St Bees School; the other, Preston Quarter, occupied most of the study area, passed into private Lordship and was acquired by the Lowther family in 1630, to simplify a complex story. The Lowthers remained dominant lords and landowners until the early 20th century; indeed, they totally dominated both the town and the industrialisation of the area despite being absentee landlords for almost all of this time, operating through a successsion of local agents.

The visible archaeology is very much dominated by industry. At the south end is a fine series of quarries in the sea-cliffs and inland escarpment of the Red Sandstone (Fig. 16.1), running from perhaps the medieval period to the 20th century. The rockfaces host a fine collection of graffiti, ranging from at least the 19th century to 2002, and including a carefully carved human face bearing a distinct resemblance to Stalin (Fig. 16.2) – if so, it forms an interesting comment (perhaps by a mid-20th-century working man) on the landscape of power on the coalfield that it overlooks. However, the landscape to the south, off the coalfield and in Sandwith township, is very different; the township boundary marks an abrupt change to an area of 'ancient countryside', with 'stone hedges' (even 'Cornish hedges' with herringbone stone revetting in places, although any outside connection is probably 'Irish Sea' rather than specifically Cornish) defining curvilinear and rectilinear (but not ruler-straight) field boundaries of various dates.

ABOVE
Figure 16.1 Quarries in the Red Sandstone at the south end of the project area (photo: Simon Roper).
BELOW
Figure 16.2 Graffiti in one of the quarries – perhaps a likeness of Stalin? (photo: Simon Roper)

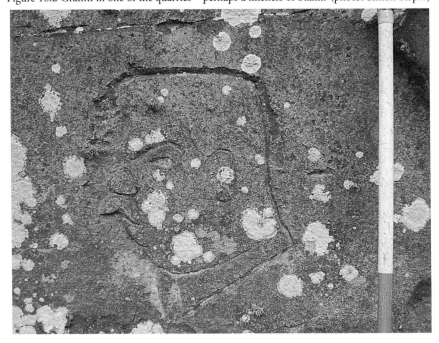

In the landslipped coastal slope of Barrowmouth Bay, on the shales between the sandstone and the underlying Coal Measures, is an area of alabaster and gypsum mining – the presence of alabaster was known by 1682, although mining is only documented from 1739, continuing intermittently until 1908. The visible features are mainly of later 19th-century date and include adits, mine buildings, an impressive engine-hauled incline, and the overgrown ruins of various domestic and industrial vernacular buildings. One of the associated houses was also used as a Victorian tea room and private museum. Remains of its collection may survive in rubbish deposits around the buildings.

The remainder of the area (all in Preston Quarter township, adjacent to the town of Whitehaven at the north end) is dominated by coal mining and associated industries and transport, and includes some magnificent 18th- to 20th-century features. However, the story is not in fact one of 'classic' industrialisation starting in the later 18th century. By about 1230, St Bees Priory and Wetheral Priory both operated saltworks on the coast, and by 1282 at the latest St Bees Priory was engaged in mining coal in the cliff for its saltworks (located either at the later Saltom Pit site, or on the south side of Whitehaven Harbour). This is one of the earliest references to coal-fuelled saltmaking, with the rocky location suggesting a form of 'direct boiling' rather than the normal medieval 'sleeching' process (which required a saltmarsh coast). If this was the case, the process was presumably not yet fully competitive with sleeching, since it did not become common for another two centuries.

The extent of coal mining and saltmaking through the later Middle Ages, and through to the Lowther acquisition of the lordship in 1630, is unclear, although there is some evidence that Sir Christopher Lowther took over existing mines and saltworks as well as building new panhouses. Sir Christopher developed both assets energetically; the coal was exported to Ireland as well as being burned in the saltworks, although the impression is that at this stage salt, rather than coal, was the core of the enterprise. From the 1660s, however, succeeding generations of the Lowther family undertook a sustained and massive programme of industrial development, centred on coal mining, transport to the harbour, the harbour itself, and on the town of Whitehaven, which was largely developed as a 'new town' at the turn of the 17th and 18th centuries. Coal mining was initially centred on the outcrops along the Pow Beck valley (outside my study area), relying on adit systems and an early Newcomen engine for drainage, and on packhorses and a specially built cartway for transport to the harbour.

In the 1730s, Carlisle Spedding (the Lowthers' agent at the time) instituted a step-change in technology and planning: he sunk Saltom Pit on the shoreline as the central drainage shaft for the whole Howgill colliery area, developed a series of pits and underground levels to operate the colliery (occupying almost the whole study area, plus the area extending east to the Pow Beck outcrops), and set out a major system of horse-drawn waggonways from the various drawing shafts to a new set of stone-built staithes dominating the south side of the harbour. The town also reached its *floruit* in terms of importance at around this time; the coal trade to Ireland was supplemented by a substantial transatlantic trade, with imports of rum and tobacco and the concomitant links to the transatlantic slave trade.

The coal industry and its infrastructure remained at the cutting edge of technology for about a century, and most of the prominent surviving features date from this period; they include the Howgill Incline (from the top of the ridge to the staithes, replacing part of the horse-hauled waggonway system), and the Saltom vertical-winder engine house of c. 1820 (Plate 5). In 1816, locomotive haulage was attempted on one of the waggonways; the locomotive worked successfully, but the trial was unsuccessful owing to problems with the track.[26] Since this waggonway was soon replaced by an incline (the Croft Incline – see below), excavation of the trackbed and formations might yield important information on the reasons for its failure.

Wellington Pit was sunk at the mouth of the harbour in a final burst of innovation around 1840. The Wellington Pit incorporated a fine 'Candlestick Chimney' (Fig. 16.3), while a very early attempt at fan ventilation was implemented at the interlinked Duke Pit. Some remains of this system may be incorporated into the surviving 1870 Guibal fanhouse (Fig. 16.4). The 1840 fan was probably the last 'cutting-edge' innovation; no new collieries were sunk for sixty years until the old Croft Pit was totally remodelled as Ladysmith Pit. The final colliery to be sunk, Haig, was up to date when constructed during the First World War, but was not groundbreaking by national standards. Its surviving engine house, winding engine and headgear nonetheless do form a survival of prime technological and iconic importance (Fig. 16.5).

The landscape of the Howgill ridge was never purely one of industry in the strictest sense. At the north end, the amenities of nearby Whitehaven included an inn (now known as Jonathan Swift's House, though the connection is apocryphal) and a bowling green on the clifftop, both dating from the early 18th century. Spedding's waggonway had to go round this bowling green, with turntables situated on the right-angle bends at its corners. The town and harbour also required defences, and a series of forts and batteries are documented continuously from the 17th century to the 1820s, with brief refortifications in the

RIGHT
Figure 16.3 Wellington Pit, 'Candlestick' Chimney (photo: Simon Roper)

LEFT
Figure 16.4 Duke Pit
fanhouse; the 1870 Guibal
fanhouse reflects the
castellated architectural
treatment of the harbour
skyline, and may
incorporate elements of
an 1840 fanhouse (photo:
Simon Roper)

1860s and during the First World War. One of the earlier forts, Old Fort, was attacked and briefly taken by John Paul Jones during in the American War of Independence (an event strangely more celebrated in American than British naval histories!). Most likely in the 1860s, gun emplacements were inserted into the west bank of the bowling green.

The agricultural landscape of the Howgill ridge, around and between the various industrial and other installations, was transformed in the 1830s from a 'traditional' landscape of enclosed fields and unenclosed grazing into a rigidly rectilinear field-system set out around the axis of the new Croft Incline along the centre of the ridge. The rear boundary between this new landscape and the 'ancient' landscape of Sandwith followed (and still follows) the historic boundary between Preston Quarter and Sandwith townships, the boundary of Lowther control – a medieval (or conceivably earlier) boundary, whose landscape significance detonated in the 1830s. Immediately afterwards, with the construction of Wellington Pit, the 'front' of this enclosed landscape was transformed into an architectural façade by a massive series of castellated revetments (Fig. 16.6), designed by Robert Smirke and extending from Wellington Pit (itself modelled by Smirke into a pseudo-castle, although also very much a functioning colliery) to the staithes and then to the Duke Pit fanhouse.

Clearly, this is not only a landscape of practical industry, but also one of power and symbolism. But what symbolism? Of feudal aristocratic power, dominating the town and harbour? Of defence against the Scots (the hills in the background of Fig. 16.7 are those of Galloway)?, or the Americans (the Tory Lowthers were strongly anti-American, and the mock-battlements tower over the genuine (if much less impressive) fortifications of Old Fort)? Or, moving from the deliberate to the subconscious, of the Lowthers' increasingly inward-looking bunker mentality, as their age of innovation began to fossilise?

Figure 16.5   Haig Pit headgear (photo: Simon Roper)

So, despite first appearances, the landscape of the Whitehaven coast is not just an 'industrial landscape' (however important and fascinating such landscapes are). It is also a landscape of fortification (both real and pretend), of leisure, of agriculture, of power and of symbolism; and, in its way, a 'designed landscape'. Returning to the industrial theme, how does this specific landscape relate to the models of the 'Industrial Revolution' discussed above? Firstly, it is *not* fundamentally a landscape of the Industrial Revolution in the narrow chronological definition of post-1750, although most of the dramatic surviving monuments do date from this period; the peak period of innovation and change arguably *ended* around 1750. In this instance the earlier phase was definitely a 'physical' rather than a 'chemical' Industrial Revolution, though it was firmly 'extractive' rather than 'manufacturing'. The lack of a chemical Industrial Revolution does not invalidate the concept (so long as this is not taken as a universal, which is not my intention) – the 'chemical Industrial Revolution' was centred in the iron and non-ferrous metals industries, and these were never important within the study area or its immediate context (despite the fact that the Lowthers and their agents were involved in an early reverberatory copper smelter at Moresby, and an unsuccessful 1690s coke-fuelled blast furnace at Cleator, both within the broader ambit of Whitehaven). However, the Whitehaven coast is very much a landscape of the 'long Industrial Revolution', in this instance taking off continuously from the 1630s onwards, with more tenuous connections (in terms of the surviving documentary evidence) back

RIGHT
Figure 16.6 Part
of the castellated
revetments between
Wellington Pit and the
staithes, taken from
Old Fort

to the 13th century. As often seems to be the case, the first phase of that 'long Industrial Revolution' seems to be related to the symbiosis of coal mining and saltmaking.

The Whitehaven coast is also a landscape of great time-depth, with developments right up to the 19th century (and perhaps beyond) being constrained by the lineaments of a medieval monastic landscape that may itself have had earlier origins. It is also a landscape of identity: an area only incorporated into England in the 12th century after a period of Scottish/Cumbric control, within clear sight of Scotland, albeit of weakly Gaelicised Galloway and Dumfriesshire rather than the Highlands, and of the firmly Gaelic Isle of Man, with hints of 'Irish Sea province' in the field boundaries of Sandwith. To what extent is the time-depth of the Whitehaven landscape 'English' as opposed to (southern) Scottish, Gaelic, Viking, or indeed proto-Welsh or simply Cumbrian? And do the revetments that tower over Whitehaven Harbour symbolise the adoption (or imposition) of a fiercely English identity over the earlier melting-pot? And, while it would be hard to characterise the study area as a 'landscape of colonialism', the links are there. The early development of coal mining and of Whitehaven depended heavily on the coal and salt trade to Ireland (whether or not British involvement in Ireland is seen as 'colonial'[27] as also discussed by O'Keeffe and Rynne, this volume), and in the early 18th century the products and profits of Caribbean and American slavery flowed into the town. Both contributed, only slightly less directly, to the growth of Lowther capital that made the industrialisation possible.

CONCLUSION

Finally, let us return briefly to the overall theme of the original conference and this publication, the 'crossing paths' or 'shared tracks' of industrial, post-medieval, and historical

Figure 16.7 Industrial, post-medieval, historical? Top of Howgill Incline (lower Right); 'Jonathan Swift's House' and bowling green (to left); Candlestick Chimney and Whitehaven Harbour (behind); and the Irish Sea with the Scottish hills on the horizon.

archaeologies. At first sight, the results of the Whitehaven coast survey offer a cogent and persuasive (I hope) argument for a holistic archaeology of the later second millennium CE, and one that takes account of the earlier background to that period – a 'long Industrial Revolution' that starts in the 17th century at the latest and whose roots can be traced back into the middle ages, and that cannot be separated fundamentally (even at its height in the 18th and 19th centuries) from the social and symbolic issues of humanities-based archaeology.

However, it was noticeable to me at the conference how few of the papers were firmly technocentric in their approach, and how few of the contributors were from the engineering-related side of 'industrial archaeology'. While the broadening of 'industrial archaeology' into more social and humanistic interests, and indeed its convergence with post-medieval and other 'mainstream' archaeologies, is very welcome and perhaps overdue, there is a real danger of losing a vital strand of our research community – and since industrialisation and the Industrial Revolution were about production at least as much as consumption (to skirt around another debate!), and the mechanical/manufacturing aspects of industrialisation (despite my strictures above) were a key element of the whole, we lose that strand at our great peril. While clearly there is a need at one level for a 'large tent' within which all those concerned with the archaeology of the later second millennium can contribute and communicate (hopefully with some mutual understanding and respect, despite what can be quite deep differences in background and perception), that tent needs to contain (and actively retain) rooms within in which each of its constituent groups can communicate at their own level and feel at home. Rather than aiming for too much 'muffling inclusivity' within an over-synthetic social archaeology, we need to celebrate our differences and the dialogue between them as a 'unity in diversity'.

ACKNOWLEDGEMENTS

The Whitehaven coast project was commissioned by the National Trust with funding support from West Lakes Renaissance, English Partnerships, the Land Restoration Trust, and the Cleaner Safer Greener Fund (Copeland Borough Council and Cumbria County Council). I am grateful to Simon Roper of Ironbridge Archaeology for his major contributons to the project, to Jamie Lund (Regional Archaeologist) and Jeremy Barlow (Property Manager) of the National Trust (Northwest Region) for commissioning the project and for friendly assistance and support throughout, and to Paul Belford for his management of the Ironbridge elements of the project, and for many enjoyable and invigorating discussions, both of Whitehaven and of broader themes. I am also grateful to Dr Peter King and to Simon Chapman for contributing their specialist expertise, respectively on medieval and legal records and on the interpretation of the Saltom Pit engine house and the Duke Pit fanhouse.

I am also grateful to Robert Baxter, Tom Robson, David Bowcock and other staff of Cumbria Record Office (Carlisle and Whitehaven), to Michelle Kelly (Museum Collections Officer, The Beacon), Pamela Telford and Toni Desovskie (Haig Colliery Mining Museum), Caroline Rhodes and Rosemary Preece (National Coal Mining Museum), David Clarke and other staff (Mining Records, Coal Authority), to Dr Richard Newman and Jo Mackintosh (Cumbria County Council historic environment section), Peter Brash (National Trust ecologist), Wayne Cocroft (English Heritage), Norman Gray, Andy Guy, Alan Routledge, Ben Russell (Science Museum) and John Todd, for their helpful assistance and discussion of various aspects of the project. In addition, Steve and Janet Pearson of Abbey Farmhouse, St Bees, provided warm, comfortable and friendly accommodation during fieldwork.

Finally, I am grateful to Dr Audrey Horning and Professor Marilyn Palmer for the opportunity to develop my ideas in this forum, to all those who contributed to discussion at the conference, and to all those who have contributed to the published debates referred to in this chapter.

NOTES

1. Barker & Cranstone 2004; Casella & Symonds 2005; Gwyn & Palmer 2005.
2. Nevell 2006.
3. Cranstone 2005a.
4. Holden 2006.
5. Fitzgerald 2007a, 2007b.
6. Cossons 2007.
7. Andren 1998; Funari *et al.* 1999.
8. Renfrew 2007, 203–22.
9. Cranstone 2000, 2001, 2004, 2005a, 2005b.
10. Tarlow & West 1999.
11. Cranstone 2001, 300; Cranstone 2004, 314–15; Cranstone 2005a, 80–4.
12. Dungworth & Paynter 2006.
13. Cranstone 2005, 79–80.
14. Trinder 2008, 19, 22.
15. Birmingham Reference Library, Boulton & Watt Papers, Box 20/2, 45.
16. Jacob 1988.
17. Flinn 1962.
18. Hatcher 1993, esp. 16–30.
19. Hatcher 1993, 430–8; Whatley 1987.
20. Cranstone 2008; Cranstone forthcoming.
21. Whatley 1987, 7, 11.
22. Gimpel 1976.
23. Cranstone 2007a (with full bibliography); Cranstone 2007b.
24. Nevell 2003, 2005a, 2005b; Nevell & Walker 2004. A 'Manchester methodology' study of the broader area would be extremely interesting, and might yield very different conclusions from those drawn by Nevell in the textile-dominated industrial landscapes of the southern Pennines.
25. Todd 2003, 101.
26. Guy 2001, 133–4; Rees 2001, 155–6; Rees & Guy 2006, 210–13.
27. Rynne 2008

BIBLIOGRAPHY

Andren, A. 1998, *Between Artifacts and Texts: Historical Archaeology in Global Perspective*. New York: Plenum Press.

Bailey, M.R. (ed.), 2006, *Early Railways 3: Papers from the Third International Early Railways Conference.* Sudbury, Suffolk: Six Martlets Publishing.

Barker, D. & Cranstone, D. (eds) 2004, *The Archaeology of Industrialization*, Society for Post-Medieval Archaeology Monograph **2**. Leeds: Maney.

Casella, E. & Symonds, J. (eds) 2005, *Industrial Archaeology: Future Directions*. New York: Springer.

Cossons, N. 2007, 'Industrial archaeology: the challenge of the evidence', *Antiquaries Journal* **87**: 1–52.

Cranstone, D. 2000, 'Reviews of Swaledale: valley of the wild river and historical archaeology: back from the edge', *Post-Medieval Archaeology* **34**: 407–8.

Cranstone, D. 2001, 'Review of *Perspectives on Industrial Archaeology* and *Archaeology and Conservation in Ironbridge*', *Post-Medieval Archaeology* **35**: 300, 304–5.

Cranstone, D. 2004, 'The archaeology of industrialisation – new directions', in Barker & Cranstone (eds), 2004, 313–20.

Cranstone D. 2005a, 'After Industrial Archaeology?', in Casella & Symonds (eds), 2005, 77–92.

Cranstone, D. 2005b 'Review of *From Farmer to Factory Owner: Models, Methodology and Industrialisation: Archaeological Approaches to the Industrial Revolution in North West England*', *Post-Medieval Archaeology* **39**:2, 450–1.

Cranstone, D. 2007b. 'Industry, image, and identity – archaeology on the Whitehaven coast', *The Archaeologist* **64**: 40–1.

Dungworth, D. & Paynter, S. 2006, *Science for Historic Industries: Guidelines for the Investigation of 17th- to 19th-Century Industries*. Swindon: English Heritage. <http://www.helm.org.uk/upload/pdf/Science-Historic-Industries.pdf>.

Fitzgerald, R, 2007a, 'Historic building record and the Halifax Borough Market Doors', *Industrial Archaeology Review* **29**(1): 51–74.

Fitzgerald, R. 2007b, 'The Stone Dam Mill engine house', *Industrial Archaeology Review* **29**(2): 115–32.

Flinn, M.W. 1962, *Men of Iron*. Edinburgh: Edinburgh University Press.

Funari, P.P.A., Hall, M. & Jones, S. 1999, *Historical Archaeology: Back from the Edge*. London & New York: Routledge.

Gimpel, J. 1976, *The Medieval Machine: The Industrial Revolution of the Middle Ages*. New York: Penguin.

Guy, A. 2001, 'North eastern locomotive pioneers 1805 to 1827; a reassessment', in Guy & Rees (eds), 2001, 117–44.

Guy, A. & Rees, J. (eds) 2001, *Early Railways*. London: Newcomen Society.

Gwyn, D. & Palmer, M. (eds) 2005, *Understanding the Workplace: A Research Framework for Industrial Archaeology in Britain* (special issue), *Industrial Archaeology Review* **27**(1).

Hatcher, J. 1993, *The History of the British Coal Industry. Vol. 1. Before 1700: Towards the Age of Coal*. Oxford: Clarendon Press.

Holden, R.N. 2006, 'Our fascination with machines', *Industrial Archaeology News* **136**: 11.

Jacob, M.C. 1988, *The Cultural Meaning of the Scientific Revolution*. New York: Alfred A. Knopf.

Nevell, M. 2003, *Farmer to Factory Owner: Models, Methodology and Industrialisation: The Archaeology of the Industrial Revolution in North-West England*, *Archaeology North West* **16**.

Nevell. M. 2005a, 'Industrialisation, ownership, and the Manchester Methodology: the role of the contemporary structure during industrialisation, 1600–1900', in Gwyn & Palmer (eds), 2005, 87–96.

Nevell. M. 2005b, 'The social archaeology of industrialisation: the example of Manchester during the 17th and 18th centuries', in Casella & Symonds (eds), 2005, 177–204.

Nevell. M. 2006, 'Industrial archaeology or the archaeology of the industrial period? Models, methodology and the future of industrial archaeology', *Industrial Archaeology Review* **28**(1): 3–16.

Nevell, M. & Walker, J. 2004, 'Industrialization in the countryside: the roles of the lord, freeholder and tenant in the Manchester area, 1600–1900', in Barker & Cranstone (eds), 2004, 53–78.

Rees, J. 2001, 'The strange story of the Steam Elephant', in Guy & Rees (eds), 2001, 145–70.

Rees, J. & Guy, A. 2006. 'Richard Trevithick and pioneer locomotives', in Bailey (ed.), 2006, 191–220.

Renfrew, C. 2007, *Prehistory: The Making of the Human Mind*. London: Weidenfeld & Nicolson.

Rynne, C. 2008, 'Technological change as a "colonial" discourse: The Society of Friends in 19th-century Ireland', *Industrial Archaeology Review* **30**(1): 3–16.

Tarlow, S. & West, S. 1999, *The Familiar Past? Archaeologies of Later Historical Britain*. London & New York: Routledge.

Todd, J.M. 2003, 'The pre-Conquest church in St Bees, Cumbria: a possible minster?', *Transactions of the Cumberland and Westmorland Antiquarian and Archaeological Society*, 3rd ser, **3**: 97–108.

Trinder, B. 2008, 'William Reynolds: polymath – a biographical strand through the Industrial Revolution', *Industrial Archaeology Review* **30**(1): 17–32.

Whatley, C.A. 1987, *The Scottish Salt Industry 1570–1850*. Aberdeen: Aberdeen University Press.

Whitley, D.S. 1998, 'New approaches to old problems: archaeology in search of an ever elusive past', in Whitley (ed.), 1998, 1–28.

Whitley, D.S. (ed.) 1998a, *Reader in Archaeological Theory: Post-Processual and Cognitive Approaches*. London: Routledge.

UNPUBLISHED SOURCES

Birmingham Reference Library, Boulton & Watt Papers, Box 20/2, 45.

Cranstone, D. 2007a, *Whitehaven Coast Archaeological Survey* (3 vols). Bound report to the National Trust.

Cranstone, D. 2008, *Anglo-Scottish Salt Survey 2007–8: Desk Assessment Report*. Report to English Heritage and Historic Scotland.

Cranstone, D. forthcoming, *Anglo-Scottish Salt survey 2007-8*. Report to English Heritage and Historic Scotland.

The Changing Countryside:
The Impact of Industrialisation on Rural Settlement in the 18th and 19th Centuries

By RICHARD NEWMAN

The little-studied topic of post-medieval rural settlement desertion and shrinkage is examined through the results of a series of disparate projects undertaken in south Wales and north-west England. It concludes that many areas of settlement of post-medieval date in both origin and abandonment are incorrectly attributed to the medieval period. One of the primary causes of post-medieval shrinkage is considered to be industrialisation.

INDUSTRIALISATION AND SETTLEMENT

Industrialisation was a primary force behind new settlement formation in the post-medieval period. Less well known and little studied is the impact of industrialisation on settlement abandonment. In various regions of Britain during the 18th and 19th centuries rural settlements went into decline as people drifted away from rural areas to seek opportunities in areas of industrial expansion. All types of rural settlement were affected, from isolated farmsteads to nucleated settlements. For the most part, nucleated settlements experienced shrinkage rather than desertion. This chapter briefly examines the phenomenon of settlement shrinkage that appears connected to industrialisation in two areas, south Wales and the north-west of England, and analyses its impact on our understanding of post-medieval rural settlement. The observations given are based in part on disparate projects undertaken over more than two decades. The investigative methodologies used vary according to the requirements of the individual projects, but recurring themes are recognisable. These include: industrialisation as a likely culprit in the process of settlement desertion and shrinkage; a lack of understanding about post-medieval rural settlement origins and abandonments; and a lack of documentary research in relation to earthwork sites leading to an often inaccurate assumption that visible earthworks are medieval in origin.

SETTLEMENT ABANDONMENT IN GLAMORGAN

In the mid-1980s, I excavated at a village called Llanmaes, in the Vale of Glamorgan in south Wales.[1] The excavation was targeted on a series of earthworks presumed to be of medieval date, though subsequent topographical analysis indicated that the excavated earthworks did not fit a regular medieval pattern of tofts and crofts (Fig. 17.1). A number of buildings were identified by the excavation and while medieval layers were encountered, these were stratigraphically earlier than the buildings whose origin dated to the later 17th century. The excavated evidence suggested that the buildings including two houses were abandoned by the end of the 18th century. An explanation for this settlement shrinkage was found in the writings of Iolo Morgannwg who, in about 1800, described the neighbouring settlements of Boverton and Llantwit Major as suffering from considerable depopulation. Around a hundred farms and cottages were said to be ruinous and abandoned. He attributed tenement desertion to farm engrossment.[2]

Corroborative evidence for Iolo's claims were found archaeologically on the edge of Llantwit Major where settlement earthworks were plotted adjacent to Ty Mawr Farm. Subsequent observations during their destruction ahead of development indicated on finds evidence that the earthworks related to occupation remains of 17th–18th-century date.[3] Analysis of population figures for Llanmaes suggests that the population declined by 10 to 19 per cent in the 18th century. Contemporary with this decline the population of the Swansea region and some of the valleys of upland Glamorgan greatly increased. Employment in copper working in particular in Swansea and iron manufacture and coal

Figure 17.1 Excavated remains at Llanmaes (© Glamorgan-Gwent Archaeological Trust).

Figure 17.2 Map of Stock in 1717 (© Lancashire County Council)

mining in the valleys attracted workers to these areas. While farm engrossment undoubtedly made some agricultural tenements unviable in the Vale of Glamorgan, the attraction of neighbouring industrialising areas must have encouraged emigration. This was certainly a process recognised in the mid-19th century when the decline in the population of Llanmaes between 1831 and 1848 was attributed to 'emigration and the removal of many families to the manufacturing districts of the north, where better wages are obtained'.[4]

SETTLEMENT AND ABANDONMENT IN LANCASHIRE

Some ten years or so after working in south Wales I reviewed the archaeological evidence for deserted and shrunken medieval settlements in Lancashire.[5] In the resultant publication, the two illustrated examples were part of Rufford and Stock, both of which were subsequently shown to be areas of later post-medieval settlement in both origin and desertion. Rufford's shrinkage was known to be a result of emparkment in the early 19th century,[6] but its origins were not recognised as being of 17th-century date.[7] Stock, however, is clearly a settlement of medieval antecedents and the earthworks present there have been scheduled as the remains of a medieval settlement. I described it in 1996 as, 'the most impressive set of medieval earthworks'[8] in Lancashire. I was very wrong. Work by John Darlington has shown that the existing settlement of five dwellings in a small scattered hamlet is very similar to the mapped settlement in 1717 (Fig. 17.2).[9] Darlington noted that by 1796, however,

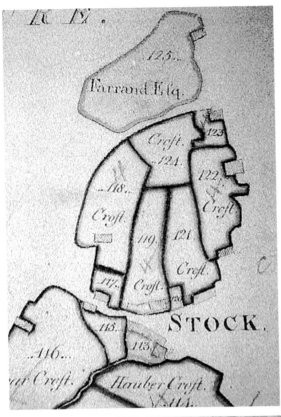

LEFT
Figure 17.3 Detail from map of Stock, 1796
(© Lancashire County Council).

BELOW
Figure 17.4 Aerial photograph of Stock
(© Lancashire County Council).

Stock was considerably larger and more nucleated.[10] By 1853 at least six of the functioning buildings shown on a 1796 estate map had been abandoned and the processes leading to the formation of today's earthworks were well under way (Figs 17.3 and 17. 4).[11]

The sequence of abandonment is a little more complex than indicated by Darlington, who attributed the creation of today's remains entirely to 19th-century desertion, with the origins of the deserted settlement area placed in the mid-18th century.[12] Comparisons between the 18th-century maps and today's earthworks indicate that one area of earthworks relates to the desertion of a freehold estate in existence by 1717 and another to desertion possibly pre-dating 1717.[13] The main area of earthworks, however, relates to two discrete enclosures that developed significantly between 1717 and 1796. These probably began as a 17th-century intake into the common pasture of Stock Hill. This resulted in the later (post-1717) development of five extra crofts, all of which had been abandoned by the mid-19th century. Darlington's plausible explanation was that Stock probably grew in the 18th century on the back of handloom weaving supplementing agricultural incomes.[14] Handloom weaving boomed in east Lancashire and on the Yorkshire border especially in the later 18th century. It declined in the earlier 19th century, however, in response to the increasing factorisation of weaving.[15] The neighbouring settlement of Barnoldswick, within easy walking distance of Stock, grew rapidly in the early 19th century, becoming a small industrial town as textile mills were established there.[16] Barnoldswick's success probably accounts for the desertion of the newly established properties at Stock. It appears that Stock's 18th-century expansion was a result of short-lived economic circumstances, largely unrelated to agriculture. This may be physically represented by the intrusion of the new properties into an existing long established field system. Their decline and abandonment seems to have had little impact on the continuing agricultural nature of the surviving settlement.

Darlington's work in Lancashire identified other areas of settlement remains that could be shown to have been abandoned in the 18th to 20th centuries, most of which were attributed to the impacts of industrialisation. These vary in size from hamlets to numerous individual farms.[17] One linking factor between most of them is that the areas of deserted settlement usually only originated in the later 16th and 17th centuries and were not of medieval origin. Not all these 18th- to early 20th-century shrinkages and desertions of earlier post-medieval settlements can be directly attributed to industrialisation. In the Forest of Bowland farmsteads were deserted following acquisition of the surrounding land for reservoir water catchments.[18] Later 16th- or 17th-century farmsteads on the fringes of Holcombe Moor were deserted because of the establishment of a military training area in 1911 and its extension in 1948.[19]

Though these examples, and that of Rufford, act as a clear warning that industrialisation should not always be attributed as the obvious cause of post-medieval abandonment, there are often compelling circumstances to suggest it as the cause of desertion in instances where no other factor can be identified as a likely cause. Recent work in Cumbria on historic landscape characterisation has identified a number of settlements for which this explanation seems the most likely reason for abandonment or shrinkage. This work has also helped to recognise some of the possible linking factors between settlements that have been noted in

Lancashire and south Wales. Moreover, it has revealed something of the range of settlement types involved and the varying likely industrial context for desertion.

SETTLEMENT ABANDONMENT IN CUMBRIA

The classic post-medieval desertion is the village of medieval origin cleared away for a landlord's estate reorganisation. Cumbria has a few examples of this process including Lowther, near Penrith. Lowther was the manorial centre of the Lowther family's holdings. In the late 17th century, it was a typical Cumbrian two-row nucleation of medieval origin, consisting of a hall, church, parsonage and seventeen tenements.[20] In 1682, it was cleared away by Sir John Lowther. The justification for the removal of crofts given in a county history 95 years later was to '*inlarge his demesne, and open the prospect to his house, for they stood just in front of it*'.[21] This Goldsmithian explanation does not reveal the entire picture. At the same time as the removal of Lowther a new settlement to the east known as Newtown was established. This is a settlement laid out on an embryonic grid plan, and initially it may have been intended for it to grow into a planned town, similar to Sir John's cousin's contemporary town of Whitehaven on the Cumbrian coast. Certainly it was intended to be a manufacturing settlement, and a linen mill was set up there and later a carpet factory,[22] though both failed and the settlement today remains a small planned estate village.

A similar desire for industrial success in part lay behind the Reverend Graham's late-18th-century Scottish-style reorganisation of his Netherby estates along the Scottish border. There, a number of farmsteads and straggling hamlets were removed as his estate was reorganised into small planned communities and a grid iron planned town at Longtown. Here success in the textiles industry was also hoped for but never achieved with the town's only long-term industrial success being a 19th-century bobbin factory. The majority of Cumbria's settlement desertions that can be associated with industrialisation, however, were far less intentional or planned than those inspired by Sir John Lowther or the Reverend Graham. Unfortunately, they are also poorly documented and archaeologically little studied.

On the northern side of the Lake District are many settlements whose origin or growth can partially be associated with coal mining. Hewerhill today consists of two farmsteads. At first sight, its place-name seems to betray its origins, but its name can be traced into the middle ages and seems to be derived from the name for a shieling on the hill. Settlement can be traced there to the 13th century.[23] Map analysis indicates that in the 18th and 19th centuries there were five separate properties there, as indicated by the number and location of wells in relation to property boundaries. The topography of the settlement indicates that it evolved as separate enclosures within or on the edge of unenclosed waste, with later enclosure of the waste fossilising the irregular layout. Two coal pits are depicted on 19th-century maps and the remains of others indicated by small spoil heaps can be identified in the field (Fig. 17.5).[24] A few kilometres to the west is Coalhole Hill. Aerial photographs reveal abandoned settlement remains there, and the First Edition Ordnance Survey map and later 18th-century county map both depict at least two blocks of buildings on the site.[25] It is likely that here a settlement of one or two properties was established by the later 18th century. Although there is no known field evidence for coal mining, the place name is clearly

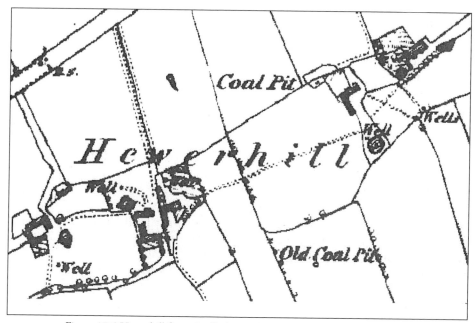

Figure 17.5 Hewerhill from the Ordnance Survey First Edition map, c. 1865

indicative of such activity. Although recorded only from 1700 the place seems to have been known as Colepitts in 1608.[26] Settlement decline is evident at both Hewerhill and Coalhole Hill by the later 19th century,[27] with the likely explanation being the concentration of coal mining in larger, better-capitalised collieries. Eventually coal mining became concentrated in west Cumbria and in the north Pennines. With only agriculture left to sustain settlement, Hewerhill shrank and Coalhole Hill was abandoned.

A settlement history more similar to that noted at Stock and Barnoldswick can be inferred for Dalston near Carlisle. Dalston was a large parish with a number of townships and manors, with the principal settlement belonging to the Bishop of Carlisle. On the later 18th-century county map the second largest nucleation after Dalston is a settlement labelled Nook.[28] This settlement was not a township or manorial centre, however. In 1774, it is depicted on the edge of waste, and a settlement is recorded there from at least the late 16th century,[29] though it may be the supposedly lost site of Cnokdentwald, which was recorded in the 14th century.[30] Its origin, history and role within Dalston's settlement hierarchy all require further investigation, but what is clear is that probably as early as 1823, the settlement shown in 1774 had shrunk considerably.[31] By the later 19th century, as today, it consisted of only three dispersed properties at the end of Nook Lane. Aerial photographs indicate that some earthworks relating to the former settlement area survive on the east side of the lane.[32]

Given the lack of research undertaken on this settlement reasons for its shrinkage can only be tentatively ascribed, but Dalston grew rapidly as a manufacturing centre from the late 18th century. By 1829 there were four cotton mills within Dalston,[33] which had developed into a large village. The main area of mill development was at Buckabank, where there were three cotton mills, a linen mill and a foundry as well as Bishop's Mill, a corn mill, and on the opposite bank of the Caldew a brewery. It seems likely that this industrial development at Dalston, and the opportunities it afforded, was linked to the shrinkage of Nook. Certainly, Dalston grew as a result of industrialisation, and today's town still retains the character of a prosperous late Georgian community. Some of this growth appears to have included bespoke workers' accommodation. To the immediate north of the centre of Dalston, in an area now largely occupied by modern industrial developments, was Low Green Mill. Probably in existence as a cotton mill by 1811,[34] it is physically associated on the First Edition OS map with a settlement formed of rows and courts known as Old Village, Village and New Village (Fig. 17.6).[35] None of these communities seem to have existed in 1774, and the settlement was largely abandoned by the 1890s, by which time Low Green Mill had gone out of operation.[36] This settlement, which owed its origins to industrial development, seems to have been abandoned as a result of such development as it presumably became a victim of the concentration of the cotton industry away from Cumbria into east Lancashire and Manchester.

At Dalton on the Cumbria/Lancashire border is the site of one of Cumbria's better-known supposed deserted medieval settlements. Until 1895, Dalton lay in Lancashire, and the parish boundary between it and neighbouring Burton-in-Kendal formed the county border. Linking earthwork survey undertaken in the 1960s and 1980s with GIS-based map analysis, aerial photographs and documentary research untangled the settlement history of the parish and greatly altered the understanding of the nature of its archaeological remains. Throughout the township there are highly visible earthworks and orthostatic stone foundations, and some of these features have been designated as scheduled monuments (Fig. 17.7).

RIGHT
Figure 17.6 Old Village, Village and New Village at Dalston from Ordnance Survey First Edition map, c. 1865.

RIGHT
Figure 17.7 Orthostatic
settlement remains at
Dalton

The designated earthworks do not represent the remains of a medieval settlement. Rather, they represent multiple-phases of post-medieval occupation, and many earthworks can be related directly to features shown on a map of 1694 (Fig. 17.8).[37] Additionally, the remains do not represent the desertion of a discrete settlement but the abandonment of an area forming part of a larger settlement. The area that was abandoned was a post-medieval extension to a medieval settlement, and in that way shares similarities with Llanmaes and Stock. The area scheduled as a deserted medieval village appears to have been thriving in 1694 but had already shrunk by 1800, though the most recent house to have been built in the area dates between 1837 and 1865 and is a still-standing ruin.[38] The last to be built, it was also the last to be abandoned. Single-storey and three-celled, it seems typical of the character of the buildings represented in the area as multi-cellular earthworks. Other than the nature of the buildings, the irregular nature of the settlement pattern and its lack of a relationship with the surrounding evidence of a medieval field system all indicate that the settlement was post-medieval in origin. This post-medieval settlement expansion can partially be explained by the possible greater availability of farm land following the opening up of a former deer park, but may also have been possible because of the presence in the parish of iron manufacturing in the 17th century.[39]

At Dalton there are a number of factors that may have contributed to settlement shrinkage from the 17th century. Iron production ceased by the 18th century. In 1661, neighbouring Burton was made a borough,[40] and during the 18th century may have acted as a local attraction, especially when in the middle of the 18th century it became a coaching stop following the opening of the turnpike. Another likely stimulus to the abandonment of tenanted farm holdings at Dalton in the later 18th century was the development of nearby Holme Mills as an industrial hamlet.[41] Later still, the remnants of an already weakened community may have been easily attracted by the industrial employment opportunities on offer in Lancaster and Kendal.

Figure 17.8 Aerial photograph of post-medieval settlement earthworks at Dalton
(© Cumbria County Council)

CONCLUSION

There are a number of conclusions that can be drawn from these disparate observations. Firstly, it is not uncommon for the remains of post-medieval shrinkages to be considered to be of medieval origin and even protected through scheduling as such, as at both Stock and Dalton. Hence a lack of understanding regarding the processes of post-medieval settlement shrinkage and desertion can lead to misdirected research and ill-informed heritage management strategies. Many of the settlement areas affected by post-medieval abandonment are of 16th- or 17th-century origin and usually associated in part with some sort of industrial activity. They are short-lived, often being abandoned in the 18th and 19th centuries, and indicative of the short duration of the favourable socioeconomic conditions that created them. Post-medieval nucleated shrinkages are often distinct in character from medieval remains as they do not fit within a medieval pattern of usually communally organised field systems and regular crofts, to an extent both a facet of strong manorial control driving the process of settlement planning. Post-medieval settlements may appear as an intrusion into this previously established pattern, and are often complex and irregular in layout. This probably reflects the lack of centralised control behind their formation. Many of these post-medieval settlement expansions are marginal in terms of physical location and/or position within the settlement hierarchy. They were physically, economically and mentally outwith the prevailing medieval-derived agrarian socioeconomic structure and thus highly susceptible to external pressures. One of the most significant of these pressures was industrialisation, which could attract migrants from these settlements at both a local and regional level. Other processes were under way too, such as estate reorganisation and farm amalgamation, and these often acted in tandem with industrialisation to bring about the demise of these rural settlements.

Finally, it is difficult to prove conclusively that industrialisation was the primary factor in the desertion or shrinkage of many post-medieval settlements, and much more work is required on this topic. Here industrialisation as a stimulus to settlement shrinkage and desertion has been inferred on the basis of likelihood. In some cases, documentary research into individual families identified as linked to abandoned holdings may help to test this inference. For the most part, however, these settlements are seldom well-documented and archaeological approaches to them are essential. That these approaches should be theoretically informed and challenge orthodoxies is crucial in order to avoid previous misconceptions and assumptions and to develop appropriately informed research and conservation strategies.

ACKNOWLEDGEMENTS

Thanks to Ken Davies (Lancashire County Council) for copies of the Stock maps and aerial photograph.

NOTES

1. Newman & Wilkinson 1996.
2. Newman & Wilkinson 1996, 229–30; National Library of Wales (NLW) MS 13152A, 233–8.
3. Information from the Glamorgan–Gwent historic environment record.
4. Lewis 1848, 80.
5. Newman 1996.
6. Neil *et al.* 1992.
7. Egerton Lea 2002.
8. Newman 1996, 118.
9. Lancashire Record Office (LRO) DDX 160/1.
10. Darlington 2003.
11. LRO DDX 160/2.
12. Darlington 2003, 80.
13. LRO DDX 160/1.
14. Darlington 2003, 81–2.
15. Turner 1992, 6.
16. Newman and Hartley 2006.
17. Darlington 2003, 83–5.
18. Lancaster University Archaeological Unit (LUAU) 1997.
19. Egerton Lea 2001.
20. Cumbria County Council aerial photograph CCC 2468, 17.
21. Nicholson & Burn 1777, 440.
22. Parsons & White 1829, 594.
23. Armstrong *et al.* 1950.
24. Ordnance Survey, First Edition Six Inches to One Mile, and Second Edition Six Inches to One Mile.
25. Donald 1774.
26. Armstrong *et al.* 1950, 331.
27. Ordnance Survey, Second Edition Six Inches to One Mile.
28. Donald 1774.
29. Donald 1774; Armstrong *et al.* 1950, 136.
30. Armstrong *et al.* 1950.
31. Greenwood 1823.
32. Information from the Cumbria historic environment record.
33. Parsons & White 1829.
34. The mill is likely to be Mr Watson's cotton-wist mill situated on the west bank of the Caldew, as described in Jollie 1811, **2**, 3.
35. Ordnance Survey, First Edition Six Inches to One Mile.
36. Donald 1774; Ordnance Survey, Second Edition Six Inches to One Mile.
37. Cumbria record Office (CRO) Kendal WPR/10 misc.
38. CRO WPR 10/1/4/22.
39. Newman 2007, 55.
40. Nicholson & Burn 1777, 237.
41. Newman 2004, 31.

BIBLIOGRAPHY

Armstrong, A.M., Mawer, A., Stenton, F.M. & Dickens, B. 1950 *The Place-Names of Cumberland*, English Place-Name Society **21**. Cambridge: Cambridge University Press.

Barker, D. & Cranstone, D. (eds) 2004, *The Archaeology of Industrialization*. Leeds: Maney.

Brooks, G. & Irwin, C. (eds) 2003 *Master of Them All: Iron Making in Cumbria*. Carlisle: Cumbria Industrial History Society.

Darlington, J. 2003, 'Industrialisation and rural desertion. Some examples from 19th- and 20th-century Lancashire', in Nevell (ed.), 2003, 79–85.

Donald, T. 1774, *Map of Cumberland*. London: J. Hodgkinson.

Greenwood, J. 1823 *Map of Cumberland*. Greenwood, London: Pringle & Co.

Jollie, F. 1811, *Jollie's Cumberland Guide and Directory*, Part **2**, Carlisle: F. Jollie & Sons.

Lewis, S. 1848, *A Topographical Dictionary of Wales* (3rd edn). London: S. Lewis & Co.

Neil, N., Quartermaine, J. & Tostevin, P. 1992, 'Rufford New Hall and Park: archaeological evaluation of a shrunken medieval village', *Medieval Settlement Research Group Annual Report* **7**: 37–40.

Nevell, M. (ed.) 2003, *From Farmer to Factory Owner: Models, Methodology and Industrialisation*, Archaeology North West **6**. Manchester: CBA North West.

Newman, C. & Hartley S., 2006, *Barnoldswick Historic Town Assessment Report*. Preston: Lancashire County Council & Egerton Lea Consultancy.

Newman, R. (ed.) 1996a, *The Archaeology of Lancashire: Present State and Future Priorities*. Lancaster: LUAU.

Newman, R. 1996b, 'Medieval rural settlement', in Newman (ed.), 1996a.

Newman, R. 2004, 'Industrial rural settlements: genesis, character and context 1550–1900', in Barker & Cranstone (eds), 2004, 25–34.

Newman, R. 2007, 'The bloomsmithies of south Westmorland and north Lancashire', in Brooks & Irwin (eds), 2007, 49–64.

Newman, R. & Wilkinson, P. 1996, 'Excavations at Llanmaes, near Llantwit Major, South Glamorgan', *Post-Medieval Archaeology,* **30**: 187–233.

Nicholson, J. & Burn, R. 1777, *The History and Antiquities of the Counties of Westmorland and Cumberland* (vol. 1). London: W. Strathan & T. Cadell.

Ordnance Survey, First and Second Edition Six Inches to One Mile maps.

Parsons, W. & White, W. 1829, *History and Gazetteer of the Counties of Cumberland and Westmorland*. Newcastle-upon-Tyne: W. White & Co.

Turner, W. 1992, *Riot! The Story of the East Lancashire Loom Breakers in 1826*. Preston: Lancashire County Books.

UNPUBLISHED SOURCES

Cumbria Record Office, Kendal, WPR/10 misc. – estate map of 1694 copied 1730.

Cumbria Record Office, Kendal, WPR 10/1/4/ – tithe map of 1837.

Egerton Lea, 2001, 'Holcombe Moor, Bury. Archaeological Assessment Report', unpub. client report.

Egerton Lea, 2002, 'Rufford Park, Lancashire. Historical Appraisal and Restoration Plan', unpub. client report.

Lancashire Record Office, DDX 160/1 Bracewell – estate map 1717.

Lancashire Record Office, DDX 160/2 Bracewell – estate map 1796.

LUAU 1997, 'North West Water's Forest of Bowland Estate, Lancashire. Archaeological Survey Report', unpub. client report.

National Library of Wales, MS 13152A, 233–8 – Iolo Morgannwg manuscript.

Understanding Landscape: Inter-disciplinary Dialogue and the Post-medieval Countryside

By CHRIS DALGLISH

This chapter explores some current traditions in post-medieval landscape archaeology and in landscape studies as practised by other relevant disciplines. It advocates an approach to landscape that aims to mediate between a well-grounded understanding of material conditions, possibilities and constraints, on the one hand, and human actions and experiences, on the other. It argues that this is best realised through a cross-disciplinary dialogue with a particular focus on the recursive relationship between the varied evidence, methods and interpretations of the different interested disciplines. However, the aim of this dialogue should not be the final resolution of dissonances between different lines of evidence and interpretation. While a common basis is required for any effective collaboration, it is argued here that the most productive way forward is to seek to value rather than erase persistent dissonance. These general issues in post-medieval landscape studies are explored in detail through a case study: the early history of the estate of the Campbells of Glenorchy in the Scottish Highlands.

INTRODUCTION

In recent decades, landscape has emerged as a subject of some importance within post-medieval archaeology, although no single approach has come to dominate the field and perspectives range from those with a strict empiricism to those seeking an understanding of past experiences and meanings. At the same time, landscape has become more of a concern for other historical disciplines, each of which has its own perspective: drawing on different evidence, employing its own methodologies and seeking to address its own interpretive concerns.

In the spirit of dialogue engendered by the *Crossing Paths or Sharing Tracks?* conference, my aim is to consider the benefits that a cross-disciplinary dialogue might have for our understanding of the post-medieval landscape, and the shape that such a dialogue should take. My starting point is a consideration of two current traditions in landscape archaeology, referred to here as evolutionary landscape history and the experiential approach. Each of these has made a significant contribution to landscape studies, but I will argue that neither is adequate in its current form.

To further the discussion, I will use the example of environmental history to exemplify the potential of a cross-disciplinary dialogue concerning landscape. This subject has brought historians, environmental scientists and others together through a common interest in the relationship between humans and the environment. To realise effective collaboration, the disciplines concerned have recognised the need to make adjustments in their diverse evidence, methods and interpretive frameworks. Developments in environmental history thus provide us with food for thought in considering how we might further our own concern for landscape.

Throughout, I will explore aspects of landscape studies with reference to the context with which I am most familiar: the post-medieval Scottish countryside. I will also consider the subject through a particular case study: the genesis and development of the estate of the Campbells of Glenorchy in the Scottish Highlands. Through this example, I hope to outline an approach to landscape that is of much wider relevance. This approach seeks to mediate between a well-grounded understanding of complex and dynamic material conditions, possibilities and constraints, on the one hand, and changing human actions and experiences, on the other. I will argue that this is best realised by integrating the evidence and interpretations of various interested disciplines. Such integration requires a cross-disciplinary dialogue that recognises that there is a recursive relationship between evidence, method and interpretation and that adjustments in one area require adjustments to be made in others. I do not believe that the final resolution of dissonances that exist between the evidence and interpretations of the different disciplines is possible, or desirable. While a common basis is required for any effective dialogue, the most productive way forward lies in taking a stance that seeks to value rather than erase persistent dissonance.

EVOLUTIONARY LANDSCAPE HISTORY

Landscape is still a relatively young subject of inquiry in Scottish archaeology. While there is no single approach to this subject, perhaps the most prominent is what I will refer to here as evolutionary landscape history and characterise through the work of its leading proponent: the Royal Commission on the Ancient and Historical Monuments of Scotland (RCAHMS).[1] For much of its history, RCAHMS has focused on the recording of individual (or 'unitary') monuments for publication in a series of County Inventories. These Inventories were intended to eventually provide a completed record of Scotland's more important monuments. However, from the 1980s, this aim came to be seen as impractical and outmoded as the concept of a finite record was challenged and the survey of unitary monuments, divorced from their landscape context, came to be seen as unsatisfactory.

Arising from these adjustments, a synthetic approach to landscape has gradually emerged. The first of RCAHMS' major landscape publications – North-East Perth (1990)[2] – marked a departure in its consideration of certain extensive groupings of archaeological remains (Fig. 18.1), but still owed much to the Inventory tradition in continuing to describe numbers of unitary monuments. Since North-East Perth, subsequent major landscape surveys have progressively moved further away from the Inventory tradition.[3]

In these surveys, the area targeted for recording has been reduced from the County to more discrete regions: portions of a county, a river catchment, an island, a glen. Meanwhile,

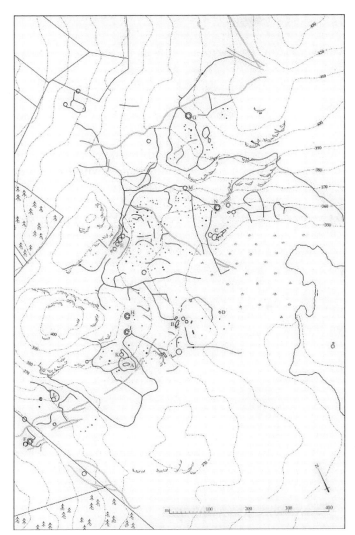

LEFT
Figure 18.1 Drumturn Burn: an
extensive archaeological landscape
lying at c. 330–430m AOD.
Most of the features date to the
late prehistoric or early historic
periods: hut circles, field systems
and Pitcarmick-type buildings
(sub-rectangular structures
probably dating to the later first
millennium AD). The plan is
an overlay of RCAHMS survey
data on an Ordnance Survey
base map (originally published as
RCAHMS 1990, fig. 124.4C).
Crown Copyright: RCAHMS;
reproduced by kind permission
of Ordnance Survey, © Crown
copyright.

the scope of survey has widened: ephemeral remains and a wider variety of monuments are
now routinely recorded, as are extensive areas of archaeological survival. Partly as a result
of an increased interest in multi-period landscapes, and of the high incidence of later-
period remains in such landscapes, the chronological scope of survey has also expanded.
The earlier Inventories adopted the Anglo-Scottish Union of 1707 as their chronological
cut-off, and even the later Inventories were selective in their post-1707 coverage. RCAHMS
now recognises no such chronological limit.

These changes in scope and subject matter are bound up with the development of a
particular perspective on landscape interpretation – evolutionary landscape history – which
seeks to locate individual archaeological features within broader evolutionary narratives.

In abstract, these narratives emerge from a three-stage process: individual monuments and areas of archaeology are identified and recorded; they are grouped by type, period and association to identify broader, synchronous patterns; and then these individual patterns are ordered in a chronology of landscape evolution. Explanations for the character of this evolution are sought in broad processes of development and major landscape events, such as settlement expansion or demographic change.

This approach is perhaps at its most impressive when dealing with landscapes with a significant upland component, with extensive areas of archaeological survival.[4] In an idealised example, the higher ground might present extensive and well-preserved prehistoric and early historic remains, representing several episodes of expansion and contraction in settlement and cultivation (Fig. 18.1). The survival of these earlier remains will have been facilitated by a subsequent contraction, perhaps evidenced today by a zone of post-medieval and occasionally medieval settlement and cultivation remains on the lower slopes (Fig. 18.2). In turn, this latter zone will have been preserved by another contraction of settlement and cultivation, and the lowest ground will be occupied today by modern farms and fields, and perhaps some isolated monuments or buried archaeological remains.

Figure 18.2 Glen Shee. Like Fig. 18.1, this plan derives from the RCAHMS study of north-east Perth (RCAHMS 1990, fig. 278). It shows an extensive area of post-medieval settlement and cultivation on the lower slopes and floor of the glen at c. 350–400m AOD. Small clusters of buildings lie among cultivation remains, separated from the hill ground by a head dyke. The remains lie just beyond the limits of modern settlement: later farmsteads are visible on the eastern and western edges of the plan. Crown Copyright: RCAHMS; reproduced by kind permission of Ordnance Survey, © Crown copyright.

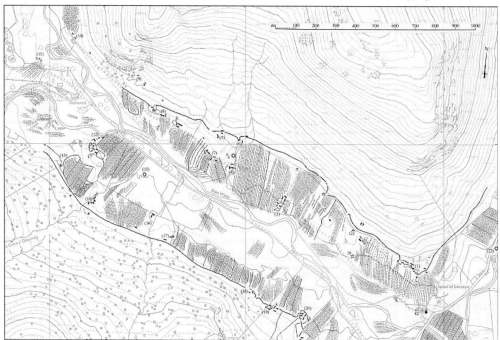

Survey of a landscape like this would identify, characterise and record its different archaeological zones, producing, in effect, a static pattern. To move from there to an evolutionary narrative, the different elements of the landscape need to be placed in chronological order by dating their origin and demise. Earlier landscape surveys tackled this issue of chronology by assigning archaeological remains to periods on the basis of their visible characteristics and by comparison with excavated examples. More recently, increasing reference has been made to documentary and environmental data in the construction of chronologies and for other purposes.[5]

In this context, the integration of environmental evidence has not been particularly successful, certainly for the medieval and post-medieval periods. The environmental analysis does often seek to identify broad patterns of evolution in geology, climate, landform, soils and vegetation.[6] However, while the archaeological and environmental studies might operate with similar conceptual frameworks, meaningful integration of the two is hindered by the millennial or sub-millennial and regional scales at which the environmental analysis operates (a point to which we will return). This problem is particularly acute for historical periods, where the environmental literature focuses on long-term and extensive trends, like the 'medieval warm period' or 'little ice age'. Meanwhile, the archaeology works with a more refined chronology of centuries, generations and decades and with more localised landscapes. As a result, the environmental evidence often provides little more than a backdrop for the archaeology, and little meaningful connection is made between the two.

For later periods, the integration of archaeological and documentary evidence has been more successful.[7] Here, archaeology maps and classifies material remains on the ground, constructing a mosaic of land-use patterns and a rough chronology of landscape development; documents allow this chronology to be refined. Documents have been used to fill gaps in the archaeological 'record' (e.g. reconstructing settlement patterns where archaeological survival is poor); to relate the archaeology to less tangible aspects of the landscape (e.g. land divisions like the estate or parish); explain settlement and land-use patterns by identifying the general processes and practices lying behind them (farming regimes, population dynamics, tenancy structures etc.); and, where possible, to identify the human agencies of change (e.g. individual landowners).

THE EXPERIENTIAL APPROACH

Evolutionary landscape history is part of a wider tradition in archaeology, which treats landscapes as palimpsests of material remains whose individual elements are to be prized apart and ordered.[8] This tradition has been challenged on a number of grounds.[9] It treats landscapes as objects: passive environments upon which people have had an effect, but which seemingly played no active part in the production of social practices and meanings. People tend to be absent from the narratives produced: the landscape is virtually uninhabited, and explanation is sought in broad and impersonal forces like settlement expansion or population change. This leaves us some way short of an understanding of past societies and their engagement with the landscape, providing only 'a history of things which have been done to the land'.[10]

In response, various approaches have been developed that seek to humanise landscape archaeology, drawing on phenomenology, practice theory and other conceptual frameworks.[11] While individual approaches may vary here, they all emphasise experience: social relationships and human understandings of the world do not develop in the abstract, but emerge from experience of the world and from routine actions within it. To understand past societies, we must understand how people moved through their world and experienced it through routine tasks, and how this experience was directed and controlled by others and by the character of the landscape itself. They also foreground the qualitative aspects of landscape: issues of meaning, memory and place. The landscape is not undifferentiated space, but a network of places; locales associated with particular cultural meanings or social memories and made meaningful through practices that take place there. The relationship between people and landscape is also recursive. Landscapes are not passive stages for action but the material conditions of and resources for action with an active role – people do not simply exploit the landscape or reshape it; they too are shaped by it. Lastly, experience and meaning are multiple and contested. Different people experience and understand a landscape in different ways. Landscapes can thus be contested, and social relationships can be contested through them.

This perspective has been adopted in various studies of the post-medieval Scottish landscape,[12] particularly focusing upon routine farming practices and drawing their inspiration from phenomenology (especially Tilley's *A Phenomenology of Landscape*)[13] and the 'dwelling perspective' advocated by Tim Ingold.[14] Such works usually depart by describing a typical landscape of the period before the Improvements and Clearances of the later 18th and 19th centuries. This landscape is characterised as one of townships set among unenclosed fields, beyond which lay open hill pastures and related shielings (transhumance sites). This landscape was experienced through routine practice. The townships were nodes within broader taskscapes formed as people ploughed the fields and tended their livestock. These practices and their associated places were dispersed throughout the landscape and linked by well-used paths. Experience of the landscape changed with the seasons, as people moved to the hill pastures in summer, for instance.

In engaging in these routines, people entered a recursive relationship with the landscape. The landscape actively shaped the practices and relationships through which communities were constituted. It embodied the social memory of the group, created and maintained through place-names, topographic folklore and recurrent activity at particular locales. This activity was sedimented onto the landscape as plough rigs, trackways or other features, providing future generations with tangible referents to their past; the experiences of these later generations were influenced by the landscape bequeathed by their predecessors.

In most cases, the narrative moves on to ask: how was the landscape contested? This question is posed in relation to the transformations associated with the Improvements and Clearances and is usually answered through an analysis of the two poles of domination and resistance. In this period, communities were severed from the landscapes that held meaning for them. They had to establish new routines and come to know new places. Meanwhile, the landscapes familiar to them were reordered through enclosure and drainage. The sediments of generations of activity were dispersed as townships decayed or were demolished, plough rigs were flattened, and connections between different places, like a township and its shielings, were broken. In resistance to such transformation, some people chose to reappropriate cleared landscapes through squatting, for example.[15] Others created new meaningful places through practices such as illicit whisky distilling at hidden locations in the hills.[16]

Such accounts seek to humanise the past by narrating how people may have experienced and understood their landscape, and they have certainly prompted us to reconsider our approach to landscape. However, the experiential tradition too has been the subject of critique.[17] Experiential analyses tend to be parochial in that they present landscapes and communities as sealed, cohesive units, quite separate from the wider world. In the Scottish case, this is most true of narratives of the pre-Improvement period. They can also be ahistorical. Experiential narratives, rather than humanising the past, can actually dehumanise it by describing static and homogenous communities: everyone experiences the same landscape in the same way, even if the potential for difference is acknowledged in theory. In the Scottish examples, discussion of different and contested experiences and understandings tends to be reduced to a friction between two internally coherent groups (the estate and the tenantry) and confined to the period of Improvement. Lastly, such narratives can seem to be divorced from the evidence. They often achieve their effect by describing idealised, abstract landscapes and experiences. The same narrative is reproduced time and again, often with only a limited correlation between it and the specific landscape to which it refers.

In broad terms, both of the two main current traditions in landscape archaeology are problematical enough to suggest that neither is adequate in its current form. This does not mean that there is nothing of value to be drawn from either. The approach advocated below draws on the body of theory that emphasises the recursive relationship between people and landscape, the centrality of routine and the potential for different and contested experiences and understandings. It also seeks to further our understanding of the people–landscape dynamic through the rigorous interrogation of the relevant material evidence. I broadly agree, therefore, with previous calls for archaeologists to value the perspective afforded by the experiential tradition *and* the empirical rigour of 'traditional' landscape archaeology.[18] However, I am suggesting more than a straightforward marriage between the theory of one and the evidence produced by the other. If we acknowledge that there is a recursive relationship between interpretation, evidence and the methods through which evidence is constructed, it follows that the effective integration of these elements may entail adjustments in all three.[19] It is thus not straightforward to approach questions developed in one conceptual context with evidence produced in another.

As we seek to pay closer attention to the variability and dynamism of our evidence, we need to discuss how this conditions the questions we might ask of it. As we reconsider what it is that we want to know, we must discuss how our evidence and methods can be reconstructed to allow the production of that knowledge. This dialogue must also extend beyond archaeology: in aiming to understand the relationship between people and landscape in some depth, we should engage those other disciplines for whom landscape is also a concern.[20] As noted above, the effective combination of archaeological, documentary and environmental analyses has often proven to be difficult – not least because of barriers erected by incompatible scales of evidence and interpretation. To better realise the potential of inter-disciplinary interpretation, we must reflect on how these barriers might be breached, both conceptually and methodologically.

Now more than ever, landscape provides a common interest for archaeology, history and many other disciplines.[21] Scotland has a long tradition of documentary landscape history, which has recently developed in new ways, most notably through the emergence of environmental history. Environmental history is significant here because of its emphasis on active inter-disciplinary collaboration, which has engendered debate on the relationships between interpretation, method and evidence.

ENVIRONMENTAL HISTORY AND CROSS-DISCIPLINARY DIALOGUE

Following its 1970s emergence outside Europe, environmental history has since become a significant concern in the Netherlands, Scandinavia and Britain.[22] Scottish historians began to show a serious interest in the subject during the 1990s.[23] The core aim of environmental history – investigation of the relationship between humans and the environment[24] – provides the basis for common cause with landscape archaeology. Within this broad human–environment nexus, Scottish environmental historians have explored a range of topics: pollution; waste; the cultural meanings of environments; land-use regimes; and others.[25] Here, woodland history will serve to exemplify the perspective adopted by environmental historians.[26]

Figure 18.3 This former royal forest in Glen Finglas still retains the characteristics of a wood pasture: a thin canopy with open ground between the trees, many of which have been cut as low pollards to place the new growth just out of the reach of grazing animals.

Woodland history tends towards a landscape scale of analysis, with its foundations laid by plotting the changing extent of Scotland's woodlands from documents and maps. Environmental historians have also characterised the diversity of the woods in terms of their species, densities and uses – oak coppices, pine timber woods, wood pastures, hunting forests and so on (Fig. 18.3). Attention has also turned to the routine practices of woodland use and management. Thus we have discussions of the uses to which timber was put (e.g. in building, in making tools and other objects, for fuel), the woods as an industrial resource (charcoal for the iron industry, bark for tanning), and the combined use of woodlands for these and other purposes, such as grazing. Much of this has been concerned with the impacts people have had on woodlands: their extent, biodiversity and other characteristics. However, the recursive relationship between people and woods has also been considered, particularly in relation to sustainability, with sustainable or unsustainable practices seen as enabling or constraining future action.

Consideration of the practices through which people engaged with the woodlands, and the recursive implications of those practices, leads to the different and competing interests in, uses and perceptions of the woods. Conflicts arose, for example, as tenants extended arable or pasture at the expense of woodlands set aside for hunting by landowners or the crown. Conversely, increasing commercial exploitation of the woods in the post-medieval period sometimes engendered protest from communities concerned for their traditional rights.

In exploring such issues, environmental history has developed in a direction that should allow, and require, closer integration with landscape archaeology. Environmental history is also relevant here because it is an explicitly inter-disciplinary endeavour, actively fostering collaboration between historians, environmental scientists and others.[27] In seeking collaboration, those who gather under the environmental history banner – perhaps most notably documentary historians and palynologists – have engaged in a dialogue about the problems of integration that stem from differences of evidential and interpretative resolution and scale.

As more generally in palaeo-environmental studies, palynology has tended to operate at the macro-scale of centuries and millennia.[28] Pollen sequences have traditionally been dated by radiocarbon assay, which presents few problems for prehistory as the other main source of knowledge for that period, archaeology, employs the same chronological tool. However, it does present a problem for the later historical periods, where documents provide a more-refined temporal resolution.[29] Palynologists have thus adjusted their methods and the nature of the evidence they produce,[30] working with short peat or sediment cores, of sufficient length to investigate the last 400–1000 years, sliced for sampling at intervals representing roughly one generation (*c.* 20 years). Palynologists have also begun to seek greater chronological resolution by employing a range of alternative dating methods (e.g. AMS radiocarbon assays, lead isotope dating, Caesium 137 dating, independently dated stratigraphic markers such as the first appearance of known-age exotic species).

Together, these methodological adjustments enable palynology to approach the temporal scale of documentary history. This allows more meaningful collaboration, but it does not mean that combined analysis is rendered unproblematic.[31] For example, detailed documentary sources tend to be confined to the period of the last four hundred years and coverage within that period is discontinuous. Documents thus provide good qualitative information for certain periods within the more recent past, but rarely support long-term quantitative analysis. Pollen diagrams, on the other hand, tend to provide a more continuous sequence and are amenable to the quantitative analysis of broader trends. The two strands of evidence retain differences of temporal coverage and resolution; and there remains an interpretative difference between the two disciplines, as historians focus on qualitative questions and environmental scientists on quantitative ones.

Running parallel has been a dialogue concerning spatial scale.[32] Many of the written records relevant to the post-medieval landscape were generated by the large estates typical of Scottish landownership. While tenancy regulations or general managerial commentary can evidence activity at specific locales, they are most often amenable to interpretation at the estate level. The documentary evidence also contains spatial discontinuities, providing little specific detail on activity away from the core farms, at shieling sites, for example. There is a more restricted spatial scale to the pollen evidence that has so far been produced with a refined temporal resolution. A peat core might have a primary pollen catchment of 50m, providing evidence more weakly for an area of up to 1km. Although it should be possible to extrapolate from the local to regional scale as more individual sequences are produced, there are presently real differences in the spatial comparability of the historical and environmental strands of evidence and interpretation, and each has its own discontinuities.

Nevertheless, the dialogue between history and environmental science has been productive. The development of common interpretive concerns and of new methods and evidence to address those concerns has facilitated greater collaboration between the two disciplines. While differences of evidential resolution and coverage and interpretative emphasis (quantitative vs qualitative) persist, these are now better understood. Furthermore – and this will be a point familiar to historical archaeologists – greater dialogue has engendered a new perspective, which sees dissonances of evidence and interpretation as something to be valued not erased.[33] This lack of concordance creates a new interpretative space, where interpretation becomes a process of movement between various contrasting standpoints, each affording a new perspective on the others. There is great potential in seeking to exploit this lack of concordance in this way – a point I will now expand with reference to a theme with great significance for our understanding of the people–landscape dynamic in post-medieval Scotland and beyond: the genesis of the landed estate.

THE EMERGENCE OF THE LANDED ESTATE

The estate is a particular relationship between people and landscape, where land is objectified as a commodity and exploited for commercial gain. The estate is also a particular set of relationships between people, where a centralised administration seeks to exercise a high degree of control over production and relates to its tenantry in an objectified and economic manner. However, this is an abstract definition and individual estates would have emerged in particular circumstances. To preserve something of the nuance of this process, I will

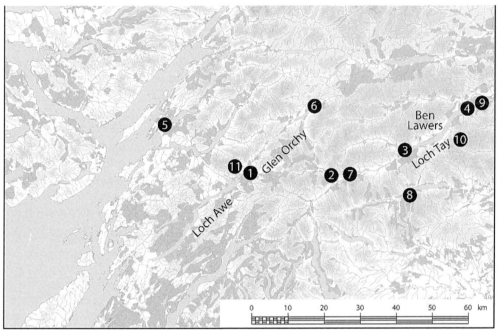

Figure 18.4 Sites mentioned in the text: the castles of Kilchurn (1), Strath Fillan (2), Finlarig (3), Isle of Loch Tay (4), Barcaldine (5), Achallader (6), Loch Dochart (7), Edinample (8) and Balloch (9); and the farms of Leadour (10) and Corries (11). The base map is © Crown Copyright/database right 2007. An Ordnance Survey/EDINA supplied service.

take one example: the estate of the Campbells of Glenorchy in the Scottish Highlands (Fig. 18.4).

The best-characterised archaeological landscape within this former estate lies on the southern aspect of Ben Lawers.[34] The later archaeology of Ben Lawers, and the surrounding region, is typical of that found in many upland parts of Scotland. Numerous ruinous 18th- and 19th-century townships and farmsteads lie on the lower ground. Some of these were established *de novo* in the period of Improvement. Others have deeper roots: although substantially remodelled *c.* 1800, the layouts of some townships betray their origins in the pre-Improvement period.

These settlements are surrounded by Improvement-era enclosed fields. Leading up from the settlements are a series of defined trackways, which pass through the enclosed fields to emerge on the hill ground above, eventually reaching peat banks and shielings. It is on this higher ground that we really begin to appreciate the time-depth of this landscape. There, a small number of medieval houses have been preserved by the later contraction of cultivation; hundreds of shieling huts have also been identified, and recent excavations have dated these to the period from the 15th century onwards.

Despite this, the present-day landscape remains most obviously a product of Improvement. Archaeologists have previously approached such landscapes in one of two ways: they have capitalised on the wealth of 18th- and 19th-century archaeology by taking the period of Improvement itself as their subject; or they have searched, often in vain, for the currently invisible core settlements of the preceding centuries.[35] However, if we abandon the idea that the core settlement is the only legitimate archaeological target – moving out from there to those places with more evident time-depth – we can begin to appreciate more of the changing and varied nature of pre-Improvement society and landscape.

The Campbells of Glenorchy established themselves in Glen Orchy and by Loch Awe in the 1430s, but rapidly spread to the west coast and to Loch Tay in the east.[36] Within this extensive territory, they held only a small amount of land in a direct way. Their position was achieved by acting as administrators for the crown and other local magnates and landowners, and by devolving local control through a network of allied kindreds. Through these offices and alliances, the Campbells exercised lordship over a much wider territory than they actually 'owned'.

Campbell engagement with the landscape in this period is most evident in the castles they built or acquired in the 15th and earlier 16th centuries.[37] These castles – Kilchurn, Strath Fillan, Finlarig and the Isle of Loch Tay – are widely dispersed throughout the area of Campbell influence and command the main routes through the mountains (Figs 18.4 & 18.5). In their pattern of dispersal and their association with churches, open-air assembly and court sites and gallows hills, these castles were placed to form a network of regional administrative centres.

Figure 18.5 Kilchurn Castle on Loch Awe: ancestral seat of the Campbells of Glenorchy. The rectangular tower in the centre dates to the first half of the 15th century.

From *c.* 1550, the Campbells moved to restructure their lordship within established geographical bounds, and sought to create a more proprietorial and direct form of lordship: an estate. They acquired extensive grants of land and sought to exclude most other local kindreds from the landholding structure. In place of these kindreds, they managed their estate through their immediate family and a body of professional staff.

The estate-building process entailed a shift in the relationship between lord and landscape. Within their established territory, the Campbells built five new castles: Barcaldine, Achallader, Loch Dochart, Edinample and Balloch.[38] Most of these were constructed on or near sites previously occupied by the chief families of other kindreds; through this castle-building programme, the Campbells sought to erase these kindreds from the landscape. Many of the existing Campbell castles also continued in use and were modified or rebuilt at this time. Together, this corpus of post-1550 castles represents a new intervention in the landscape, now more densely populated by and closely monitored from these centres.

Not least through a restructuring of the material components of their lordship, the Campbells sought to achieve more direct and centralised control of a territory they had formerly occupied as heads of a kin network. This centralising process is also evident in the documentary archive of the estate: records become more numerous and detailed from the late 16th century onwards.[39] These documents, like the castles of the same period, were a material resource for action; a technology through which a lordship based in personal relationships was replaced by one exercised at a remove.

The estate archive also has a lot to tell about the early operation of the estate and its owners' attitudes towards the landscape. Rentals suggest that most farms had a mixed economy, but were subject to significant relative differences in the balance of their rent bundle.[40] In general, farms in the more fertile districts – on the west coast and by Loch Tay – owed relatively large amounts in grain. In rentals for the interior parts of the estate, cattle or dairy produce feature much more prominently. The estate appears to have drawn a distinction, then, between stock or dairy farms and arable farms. While this distinction might have been less evident in the subsistence economy of a farm, it appears to have mattered in terms of its rental economy. The estate's differing expectations of its component landscapes would thus have had a real impact on the daily practices of the tenantry and their own engagement with those landscapes.[41]

Alongside this spatial variation, we also see change through time. While, traditionally, pre-Improvement farming has been seen as organised through largely unchanging routines, the economies of farms in this period actually underwent significant change.[42] Before *c.* 1600, farms typically had a balanced emphasis on arable and pasture, both geared to the provision of all-round subsistence for the tenants themselves and the chiefly household.[43] Rents in kind were consumed directly by chiefs in supporting their kinsmen and tenants in hard times, maintaining a retinue, hosting feasts and building alliances.[44] These food rents were thus charged with a social rather than an economic value.[45] From *c.* 1600, a more commercial attitude to production and rent began to emerge. For the Highlands as a whole, there were two broad strategies whereby the produce of an estate was transformed into a cash income: landlords began to market the produce they had accumulated as rent; and/or they replaced rents in kind with rents in cash.[46]

Although cash rents first appeared in the Highlands in the 16th century, they were slow in replacing rents in kind in many areas.[47] Where they were introduced, they allowed tenants to determine the balance of their economy with some freedom.[48] Some tenants chose to market grain, or higher-value whisky, to provide for their rent. More commonly, tenants began to market livestock, allowing them to increase the arable that was central to their subsistence needs by shifting their rental burden from arable (which was scarce) to pasture (which was abundant). This created a potential tension between the subsistence and rental sectors of the farm; between the desire to expand arable at the expense of winter pasture and meadow.

The Glenorchy estate continued, if not exclusively, to expect rents in kind, which they marketed themselves. They continued to receive large quantities of grain into the 18th century, particularly from the estate's select arable districts.[49] However, livestock, especially cattle, were perhaps the most marketable of the estate's products and, certainly for the inner districts, the estate focused increasingly on commercial cattle production. The Campbells were regularly marketing stock from at least the late 16th century.[50] By that time, they had also moved beyond the simple marketing of stock acquired as rent to institute an estate-wide system of livestock production.[51] While tenants did maintain their own stock and pass these on as rent, many also herded stock on behalf of the estate under a system known as steelbow tenure. Under steelbow, tenants were charged with raising estate-owned livestock and encouraged to specialise in livestock production at the expense of arable farming. The co-ordinated, commercial production of livestock is also evident in references to bowhouses – central farms where livestock were grazed after they had been collected in from the tenants for marketing.

Beyond the fields and pastures of the farms, the emergence of the estate also created new relationships between landlord, tenant and other parts of the landscape – perhaps most notably the woodlands. From *c.* 1600, the estate increasingly perceived these woods as a commercial resource and sought to specialise their use. The Campbells were renowned planters and actively sought to increase the commercial usefulness of their woods.[52] Through the local baron court, they attempted to restrict the actions of their tenants and establish practices amenable to woodland vitality – tenants' grazing and timber rights were limited; shielings seen to be impinging on valuable woodland were removed; muirburn was regulated; and tree planting was encouraged.[53] In the early 18th century, the estate also began to lease woods to non-local, often English or Irish, entrepreneurs for their timber or for the production of charcoal to fuel industry.[54]

These are some of the more important developments in the early history of the estate. The Glenorchy archive is exceptionally rich and is most amenable to the analysis of such broad, estate-wide trends. The documents raise questions concerning the implications of the new estate economy for farming practices in specific locales, and suggest some of the tensions that would have arisen: between subsistence and commercial production; between arable and pasture; between traditional use rights and commercial pressures on the woodlands. However, the archive provides us with little material with which to explore these tensions.

Changing practices and the tensions they engendered brought the estate and its tenants into conflict. Tensions would also have arisen within communities as people sought to accommodate different needs in their engagement with a single landscape. As such, to fully understand the early history of the estate, we need to find ways to approach this history at the scale of the farm. It is here that a combined documentary, archaeological and environmental analysis perhaps has its greatest potential. To expand, we can consider two recently studied locales: Leadour and Corries.

Leadour is a former farm and associated shieling on the south side of Loch Tay.[55] The farm survives as a small group of ruinous buildings and enclosures, all probably dating to the period of Improvement (Fig 18.6). The shieling lies some 2km distant and is evident today as a series of ruinous structures. Documentary evidence for Leadour only becomes available from the late 16th century, but recent pollen analysis has detailed land use in the preceding centuries.[56] In the medieval period, the farm was partly cultivated and partly under pasture. The shieling was characterised by a heather–grass mosaic typical of such high pastures. However, there is evidence for cultivation there, suggesting that use of the shieling was more varied than might normally be assumed; such sites are typically characterised as single-use transhumance pastures. The wider landscape was largely open, although there was some tree cover at specific locales. Around 1400, the few remaining trees at the shieling died out, but a new wood was established near the farm. The latter reached its maximum extent or density between 1540 and 1620, and was probably actively maintained as cultivation with

Figure 18.6 The farmstead at Leadour, in Gleann a' Chilleine on the south side of Loch Tay. The gable-ended building on the right is typical of abandoned Improvement-era houses in this area. The structure in the foreground, although more ruinous, is probably of similar age.

grazing continuing nearby. The trees were cleared *c.* 1620, consistent with a high number of court book entries regarding the destruction of this wood at that time.

The pollen evidence for the period after 1620 indicates further changes in land use.[57] In the mid 17th century, stock-raising was intensified at the farm and use of the shieling also intensified, with a peak in both pastoral and arable activity *c.* 1680 and a decline in vegetation diversity there between *c.* 1650 and *c.* 1760.

The pollen thus suggests a series of significant and probably related land-use changes in the 17th century: the woods near the farm were cleared by 1620; this was followed by (associated with?) more intense livestock rearing at both the farm and shieling; and, contemporaneously, cropping seems to have displaced from the farm to the shieling. All of this implies much greater dynamism in practice at both locales than we would normally assume. The environmental narrative also concords well with aspects of the archive evidence. The estate's bow books, which detail livestock and seed provided to tenants by the estate, indicate that Leadour specialised in cattle from the 1650s; they also describe some of the cattle provided to Leadour as 'English', suggesting that the estate was experimenting with different breeds.[58]

At Leadour, then, we have a good specific example of the changing practices associated with the emergence of the estate. Here, though, the environmental evidence allows us to go beyond the general trend towards intensified and specialised stock production to understand something of the tenants' actions in addressing the conflicts arising from this changing economy. As stocking increased around the farm and shieling, cultivation also intensified – something not evident from the documentary sources.[59] The tenants appear to have approached the developing tension between the demands of the wider estate economy and their own subsistence needs by bringing the shieling more fully into cultivation, maintaining something of a mixed economy under the pressure to specialise. Cultivation came to be identified more with the locale of the shieling than with that of the farm, with implications for tenants' daily routines, patterns of movement and understandings of their landscape. Here we also see something of the recursive people–landscape dynamic: previous generations, in grazing their cattle at the shieling, increased its fertility and provided an opportunity for their 17th-century descendents when they came under pressure to turn lower-lying cultivated ground over to pasture.

In changing circumstances, Leadour's tenants did not simply and passively react but made active choices, albeit constrained ones. This point is underlined when we turn to changing land use at Corries, which lies to the north of Loch Awe (Fig 18.7).[60] As at Leadour, the archaeology at Corries comprises the ruinous buildings and enclosures of a small farm with associated cultivation remains on the lower ground and stone footings representing shieling structures on the higher ground.[61] Pollen evidence from the shieling indicates that it lay within a long-standing wood pasture landscape.[62] Again, this mixed use would not normally be considered in standard accounts of such a site. Relatively open woods were present here as early as the period when sediment accumulation began *c.* AD 940. From the early 13th to late 15th centuries, there was a series of reductions and increases in tree growth and related changes in open grassland. However, throughout this period, the broad character

Figure 18.7 The shieling at Corries, to the north of Loch Awe. The denuded remains of a former shieling hut lie in the foreground. The shieling ground occupies a steep-sided natural bowl at the head of a glen, through which runs the tree-lined burn in the middle ground of the photograph (photo: Katinka Stentoft).

of the wood pasture appears to have been maintained; even when woodland composition appears to have been altered through selective management and planting between 1440 and 1490, areas of open pasture were retained. In the 16th and 17th centuries, local tree cover remained relatively stable and formed one element of an open or patchy mosaic that also included areas of grass, heath and mire. After *c.* 1680, the character of this wood pasture was transformed as local activity intensified; the removal of trees became more rapid after *c.* 1720, when grazing and burning also increased.

The surviving documentary evidence for Corries begins in the late 16th century.[63] By *c.* 1600, the farm's tenants appear to have had a long-standing interest in livestock. By the mid-17th century, evidence suggests that they were making significant cash profits from cattle sales.[64] The tenurial position of Corries' inhabitants also changed in the mid 1600s. Partly as a result of the civil wars and subsequent Commonwealth of the 1640s and 1650s, the Glenorchy Campbells began to experience financial difficulty. In 1656, they wadset Corries and several neighbouring farms to the tenants of the former: a wadset was a form of mortgage whereby lands were granted out by their owner in return for a sum of money. Corries' tenants thus acquired control of their farm, and others adjacent, until the principal sum that they had lent to their landlord was repaid. This becomes particularly interesting when we return to the pollen evidence. Although the tenants of Corries were marketing cattle by at least the mid-17th century, the balance of vegetation at the wooded shieling appears to have changed little as a result of grazing. However, around 1680, when the farm was wadset and cattle were increasing in market value, grazing intensified, making a significant impact on the local woodland.

The circumstances at Corries differed from those at Leadour: the stock at Corries belonged to the tenants, while much of the stock at Leadour belonged to the estate; and grazing at Corries intensified in a period when the tenants there had assumed greater control of their farm. Unlike those at Leadour, the tenants at Corries thus appear to have made the move towards specialised and intensified livestock farming with less direct pressure from the estate. At Leadour, the onset of commercial livestock farming created a tension between the tenants' need for subsistence arable and the estate's requirements for grazing; at Corries, the same development created a tension between the grazing demands of the tenants and the estate's expectations regarding the farm's woodlands. While the livestock belonged to the tenants and they had a significant degree of control over their farming practices, the woods at Corries continued to belong to the estate and were regulated through the local court.[65] The detrimental impact of intensified grazing on the woods at Corries was thus potentially contrary to the estate's interests: woodland grazing at Corries increased despite, and perhaps resulted in, renewed estate regulations on the protection and planting of trees there.

CONCLUSION

Drawing on the strengths of two traditions in landscape archaeology – evolutionary landscape history and the experiential approach – but recognising some of their limitations, I have argued for an approach to the post-medieval landscape that aims to mediate between a well-grounded understanding of complex and dynamic material conditions, possibilities and constraints, on the one hand, and changing human actions and experiences, on the other. To achieve this, we need to rethink our approach to landscape at both a conceptual and an operational level, and creating a dialogue between various disciplines is essential to this process. We must construct a more solid evidential base and give full regard to the complexities and dynamism of this evidence. To do this, we undoubtedly need to reconsider our methods of analysis – those methods that allow us to construct the evidence appropriate to the questions we seek to answer.

These questions, and our conceptual framework as a whole, will also change in recursive dialogue with our changing evidence and methods. An explicit consideration of the relationship between evidence, method and interpretation can resolve certain dissonances, such as hitherto-incommensurable differences in chronological resolution. However, it can also reveal other, more persistent dissonances; but these need not be debilitating – they can be productive. For this to be so, it is necessary to approach interpretation not with the aim of achieving the final resolution of these dissonances, but as a process of moving backwards and forwards through the space they create. In other words, the key is to explore the relationships between different and contrasting lines of evidence and interpretation. We might move, for example, between the small-scale and local, on the one hand, and wider historical processes, on the other. In doing so, we create what Charles Orser has referred to earlier in this volume as a 'dialectics of scale'.[66]

Through a case drawn from the central Scottish Highlands, I have endeavoured to sketch out how a dialectical approach to landscape that seeks to integrate different disciplinary perspectives might benefit our understanding of the post-medieval countryside. The pre-Improvement period was not one of static experiences, routines and landscapes. Rather, as the estate emerged and developed, its component landscapes and people's experiences of those landscapes changed, and did so in complex, contingent and contested ways. The nature of these changes was conditioned at the macro-scale by the estate and by changing economic circumstances, but it was also determined by tenants acting with reference to their own particular circumstances, including the possibilities and constraints established by specific landscapes. The routines and experiences of individual tenants were thus actively created by them, but always and at the same time with reference both to the specific nature of their landscape *and* the wider world. By moving between these contexts, we can begin to appreciate rural society and the human–landscape nexus in the post-medieval period in a more nuanced way.

ACKNOWLEDGEMENTS

My thanks to Audrey Horning for inviting me to contribute to the *Crossing Paths* conference and for her patience as an editor; and to Katinka Stentoft for Figure 18.7 and for her help in processing the other illustrations.

NOTES

1. cf. RCAHMS 1990, vii; RCAHMS 2004.
2. RCAHMS 1990.
3. cf. RCAHMS 1994; 1997; 2001; 2007.
4. e.g. RCAHMS 1990; 1997; 2001.
5. Especially RCAHMS 1997; 2001; 2007.
6. e.g. Tipping 1997; 2007.
7. cf. in particular RCAHMS 2001; 2007.
8. cf. Thomas 2001, 165; cf. also English Heritage 2007; Fleming 2006, 267.
9. e.g. Holtorf & Williams 2006, 236–7, 253–4; Thomas 2001, 165.
10. John Barrett quoted in Thomas 2001, 165.
11. For a general review, cf. Brück 2005; for reviews specific to historical archaeology, cf. DeCunzo & Ernstein 2006; Holtorf & Williams 2006; Pauls 2006.
12. e.g. Atkinson 2000; Given 2004, ch. 8; Lelong 2000; Symonds 1999; 2000; my own work (e.g. Dalglish 2003) has also placed an emphasis on routine and the mutual structuring of landscape and society, but has no explicit reliance on phenomenology or Ingold's 'dwelling perspective'.
13. Tilley 1994.
14. Ingold 1993.
15. cf. e.g. Fairhurst 1968, 143, 155–6, 163.
16. cf. Given 2004, ch. 8.
17. cf. Brück 2005; Fleming 2006; cf. Johnson 2005; 2006 for a relevant discussion of particularism in landscape archaeology.
18. e.g. Fleming 2006, 279.
19. cf. Hodder 1999; Jones 2002.
20. cf. Mrozowski 2006 on integrating the environment into our historical archaeologies.
21. Smout 2002, 9–10.
22. Smout 2000, 1.
23. cf. <http://www.st-andrews.ac.uk/envhist/> [last accessed May 2008]; <http://www.cehp.stir.ac.uk/> [last accessed May 2008].
24. Hamilton & Davies 2007, 25.
25. cf. <http://www.st-andrews.ac.uk/envhist/> [last accessed May 2008]; <http://www.cehp.stir.ac.uk/> [last accessed May 2008]; on specific topics, cf. Hingley & Ingram 2002; Davies & Watson 2007; Hamilton & Davies 2007; Ross nd; Tipping 2000; papers in Foster & Smout (eds) 1994.
26. cf. Hampson & Smout 2002; papers in Smout (ed.) 2003; Smout, MacDonald & Watson 2005.
27. cf. <http://www.st-andrews.ac.uk/envhist/> [last accessed May 2008]; <http://www.cehp.stir.ac.uk/> [last accessed May 2008].

28. Davies & Watson 2007, 1778; Hamilton & Davies 2007, 26.
29. Tipping 2000, 130.
30. cf. Davies & Watson 2007, 1779–80; Hamilton & Davies 2007, 26; Tipping 2000, 131.
31. Davies & Watson 2007, 1778, 1785.
32. Davies & Watson 2007, 1785–7; Hamilton & Davies 2007, 26–7.
33. Davies & Watson 2007, 1786–8; Hamilton & Davies 2007, 26–7, 32.
34. cf. Atkinson 2000; Boyle 2003; <http://www.benlawers.org.uk/> [last accessed 24 May 2008].
35. cf. Dalglish 2003, ch. 2; Lelong 2003.
36. cf. Dalglish 2005 for a summary and MacGregor 1989 for the analysis on which this is based.
37. cf. Dalglish 2005, 249–52.
38. cf. Dalglish 2005, 252–61.
39. Dodgshon 1998, 76.
40. Dodgshon 1998, 60, 62, 64–5, 76–7, 109, 174–6, 185.
41. Dodgshon 1998, 62, 76, 185.
42. Dodgshon 1998, 195-6.
43. Dodgshon 1998, 107–8, 196.
44. Dodgshon 1998, chapters 3 & 4.
45. Dodgshon 1998, 93.
46. Dodgshon 1998, 108.
47. Dodgshon 1998, 59–60, 68–9.
48. Dodgshon 1998, 110–12, 196–7.
49. Dodgshon 1998, 111.
50. Dodgshon 1998, 113.
51. Dodgshon 1998, 76–7, 107, 113, 162.
52. Smout et al. 2005, 160, 176.
53. Smout et al. 2005, 99 n.60, 110, 135, 160.
54. Smout et al. 2005, 179, 202–3, 246, 340–63; Stewart 2003, 108, 110–12.
55. cf. Hamilton & Davies 2007.
56. Hamilton & Davies 2007, 27.
57. Hamilton & Davies 2007, 28.
58. Hamilton & Davies 2007, 27–8.
59. Hamilton & Davies 2007, 28.
60. cf. Davies & Watson 2007.
61. Davies & Watson 2007, 1779.
62. Davies & Watson 2007, 1781–2, 1786.
63. The historical evidence for Corries is detailed in Davies & Watson 2007, 1782–5.
64. Davies & Watson 2007, 1783–4.
65. Davies & Watson 2007, 1787.
66. cf. Johnson 2006.

BIBLIOGRAPHY

Atkinson, J.A. 2000, 'Rural settlement on north Lochtayside: understanding the landscapes of change', in Atkinson *et al.* (eds), 2000,150–60.

Atkinson, J.A., Banks, I. & MacGregor, G. (eds) 2000. *From Townships to Farmsteads: Rural Settlement Studies in Scotland, England and Wales.* Oxford: Archaeopress.

Boyle, S. 2003, 'Ben Lawers: an improvement-period landscape on Lochtayside, Perthshire', in Govan (ed.), 2003, 17–29.

Brück, J. 2005, 'Experiencing the past? The development of a phenomenological archaeology in British prehistory', *Archaeological Dialogues* **12**(1): 45–72.

Dalglish, C. 2003, *Rural Society in the Age of Reason: An Archaeology of the Emergence of Modern Life in the Southern Scottish Highlands.* New York: Kluwer/Plenum.

Dalglish, C. 2005, 'An age of transition? Castles and the Scottish Highland estate in the 16th and 17th centuries', *Post-Medieval Archaeology* **39**(2): 243–66.

Davies, A.L. & Watson, F. 2007, 'Understanding the changing value of natural resources: an integrated palaeoecological-historical investigation into grazing–woodland interactions by Loch Awe, Western Highlands of Scotland', *Journal of Biogeography* **34**: 1777–91.

De Cunzo, L.A. & Ernstein, J.H. 2006, 'Landscapes, ideology and experience in historical archaeology', in Hicks & Beaudry (eds), 2006, 255–270.

Dodgshon, R.A. 1998, *From Chiefs to Landlords: Social and Economic Change in the Western Highlands and Islands, c.1493–1820.* Edinburgh: Edinburgh University Press.

English Heritage 2007, *Understanding the Archaeology of Landscape: A Guide to Good Recording Practice.* Swindon: English Heritage.

Fairhurst, H. 1968, 'Rosal: a deserted township in Strath Naver, Sutherland', *Proceedings of the Society of Antiquaries of Scotland* **100**: 135–69.

Fleming, A. 2006, 'Post-processual landscape archaeology: a critique', *Cambridge Archaeological Journal* **16**(3): 267–80.

Foster, S. & Smout, T.C. (eds) 1994, *The History of Soils and Field Systems*. Aberdeen: Scottish Cultural Press.

Given, M. 2004, *The Archaeology of the Colonized*. London: Routledge.

Govan, S. (ed.) 2003, *Medieval or Later Rural Settlement in Scotland: 10 Years On*. Edinburgh: Historic Scotland.

Hall, M. & Silliman, S.W. (eds) 2006, *Historical Archaeology*. Oxford: Blackwell Publishing.

Hamilton, A. & Davies, A. 2007, '"Written in the hills": an environmental history project in the Scottish uplands', *History Scotland* **7**(3): 25–32.

Hampson, A. & Smout, T.C. 2002, 'Trying to understand woods', in Smout (ed.), 2002, 87–95.

Hicks, D. & Beaudry, M.C. (eds) 2006, *The Cambridge Companion to Historical Archaeology*. Cambridge: Cambridge University Press.

Hingley, R. & Ingram, H.A.P. 2002, 'History as an aid to understanding peat bogs', in Smout (ed.), 2002, 60–86.

Hodder, I. 1999, *The Archaeological Process: An Introduction*. Oxford: Blackwell.

Holtorf, C. & Williams, H. 2006, 'Landscapes and memories', in Hicks & Beaudry (eds), 2006, 235–54.

Ingold, T. 1993, 'The temporality of the landscape', *World Archaeology* **25**(2): 152–74.

Johnson, M. 2005, 'On the particularism of English landscape archaeology', *International Journal of Historical Archaeology* **9**(2): 111–22.

Johnson, M. 2006, 'The tide reversed: prospects and potentials for a postcolonial archaeology of Europe', in Hall & Silliman (eds), 2006, 313–31.

Jones, A. 2002, *Archaeological Theory and Scientific Practice*. Cambridge: Cambridge University Press.

Lelong, O 2000, 'The prospect of the sea: responses to forced coastal resettlement in nineteenth century Sutherland', in Atkinson *et al.* (eds), 2000, 217–24.

Lelong, O. 2003, 'Finding medieval (or later) rural settlement in the Highlands and Islands: the case for optimism', in Govan (ed.), 2003, 7–16.

Mrozowski, S.A. 2006, 'Environments of history: biological dimensions of historical archaeology', in Hall & Silliman (eds), 2006, 23–41.

Pauls, E.P. 2006, 'The place of space: architecture, landscape, and social life', in Hall & Silliman (eds), 2006, 65–83.

RCAHMS 1990, *North-East Perth: An Archaeological Landscape*. Edinburgh: HMSO.

RCAHMS 1994, *South-East Perth: An Archaeological Landscape*. Edinburgh: HMSO.

RCAHMS 1997, *Eastern Dumfriesshire: An Archaeological Landscape*. Edinburgh: The Stationery Office.

RCAHMS 2001, *'Well Shelterd & Watered': Menstrie Glen, a Farming Landscape Near Stirling*. Edinburgh: RCAHMS.

RCAHMS 2004, *Survey and Recording Policy* <http://www.rcahms.gov.uk/RCAHMS_surveyandrecordingpolicy_2004.doc> [last modified April 2004].

RCAHMS 2007, *In the Shadow of Bennachie: A Field Archaeology of Donside, Aberdeenshire*. Edinburgh: Society of Antiquaries of Scotland/RCAHMS.

Ross, A. nd, *Assessing the Impact of Past Grazing Regimes: Transhumance in the Forest of Strathа'an, Banffshire*, AHRC Centre for Environmental History (Universities of Stirling & St Andrews) Short Report **3**. <http://www.cehp.stir.ac.uk/resources/documents/ross-transhumance.pdf>[last accessed May 2008].

Smout, T.C. 2000, *Nature Contested: Environmental History in Scotland and Northern England Since 1600*. Edinburgh: Edinburgh University Press.

Smout, T.C. 2002, 'Introduction', in Smout (ed.), 2002, 9–12.

Smout, T.C. (ed.) 2002, *Understanding the Historical Landscape in its Environmental Setting*. Dalkeith: Scottish Cultural Press.

Smout, T.C. (ed.) 2003, *People and Woods in Scotland: A History*. Edinburgh: Edinburgh University Press.

Smout, T.C., MacDonald, A.R. & Watson, F. 2005, *A History of the Native Woodlands of Scotland, 1500–1920*. Edinburgh: Edinburgh University Press.

Stewart, M. 2003, 'Using the woods, 1600–1850: (2) managing for profit', in Smout (ed.), 2003, 105–27.

Symonds, J. 1999, 'Toiling in the Vale of Tears: everyday life and resistance in South Uist, Outer Hebrides, 1760–860', *International Journal of Historical Archaeology* **3**(2): 101–22.

Symonds, J. 2000, 'The dark island revisited: an approach to the historical archaeology of Milton, South Uist', in Atkinson *et al.* (eds), 2000, 197–210.

Thomas, J. 2001, 'Archaeologies of place and landscape', in Hodder, I. (ed.) *Archaeological Theory Today*. Cambridge: Polity Press, 165–86.

Tilley, C. 1994, *A Phenomenology of Landscape: Places, Paths and Monuments*. Oxford: Berg.

Tipping, R. 1997, 'The environmental history of the landscape', in RCAHMS 1997, 10–25.

Tipping, R. 2000, 'Palaeoecological approaches to historical problems: a comparison of sheep-grazing intensities in the Cheviot Hills in the Medieval and later periods', in Atkinson *et al.* (eds), 2000, 130–43.

Tipping, R. 2007, 'Environmental history', in RCAHMS 2007, 25–44.

UNPUBLISHED SOURCES

MacGregor, M.D.W. 1989, 'A Political History of the MacGregors before 1571', unpublished PhD thesis, University of Edinburgh.

Part Three

Of People and Things

Of People and Things
INTRODUCTION

By AUDREY HORNING and MARILYN PALMER

The nine chapters in this section all reflect, in one way or another, upon the relationship between 'people and things'. Moving beyond a simple dichotomous relationship between the two, wherein we somehow have to prioritise the agency and importance of one over the other, each of these chapters provides us with a statement on the current practice of archaeology (be it defined as industrial, post-medieval, historical, contemporary, avocational, academic or commercial). Each author employs a variety of case studies not only to illustrate the range of contemporary practice, but to ground thoughtful suggestions about the future. Following on from Chris Dalglish's call for more engaged interdisciplinary research in chapter 18, the final contribution in Section Two, many of the chapters in this section also engage with the need for increased discourse between specialists and scholars, with the concluding chapter by Steve Mrozowski defining this aim as the most important goal for the future development and enhancement of the study of the archaeology of the past five hundred years.

In chapter 19, Roger Holden opens the section with a concise argument in favour of the continued incorporation of technological and engineering insights in the interpretation of industrial archaeology. Just as Nevell (this volume) acknowledged his greater interest in social approaches to industrial archaeology, Holden freely admits that he personally is 'more interested in the movement of cogs than the passage of clogs'. Taking 'power' as his theme, he first examines the engineering principles behind the increasing speeds, and thus energy, used in 19th-century mills, and then considers the physical size of power plants. Holden reminds us that 'understanding the technology is essential to understanding the work the workforce has to do', noting that while improvements in loom technology meant that the machines did not have to be continually monitored, the danger of being injured by a shuttle flying off the loom increased exponentially with the speed of the machine. Holden then questions the tendency of some archaeologists to interpret the appearance of mill buildings only in relation to the social motivations of the owners. Rather than seeing power in its ideological sense as the driving force between the appearance of such industrial structures, Holden reminds us that power plants housed engines and ultimately, the function of those engines was more closely linked to the success or failure of an industrial enterprise than were any flamboyant efforts at architectural display. While he does not use these terms, his discussion of the active role of looms and of engine houses in effecting and affecting human behaviour clearly articulates with current archaeological considerations of materiality and the recursive relationship between people and things.

Then, in chapter 20, Geoff Egan considers the centrality of finds research to post-medieval archaeology, past and present. Just as Holden reminds us that an understanding of the function of machines must remain core to efforts to understand the relationship between people and things in an industrial workplace, Egan reminds us that it is very difficult to draw any conclusions about the use of portable material culture by people in the past if we lack even a basic understanding of the production and distribution of such objects. Egan's overview of the current state of knowledge about non-ceramic artefactual materials should convince anyone who argues that finds research is somehow passé that the opposite is, in fact, true. In spite of decades of research and analysis, comparatively little is known about a wide range of objects, with a particularly glaring absence of solid studies of 19th- and 20th-century objects from archaeological contexts. Just as Holden questions the characterisation of 'technocentric' approaches to industrial archaeology as somehow old-fashioned, Egan laments what he sees as a lack of academic attention paid to basic instruction in finds recognition and a consequent devaluing of specialist knowledge.

Ceramics serve as the focus of chapter 21, by Alasdair Brooks. Broadening from artefact-specific studies, Brooks instead focuses upon the impacts of international economic and political conflicts on the distribution of post-medieval ceramics. His study exemplifies Orser's call for a multi-scalar analytical archaeology, as it tacks between site-specific assemblage data to the global impact of events including the Napoleonic Wars and the American Civil War. Noting cultural preferences for certain Staffordshire products, such as the popularity of colourful transfer prints in Britain versus the wider appeal of plain white granite wares in North America, Brooks convincingly argues for the 'potential interpretive impact of considering the relevance of international events to the distributions of material culture to our analysis of post-1750 domestic assemblages within Britain and Ireland'. His evidence from Australia in particular highlights how the preferences of consumers were to an extent overridden by the needs of the Staffordshire producers to compensate for the lack of an American market during the Civil War. Australia became a dumping ground for unwanted white granite ceramics – an insight only gained through the careful recording and consideration of 19th-century archaeological assemblages.

The next four chapters take us into the field, each grappling with the challenge of not only convincing the wider archaeological community of the need to take post-medieval archaeological deposits as seriously as those dating to earlier periods, but also with the challenge of dealing with the greater complexity (and volume) of post-medieval assemblages and related documentary sources. In chapter 21, a forceful presentation of the realities of conducting developer-funded urban excavations in Britain, Craig Cessford of the Cambridge Archaeological Unit challenges archaeologists to move away from rigid period divisions that seldom express themselves in urban deposits, and to cease looking at the often large assemblages from sizable post-medieval features as simply 'time capsules' of interesting objects. Like Holden and Egan, Cessford has little time for archaeological narratives that are not clearly grounded in data. Cessford castigates academic archaeologists for what he sees as a 'lack of understanding' of complex urban excavations, 'characterised by a level of interpretive naiveté'. Cessford then uses his own experience in directing and interpreting the large-scale Grand Arcade project in Cambridge to argue for a more sophisticated and integrated approach to developer-funded urban archaeology that, on the one hand, acknowledges the complexity of human actions that contributed to the creation of archaeological deposits and, on the other, recognises that any effective investigation of the lives of those people must venture well beyond individual site boundaries and artefact assemblages.

Many of the contributors to this volume, Cessford included, advocate the use of interdisciplinary approaches to interpreting the material legacy of post-1550 Britain and Ireland. The next chapter in particular highlights the potential of such an integrated approach to the interpretation of preciously excavated assemblages from London. Authored by Nigel Jeffries, Alastair Owens, Dan Hicks, Rupert Featherby and Karen Wehner, chapter 23 capitalises upon the vast, if mainly untapped, resources of the London Archaeological Archive and Research Centre to investigate the 'ways in which the analysis of these sources might be used in interdisciplinary urban historiography, especially in the light of methodological approaches developed in North American and Australian urban archaeology'. Opening with a sobering overview of the general lack of attention paid to post-1750 archaeological deposits in Britain, the authors then detail their preliminary results from a multi-source examination of 19th-century working-class households in Bell Green, Sydenham. Echoing Cessford's comments on the complexity of the urban archaeological record, the authors note that 'in a city that was constantly on the move, it is often difficult for archaeologists to bring together people with their things'. They nevertheless present a convincing demonstration of the kinds of insights that can be derived from considering archaeological assemblages from urban households in both their local and broader historical contexts. Here again we see a recognition of the need to approach archaeology in a multi-scalar fashion.

Remaining in London, in chapter 24 Emma Dwyer picks up on the theme of the interpretive potential of post-1750 urban archaeology. Building on James Dixon's earlier discussion of contemporary archaeology, Dwyer focuses upon lesser-appreciated aspects of the archaeological significance of a piece of industrial heritage, the Great Eastern Railway Viaduct in Pedley and Grimsby Streets, East London, by focusing upon the unofficial uses of the spaces under the viaduct, taking her examination up to the present. The viaduct comes to life as far more than a piece of 19th-century industrial heritage to feature as an active element in people's everyday lives. Over the past 160 or so years, the railway arches served a variety of functions, from legitimate business locale to zones of liminality and criminality, to spaces for shelter and of war-time refuge, to canvases for street art. As Dwyer notes, 'the construction of the railway viaduct in the 1830s divided streets and communities, but the spaces underneath the arches were successfully reclaimed'. Historic structures such as the viaduct, built to carry trains rushing in and out of the capital city, both constrain and facilitate human action in the past and in the present.

Past and present dynamically intersect in chapter 25 by Eleanor Casella, which incorporates archaeological, documentary and oral historical evidence to flesh out working-class life at Alderley Edge, Cheshire. Casella's chapter also exemplifies the importance of an interdisciplinary, multi-scalar approach to historical archaeology. As in the chapters by

Cessford, Brooks, and Jeffries *et al.* it is the kind of detailed information on 19th- and 20th-century material culture, as advocated by Egan, that provides a firm support for Casella's interpretations. For example, decorative ceramic figurines form an integral part of Casella's consideration of the intersection of individual identities with the sometimes constraining structures of community and class identity, as they allow for a nuanced consideration of the meanings attached to the ownership and display of such items. Discussion of the meaning of material culture is made far richer, if less straightforward, by the incorporation of ethnographic and documentary sources. As noted by Casella, 'by juxtaposing diverse sources of evidence, the situated, multiscalar, and frequently dissonant patterns of community life can be illuminated'.

Finally, in chapter 26, Stephen Mrozowski wraps up our consideration of people and things by reflecting back upon the themes of analytical approaches and the relationship between theory and practice. Drawing upon his considerable experience in running interdisciplinary archaeological projects in both urban and rural contexts, he reiterates a point made earlier in this volume by Thomas, which is the need for 'greater attention to environmental analysis on post-medieval sites: the biological sides of large-scale processes such as colonialism, industrialisation, urbanisation, the growth of capitalism and the construction of empire are absolutely essential if we are to understand the world we have inherited'. Mrozowski focuses upon three principal points in his discussion; 'the importance of theory, the centrality of archaeological practice, and the connections between interrelated historical processes of colonialism, industrialisation, urbanisation, the rise of capitalism, and the construction of empire'. Mrozowski strongly argues for the value of theoretically informed research that does not eschew the kinds of solid empirical study of objects and technological processes such as those discussed by Holden and Egan in this section, but rather integrates those insights to facilitate the range of multiscalar, holistic considerations of past experiences that have emerged as a central aim of all the contributors to this volume, no matter from which direction they approach their own researches.

Lancashire Cotton Mills and Power

By ROGER N. HOLDEN

The recent debate in industrial archaeology has been presented as one of 'things' versus 'people', but this is not really the issue. The question is whether an understanding of technology and its development in all its contexts is central to the subject or whether this should be superseded by a programme asking specifically social questions derived from the theoretical social sciences. Using some specific examples relating to the power requirements of Lancashire cotton mills, this chapter suggests that an understanding of technology must remain central to the task of understanding industrial buildings.

INTRODUCTION

Although James Symons may be 'more interested in the passage of clogs than the movement of cogs', some of us would have to admit that we are more interested in the movement of cogs than the passage of clogs.[1] This observation has no doubt led to the recent debate in industrial archaeology being presented as one of 'things' versus 'people', perhaps with an implication that those interested in 'people' occupy the moral high-ground over those interested in 'mere machines', but this is not really the issue. The question is whether an understanding of technology and its development in all its contexts is central to the subject or whether this should be superseded by a programme asking specifically social questions derived from the theoretical social sciences, as some recent publications purporting to provide a research agenda for the subject seem to suggest.[2] Subsequently Ron Fitzgerald has argued forcibly that industrial archaeology should have a technological focus and that archaeological evidence can be used to answer questions about technological development.[3] Using some specific examples relating to the power requirements of Lancashire cotton mills, this chapter suggests that an understanding of technology must remain central to the task of understanding industrial buildings.[4]

My 1999 paper on 'Water-supplies for steam-powered textile mills' showed that an understanding of steam engineering and some elementary thermodynamic theory leads to an understanding of why mills were located where they were.[5] The clustering along canals and other water-courses was because of the need for cold water to supply the engine condensers (Fig. 19.1). If such a ready water supply was not available then it was necessary to construct a reservoir (Fig. 19.2). In concluding this article I responded to a paper by Shane Gould,

ABOVE
Figure 19.1 Mills along the Leeds & Liverpool Canal at Nelson, Lancashire. Lomeshaye Bridge Mill
(foreground) and Whitefield Shed (background), 14/4/2007
BELOW
Figure 19.2 Mill reservoir at Moses Gate, Bolton, Lancashire. Cobden Mill (left), Bolton Textile Mill No. 2
(right), 16/2/2008

presented at a previous conference in Leicester, provocatively titled 'Industrial Archaeology and the neglect of humanity'.[6] In this paper, the author seemed to be claiming that only questions relating to social relations were intellectually and academically acceptable; moreover, anything else was neglecting humanity!

This would, of course, rule out of court my studies on steam technology, yet the conclusions arrived at, which have implications beyond the technological, could not have been arrived at from a social relations direction. At the time one might have dismissed this as a one-off minority viewpoint, but as time went on it became clear that this was not so. Many of the contributors to the special issue of *Industrial Archaeology Review* 'Understanding the Workplace' and also to *Industrial Archaeology: Future Directions*, which were originally given at a Theoretical Archaeology Group conference, seemed to be pointing in the same direction.[7] At the same time, as one correspondent to *Industrial Archaeology News* complained, papers began to appear in *Industrial Archaeology Review* with 'esoteric verbiage' from the field of the theoretical social sciences and cultural criticism, indeed readers may have felt that they had picked up *Archaeological Dialogues* by mistake.[8] Shane Gould accused industrial archaeologists of having been 'locked in a techno-centric paradigm', and rhetoric about 'paradigm shifts' is frequently encountered. But the concept of rival and incommensurable paradigms striving for supremacy is not appropriate, as we are not looking at different, rival, theoretical frameworks that can explain the same set of data but at complementary explanations.[9] Much of this change of direction seems to be coming from professional archaeologists, seeking to fit the subject into their understanding of what is 'archaeological', rather than the non-professionals who had previously formed the core of industrial archaeology as a subject focused on technological matters. Many of these non-professionals have backgrounds in other fields, for example, professional engineering.

The present author raised his concerns about this change of direction in a letter to *Industrial Archaeology News*, arguing that understanding the technology and engineering of industrial buildings and processes is non-trivial, and it is perfectly valid for a group of people to make this the focus of their studies.[10] Perhaps this is more a field for non-professionals, although it is not really clear why this should be so. Traditionally these people have operated under a heading of 'Industrial Archaeology' and have been supported by the Association for Industrial Archaeology (AIA). If professionally trained archaeologists tend to focus on social questions, then our knowledge and interest in technological matters is what makes a distinctive contribution to the historical and archaeological enterprise. None of this is to say that we should study these things out of context, but there is a variety of contexts that depend on the questions being asked. Economic and business history has perhaps been the traditional context for industrial archaeology, and there is nothing wrong with this. I tend to operate in this area, but another possible context is architectural history; perhaps an interest in the passage of patent leather shoes than the passage of clogs would be more appropriate in this case.[11] Some writers give the impression that technological matters are purely descriptive and trivial. For example, Stephen Mrozowski, writing in *Industrial Archaeology: Future Directions*, says:

> By concentrating on processes that are governed explicitly by principles of engineering and science industrial archaeologists have escaped many of the interpretive dilemmas that have preoccupied

archaeological theorists. As a result industrial archaeologists have yet to explore some of the more interpretively challenging issues such as the role of industrial products in the reification of class identities.[12]

Certainly some of us have no wish to get involved in the interpretive dilemmas that have preoccupied archaeological theorists nor to explore the questions discussed by Mrozowski, but there are plenty of 'interpretively challenging' issues within the technological field. Two examples follow, both concerned with 'power'. 'Power' is of course an ambiguous word, and it is listed among the 'weighty issues' that the editors of *Industrial Archaeology: Future Directions* considered we should be engaging with. But I am sure that having read this far any readers initially deceived by my title will have realised that I am not talking about 'power' in the political or social sense but in the physical sense, the entity that today we measure in Watts (W) but historically in horsepower (hp). To put it another way, 'power' in the sense used by Richard Hills in the title of his book *Power in the Industrial Revolution*, not as used by Thomas Markus in *Buildings and Power*.[13]

EXAMPLE 1: POWER REQUIRED TO DRIVE LOOMS

Referring to the cotton industry, the economic historian Von Tunzelmann poses the following query:

... before beginning some of the present work I had imagined that one way to gauge technical advance in steam-power was by calculating the number of machines that could be driven by unit of power. But after doing that for spindles in the cotton industry I was surprised to find that the number of spindles per horsepower seemed to have fallen drastically over the observation period. The neo-classical economist might retort that this would result if the price of power was falling relative to the price of machinery. Indeed, this appears to be the case. However, the question is, what meaning can be given to the decline in the number of machines driven by a unit of power? Is this historical fact some form of regress?[14]

LEFT
Figure 19.3. Engine-house at Alma Mill, Blackburn, built 1859. This accommodated a beam engine of 25hp to drive 400 looms, 3/3/2007

LEFT
Figure 19.4
Engine-house at Bancroft
Mill, Barnoldswick,
15/8/1993

Von Tunzelmann is referring to spinning but the same phenomenon can be seen in weaving branch of the industry. Alma Mill, Blackburn, built in 1859, had a 25hp (17kW) steam engine to drive 400 looms, this is sixteen looms per horsepower (Fig. 19.3).[15] Note the small size of its beam engine house facing the canal. By contrast, the engine at Bancroft Mill, Barnoldswick (Fig. 19.4), completed as late as 1920, developed 500hp (373kW) to drive 1,200 looms, that is 2.4 looms per horsepower.[16] Indeed, this is on the high side as after 1900, mill designers seem to have worked to a 'rule-of-thumb' of two looms per horsepower; this would have covered the power to drive the loom itself as well as that needed for the associated preparation machinery; that is, winding, beaming, sizing and looming.

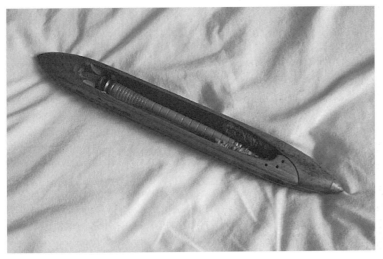

LEFT
Figure 19.5 A Lancashire
loom shuttle

So is Von Tunzelmann right? Is this a historical regress? The short answer is no, he has forgotten his elementary physics. The reason for the increase in power consumption is increasing machinery speeds, power increasing according to the square of the velocity since the kinetic energy, E, of a moving body is given by the equation

$$E = \tfrac{1}{2}mv^2$$

where m = mass (kg)

v = velocity (m/s).

For example, the weaving loom shuttle illustrated (Fig. 19.5) is 16 inches (406.4mm) long and weighs exactly 1lb (0.45kg). Loom speed is measured in picks per minute (ppm), that is, the number of weft threads inserted in one minute, which is the same as the number of throws of the shuttle. Assuming a loom of 28-inch reed space and making various other assumptions, which we will not detail here, leads to the following observations: To throw this shuttle at

50ppm requires 0.005hp (0.004kW)

100ppm   0.047hp (0.035kW)

200ppm   0.35hp (0.261kW).

Shuttle throwing was of course not the sole power requirement of a loom, but these figures suggest of the order of twenty looms per horsepower could be run at 100ppm, but doubling the speed reduces this to the order of two looms per horsepower. It is difficult to provide precise figures on increases in loom speeds during the 19th century, partly because it is not always clear if like is being compared with like, loom speeds varying according to the type of loom, the width of the loom and type of cloth being woven. Although there are reports in the 1830s of looms running at 180ppm, 100–120ppm seems more common, increasing to 200–220ppm by the end of the century. We can now see how Von Tunzelmann's surprising fact arises. Really he is looking at the wrong question. Faster machines produce more output in a given time, so the real issue is power to produce unit output, that is, unit length of yarn or unit area of cloth. But there are no readily available figures on this question. Because of the square law, it may still be found that the power requirement has increased, but not by such a great factor, so Von Tunzelmann's raising of the question of power costs is not irrelevant.

This may look like a pure exercise in engineering history, but of course increasing loom speeds does have significance for the workforce. It should not be simply assumed, however, that increasing speeds meant intensification of labour because over the 19th century improvements in the engineering of looms meant that they needed less attention. But understanding the technology is essential to understanding the work the workforce has to do as well as wage payment systems.[17] It is also important for understanding of health and safety issues, which have attracted the attention of labour and social historians, such as Fowler, recently.[18] Increasing shuttle speeds increased the hazard from shuttles failing to enter the shuttle box at the end of a pick and flying out of the loom, with potentially fatal consequences for anybody they hit. Despite its title, Fowler's book has very little to say about the actual work that the cotton operatives did, and traditional labour history has concerned itself with political and ideological questions, particularly in trade union activity.[19] So there is clearly scope here for the technologically oriented industrial archaeologist to make a contribution to the understanding of the workforce.

EXAMPLE 2: SIZE OF POWER SYSTEMS

A related issue is the physical size of power plant; that is, engine houses, boiler houses and chimneys. India Mill, Darwen, was widely publicised at the time of its construction, being depicted in Evan Leigh's *Science of Modern Cotton Spinning* of 1871 (Figs. 19.6 & 19.7).[20] The mill was built to impress and fortunately still survives largely intact. The power plant was particularly grand, with a huge decorative chimney 300 feet (91m) tall, one of the great Victorian chimneys, ranking alongside that at Lister's Manningham Mills in Bradford and 'Cox's Stack' at Camperdown Works in Dundee, together with a range of six boilers behind a grand colonnade and a tall engine house with decorative stonework. The engine house had to be tall to accommodate a pair of beam engines; there is no suggestion that it was unnecessarily large, and its volume from engine floor to the eaves was 49,500 ft³ (1,435m³). The elegantly attired Victorian gentleman with his lady admiring the engine stands exactly six feet (1.83m) high to the brim of his top hat. This pair of beam engines generated 250hp (186kW). The six boilers were said to have been tested to 100psi (690kPa), their actual working pressure is not stated but probably 60psi (413kPa).

Figure 19.6 India Mill, Darwen, Lancashire. From Leigh, *The Science of Modern Cotton Spinning*, Manchester, 1871–2, plate 9

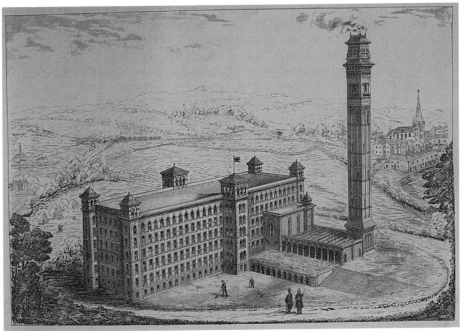

But if this looks impressive, again consider Bancroft Mill in Barnoldswick, admittedly not quite comparing like with like because it was a weaving mill, whereas India Mill was a spinning mill (see Fig. 19.4). Bancroft Mill is far less impressive, the engine house is only 36,000 ft³ (1,019m³) in volume. There is only a single boiler located in a boiler house hidden from public view, and the chimney, although not unimpressive, is nothing like that at India Mill, being a mere 120 feet (36.5m) high. The whole lacks decoration, even the corbels under the over-sailer of the chimney have a practical purpose. But the engine is a horizontal compound engine (Fig. 19.8), which develops twice the power, 500hp (373kW), of the India Mill engine.

What we are looking at here, of course, are improvements in steam technology.[21] The boiler at Bancroft worked at the much higher pressure of 160psi (1,103kPa) but this is not the whole story. The basic formula for power, P, generated in a steam cylinder is

$$P = pv$$

where   p = average pressure in the cylinder (Pa)

v = volume of the cylinder swept by the piston in unit time (m³/s).

The actual cylinder volume at Bancroft is smaller than that at India Mill so it achieves higher output by higher pressure and higher speed: 144 strokes per minute as against 23. Higher speeds also required developments in valve gear and governors. India Mill had a crude fly-ball governor, Bancroft originally had a Whitehead governor, subsequently replaced by

Figure 19.7 Cross-section of the engine-house, India Mill, Darwen, Lancashire. From Leigh, *The Science of Modern Cotton Spinning*, Manchester, 1871–2, plate 12

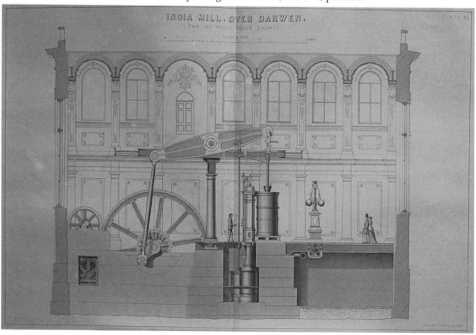

Figure 19.8 The engine at Bancroft Mill, Barnoldswick, in steam specially for members of the Association for Industrial Archaeology. The Secretary of the AIA, Barry Hood, provides the scale, 13/8/2007

the Porter governor now seen, illustrating developments in governors necessary to control faster engines.[22] The India Mill engine has slide valves, the Bancroft engine has Corliss valves, again an important development in raising engine speeds.[23] Less is understood about boiler development; clearly the steam-raising power of boilers had increased, although the India Mill engine seems to have consumed prodigious amounts of steam. Certainly answering this question lies in the field of steam technology, not social theory.

Ian Mellor, in his contribution to *Understanding the Workplace*, draws attention to the often ornate, non-functional, nature of structures associated with power plant in mills, suggesting this tells us something about the social relations of mills.[24] This may be true, but despite rhetoric about 'challenging existing narratives' this has been noted before.[25] India Mill fits in with this, but is definitely 'over the top' for its date. It is unclear who exactly Eccles Shorrock were trying to impress. But its grandeur is rather contradicted by economic reality, since it took a very long time to build, from 1859 to 1871, bankrupted the company and was arguably obsolete by the time it went into operation. Certainly in weaving mills, where engines tended to be smaller, there was a rapid changeover from beam to horizontal engines in the early 1860s, although this process took about a decade longer in spinning mills. At some unknown date, the India Mill engine was 'McNaughted', that is, converted to compound operation. This conversion suggests that its power output was too low to drive faster machinery. It was then replaced altogether in 1890 when a new engine of 1,800hp (1,342kW) was installed in a new engine house on the opposite side of the mill.[26]

Nineteen years is a very short lifetime for a steam engine; the Bancroft engine remained in use for fifty-eight years. This makes the survival of the original engine house at India Mill all the more remarkable, although it has been somewhat disfigured by an extension being placed on its roof.

By comparison Bancroft Mill, also built by a private firm, was very plain. It may be thought that this reflects the difference in date; after all, Bancroft Shed was completed after the First World War when austerity might be expected. However, weaving mill engine houses, whether built by private or public firms, generally were plain compared with spinning mill engine houses, as can be seen by studying photographs by George Watkins.[27] In part, this difference may reflect the much higher capitalisation of cotton-spinning companies. During the Edwardian period, in order to build a spinning mill, a company would typically have a nominal capital of £100,000, so a little extra expenditure on decoration would have seemed a small matter compared with a weaving mill building company with capital of £12,000. In addition, many spinning companies were heavily influenced by their architects, who were often among the company promoters, whereas weaving mills, particularly in the Blackburn area, were often designed by engineering companies. Bancroft was designed by an architect, W.H. Atkinson of Colne. As this was a private company, he would have had no other financial interest in the mill.

CONCLUSION

In conclusion I should simply like to turn on its head Shane Gould's argument that if industrial archaeology is to gain intellectual credibility it has to embrace social theory. On the contrary, I would suggest that if traditional archaeology is to get to grips with the buildings of industry it must embrace technological and engineering understanding. Although one contributor to *Industrial Archaeology News* was concerned that I might be diminishing the importance of social, economic and political factors, this was certainly not my intention; my concern was the opposite, that the importance of technology might be diminished by emphasising an agenda focused on social questions.[28] Traditionally people called 'industrial archaeologists' have pursued this technological agenda, and it is important that the AIA continues to support this perspective and adequately represent it in its research agenda. The idea that industrial archaeology has neglected humanity is hardly a view that can be seriously maintained, given that the founders of the subject, whose writings inspired many of us, include L.T.C. Rolt and Arthur Raistrick, neither of whom could be guilty of such an accusation.

NOTES

1. Symonds 2005.
2. Casella & Symons 2005; Gwyn & Palmer 2005.
3. Fitzgerald 2007a, 2007b.
4. This discussion includes insights from a study in progress of weaving mills in Lancashire, which it is hoped will be published.
5. Holden 1999.
6. Gould 1995.
7. Gwyn & Palmer 2005; Casella & Symonds 2005.
8. Hughes 2006. One can guess that two of the offenders were Taylor 2003 and Lamb 2004.
9. While lacking in clarity and doubtful as an explanation for the history of science (see Losee 1993, 223–8), Thomas Kuhn's concept of 'paradigm shifts' has somehow entered into popular consciousness but is frequently misused; personally I avoid using the term 'paradigm'.
10. Holden 2006.
11. See, for example, Holden 1998; Holden 2003; Holden 2004.
12. Mrozowski 2005.
13. Hills 1970; Markus 1993. Markus, in a book written for architects rather than archaeologists, sees 'power' as a negative as opposed to 'bonds', which are a positive. This is in keeping with postmodernist thinking, which sees even knowledge as constructed for purposes of 'power'. Some would argue that even technological knowledge as presented here is 'socially constructed' and therefore argue for the primacy of social theory. In the extreme this would reduce Richard Hills's 'power' to Thomas Markus's 'power'. For a critique of constructivism and a defence of the view that there are mind-independent facts, which starts by considering an example from archaeology, see Boghossian 2007.
14. Von Tunzlemann 1978, 10.
15. Rothwell 1985, 39. Note that imperial units are used here because these mills were designed in imperial units and using metric units, which appear as 'funny numbers', can obscure important points. Metric equivalents are given.
16. Shackleton 2006, 51–5.
17. Holden 2005.
18. Fowler 2003.
19. See, for example, Firth 2003, which is concerned with placing powerloom overlookers within theoretical concepts of 'labour aristocracy' and whether they identified with working class ideologies and politics. The front cover of Fowler 2003 shows a trade union demonstration, a rare event in the life of a cotton operative, rather than cotton operatives at work.
20. Leigh 1871–2, 26–9.
21. Hills 1989.
22. Hills 1989, 193–212; Bennett 1979, 7–95.
23. Hills 1989, 178–88.
24. Mellor 2005.
25. Jones 1985, 183–94; Holden 1998, 119–36.
26. Rothwell 1992, 22–3.
27. Watkins 1999; Watkins 2001a; Watkins 2001b.
28. West 2006.

BIBLIOGRAPHY

Bennett, S. 1979, *A History of Control Engineering 1800–1930*. London: The Institution of Electrical Engineers.

Boghossian, P. 2007, *Fear of Knowledge: Against Relativism and Constructivism*. Oxford: Clarendon Press.

Casella, E.C. & Symonds, J. (eds) 2005, *Industrial Archaeology: Future Directions*. New York: Springer.

Firth, P. 2003, 'Powerloom overlookers: labour aristocracy of north-east Lancashire cotton weaving 1890-1920', *Transactions of the Lancashire and Cheshire Antiquarian Society* **99**: 177–89.

Fitzgerald, R. 2007a, 'Historic building record and the Halifax Borough Market Doors' *Industrial Archaeology Review*, **29**(1): 51–74.

Fitzgerald, R. 2007b, 'The Stone Dam Mill engine house', *Industrial Archaeology Review* **29**(2): 115–32.

Fowler, A. 2003, *Lancashire Cotton operatives and Work, 1900–1950: A Social History of Lancashire Cotton Operatives in the Twentieth Century*. Aldershot: Ashgate.

Gould, S. 1995, 'Industrial archaeology and the neglect of humanity', in Palmer & Neaverson (eds), 1995, 49–53.

Gwyn, D. & Palmer, M. (eds.) 2005, *Understanding the Workplace* (special issue), *Industrial Archaeology Review* **27**(1).

Hills, R.L. 1970, *Power in the Industrial Revolution*. Manchester: Manchester University Press.

Hills, R.L. 1989, *Power from Steam*. Cambridge: Cambridge University Press.

Holden, R.N. 1998, *Stott & Sons: Architects of the Lancashire Cotton Mill*. Lancaster: Carnegie.

Holden, R. N. 1999, 'Water supplies for steam-powered textile mills', *Industrial Archaeology Review* **21**(1): 41–52.

Holden, R.N. 2003, 'Ring and mule spinning in the nineteenth century: a technological perspective', *Journal of Industrial History* **6**: 34–60.

Holden, R.N. 2004, 'The end of an era: Elk Mill 1926–1999', *Industrial Archaeology Review* **26**(2): 113–27.

Holden, R.N. 2005, 'Culture and know-how in the "Satanic Mills": a response', *Textile History* **36**: 86–93.

Holden, R.N. 2006, Letter: 'Our fascination with machines', *Industrial Archaeology News* **136**: 11.

Hughes, P.M. 2006, Letter: 'Hooray for Roger Holden!'[*sic*], *Industrial Archaeology News* **137**: 7.

Jones, E. 1985, *Industrial Architecture in Britain 1750–1939*. London: Batsford.

Lamb, J. 2004, 'The "Contemporary Archaeology" of Mell Square: developing an interpretive theoretical framework and research strategy for the "Preservation by Record" of a 1960s shopping precinct in the West Midlands', *Industrial Archaeology Review* **26**(2): 129–40.

Leigh, E. 1871–2, *The Science of Modern Cotton Spinning* (vol. 1). Manchester: Palmer & Howe.

Losee, J. 1993, *A Historical Introduction to the Philosophy of Science*, 3rd edn. Oxford: Oxford University Press.

Markus, T.A. 1993, *Buildings & Power: Freedom & Control in the Origin of Modern Building Types*. London: Routledge.

Mellor, I. 2005, 'Space, society and the textile mill', *Industrial Archaeology Review* **27**(1): 49–56.

Mrozowski, S. 2005, 'Cultural identity and the consumption of industry', in Casella & Symonds (eds), 2005, 243–60.

Palmer, M. & Neaverson, P. (eds) 1995, *Managing the Industrial Heritage*. Leicester: School of Archaeological Studies, University of Leicester.

Rothwell, M. 1985, *Industrial Heritage: A Guide to the Industrial Archaeology of Blackburn. Part One: The Textile Industry*. Accrington: Hyndburn Local History Society.

Rothwell, M. 1992, *Industrial Heritage: A Guide to the Industrial Archaeology of Darwen*. Accrington: Bridgestone Press.

Shackleton, G. 2006, *The Textile Mills of Pendle and their Steam Engines*. Ashbourne: Landmark Publishing.

Symonds, J. 2005, 'Dirty old town? Industrial archaeology and the urban historic environment', *Industrial Archaeology Review* **27** (1): 57–66.

Taylor, V.J. 2003, 'Structuration revisited: a test case for an industrial archaeology methodology for far north Queensland', *Industrial Archaeology Review* **25**(2): 129–46.

vonTunzelmann, G.N. 1978, *Steam Power and British Industrialization to 1860*. Oxford: Clarendon Press.

Watkins, G. 1999, *The Textile Mill Engine*, 2nd edn. Ashbourne: Landmark Publishing.

Watkins, G. 2001a, *Stationary Steam Engines of Great Britain, Vol. 3.1: Lancashire*. Ashbourne: Landmark Publishing.

Watkins, G. 2001b, *Stationary Steam Engines of Great Britain, Vol. 3.2: Lancashire*. Ashbourne: Landmark Publishing.

West, I. 2006, Letter: 'Our fascination with machines', *Industrial Archaeology News* **137**: 7.

Material Concerns: The State of Post-Medieval Finds Studies

By GEOFF EGAN

The study of finds, long central to post-medieval archaeology, has developed unevenly. This is in part because of biases in the buried record, resulting in an established wisdom that is in some areas arguably top-heavy with data and in others surprisingly lean and simplistic through lack of basic information. The present discussion, concentrating on non-ceramic items, considers the present state of the art, some of the reasons for its having come to the point it has now reached and some potential future directions. There is below inevitably an emphasis on urban archaeology in areas that have been the focus of the writer's work over the past thirty years to illustrate points raised, but material elsewhere has also been used to present wider perspectives.

INTRODUCTION: SOME BASICS THAT DETERMINE THE PRESENT POSITION

The single volume that is Ivor Noël Hume's *Guide to the Artifacts of Colonial America*, first published in 1970[1] and still in print without major alteration after almost forty years, is probably, for most students and practitioners, the best starting point for gaining a rounded view of the scope of regularly unearthed material culture from the 17th and early 18th centuries. The title can be slightly misleading in that several items included in the volume were found in London rather than America. This is the only introduction to post-medieval finds across the board within one book. Other attempts to cover a similar range of material are few. Kathleen Deagan's publications of finds in America of Spanish origin, with two volumes available,[2] comes closest, but there is – remarkably, in view of the amount of work undertaken in Europe[3] – still no equivalent work undertaken on the Old World side of the Atlantic.

The 16th century was, until very recently, surprisingly poorly served in terms of detailed assimilation of everyday material culture for a period so familiar in historical terms with its memorable events and personalities. A series of publications in the early 2000s has made this problem less acute. The published finds from the wreck of the *Mary Rose*[4] (which sank in 1545) include a number of 'voucher' objects (first-time published with close dating), some of them apparently otherwise unknown until the early 1600s (the non-survival of iron from the wreck is a limiting factor on what is otherwise an outstanding marker for 16th-century material). From London, a range of finds from a cluster of waterlogged, Thames-side sites, especially from the early 1500s and covering a wide social spectrum as well as waste from several industries, is now available,[5] as is a less extensive group from the moat at the high-status site of Acton Court outside Bristol.[6] Several military sites have produced Tudor-period finds that are now in print.[7] Some of the urban finds monographs that have become standard works of first resort for comparanda, like those for Norwich and Winchester,[8] deal with material that sometimes appears to have been disturbed in the ground and which ended up in mixed deposits also including somewhat later items.

A lack of basic material for study still applies to the second half of the 15th century, if one includes that as post-medieval. There are sound reasons for doing so in several branches of material culture in which clear breaks with 'medieval' traditions are evident during those years; the logic comes from each category of objects. Extraordinarily, there is still no broad-ranging assemblage of non-ceramic finds from a tight excavation sequence anywhere in Britain from the generation from *c.* 1450 to *c.* 1480, a crucial period in terms of the shift from 'gothic' towards 'renaissance' style, which still lacks basic raw material to chart in detail these and other changes. The first decade of the 17th century is also poorly served, though not quite as markedly so. The relative lack of full, well-preserved assemblages from the very early 1600s in Britain is to some extent mitigated by the tightly dated and very varied, though not yet fully published, finds from the colonial site of Jamestown in Virginia. Most of the objects unearthed there were imported from London and elsewhere in England. There are also several other very useful reports from the United States and Canada.[9] Of course, there are many other specific lacunae in the received and assimilated record of material culture, but the preceding ones need further raw material or work to clarify the sometimes flimsy basis of the present state of knowledge.

Along with shipwreck finds groups,[10] some of the fullest assemblages, which often include unusual survivals, come from scenes of disasters including major conflagrations. The 1507 fire at Pottergate in Norwich and the 1666 Great Fire of London[11] have both produced finds groups of great interest, but there are many other recorded major fires that might furnish similarly useful assemblages elsewhere. For example, part of Southwark was burnt in 1676, a decade later than the more famous event in the City, but so far no archaeological trace seems to have been recognised of an event that might provide very helpful assemblages to compare with those from the earlier event to help chart any significant changes in the capital.

It is noticeable to those who have been practitioners for a quarter of a century or more that whereas when they started working there was often debate about whether or not to deal with evidence from the 17th century, fieldworkers who have graduated over the past two decades routinely collect finds from throughout the 18th century. The most recently trained excavation staff regularly also pick up those from the 19th and sometimes 20th century too. This is part of a welcome, broad trend over recent years to take the potential of the latest archaeology much more seriously. So far, however, there is little evidence of a broad agenda for routinely dealing with the material culture of the 1800s and 1900s, with site-by-site priorities and research aims having produced very useful and stimulating results, but relatively little sense of any national programme comparable to those devised for comparable finds from the 16th to 18th centuries.[12]

For just over a decade, the Portable Antiquities Scheme (PAS) has been recording mainly metal finds discovered in England and Wales other than during the course of archaeological excavations.[13] This is, for the first time, beginning to fill in a picture of consumption of all manner of goods in the previously neglected rural areas. The majority of excavations that have produced varied finds assemblages of large numbers of post-medieval date have tended to be urban redevelopments. What seems to be emerging now is more a nationwide distribution from the later medieval period onwards of items of portable material culture rather than multiple smaller, regional varieties. This situation contrasts with the picture for ceramics in the pre-1750 era, which were long the most fully studied goods that are regularly unearthed.

Aside from all other considerations, most worrying for the long-term health of the studies considered here is the lack of younger practitioners in secure jobs with access to fresh assemblages and the resources to study them. Neither archaeological units nor museums have retained the numbers of posts in this specialism that they had in the late 1970s and 1980s, and this shrinkage is only to a small extent compensated by a recent growth in university posts that could provide a home for such expertise. Higher-educational institutions, however, rarely have direct access, let alone first call, on the assimilation of and research into newly excavated material. These tasks usually fall to the few still employed or brought in as external consultants by the excavating organisation, who can only rarely rise to the challenge of making material culture in all its complexity available to a wide public through full publication. Without adequately funded fresh minds to develop over the course of working lives the art of looking in new ways at the rich material culture of the post-medieval period, the tradition of study is in danger of gradually withering away.

CLAY PIPES

After pottery, clay pipes are perhaps the most obvious category of post-medieval finds. They have long been the subject of intensive study by committed enthusiasts, with a couple of general key works (currently in need of revision) and almost twenty volumes in the *British Archaeological Reports* series.[14] Clay pipe specialists also have their own journal.[15] This study is soundly established, with its own momentum.

METALWORK

Inevitably, a fuller picture of the range of metal items, technological and stylistic developments, and regional and international trade patterns is constantly emerging. Metallic structural fixtures that must have once been extremely common are, in some cases, surprisingly elusive among excavated material that is still in a recognisable state.[16]

The history of pewterware would be much the poorer if it had to rely only on above-ground survivals.[17] The *Mary Rose* wreck assemblage of 1545 has produced several unique pieces – a range of tankards, flasks, plates and spoons with makers' stamps and owners' marks. The *Mary Rose* also included some cast copper-alloy tripod cooking cauldrons. This category of vessel was common up to the early 19th century. Along with long-handled versions (skillets), these have been the subject of a multidisciplinary study of above-ground survivals from private collections and museums, excavated pieces and evidence from production sites, with scientific analyses. These studies encompass the entire period of use of copper cauldrons and skillets, concentrating particularly on the important West Country producers. This valuable work has revolutionised understanding of two already familiar forms of domestic vessel.[18] We may finally have become less dependent on a book originally written in the 1920s from the metalware collectors' ambit for our understanding of these items, although work from the collectors' quarter remains very useful for a range of other domestic items.[19]

It has only become clear over the past decade just how much the range of dress accessories changed from centuries-old 'medieval' traditions to new 'post-medieval' ones over the period from the late 15th to the mid-16th centuries.[20] In silver, not only the basic forms of accessories changed, but hallmarking in the form of stamped makers' initials was extended to light-weight items of dress known as 'smallwares'. Hallmarking had been routine on large items for some time. This development has been traced in the hooked clasps (Fig. 20.1), which were briefly in fashion through this period.[21] A fairly plain circular brooch is so far unique among the very few excavated items recognised as being of this category and date in having the maker's initials stamped on the pin.[22] It remains very difficult if not impossible to trace in detail the typological progress of brooches through the 15th, 16th and 17th centuries from excavated material. They had plainly lost the popularity they had enjoyed throughout the high Middle Ages but it seems unlikely that they should have almost completely disappeared as the present archaeological record seems to suggest.

Excavated buttons, by contrast, are the subject of a very useful study.[23] A brief flowering of buckles together with the latest strap ends, both made almost entirely (including the buckle frames and occasionally the pins, too) from folded brass sheeting is recognised from finds across England and on the Isle of Man. A single manufacturing assemblage is known for these distinctive early 16th-century products, found in London.[24] It is possible further production evidence may in due course come to light in other towns.

Starkly isolated, with very few comparable items, is the Cheapside Hoard of jewellery, which appears to have been abandoned in the centre of the jewellery-making quarter of

Figure 20.1 Copper alloy hooked clasp, from Wharram Percy (Goodall 1981, fig. 66 no. 21). Length 44 cm.

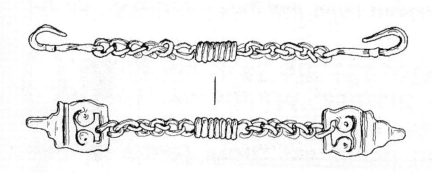

London in the early 17th century.[25] This remarkable assemblage is from a very specific social level – high enough to use precious metals and real stones but with a few exceptions not so high that the components are particularly heavy or of the best quality that marks out the weighty jewellery of the real elite. These are the objects that occasionally survive in aristocratic and institutional collections. The Cheapside jewels are the rarest survivals, being of a level generally not from a milieu affluent enough to ensure they would survive their financial attraction of recycling when they went out of fashion, to become heirlooms.

Recent developments in the study of metallic dress items also include the recognition that enamelled brass dress accessories, using a limited palette of blues, blue-green, black and white (perhaps with occasional red), were produced in the mid 17th century in London. These are from the industry that used to be known (erroneously) in the art world as 'Surrey Enamels'.[26] The reason for the restricted colours, with black and white a prominent combination, presumably lies in the puritan ethic of the times. So far buttons, buckles and mounts are known, mainly from finds recorded on the Portable Antiquities Scheme database (Fig. 20.2), although a couple of the buttons have been found in the course of formal excavations.[27] These accessories seem, like most others, to have had a nationwide distribution. The 18th-century fashion for prominent, ornate shoe buckles has left a considerable legacy in the ground, but so far synthesis has been from the art history/ collectors' viewpoint, concentrating on the more expensive end of a very wide range.[28] There is a considerable amount of documentary evidence pertinent to the makers' marks that could be considered against finds from the ground.

Much metalwork from the 18th century onwards seems regularly to suffer in the soil from corrosion to a greater extent than that from the immediately preceding and earlier periods. This surprising trend (not universally evident) may be the result of more aggressive chemicals in the later soils, or there may be other factors (new, less robust alloys?), but the

Figure 20.2 Copper alloy buckle with black and white enamel from Wiltshire, mid-17th century
(PAS database SOM-BB0BB4)

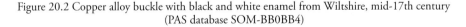

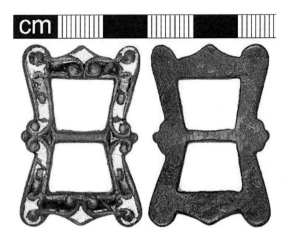

effect is to limit significantly the detailed examination of a proportion of excavated recent metal finds. Copper-alloy small change from the 18th century seems to be particularly susceptible in many soils.

GLASSWARE

Until the publication of Hugh Wilmott's 2002 study of 16th- and 17th-century glassware,[29] the study of post-medieval English glassware vessels up to the development of lead glass (*c.* 1670) lacked a basic textbook. There is also a new synthesis of production evidence in England over the same crucial period,[30] during which the manufacture of 'crystal' glass using Italian technology was introduced from the Continent. There is also now a detailed, science-based investigation of the transfer of manufacturing knowledge from southern to northern Europe.[31] Investigation of glass-manufacturing sites continues, with the complex sequence and details of the formulae used is gradually becoming clearer (see Bayley, Dungworth & Paynter, this volume). Attributions of products to specific furnaces is becoming more a matter of chemical investigation than simple visual judgement. The past heavy dependence on the part of archaeologists on historical accounts of the development of glassmaking in post-medieval England is a thing of the past, although the principal historical syntheses still provide a very useful framework.[32] The discovery in west London of glass bead manufacturing in the early 17th century on the private estate of one of the leading international entrepreneurs, Nicholas Crispe, was a surprise (Fig. 20.3). The discovery revealed an alternative source to those of the Netherlands for glass beads, which were traded to the Americas, Africa and the Far East.[33]

NUMISMATIC ITEMS

In contrast with earlier periods, finds of British coins have relatively little basic new information to offer numismatic studies given that the great majority of regular issues having long been known. However, a variety of details of unofficial issues and foreign coins used in Britain when the coin of the realm was not available in adequate numbers can be elucidated. Also worthy of study are the ubiquitous, often very crude lead/lead-alloy tokens thought to have served as fractions of pence for small purchases for which the official coins were too large. Most of these tokens fall outside readily defined series and defy useful categorisation. Even regional distributions are proving difficult to establish.

Another category of numismatic items is copper-alloy jettons, ubiquitous up to the mid-17th century. The variety of jettons have yet to be fully established,[34] however, for many of the early 16th-century Nuremberg issues production values were so low that legends are frequently completely nonsensical jumbles of letters and sometimes other characters, including occasional reversals and upside-down placings. Minute differences on often poorly preserved items and the lack of foreseeable inference, even if correctly read, mean that it is questionable whether further efforts are necessarily a worthwhile use of resources. Interest can, however, be found in the move from using Catholic religious mottoes to Protestant ones for the legends, and in the background entrepreneurial skill that saw these humble, often poorly made items, which could have been produced almost anywhere, traded for

Figure 20.3 Glass beads made in the grounds of Sir Nicholas Crispe's out-of-town villa in Hammersmith, West London, second quarter of the 17th century (photo Museum of London Archaeological Service)

almost the first century and a half of the early modern era from southern Germany across northern Europe.[35]

LEATHER

Survival in the field inevitably limits our understanding of post-medieval leather objects. Once again, the *Mary Rose* assemblage (1545) of shoes, jerkins, mittens, buckets, costrels and pouches has transformed ideas about what was available in the first half of the 16th century.[36] However, there remains a great deal of research and compilation to accomplish in order to bring the scattered, later archaeological finds towards synthesis.

TREEN

For wooden objects, too, the *Mary Rose* assemblage of 1545 is a revelation, as it includes stave-built and turned vessels (barrels, bowls, boxes, a spice grinder and a ladle), remains of wicker containers to protect glass and other vessels, and baskets. The generally humble furniture recovered from the shipwreck, including benches, stools and chests, comprises a unique and highly informative assemblage alongside the sometimes very sophisticated wooden musical instruments also recovered. Unparalleled and from the same source is an intriguing series of individually decorated wooden knife holders.[37]

Poor survival in the ground is again partly responsible for the current scant understanding of the demise of wooden tableware in the post-medieval period. For example, the almost universal use of boxwood for making combs at the beginning of the 16th century changed to a similarly dominant use of ivory by the early 17th century, reflecting wider trade patterns.[38] Very little archaeological work has yet been undertaken on the introduction of exotic woods for a wide variety of routine and less common uses throughout the period.

BONE AND IVORY

A fairly comprehensive synthetic work first published in 1985 still covers most of the ground for the post-medieval period.[39] There are, inevitably, some additions and new variations noted in recent years. The range of decoration on knife handles, for example, seems almost infinite, with previously unrecorded forms continuing to emerge. The focus in London on manufacture of humble items like dice and small figurines at the sites of prisons, presumably representing inmates creating an income out of meal waste, has been recognised, and it may be found to have been manifest elsewhere.[40] Study of potential coloured stains/dyes on some small bone and ivory objects (suspected to have been far more widespread than is evident from most finds) is still needed.

TEXTILES

The study of textiles remains a highly specialised field. Relatively limited survival in the soil is arguably exacerbated by a general lack of appreciation of the significance of this rare evidence for basic clothing and furnishings. The *Mary Rose* assemblage again illustrates the potential information to be gleaned through textile study, with its woollen caps, the barber surgeon's coif, as well as a series of body garments.[41] Textile assemblages recovered from the Newcastle town ditch have also been analysed.[42] One of the few studies of a group of surviving textile fragments that incorporated scientific dye analysis revealed the use of lichens, among other natural materials, for colouring 16th-century fabrics recovered from London.[43] Burial clothing, shrouds and textile coffin linings have recently provided a great deal of information about a particular aspect of the broad study of post-medieval textiles. There is great scope for analysis when preservation is adequate. Given that a number of opportunities have been lost in the past, vigilance is needed to capitalise on future chances for study. The important national and international trade in textiles is also charted in the archaeological record by seals of lead, which were put on each newly woven length to indicate who was responsible for weaving and other processes, to certify that the fabric was of good quality and the dye fast and even, and indicate the textile's origin.[44]

OTHER GOODS

Progress has also been made with several specialised categories of material culture. These include the study of children's playthings,[45] of musical instruments,[46] and of medicinal provision.[47]

PRODUCT MARKING

Strands of evidence from several different fields converge to point to the value of an archaeology of regulation as a potential theme in finds studies. The post-medieval period saw the high point in use of industrial control marks, and thus a significant amount of fresh information, not available from other sources, comes from those marks found actually on or applied to a surprising variety of consumer goods. Marks were employed (not universally) on particular products among textiles (see above), raw flax and its products, pewterware, brassware, tin-plate ironware, precious metals, armour, ingots of various metals, knives and other blades, glass vessels, window leads, commercial seeds and crops, manure, wire, humble nails, and even kosher foods prepared and consumed by the Jewish community,[48] all in addition to the well-known marks on clay pipes and some ceramics.

RECENT FINDS

Now that finds from the later 18th, 19th and 20th centuries are beginning to be taken seriously both in rescue/development archaeology and by academics (see, for example, Casella, this volume, and Jeffries *et al.*, this volume) the general lack of a broad framework in which to fit many of these objects has become evident. There are, of course, many exceptions, where collectors and other enthusiasts have brought a mass of pertinent information together on various categories of later objects, though different emphases may be more appropriate for archaeologists.[49] The almost inevitable course will be the collation and assimilation of information about similar items from several sites, and from this the development of research questions across a range of fronts will emerge, including manufacture, usage, development through time, social and other implications, as has been evolved for earlier post-medieval finds and those from previous periods. Something as regionally varied as milk and soda bottles may not seem a particularly attractive subject for serious, in-depth research, but precisely these items are going to keep on cropping up with the investigation of later deposits. The marmite jar from the last days of St Kilda's occupation[50] will recur elsewhere. Bottle enthusiasts, whom many archaeologists may despise because of their focus on collecting, may already have got some of the way towards assimilation, while archaeologists working in North America and Australia have produced a range of studies focusing upon 19th- and 20th-century material culture.

Over the past year the writer has examined parts of excavated 19th-century umbrellas and sunshades on three separate occasions. One site in London, which produced multiple finds of several umbrella components, emerged from documentary sources to have been the shop of an umbrella seller.[51] From this experience it was possible to identify a much-discussed, carved U-shaped bone object reported under the Portable Antiquities Scheme as another umbrella handle of similar date.[52] One of the initially plausible suggestions for this object saw it as part of a very unusual wind instrument, perhaps like a crumhorn, its Romanesque-style carving pointing *prima facie* to a date around the 12th century! Part of the frame of another umbrella, found among the interments in an urban graveyard,[53] was readily enough identified as such with broad dating provided from other finds. The reason for its presence in this context remains unclear (there was tempting scope for speculation following the tradition of Gothic novels, but others may go down that route if they wish).

The suggestion that someone (?possibly the sexton) may have been systematically removing jewellery left on corpses for recycling on a modest industrial scale arose from the recovery of a small number of bone-ash cupels (specialised vessels used for refining silver from impurities) during archaeological investigations of more than one London 19th-century graveyard, although this theory will remain speculative depending upon support from future finds at other cemeteries. Some remarkably early, highly specialised work by Francis Celoria on a range of 19th-century objects that are still routinely ignored by archaeologists who encounter them (from London or Exeter hammers through London coopers' hollowing knives to London pulley blocks) should be taken up and further built on.[54] There are innumerable other questions beginning to be formulated, wherever stimulating material of 'recent' date is encountered.

CONCLUSIONS

The cumulative efforts of past and current archaeological researchers continues to develop understanding of material culture, from basic identifications, definitions and dating, to a wide range of technological, social, political and other perspectives. It is possible to be impressed either by what has been achieved to date or by what has not been achieved. Some of the most stimulating recent work is coming from strange alliances – joint efforts by archaeologists with collectors and detectorists, each with something unique to contribute. What is certain is that the excavated material culture of the post-medieval period comprises a body of stimulating, varied evidence that has many different stories to tell both independently of and in conjunction with the written record. Finds analysis and material culture studies are not simply subservient nor some kind of an add-on to history.

NOTES

1. Noël Hume 1970.
2. Deagan 1987 & 2002.
3. There are, of course, very many useful publications from Continental Europe; few of these match the scope of one of the earliest – Baart *et al.* 1977.
4. Gardiner 2005.
5. Egan 2005a.
6. Courtney 2004.
7. e.g. Biddle *et al.* 2001; Ellis 1993; Mayes & Butler 1983.
8. e.g. Margeson 1993; Biddle 1990.
9. Kelso *et al.* 1995–2001; Straube 2006; see Noël Hume & Noël Hume 2001 for finds from another nearby colonial site; see Stone 1974 for 18th-century finds.
10. Redknap 1997.
11. Margeson 1993; Egan 2007a.
12. See SPMA 1988.
13. Portable Antiquities Scheme Database <finds.org.uk>.
14. Higgins 2002; Davey 1979 etc.
15. *Soc. for Clay Pipe Research Newsletter.*
16. cf. Alcock & Hall 1994; Goodall 1981.
17. Hornsby *et al.* 1989; Hilton Price 1908; Homer 1975.
18. Butler & Green 2003.
19. Seymour Lindsay 1970.
20. Egan & Forsyth 1997.
21. e.g. Gaimster *et al.* 2002; Thornton & Mitchell 2003.
22. Treasure case no. 2008 T366.
23. Read 2005.
24. Egan forthcoming a.
25. Wheeler 1928; Forsyth 2003.
26. Blair 2005; Blair & Patterson 2006.
27. Buttons recorded by PAS database: LANCUM-BOD5C3 from Lancashire; CORN-87AA74 from Corbwall; NMS-DE1042 from Norfolk; LANCUM-C7E331 from Cumbria; Buckle SOM-BB0BB4 from Wiltshire.
28. Abbitt 1973; Hughes & Hughes 1972; Egan 2007b.
29. Willmott 2002.
30. Willmott 2005.
31. Veeckman 2002.
32. Powell 1923; Godfrey 1975.
33. Egan forthcoming b.
34. Mitchiner 1988.
35. Egan 2005a, 272.
36. Evans & Mould 2005; Nailer 2005.
37. Every & Richards 2005; Chinnery & Gardiner 2005.
38. Egan 2005a, 64–5.
39. MacGregor 1985.
40. Egan 1997.
41. Gardiner 2005.
42. Walton 1981 & 1987.
43. Pritchard 1992.
44. Endrei & Egan 1982; Egan 1995.
45. Forsyth & Egan 2005; Egan 1996; marbles have their own study with Gartley & Carskadden 1998.
46. Montagu 1963.
47. Most notably Castle 2005.
48. e.g. Sullivan 2000; Egan *et al.* 1986; other categories of finds currently lack detailed syntheses.
49. The excellent publications of Brian Read, who comes from the detecting fraternity, show the way here – Read 1995, 2001 & 2005 (archaeologists cannot ignore his key contributions).
50. Emery 1996.
51. Egan forthcoming c (SQR00 site).
52. PAS Database SUR-22F3C4.
53. Egan forthcoming d.
54. Celoria 1974 (which includes regionality in tools from the 1800s) & 1978.

BIBLIOGRAPHY

Abbitt, M.W. 1973, 'The colonial shoe buckle', in Noël Hume, A. (ed.), *Five Artefact Studies*, Colonial Williamsburg Occasional Paper **1**. Williamsburg, Virginia: Colonial Williamsburg Foundation, 25–33.

Alcock, N.W. & Hall, L. 1994, *Fixtures and Fittings in Dated Houses 1567–1763*, CBA Practical Handbook in Archaeology **11**. York: Council for British Archaeology.

Baart, J.M. *et al.* 1977, *Opgravingen in Amsterdam.* Haarlem: Amsterdam Historisch Museum.

Biddle, M. 1990, *Object and Economy in Medieval Winchester*, Winchester Studies **7**:2, 2 vols. Oxford: Oxford University Press.

Biddle, M., Hiller, J., Scott, I. & Streeten, A. 2001, *Henry VIII's Coastal Artillery Fort at Camber Castle, Rye, East Sussex.* Oxford: Oxford Archaeological Unit for English Heritage.

Bird, J., Chapman, H. & Clark, J. (eds) 1978, *Collectanea Londiniensia: Studies Presented to Ralph Merrifield.* London & Middlesex Arch. Soc. Special Paper **2**.

Blair, C. 2005. '"Surrey" enamels reattributed, part 1', *Journal of the Antique Metalware Society* **13**: 2–9.

Blair, C. & Patterson, A. 2006, '"Surrey" wares reattributed, part 2: an illustrated list of known types', *Journal of the Antique Metalware Society* **14**: 10–21.

Blair, I. & Sankey, D. 2007, *A Roman Drainage Culvert, Great Fire Destruction Debris and other Evidence from Hillside Sites north east of London Bridge*, MOLAS Archaeology Studies **27**.

Butler, R. & Green, C. 2003, *English Bronze Cooking Vessels and their Founders 1350–1830*. Honiton: Roderick & Valentine Butler.

Castle, J. 2005, report on medicinal provision, in Gardiner (ed.), 2005, 171–225.

Celoria, F. 1974, *London Studies: Topography, Archaeology, Folklife* **1**, Stafford.

Celoria, F. 1978, 'Early Victorian telegraphs in London's topography, history and archaeology', in Bird, J., Chapman, H. & Clark, J. (eds), 1978, 415–35.

Chinnery, V. & Gardiner, J. 2005, reports on furniture, in Gardiner (ed.), 2005, 377–409.

Courtney, P. 2004, 'Vessel glass/small finds', in Rodwell, K & Bell, R. (eds), *Acton Court: The Evolution of an Early Tudor Courtier's House*. London: English Heritage, 331–49, 365–97.

Crossley, D.W. (ed.) 1981, *Medieval Industry*, CBA Research Report **40**. London: Council for British Archaeology.

Davey, P. (ed.) 1979 onwards, *The Archaeology of the Clay Tobacco Pipe* (British Archaeological Reports **63** onwards), Oxford.

Deagan, K. 1987, *Artifacts of the Spanish Colonies of Florida and the Caribbean 1500–1800*, 1: *Ceramics, Glassware and Beads*. Washington, DC: Smithsonian Institution.

Deagan, K. 2002, *Artifacts of the Spanish Colonies of Florida and the Caribbean 1500–1800*, 2: *Portable Personal Possessions*. Washington, DC: Smithsonian Institution.

Egan, G. 1995, *Lead Cloth Seals and Related Items in the British Museum*, British Museum Occasional Paper **93**. London: British Museum.

Egan, G. 1996, *Playthings from the Past*. London: Jonathan Horne.

Egan, G. 1997, 'Dice', *Finds Research Group 700–1700 Datasheet* **23**.

Egan, G. 2005, *Material Culture in an Age of Transition: Tudor and Stuart Period Finds c1450–1700 from Excavations at Riverside Sites in Southwark*, Museum of London Archaeological Monograph **19**. London: Museum of London.

Egan, G. 2007a, 'Accessioned finds,' in Blair & Sankey, 2007, 41–7.

Egan, G. 2007b, 'Shoe buckles', in Griffiths *et al.* (eds), 2007, 217–21.

Egan, G. forthcoming a, 'Evidence for the manufacture of early 16th century sheet strap accessories from the City of London', *Transactions of the London & Middlesex Archaeological Society.*

Egan, G. forthcoming b, 'The manufacture of glass beads in west London: Nicholas Crispe and the early colonial trade', *MOLAS Archaeological Studies.*

Egan, G. forthcoming c, 'Report on finds', in Jeffries, N. (ed.) *Report on Excavations at Spitalfields*. London: Museum of London.

Egan, G. forthcoming d, 'Report on finds', in Miles, A. (ed.) *Excavations at St Marylebone School, London*. London: Museum of London.

Egan, G. & Forsyth, H. 1997, 'Wound wire and silver gilt', in Gaimster & Stamper (eds), 1997.

Egan, G. & Michael, R.L. (eds), *Old and New Worlds*. Oxford: Oxbow.

Egan, G., Hanna, S.D. & Knight, B. 1986, 'Marks on milled window leads', *Post-Medieval Archaeology* **20**: 303–9.

Ellis, P. (ed.) 1993, *Beeston Castle, Cheshire: Excavations by Laurence Keen and Peter Hough 1968–85*, English Heritage Archaeological Report **23**. London: English Heritage.

Endrei, W. & Egan, G. 1982, 'The sealing of cloth in Europe with special reference to the English evidence', *Textile History* **13**(2): 47–75.

Emery, N. 1996, *Excavations on Hirta 1986–90*, The Archaeology and Ethnography of St Kilda **1**. Edinburgh.

Evans, N. & Mould, Q. 2005, reports on leather finds, in Gardiner (ed.), 2005.

Every, R. & Richards, M. 2005, reports on knives and knife sheaths, in Gardiner (ed.), 2005, 144–52.

Forsyth, H. 2003, *The Cheapside Hoard*. London: Museum of London.

Forsyth, H. & Egan, G. 2005, *Toys, Trifles and Trinkets: Base Metal Miniatures from London 1200–1800*. London: Unicorn Press, Museum of London.

Gaimster, D. & Stamper, P. (eds) 1997, *The Age of Transition: The Archaeology of English Culture c1400–c1600*, Soc. for Med. Arch. Monograph 15/Oxbow Monograph **98**. Oxford: Oxbow.

Gaimster, D.R.M., Haywood, M., Mitchell, D. & Parker, K. 2002, 'Tudor silver gilt dress hooks: a new class of Treasure find in England', *Antiquaries Journal* **82**: 157–96.

Gardiner, J. (ed.) 2005, *Before the Mast: Life and Death aboard the* Mary Rose, The Archaeology of the *Mary Rose* **4**. Portsmouth: *Mary Rose* Trust.

Gartley, R. & Carskadden, J. 1998, *Colonial Period and Early 19th Century Children's Toy Marbles: History and Identifications for the Archaeologist and Collector*. Zanesville, OH: The Muskingum Valley Archaeological Survey.

Godfrey, A. 1975, *The Development of English Glassmaking 1560–1640*. Oxford University Press.

Goodall, A.R. 1981, 'The medieval bronzesmith and his products', in Crossley (ed.), 1981, 63–71.

Griffiths, D, Philpott, R & Egan, G (eds) 2007, *Meols: The Archaeology of the North Wirral Coast: Discoveries and Observations with a Catalogue of Collections. Oxford University School of Archaeology Monograph* **68**.

Higgins, D.A. 2002, 'Little tubes of mighty power: a review of British clay tobacco pipe studies', in Egan & Michael (eds), *Old and New Worlds*. Oxford: Oxbow, 310–21.

Hilton Price, F.G. 1908, *Old Base Metal Spoons*. London: Batsford.

Homer, R.F. 1975, *Five Centuries of Base Metal Spoons*. London: privately printed.

Hornsby, P.R.G., Weinstein, F.R. & Homer, R.F. 1989, *Pewter: A Celebration of the Craft 1200–1700*. London: Museum of London.

Hughes, B. & Hughes, H.T. 1972, *Georgian Shoe Buckles*. London: Greater London Council.

Kelso, W. *et al.* 1995–2001, *Jamestown Rediscovery* **1–7**. Richmond, VA: Association for the Preservation of Virginia Antiquities and Dietz Press.

MacGregor, A. 1985, *Bone, Antler, Ivory and Horn*. London: Croom Helm.

Margeson, S. 1993, 'Norwich households: medieval and post medieval finds from Norwich Survey Excavations 1971–78', *East Anglian Archaeology* **58**.

Mayes, P. & Butler, L.A.S. 1983, *Sandal Castle Excavations 1964–73*. Wakefield: Wakefield Historical Publications.

Mitchiner, M. 1988, *Jetons, Medalets and Tokens* 1: *The Medieval Period and Nuremberg*. London: Seaby.

Montagu, J. 2005, report on musical instruments, in Gardiner (ed.), 2005, 226–49.

Nailer, A. 2005, reports on various leather finds, in Egan, 2005.

Noël Hume, I. 1970, *A Guide to Artifacts of Colonial America*. New York: Knopf.

Noël Hume, I. & Noël Hume, A. 2001, *The Archaeology of Martin's Hundred*, 2 Artifact Catalog. Philadelphia/Williamsburg: University of Pennsylvania Museum of Archaeology and Anthropology/Colonial Williamsburg Foundation.

Powell, H.J. 1923, *Glassmaking in England: A Historical Investigation*. Cambridge: Cambridge University Press.

Pritchard, F. 1992, 'Dyes on some 16th and 17th-century textiles excavated in London', in *Dyes in History and Archaeology* **10**. York: Textile Research Associates, 38–41.

Read, B. 1995, *History Beneath Our Feet*, 2nd edn. Langport: Portcullis Publications.

Read, B. 2001, *Metal Artefacts of Antiquity: A Catalogue of Small Finds from Specific Areas of the United Kingdom*, 1. Langport: Portcullis Publications.

Read, B. 2005, *Metal Buttons c900BC–cAD1700*. Langport: Portcullis Publications.

Redknap, M. (ed.) 1997, *Artefacts from Wrecks: Dated Assemblages from the Late Middle Ages to the Industrial Revolution*, Oxbow Monograph **84**. Oxford: Oxbow.

Seymour Lindsay, J. 1970, *Iron and Brass Implements of the English House*, rev. edn. London: Tiranti.

Society for Post Medieval Archaeology 1988, *Research Priorities for Post Medieval Archaeology*. London: National Army Museum (privately distributed).

Stone, L.M. 1974, *Fort Michilimackinac 1715–1781: An Archaeological Perspective on the Revolutionary Frontier*. East Lansing, MI: Michigan State University Museum/Mackinac Island State Park Commission.

Straube, B. 2006, '"Unfitt for any modern service": arms and armour from James Fort', *Post Medieval Archaeology* **40**(1): 33–6.

Sullivan, J. 2000, 'Lead seals of Russian origin in Fife', *Tayside and Fife Archaeological Journal* **6**, 211–27.

Thornton, D. & Mitchell, D. 2003, 'Three Tudor dress hooks', *Antiquaries Journal* **83**, 486–91.

Veeckman, J. 2002, *Majolica and Glass from Italy to Antwerp and Beyond*. Antwerp.

Walton, P. 1981, 'The textiles', in Harbottle, B. & Ellison, M. (eds), 'An excavation in the Castle Ditch, Newcastle upon Tyne, 1974–1976', *Archaeologia Aeliana* 5th series **9**,190–228.

Walton, P. 1987, 'Medieval and 17th-century textiles from High Street/Blackfriargate', in Armstrong, P. & Ayers, B. (eds), *Excavations in High Street and Blackfriargate, Hull*, East Riding Archaeology **8**, 227–31.

Wheeler, D.R.M. 1928, *The Cheapside Hoard of Elizabethan and Jacobean Jewellery*, London Museum Catalogue **2**). London: HMSO.

Willmott, H. 2002, *Early Post Medieval Vessel Glass in England 1500–1670*, CBA Research Report **132**. York: Council for British Archaeology.

Willmott, H. 2005, *A History of English Glassmaking AD43–1800*. Stroud: Tempus.

The View From Afar: International Perspectives on the Analysis of post-1750 Ceramics in Britain and Ireland

By ALASDAIR BROOKS

The concept of a globally aware historical archaeology is not itself new, but the implications of such a perspective on the historical archaeology of Britain and Ireland have yet to be fully explored. Later post-medieval ceramics, specifically those dating after the advent of industrial mass production in the mid-18th century, offer one means of exploring these implications through material culture analysis. Global conflicts, such as the Napoleonic Wars and the American Civil War, are also shown to have relevance to internationally aware interpretations of domestic ceramic distributions in Britain and Ireland.

INTRODUCTION

The implications of a globally aware international perspective on the analysis of post-1750 British material culture, particularly ceramics, are still imperfectly understood. In this chapter, a 'globally aware perspective' does not mean a discussion of whether North American and Australian historical archaeology analytical techniques are applicable outside their home regions, but rather how an awareness of international events and the increasing globalisation of trade might impact our interpretations of domestic material culture assemblages within Great Britain and Ireland.

The observation that historical archaeology deals with an increasingly globalised world, and that a by-product of this phenomenon is an increasingly globalised international trade market, has become a major point of discussion in the discipline, whether through general theoretical overviews of the topic[1] or more focused studies of maritime trade[2] or even more specific studies of individual material culture types, such as ceramics.[3] British ceramics of the industrial era have been recovered from archaeological sites in Iceland,[4] the Mediterranean,[5] the Falkland Islands,[6] Australia,[7] South American nations,[8] various regions of Africa,[9] and many other countries and regions.

Despite an increasingly broad literature on the analysis of domestic, rather than industrial, post-1750 ceramics assemblages in Britain and Ireland, including south-west Wales,[10] London,[11] St Kilda[12] and Cheshire,[13] our understanding of the impact of the global market and global events on domestic assemblages within Britain remains incomplete. This in turn has implications for our ability to examine a range of interpretive issues relevant to our developing understanding of the archaeological record of the more recent British past, particularly as regards socioeconomic and geographical variation. The general impact of the end of the Napoleonic Wars on international trade, and the specific impact of the American Civil War on the global distribution of the white granite ceramic type across the world, both offer a means by which to engage in a preliminary examination of different aspects of this issue.

INTERNATIONAL VARIATION IN CERAMICS DISTRIBUTION

While the impact of international events on British domestic assemblages may be poorly understood, past research both within and outside the United Kingdom has identified clear differences in ceramics preferences and distributions between the United States on the one hand, and the British Empire on the other. Past research on different aspects of this issue by, among others, Ewins, Lawrence, Klose & Malan, and the present author,[14] has demonstrated that while domestic assemblages within these two blocs maintain certain broad similarities from the introduction of mass production through to the first couple of decades of the 19th century, decorative and ware distributions between the two increasingly diverge over the course of the 19th century. Perhaps most obviously, while the United States market gives more prominence to lightly decorated or undecorated materials by the mid-19th century, distributions of mass-produced materials within the Empire seem to favour more brightly decorated materials.[15]

There is scope for variation within this broad observation, notably within Canada, where Western assemblages tend to be closer to the 'American' model and Eastern assemblages tend to be closer the 'British Empire' model,[16] and it perhaps underestimates the presence of flow blue transfer prints within American assemblages. This general overview of international variation also does not attempt to grapple with the complex interaction between consumer choice and market forces, something perhaps best addressed on a case-by-case basis. The general point about differences between the United States and the British Empire nonetheless holds true enough across enough assemblages internationally to serve as a starting point for discussion.

THE NAPOLEONIC WARS

The examination of the impact of international conflicts on ceramics trade and international ceramics distributions provides a useful starting point for studying the themes outlined in the introduction. The Napoleonic Wars, the first major Western European conflict of the 19th century, are particularly relevant as the impact of the end of the Napoleonic and French revolutionary conflicts on a variety of British industries is well understood, and this has been implicitly addressed through British archaeology.

In the Outer Hebrides, for example, an understanding of the impact of the Napoleonic Wars has informed part of the general background of archaeological research, particularly as regards the rise of the kelp industry during the Wars, and the clearances and emigration that occurred after those wars. Both Symonds and Webster, for example, have used these events to inform archaeological discussions of domination and resistance in the Outer Hebrides,[17] in Webster's case using the specific example of ceramics, and the display thereof on dressers, to examine past and present conceptions of Hebridean poverty. Yet past archaeological analysis has tended to acknowledge the role of the Napoleonic Wars through its impact on the broader socioeconomic environment rather than on the specific impact on assemblage distribution. This is a subtle but important distinction, because the war with France also clearly impacted the manufacture and distribution of domestic material culture, including ceramics. To properly explore this point requires a more detailed understanding of the economic impact of the wars within the United Kingdom; the rise and fall of the Hebridean kelp industry is particularly informative in this regard.

Kelp is an alkaline by-product of seaweed used in the production of soap and glass. Prior to the second half of the 18th century, seaweed was chiefly used in the Hebrides for manuring the barley crop,[18] but the emphasis would change dramatically in the following decades. During the Napoleonic Wars, the Hebridean kelp industry was suddenly converted into a vital part of the British war effort when the Spanish supply of alkalis was cut off in the 1790s. The price of kelp doubled between 1790 and 1810, while production more than tripled between 1770 and 1810.[19] The effect of this shift in the kelping industry on the local population was dramatic, as communities were increasingly transformed by the introduction of crofting. The primary motivation behind this transformation was to turn the local population into labourers, with agriculture only a secondary concern. The crofts were intentionally reduced in size in order to force the family into dependence on outside labour, while landlords raised rents to artificially high levels, mechanisms that both served to force tenants to turn to kelping to supplement their income. Meanwhile the population of the Islands increased dramatically, a process facilitated by the potato crop, as the landlords realised that more people translated into more labour and thus more production. South Uist's population, for example, increased by a staggering 211 per cent between 1755 and 1831.[20]

As traumatic as the changes outlined above undoubtedly were to the Hebridean communities involved, the socioeconomic system based on kelping rapidly came apart. With the end of the Napoleonic Wars in 1815, the markets for foreign alkali sources were reopened. Almost simultaneously, a chemical process perfecting the extraction of alkali from salt was perfected. The Highland landlords battled to maintain high tariffs on foreign alkali sources, but by 1825, the British soap and glass manufacturers convinced the government to lower or even abolish import duties. In the face of these pressures, the market price of kelp collapsed.[21] Unfortunately, the Island estates had been organised in the assumption that the kelp boom would be permanent. The crofters and landlords both felt the consequences of this drastic fall in prices, but kelping was by now so integral to the crofting communities that it could not be abandoned without causing the entire financial structure of the islands to collapse. The value of commodities that might have cushioned the blow to kelp also suffered. Cattle prices halved and herring bounties were withdrawn – the latter occurring just as over-fishing eliminated herring from coastal regions. Of the Highland staples, only sheep and wool remained profitable.[22]

Further social disruption across the Highlands was caused by demobilisation following the end of the long struggle with France. Estimates of the total number of men demobilised vary,[23] but even recognising that demobilisation was far from total, it was impossible for an economically marginal society on the verge of economic collapse to absorb tens of thousands of suddenly unemployed men.   Under these circumstances, the crofters were no longer an irreplaceable labour force working in a highly profitable industry, but rather a redundant population taking up valuable land and unable to pay a viable rent. As a result, restrictions on emigration were lifted, and the Hebridean sheep clearances began in earnest.[24] Given the direct connection between the Napoleonic Wars, the shifts in Spanish alkali imports, and the development and collapse of the kelp industry, it is not entirely unreasonable to see the Napoleonic conflict as one of the causes of the introduction of crofting and the Hebridean clearances.

Post-Napoleonic economic developments have also been considered in archaeological analysis in south-west Wales,[25] though the specific impact inevitably differed somewhat from that observed in the Hebrides. In the wake of the end of the Napoleonic Wars, market prices for the agricultural goods of north Pembrokeshire collapsed, reaching rock bottom in 1842 following Peel's tariff reforms and the temporary collapse of the Merthyr Tydfil mining industry. Every bank in Pembrokeshire closed in the banking crisis of 1825–6, causing many farmers to lose their savings.[26] The 1839–41 growing season was a disaster, and corn had to be imported, further stretching farmers' limited resources[27] and leading to 'a state of semi-starvation and spiritual malaise'.[28] The Rebecca riots of the late 1830s and 1840s were ostensibly over turnpike abuses, but they should be seen as a reaction against the post-Napoleonic disintegration of rural conditions in general[29] – though the expansion of the south Wales coalfields in the early 19th century (themselves subject to a post-Napoleonic economic depression) additionally encouraged massive internal migration from depressed rural areas to the new industrial areas.[30]

These examples from Scotland and Wales may initially seem of limited relevance to ceramic distributions, but they clearly indicate the often transformative impact that the Napoleonic conflict and its aftermath had within the British Isles. Yet while the histories of the Hebridean kelp industry and 19th-century agriculture in Pembrokeshire offer examples of negative Napoleonic impact, some British industries profited through the end of the conflict, and the opening up of newly secure international markets for industrially mass-produced goods. The British ceramics industry was one of the real beneficiaries.

The extent to which British ceramics manufacturers actively benefited from the end of the Napoleonic Wars has perhaps been obscured in the broader international archaeological literature by a natural and understandable American-centrism on the part of colleagues focused on the dynamics of trans-Atlantic trade.   Those colleagues, by no means unreasonably, tend to think of the changes in American later 18th- and early 19th-century domestic assemblages as being part of the maturation of the American domestic market in the wake of the War of Independence and the War of 1812. Difference have been observed between the types of materials contained within American assemblages before and after the latter conflict, though there is also regional variation.[31] From a globally-aware British-centred perspective, however, this perhaps misses the importance of the combination of changes in ceramics technology coinciding with the Napoleonic Wars, the last few years of which themselves coincided with the 1812–15 conflict between the United States and United Kingdom. What an Atlanticist perspective might see solely as a maturing domestic American market, a broader perspective might instead see as part and parcel of a wider international process whereby the industrialised British potters were taking advantage of an ability to expand to a variety of international markets once a series of interlocking conflicts, of which the long conflict with France was the most prominent, come to an end. The decision by the J. & M.P. Bell firm of Glasgow to produce transfer prints specifically designed for and exported to, south-east Asia[32] can hardly be understood as a matter of catering to an American market. Sarah Croucher has also shown how cut-sponged vessels made for a general 'Asian' market occur in Zanzibar, but were also tied to wider Indian Ocean patterns of rice-based dishes.[33] Again, this is not a distribution of materials that can in any way be understood as catering to the American market.

South America provides a particularly instructive example, as here the end of the Napoleonic Wars also roughly coincides with the end of the South American wars of independence; indeed, the conflicts are not unrelated, as Napoleon's insecure conquest of Spain and the consequent weakening of Spanish rule in South America are directly linked. Recent research by Rodriguez in the Venezuelan colonial city of Barcelona shows an even sharper difference in ceramics distributions between the pre-and post-independence period here than exists before and after the War of 1812 in the United States. While quantification of the materials is still ongoing, Rodríguez has noted that ceramics are largely of Spanish manufacture prior to independence, while after the Venezuelan War of Independence those domestic assemblages are mostly of British manufacture.[34]

Given the mercantilist nature of trade within the Spanish Empire, the dominance of Spanish materials in the colonial period is unsurprising in and of itself, but the consistency with which British ceramics manufacturers expand into new trans-Atlantic markets within a decade of the Napoleonic Wars ending is remarkable. Whether the United States or Latin America – and the discussion of white granite later in this chapter will show that the latter was the second largest market for British ceramics by the middle of the 19th century – the end of international warfare permits the expansion of the British ceramics industry's exports. The fact that the 1820s is also the decade where the creamware and pearlware of the immediate post-1750 period give way to whiteware should also perhaps be considered in this international shift. Is it just coincidence that the post-Napoleonic expansion in the international market for British ceramics coincides with the final phasing-in of true white-bodied ceramics, or is there a more direct connection between ceramics innovation and international expansion? This particular point requires deeper consideration. In the longer run, it will prove instructive to compare British, American and South American assemblages from the period 1780 to 1880 to properly examine the extent to which these shifts are local market-based, producer-based, technological, or were indeed caused by some combination of the three.

Dellino-Musgrave's comparisons of late-18th-century British shipwreck assemblages off the Falkland Islands and Australia certainly suggest significant differences in British attempts to engage in local markets before and after the end of the Napoleonic Wars. She argues that non-American British trade in late-18th-century mass-produced goods (including ceramics) was centred on important and strategic (to the British) military sites.[35] The sudden rise in exports to South America (and, anecdotally, post-Ottoman European nations in the Mediterranean) in the early 19th century suggests that this dynamic significantly shifted in the wake of Napoleon's defeat, instead of concentrating on strategic British sites. The crucial question here is whether that dynamic is also reflected within British domestic assemblages. If post-Napoleonic developments in the international archaeological record are so clearly visible, are they similarly visible in the British archaeological record? What might be the implications for British archaeological analysis? Only by comparing shifts in British material culture distributions with those from other regions can this point be fully understood, but these comparisons cannot be made until 19th-century materials are treated more seriously – and collected more consistently – within the United Kingdom.

The post-Napoleonic presence of British ceramics in Venezuela also raises intriguing questions of ideological interpretation that potentially impact similar research in the United Kingdom. These questions also serve to emphasise that an awareness of international issues need not solely be restricted to studying economy, trade, and consumption. The role of transfer prints as a means of transmitting ideological perspectives is well understood, whether from a general perspective,[36] or through a more specific analysis of literary associations[37] or – perhaps most relevant to the present discussion – transmitting British conceptions of nationhood, whether associated with 'Celtic Myth' or the creation of British identity during the Napoleonic Wars.[38] The role of ceramic vessel form in the transmission of British ideology is perhaps less fully explored, though studies of form enjoy a long tradition in American research on African-American sites.[39] Within the United Kingdom, past research on the ideology of form has largely been restricted to a study of the interaction between traditional Welsh and emerging metropolitan British ideologies in the 19th century.[40]

Within the Venezuelan context, Ana Cristina Rodríguez Yilo has posited that the ideological content of British transfer prints was actively manipulated by the elite of the newly independent state.[41] This elite intentionally associated itself with European ideology, as displayed on British transfer prints of Georgian mansions and a bucolic countryside, while excluding South American – whether indigenous or creole (or indeed African) – cultural imagery. Those very same Georgian mansions were replicated in the Venezuelan countryside in the post-independence period, right down to the inclusion of purely ornamental chimneys (as opposed to those associated with 'summer kitchens') with no function beyond replicating the appearance of their European counterparts. Rodríguez has also noted how the flora and fauna displayed on British transfer prints were wholly alien to the South American experience, further reinforcing the elite's ideological connection with European – in this case British – material culture once independence had been achieved in the wake of the Napoleonic Wars.

This South American example is potentially instructive for the United Kingdom and Ireland through its demonstration of how meaning can be manipulated by geographically based sociocultural groups. Taking Ireland as an example, several transfer-printed pattern sets were produced in the 19th century that explicitly included Ireland as both part of the United Kingdom (as is indeed it was *de jure* from 1801 through to the early 20th century) and culturally British (which is far more disputable). Particularly relevant to the discussion of the presence in Venezuela of plates displaying British stately homes are the presence of Castle Freke (County Cork) in the 'Titled Seats' series,[42] and Holywell Cottage (County Cavan) in the 'Grapevine Border' series, itself based on a series of prints of 'Seats of Noblemen and Gentlemen in England and Wales, Scotland and Ireland'.[43]

If this type of pattern were ever to be excavated in Ireland, it would be reasonable to ask how it might be understood, and what the implications might be from both a local and international perspective. Would the use of the pattern indicate an intentional attempt by the governing elite to identify themselves with the new United Kingdom? Might it indicate a more subconscious process whereby metropolitan British ideologies filter through to the 'Celtic fringe'? Might there be class- or regional-based divisions in pattern distributions that could inform research on differing perceptions of the political union between Great Britain and Ireland across the 19th century? How might the distributions of these patterns compare to other regions of the 19th-century United Kingdom or other regions where they have been found, such as Venezuela? What might this tell us in turn about how these vessels are used to transmit metropolitan British ideology in the post-Napoleonic period? Regrettably, the lack of a systematic approach to saving 19th-century material in Ireland makes it difficult to identify at present whether relevant patterns occur, but the potential for using international research to help frame these important research questions is clearly there.

THE AMERICAN CIVIL WAR

The topics outlined in the discussion of the impact of the Napoleonic Wars were somewhat general and speculative. A more specific and developed analysis of the impact of international conflict on 19th-century ceramic distributions can be offered through an examination of the impact of the American Civil War, particularly as relates to the occurrence in some Australian assemblages of a 19th-century pottery type called 'white granite'.

White granite is a fairly plain earthenware with a bluish-grey body, which usually features little more in the way of decoration than a lightly moulded body;[44] the collecting community often refers to the ware type as 'white ironstone china',[45] but this is typologically misleading for a number of reasons, and 'white granite' is usually preferred by archaeologists.[46] White granite occurs in range of tableware forms, though plates seem to be the most common form recovered archaeologically, with cups the second most common form. Similar materials were also produced in the United States, most famously in the East Liverpool, Ohio region, though not necessarily under the 'white granite' name.[47] It was manufactured in the United Kingdom, however, specifically to cater to the American market, where it had became popular in the 1840s owing to an American vogue for the French porcelain white granite was supposed to resemble. French goods had been considered sophisticated and genteel in the upper echelons of American society since the 18th century; the popularity of white granite in the mid-19th century seems to have been connected to this broader desire to emulate French 'good taste'.[48]

Until fairly recently, most archaeologists and ceramicists who were familiar with the ware type assumed that white granite remained a material that, where it was produced in the

United Kingdom, was manufactured exclusively for the American market. Recent research has shown that the situation is more complex than was at first apparent, and the question might reasonably be asked as to whether new evidence on the international distribution of these materials might be relevant to studies of 19th-century assemblages within Great Britain and Ireland. Of particular relevance here are distributions of white granite in Australian assemblages, where the material has been identified, but where distribution appears to be inconsistent. At a site called 'Viewbank', on the outskirts of modern Melbourne, it formed a significant part of the assemblage, perhaps over 10 per cent.[49] Much smaller amounts have been recovered from a range of other sites across eastern Australia, and at other sites it is absent entirely. No white granite was identified in the period-relevant materials at the Lake Innes estate in New South Wales,[50] and unpublished research by the present author suggests that it is also absent from relevant assemblages at the Port Arthur historic site in Tasmania. The latter was a military-run convict station during the period in question, which perhaps presents a different supply and demand mechanism than that encountered at domestic sites, but differences nonetheless clearly exist in the distribution of white granite in Australia.

As has been discussed in more detail elsewhere,[51] the occurrence of white granite within Australia appears to be closely tied to the closure and collapse of American markets in the American Civil War of 1861–5. According to figures collated from the *Staffordshire Advertiser*, ceramics exports from Liverpool to the United States collapsed by approximately 32,000 crates between the last six months of 1860 and the last six months of 1861, from slightly over 40,000 crates to only 8,000 crates; this represents an 80 percent collapse in the American market. Of the ports listed by the *Advertiser*, the Confederate ports of New Orleans and Charleston were under a total embargo, while even the major Northern ports of Boston, Philadelphia and New York featured massive declines in imports of British ceramics. Of the six American ports for which figures are available, only San Francisco – on the Pacific coast, and well away from the war – recorded an increase in imports during the period in question. This decline also impacted American market share; whereas the United States was the destination for nearly 60 percent of Liverpool ceramic exports in the second half of 1860, it only had a 20 percent market share in the second half of 1861. South America meanwhile went from taking 21 percent of Liverpool ceramics exports at the end of 1860 to just over 38 percent at the end of 1861, becoming the largest market for those exports in the process.

Australia went from a comparatively minor 1 percent of the market to 3 percent of the market in the same period, though this represents an increase of nearly 50 percent in exports to the Australian market. As the *Staffordshire Advertiser* noted in October 1861: 'It will be seen from the above that there is an increase of exports in almost every quarter, with the important exception of the "United States." Here the decrease is unfortunately too manifest, and still continues to supply the reason why many houses in the Potteries are finding their hands so little employment.' The *Advertiser* also directly addressed the impact of increased exports to Australia over the course of the Civil War. In April 1863, the newspaper notes that 'to some other countries the exports show a very considerable increase … to Australia and New Zealand 164 crates'. So great was the relative increase in exports to Australia that by November 1864 the *Advertiser* stated: 'For some years past the exports to Australia have been excessive, and this has led to a glut in the market, and a consequent deprecation in value.' The Staffordshire potters therefore compensated for the difficulties in the American market, and the total embargo on Confederate ports, by expanding exports to other markets, of which Australia was one.

This evidence is documentary, but there is also clear evidence of just the type of period-appropriate dumping of white granite in Australia that might be expected from this evidence. To take but one example, some of the 'Berlin Swirl' pattern white granite vessels recovered from the Viewbank site in Melbourne feature a maker's mark from 'Liddle, Mayer and Elliot',[52] a firm not listed in Godden's standard guide to British pottery marks,[53] but which, from information on predecessor and successor firms in Godden, could only have operated between 1861 and 1862 – precisely when the American market had collapsed owing to the Civil War. Otherwise, the most common 'Berlin Swirl' mark is for the 1862–71 successor firm 'Liddle, Elliot and Son'. No white granite has yet been identified at any site in Australia with a mark pre-dating 1861. Further evidence from the Viewbank assemblage is provided by a jug base printed with the Latin motto *e pluribus unum*,[54] the then national motto of the United States of America.

Viewbank was the residence of a comfortably well-off respectable middle-class doctor and his family, perhaps reflecting what Hayes has suggested about class and status impacting distributions of white granite in Australia.[55] Despite Hayes's recent work on this issue, Australian studies are still to fully address the potential status implications of white granite in local assemblages, or the extent to which domestic demand may have existed for the material, whether following its introduction in the wake of the Civil War or through trans-Pacific gold rush connections pre-dating the War. These issues require further study. When the documentary and archaeological evidence are combined, the presence of British-made, but American-market, materials on at least some Australian sites would appear to be the by-product of a fratricidal conflict on the other side of the world.

While this may seem to be an interesting but nonetheless fairly abstract conclusion from a British perspective, there are direct implications for the interpretation of domestic assemblages recovered from mid-19th century sites within the United Kingdom. Of particular relevance are two further observations from the *Staffordshire Advertiser*. In June 1861, the newspaper noted that while the 'civil discord' in the United States has blighted trade with that country, 'the houses engaged in the home, colonial and continental trade are somewhat better off'. In November 1864, the newspaper similarly noted that 'the outbreak of war in America has led to a great expansion of the home and continental markets'. Given this apparent expansion of the home market in this period, we turn to the question as to whether the close of American markets had any impact on domestic distribution within the 19th-century United Kingdom.

To fully answer this point would require more in-depth analysis of the documentary evidence than has currently taken place. While the *Staffordshire Advertiser* offers quite detailed figures for exports, no such figures are given for the internal market, and a more detailed examination of local merchants' records within the United Kingdom is probably necessary before the question can be looked at quantitatively. A more robust collection policy towards

19th-century materials excavated in Britain and Ireland is also necessary (*contra* O'Keefe, this volume); it remains impossible to fully investigate either domestic or international research issues unless these materials are excavated, retained and analysed more consistently. It is nonetheless possible to offer more qualitative research questions for future work, based on past archaeological research in Britain, in order to demonstrate how an awareness of these international issues might potentially impact on British and Irish analysis. As noted, white granite was very much an American-market material produced for export, but small quantities of the wares have been identified within British domestic assemblages; while most of these identified items remain unpublished, they are known to have been recovered from the 19th-century cottages of transient farm workers in Pembrokeshire, Wales.[56] White granite wares have also been observed in Ireland, though a lack of a robust collection policy towards later materials in either the Republic or the North means that any attempt to quantify the volume of material remains problematic as of this writing.[57]

That this material does occur in the 19th-century United Kingdom leads us to consider a series of interpretive hypothesis regarding its presence. Is it widespread? Does its presence in British and Irish assemblages indicate a dumping mechanism similar to that observed in Australia? Is its distribution more restricted, whether on a class or regional basis? If class-based, might this indicate that these American-market materials are being dumped on poorer markets? If regionally based, might this indicate that these American-market materials are being dumped on a Celtic Fringe that, as distasteful as we might consider this view today, was still, in the 19th century at least, often considered by the United Kingdom's metropolitan core to be an unsophisticated cultural backwater?[58] This discussion is no doubt more focused on asking questions rather than supplying answers, but these questions serve to point towards the potential interpretive impact of considering the relevance of international events to the distributions of material culture to our analysis of post-1750 domestic assemblages within Britain and Ireland.

CONCLUSION

This chapter has ranged over some considerable geographical ground, but the conclusion must return us to Great Britain and Ireland in order to summarise what an awareness of global issues might mean to the archaeological interpretation of domestic assemblages of post-1750 pottery – and potentially other material culture – both within and without these islands. As was noted in the introduction to this chapter, the idea of global interconnectedness in historical archaeology is not in itself new. What is new is a detailed exploration of the potential of global interconnectedness for the analysis of domestic assemblages within the archaeology of post-1750 Britain and Ireland. As noted in the discussion of the American Civil War and Australian assemblages, Britain and Ireland existed within a global market where international events potentially impact assemblage distribution even within nations where the ceramics were originally manufactured.

Just as an awareness of global events might occasionally give us reason to consider our interpretations within Britain and Ireland, so too might a global ceramics perspective centred on Britain cause us to reassess some interpretations undertaken by our colleagues abroad. For example, are shifts in American distributions in the first two decades of the 19th century the product of a shifting American market, the product of a newly confident British ceramics industry taking advantage of a range of newly available international markets following a series of international wars, or indeed a combination thereof? The answer might have a bearing on our interpretations of assemblages within Britain and Ireland once we better understand the dynamics.

A further sub-theme throughout this chapter has been the problems caused to interpretation by the uneven approaches to saving 19th-century materials within Britain and Ireland. While there are many colleagues in universities, museums and commercial units prepared to give these materials their due, the post-1750 period – and the 19th century in particular – still struggles to be considered seriously by the majority of archaeologists working in Britain and Ireland. This chapter has used international examples to help emphasise that important and relevant archaeological research questions exist for the archaeological study of our ceramics – and, by implication, other materials – from this period. It is one of the paradoxes of historical archaeology internationally that the archaeological study of industrially produced British-made material culture is arguably far more advanced in export markets, such as the United States, Canada and Australia, than it is in the country where these materials were produced. We understand the periphery far better than we understand the core, and the time has surely come to pay closer attention to that core, even while continuing to appreciate the importance of the periphery.

Despite the somewhat speculative nature of elements of this chapter, one thing remains clear. Whether we consider ourselves historical archaeologists, post-medieval archaeologists, or industrial archaeologists, the material culture of post-1750 Britain and Ireland exists within a global, interlocked world that potentially impacts on all of our interpretations, no matter where we work.

ACKNOWLEDGEMENTS

I am very grateful to Ana Cristina Rodríguez Yilo for sharing with me her research on her Venezuelan assemblage – more detailed co-authored English-language publication of which is hopefully forthcoming. I would also like to thank volume co-editor Audrey Horning for her editorial patience, not least when gently pointing out that I had spectacularly failed to follow SPMA's endnote citation system in my 'final' draft. Audrey and my anonymous referee also made helpful comments about restructuring the chapter, notably as regards switching the order of the Napoleonic War and Civil War discussions. Any errors of fact and perceived errors of interpretation remain, of course, entirely my own responsibility.

NOTES

1. Orser 1996.
2. Dellino-Musgrave 2006; Staniforth 2003.
3. Brooks 2002; Ewins 1997.
4. Sveinbjarnardóttir 1996.
5. Amouric *et al.* 1999.
6. Barker 1996.
7. Brooks 2005.
8. Schávelzon 2005; Rodríguez Yilo 2007.
9. Croucher 2008; Klose and Malan 2000.
10. Brooks 2003.
11. Pearce 2000.
12. Emery 1996.
13. Matthews 1999.
14. Brooks 2005; Ewins 1997; Klose & Malan 2000; Lawrence 2003.
15. Lawrence 2003, 23–9.
16. Lawrence 2003, 26.
17. Symonds 1999; Webster 1999.
18. Fenton 1986, 77.
19. Devine 1994, 42–3; Hunter 1976, 16.
20. Hunter 1976, 31.
21. Devine 1994, 51–2; Hunter 1976, 35.
22. Devine 1994, 51–2.
23. See, for example, the different estimates in Devine 1994, 43; MacInnes 1988, 43.
24. Hunter 1976, 39–42.
25. Brooks 2003.
26. Davies 1993, 355.
27. Howell 1993, 83–4.
28. Williams 1955, 185.
29. Davies 1993, 379.
30. Davies 1993, 351.
31. Ewins 1997, 18–25.
32. Kelly 1999, 105, 127–8.
33. Croucher 2008.
34. Rodríguez Yilo 2007.
35. Dellino-Musgrave 2006.
36. Brooks in press; Smart Martin 2001.
37. Lucas 2003.
38. Brooks 1997; 1999.
39. Of which one of the better-known examples is Ferguson 1992, 106–7.
40. Brooks 2003.
41. Rodríguez Yilo 2007.
42. Coysh & Henrywood 1982, 363.
43. Coysh & Henrywood 1982, 161–2.
44. Brooks 2005.
45. Dieringer & Dieringer 2001.
46. Brooks 2005.
47. Gates and Ormerod 1982, 8.
48. Ewins 1997, 49.
49. Brooks 2005, 59; Hayes 2007, 95.
50. Brooks & Connah 2007.
51. Brooks 2005, 56–60.
52. Brooks 2005, 59.
53. Godden 1991.
54. Hayes 2007, 95.
55. Hayes 2007, 95.
56. Brooks 2003, 124.
57. Audrey Horning pers. comm. 23 May 2008.
58. Brooks 2003, 131; Curwen 1938.

BIBLIOGRAPHY

Amouric, H., Richez, F. & Vallauri, L. 1999, *Vingt Mille Pots Sous Les Mers; Le Commerce de la Céramique en Provence et Languedoc du Xe au XIXe Siècle*. Aix-En-Provence: Edisud.

Barker, D. 1996, 'A note on the surface finds from Port Egmont', in Philpott, 1996, 54–5.

Brooks, A.M. 1997, 'Beyond the fringe: transfer-printed ceramics and the internationalisation of Celtic myth', *International Journal of Historical Archaeology* **1**(1): 39–55.

Brooks, A.M. 1999, 'Building Jerusalem: transfer-printed finewares and the creation of British identity', in Tarlow & West (eds), 1999, 51–65.

Brooks, A.M. 2002, 'The cloud of unknowing: towards an international comparative analysis of eighteenth- and nineteenth-century ceramics', *Australasian Historical Archaeology* **20**: 48–57.

Brooks, A.M. 2003, 'Crossing Offa's Dyke: British ideologies and late eighteenth- and nineteenth-century ceramics in Wales', in Lawrence (ed.), 2003, 119–37.

Brooks, A.M. 2005, *An Archaeological Guide to British Pottery in Australia, 1788–1901*. Sydney: Australasian Society for Historical Archaeology, and Melbourne: La Trobe University Archaeology Program.

Brooks, A.M. in press, 'A not so useless beauty – economy, status, function, and meaning in the interpretation of transfer-printed tablewares', in Symonds in press.

Brooks, A.M. & Connah, G. 2007, 'A hierarchy of servitude: ceramics at Lake Innes Estate, New South Wales', *Antiquity* **81**: 133–47.

Coysh. A.W. &. Henrywood, R.K. 1982, *The Dictionary of Blue and White Printed Pottery 1780–1880, Volume 1.* Woodbridge: Antique Collectors' Club.

Croucher, S. 2008, 'Exchange values: commodities, colonialism, and identity on nineteenth-century Zanzibar', paper presented at the annual meeting of the Society for Historical Archaeology, Albuquerque, New Mexico.

Curwen, E.C. 1938, 'The Hebrides: a cultural backwater', *Antiquity* **12**: 261–89.

Davies, J. 1993, *A History of Wales.* Harmondsworth: Allen Lane.

Dellino-Musgrave, V. 2006, *Maritime Archaeology and Social Relations: British Action in the Southern Hemisphere.* New York: Springer.

Devine, T.M. 1994, *Clanship to Crofter's War: The Social Transformation of the Scottish Highlands.* Manchester: Manchester University Press.

Devine, T.M. & Micheson R. (eds) 1988, *People and Society in Scotland, Volume 1: 1760–1830.* Edinburgh: John Donald.

Dieringer, E. & Dieringer, B. 2001, *White Ironstone China.* Atglen: Schiffer.

Emery, N. 1996, *Excavations on St Kilda.* Edinburgh: HMSO.

Ewins, N. 1997, '"Supplying the present wants of our Yankee Cousins": Staffordshire ceramics and the American market 1775–1880', *Journal of Ceramic History* **15**.

Fenton A. 1996, *The Shape of the Past: Essays in Scottish Ethnology, Vol. 2.* Edinburgh: John Donald.

Ferguson, L. 1992, *Uncommon Ground: Archaeology and Early African America 1650–1800.* Washington, DC: Smithsonian Institution Press.

Gates, W. & Ormerod, D. 1982, 'The East Liverpool pottery district: identification of manufacturers and marks', *Historical Archaeology* **16**(1) & **16**(2).

Godden, G.A. 1991, *Encyclopaedia of British Pottery and Porcelain Marks*, corrected edn. London: Barrie & Jenkins.

Hayes, S. 2007, 'Consumer practice at Viewbank Homestead', *Australasian Historical Archaeology* **25**: 87–104.

Howell, D.W. 1993, 'Farming in Pembrokeshire, 1815–1974', in Howell (ed.), 1993, 77–110.

Howell, D.W. (ed.) 1993, *Pembrokeshire County History, Volume IV: Modern Pembrokeshire 1815–1974.* Haverfordwest: The Pembrokeshire Historical Society.

Hunter, J. 1976, *The Making of the Crofting Community.* Edinburgh: John Donald.

Kelly, H. 1999, *Scottish Ceramics.* Atglen: Schiffer Publishing.

Klose, J. & Malan, A. 2000, 'The ceramic signature of the Cape in the nineteenth century, with particular reference to the Tennant Street Site, Cape Town', *South African Archaeological Bulletin* **55**: 49–59.

Lawrence, S. 2003, 'Exporting culture: archaeology and the nineteenth-century British Empire', *Historical Archaeology* **37**(1): 20–33.

Lawrence, S. (ed.) 2003, *Archaeologies of the British.* London: Routledge.

Lucas, G. 2003, 'Reading pottery: literature and transfer-printed pottery in the early nineteenth century', *International Journal of Historical Archaeology* **7**(2): 127–43.

MacInnes, A. 1988, 'Scottish Gaeldom: the first phase of clearance', in Devine & Micheson (eds), 1988, 43–51.

Matthews, K. 1999, 'Familiarity and contempt; the archaeology of the "modern"', in Tarlow & West (eds), 1999, 155–79.

Orser, C.E. 1996, *A Historical Archaeology of the Modern World.* London, Springer.

Pearce, J. 2000, 'A late 18th-century inn clearance assemblage from Uxbridge, Middlesex', *Post-Medieval Archaeology* **34**: 144–86.

Philpott, R. 1996, 'An archaeological survey of Port Egmont, the first British settlement in the Falkland Islands', *Post-Medieval Archaeology* **30**: 1–62.

Rodríguez Yilo, A.C. 2007, 'Hablamos Espanol, Comemos en Ingles', paper presented at the 23rd Annual Congress of the International Association for Caribbean Archaeology, Kingston, Jamaica.

Schávelzon, D. 2005, 'When the revolution reached the countryside: use and destruction of imported wares in Alta Gracia, Córdoba, 1810', *International Journal of Historical Archaeology* **9**(3): 195–207.

Staniforth, M. 2003, *Material Culture and Consumer Society: Dependent Colonies in Colonial Australia*. New York: Plenum.

Sveinbjarnardottir, G. 1996, *Leirker á Íslandi – Pottery found in excavations in Iceland*. Reykjavík: Þjódminjasafn Íslands.

Symonds, J. 1999, 'Toiling in the Vale of Tears: everyday life and resistance in South Uist, Outer Hebrides, 1760–1860', *International Journal of Historical Archaeology* **3**(2): 101–22.

Symonds, J. (ed.) in press, *The Table*. Oxford: Oxbow Books.

Tarlow, S. & West, S. (eds) 1999, *The Familiar Past? Archaeologies of Later Historical Britain*. London: Routledge.

Webster, J. 1999. 'Resisting traditions: ceramics, identity, and consumer choice in the Outer Hebrides from 1800 to the present', *International Journal of Historical Archaeology* **3**(1): 53–73.

Williams, D. 1955, *The Rebecca Riots: A Study in Agrarian Discontent*. Cardiff.

Post-1550 Urban Archaeology in a Developer-funded Context: An Example from Grand Arcade, Cambridge

By CRAIG CESSFORD

The amount of post-1550 developer-funded urban archaeology has expanded exponentially in recent years. Based upon the author's recent experience of directing excavations at the Grand Arcade site, Cambridge, some of the implications of this expansion are explored, with particular reference to how such material should be published. Existing models of publication are problematic, but the potential exists for developer-funded urban archaeology to make a substantive contribution to our understanding of the period.

INTRODUCTION

Since the introduction of PPG16 Archaeology and Planning in November 1990 a vast amount of developer-funded archaeology has been undertaken in the United Kingdom. The extent of such work is impossible to quantify precisely, but certainly runs into millions of pounds, with a significant proportion of this directed towards the post-1550 period. This has led to the investigation of thousands of features and the creation of huge assemblages of material. Yet in most instances this work has not been undertaken by organisations or individuals with a specific interest in the post-1550 period, but by 'generalists' or 'urban specialists' who must frequently deal with the Roman, Saxon, medieval, post-medieval and modern periods on a single site. From this perspective the fragmentation of the post-1550 period into 'post-medieval', 'industrial' and 'contemporary and historical' archaeologies is simply part of a wider disciplinary malaise of factionalisation and specialism, which is the antithesis of what high quality urban archaeology should be about, as 'sequence is all'.[1] The scale of developer-funded urban archaeology being undertaken clearly has the potential to inform us about both 'questions that count' and 'stories that matter'[2] for the post-1550 period, although this potential remains largely untapped.

Some of the issues surrounding developer-funded archaeology of the post-1550 period will be addressed in this chapter. These primarily relate to an inherent contradiction, for while on the one hand it is desirable to treat all periods on a site in as similar a manner as possible in order to promote comparability, on the other it is also important to recognise the particular strengths and weaknesses of each individual phase. With regard to the post-

1550 period, it is both the nature and variety of the available evidence that are striking, and which often comprise an undervalued and underused resource.

GRAND ARCADE, CAMBRIDGE

In 2005 and 2006 the Cambridge Archaeological Unit (CAU) undertook large-scale excavations at the Grand Arcade site in central Cambridge (Figs 22.1 & 22.2). This site represents a breakthrough regionally in terms of both its size at 1.5 hectares, which took a team of around twenty-five over a year to excavate, and the fact that archaeological features and deposits of all periods up to and including the 20th century were treated as 'proper' archaeology and investigated as thoroughly as earlier periods. Allowing for a few methodological nuances, largely related to the recording of masonry, post-1550 features were excavated and recorded in roughly the same manner as the earlier features at the site. In common with most developer-funded archaeology in Britain, the work was carried out following a brief from the County Archaeological Office, plus a statement of archaeological strategy and a written scheme of investigation by the CAU, all of which took account of the regional resource assessment[3] and research agenda and strategy.[4] The post-1550 period was specifically recognised in the written scheme of investigation, which stated that 'Attention will be paid to remains of the 16th–20th centuries where they are sufficiently well preserved'; this, combined with a sympathetic developer and the commitment of the CAU and the County Archaeological Office to post-1550 archaeology, is what allowed the detailed treatment of the later periods at the site. This would not have happened a decade or so earlier, when post-1550 archaeology was dealt with much more summarily in Cambridgeshire.

The CAU, like the majority of organisations involved in developer-funded archaeology, undertakes work on sites of all periods, although later prehistoric and Roman sites

LEFT
Figure 22.1 Aerial view of the Grand Arcade archaeological excavations during April 2005 in the midst of demolition and construction (courtesy of Bovis Lend Lease Ltd)

RIGHT
Figure 22.2 General
view of Grand Arcade
excavations (photo: Dave
Webb)

predominate. It also works in both urban and rural contexts, although rural work is by far the most common. Only a relatively small minority of post-1550 investigations are conducted by organisations with a strong period-specific focus (notably ARCUS and Ironbridge Archaeology), and the majority are undertaken by organisations whose principal focus is rural rather than urban (exceptions include the Museum of London Archaeology Service and Pre-Construct Archaeology in London). While not problematic *per se*, these factors do have an impact, not necessarily upon the quality of the work undertaken in the field but on the degree of engagement with the material recovered.

Large and complex urban excavations have a tendency to render all disciplinary boundaries, temporal or otherwise, ridiculous when faced with the reality of the archaeological record. The post-1550 boundary adopted by the conference enshrines another temporal distinction, the 'Age of Transition' between medieval and post-medieval that is itself problematic.[5] At Grand Arcade, as at many sites, there is little archaeological evidence for such transitions; instead there is a long continuum with just as much change apparent in the 14th or 18th centuries as in the 16th. Indeed, some aspects of the site appear to mock any attempt at defining boundaries. Dendrochronology indicates that a cask used to line a well was built using Greek oak, felled between 1542 and 1555 (Fig. 22.3), and it is impossible to tell if the well was constructed before or after 1550. While trite, this example aptly demonstrates the futility from a field archaeology perspective of the academic tendency to draw lines in the sand.

DEVELOPER-FUNDED ARCHAEOLOGY

In certain respects the history of British urban archaeology since World War Two is a success story, with later and later periods being treated as 'proper' archaeology, from Roman to Saxon to medieval to post-medieval to modern. While it would be possible to present this

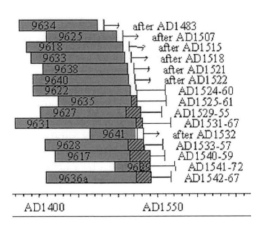

Figure 22.3 Cask-lined well built using Greek oak felled between 1542 and 1555

in terms of an inevitable triumphalist narrative, post-1550 archaeology has still not been entirely accepted, both inside and outside the discipline. It is still viewed by some as the 'handmaiden to history'[6] or 'a very expensive demonstration of the obvious',[7] and unless the archaeology of the post-1750 period in particular actively demonstrates that it has an important contribution to make, it is probable that resources will be directed elsewhere.

The roots of British urban archaeology lie in an academic context. Grand Arcade is no exception, with earlier work at the site having been undertaken by Thomas McKenny Hughes[8] and Peter Addyman and Martin Biddle.[9] Currently, however, the vast majority – indeed probably all – British urban archaeology now occurs within a PPG16 developer-funded context. The last two decades, when the great expansion of post-1550 urban archaeology has occurred, has seen a growing gulf between the worlds of academic and developer-funded archaeology. Although largely due to the exponential growth of developer-funded archaeology, it is also partly due to the contemporary major changes in how universities work. This gulf has been recognised as divisive and unhelpful in a prehistoric context[10] and is probably even more profound in post-1550 urban archaeology for a number of reasons. The majority of individuals directing the major excavations have probably been working in developer-funded archaeology for a decade or more, meaning that they studied archaeology at a time when post-1550 archaeology was not covered in detail at most universities. For example, my undergraduate degree at Newcastle University between 1987 and 1990 consisted mainly of the prehistoric and Roman periods, with the small amount of later material that was taught dating before the Norman Conquest; I certainly learnt more about the Secondary Products Revolution than I did of the Industrial Revolution. Despite the progress that has been made since, post-1550 archaeology is still clearly a minority interest in British academia.

From the other side of the divide, the excavation experience of most academics includes little if any urban work. Few urban research excavations of any scale take place in Britain, although this was not true in the past. Most university training excavations and research projects tend now to be rural in nature and relatively small scale, given practical considerations of site availability, timing, finances and resources. While most academics may feel that they possess an adequate theoretical grasp of the complexities of urban archaeology, there is no substitute for intensive and long-term experience. Yet in a sense, developer-funded and academic archaeology are complementary; developer-funded archaeology tackles sites that are by and large impractical to excavate in an academic context, whilst academics often tackle types of sites that are rarely threatened by development, such as cemeteries. With some notable exceptions, often relating to older archaeologists who were involved in urban archaeology prior to the advent of PPG16, the academic lack of understanding of urban archaeology is characterised by a level of interpretive naiveté.

British developer-funded archaeology varies markedly on a county-by-county basis. What periods constitute 'real' archaeology is largely determined by the development control archaeologists attached to local councils, although they only provide advice to elected representatives. So while in some towns all periods constitute archaeology, in others there is still a reluctance to take post-1750 or in some cases even post-1550 archaeology seriously. Indeed, there are still towns in which the Roman period remains the main focus of attention, with scant lip service paid to later periods.

There are usually several stages in the acceptance of a period as 'real' archaeology: (1) 'Ignore it': remove archaeological deposits after a certain date by machine and don't record anything or keep any material. (2) 'Rescue': officially archaeologists are supposed to ignore deposits after a certain date, but those on site try to rescue any significant material where practical. The lack of budget and resources assigned to these later periods means that they will largely be ignored during post-excavation and publication. (3) 'Intrusive': remove all archaeological deposits after a certain date by machine but excavate intrusive features that cut into earlier deposits, recording these and retaining the material from them. As with the 'rescue' stage, limited budget and resources mean that this material will usually be largely ignored during post-excavation and publication. (4) Special sites: deal properly with the archaeology of certain sites, particularly those related to production, such as pottery kilns, but also religious and military sites. 'Ordinary' domestic and commercial sites are still treated as 'rescue' or 'intrusive' archaeology. (5) 'Normality': treat the material just like all other periods, including 'ordinary' domestic and commercial premises during excavation and in later post-excavation and publication phases.

The current situation in Britain with regard to post-1550 urban archaeology varies widely; in general the range is between the 'intrusive' and 'normality' stages, but there are examples where 'ignore it' and 'rescue' still apply. The exact situation is difficult to gauge, as the inherent delay of several years between excavation and publication means that such impressions are often slightly dated. This delay also means that here are still relatively few publications of large-scale British urban excavations of post-1550 urban domestic and residential sites.

It needs to be acknowledged that post-1550 urban British archaeology does have some fundamental differences from earlier periods. Its proximity to the surface means that it has often been badly disturbed by 20th-century activity, and while this activity is itself archaeology, the nature of 20th-century construction – particularly its increasing mechanisation – means that its impact on immediately preceding deposits is often much greater. Furthermore, 18th-century and later deposits in particular often lie directly beneath concrete surfaces that are typically removed by machine, often resulting in the destruction of the uppermost elements of the underlying archaeological sequence so that only deeper features survive.

As post-1550 archaeological features are the latest in a sequence, there is great pressure to deal with them as rapidly as possible, leaving the maximum time for earlier phases. This situation is exacerbated by the fact that constraints, such as standing buildings, roads and live services, mean that it is impossible to evaluate urban sites as thoroughly as would be wished beforehand. At Grand Arcade, for example, less than 0.2 per cent of the site was evaluated prior to excavation, a much lower percentage than the 2 to 5 per cent sample generally considered appropriate, although such figures are largely derived from the requirements of rural site identification.[11] This relative lack of evaluation increases the desire to deal with the post-1550 material rapidly, as the likelihood of encountering significant unknown material of earlier date is commensurately higher. The high variability of urban deposits means that the nature of the archaeology can frequently change character radically over a distance of just a few metres, making extrapolation of evaluation results highly problematic. Evaluation, which often removes important stratigraphic relationships, can be a highly destructive event in an urban context; although the evaluation records may allow these stratigraphic relationships to be reconstructed later, this does not always prove possible, and the evaluation process can often compromise the results of the subsequent excavation.

These negative factors are partially counteracted by the fact that the excavation of post-1550 features is often relatively simple in comparison with those of earlier periods. Many features are wholly or partially lined with brick or stone, making them easier to recognise, quicker to excavate and reducing issues of residuality. Indeed, it is not unknown for archaeologists to dislike excavating such features, not out of period-based prejudice but because they do not represent a sufficient 'challenge'.

PUBLICATION MODELS

The initial Grand Arcade assessment report was completed in December 2007,[12] adding over 950 pages and half a million words to the mountain of grey literature created by developer-funded archaeology annually. While there are clearly some examples of poor-quality grey literature, the majority is produced to a reasonable standard and some is of excellent quality. A misunderstanding sometimes arises in certain quarters about the function of grey literature; such work is produced as part of the development control and planning process, and needs to be fit for purpose in that context. Criticising grey literature for not fulfilling other purposes as well as might be desired is therefore largely inappropriate. Following the production of the Grand Arcade grey report an updated project design for analysis and publication was also created;[13] the budget for this was rapidly agreed with the client, and the project has moved into a two-year publication phase. While the production of the grey literature report was to a large extent formulaic, it was clear that the nature of the publication would require more thought. In general, publication of post-1550 archaeological excavations largely falls into two 'genres': publications concentrating upon the material derived from individual features, or small groups of features and publications of entire sites.

FEATURE GROUPS

Perhaps the most common form or 'genre' of publication of post-1550 archaeology is the discussion of the material from a single feature or small group of features that contained large assemblages of material. This is certainly true locally in Cambridge[14] and regionally,[15] while nationally there are numerous examples in the journal *Post-Medieval Archaeology*, including examples from some of the earliest and most recent volumes.[16] The post-1550 and particularly post-1750 periods are archaeologically distinctive in that individual features often contain significantly larger and more varied assemblages of material culture than earlier periods, often consisting of nearly complete, reconstructable vessels. At Grand Arcade over 95 per cent of the nearly 500kg or 23,000 sherds of post-1700 pottery and over 180kg of vessel glass recovered comes from just forty-one features. The majority of these represent short-term deliberate depositional events that can broadly be interpreted as 'clearance groups' or 'pit groups', closed assemblages of domestic artefacts discarded as a single deposit;[17] the term 'feature group' is probably preferable as 'clearance' has connotations that are probably not appropriate for all such groups and the assemblages derive from a range of features, not just pits.

Quantification of this material is still ongoing, but it is already clear that each 'feature group' at Grand Arcade represent the remains of dozens and sometimes hundreds of ceramic vessels and other items. The discard of large groups of material, although not unknown during earlier periods in Cambridge, appears not to occur with any frequency prior to the 16th century and only becomes a regular occurrence in the mid-18th century. A single such assemblage frequently contains more material than was deposited in an entire property over a period of several centuries during the medieval and earlier periods. These large single-event depositional groups offer a host of interpretive and analytical possibilities that simply do not exist for earlier periods.

Such 'feature groups' can be considered one of the dominant 'genres' in post-1550 archaeological publication. Publications of feature groups are often highly interesting and exemplary in terms of their presentation and quantification of material, but their focus on a single feature provides a poor model for how to deal with the much greater level of complexity presented by larger sites. Additionally, the lengthy description and numerous illustrations that frequently characterise such publications render them impractical for larger sites. There are also some more deep-rooted interpretive issues with these types of publications that render traditional interpretations problematic for a number of reasons, most of which derive from the fact that they are primarily artefact-driven.

Studies of 'feature groups' often reduce the role of the feature in which the material was recovered to that of passive container or receptacle. The cellars, wells and other features that typically produce such assemblages were not created for that purpose and often possess rich histories of construction, use and abandonment that are usually ignored, as the studies appear only to be interested in the short-lived final abandonment stage. The process of depositing the pottery, glass and other material is also usually treated passively. It simply happened, but if material culture is significant then the act of physically destroying so much of it deserves more attention. Typically ceramic vessels, glass bottles, clay pipes and animal bone were thrown in by the armful from the top of a feature, noisily smashing on its base below again and again and again.[18] This act in many instances probably followed relatively soon after a death, the end of a business or other traumatic event. To ignore this emotive context and simply objectively quantify material is frankly ludicrous.

A focus solely on large 'feature group' assemblages means that others, which are often nearly identical in all respects apart from the nature of their backfilling, are ignored. This typically constitutes around three-quarters of the cellars, cesspits etc., at many sites. Such features are significant in their own right, but are also important in generating a more nuanced consideration of the features that do contain large assemblages, as they raise the issue of why some features contain lots of material and others have nearly none. Discussions of features backfilled with rich material culture assemblages often appear to implicitly assume that this is almost a natural or automatic process, whereas a wider view covering all features indicates that it is not. At a more general level it is clear that many theoretically inclined publications indulge in highly selective 'cherry picking' of data, choosing examples that suit a particular proposition rather than attempting to engage with larger and generally more ambiguous bodies of data.

Discussions of such assemblages often seem rather naïve and simplistic. They implicitly employ the 'Pompeii Premise',[19] assuming that the assemblages of material culture found in features directly reflect the material originally owned and used by whoever dumped the material, frozen at a single moment in time. Once quantified these assemblages are used as the raw material for discussions of a host of themes, including social status and gender relations. Little if any consideration is usually given to the fact that the dumped material has probably been carefully selected. Still-fashionable or valuable material was probably saved for further use, either on the same site or elsewhere.[20] This becomes apparent when the material from large assemblages is compared to that derived from other types of context, such as those related to middening and nightsoiling. The relative proportions of different material types and wares in the different types of deposit vary markedly, demonstrating that discard in 'feature groups' was carefully organised.

The power structure in British developer-funded archaeology means that there is frequently an issue of 'the interpretation of artefacts and the tyranny of the field archaeologist',[21] but in the publication of large assemblages of post-1550 material there often appears to be the opposite issue of 'the interpretation of features and the tyranny of the finds specialist'. What is required is a more holistic approach that considers both features and artefacts in conjunction. More recent publications of such groups have certainly gone some way towards this, such as the comparison of inn or tavern groups.[22] A much more innovative recent discussion comparing the mid-19th-century backfilling material in wells and cesspits in Lambeth linked it to sanitary reform and the idea of 'dry and proper rubbish' being selected as backfilling material.[23] This study demonstrates several ways in which studies of 'feature groups' can develop to become more meaningful.

SITES

Publications of post-1550 urban sites, as opposed to individual features, are rarer but do exist and form another distinct publication 'genre' that exists locally,[24] regionally[25] and nationally.[26] When it comes to publication, the dominant model applied is to use the traditional approach that has been employed in British urban archaeology for several decades. This approach is essentially additive and 'bolts on' later periods, treating them in much the same manner as earlier ones. Such an approach is eminently understandable, as it mirrors both the dominant academic model of period-based specialisms and the incremental way that later and later periods have come to be treated archaeologically in Britain. Such a publication will typically have sections on the Roman, Saxon, medieval, post-medieval and modern periods presented one after the other in chronological order, although the post-1750 period is often dealt with in a noticeably more cursory manner, with far fewer words per feature than are deemed necessary for earlier periods.

There are several difficulties with this approach to data presentation, particularly when it is applied to the post-1550 and particularly the post-1750 period. The existence of various sources of evidence such as maps, documents and photographs that either do not exist for earlier periods or are much rarer is usually acknowledged, but does not fundamentally alter the approach adopted. Such publications typically list the names, dates and occupations of individuals who lived at a site, and have some comparison between the features that were identified archaeologically and with historic maps. This approach falls far short of the level of integration that should be possible, and it is also clear that the documentary and cartographic research frequently fails to achieve what is possible and desirable. One obvious shortcoming of most documentary research is that it is site-focused and only relates to the period when someone lived or worked in the area investigated; in more recent periods, in particular, this is unlikely to have represented their whole life (see below).

A major failing of most site publications is that, in dealing with large numbers of features, the individual large 'feature groups' are not dealt with properly. Traditionally in site publications finds and environmental evidence are presented as a series of separate specialist reports. Integration of the different types of artefactual and environmental evidence and the description of the features that produced them is frequently facile, minimal or non-existent in publications of larger sites, as also considered by Berry and by Mrozowski, this volume. In some instances it is possible to laboriously reconstruct 'feature groups' from the various specialist reports, although in some cases such reports deal solely with the material at the level of the entire assemblage, rendering this impossible. It is paradoxical that large assemblages from single isolated features are often published in great detail, while similar assemblages from more extensive sites are usually dealt with in a much more cursory manner.

Assemblages from larger sites are often much better contextualised and provide richer interpretive possibilities than isolated groups of material. There are obvious underlying practical issues, for instance, when published in detail, a single 'feature group' can frequently run to twenty or thirty pages. Utilising this model the 'feature groups' from Grand Arcade would occupy around 800 pages, a wholly impractical proposition. Much of the length of publications derives from the copious illustration of artefacts, particularly pottery. The mass-produced nature of much later pottery and the fact that complete or nearly complete vessels become a commonplace rather than the rarity they are in earlier periods, means that at a practical level the fetishisation of artefact illustration will probably have to be challenged, perhaps involving CD or web-based alternatives or simply an acceptance that it is unnecessary to illustrate items simply because their entire profile survives.

OTHER PUBLICATIONS

Other publication 'genres' do exist, one particularly useful one being the review of work in an entire town such as Gloucester [27] or Norwich.[28] Such reviews are a useful mechanism for presenting the results from small-scale fieldwork, which is often the norm in urban contexts but usually does not warrant individual publication. Unfortunately, such publications are now a rarity, owing to the fragmentation of archaeological fieldwork in most urban centres resulting from PPG16. Only in the relatively rare instances where a single organisation retains a dominant position, undertaking the majority of archaeological investigations in a town, do they remain a realistic possibility.

THE INTERNATIONAL CONTEXT

Internationally there are of course numerous publications of post-1550 sites, particularly from North America but also Australia and elsewhere, where the archaeological study of the post-1750 period in particular has a longer history. An in-depth critique of this literature is beyond the scope of this discussion, but certain contrasts are worth noting. From a British perspective, the main difference is the inherent lack of time-depth. The urban archaeology of sites occupied for only decades or even a few hundred years is profoundly different in character from those occupied for much longer periods of perhaps a thousand years or more. At Grand Arcade, by the time we reach the post-1750 period this area of townscape has evolved over about 800 years. Although the area began as a series of regularly laid out plots in the 11th or 12th centuries, these divisions went through a complex series of modifications. Some properties had gained space from neighbours, while conversely others had lost. In some cases institutions managed to acquire blocks of adjacent plots over time and amalgamated parts of them. Eventually, each property plot acquired its own set of distinctive characteristics, profoundly affecting its appeal to various types of potential occupiers and the nature of activities that could take place. In contrast, a similar block in a contemporary North America or Australian town would tend to consist of a much more homogenous set of plots, although some variation would undoubtedly exist. This makes a profound difference to the type of archaeology that should be written; the dominant British narrative should be about the individual long-term trajectories of a series of plots whereas a North American or Australian narrative must be more short-term and concerned more with a comparison of how similar plots are used. This does not mean that British sites should not seek to contribute to a temporally specific global historical archaeology, merely that this should not be their sole or perhaps even main *raison d'être*.

RIGHT
Figure 22.4 Seventeenth-century well, incorporating contemporary timber and tile plus 14th-century timber and 13th-century moulded stone in its construction

The time-depth of occupation at British sites does have direct, discernible archaeological impacts. Features such as wells or walls that were constructed in the post-1550 period at Grand Arcade frequently reused much earlier material. There is dendrochronological evidence for the reuse of timber that was several centuries old and stylistic evidence for the reuse of even older moulded stone. In some cases the timber and stone bear the traces of three or four distinct phases of use and reuse prior to their context of discovery.

One particular well (Fig. 22.4) has a timber baseplate that utilises early 17th-century English oak alongside late 14th-century Baltic pine. Placed on this was moulded stonework derived from early 13th-century arcading and above this early 17th-century red bricks. The well itself appears to have had a short life of perhaps half a century, between the early and late 17th century. The story contained in the structure of the well covers a period of five hundred years, around ten times as long as its actual use. The narrative of the well should incorporate the much longer story and the fact that in towns that have been in existence for a long period, construction in one location is frequently linked to destruction elsewhere. It is worth noting that the backfilling deposits in this well contained relatively little material culture and are among the least interesting elements in the well's narrative, in contrast to the usual artefact-driven approach for this period.

THE WAY FORWARD?

Given the scale of fieldwork being undertaken, there should be an exponential rise in the number of publications of British post-1550 urban sites over the next few years. Currently the field feels particularly exciting and interesting as things are in a state of flux and transition; however, to make a truly substantive contribution to our understanding of the period it is vital that things need to 'bed in' to an extent. As part of this process it is urgent that minimum standards need to be agreed, otherwise the results from different excavations will not be comparable. In particular it is vital that the apparent methodological distinctions between the publications of large assemblages from individual features and whole sites are broken down.

A good site publication should discuss all the archaeological features present, although with a variable level of detail depending upon the significance of the feature. While significance may be partly determined by the quantity of material culture utilised to backfill the feature this should not be the only factor. The material needs to be well quantified, with all material types from large assemblages quantified by some form of minimum number of individuals (MNI) count. This is relatively straightforward, although not entirely unproblematic, for certain types of material such as ceramics,[29] glass[30] and clay pipes. Other material such as animal bone is more difficult, but the minimum number of butchering units[31] and probable unit of acquisition[32] methods offer possibilities for at least comparing features.

Standardised quantification of the various large assemblages at the Grand Arcade site should allow comparative analysis at a local level, and the potential exists for global comparisons. This type of quantitative analysis should, however, not blind us to more qualitative or personal insights. This is most obvious in the case of the selection of vessels with particular transfer-printed designs in preference to other available patterns.[33]

It is also apparent that standards of documentary and cartographic analysis need to be raised, as also argued by Paul Courtney in this volume. The sheer volume of material available, particularly for the 19th and 20th centuries, is daunting and it is perhaps unfeasible to examine every potentially relevant document. Nonetheless it is clear that more resources need to be directed to this area; the sums involved are relatively low in comparison to excavation costs, especially given the contribution that proper documentary and cartographic analysis can make.

Even if standards are raised there is a case to be made for arguing that a period-based approach is not necessarily the most appropriate in urban archaeology. Period-based approaches tend to obscure the story of individual properties or tenements. In many cases I would advocate the idea that the principal approach should be spatial, where individual properties are discussed one after the other from the onset of activity to the latest archaeological features. Temporal comparisons should then form a secondary level of discussion. This is the reverse of the standard approach where temporal organisation is usually given primacy and the spatial element is secondary.

It is also crucial that we move beyond the excavated site boundaries. These are usually an arbitrary construct related to modern developments that are nonetheless frequently allowed to impose some form of reality upon the past. While we are forced to dig arbitrarily defined sites, surely analysis must relate to entities that existed in the past such as individual properties, larger blocks of land or the whole town? At the most basic level no property at Grand Arcade was excavated in its entirety, but any reasonable interpretation of the site must at least consider what was happening in those areas that fell outside the site boundaries. At a slightly wider scale, the site did not include the local parish church of St Andrew the Great, where the majority of those who lived at the site worshipped, or the cemetery at Mill Road where they were buried. These are crucial aspects of the lives of the people that we seek to study. It would be easy to study the Grand Arcade site with relatively little reference to religion, but the inclusion of unexcavated but relevant 'off-site' locales can counteract this. This applies not just to religion but to other aspects of life, such as places where individuals who lived at Grand Arcade worked or where people who worked at Grand Arcade lived.

Most of these points are not new; that it is possible to combine the publication of 'feature groups' and larger sites was demonstrated several decades ago at the site of Sewardstone Street, Waltham Abbey, Essex.[34] The site as a whole is well-presented, and the development of one 16th-century town house was studied with the aid of documentary evidence. A substantial quantity of material was recovered from a latrine, which it was suggested was backfilled in 1669 after the indictment of the owner Thomas Winspear II for sodomy, while some of the contents are compared to a meal described by Samuel Pepys. Whether the actual interpretation of the deposit is correct is debatable; nonetheless, it must be recognised that this publication successfully discusses both the overall site and the individual large assemblage at different levels of detail in a manner that works. Documentary sources are well used, and something of the possible nature and circumstances of the backfilling process is presented.

SARAH DOBSON, A CASE STUDY

One particular 'feature group' from Grand Arcade is a planting bed in the garden of No. 22 St Andrew's Street associated with Sarah Dobson, who ran a school there between at least 1841 and 1866 (Fig. 22.5). This feature group contained a minimum of 54 ceramic vessels, 23 glass vessels and three clay tobacco pipes, along with over 1,100 animal bones, 43 oyster shells, 48 brick and tile fragments and a small quantity of unidentifiable copper alloy and iron objects. This material was deliberately introduced into the base of the planting bed, presumably to improve its drainage, and does not appear to have been disturbed by later horticultural activity. So although this was a long-lived feature, the end of its life being dated by a farthing minted between 1895 and 1936, the assemblage relates solely to its construction probably in the second quarter of the 19th century. Even prior to more detailed analysis of the assemblage, it is clear that it is distinct for a number of reasons. Several children's cups were recovered, along with elements of several identifiable ceramic services, which may indicate gentility; a large number of animal bones were also present, in direct contrast to the majority of features of this date.

While the adult-sized ceramic vessels are decorated with blue and white transfer-printed designs, there are also some pink transfer-printed children's cups bearing illustrations and text from the work of Isaac Watts, a leading early 18th- century nonconformist. There are two cups with the text *'For I have food, while others starve, Or beg from door to door'*, from Watts's song 'Whene'er I take my walks abroad', part of his collection of 'Divine and Moral Songs for Children' (Fig. 22.6). This material therefore presents an opportunity to try and understand aspects of the lives of Sarah Dobson and her household, which included various relatives, members of staff, servants and children who were taught at the school (some of whom lived at the premises and some of whom did not). This is all largely conventional, however; to more fully understand Sarah Dobson and her choice of ceramics, we need to try

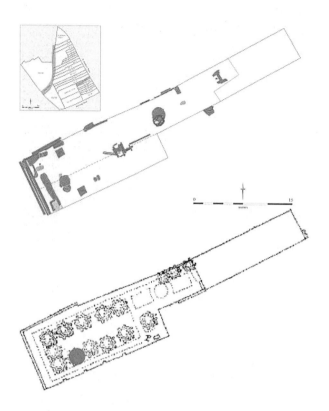

LEFT
Figure 22.5 No. 22 St Andrew's Street
showing plan of excavated post-1550
features, First Edition Ordnance Survey
map surveyed in 1885 and garden feature
with material in its base associated with
Sarah Dodson

and understand her origins. Sarah was the daughter of George and Dinah Dobson, and was baptised at the nearby village of Stow cum Quy in 1796. Her father was a farmer and would have worked in the southern part of the parish, which was used for arable farming.[35] He died in 1818, and the farm was taken over by her brother Joseph, who himself died in 1840, after which there is no further evidence of the family living in the village although some members continued to be buried there. The population of Stow cum Quy was expanding rapidly during the late 18th and early 19th centuries, nearly doubling in size. This led to a high degree of movement away from the village, including some emigration to Australia. Although unemployment was relatively low, there were few opportunities outside farm

Figure 22.6 Near-complete pink transfer-printed child's cup with text and image derived from Isaac Watts's 'Whene'er I take my walks abroad' from garden feature associated with Sarah Dobson. Plus sherd from a second identical vessel from the same feature and part of a third child's cup from a nearby feature, with text from Watts's ' Innocent Play' (image partly by Dave Webb)

labouring. Thus, by understanding her family circumstances and the village from which she came, we can begin to understand why Sarah Dobson moved to Cambridge.

By 1818, there was a 'dame school' in Stow cum Quy, where twelve children were taught and the lord of the manor paid for three poor girls to learn to read.[36] Such schools were usually taught by women, often in their own home, and were of highly variable quality. A survey of 1838 found nearly half of all pupils were only taught spelling, with only a small number learning mathematics and grammar. It is likely that the Stow cum Quy dame school existed while Sarah Dobson was a child in the early 19th century and that she received her initial education there, which must have had a major impact upon her later career as a teacher. Although Sarah was an Anglican, there is some evidence for nonconformity at Stow cum Quy, with a house registered for worship in 1839.[37] The curates during Sarah's time were James Hicks of Wilbraham Temple (*c.* 1784 to 1826) and Edward Ventris of Cambridge (1826 to 1886), both of whom were non-resident and only performed morning services.[38] The potential exists to research the religious views of both Hicks and Ventris, to determine what they might have felt about Watts's work. While this background does not necessarily explain Sarah's later interest in Isaac Watts (as evinced by the children's cups) it certainly provides useful hints towards an explanation.

Although the transfer-printed ceramics offer the most obvious interpretive potential, other material from the feature also raises possibilities. There are a number of complete blacking bottles, which are suggestive of attitudes to cleanliness and hygiene, as well as a glass bottle of Dalby's carminative, a popular opium-based medicine given to babies and small children with stomach disorders such as colic. The large faunal assemblage has not yet been fully analysed, but must represent a considerable quantity of meat, and the assemblage is notable for the large number of bird bones, mostly chicken but also duck, turkey, pigeon and swan.

Although this planting bed was the only feature associated with Sarah Dobson that produced a large 'feature group', there are a range of other broadly contemporary features that can further enrich our understanding of her life. A nearby planting bed contained part of another child's cup with the text of a different work by Isaac Watts entitled 'Innocent Play' (Fig. 22.6), while other garden features produced considerable numbers of slate pencils, which are intriguingly absent from the large 'feature group'. The material in these smaller assemblages is clearly still significant in understanding the Dobson household. There are also features that produced no significant artefacts but indicate substantial investment in the garden of this property in the 18th and 19th centuries, including a large brick-lined cistern, a substantial brick-lined well with an oak baseplate and several boundary walls that indicate at least two phases of expansion. Taken in totality, these indicate that the garden was a considerable focus of this property, much more so than in most of the adjoining plots.

In the late 1860s or early 1870s, Sarah moved to much smaller premises a short distance away at No. 7 St Andrew's Hill; these premises lacked the pleasant garden of No. 22 St Andrew's Street where the archaeological evidence relating to Sarah was discovered. This move was probably a result of the 1870 Elementary Education Act, which legislated for the education of all children aged 5 to 13 and led to massive changes in the provision of education. Sarah's school would have come under the control of the elected members of a school board and would have been partly funded by either the local poor rates or municipal rate. In this context, the movement to No. 7 St Andrew's Hill can potentially be seen as a cost-cutting measure. Sarah died in 1886 and was buried in the Mill Road cemetery. Until 1860, family members (including her brother George) had been buried in Stow cum Quy, but between 1870 and 1913 the family were buried in Mill Road where they are commemorated by a headstone. This change suggests a break from familial tradition and origins.

The life story that can be reconstructed for Sarah Dobson is not extraordinary and represents the level of detail that can be relatively easily discovered for many 19th-century individuals. While it could be argued that it is not directly relevant to the archaeology of No. 22 St Andrew's Street, by looking at Sarah's life as a whole we can gain a better understanding of the archaeological remains associated with her at the site. Sarah Dobson, born 1796 and died 1886, is a much more 'complete' individual than Sarah Dobson defined solely as school teacher at No. 22 St Andrew's Street between 1841 and 1866. If archaeology is primarily about people, then it is their entire lives that should have primacy rather than a narrow site-based and archaeologically defined agenda.

The range and type of documentary sources available for the 19th century in particular allows linkages between individuals at different sites such as Stow cum Quy, No. 22 St Andrew's Street, No. 7 St Andrew's Hill and the Mill Road cemetery to be explored. These documented connections only really exist in earlier periods for elite individuals, such as monarchs or members of the nobility. There are also other kinds of linkages. At the time of the 1861 census, for example, one of Sarah Dobson's pupils was Albert Bone, who was born in Sydney, Australia, in 1854 and who may have used some of the items discovered at the Grand Arcade excavations. The ceramics included several parts of a blue and white transfer-printed Sicilian pattern service (Fig. 22.7). The Sicilian pattern has been found on several sites in Australia, such as the Lake Innes Estate.[39] Given the global nature of post-1550, and particularly post-1750, archaeology, it is possible that one day archaeologists working on different continents will have excavated identical vessels in Cambridge and Sydney on sites linked to Albert Bone; indeed, it may already have occurred. This would potentially raise numerous issues, such as what impact would the similarities in global material culture have had in terms of defining things as 'familiar' or 'other' for those who travelled the globe at this time.

Another example of linkage is the excavation of Polymond Hall in Southampton, where Isaac Watts lived as a child and young man. These excavations revealed the building used as a boarding school run by Watts's father, the garden of the property and a garderobe

backfilled while Isaac Watts lived there. This feature contained ceramics and a rare find of Brazil nut shells. Potentially, we can compare the material associated with the childhoods of Watts and those over a century later of children who used cups inspired by his work. This surely invites us to consider Watts's early 18th-century nonconformist religious and moral beliefs, and wonder what he would have thought about the Anglican beliefs of the mid-19th century and the incorporation of his work into the religious mainstream.

LEFT
Figure 22.7 Near-complete blue transfer-printed Sicilian pattern plate and large dish (image partly by Dave Webb)

CONCLUSION

Post-1550 developer-funded archaeology in Britain stands on the threshold of making great contributions at both a local level, where it contributes to the long-term story of how particular locales developed over perhaps a thousand years, and as part of a more temporally specific global historical archaeology. Whether this potential is realised or not depends upon how we address the challenges and opportunities that the archaeological remains of this period present. We need to develop strategies and methodologies that deal adequately with both whole sites and substantial 'feature groups', and which fully integrate the archaeological, documentary, cartographic and other evidence as well as challenging the arbitrary spatial and temporal boundaries that the nature of developer-funded archaeology can impose, replacing them with more archaeologically valid ones. What these strategies and methodologies would involve is still uncertain, although hopefully this chapter has suggested some possibilities.

ACKNOWLEDGEMENTS

This chapter builds upon the dedicated work of the entire team involved in the work at Grand Arcade, which has been funded by the Grand Arcade Partnership consisting of the Universities Superannuation Scheme and Grosvenor Developments Ltd. In particular I would like to thank my project manager, Alison Dickens, for her support and Richard Newman for reading a draft of the text. Specific aspects of this chapter draw upon the specialist work of Richard Darrah (timber), Andy Hall (post-1700 pottery), Vicki Herring (post-1700 glass), Mark Samuel (moulded stone) and Ian Tyers (dendrochronology). The illustrations utilise work by Andy Hall and Dave Webb.

NOTES

1. cf. Reece 1984.
2. cf. Hicks 2004.
3. Glazebrook 1997.
4. Brown & Glazebrook 2000.
5. cf. Egan 2005; Gaimster & Stamper 1997; Dyer 2005.
6. Noël Hume 1964
7. Sawyer 1983, 44.
8. Hughes 1906; Hughes 1915.
9. Addyman & Biddle 1965, 77–80 and 85–8.
10. Bradley 2006
11. cf. Hey & Lacey 2001.
12. Cessford 2007.
13. Dickens & Cessford 2007.
14. e.g. Edwards & Hall 1997; Hall 2002; McCarthy 1974.
15. e.g. Walker 2002; Walker 2004.
16. e.g. Barton 1969; Matthews & Green 1969; Boothroyd & Higgins 2005; Pearce 2007.
17. cf. Barker & Majewski 2006, 207; Fryer & Shelley 1998; Pearce 2000.
18. cf. Johnson 1996, 182–3.
19. cf. Binford 1981; Schiffer 1985.
20. cf. Johnson 1996, 182–3.
21. Blinkhorn & Cumberpatch 1998.
22. Pearce 2000.
23. Jeffries 2006.
24. e.g. Addyman & Biddle 1965, 82.
25. e.g. Shelley 2005.
26. e.g. Fox et al. 1986.
27. Atkin 1987.
28. Ayers 1991.
29. cf. Brooks 2005.
30. cf. Willmott 2002.
31. Lyman 1979.
32. See Huelsbeck 1991.
33. Brooks 1997; Brooks 1999; Lucas 2003.
34. Huggins 1969.

35. Wright 2002, 230–1.
36. Wright 2002, 246.
37. Wright 2002, 245.

38. Wright 2002, 244.
39. Brooks & Connah 2007, 140.

BIBLIOGRAPHY

Addyman, P. & Biddle, M. 1965, 'Medieval Cambridge: recent finds and excavations', *Proceedings of the Cambridge Antiquarian Society* **63**: 74–137.

Atkin, M. 1987, 'Post-medieval archaeology in Gloucester: a review', *Post-Medieval Archaeology* **21**: 1–24.

Ayers, B. 1991, 'Post-medieval archaeology in Norwich: a review', *Post-Medieval Archaeology* **25**: 1–23.

Barker, D. & Majewski, T. 2006, 'Ceramic studies in historical archaeology', in Hicks & Beaudry (eds), 2006, 205–31.

Barton, K.J. 1969, 'The contents of an eighteenth-century well at Bishops Waltham, Hants', *Post-Medieval Archaeology* **3**: 166–87.

Binford, L.R. 1981, 'Behavioural archaeology and the "Pompeii Premise"', *Journal of Anthropological Research* **37**: 195–208.

Blinkhorn, P.W. & Cumberpatch, C.G. 1998, 'The interpretation of artefacts and the tyranny of the field archaeologist', *Assemblage* **4**, <http://www.shef.ac.uk/~assem/4/4bln_cmb.html>.

Boothroyd, N. & Higgins, D. 2005, 'An inn-clearance group, c. 1800, from the Royal Oak, Eccleshall, Staffordshire', *Post-Medieval Archaeology* **39**: 197–203.

Bradley, R. 2006, 'Bridging the two cultures – commercial archaeology and the study of prehistoric Britain', *Antiquaries Journal* **86**: 1–13.

Brooks, A. 1997, 'Beyond the fringe: transfer-printed ceramics and the internationalisation of Celtic myth', *International Journal of Historical Archaeology* **1**: 39–45.

Brooks, A. 1999, 'Building Jerusalem: transfer-printed finewares and the creation of British identity', in Tarlow & West (eds), 1999, 51–65.

Brooks, A. 2005, *An Archaeological Guide to British Ceramics in Australia, 1788–1901*. Sydney: Australasian Society for Historical Archaeology.

Brooks, A. & Connah, C. 2007, 'A hierarchy of servitude: ceramics at Lake Innes Estate, New South Wales', *Antiquity* **81**: 133–47.

Brown, N. & Glazebrook, J. 2000, *Research and Archaeology: A Framework for the Eastern Counties 2: Research Agenda and Strategy*, East Anglian Archaeology Occasional Paper **3**.

Dyer, C. 2005, *An Age of Transition? Economy and Society in England in the Later Middle Ages*. Oxford: Clarendon Press.

Edwards, D.N. & Hall, D. 1997, 'Medieval pottery from Cambridge', *Proceedings of the Cambridge Antiquarian Soc.* **86**: 153–68.

Egan, G. 2005, *Material Culture in London in an Age of Transition: Tudor and Stuart period finds c.1450–c.1700 from Excavations at Riverside sites in Southwark*. London: Museum of London Archaeology Service.

Fryer, K. & Shelley, A. 1998, 'Excavation of a pit at 16 Tunsgate, Guildford, Surrey, 1991', *Post-Medieval Archaeology* **31**: 139–230.

Gaimster, D.R.M. & Stamper, P. 1997, *The Age of Transition: The Archaeology of English Culture 1400–1600*. Oxford: Oxbow Books.

Glazebrook, J. 1997, *Research and Archaeology: A Framework for the Eastern Counties 1: Resource Assessment*, East Anglian Archaeology Occasional Paper **3**.

Fox, R. Barton, K. J. and Hoad, M.J. 1986, 'Excavations at Oyster Street, Portsmouth, Hampshire, 1968–71', *Post-Medieval Archaeology* **20**: 31–255.

Hall, A. 2002, 'A late 16th-century pit group from Pembroke College, Cambridge', *Proceedings of the Cambridge Antiquarian Society* **91**: 89–101.

Hey, G. & Lacey, M. 2001, *Evaluation of Archaeological Decision-making Processes and Sampling Strategies.* Canterbury: Kent County Council.

Hicks, D. 2004, 'From "questions that count" to stories that "matter" in historical archaeology', *Antiquity* **78**: 934–9.

Hicks, D. & Beaudry, M. (eds), 2006, *The Cambridge Companion to Historical Archaeology.* Cambridge: Cambridge University Press.

Hinton, D.A. (ed.) 1983, *25 years of Medieval Archaeology.* Sheffield: Department of Prehistory & Archaeology, University of Sheffield and Society for Medieval Archaeology,

Huelsbeck, D.R. 1991, 'Faunal remains and consumer behavior: what is being measured', *Historical Archaeology* **25**: 62–76.

Huggins, P.J. 1969, 'Excavations at Sewardstone Street, Waltham Abbey, Essex, 1966', *Post-Medieval Archaeology* **3**: 47–99.

Hughes, T. McK. 1906, 'On the section seen and the objects found during excavations on the site of the Old Bird Bolt Hotel', *Proceedings of the Cambridge Antiquarian Society* **17**: 424–45.

Hughes, T. McK. 1915, 'On some objects found in the King's Ditch under the Masonic Hall', *Proceedings of the Cambridge Antiquarian Society* **19**: 16–27.

Jeffries, N. 2006, 'The Metropolis Local Management Act and the archaeology of sanitary reform in the London Borough of Lambeth 1856–86', *Post-Medieval Archaeology* **40**(2): 272–90.

Johnson, M. 1996, *An Archaeology of Capitalism.* Oxford: Blackwell.

Lucas, G. 2003, 'Reading pottery: literature and transfer-printed pottery in the early nineteenth century', *International Journal of Historical Archaeology* 7: 127–43.

Lyman, R.L. 1979, 'Available meat from faunal remains: a consideration of techniques', *American Antiquity* **44**: 536–46.

Matthews, L.G. & Green, H.J.M. 1969, 'Post-medieval pottery of the Inns of Court', *Post-Medieval Archaeology* **3**: 1–17.

McCarthy, M. 1974, 'An early seventeenth-century pit group from Bene't Street, Cambridge', *Proceedings of the Cambridge Antiquarian Society* **65**: 79–92.

Noël Hume, I. 1964, 'Archaeology: handmaiden to history', *The North Carolina Historical Review* **41**: 215–25.

Pearce, J.I. 2000, 'A late 18th-century inn clearance assemblage from Uxbridge, Middlesex', *Post-Medieval Archaeology* **34**: 144–86.

Pearce, J.I. 2007, 'An assemblage of 17th-century pottery from Bombay Wharf, London SE16', *Post-Medieval Archaeology* **41**: 80–99.

Reece, R. 1984, 'Sequence is all: or archaeology in an historical period', *Scottish Archaeology Review* **3**: 113–15.

Sawyer, P. 1983, 'English archaeology before the Conquest, a historian's view', in Hinton (ed.), 1983, 44–7.

Schiffer, M.B. 1985, 'Is there a "Pompeii Premise" in archaeology?', *Journal of Anthropological Research* **41**: 18–41.

Shelley, A. 2005, *Dragon Hall, King Street, Norwich: Excavation and Survey of a Late Medieval Merchant's Trading Complex,* East Anglian Archaeology **112**.

Tarlow, S. & West, S. (eds) 1999, *The Familiar Past? Archaeologies of Later Historical Britain.* London: Routledge,

Walker, H. 2002, 'An 18th-century assemblage from a well in the garden of 4 Falcon Square, Castle Hedingham', *Essex Archaeology and History* **33**: 288–309.

Walker, H. 2004, 'Finds from a well behind 2 High Street, Kelvedon, formerly the White Hart', *Essex Archaeology and History* **35**: 233–40.

Wareham, A.F. & Wright, A.P.M. (eds), 2002, *The Victoria County History of the County of Cambridgeshire and the Isle of Ely: Volume X, North-Eastern Cambridgeshire.* London: Institute for Historical Research.

Willmott, H. 2002, *Early Post-medieval Vessel Glass in England, c.1500–1670,* Council for British Archaeology Research Report **132**.

Wright, A.P.M. 2002, 'Stow cum Quy', in Wareham & Wright (eds), 2002, 230–47.

UNPUBLISHED SOURCES

Cessford, C. 2007, *Grand Arcade, Cambridge: An Archaeological Excavation*, CAU Report **800**.

Dickens, A. & Cessford, C. 2007, *Updated Project Design for Analysis and Publication of Archaeological Excavations at the Grand Arcade, Cambridge*, CAU

Rematerialising Metropolitan Histories?
People, Places and Things in Modern London

By NIGEL JEFFRIES, ALASTAIR OWENS, DAN HICKS,
RUPERT FEATHERBY & KAREN WEHNER

*In recent years historians have begun to show renewed interest in studying 'the material'
dimensions to urban life. This shift has opened up a space for new dialogues between
historians and post-medieval archaeologists working on British cities. It offers the potential
for reassessing approaches to studying the urban past and for experimenting with fresh
methodologies. Noting that archaeological perspectives have been largely absent from recent
historical accounts of the modern metropolis, in this chapter we explore the potential for
pursuing collaborative research that fuses archaeological evidence and thinking with other
forms of historical practice to write material histories of London. The discussion divides into
three parts. First, we sketch the post-war development of urban post-medieval archaeology
in London, and the range of archaeological collections and excavation sites that relate
to the Georgian and Victorian city. Second, we consider some of the ways in which the
analysis of these sources might be used in interdisciplinary urban historiography, especially
in the light of methodological approaches developed in North American and Australian
urban archaeology. Third, we present a case study that explores how nineteenth-century
household archaeologies in London might be developed, examining some of the complexities
and challenges of integrating archaeological methods into the study of households and
localities in the nineteenth-century metropolis. In conclusion we consider the prospects
for the development of interdisciplinary approaches to the material remains of London's
modern past.*

INTRODUCTION

Over the course of the 17th, 18th and 19th centuries, London developed to become one
of the largest and most powerful cities in the world. According to some recent historical
accounts, it can be characterised as a birthplace of modernity: a city where new identities,
practices and power relations were forged and experienced.[1] London was increasingly bound
into mercantile, political and social networks that were global in scope, yet at the same time
its local landscapes became evermore distinctive, as dramatic demographic and economic
changes transformed the city. Whether as a place of shocking social and material inequality,
as a centre of industrial production, as a nexus of imperial power and commerce, or as a
site for experiencing new forms of consumption, leisure and pleasure, the metropolis has

long provided historians with a means of peering into and making sense of much of that which is deemed to constitute modern life. But if the processes that constituted London's emergent modernity loom large in recent historical writing about the city, they feature less in archaeological investigations of the post-medieval metropolis. Indeed, archaeologies of modern London that seek to engage simultaneously with evidence derived from site-based excavations and with wider historical processes and contemporary narratives are notable by their absence.

How might archaeological evidence and archaeological thinking contribute to the historiography of post-medieval London? Whether clay tobacco pipes smoked by the 17th-century audiences of Shakespearean plays at the Rose Theatre,[2] or cylindrical glass beads manufactured in Hammersmith for trading on the west African coast,[3] or the vast quantities of blue-and-white transfer-printed whitewares that would have been found on dining tables of households across the 19th-century city, a diverse range of post-medieval material has been recorded and recovered. The scale and complexity of London's post-medieval archaeological material is formidable, particularly when compared with urban archaeologies in the New World, since it derives from the most recent elements of complex stratigraphic sequences that begin with early medieval or Romano-British activity. But while the past fifty years have witnessed enormous quantities of archaeological fieldwork in the context of urban development in London, the use of post-medieval materials to write urban archaeological histories remains little explored. In Britain, Tadhg O'Keeffe and Rebecca Yamin's verdict that 'the contribution of historical archaeologists to … historical urban research remains largely unrecognised' is felt particularly sharply.[4] Commercially funded projects have often excluded post-1500 material from analysis and publication.[5] But while some bemoan the limited ambitions of 'most [professional] archaeologists working in this period to interpret their work in terms of wider social and cultural change',[6] we believe that it is the responsibility of all British historical archaeologists, whether working in public, private or university environments, to begin to make use of the 'grey literature' (unpublished excavation reports) and objects that fill city museums across the United Kingdom.[7]

This chapter begins to explore how such collaborative research might be developed in practice. It presents some of the results of a recently completed pilot study that used cross-disciplinary collaboration between archaeology, historical geography and the museum sector in order to develop historical studies of 19th-century household archaeological assemblages curated by the London Archaeological Archive and Research Centre (LAARC), which forms part of the Museum of London.[8] The study focused on the analysis of mid-19th-century assemblages from three socially and geographically contrasting sites across the city: a group of multiple occupancy houses in Regent Street, Limehouse (a poor dockside community in the city's East End); a residential/professional property located in New Palace Yard, Westminster (adjacent to the Houses of Parliament); and cottages occupied by labouring families at Bell Green in Sydenham (to the south-east of London).

Our discussion divides into three sections. Firstly, we sketch the post-war development of urban post-medieval archaeology in London, and the range of grey literature reports, articles in specialist periodicals, and archaeological collections and excavation sites that relate to the Georgian and Victorian city. Secondly, we consider some of the ways in which the analysis of these sources might be used in interdisciplinary urban historiography, especially in the light of methodological approaches developed in North American and Australian urban archaeology and specifically with the 'ethnographies of place' research programme developed by historians and historical archaeologists working on 19th-century Australian cities.[9] Thirdly, we present a case study from our Bell Green, Sydenham site that explores how 19th-century household archaeologies in London might be developed, examining some of the complexities and challenges of integrating archaeological methods into the study of households and localities in the 19th-century metropolis. In conclusion, we consider the prospects for the development of interdisciplinary approaches to the material remains of London's modern past.[10]

GEORGIAN AND VICTORIAN LONDON: AN INVISIBLE ARCHAEOLOGY?

While the identification and description of archaeological remains in urban contexts occurred in London and other British cities from the 18th century, the scale of the urban rebuilding programmes in the period after the Second World War led to radical changes in the practice of British field archaeology. From 1947, under the direction of Professor William F. Grimes of the Institute of Archaeology (which had been founded a decade earlier), the Roman and Medieval London Excavation Committee (RMLEC) recorded archaeological remains exposed during urban clearance after bombing. Until 1962, Grimes developed research excavations that focused especially upon Romano-British and medieval remains in the City of London: most famously in the excavations of the Temple of Mithras.[11] From 1949, archaeologists based at the Guildhall Museum also operated under 'rescue' situations in the City – including the historical archaeologist Ivor Noël Hume who ran excavations for the Guildhall between 1949 and 1957.[12] In 1962 the responsibility for rescue archaeology in the City of London passed entirely to the Guildhall Museum,[13] until the formation of the Department of Urban Archaeology (DUA) in 1973. The DUA continued to carry out almost all of the development-related archaeology in the City of London until the national implementation of the Department of Environment's Planning Policy Guidance Note 16 (PPG16) in 1990.[14]

With the widening-out of competition in archaeology as a consequence of the PPG16 guidance, the DUA merged with the various regional Department of Greater London Archaeology (DGLA) sections to form the Museum of London Archaeology Service (MoLAS) in 1991. Since 1991, the number of commercial archaeological contractors operating in London has grown rapidly. The quantities of archaeological materials that have been recovered and recorded for all periods of London's history have increased markedly, and archaeological curators across the United Kingdom have been increasingly willing to include the recording of post-medieval material as part of their briefs for the mitigation of the impact of development upon buried archaeological remains. Often the pressures to excavate and record Romano-British and medieval remains between the 1950s and 1980s led to the swift removal of later horizons filled with the ubiquitous assemblages of creamwares, pearlwares or clay pipes.[15] Nevertheless, though major post-medieval excavations were carried out throughout the post-war period in London (especially Aldgate High Street sitecode AL74, Cutler Street sitecode CUT78, and the Fleet Valley sitecode VAL88), these have increased markedly since the early 1990s, with the upsurge in developer-funded excavation work outside London's Roman and medieval core into areas such as the East and West End and large parts of south London.

Despite this growth of post-medieval fieldwork, integrative studies of urban archaeology in London continue to reflect the Romano-British and medieval focus of the immediate post-war period. For London, while summaries of the Romano-British town have been produced at regular intervals since the 1950s,[16] and more recent studies have brought together the evidence for Saxon[17] and medieval London,[18] the results of fieldwork at post-medieval sites remain almost entirely fragmented and recorded only in grey literature reports. While modern material has featured in some published accounts of excavations in London,[19] in strategic documents such as *The Future of London's Past* (published 1973),[20] and in collections of themed, integrative essays on the city's archaeology such as *London Under Ground: The Archaeology of a City?* (published in 2000)[21] – there is limited analysis of the post-medieval period (apart from some discussion of mortuary archaeology) and virtually no mention of material dating from after AD 1800. The Research Framework for London's Archaeology developed by English Heritage, the Museum of London and other stakeholders for London, published in 2002, considered the potential of the post-1800 era in the shortest of all the sections in the book; this reflected the unease that many urban archaeologists feel about the significance of the remains of this recent period.[22]

The situation in London mirrors that in other British cities with similarly complex archaeological sequences, where surveys of urban archaeology and of excavations in particular towns or cities have focused almost exclusively upon Romano-British and medieval remains.[23] Indeed, the only major integrative study of post-Roman urban archaeology in Britain is restricted to the period before c. AD 1350.[24] While post-medieval archaeology in Britain has seen remarkable expansion over the past decade,[25] academic studies of post-medieval archaeology have been criticised for their neglect of urban contexts.[26] Commercial archaeological field units have arguably done more, particularly in retrieving material evidence of the past for British industrial cities, such as the Archaeology Research Consultancy at the University of Sheffield (ARCUS) and the Greater Manchester Archaeological Unit whose investigations have focused on the south Yorkshire and the North West region respectively.[27] London's somewhat uncertain status as a manufacturing city – the social historian John Hammond once claimed that the industrial revolution 'was like a storm that passed over London and broke elsewhere' – has meant that interest in the city's industrial archaeology has been more limited.[28]

Historical archaeologist James Symonds has observed that the scale of British urban regeneration in the first years of the new millennium represented a major opportunity for archaeological research.[29] In London, since the late 1990s, the previous neglect of modern-period archaeology has been increasingly acknowledged.[30] The changes in the structure and funding of archaeology since the implementation of PPG16, and the increasing redevelopment of 'brownfield' urban sites (an urban planner's term that for the archaeologist often indicates the presence of post-medieval remains), has witnessed a proliferation of post-medieval excavations in London, often in previously little-studied boroughs, such as Lambeth and Tower Hamlets.

During the 1990s the post-medieval period produced the highest number of archaeological 'results' in the London boroughs than in any earlier period.[31] Excavations at Spitalfields to the west of the present-day market and to the east of Bishopsgate (sitecodes SQU94, STE95, SRP98, SQR00 and SSA01), in what might be considered as the beginning of London's 'East End', revealed unparalleled survival of aspects of this area's suburban development after AD 1680.[32] This has provided an important opportunity to develop approaches for analysing and interpreting 18th- and 19th-century household archaeologies for the East End. Some of the methods and techniques used in this study will be explored further in the case study below. The subsurface remains of working-class housing and backyard features demolished and filled during the 1880s by the Metropolitan Board of Works programme of slum clearances around Covent Garden, in central London, at Wild Court[33] and St Giles,[34] and Jacob's Island in Bermondsey[35] have been investigated, together with large areas of north Lambeth's Victorian landscape.[36] The archaeological record of these neighbourhoods provides fertile ground for integrative initiatives in historical archaeology, building upon the historical and geographical approaches used to consider the 'civilising' Brady Street Scheme in Bethnal Green[37] and other late Victorian and inter-war housing improvement schemes.[38]

Despite such promising developments in fieldwork, the post-excavation analysis of archaeologically derived material culture of post-medieval London largely remains isolated from broader accounts of the archaeological sequence and of historical processes.[39] Recent studies have described the production of domestic and other consumer goods, including tin-glazed ware ceramics,[40] glass,[41] porcelain (manufactured in the pothouses of Limehouse and Isleworth),[42] and other pottery (particularly Surrey–Hampshire border wares).[43] But while important integrative studies of London's post-medieval material culture, such as Geoff Egan's study of Tudor and Stuart small finds,[44] are beginning to appear, the study of the archaeological material culture of this period focuses almost exclusively on the details of industrial manufacture.

Much of the post-excavation analysis of London's archaeology for all periods is accessible through the Museum of London Archaeology Service's Monograph and Study Series, which reports the detailed findings of the more recent excavation projects, and through contributions to *Transactions of the London and Middlesex Archaeological Society* and *London Archaeologist*, which detail the significant archaeological investigations carried out over the past thirty years. But again, these often yield little to those interested in the Georgian and Victorian periods. Despite the potential of excavations such as those at Richmond and Mortlake,[45] the remains of early modern and modern London are often treated as beyond the scope of many post-excavation analysis reports and monographs.[46] Alternatively, when chronologies beyond 18th century are included, they are limited to the details of architectural sequences.[47]

However, a small number of post-excavation analyses have explicitly focused on the 19th-century metropolis. The application of a household archaeology approach to study sites in Victorian London's East End can be traced to the early 1970s, which included a detailed description of the clay tobacco pipes and the local pipe makers present among the backyard rubbish pits belonging to properties in Malverton Road, Bow.[48] Later excavations in Lambeth at Norfolk House uncovered a series of cesspits serving properties fronting Church Street (now Lambeth Road) that were similarly rapidly filled with large quantities of mid 19th-century rubbish.[49] Both sites remain as important, but narrowly disseminated, resources for understanding the material histories of documented households. Similarly, London's recent maritime past has been presented in the detailed accounts of the constructional techniques applied to various waterfronts that have not made the transition to being cited by historians of London.[50]

The archaeology of London's recent past is therefore largely a contradictory one: while it is clear that this period is very often the focus of development-funded archaeology – and the yearly summaries provided in the journals *London Archaeologist* and *Post-Medieval Archaeology* offer only a glimpse of the breadth of desk-based studies, fieldwork and post-excavation analysis conducted each year – archaeologists remain uncertain over how to deal with the complexity, diversity and sheer quantity of excavated post-medieval material remains from London.[51] Relatively few attempts have been made to interpret archaeological evidence in relation to the broader intellectual agendas that currently exercise historians of the modern metropolis. Having recognised the sheer volume of Georgian and Victorian materials that are stored, unstudied, in the LAARC and other repositories, what approaches might we call upon to develop research that contributes to current studies of the historiography and heritage of London?

DESCRIPTION, INTERPRETATION AND ARCHAEOLOGY

In the 1990s, a new wave of British post-medieval archaeology, represented especially by Sarah Tarlow and Susie West's edited volume *The Familiar Past?*,[52] recognised the importance of moving beyond the conventional descriptive accounts in 'industrial and traditional artefact studies … in post-medieval archaeology' that had dominated the field since its emergence in the 1960s.[53] The notion of 'interpretation', especially in relation to transatlantic intellectual exchanges in historical archaeology, was central to this critique.[54] Alisdair Brooks hoped 'to demonstrate ways of expanding ceramics analysis to include a more interpretive and contextual approach'.[55] Sarah Tarlow suggested that the presence of 'documentary and interpretative texts, art, architecture, music and artefacts' enabled the production of 'subtle, sophisticated and nuanced archaeologies'.[56] Most explicitly, Susie West criticised 'the low level of interpretation, usually no more than a summary description of results, required of most rescue projects', arguing that

> Most published post-medieval archaeology does not rise to the interpretive challenges that are posed by a social archaeology able to consider social identities and multiple meanings. What have we most to gain from adopting American modes of producing historical archaeology? How do British traditions help us develop a new formulation of the recent past?[57]

However, as Dan Hicks has recently argued, the 'Interpretive Critique' in British historical archaeology often served to 'weaken [researchers'] engagement with materiality, critiquing previous uses of archaeology to illustrate processes defined by social and economic history but replacing such studies with similar illustrations of social theory'.[58] At the same time, in practice the Interpretive Critique – which Matthew Johnson termed

Britain's 'new post-medieval archaeology'[59] – tended to downplay the usefulness of drawing from approaches developed in the 'different contextual circumstances' of North America or Australia.[60] Hicks challenges the distinction between descriptive and interpretive approaches as leading to a 'division of disciplinary labour' in the practice of historical archaeology,[61] and has called instead for studies that work between material detail and broader historical and geographical narratives, and that simultaneously draw from international traditions of historical archaeology, so as to 'decentre the Britishness in British historical archaeology':

> Such decentring involves moving away from a focus on human identities and ideas that neglects the complex affordances of material things, while also relocating our narratives of historical process to accommodate the unceasing mobilities of objects and people: mapping human and material movements onto one another.[62]

In London, this task of decentring has begun in discussions of the archaeology of ethnicity in studies of the material remains of Huguenot households in Spitalfields,[63] and in John Schofield and Richard Lea's reconsideration of Jacqui Pearce's[64] study of a tin-glazed plate painted with a Hebrew inscription recovered from a late-17th-century context in Aldgate, in relation to the history of Jewish immigration to this part of London during this period.[65] The global contexts of the circulation of objects in the past and the exchange of perspectives in their study in the present have also been increasingly acknowledged, for example in Pearce's study of a late-18th-century tavern assemblage from Uxbridge in relation to alternative approaches to the interpretation of tavern assemblages in British and North American archaeology.[66] What do the lead seals depicting the symbol of the little-known Company of Royal Adventurers to Africa found on the Thames foreshore tell of London's role in the slave trade?[67] Indeed, capturing London's role as the warehouse of an empire and its central position within global urban historical archaeology has been acknowledged in recent, multidisciplinary, perspectives relating to Australian practices in urban archaeology, such as the 'Exploring the Archaeology of Early Modern City' project (EAMC) established for Sydney in 2001 and the subsequent *Exploring the Modern City* volume.[68] A significant challenge therefore remains in firstly connecting the archaeology of London as a centre of global empire (rather than its peripheral geographical role when *Londinium*) and then communicating this within the frameworks and dialogues presented in the *Archaeology of the British* volume.[69]

The process of decentring has also begun at other scales. The urban geographies of industrialisation have informed Killock, Brown & Jarrett's archaeological study of mid-19th-century north Lambeth, and Brown's study of the Royal Doulton stoneware factory, which explored the sanitary reform movement through an examination of the relationships between the industrialists Henry Doulton and Joseph Cowen and the social reformer Edwin Chadwick.[70] Jeffries has investigated the processes and then demonstrated the correlation between the backfilling of cesspits in north Lambeth during the mid-to-late 19th century with changing attitudes towards rubbish disposal as a consequence of the Metropolis Local Management Act of 1855.[71] Yeomans has presented a much-needed fresh interpretation of London's post-medieval animal bone assemblages in relation to 'co-operative supply networks'.[72] A biographical account of a ginger beer bottle, tracing its life histories and use in the mineral water industry by two Swiss-Italian brothers in late-19th-century London, has also been considered.[73] Publications on materials derived from documented households, however, remain elusive, with the largely descriptive account of one late-17th- and one mid-18th-century dated finds-rich assemblage from the National Gallery site in Westminster representing the first output in twenty-five years,[74] since the consideration of the mid-18th-century finds assemblage discarded by the occupants of Crosswall in the City of London.[75]

Over the past decade, historical archaeology in North America and Australia has witnessed the emergence of a remarkable range of highly sophisticated studies of urban material. Foundational research such as Grace Karskens' study of the Rocks neighbourhood in Sydney, Australia,[76] the work of Steve Mrozowski, Grace Zeising and Mary Beaudry at the 19th-century Boott Mills Boardinghouses in Lowell, Massachusetts (see Mrozowski, this volume), have combined archaeological and documentary sources to present highly textured accounts of human social relationships in relation to built structures, landscapes or durable artefacts in the recent past.[77] Initiatives such as Alan Mayne and Tim Murray's edited volume *The Archaeology of Urban Landscapes: Explorations in Slumland* (2001) have brought together archaeologists with historians, aiming to develop alternative accounts of urban poverty and to 'trace the actualities of working-class lives' by focusing upon material remains.[78] Historical archaeologists have begun to produce integrative, long-term urban histories, such as the monumental populist study of 11,000 years of occupation at New York produced by Anne-Marie Cantwell and Diana diZerega Wall.[79] Developer-funded archaeological reports have begun to tell new stories with their material, notably with Rebecca Yamin's work in the Five Points district in New York,[80] and Adrian and Mary Praetzellis's report on the Cyprus Freeway replacement project in West Oakland, California.[81]

Such approaches hinge on a detailed engagement with the material culture. Yet by relying on 'intensely collaborative' working methods, the processes of recording, identifying and describing archaeological artefacts are never divorced from that of interpretation. This working model brings both the labour of the research process – fieldwork specialists, professional post-excavation analysts, academic archaeologists and historians – and its raw materials – the material artefacts, documentary and oral historical evidence, theoretical frameworks and interpretative narratives of historical change – into a close and 'democratic' dialogue. Sharing parallels with some of the traditions in documentary archaeology, such research projects involve 'tacking back and forth' between different kinds of evidence.[82] This is not a matter of privileging one kind of historical evidence over another, or of subordinating such evidence to the demands of certain kinds of social theory or narratives of historical change. By bringing multiple sources together, the 'ethnographies of place' approach tackles the complexity of lived experience and points to the fragility and contingency of all historical interpretation.[83] Social theory and an awareness of narrative voice remain important here, but are made to be 'responsive to an active engagement with material culture and archaeological contexts'.[84]

We have much to learn from such collaborative urban historical ethnographies in exploring the material history of modern London.[85] One important practical context here is the opening of the London Archaeological Archive and Research Centre (LAARC) in 2002. Where the thousands of boxes accumulated from London's excavations had previously been stored in an *ad hoc* fashion spread in many different locations – in warehouses and in lockups underneath railway arches or in the Museum of London rotunda and car park – the new LAARC brought together the 120,000 boxes of artefacts on over 10km of shelving in a single location. The site records, grey literature reports, artefacts and environmental remains from over 5,000 archaeological investigations in Greater London – the City of London and its thirty-two boroughs – are now held in this single location, providing access for researchers to the largest collection of excavated post-medieval material in the world. Post-medieval material accounts for a greater proportion of the archived archaeological material from the Greater London area.[86]

To encourage new engagements with the contents of the LAARC, the Museum launched a research programme into the 'archive archaeology' of post-medieval London, and a discussion document titled 'Biographies of London Life'.[87] This led to new curatorial work on quantifying and identifying the LAARC's archaeological collections for this period, partly through a number of funded student placements, financed by the Higher Education Funding Council for England (HEFCE FTDL5, led by Clive Orton, Gustav Milne, Dan Hicks and Robin Skeates). This enabled graduate students from Bristol University and the Institute of Archaeology, University College London, to work under the supervision of Museum of London Archaeology Service staff to 'rediscover' a range of important assemblages relating to the Georgian and Victorian metropolis.[88]

The present project builds upon these initiatives. Using some of collections of the LAARC, it aims to develop the research agendas proposed by Dan Hicks and Nigel Jeffries.[89] It involves collaboration between Alastair Owens (an academic historical geographer), Karen Wehner (an academic archaeologist and social anthropologist) and Rupert Featherby and Nigel Jeffries (professional archaeologists and material culture experts at the Museum of London Archaeology Service). Drawing upon the complementary skills of the research team (and some of the wider resources and expertise of the Museum of London Archaeology Service), the project applies the 'ethnographies of place' approach utilised by Australian and North American historical archaeologists, to investigate the material history of everyday domestic life in early-Victorian London. As well as providing a working model that refuses to separate the description of archaeological artefacts from their interpretation, such collaborative arrangements offer other benefits. In terms of attracting research funding (in our case the United Kingdom's Arts and Humanities Research Council) the project offers a credible example of 'knowledge transfer' between the academic and professional sectors and addresses recent calls for greater interdisciplinary collaboration.[90] Working with part of the Museum of London group also enables the dissemination of research findings beyond professional and academic archaeologists and historians, to others with an enthusiasm for London's history.

The project has begun to explore the social and geographical diversity of 19th-century London's material culture, and to consider patterns of consumption and disposal, the organisation and use of domestic space and the relationship between the home, economic activities and the wider urban world. In examining these themes, it seeks to assess how far it is possible to add a material dimension to historical understandings of life in the modern metropolis. For each of the study sites (Limehouse, Westminster and Sydenham), analysis of the surviving material artefacts has been undertaken alongside detailed investigations of a range of documentary historical sources – such as census records, rate books, street directories, civil registration records, personal papers, legal and administrative records – in order to explore the nature of everyday domestic life.

In the next section, we focus on the Sydenham site as a detailed case study that starts to interweave archaeological and documentary evidence in order to address questions about how people 'construct power and identity in their everyday lives'.[91] Yet in developing such an approach, we also emphasise the complexities and challenges of moving between the historical and archaeological evidence, and in particular examining the material culture and 'minute' details from transitory working-class households in multiple occupancy.

CASE STUDY: HOUSEHOLD ARCHAEOLOGY IN BELL GREEN, SYDENHAM

Over the middle decades of the 19th century, the area of Sydenham in south-east London was transformed from a satellite village of the growing metropolis into a fashionable new suburb. An important catalyst for this transformation was the relocation of Joseph Paxton's celebrated Crystal Palace – built to house the 1851 Great Exhibition – to Penge Place (to the west of Sydenham) in the mid-1850s. The enlarged building was surrounded by a new park with pleasure gardens, sports grounds, and even a mock prehistoric swamp with model dinosaurs.[92] Several local speculative developers constructed new middle-class housing estates close to the Palace, consisting of grand detached and semi-detached villas and substantial terraces: buildings that apparently represented 'a spiritual safe haven for the successful middle-class Victorian family' where 'realistic attempts could be made to balance the corrupting influences of the marketplace, money and the temptations of life beyond the doorstep'.[93] With the further development of south London's suburban rail network, much of Sydenham became (or aspired to become) a middle-class suburb.

The social composition and fortunes of Bell Green (to the east of the Crystal Palace, down the hill in Lower Sydenham) were rather different. Originally common land, Bell Green was enclosed in 1810 (Fig. 23.1). In the areas of Bell Green fronting Sydenham Road, terraced brick-built cottages were constructed sometime over the following decade. A brewery, converted and expanded from an old farm building and owned and operated by the Verey family, covered a considerable portion of the land to the south. In the 1830s and 1840s, this part of Lower Sydenham was not a bourgeois enclave, but a mixed neighbourhood, not fully overtaken by the suburban wave until the 1880s. Census records reveal that it provided a site of residence for the independently wealthy (fund holders), professionals (a solicitor, librarian, insurance broker) and tradespeople (a printer, press maker, carpenter).[94] Employing servants, many of these people evidently lived in modest comfort. Several, such as the Cowburn family who lived in Home Park Lodge (of whose estate Bell Green was part), had strong London connections. William Cowburn was a solicitor at Lincoln's Inn Fields in inner London, where he also maintained a second residence. Home Park Lodge was the family home and William's weekend retreat; it boasted a sizeable staff of domestic servants including a butler and page boy.[95] Cowburn might well have considered himself one of the urban gentry.[96]

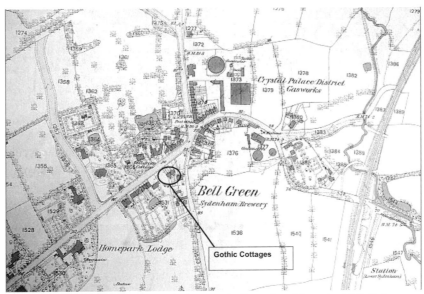

Figure 23.1 Map of Bell Green, Sydenham, 1863. Reproduced from the 1863 Ordnance Survey Map

Alongside these wealthier inhabitants, who often had long-standing connections with the locality, many of the cottages that were part of, or adjacent to, the Home Park estate were occupied by a poorer population of labourers and market gardeners. Between the 1830s and 1850s the 'Gothic cottages' that fronted Sydenham Road on the northern edge of Bell Green were inhabited by a succession of families and individuals – often migrants from other parts of the country – who sought to make a living on the fringes of the metropolis. They worked in the market gardens and farms that met the city's growing consumption needs and offered their labour to local trades: bricklayers, breweries and the nearby gasworks. Indeed, the construction of the Crystal Palace and District Gas Company's works on the land to the north east of Bell Green between 1852 and 1854 had a significant effect on the immediate locality. While the gas works themselves reflected the burgeoning demand for the modern domestic technologies of light and heat in the luxury middle-class housing rapidly being built close to the Crystal Palace, they transformed Bell Green into one of Sydenham's less desirable districts. The presence of the works discouraged the development of quality housing so that Bell Green became one of the area's 'few slums'.[97]

During the middle decades of the 19th century, then, Bell Green's history was distinct from, but shaped by, the development of middle-class Sydenham Hill and Crystal Palace.[98] It would be tempting to narrate the history of Bell Green as one of progressive urban degeneration. Its apparent contrast with the wealth and consumer spectacle of Upper Sydenham would seem to replicate in miniature the patterns of social segregation that characterised modern London as a whole: between the wealthy west end and the poor east; between the ordered stability of the suburbs and the transient chaos of the inner city. Bell Green's emergence as a 'slum' by the end of the century could be situated within what has become a compelling historical narrative for understanding the relationships between poverty and the built environment in the Victorian metropolis.[99] Yet, as Alan Mayne and Tim Murray have argued, such historical interpretations are often uncritical, reproducing 'a stereotype that was fashioned in the early nineteenth century by bourgeois entertainers and social reformers and that obscured and distorted the varied spatial forms to which it [the label 'slum'] was applied'.[100] They insist on the potential for fine-grained archaeological analyses to provide alternatives to 'slum myths'.[101]

In 1992, Verey's brewery, located on Bell Green, provided the principal focus for an excavation by the Museum of London Archaeology Service (sitecode: SYB92). In the north-west corner of the site were the partial remains of an external wall and a circular brick-lined soakaway located in the back yard of one of the 'Gothic Cottages.' The archaeological sequence revealed that the soakaway – designed to drain excess surface, household and gutter water from the yard – became a rubbish pit and was rapidly filled in one event, or in a series of closely related events (context [27]), with household refuse. The evidence from the material culture within the feature suggests that this occurred shortly after 1851: the most recent dated item is a glass inkwell with a registration mark suggesting its manufacture in 1851, while the makers' marks present on the crockery are mostly dated to the 1830s. The pit was then partially capped with a slab and the rear wall modified to take a run-off drain, completing a process of modification that appears to be linked to the widespread drainage improvement works known to have taken place in the area in 1854.[102]

The assemblage (Table 23.1) is dominated by pottery and glass items retrieved in a good condition (totalling a minimum of 328 vessels weighing nearly 50kg).[103] This fits well with the 'proper dry rubbish' often employed to fill holes in the ground across London from the 1840s.[104] The presence of both complete and reconstructable crockery and glassware here, together with more fragmented examples, strongly suggests that materials were directly sourced from a household clearout, and mixed with stockpiled domestic rubbish.

Table 23.1 SYB92: Context [27] by material and statistical counts

Material	Fragment count	Fragment count %	Vessel count	Vessel count %	Weight (grammes)
Glass	59	6.9	54	16.4	10,503
Other	1	0.1	1	0.2	-
Pipes	4	0.1	4	1.2	-
Pottery	789	92.5	270	82.1	39,351
Total	853	100.0	329	100.0	49,854

Linking individual archaeological contexts such as this infilled-soakaway with historical documentation of the households that created them is 'one of the most challenging aspects of urban archaeology',[105] as discussed also by Cessford, this volume. It becomes a particularly difficult task when interpreting assemblages related to properties that witnessed a rapid turnover of tenants. A historic map regression exercise, using a geographic information system (GIS), nevertheless located the soakaway at the rear of the end terrace cottage that formed one of the four properties in the row of 'Gothic Cottages'. As noted above, the censuses covering the period 1841 to 1871 (from which it is possible to extract detailed information on households) show that the inhabitants of the cottages were mainly employed as skilled labourers.[106] Rate books from the late 1840s suggest the rentable value of such property to be relatively low at £11 per annum, per cottage.[107] As with most working-class neighbourhoods of the period, significant levels of residential mobility led to a high turnover of occupants in these tenanted households. The censuses provide decennial snapshots of who lived in the 'Gothic Cottages'; other sources (such and rate books and trade directories) reveal inter-censual mobility of occupants suggesting that the 'Gothic Cottages' were inhabited by transitory, poorer inhabitants, with household structures that bore little resemblance to the newly constructed middle-class villas elsewhere in Sydenham.

Unlike many North American studies that successfully tie archaeological assemblages to specific families or household inhabitants, it is difficult to establish a group of individuals to whom the contents of the soakaway may have belonged. However, the composition of the assemblage – which includes a number of children's ceramic objects – suggests the presence of a family. From the late 1840s through to the early 1850s, the Anthony family lived at the cottage that adjoined the end of terrace. In 1851, the recently widowed Charlotte Anthony was listed as the household head along with her four children, aged between 2 and 12 years. Since the timing of the deposition appears to coincide with the moment the Anthony family moved away from Bell Green (to elsewhere in the locality), it is possible that the objects might represent the breaking up of the household. The presence of a Christening cup bearing the name William – possibly William Anthony, aged 10 in 1851 – also points towards the assemblage's association with the Anthony household (Plate 6). A key challenge, therefore, both in interpreting the archaeology of Bell Green's 'Gothic Cottages' and in developing a household archaeology approach in London more generally, comes in trying to map specific assemblages onto historically documented people. In a city that was constantly on the move, it is often difficult for archaeologists to bring together people with their things.

The soakaway yielded a range of objects that will be familiar to anyone who has excavated 19th-century urban sites in Britain. Just over a third of the pottery (up to 98 vessels) comprises transfer-printed wares. The most popular design is the ubiquitous 'Willow Pattern' on dining wares, and a formalised setting is apparent through the sauceboat and eighteen dinner, two dessert and two meat plates decorated with this pattern. Though this might be seen as reflecting a 'set', the range of makers' marks and quality of the prints indicate a more gradual and piecemeal acquisition in order to build up a stock of 'Willow Pattern' crockery and mitigate breakages.

A similar pattern is visible in the tea sets present. A few slightly more expensive bone china moulded teacups with Chelsea sprig decoration provided the largest tea set, supplemented by some individually matched teacup and saucer sets in both blue and green transfer-printed whiteware. Lower-quality and costed items, whiteware cups and saucers with cut-sponged decoration, complete this functional group.

A significant proportion of the pottery was derived from a kitchen or storeroom, with a group of up to ten complete stoneware black leading bottles (vessels used to contain polish for kitchen and window ranges, and boots) and up to sixteen different-sized plain refined whiteware cylindrical jars employed as food containers. Yellow wares provided the rounded bowls used to eat sloppy foods, pitchers for decanting drinks and chamber pots for hygiene. The glass items included a series of individual pharmaceutical and gendered scent/perfume bottles and a glass tumbler engraved with the initials of its owner – 'GR' – an attempt to mark possession.[108]

Few of these superficially familiar items by themselves are particularly unusual in the archaeological record of this period and many were common to all three sites that were investigated as part of the project. Indeed, one of the themes we aim to develop is to underline the frequency with which certain types of crockery and glass items regularly turned up in assemblages relating to a wide variety of social and geographical contexts from around the metropolis, elsewhere in Britain, and far beyond: Willow Pattern was traded across the Atlantic world and further afield and represented the cheapest of all the transfer-printed patterns available in Staffordshire potters' price-fixing lists (see further consideration in Brooks, this volume).[109] Notwithstanding differences in quality and quantity, the repetitive, mundane and (above all) banal nature of much of the archaeological evidence recovered from a variety of locations across Georgian and Victorian London demonstrates that it is not always possible to read artefacts from poor neighbourhoods simplistically as 'the material residues of inequality'.[110]

However, the excavated artefacts, when interwoven with a range of documentary historical sources, do allow us to begin to explore the material life of the working-class residents who occupied the 'Gothic Cottages' over the mid-19th century amid the surrounding bourgeois prosperity and associated ideals of moral propriety.[111] Among the banal and everyday fragments, a number of the ceramic artefacts were display items and personalised possessions. A small but significant group of the transfer-printed wares provide several examples of 'moralising china', comprising a number of toy plates and mugs adorned with maxims, religious inscriptions and children's rhymes (Plate 7).

While 'moralising china' is not necessarily uncommon in London's Victorian ceramic assemblages, such a varied collection from the Sydenham site is unusual and distinctive.[112] A black transfer-printed refined whiteware toy plate with overglaze painted decoration and moulded daisy rim included the Benjamin Franklin maxims (taken from *Poor Richard's Almanac*, 1737): 'There are no gains with out pains' and 'Industry pays debts'. Another, red-transfer printed refined whiteware plate with similar moulded daisy rim has an equally insistent Franklin-inspired inscription proclaiming the virtues of hard work: 'At the working man's house hunger looks in but dares not enter.' Other items emphasised the value of family relationships. A further black-transfer printed refined whiteware toy plate carried a short poem, written by Jane Taylor (1783–1824) in honour of grandmother:

> Who came to see me far and near. With cakes and toys throughout the year and called me her 'sweet little dear' my grandmother.

Another toy plate carried an image of a mother and daughter hugging one another. A green transfer-printed whiteware small cylindrical mug depicted young children playing together. Evidence of a religious influence was found in the form of a plate depicting angels with harps and reading from a book on a table, with the inscription 'How glorious is our heavenly King who reigns above the sky' (an excerpt from Isaac's Prayer). There was also a bone china Christening cup enamelled with the name 'William', which, as mentioned above, possibly belonged to William Anthony, born in 1841 and recorded in the 1851 census as a 'scholar'.

Surveying the recorded patterns in Coysh and Henrywood – a 'dictionary' of transfer-printed pottery designs – reveals a series of different prints that were used to convey Christian and other moral values.[113] These included the depiction of Biblical images,[114] prayers or passages from the Scriptures,[115] and Benjamin Franklin's maxims.[116] Colour was also significant: most 'moralising china' utilised 'new coloured' transfer prints (particularly mulberry and green) or was decorated with black or brown transfer-prints that are often further embellished with garish underglaze painting. The borders of plates were frequently moulded with a daisy pattern. Further transfer-printed patterns also have children at their centrepiece. These are nearly always linked to pastoral scenes depicting either rural pastimes (for example, 'Boys Fishing', 'Boy Piping' or 'Girl at the Well'), occupations (including 'Mushroom Picker', 'The Errand Boy' or 'The Young Philosopher'), or distress (such as 'Shepherd Boy Rescued' or 'The Impatient Child'). Children are also frequently depicted together with adults in numerous other pastoral scenes (for example, 'May Morn' or 'Milking Time').[117] In investigating the implied status of owning such 'moralising china', the relative value of these wares can be partially assessed through American historical archaeologist George L. Miller's 'CC' (Cream-Coloured ware) index.[118] Miller's work demonstrates that in the early 1870s 'children's ABC and Motto plates printed and coloured' cost considerably more than other transfer-printed pottery available in the Staffordshire potter's price-fixing agreements, individual potter's lists and their invoices.[119]

Moralising china similar to that from Bell Green has been the focus of historical archaeologies of 19th-century households elsewhere in the Anglophone world.[120] For instance, at Sydney's Rocks neighbourhood, Australian historical archaeologist Grace Karskens has argued that such ceramics 'reveal a clear interest in educating children, in inculcating them with moral principles of self-control, self improvement and hard work'.[121] In the United States, Steve Brighton has argued that its presence represents evidence of a deep concern with the education and moral upbringing of children and of working-class aspiration for bourgeois material culture.[122] This parallels Karskens' focus on these objects as a material trace of middle-class attempts to morally indoctrinate the poor.[123]

In the case of the 'Gothic Cottages', one possibility would be to understand such artefacts as evidence of an embracing of the popular trope of 'self-improvement': a material dimension of a theme recently explored by Sarah Tarlow.[124] Benjamin Franklin's writings have often been seen by historians as 'favourite reading for aspiring working men' of the mid-19th century.[125] Certainly, the use of his maxims to decorate pottery was common from the 1820s.[126] The purchase and use of such ceramics may have represented an attempt by the working poor to transmit such values to a younger generation – an aspirational expression of identity; an outward expression of gentility. The presence of nine stoneware inkwells within the assemblage perhaps also hints at a belief in the principles of 'self-improvement' here, the material remains of a desire to become members of the expanding reading populace.

The eldest four children of the Anthony family, headed by the recently bereaved dressmaker Charlotte Anthony (including 10-year-old William to whom the Christening cup may have belonged) are listed as 'scholars' in the 1851 census.[127] But can we generalise from this to suggest, for example, that such personalised items promoted ideas of individuality and reinforced the perception of private property?[128]

The moralising china may equally reflect the inhabitants' engagement with another key social and political issue of the time: drink. Franklin's writings are often associated with the 19th-century English temperance movement, not least as they strongly influenced the 'pioneer teetotaler', Joseph Livesey.[129] The 1830s and 1840s were a key time in relation to debates about the moral misfortunes of alcohol consumption, and many working men and women pledged a commitment to moderation or teetotalism.[130] The London Temperance Society (later renamed the British and Foreign Temperance Society) was founded in 1831 and was supported, albeit with varying degrees of commitment, by the Church of England (its patron was the Bishop of London) and the nonconformist churches.[131] Thus the ownership of these items may have been shaped by religious beliefs and influences.

Indeed, in explaining the presence of objects with a more explicitly religious dimension, there is evidence that several of the cottages' inhabitants were involved with local ecclesiastical institutions. James and Harriet Ailing, who lived at one of the cottages in 1841, baptised two of their children at nearby St Bartholomew's church (opened in 1832) in the 1840s, as did many other families resident over the next two decades.[132] Thus, these items might be taken as evidence of positive attempts by working-class people to express a set of ethics and values associated with hard work and religious observance.

An alternative interpretation would be to argue that these items of moralising china represent an imposed (material) culture of improvement: tangible remains of middle-class attempts to guide and chastise the poor. The paternalistic nature of the relationship between Bell Green's labouring populations and their landlords, coupled with the wider development of Sydenham as a suburb that supposedly embodied bourgeois values and ways of life, would lend credibility to this interpretation.[133] William Cowburn, who took up the lease of Home Park lodge and who became landlord to the 'Gothic Cottages', proclaimed in a letter to his new tenants in December 1836 that he intended to 'build more comfortable cottages at Bell Green, for industrious and deserving labourers, and … to make my little property there the means of usefulness, and for the bettering of the condition of the Poor, and so in every respect and advantage to myself'.[134] Indeed, Cowburn was a keen advocate of working-class self-improvement. Prior to moving to Sydenham he had lived in the village of Selborne in Hampshire, the scene of a notorious rural riot in November 1830. Sensing the growing unrest, Cowburn had written to the 'Cottagers of Selborne' in February 1830, suggesting ways that they could improve their lot and secure independence from parochial relief. His letter provided heart-rending examples of struggles against adversity, illustrating 'the many advantages to be derived from industry'.[135] Could the plates and other items found among the assemblage have been a gift from the Cowburn family to their tenants?

Although much later, glimpses of an ongoing 'moralising mission' in Sydenham can be seen in the local parish magazine, copies of which survive from the 1860s. These describe 'lectures for the poor on the Gospel according to St. Matthew', evening schools for poor boys and girls, and various subscription societies in aid of the poor, including ones for clothing, shoes, coal and a library. They also include discussion of plans for the establishment of a 'working man's club' where the virtues of self-improvement might be extolled directly to the poor.[136]

While an assemblage of this kind cannot be reduced to single historical narratives, it is suggestive of the manner in which bourgeois ideals were experienced by the urban poor through material things, adding an alternative dimension to historical studies of metropolitan middle-class discourses of poverty and attitudes towards the poor.[137] Rather than engaging only superficially with archaeological materials – using them to illustrate a narrative focused on conventional documentary history – such materials can evoke how both the poor and the middle classes encountered these contemporary values and ethics in their everyday lives.

Other items found within the soakaway feature raise questions about the extent to which the inhabitants of the 'Gothic Cottages' either embraced or were coerced into the moral habits and behaviours suggested by the moralising china and other documentary evidence. In particular, the presence of a large number of glass wine bottles would seem to be at odds with the values of temperance and abstemious frugality hinted at by the decorative plates and counselled by the insistent voices of the local bourgeoisie. In total there were twenty-one free-blown, common English cylindrical wine bottles and a further six imported, continental, Burgundy-shaped glass bottles within the assemblage. Discarded intact, these vessels obviously suggest that alcohol consumption was common among these households, meaning that calls to temperance were either resisted or ignored; an outward pledge of abstention from alcohol (expressed through some Franklin-inspired ceramic toys) was not always followed in practice.

In interpreting working-class ceramics in 19th-century New York, Steve Brighton observes that the ownership of moralising china and fancy display items 'created the outward appearance of gentility and temperance in opposition to the popular culture's oppressive judgements, while at the same time maintaining ethnic and working-class customs'.[138] But alternatively, the evidence could suggest a more moderate observance of temperance. The modest consumption of wine and certain spirits was not always seen to conflict with a stand against drunkenness and the 'insensibility' caused by excessive beer or gin drinking (the self-interest of middle-class advocates of temperance is evident in this stance!).[139] And as the example of many middle-class Victorian clergyman would attest, leading a godly existence and enjoying the occasional drink were not mutually exclusive activities.[140]

The complex ambiguities of the artefactual evidence must be acknowledged here. The consumption of wine would have been unusual among working-class households at this time.[141] There are always ambiguities present in interpreting glass assemblages of the period, linked to the ideals of thrift, recycling and resale value. Perhaps the 'Gothic Cottage' bottles were being used for a different function – recycled in order to store other liquids? There are only a few glass-related items that were thrown away that can be linked to the taking of alcohol, with just a few mismatched wine glasses present. Perhaps they were not disposed of by the occupants of the 'Gothic Cottages', but by the neighbouring Cowburn household or the 'respectable' Verey family who made a living from alcohol by running a brewery next door? Were they simply a convenient durable substance with which a redundant soakaway could be rapidly filled?

There are, however, other hints from documentary sources that the labourers of Bell Green did not acquiesce to the moralising ambitions of the middle class. The Sydenham Parish Magazine (published in the 1860s) hints at the ongoing challenges that St Bartholomew's 'respectable' church officers and congregation faced in persuading the local poor to engage with the 'rational' and godly pursuits that they sought to offer. The May 1868 edition of the magazine gave notice of a meeting to discuss the establishment of a working men's club; the need for which, it was reported, was 'greatly felt'. However, the June edition of the magazine bemoaned the small attendance, comprised of local 'gentlemen' who, in a rather desperate tone, declared their 'readiness to support any scheme that might find favour with the working men themselves.'[142] But perhaps the strongest evidence that the residents of the 'Gothic Cottages' did not fully subscribe to bourgeois attempts to shape their economic and moral behaviour comes in the form of the 'moralising china' itself: items that that were thrown away. Rather than cherished objects, displayed on a mantle piece or kitchen dresser, they were discarded, evidently no longer wanted, into a hole in the backyard. Whatever their one-time significance to their owners, they no longer mattered: people's relationships to objects and the role that material culture plays in the construction of personal and collective identities changes.

CONCLUSION

As the above discussion of a dumped household assemblage from mid-19th-century London reveals, the challenges raised by seeking to make use of archaeological materials to write modern history relate to the forms of historiography that are used or adopted. The sheer complexity and diversity of the materials means that we must resist reductive interpretations of historical change in preference to grappling with the fluidity of metropolitan life. The material traces left by the inhabitants of Bell Green's 'Gothic Cottages' are fragmented, and undoubtedly ambiguous. They survive in the present, and will always fail adequately to illustrate their time of deposition (which was just one moment in their long life-histories). For many historians, this ambiguity would be problematic, especially when compared with the apparent certainties of much documentary evidence. But in a recent review article exploring the place of historical archaeology within modern historical studies, historian Alan Mayne has argued that it is precisely the ambiguity of archaeological evidence that forms one of its key contributions to historical practice. He claims that detailed archaeological inquiry is a trigger of 'innovative analysis', since it forces scholars to the 'edges of history's comfort zones', highlighting dissonances, contradictions and diversity in preference for a 'smoothed out' history that concentrates on the 'normal' and the 'representative'.[143] Mayne further argues that 'historical archaeologists' study of materiality', has the potential 'to emphasize and recalibrate ambiguity as a powerful tool with which to extend cross-disciplinary interpretation of modern history'.[144] To this we would add the significance of historical archaeology as a contemporary practice – an observation that includes not only fieldwork but also writing archaeological histories. Archaeology can never write the human past on its own terms. Instead, all historical evidence – documentary and material – provides a partial, often only fleeting, glimpse of the past; the fragmented, everyday, banal contents of 19th-century London soakaways and privies are a valuable reminder of this observation.

The approaches and perspectives described in Mayne's review article and developed in this chapter offer the potential for enriching our understanding of Georgian and Victorian London and for shifting the nature of historical and theoretical debate and the axis of empirical enquiry. Firstly, historians' culturally inflected emphasis on studying representations of London life during this period and charting the discursive construction of social relationships and urban topographies could usefully be counterbalanced with approaches that attend to the material dimensions of metropolitan life.[145] As Dennis neatly puts it, this directs greater attention to practice: to 'how things work rather than … what things mean'.[146] Secondly, historical archaeology offers a distinctive set of methods and concepts for grappling with the lives of 'modern' London. The idea of modernity, as Nigel Thrift has argued, affords too much importance to apparently large-scale processes such as social segregation, commodification and alienation that were more complex, tentative and uncertain in the ebb and flow of everyday life.[147] The approaches described in this chapter direct attention to precisely such material complexities and the messy inconsistencies of historical change as played out in London's varying localities, households and parlours. In this way, archaeological knowledge of the recent past can be used to follow historical geographer Miles Ogborn's desire to avoid the totalising ambitions of modernity and provide carefully contextualised histories of the modern, attentive to questions of difference, hybridity and contestation.[148]

London, like many other British cities, has the archaeological resources for pursuing such goals. The collections of the LAARC remain underused, and the scope for building imaginative collaborations between historians, academic and professional archaeologists and the museums and archives charged with curating the city's past are many. Historical archaeologists should seize this opportunity to draw upon and develop approaches that collapse apparent distinctions between the descriptive and the interpretive, in order to rematerialise the history of modern London.

ACKNOWLEDGEMENTS
This chapter draws upon research undertaken for an Arts and Humanities Research Council (AHRC) funded project 'Living in Victorian London: material histories of everyday life in the nineteenth-century metropolis' (Award number: AH/E002285/1, July 2007–March 2008). This support is gratefully acknowledged. We also thank the editors of this book and the anonymous referee for their encouragement and suggestions.

NOTES

1. See, for example, Dennis 2008; Ogborn 1998 and Nead 2000. See also Griffiths & Jenner 2000.
2. Bowsher & Miller nd.
3. Jamieson 2006.
4. O'Keeffe & Yamin 2006, 91.
5. West 1999, 11.
6. Tarlow 2007, 164–5.
7. Hicks 2008, 114.
8. 'Living in Victorian London: Material Histories of Everyday Life in the Nineteenth-Century Metropolis', funded by the UK's Arts and Humanities Research Council (Award AH/E002285/1, July 2007–March 2008). The project involved collaboration between Alastair Owens (Principal Investigator) of the Department of Geography at Queen Mary, University of London and Nigel Jeffries, Rupert Featherby and other staff at the Museum of London Archaeology Service. Karen Wehner was the project's Postdoctoral Research Assistant.
9. Mayne & Lawrence 1999; Mayne & Murray 2001a, 2.
10. In this sense the chapter further develops ideas and agendas relating to the potential use of the LAARC's collections set out in Hicks & Jeffries 2004.
11. Grimes 1968; Shepherd 1998.
12. After 1957 Noël Hume moved to Virginia to take up the position of Chief Archaeologist at Colonial Williamsburg.
13. Ottaway 1992, 59.
14. cf. McCracken & Phillpotts 1995.
15. See Thompson et al. 1998 for a summary of pre-1990 excavation.
16. See, for example, Merrifield 1965; Milne 1995.
17. Vince 1990.
18. Thomas 2002.
19. See, for example, Rowsome 2000.
20. Biddle et al. 1973.
21. Haynes et al. 2000.
22. Museum of London 2002.
23. For overviews of urban archaeology in Britain, see Carver 1990; Schofield & Leech 1987; for a standard example of studies of specific towns, see Platt & Coleman-Smith 1975.
24. Ottaway 1992.
25. Johnson 1996; Tarlow & West 1999; Hicks & Beaudry 2006; Tarlow 2007.
26. Broad 1998, 117; Egan 1999, 61.
27. For Sheffield, see Symonds 2002. For the North West, see Nevell 2004. More generally, see Symonds & Casella 2006.
28. Hammond 1925, cited in Lee 1986, 125. This statement is not intended to downplay the important role that the Greater London Industrial Society has played in raising the profile of London's recent industrial past since its foundation in 1968. However, their interests are generally excluded in PPG16-funded archaeology.
29. Symonds 2004, 37.
30. Hicks & Jeffries 2004; cf. Museum of London 2002, 68.
31. Egan 1999, 61.
32. Holder et al. forthcoming.
33. Jeffries & Watson forthcoming, Museum of London Archaeology Service (MoLAS) sitecode KEL00.
34. MoLAS sitecode SIC06.
35. MoLAS sitecode JAC96.
36. Webber 1991, Killock et al. 2003, Tyler 2004, Tyler 2005a; Jeffries 2006.
37. Bentley 2000.
38. Cox 1995; Bailey 1987; Yelling 1995.
39. Brooks 2005, 3; Hicks 2007, 1320.
40. Stephenson 1999, 265–8; Tyler et al. 2008.
41. Tyler 2005b.
42. Tyler et al. 2000; Pearce 2000.
43. Pearce 1992; Pearce 2007.
44. Egan 2005.
45. Sloane et al. 2003.
46. Bluer et al. 2006, 140.
47. Thomas et al. 2005; Bowsher et al. 2007.
48. Atkinson 1977.
49. Webber 1991. Sitecode NOR90.
50. Divers 2002, 2004; Heard with Goodburn 2003; Wood & Munby 2003.
51. See also Schofield & Maloney 1998.
52. Tarlow & West 1999.
53. Johnson 1996, 187.
54. Hicks 2007, 1324.
55. Brooks 1999, 51.
56. Tarlow 1999, 266.
57. West 1999, 2.
58. Hicks 2007, 1324.
59. Johnson 1999.
60. West 1999, 8; see Hicks 2000, par 1.
61. Hicks 2008, 114.
62. Hicks 2008, 115.
63. Jeffries 2001; Oleksy 2006.
64. Pearce 1998.
65. Schofield & Lea 2005, 188–9.
66. Pearce 2000.
67. Egan 1994, fig 38, no. 291, 189.

68. Murray 2003; Murray *et al.* 2003, especially 133–4.
69. Lawrence 2003.
70. Killock *et al.* 2003.
71. Jeffries 2006.
72. Yeomans 2005.
73. Jeffries forthcoming.
74. Telfer *et al.* 2006.
75. Vince & Egan 1981.
76. Karskens 1999.
77. Mrozowski *et al.* 1996.
78. Mayne & Murray 2001a, 1.
79. Cantwell & Wall 2001.
80. Yamin 1998.
81. Praetzellis & Praetzellis 2004. Reviews of many of the above works can be found in Hicks & Beaudry 2006: O'Keeffe & Yamin 2006; Symonds & Casella 2006.
82. Wilkie 2006, 25.
83. On the ethnography theme, see Hirsch & Stewart 2005.
84. Murray & Crook 2005, 93. For further discussion of narrative voices, see Praetzellis 1998.
85. This echoes a similar claim made by Murray & Crook 2005.
86. Roy Stephenson (LAARC), pers. comm.
87. Hicks & Jeffries 2004. See also Hoskins 1998.
88. For an example of work arising from this collaboration, see Gooch 2007.
89. Hicks & Jeffries 2004.
90. AHRC 2007, 5.
91. Beaudry & Mrozowski 2001, 118.
92. On the relocation of the palace and the development of Sydenham as a suburb, see Kay 2008; Piggott 2004; Hassam 1999. However, Lower Sydenham (and indeed large parts of south London) lacks any scholarly history, but a good local history of Sydenham is provided by Coulter 1999.
93. Kay 2008, 29.
94. 1841 Census: Bell Green, Sydenham. Enumerated 7 June 1841 HO 107/484/11, pp. 20–1; 1851 Census HO 107/1591, pp. 493–495b; 1861 Census: Bell Green, St. Bartholomew's Sydenham. Enumerated 8 April 1861 RG 9/416 13–14, pp. 16–19; 1871 Census: Lewisham, Bell Green, Village of Sydenham RG10/768, pp. 1–8.
95. 1851 Census HO 107/1591, fols 493–493b, pp. 22–3.
96. He is described among the gentry in *Kelly's Directory of the Home Counties*: Kent (Sydenham), 1852.
97. Coulter 1999.
98. Dennis 2008, chapters 7 and 8.
99. Dyos 1967; Green & Parton 1990; Wohl 1977.
100. Mayne & Murray 2001a, 1. See also Mayne 1993. There is now a voluminous literature on the representation of urban life in Victorian London. See, for example: Driver 2001; McLaughlin 2000; Robinson 2004.
101. Mayne & Murray 2001a, 2.
102. London Metropolitan Archive (LMA) MCS/215 Original Contracts, Metropolitan Commission of Sewers, 1847–1862. 1854 Brick Sewers in Deptford, Lewisham and Bell Green.
103. Reports detailing the full assemblages can be downloaded via <http://www.geog.qmul.ac.uk/victorianlondon/publications.html> [site accessed 22 July 2008].
104. Jeffries 2006, 275.
105. Mrozowski 2006, 38.
106. See note 94.
107. St Mary's Poor and Highway Rate Book, LLHAC SM/1/4/4/, 11 December 1849, fol. 74.
108. No individual with the initials 'GR' could be traced in the census or other documents. Initialled tumblers were also found excavated at the Rocks in Sydney: see Karskens 2001, 77.
109. Barker & Majewski 2006.
110. Mayne & Murray 2001a, 3. It may be that what was eaten off 'Willow Pattern' plates (or similar) would be a better marker of inequality. As noted, evidence of animal bone or other foodstuffs was limited for our sites. Karskens 2001, 76–7, also makes the point that at first glance 'material culture can be indistinguishable from one class to another'. A study like Brighton's 2001 analysis of the procurement and availability of 'fancy ceramics' at nineteenth-century New York's 'Five Points' would greatly aid interpretation of London's pottery assemblages.
111. Evidence from enclosure maps held at Lewisham Local History and Archives Centre (LLHAC) suggest that the cottages were constructed sometime between 1812 and 1819. The name 'Gothic Cottages' was not used until the 1860s. Whether this name perhaps reflects their architectural style remains unclear.
112. Although it is dwarfed by the 'moralising china' assemblage dumped in the cellar of a property from Church Street, Isleworth: sitecode CSI86.
113. Coysh & Henrywood 1982.
114. Coysh & Henrywood 1982, 91.
115. Coysh & Henrywood 1982, 197, 247, 253, 282 and 325.
116. Coysh & Henrywood 1982: 108, 132, 264.
117. Coysh & Henrywood 1982: 53, 95, 130, 154, 186, 241, 247, 255, 334 and 412.
118. Miller 1991.
119. Miller 1991, 13. However, while Miller's work on cost/value was based on British source materials, the interpretation of those values is weighted to the North American market. Whether his work can be

recalibrated and applied to ceramics excavated from London or elsewhere in the British Isles in order to determine cost remains doubtful.

120. See, for example, Brighton 2001; Praetzellis & Praetzellis 1992.
121. Karskens 2001, 76.
122. Karskens 2001, 77.
123. Karskens 2001, 77.
124. Tarlow 2007.
125. Harrison 1971, 120.
126. See Lucas 2003 for a wider discussion of how the production and consumption of 'literary ceramics' in the early 19th century was connected with wider social changes in reading practices and perceptions of fiction.
127. 1851 Census HO 107/1591, p. 495b.
128. Brighton 2001, 27.
129. Harrison 1971, 120.
130. Shiman 1988. The temperance theme is also present in mottoes used on the ceramics of the period, in particular the products of the Sunderland potteries (cf. Baker 1984, Appendix IV, especially catalogue no. 28), which also made a large range of 'moralising china'.
131. Shiman 1988, 12–13.
132. Parish Records on Microfilm: St Bartholomew's chapel in the County of Kent: 1/9/1832–10/12/1844, 1845–1858, 11/4/1858–20/10/1867 (Baptism Records) LLHAC.
133. On the latter theme see Kay 2008.
134. Coulter 1999, 23.
135. The full text of William Cowburn's letter is available from <http://www.johnowensmith.co.uk/riot/personal.htm#cowburn> [site accessed 24 July 2008].
136. 136 Parish Magazine, Sydenham, Volume 1 (1868), LLHAC.
137. For example, Driver 2001; Englander & O'Day 1995.
138. Brighton 2001, 23.
139. Shiman 1988, 21.
140. Harrison 1971, 44.
141. Harrison 1971, chapter 2.
142. Parish Magazine, Sydenham, Volume 1 (1868), May and June, LLHAC.
143. Mayne 2008, 111–12.
144. Mayne 2008, 94.
145. A raft of recent publications illustrates this enthusiasm for studying representation: Freeman 2007; Gilbert 2002; Phillips 2007; Robinson 2004.
146. Dennis 2008, 3.
147. Thrift 2000.
148. Ogborn 1998.

BIBLIOGRAPHY

AHRC (Arts and Humanities Research Council) 2007, *Vision and Strategy, 2007–2012*. Bristol: Arts and Humanities Research Council.

Atkinson, D.R. 1977, '19th century marked pipes from Maverton Road, Bow, East London', *Transactions of the London and Middlesex Archaeology Society* **28**: 258–68.

Bailey, K. 1987, 'Estate development in Victorian London: some examples from Battersea', *Transactions of the London and Middlesex Archaeology Society* **38**: 187–202.

Baker, J.C. 1984, *Sunderland Pottery*, 5th edn. Newcastle upon Tyne: Tyne and Wear County Museums.

Barker, D. & Majewski, T. 2006, 'Ceramic studies in historical archaeology', in Hicks & Beaudry (eds), 2006, 205–34.

Beaudry, M. & Mrozowski, S. 2001, 'Cultural space and worker identity in the company city: nineteenth-century Lowell, Massachusetts', in Mayne & Murray (eds), 2001b, 118–81.

Bell, D. & Haddour, A. (eds) 2000, *City Visions*. Harlow: Pearson.

Bentley, C. 2000, 'The Brady Street Scheme: homes for the poorest Londoners in early 20th century', *Transactions of the London and Middlesex Archaeological Society* **51**: 189–207.

Biddle, M., Hudson, D. & Heighway, C. 1973, *The Future of London's Past*. Winchester: Rescue Publications.

Bluer, R., Brigham, T. with Neilson, R. 2006, *Roman and Later Development East of the Forum and Cornhill: Excavations at Lloyd's Register, 71 Fenchurch Street, City of London*. London: Museum of London Archaeology Service Monograph Series.

Bowsher, D., Dyson, T., Holder, N. & Howell, I. 2007, *The London Guildhall: An Archaeological History of a Neighbourhood from Early Medieval to Modern Times*. London: Museum of London Archaeology Service Monograph Series.

Bowsher, J.M.C. & Miller, P. nd, *The Rose and the Globe: Playhouses of Tudor Bankside, Southwark: Excavations 1988–1991*. London: Museum of London Archaeology Service Monograph Series.

Brighton, S.A. 2001, 'Prices that suit the times: shopping for ceramics at The Five Points', *Historical Archaeology* **35**(3): 16–30.

Broad, J. 1998, 'Review of M. Johnson 1996: *An Archaeology of Capitalism*. Oxford: Blackwell', *English Historical Review* **113**(450): 177–9.

Brooks, A. 1999, 'Building Jerusalem: transfer-printed finewares and the creation of British identity', in Tarlow & West (eds), 1999, 51–65.

Brooks, A. 2005, *An Archaeological Guide to British Ceramics in Australia 1788–1901*. Sydney: The Australasian Society for Historical Archaeology and The La Trobe University Archaeology Program.

Cantwell, A.M. & Wall, D. diZerega 2001, *Unearthing Gotham: The Archaeology of New York City*. New Haven: Yale University Press.

Carver, M. 1990, *Underneath English Towns: Interpreting Urban Archaeology*. London: Batsford.

Coulter, J. 1999, *Sydenham and Forest Hill Past*. London: Historical Publications.

Cox, A. 1995, '"An example to others": public housing in London, 1840–1941', *Transactions of the London and Middlesex Archaeology Society* **46**: 145–66.

Coysh, A.W. & Henrywood, R.K. 1982, *The Dictionary of Blue and White Printed Pottery 1780–1880*, Vol. 1. Woodbridge: Antiques Collectors' Club.

Dennis, R. 2008, *Cities in Modernity: Representations and Productions of Metropolitan Space, 1840–1930*. Cambridge: Cambridge University Press.

Divers, D. 2002, 'The post-medieval waterfront development at Adlards Wharf, Bermondsey, London', *Post-Medieval Archaeology* **36**(1): 39-117.

Divers, D. 2004, 'Excavations at Deptford on the site of the East India Company dockyards and the Trinity House almshouses, London', *Post-Medieval Archaeology* **38**(1): 17–132.

Driver, F. 2001, *Geography Militant: Cultures of Exploration and Empire*. Oxford: Blackwell.

Driver, F. & Gilbert, D. (eds) 1999, *Imperial Cities: Landscape, Display and Identity*. Manchester: Manchester University Press.

Dyos, H.J. 1967, 'Slums of Victorian London', *Victorian Studies* **11**(1): 5–40.

Egan, G. 1994, *Lead Cloth Seals and Related Items in the British Museum*, British Museum Occasional Paper **93**, with contributions by M. Cowell and H. Granger-Taylor. London: British Museum.

Egan, G. 1999, 'London, axis of the Commonwealth? An archaeological review', in Michael & Egan (eds), 1999, 61–78.

Egan, G. 2005, *Material Culture in an Age of Transition: Tudor and Stuart Period Finds c1450–c1700 from Excavations at Riversides in Southwark*. London: Museum of London Archaeology Service Monograph Series.

Englander, D. & O'Day, R. (eds) 1995, *Retrieved Riches: Social Investigation in Britain 1840–1914*. Aldershot: Scolar Press.

Freeman, N. 2007, *Conceiving the City: London, Literature and Art, 1870–1914*. Oxford: Oxford University Press.

Gaskell, M. (ed.) 1990, *Slums*. Leicester: University of Leicester Press.

Gilbert, P. (ed.) 2002, *Imagined Londons*. New York: State University of New York Press.

Gooch, T. 2007, 'Hinton's: A nineteenth century eating house in Southwark. Social history from discarded pottery', *London Archaeologist* **11**: 10.

Green, D.R. & Parton, A.G. 1990, 'Slums and slum life in Victorian England: London and Birmingham at mid-century', in Gaskell (ed.) 1990, 17–91.

Griffiths, P. & Jenner, M.S.R. (eds) 2000, *Londinopolis, c.1500–c.1750: Essays in the Cultural and Social History of Early Modern London*. Manchester: Manchester University Press.

Grimes, W.F. 1968, *The Excavation of Roman and Medieval London*. London: Routledge & Kegan Paul.

Harrison, B. 1971, *Drink and the Victorians: The Temperance Question in England, 1815–1872*. London: Faber & Faber.

Hassam, A. 1999, 'Portable iron structures and uncertain colonial spaces at the Sydenham, Crystal Palace', in Driver and Gilbert (eds) 1999, 174–93.

Haynes, I., Sheldon, H. & Hannigan, L. 2000, *London Underground: The Archaeology of a City*. Oxford: Oxbow.

Heard, K. with Goodburn, D. 2003, *Investigating the Maritime History of Rotherhithe Excavations at Pacific Wharf, 165 Rotherhithe Street, Southwark*. London: Museum of London Archaeology Service Archaeology Study Series.

Hicks, D. 2000, 'Ethnicity, "race", and the archaeology of the Atlantic slave trade', *Assemblage* **5** <http://www.shef.ac.uk/assem/5/hicks.html> [site accessed 25 July 2008].

Hicks, D. 2007, 'Historical archaeology in Britain', in Pearsall (ed.), 2007, 1318–27.

Hicks, D. 2008, 'Improvement: what kind of archaeological object is it?', *Journal of Field Archaeology* **33**(1): 111–16.

Hicks, D. & Beaudry, M.C. (eds) 2006, *The Cambridge Companion to Historical Archaeology*. Cambridge: Cambridge University Press.

Hicks, D. & Jeffries, N. 2004, *Biographies of London Life: The Archaeology of Londoners and their Things (1600–2000)*. London: Museum of London Research Matters Series.

Hirsch, E. & Stewart, C. 2005, 'Introduction: ethnographies of historicity', *History and Anthropology* **16**(3): 261–74.

Holder, N. & Jeffries, N. with Daykin, A., Harward, C. & Thomas, C. forthcoming, *Spitalfields: The Archaeology of a London Suburb 1539-1880s*. London: Museum of London Archaeology Service Monograph Series.

Hoskins, J. 1998, *Biographical Objects: How Things tell the Stories of People's Lives*. London: Routledge.

Jeffries, N. 2001, 'Historically visible but archaeologically invisible? The Huguenots of Spitalfields', *Medieval Ceramics* **25**: 54–64.

Jeffries, N. 2006, 'The Metropolis Local Management Act and the archaeology of sanitary reform in the London Borough of Lambeth 1856–86', *Post-Medieval Archaeology* **40**(2): 272–90.

Jeffries, N. forthcoming, '"There is an immense trade nowadays in ginger beer in cashes": The Biucchi brothers and their role in the mineral water and ginger beer industry in late 19th-century London', in White forthcoming.

Jeffries, N. & Watson, B. forthcoming, 'From Saxon *Ludenwic* to Victorian Rookery: excavations at City Lit, Keeley Street, Camden London EC2', *Transactions of the London and Middlesex Archaeology Society.*

Johnson, M.H. 1996, *An Archaeology of Capitalism*. Oxford: Blackwell.

Johnson, M. 1999, *Archaeological Theory: An Introduction*. Oxford: Blackwell.

Karskens, G. 1999, *Inside the Rocks: The Archaeology of a Neighbourhood*. Sydney: Halle & Iremonger.

Karskens, G. 2001, 'Small things, big pictures: new perspectives from the archaeology of Sydney's Rocks neighbourhood', in Mayne & Murray (eds), 2001b, 69–88.

Kay, A.C. 2008, 'Villas, values and the Crystal Palace Company', *The London Journal* **33**(1): 21–40.

Killock, D., Brown, J. & Jarrett, C. 2003, 'The industrialization of an ecclesiastical hamlet: stoneware production in Lambeth and the sanitary revolution', *Post-Medieval Archaeology* **37**(1): 29–78.

Lawrence, S. (ed.) 2003, *Archaeologies of the British: Explorations in Identity in Great Britain and its Colonies, 1600–1945*. London: Routledge.

Lee, C. 1986, *The British Economy since 1700*. Cambridge: Cambridge University Press.

Lucas, G. 2003, 'Reading pottery: literature and transfer-printed pottery in the early nineteenth century', *International Journal of Historical Archaeology* **7**(2): 127–43.

McCracken, S. & Phillpotts, C. 1995, 'Archaeology and planning in London: assessing the effectiveness of PPG 16', *Standing Committee on London Archaeology* **10**: 143–47.

McLaughlin, J. 2000, *Writing the Urban Jungle: Reading Empire in London from Doyle to Eliot*. Charlottesville: University Press of Virginia.

Mayne, A. 1993, *The Imagined Slum: Representation of Three Cities in Newspapers, 1870–1914*. Leicester: Leicester University Press.

Mayne, A. 2008, 'On the edges of history: reflections on historical archaeology', *American Historical Review* **113**(1): 93–118.

Mayne, A. & Lawrence, S. 1999, 'Ethnographies of place: a new urban research agenda', *Urban History* **26**(3): 325–48.

Mayne, A. & Murray, T. 2001a, 'The archaeology of urban landscapes: explorations in slumland', in Mayne & Murray (eds), 2001b, 1–7.

Mayne, A. & Murray T. (eds) 2001b, *The Archaeology of Urban Landscapes: Explorations in Slumland*. Cambridge: Cambridge University Press.

Merrifield, R. 1965, *The Roman City of London*. London: Ernest Benn.

Michael, R.J. & Egan, G. (eds) 1999, *Old and New Worlds*. Oxford: Oxbow Books.

Miller, G.L. 1991, 'A revised set of CC index values for classification and economic scaling of English ceramics from 1787 to 1880', *Historical Archaeology* **25**(1): 1–25.

Milne, G. 1995, *The English Heritage Book of Roman London*. London: Batsford/English Heritage.

Mrozowski, S. 2006, *The Archaeology of Class in Urban America*. Cambridge: Cambridge University Press.

Mrozowski, S., Zeising, G.J. & Beaudry, M.C. 1996, *Living on the Boott: Historical Archaeology of the Boott Mills Boarding Houses, Lowell, Massachusetts*. Amherst, MA: University of Massachusetts Press.

Murray, T. (ed.) 2003, *Exploring the Modern City Recent Approaches to Urban History and Archaeology*. Melbourne: Historic Houses Trust of New South Wales and La Trobe University.

Murray, T. & Crook, P. 2005, 'Exploring the archaeology of the modern city: issues of scale, integration and complexity', *International Journal of Historical Archaeology* **9**: 89–109.

Murray, T., Crook, P. & Ellmoos, L. 2003, 'Understanding the archaeology of the modern city', in Murray (ed.), 2003, 112–35.

Museum of London 2002, *A Research Framework for London Archaeology 2002*. London: Museum of London.

Nead, L. 2000, *Victorian Babylon: People, Streets and Images in Nineteenth-Century London*. New Haven: Yale University Press.

Nevell, M. 2004, *Farmer to Factory Owner: Models Methodology and Industrialisation. Archaeological Approaches to the Industrial Revolution in North West England*. Manchester: University of Manchester Field Archaeology Centre.

Ogborn, M. 1998, *Spaces of Modernity: London's Geographies, 1680–1780*. New York: Guilford Press.

O'Keeffe, T. & Yamin, R. 2006, 'Urban historical archaeology', in Hicks & Beaudry (eds), 2006, 87–103.

Ottaway, P. 1992, *Archaeology in British Towns: From the Emperor Claudius to the Black Death*. London: Routledge.

Pearce, J. 1992, *Border Wares*. London: HMSO.

Pearce, J. 1998, 'A rare delftware Hebrew plate and associated assemblage from an excavation in Mitre Street, City of London', *Post-Medieval Archaeology* **32**(1): 95-112.

Pearce, J. 2000, 'A late 18th-century inn clearance assemblage from Uxbridge, Middlesex', *Post-Medieval Archaeology* **34**(1): 144-186.

Pearce, J. 2007, *Pots and Potters in Tudor Hampshire: Excavations at Farnborough Hill Covent 1968–72*. Guildford: Guildford Museum.

Pearsall, D. (ed.) 2007, *Encyclopedia of Archaeology*. Oxford: Elsevier.

Phillips L. (ed.) 2007, *A Mighty Mass of Brick and Smoke: Victorian and Edwardian Representations of London*. Amsterdam: Rodopi.

Piggott, J.R. 2004, *Palace of the People: The Crystal Palace at Sydenham 1854–1936*. London: Hurst Publishers.

Platt, C. & Coleman-Smith, R. 1975, *Excavations in Medieval Southampton, 1953–69*, 2 vols. Leicester: University of Leicester Press.

Praetzellis, A. 1998, 'Introduction: why every archaeologist should tell stories once in a while', *Historical Archaeology* **32**(1): 1–3.

Praetzellis, A. & Praetzellis, M. 1992. 'Faces and facades: Victorian ideology in early Sacramento', in Yentsch & Beaudry (eds) 1992, 75–100.

Praetzellis, M. & Praetzellis, A. (eds) 2004, *Putting the 'There' there: Historical Archaeologies of West Oakland, 1-880 Cypress Freeway Replacement Project*. Sonoma: report prepared by Anthropological Studies Center, Sonama State University, California <http://www.sonoma.edu/asc/cypress/finalreport/index.htm> [site accessed 24 July 2008].

Robinson, A. 2004, *Imagining London, 1770–1900*. Basingstoke: Palgrave.

Rowsome, P. 2000, *Heart of a City: Roman, Medieval and Modern London Revealed by Archaeology at 1, Poultry*. London: Museum of London.

Schofield, J. & Lea, R. 2005, *Holy Trinity Priory, Aldgate, The City of London: An Archaeological Reconstruction and History*. London: Museum of London Archaeology Service Monograph Series.

Schofield, J. & Leech, R. (eds) 1987, *Urban Archaeology in Britain*. London: Council for British Archaeology.

Schofield, J. & Maloney, C. (eds) 1998, *Archaeology in the City of London, 1907–91: A Guide to Records of Excavations by the Museum of London and its Predecessors*. London: Museum of London Archaeological Gazetteer Series.

Shepherd, J.D. 1998, *The Temple of Mithras, London: Excavations by W.F. Grimes and A. Williams at the Walbrook*. London: English Heritage.

Shiman, L.L. 1988, *Crusade Against Drink in Victorian England*. Basingstoke: Macmillan.

Sloane, B. & Hoad, S. with Cloake, P., Pearce, J. & Stephenson, R. 2003, *Early Modern Industry and Settlement: Excavations at George Street, Richmond, and High Street, Mortlake, in the London Borough of Richmond upon Thames*. London: Museum of London Archaeology Service Study Series.

Stephenson, R. 1999, 'The tin glazed ware in London: a review', in Michael & Egan (eds), 1999, 265–8.

Symonds, J. (ed.) 2002, *The Historical Archaeology of the Sheffield Cutlery and Tableware Industry 1750–1900*. Sheffield: ARCUS Studies in Historical Archaeology.

Symonds, J. 2004, 'Historical archaeology and the recent urban past', *International Journal of Heritage Studies* **10**(1): 33–48.

Symonds, J. & Casella, E.C. 2006, 'Historical archaeology and industrialisation', in. Hicks & Beaudry (eds), 2006, 87–103.

Tarlow, S. 1999, 'Strangely familiar', in Tarlow & West (eds), 1999, 263–72.

Tarlow, S. 2007, *The Archaeology of Improvement in Britain, 1750–1850*. Cambridge: Cambridge University Press.

Tarlow, S. & West, S. (eds) 1999, *The Familiar Past? Archaeologies of Later Historical Britain*. London: Routledge.

Telfer, A., Blackmore, L., Jackson, C., Pearce, J., Whittingham, L. & Willmott, H. 2006, 'Rich refuse: a rare find of late 17th-century and mid-18th-century glass and tin-glazed wares from an excavation at the National Gallery, London', *Post-Medieval Archaeology* **40**(1): 191–213.

Thomas, C. 2002, *The Archaeology of Medieval London*. Stroud: Sutton.

Thomas, C., Cowie, B. & Sidell, J. 2005, *The Royal Palace, Abbey, and Town of Westminster on Thorney Island: Archaeological Investigations (1991–8) for the London Underground Jubilee Line Extension Project*. London: Museum of London Archaeology Service Monograph Series.

Thompson, G.A., Westman, A. & Dyson, T. (eds) 1998, *Archaeology in Greater London 1965–1990: A Guide to the Records of the Excavations by the Museum of London*. London: Museum of London Archaeological Gazetteer Series.

Thrift, N. 2000, '"Not a straight line but a curve", or, cities are not mirrors of modernity', in Bell & Haddour (eds), 2000, 233–63.

Tyler, K. 2004, 'Two centuries of rubbish: excavations at an 18th- and 19th-century site at 12–18 Albert Embankment, Lambeth', *Surrey Archaeological Collections* **91**: 105–36.

Tyler, K. (ed.) 2005a, *The Doulton Stoneware Pothouse in Lambeth, Excavations at 9 Albert Embankment* (with contributions from J. Brown, T. Smith and L. Whittingham). London: Museum of London Archaeology Service Studies Series.

Tyler, K. (ed.) 2005b, *John Baker's Late 17th-Century Glasshouse at Vauxhall* (with contributions from H. Willmott). London: Museum of London Archaeology Service Monograph Series.

Tyler, K., Betts, I. & Stephenson, R. 2008, *London's Delftware Industry: The Tin-Glazed Potteries of Southwark and Lambeth*. London: Museum of London Archaeology Service Monograph Series.

Tyler, K., Stephenson, R., Owen, J.V. & Philpotts, C. 2000, *The Limehouse Porcelain Manufactory: Excavations at 108–116 Narrow Street, London, 1990*. London: Museum of London Archaeology Service Monograph Series.

Vince, A. 1990, *Saxon London: An Archaeological Investigation*. London: Seaby.

Vince, A.G. & Egan, G. 1981, 'The contents of a late 18th-century pit at Crosswall, City of London', *Transactions of the London and Middlesex Archaeology Society* **32**: 159–82.

Webber, M. 1991, 'Excavations on the site of Norfolk House, Lambeth Road, SE1', *London Archaeologist* **6**: 343–50.

West, S., 1999, 'Introduction', in Tarlow & West (eds), 1999, 1–16.

White, C. (ed.) forthcoming, *The Materiality of Individuality*. New York: Springer.

Wilkie, L. 2006, 'Documentary archaeology', in Hicks & Beaudry(eds) 2006, 13–33.

Wohl, A.S. 1977, *The Eternal Slum: Housing and Social Policy in Victorian London*. London: Edward Arnold.

Wood, D. & Munby J. 2003, 'The historical development of Somerset House: an archaeological investigation', *Transactions of the London and Middlesex Archaeology Society* **54**: 79–110.

Yamin, R. (ed.) 1998, *Tales of Five Points: Working-Class Life in Nineteenth-Century New York*. West Chester, Pennsylvania: John Milner Associates.

Yelling, J.A. 1995, 'Banishing London's slums: the inter-war cottage estates', *Transactions of the London and Middlesex Archaeology Society* **46**: 167–74.

Yentsch, A.E. & Beaudy, M.C. (eds) 1992, *The Art and Mystery of Historical Archaeology: Essays in Honour of James Deetz*. Boca Raton, FL: CRC Press.

Yeomans, L. 2005, 'Spatial determinants of animal carcass processing in post-medieval London and evidence for a co-operative supply network', *Transactions of the London and Middlesex Archaeology Society* **55**: 69–83.

UNPUBLISHED SOURCES

Jamieson, D. 2006, *Hammersmith Embankment Phase 3: A Post-Excavation Assessment and Updated Project Design (Sitecode WIZ05)*. London: Museum of London Archaeology Service (unpublished archive report).

Oleksy, V., 2006, 'Buildings and ethnicity: two examples from Spitalfields, London', unpublished University of Bristol MA thesis.

Underneath the Arches: The Afterlife of a Railway Viaduct

By EMMA DWYER

The Great Eastern Railway Company's viaduct in east London was one of the earliest, and most substantial, railway structures in London, transporting huge quantities of goods and people entering and leaving central London. Rather than considering the official use of the viaduct, however, this chapter will focus on the unofficial, parallel uses of the spaces underneath the arches, long used as a sanctuary and shelter, a series of secluded places where independent businesses and illicit activities thrived.

INTRODUCTION

Understanding the history of London's earliest railways would be one way of assessing the significance of the former Great Eastern Railway Company's viaduct in Pedley Street and Grimsby Street, situated to the east of Brick Lane, in the London Borough of Tower Hamlets. One could consider the linkages between the increasing importance of London as a world commercial centre during the 19th century and the expansion of the railway network, and technological advances in locomotives and railway infrastructure. One might also wish to examine the architectural qualities of the brick and stone viaduct and its elliptical arches. However, this chapter moves away from these more pragmatic considerations to examine the non-railway-related use (with the exception of the Great Eastern Railway's Horse Infirmary) of the railway viaduct and the arches underneath.

The mainly non-railway uses of the viaduct has been chosen as a theme for this discussion in the hope that it will demonstrate the potential for an holistic approach to industrial sites, which looks beyond the context of intended function, and examines the role that such a structure can have in everyday life. An increasing body of literature has been concerned with the importance of thinking about the social significance of aspects that have been traditionally associated with industrial archaeology,[1] and this chapter is a contribution to that debate.

CONTEXT OF THE PROJECT: THE EAST LONDON LINE TUBE EXTENSION

The East London line of the London Underground, coloured orange on the well-known 'tube' map, was closed in November 2007 to allow for its extension northwards, and its integration into the London Overground rail network. When the line reopens in 2010,

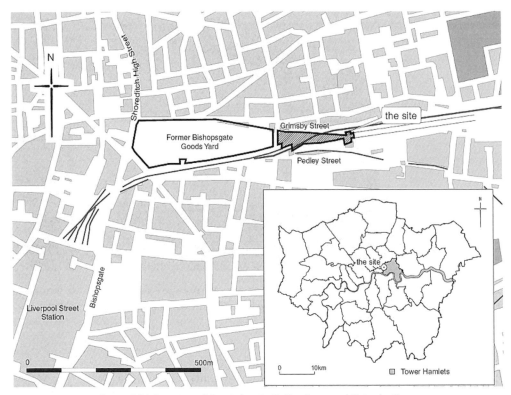

Figure 24.1 Location of the viaduct in Pedley Street and Grimsby Street

trains will serve the area from Crystal Palace in the south to Highbury and Islington in the north. The construction works involved with the extension of the East London line have involved excavation and standing building recording along its route, from New Cross in the south to Dalston in the north. The brief for archaeological fieldwork for this project was set by English Heritage, which in London provides advice on archaeological matters to planning departments in most of the London boroughs. A full drawn and photographic survey of the Pedley Street/Grimsby Street viaduct was required, with a specific condition that the full history and use of the structure be recorded and analysed prior to its demolition and the construction of a new bridge and ramp, which will direct the extended railway line below ground and onto the tracks of the existing East London line (Fig. 24.1).

The viaduct formed part of the Eastern Counties Railway line from Romford in Essex to the Bishopsgate terminus in Shoreditch High Street, outside the jurisdiction of the City of London, and was constructed between 1836 and 1840. Much of the railway line passed through land that was occupied by large mansions or estates, or was under cultivation, but once the railway line entered the crowded core of east London, it was mostly carried on a brick viaduct.[2] This structure was costly to build; it was a mile and a quarter in length and comprised 160 arches, but had the advantage of minimising the number of buildings that would have to be demolished, raising the railway line above adjacent properties in a

RIGHT
Figure 24.2 The railway
arches in Pedley Street
(© MoLAS)

congested district and providing a source of income for the railway company. To that end, many of the arches underneath the viaduct were let out as warehouses and workshops (Fig. 24.2).

The Eastern Counties Railway merged with a number of smaller companies in 1862 to form the Great Eastern Railway Company. At around this time, the viaduct was widened to provide additional capacity for trains and the opportunity was taken to convert the arches into usable spaces, where previously they had been open to the street. The ends of the arches were closed off, with doors and windows inserted in the walls at either end. The arches subsequently housed the Great Eastern Railway Company's Horse Infirmary; the standing

LEFT
Figure 24.3 A railwayman
at the Great Eastern
Railway Company's Horse
Infirmary in Pedley Street,
c. 1911, demonstrating
the level of injuries to
the company's horses;
nails recovered from their
hooves were annually
hung in strips of leather
(© National Railway
Museum, York)

building survey showed evidence for the stalls, tethering rings and farriers' workshops that the railway company erected (Fig. 24.3). The viaduct was further modified in the 1870s when the railway terminus was relocated to Liverpool Street, in the City of London; a tunnel and ramp was cut through the viaduct to direct trains to the new station, and the former terminus in Shoreditch High Street was demolished and rebuilt as a goods yard.

Mapping from the 18th century, such as John Rocque's map of 1746 (Fig. 24.4), shows how the site of the viaduct was situated on the edge of the city, the yards and alleys leading off Shoreditch High Street and Bishopsgate to the west, market gardens and pasture to the east. An archaeological evaluation on the site of the southern side of the viaduct in Pedley Street showed that the deposits relating to the earlier use of the site had been heavily truncated in order to make up the ground level for the construction of the viaduct; however, a higher level of preservation was found on the site of the arches in Grimsby Street. Water-lain deposits suggested boggy ground in the area during the earlier post-medieval period, and a 'raft', mostly comprising lumps of chalk and containing some residual Roman material, was deposited to provide a stable building platform. The site contained the remains of two cellars, probably early- to mid-18th century in date, which belonged to buildings on the southern side of St John Street, later renamed Grimsby Street.

Figure 24.4 Extract from John Rocque's Map of London of 1746, showing the future site of the viaduct

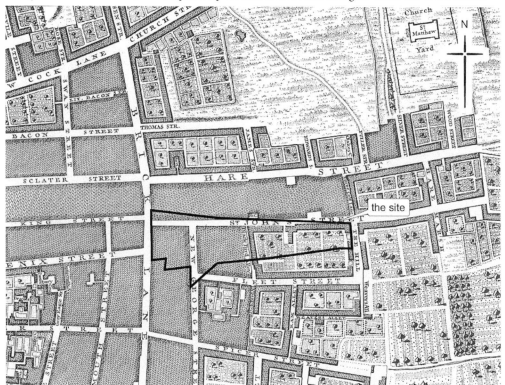

THE SPATIAL FORM OF POVERTY

Edward Stanford's *Library Map of London and its Suburbs* of 1862 (Fig. 24.5) was the earliest widely available map that showed the Eastern Counties Railway line. Bishopsgate Railway Station (which had changed its name from Shoreditch in 1847) was located to the west of the site, and Brick Lane goods depot, which opened along with the rest of the railway line in 1840, was situated immediately to the east. The railway had cut through a number of streets and alleys; the construction of the Eastern Counties Railway viaduct through Shoreditch necessitated the demolition of homes and workshops in courts on either side of Brick Lane.

In 1886, Charles Booth, philanthropist and social campaigner, began a survey of living and working conditions in London, a project that continued until 1903. The results of the fieldwork undertaken by Booth and his team of researchers were expressed in his *Descriptive Map of London Poverty*, which used a system of colour coding residential properties to identify the economic and social make-up of each street in London. Booth's study indicated that in 1889 the area through which the railway viaduct passed was mainly occupied by poor and very poor households. More economically and socially mixed households, some financially comfortable and others poor, were concentrated along the main roads, including Brick

Figure 24.5 Extract from Edward Stanford's Library Map of London and its Suburbs, 1862

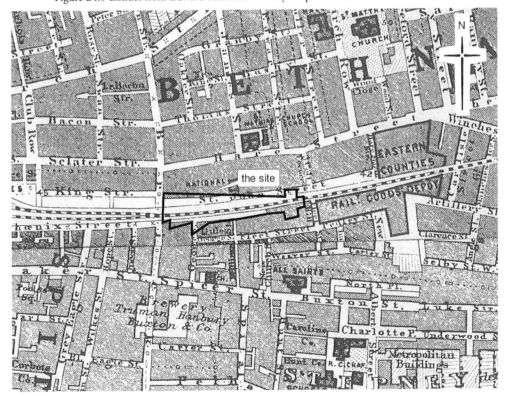

Lane. Booth's maps of poverty in London were presented as an objective statement, yet can be seen as embodying the subjective attitudes of a middle-class, evangelical social reformer.[3] The information contained in the maps and accompanying reports was gathered by a team of investigators who were recruited largely from Toynbee Hall, a university settlement in Whitechapel. The investigators accompanied School Board Visitors, who had a detailed knowledge of families with children, and policemen on their beats. The notebook of the investigator who accompanied Sergeant French from the Commercial Street Police Station on 22 March 1898 commented on the dirty appearance of the children in Fleet Street (now the western end of Pedley Street) and that he saw one child who was wearing only one shoe.[4] Thieves and prostitutes who operated in Boundary Street, in the Old Nichol area, congregated at the eastern end of Pedley Street; the Old Nichol was located further west, to the north of Bishopsgate Goods Station, and was presented in contemporary newspaper accounts and thinly disguised in fiction, as a notorious slum.[5]

The effect that the insertion of linear features such as roads and railways has on the functioning of a landscape and the people who populate it has been researched by several authors. Urban historian David Reeder pointed out how Charles Booth's *Descriptive Map of London Poverty* provides information on the impact that spatial forms in London had on the location of economically poor areas. He noted that the map

> points to the significance especially of innumerable dead ends, closed up vistas and backwaters in the layout of streets ... a more careful reading indicates how some new addition to the ground plan – a dock or canal, for example, a gas works or waterworks, a railway line, or just the alignment of a new street – seems to have served to reinforce slum tendencies.[6]

Booth and his team were repeatedly to draw attention in later volumes to the importance of physical barriers. For example, to the north of Shoreditch 'another dark spot of long-standing poverty and extremely low life ... is wedged in between the Regent's Canal and the gas works'.[7]

The effect of linear barriers on the functioning of the modern landscape has also been a subject of research. Sefryn Penrose's study of the contemporary landscape beneath and surrounding Junction 3 of the M32 motorway in Bristol, the construction of which bisected the inner city suburbs of St Pauls and Easton, analysed the experiences of those who try to negotiate it: 'our experience of the city is dependent on its layout, and more and more often in the contemporary urban setting, severe alterations have been enacted on this landscape which in turn alter our experience'.[8] The altered landscape is 'not passive and reflective but can act back upon us in different ways'.[9] The motorway flyover and the pedestrian subway beneath it 'fulfil a function for users of the motorway in its routing of traffic from the motorway onto city roads, but for pedestrians, local residents who wish to move between St. Pauls and Easton, it is a problem to be negotiated'.[10] How was the population of 19th-century Shoreditch able to negotiate the railway viaduct?

SHELTER

While the construction of the railway viaduct created a physical barrier, the structure provided a refuge too, in the spaces underneath the arches. There were few restrictions on the activities that could be carried out underneath them (and the few restrictions that were in place were difficult to enforce), and they provided large spaces at little or no financial cost.

The railway arches, particularly those in Grimsby Street, provided shelter for the East End's homeless, and across London, railway arches and vaulted spaces afforded shelter for the city's vagrants.[11] For many years, the bridges across the Thames served as what were called 'Dry Arch' Hotels for the city's vagrants, and the arches under the Adelphi Buildings, a late-18th-century speculative residential development between the Strand and the Thames, was described as 'a little subterranean city',[12] where 'no sane person would have ventured out to explore them without an armed escort'.[13] Closer to our site, Arthur Harding, a reformed petty criminal and contemporary of the Krays, recalled vividly the nights spent sleeping under the Brick Lane bridge as a child (Fig. 24.6):

> We got slung out of Drysdale Street because we were three children, and a fourth coming, and there wasn't supposed to be any at all. I remember that quite well. It was rainy, a January day. The first night we were homeless and settled down under Brick Lane arch for the night. There were others laying there, with sheets of newspaper on the pavement and old coats to cover them. It was a common thing both at Brick Lane arch and Wheler Street, the two railway arches. The Wheler Street arch was more crowded because it was longer and bigger. The police walked down the right-hand side, the people slept on the left.[14]

Figure 24.6 The railway bridge over Brick Lane, c. 1976 (© J. E. Connor)

Railway arches also provided a refuge on a more formal, organised basis, such as during the Second World War, when many were converted to act as air-raid shelters. Railway arches were not indestructible, however, and when the air-raid shelter in an arch in Stainer Street, on the approach to London Bridge railway station, suffered a direct hit in February 1941, over sixty people were killed.[15] None of the arches at Pedley Street or Grimsby Street were ever officially used as air-raid shelters. Instead, they provided more permanent accommodation. The close proximity of the Brick Lane Goods Depot and Bishopsgate Goods Yard made Pedley Street the ideal location for the Great Eastern Railway Horse Infirmary, which cared for some of the 6,000 horses the railway company owned in London in 1890.[16]

THE SHOREDITCH FURNITURE TRADE

Industry in London has had a complex geography, with some industries concentrated in specific areas, and others more widely distributed across the city. There was a diverse range of industries in London, and none predominated, unlike metal-working in Birmingham and Sheffield, or textile milling in Lancashire and West Yorkshire. London was a centre for the furniture trade, however, and by the end of the late 18th century the City of London and the West End were home to many bespoke manufacturers. During the late 19th century, as the mass market for cheap goods emerged, Shoreditch, on the eastern fringe of the City, became a focus for the trade in low-priced, ready-made furniture. While a few large furniture factories were constructed to meet the need for cheap furniture, manufactured on something approaching a production line, the character of the trade required a larger number of small workshops, which carried out specialised tasks. This smaller-scale manufacturing could meet fluctuations in demand and was more responsive to changing fashions and forms. The various processes involved in production were broken down into stages, each undertaken by a specialised firm. This resulted in a kind of assembly line that ran through the streets of Shoreditch, supplied by a host of ancillary trades that contributed raw materials, machinery, accessories, finishes and warehouses for distribution.[17]

The Second World War brought great disruption to the East End, and the furniture trade went into further significant decline in the 1980s. Firms were unable to keep up with the import of cheaper furniture from overseas, and most of the businesses associated with the Shoreditch furniture trade closed, or relocated to cheaper premises. The few small firms that have remained in the area are run by designers, many of whom are graduates of the London College of Furniture in Whitechapel, or specialise in high-quality reproduction furniture,[18] such as Barley Reproduction, based in one of the railway arches in Pedley Street until January of 2007 (Fig. 24.7).

ILLICIT BEHAVIOUR

The railway arches in Pedley Street and Grimsby Street have had a long history as a place of relative safety and shelter, but their seclusion has also attracted illicit behaviour. Grimsby Street was described by the graffiti artist Banksy as 'a bulletin board for a community', albeit a 'slippery, elusive anonymous one', mainly for reasons of illegality.[19]

Figure 24.7 The premises of Barley Reproduction, furniture manufacturers, in one of the arches in Pedley Street (© MoLAS)

In New York and Philadelphia there was a proliferation of graffiti writing on the subways and trains in the late 1970s and early 1980s. The sides of trains made excellent canvases for graffiti, and their mobility meant that graffiti could traverse the city. This 'tagging', a seemingly simple act of spraying one's name, usually takes the form of a stylised signature or logo, which forms a language for those who undertake it, with its own grammar and syntax.[20] By the mid-1980s, most major European cities, notably Berlin, Paris and Amsterdam, had their own flourishing street art movements, while graffiti emerged from indigenous art forms in South America, particularly Brazil, and later south-east Asia. Other forms of street art emerged. In 1981, a French graffiti writer named Blek le Rat began to use the utilitarian method of spraying through stencils, and his spray-painted black rats began to appear on the streets of Paris.[21]

The anthropologist Nancy Macdonald has studied the syntax and grammar of tagging, and found, perhaps not surprisingly, that graffiti attracts graffiti. 'As writers' names hit the wall a form of interaction begins to develop, one which mirrors, on the wall, the activities that might occur in front of it.'[22] Placing one's tag near someone else's is a means of saying 'hello', but writing over the top of another person's tag is a cardinal sin, a violent act. Macdonald suggests that little attention has been paid to the divides that operate within the 'graffiti subculture' – a fractured group that offers its members a diversity of standpoints and realities; its main division centres on how it should present itself to the world. Much of the graffiti in Grimsby Street was more complex than seemingly simple tagging, and involved much larger pieces of contemporary art. During her fieldwork among graffiti writers in London and New York, Macdonald found that professionally undertaken pictorial or abstract work was often discredited for sacrificing the traditional essence of graffiti, as expressed by the graffiti writer Teck:

> I made a fair amount of work doing legal art for TV commercials and other film endeavours. In actuality, all of this paled to the thrill of being chased through back streets and narrowingly [sic] escaping the beam of police headlights. Living precariously against the grain took precedence in my daily routine.[23]

The artworks in Grimsby Street transcended traditional graffiti methods, and towards the end of the structure's life it was used as a canvas by a wider range of artists, beyond the more 'traditional' spray painters. Many of the artistic interventions took the form of stickers, posters and collages, undertaken within the safe (and legal) confines of a studio and then fixed to the walls in Grimsby Street. Some graffiti writers disapprove of such 'non-conformist' activities. Nancy Macdonald's interviews with graffiti writers in New York showed there was significant antipathy towards Adam Cost and Revs, two graffiti writers who began producing slogans on stickers and posters, which they pasted on walls and street furniture in New York throughout the late 1980s and 1990s. Such measures, which minimise the amount of work one has to undertake, or which offer a shortcut to fame, are frowned upon, unless the graffiti writer has considerable experience.[24] Despite this, Grimsby Street remained a popular canvas for local and visiting artists (Plate 8).

Grimsby Street continued to be appropriated for commercial artistic endeavours; the street and those around it became a popular place for fashion photography shoots and film-makers, and with so many works by famous (or notorious) contemporary artists covering its walls, Grimsby Street was a regular stop for organised walking tours of London's graffiti, and a key site to visit in published guides to east London.[25]

The top of the viaduct, conversely, functioned as a different kind of space. The railway line that used the viaduct was closed following a fire at Bishopsgate Goods Yard in 1964 and the closure of the Brick Lane Goods Depot in 1967.[26] Appropriation and illicit use of the top of the viaduct was limited to one highly visible structure. Erroneously called a signal box on the various websites devoted to this building, and to other derelict structures in London, the structure was an inspection tower, or 'sludge house' for the water softening plant that was constructed next to the viaduct in the 1930s (Fig. 24.8).

The Office for Subversive Architecture (OSA) is a loose collective of architects who are exploring the ways in which people use and interact with public spaces, and address issues relating to urban regeneration by provoking debate and creating awareness of the structures in the built environment. The OSA focuses on areas that tend to be overlooked, forgotten or abandoned; one such project undertaken by the OSA was a refurbishment of the sludge house, which commenced in 2004. The structure reminded the OSA of a stereotypical country cottage, so they decided to restore it as one, painting the exterior of the structure, wallpapering and furnishing the interior and installing window boxes in time for London Open House weekend in September 2006. The popularity of the project was such that a short film was made for broadcast on Channel 4.[27]

Figure 24.8 The sludge house on the top of the railway viaduct (© MoLAS)

CONCLUSION

There is, then, a long history of appropriation of the Great Eastern Railway Company viaduct in Grimsby and Pedlar Streets and of the spaces beneath the structure. It offered a place of relative safety and shelter for the homeless, for struggling independent businesses and for illicit activity. The seclusion offered by the arches was subverted by a wider artistic community, using Grimsby Street in particular as a billboard. These parallel uses, both official and unofficial, run throughout the history of the viaduct, and include common, persisting themes. The construction of the railway viaduct in the 1830s divided streets and communities, but the spaces underneath the arches were successfully reclaimed. Yet this London viaduct is not unique, and it is hoped that this research project will encourage others to look at the ways in which similar structures can be appropriated and subverted for uses for which they were not intended but which then become part of the life of a local community. As David Gwyn has said elsewhere in this book, 'there is no archaeology that is not social archaeology and that recognition of this may open the way to a more holistic understanding of the ways in which industrial archaeologists can contribute to understanding the world as it has evolved from the 16th century'. This investigation underneath the arches of a railway viaduct is another contribution to that debate.

ACKNOWLEDGEMENTS
The author would like to express her gratitude to Jon Colclough and Transport for London, Balfour Beatty Carillion Joint Venture, David Divers of English Heritage and Steve Haynes of Arup. The staff of the London Metropolitan Archive, Essex Records Office and the Tower Hamlets Local History Library (in particular Malcolm Barr-Hamilton) provided access to historic maps, plans and photographs. The author is especially grateful to the National Railway Museum and Jim Connor for granting permission to reproduce the images in Figs 24.3 and 24.6. George Dennis, Nick Elsden and Nicky Powell provided project management and invaluable advice, and Andrew Westman and an anonymous reviewer made helpful comments on the text. The geomatics survey was undertaken by Eamonn Baldwin, Mark Burch, Neville Constantine, Simon Davis and Catherine Drew, the photography was carried out by Maggie Cox and the figures accompanying this text were produced by Sandra Rowntree. The standing building recording was undertaken by the author and Al Telfer.

NOTES

1. Casella & Symonds 2005; Gwyn & Palmer 2005.
2. Allen 1975, 5.
3. Symonds 2006, 240.
4. <http://booth.lse.ac.uk/>.
5. Morrison 1896.
6. Hyde & Reeder, 1984, cited in Vaughan 2005, 6–7.
7. Pfautz 1967, 113, citing Booth.
8. Penrose, forthcoming.
9. Buchli & Lucas 2001, 5.
10. Penrose & Trickett 2004.
11. Samuel 1973.
12. Miller 1852, 207.
13. Shaw 1914, 61–2.
14. Samuel 1981, 53–4.
15. <http://www.portcities.org.uk/london/server/show/ ConNarrative.54/chapterId/802/Defending-the-East-End.html>.
16. <http://www.gersociety.org.uk>.
17. Smith & Rogers 2006.
18. Smith & Rogers 2006, 57.
19. Addley 2006.
20. Best 2003, 835.
21. Addley 2006.
22. Macdonald 2001, 203.
23. Interview with graffiti writer 'Teck' – *Urb* Magazine 37, 1994, cited in Macdonald 2001, 73.
24. 'Revs used to get up on the trains and he did some nice pieces [labour-intensive graffiti paintings]. Cost never really did trains, the little bit he did was considered a toy [an incompetent artwork] by the older generations.' Interview with graffiti writer 'Smith', Macdonald 2001, 132.
25. Bull 2007.
26. Site Record for Bishopsgate Goods Station, <http:// www.disused-stations.org.uk/>.
27. <http://www.osa-online.net/de/flavours/up/intact/a/ index.htm>.

BIBLIOGRAPHY

Addley, E. 2006, 'The story of a wall', *The Guardian*, 30 September 2006. <www.guardian.co.uk/artanddesign/2006/sep/30/art.streetart>.

Allen, C.J. 1975, *The Great Eastern Railway*. Shepperton: Ian Allan.

Best, C. 2003, 'Reading graffiti in the Caribbean context', *Journal of Popular Culture* **36**: 828–53.

Buchli, V. & Lucas, G. 2001 *Archaeologies of the Contemporary Past*. London: Routledge.

Bull, M. 2007, *Banksy Locations and Tours: A Collection of Graffiti Locations and Photographs in London*. London: Shell Shock Publishing.

Casella, E.C. & Symonds, J. (eds) 2005, *Industrial Archaeology: Future Directions*. New York: Springer.

Disused Stations website: <http://www.disused-stations.org.uk/> [accessed March 2008].

Dyos, H.J. & Wolff, M. (eds) 1973, *The Victorian City: Images and Realities*. London: Routledge & Kegan Paul.

Great Eastern Railway Society website: <http://www.gersociety.org.uk> [accessed March 2008].

Green, A. & Leech, R. (eds) 2006, *Cities in the World*, Society for Post-Medieval Archaeology Monograph **3**. Leeds: Maney.

Gwyn, D. & Palmer, M. (eds) 2005 *Understanding the Workplace: A Research Framework for Industrial Archaeology in Britain* (special edition), *Industrial Archaeology Review* **27**(1).

Hyde, R. & Reeder, D. 1984, *Charles Booth's Descriptive Map of London Poverty, 1889, with introduction by Dr David Reeder*. London: London Topographical Society.

Macdonald, N. 2001, *The Graffiti Subculture: Youth, Masculinity and Identity in London and New York*. Basingstoke: Palgrave Macmillan.

Miller, T. 1852, *Picturesque Sketches of London*. London: Office of the National Illustrated Library.

Morrison, A. 1896, *A Child of the Jago*. London: H S Stone & Co.

Office for Subversive Architecture: <http://www.osa-online.net/de/flavours/up/intact/a/index.htm> [accessed March 2008].

Penrose, S. & Trickett, P. 2004, 'Peds versus Pods: conflict and the M32', paper presented at Contemporary and Historical Archaeology in Theory conference, Leicester University, 19 November 2004.

Pfautz, Harold W. 1967, *Charles Booth on the City: Physical Pattern and Social Structure*. Chicago: University of Chicago Press.

Port Cities website: <http://www.portcities.org.uk/london/server/show/ConNarrative.54/chapterId/802/Defending-the-East-End.html> [accessed March 2008].

Samuel, R. 1973, 'Comers and Goers', in Dyos & Wolff (eds), 1973, 123–60.

Samuel, R. 1981, *East End Underworld: Chapters in the Life of Arthur Harding*. London: Routledge & Kegan Paul.

Shaw, D. 1914, *London in the Sixties, by 'One of the Old Brigade'*. London: Everett & Co.

Smith, J. & Rogers, R. 2006, *Behind the Veneer: The South Shoreditch Furniture Trade and its Buildings*. Swindon: English Heritage.

Symonds, J. 2006, 'Tales from the City: brownfield archaeology – a worthwhile challenge?', in Green & Leech (eds), 2006, 235–48.

Urb Magazine **37**, 1994.

Vaughan, L. 2005, 'The relationship between physical segregation and social marginalisation in the urban environment', *World Architecture* **185**: 88–96.

Vaughan, L. 2007, 'The spatial form of poverty in Charles Booth's London', *Progress in Planning* **67**: 231–50

MAPS

Rocque, J. 1746, *Map of London*.

Stanford, E. 1862, *Library Map of London and its Suburbs*.

'You knew where you were': An Archaeology of Working Households in Turn-of-century Cheshire

By ELEANOR CASELLA

The Alderley Sandhills Project was designed to illuminate the transformative roles of industrialisation and de-industrialisation on the working households of rural England. By focusing on a domestic site, we sought to examine how the men, women and children of this ordinary working neighbourhood both maintained and improved their conditions of everyday life in the face of the rapid socioeconomic revolutions of the 18th to 20th centuries. Community outreach was an intrinsic component of this fieldwork programme, with project participants including former residents and neighbours of the excavated cottages. Their oral histories provided a crucial source of information for understanding the social meanings of archaeological objects and places within the study site. Drawing from results of this narrative source, this chapter explores the material nature of class mobility and community life within the working households of Alderley Edge, Cheshire.

'But I mean … I mean, that's just a family thing, you know.'
(Mrs Molly Pitcher, ASP Interviews, August 2003)

INTRODUCTION

Since its earliest years of practice, our discipline has maintained a long-standing tradition of 'household archaeology'. Current directions have begun to explore the material implications of domestic sites as venues for labour,[1] as arena for inter- and intra-gendered relations,[2] and sites of consumption.[3] These approaches have encouraged historical archaeologists to consider how the growing tide of mass-produced industrial commodities – the 'stuff' of empire – inextricably transformed the ways ordinary people lived and worked within their own homes from the 18th century onwards.

Further, by recognising that the material world of a household operates simultaneously on multiple geographic scales, these studies have demonstrated how the familiar process of 'making home'[4] is at once an internal and external dynamic, as also discussed by Charles Orser, this volume. It is both an experience of intimate social relationships, and a reflection of transnational economic forces. Accepting this paradox encourages us to 'think globally, dig locally'[5] in order to grasp the material articulations of class mobility and community life within the archaeological household.

ON MEMORY AND MATERIALITY

Oral histories offer a powerful means for engaging with this crucial dialectics of scale – for understanding how global products enter into regional domestic patterns, and how they inform local processes of community building and social belonging. Indeed, scholars have long acknowledged the central role of these narratives in forging collective identities, allowing people to not only represent their world, but mobilise their social ties and maintain their local networks. Operating as a circular process, these social ties also equally shape the narratives, with memories invoked and reconstructed through the active process of storytelling.[6] Drawing from the work of Graham Dawson,[7] Penny Summerfield adopted the term 'composure' to describe the production of memory.[8] Playing on the double meaning of the verb 'to compose', her study examined the dual process of crafting accounts of past experiences and achieving personal composure (or equilibrium). Crucially, the production of oral histories is not indiscriminate – the story told is always 'the one preferred amongst other possible variations'.[9] Composition, in other words, necessarily requires the inclusion *and* omission of specific memories to produce both a coherent narrative, and a comfortable version of one's self. Further, individual narratives are composed as 'social memory' through their association with broader collective contexts – ranging from kin affiliations to regional or national identity groups.[10] These personal stories draw upon, and thereby reinforce, broader social themes of gender, age, nationality, locale and class to echo (and sometimes critique) their underlying social meanings.[11]

This metaphor can be extended to material culture on both personal and collective scales of analysis. Through their dwellings and possessions, each community resident actively cultivates a constellation of social meanings that in turn establish an 'acceptable self'.[12] However, these acts of material 'composition' also serve as a communal process, with individual residents habitually linking their personal memories and memorabilia to their deeper understandings of local norms and shared narratives. Thus, the community group belongs to a 'memoryscape',[13] a patterned collective of stories and recollections materially anchored together through the architecture and artefacts of the local settlement. This chapter will turn to consider how an integration of both excavated and ethnographic sources illuminates the turn-of-century dynamics of class mobility and community life within the ordinary working households of The Hagg, a rural hamlet in northern Cheshire.

THE HAGG COTTAGES OF ALDERLEY EDGE

Located approximately 25km south of Manchester, Alderley Edge is a natural sandstone outcrop with views across both Greater Manchester and the Cheshire plain. From 1842, an early rail link joined central Manchester to a new terminus at Alderley Edge. This route established a growing service town as one of the earliest commuter suburbs of Great Britain. During the 1850s, a series of Italianate 'Villas' were constructed at this new commuter town of Alderley Edge, and sold to the newly wealthy mill barons desperate to escape the urban grime and crowding of industrial Manchester. Parodied as 'Cottentots' by the established Stanley and DeTrafford families of the old landed gentry, these industrial 'nouveau-riche' urban incomers provided new sources of income for the working classes of Alderley Edge. Finally, from the 1780s to the 1890s, the Edge was industrially mined for copper, lead and cobalt deposits. Thus, from the late 18th century, the region supported a complex mix of agricultural, industrial and service-based economies.

The study area became locally known as the Sandhills because of the large quantities of acidic sand dumped outside West Mine as a by-product of the 19th-century copper mining activities. The pH of the remnant Sandhills continues today to discourage regrowth of plant species, thereby maintaining these features as a dominant landscape marker within the study area. The site itself contained the remains of two brick and sandstone cottages (Fig. 25.1). Parish records indicated that the eastern cottage was built during 1747 on Lord Stanley's Estate in a local architectural style named after his lordship. As a mid-century 'improvement' of his estate holdings, Lord Stanley had sponsored the erection of identical workers' cottages across his property, with surviving two-storey houses offering a built reflection of his paternalistic efforts.

The date of construction and original function of the southern building was initially unknown, although post-excavation analysis later indicated a possible late 17th-century origin. Excavated features suggested the orientation of the southern house had been likely reversed in 1747 when Lord Stanley added his 'improved' Georgian cottage to the hamlet.[14] Thus, the 'rear' brick coal cellar may have originally acted as an early entrance porch for this southern structure. When reoriented with a southern entrance, the position of the remnant brick chimney foundations suggested a classic 'baffle-entrance' layout, identified by Ronald

LEFT
Figure 25.1 Hagg Cottages in the 1920s (photo courtesy of R. Barber)

Brunskill[15] as a signature for English rural housing over the mid- to late 17th century. Additionally, a white clay pipe bowl was recovered from the bottom of a wall trench, with specialist analysis yielding a manufacture date range of 1650–70.[16] Both structures appeared for the first time on the 1787 Lord Stanley Estate plan. Since they were built on Hagg Lane, the houses became known as the Hagg Cottages. A local word derived from an Old Saxon term for 'clearing in the woods', the 'Hagg' encompassed a region of biotic transition, where woods gave way to open pastureland.

During the early 19th century, the cottages were internally subdivided and leased to four separate households of workers from the Alderley Edge Mining Company. By the turn of the 20th century, industrial mining industry had completely ceased, and the occupants of the cottages were primarily attached to the service economy of Alderley Edge village. Residents of the four households consisted of the locally established Barrow, Ellam, Perrin, and Barber families. The Hagg Cottages were occupied until after the Second World War, and were demolished by the mid-1950s.

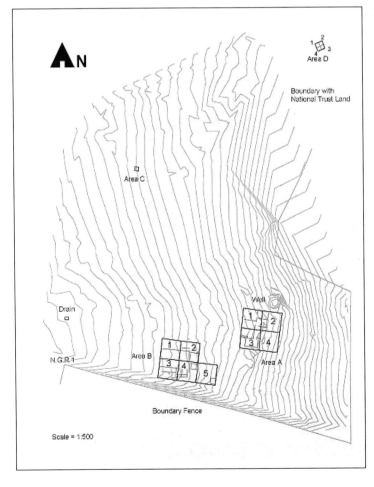

LEFT
Figure 25.2 Alderley Sandhills Project 2003, site plan. Topographic contours set at 50cm intervals

THE ALDERLEY SANDHILLS PROJECT

Following geophysical and topographic surveys of the Sandhills site, four excavation trenches were opened during the summer 2003 field season. Areas A and B initially consisted of two 10 x 10m open area trenches, positioned over structural remains of Hagg Cottages (Fig. 25.2). Area C consisted of a 1 x 1m test trench that ultimately did not contain any significant material deposits. Finally, a 2 x 2m trench was opened on the adjoining National Trust property to investigate an eroding artefact scatter at the end of Hagg Lane. Post-excavation analysis identified this feature as a late-19th to mid-20th-century garbage dump related to Areas A and B.[17]

In addition to excavation and archival research, the Sandhills Project benefited from the generous involvement of the local community of Alderley Edge. During excavations, former residents Mrs Edna Younger (née Barrow), Mr Roy Barber and Mrs Molly Pitcher (née Barber) visited to see the traces of their childhood homes emerge from the soil (Fig. 25.3). Their memories, stories and family photographs provided a unique personal perspective, as well as valuable ethnographic and historical data.[18]

Returning to the underlying research questions on class mobility and community life, we must consider whether the presence of consumer goods within this rural English settlement *necessarily* communicated aspirations towards what Bob Paynter[19] has called 'the etiquette and equipage of upward socio-economic mobility'. Or perhaps they reflected a far more complicated, if not contradictory, role as objects of both individual aspiration and community hierarchy?

LEFT
Figure 25.3 Roy Barber, Edna Younger (née Barrow), Molly Pitcher (née Barber), site visit September 2003. Inset: Edna Barrow, Roy Barber and Molly Barber at the Hagg, c. 1928 (photo courtesy of E. Younger)

ON RURAL LIFE AND SOCIAL BELONGING

First, it is important to recognise that rural workers' housing in Europe (as opposed to the New World or Australasia) tends to materially represent a *durability* of presence within the landscape. As observed by the English historian John Rule, working populations of rural districts occupied the old homes built by their ancestors, and repaired and extended over generations by the labourers themselves. As a result of the long-term continuity of these durable settlements, the community-wide scale of social belonging retained a pivotal role within workers' households.

Characterising small agricultural settlements as 'complete and integrated' communities, John Rule classically described the 'intermingling of neighbourhood, friendship and kin links developed over time'[20] as a product of the reciprocal relationships that structured these worlds. Importantly, this sense of 'community belonging' emerged from the ability of inhabitants to 'know' each other both *socially* in the present, and *temporally* through the dimension of previous generations. During an interview, Mrs Edna Younger explained:

> You felt part of a very big family. That's gone now, hasn't it? I mean, if you live in a town, you don't belong to anyone but your own few people, do you. Whereas, you felt belonging to everybody in the parish. You felt safe with everybody.[21]

Or, as she said during another site tour, 'You knew where you were.' Thus, complicated relationships of affiliation, support, kinship, competition and obligation interlaced the Sandhills occupants both to each other, and to the wider Alderley community. When asked about her family history, Mrs Edna Younger invoked memories of her great-grandmother:

> EY: … [S]he was a great worker. She went and cooked dinners at the school at one point, 'cause she'd heard they'd no cook. And I heard one story of her, coming from Alderley village. And, of course, they always walked from Alderley village to the Welsh Row. Two miles. We walked two miles to school from here. And she met this gentleman who worked for the coal people in the village. Oh, what did they call it – coal merchant. And she met this old chap coming up the hill, and he looked terribly ill. She said, he'd got flu. And she asked him where he was going, and he said, oh, so-and-so. So she pushed the barrow while he carried her shopping up.[22]

'A VERY ASTUTE LADY'

However, a sense of community, of social belonging, did *not* create egalitarian social structures, but rather quite the opposite. Life within a 'complete and integrated' community meant a life of rigid social hierarchies – a life where everyone else knew your ancestors, and everyone else knew where you belonged. Despite their adoption of the 'etiquette and equipage' of upward socioeconomic standing, mobility within this Alderley community appeared elusive. Community residents knew their relative status, and could (and did) perform that hierarchy through their material world.

During excavation of the Georgian-style 'Stanley Cottage', we recovered a ceramic assemblage that, at first, suggested efforts towards domesticity and bourgeois sensibilities, specifically concentrated in the northern half of the Area A trench. Results from secondary analysis of Trench A, Unit 1 indicated that tablewares constituted the largest single

Table 25.1: Ceramic Assemblage, Area A/Unit 1. Alderley Sandhills Project.

	Bottle	Hollow cup/bowl	Hollow jug, jar	Flat dish, plate	Service platter, lids	Stopper	Teapot	Flowerpot	Unidentified	Totals
Terracotta								14		**14**
Coarse earthenware									11	**11**
Earthenware (various)		16	3	10	1		12		102	**144**
Transfer-printed whiteware	1	12	2	33	3				82	**133**
Undecorated whiteware		71	4	63	2	1			316	**457**
Stoneware	1	1	3	1					21	**27**
Porcelain		28	1	26	2				101	**158**
Unidentified									3	**3**
Totals	**2**	**128**	**13**	**133**	**8**	**1**	**12**	**14**	**636**	**947**

identifiable category of ceramics within this excavation area (Table 25.1). These occurred in both hollow (cup, bowl, mug, eggcup) and flat (plate, dish, saucer) forms. While coarse earthenwares did appear in small quantities, the sample was characterised by its relative lack of these locally produced artefacts, particularly in comparison with other regional sites.[23] Additionally, the assemblage was characterised by a general lack of ceramics associated with food preparation and service (platters, lids, large bowls, storage vessels). Since this excavation trench exposed both the parlour and kitchen associated with the northern half of the internally subdivided cottage, this absence piqued our curiosity.

The tablewares recovered from Area A/Unit 1 were further distinguished by an absence of high-quality wares, and a concentration of cheap mass-produced items, particularly whitewares. These artefacts were either undecorated or displayed a limited range of standard decorative motifs, including the ubiquitous 'Asiatic Pheasant' and 'Willow Pattern' that represented the lower end of tablewares available to consumers from the early 19th century.[24] Thus, the inexpensive mass-produced tablewares that constituted the bulk of this ceramic assemblage told a story of frugal domestic life, not of aspirational gestures of upwards mobility.

Nonetheless, a surprising quantity of highly decorative items was also recovered, including Jasperware display ceramics, hand-blown glass decanter fragments, and faux-Coalport figurines in both historic and pastoral themes. When these curious decorative artefacts were shown to our oral history participants, they invariably linked the items to a specific resident, Mrs Lena Perrin, the final occupant of the Hagg Cottages.

Through these stories, Mrs Perrin emerged as quite a formidable character within the community (Fig. 25.4). A member of the local Cheshire clan of Barbers, she was the great-aunt of former residents Molly Pitcher and Roy Barber. From 1912, Mrs Perrin had lived in the northern side of the Stanley Cottage of Area A. Ostensibly, she had moved there to

LEFT
Figure 25.4 Mrs Lena Perrin (far right), pictured in costume jewellery atop the Sandhills, c. 1928 (photo courtesy of M. Pitcher)

care for her nephew George Barber (father of our participants), who occupied the southern half of the internally divided cottage with Mrs Perrin's recently widowed brother Ernest. However, during an interview session, Molly Pitcher (MP) questioned her great-aunt's suitability as a homemaker:

> MP: Yes now, my grandma, which er, she died when my father was very little… she [Mrs. Perrin] took over… kind of she was supposed to be looking after us. He got fed at Brindlow Farm over there because she wasn't very good at it.[25]

Later in the same interview, Molly Pitcher explicitly referred to 'Mrs Perrin who didn't cook', a characterisation potentially reflected in the curious lack of food preparation and serving vessels within the recovered ceramic assemblage. In effect, Mrs Pitcher's memory had not only relocated cooking activities *outside* the archaeological household, thereby relegating the excavated 'kitchen' to a different category of activity, but also situated this particular study site within an extended regional network of Barber households.

Mrs Perrin's husband, Jack Perrin, held casual local agricultural employment, as observed by his grand-nephew Mr Roy Barber (RB):

> RB: I've never known him to work, as such. I suppose he did at one time. But he was the one who used to go round the farms assisting in the pig killing.[26]

Mr Perrin also delivered the local newspaper by bicycle, with Roy Barber describing how he enjoyed riding on the rear frame as company during delivery routes. When day-trippers from Manchester began visiting Alderley Edge to explore the disused mine shafts, Jack Perrin developed an ingenious source of supplementary income:

> RB: They made him … custodian of the [disused] mines and he used to sit on a rock just before the mine entrance … he used to sit there, selling these candles.
>
> Edna Younger (EY): Ha'penny each.
>
> RB: These candles he bought in Alderley Edge … He used to cut them in half and sell them for about, one half for about four times what he paid for them.
>
> [Laughter]
>
> RB: And that was a little income for him….[27]

Thus, Jack Perrin emerged from these interviews as a man of frugal means, a well-connected fellow who resourcefully drew from local agricultural, service and emerging tourist industries to generate his livelihood. Curiously, a very different story unfolded when former residents were asked about the nature of Mrs Perrin's employment:

> RB: Oh, she didn't do anything. She went and bought at sales, auction. This sort of thing. And she bought five houses … Over a period of time. She bought therein – one, two, three in Wilmslow, and two in Alderley Edge. I know there's one down Moss Lane, but I don't know where the others were.
>
> EY: Yes, she was a very astute lady.[28]

These memories offered one explanation for the unusual concentration of decorative household ornaments recovered from Area A. More importantly, they suggested a rather contradictory perspective on the socioeconomic status of this elderly couple. Dwelling in half of a damp, internally divided, and increasingly dilapidated 18th-century worker's cottage, Jack Perrin earned his primary casual income as a 'pig sticker' on local Alderley farms. Meanwhile, his wife attended auctions and invested in local property. Following the death of her husband in the mid-1930s, Mrs Perrin continued to occupy the northern half of the Stanley Cottage as its solitary resident. Molly Pitcher recalled travelling as a teenager by bicycle up to the crumbling cottage to deliver dinners prepared by her mother. She described the northern 'parlour' room as filled with exotic ornaments, display figurines and memorabilia.

Oral history participants generally remembered Mrs Perrin as 'a bit frightening'. Mrs Edna Younger and Mrs Molly Pitcher both described her 'big flashing eyes' and her dramatic emotional outbursts. And all former residents commented on Mrs Perrin's love of costume jewellery – the 'spangly-dangleys' she inevitably wore to accompany her Edwardian-era dress. While her presentation of self might appear a direct example of bourgeois aspirations, a closer material analysis of the excavated ceramic and glass assemblages revealed something rather unusual.

MRS PERRIN'S 'TRANKLEMENTS'

Both the glass and ceramic collections of Area A/Unit 1 were characterised by not only the sheer quantity of display items recovered, but the rather spectacular aesthetic they embodied. Further, these non-functional display items were also characterised by their unexpected age, particularly compared to the functional tablewares, condiment bottles and medicinal vessels that constituted the bulk of glass and ceramic assemblages from Areas A and B. The vast majority of artefacts recovered from the Hagg Cottages were of 20th-century origin, typically spanning the 1920s to the 1950s. In stark contrast, post-excavation analysis dated the display assemblage to the mid- to late19th century. For example, one particularly arresting decorative figurine depicted a white infant hand supporting an egg-shaped orange object, encrusted with fine chips of ceramic and applied polychrome flowers (Fig. 25.5). Dated by its base registration stamp to 1870, the wrist of this hand was also encrusted and adorned with a floral wreath. A highly similar ornamental vase – its exterior described as 'textured frit chipping finish, [with] applied ceramic roses and leaves'[29] – was identified as a turn-of-century family heirloom in Grace Karskens' study of 'The Rocks', a working urban neighbourhood of Sydney, Australia.

Another figurine within this assemblage depicted a creature first identified as a horse. However, upon closer examination, the project ceramic specialist determined that black horizontal stripes along the neck and body fragments identified the animal as a zebra – although one portrayed with the mane of a horse.[30] Further comparative research suggested the specimen dated to the first half of the 19th century, when depictions of exotic animals gained wide popularity across England as a result of touring fairs, circuses and wild beast shows.

Specialist analysis of the glass assemblage produced similar results, with the collection distinguished by a remarkable number and variety of non-functional display items.

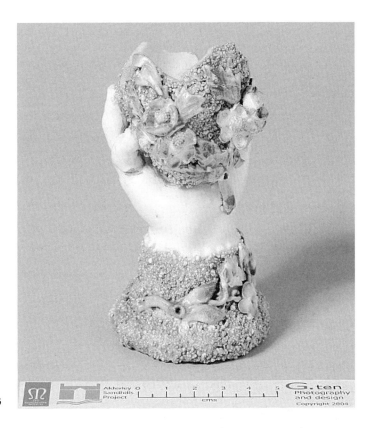

RIGHT
Figure 25.5 Hand figurine,
Alderley Sandhills Project 2003

Example included two early 20th-century press-moulded vases, three opaque white vases, and a particularly spectacular 'lustre' pedestal bowl. Popular over the later Victorian era, this artefact was moulded of opaque blue glass, decorated with a worn band of gilding, and retained seven of the eight original cut and faceted glass drops hung from small holes drilled through its central body. Dated from 1860 to 1880,[31] the specimen probably represented one of an identical pair, typically displayed as a matched set of mantelpiece ornaments. Thus, these display artefacts exhibited a manufacture date of up to two generations *before* the main occupation period represented by the majority of artefacts at the site.

But did these curious material acquisitions indicate an achievement of middle-class standing? Had Mrs Lena Perrin managed to elevate her social position within the hierarchical world of Alderley Edge? Did these objects hold nostalgic or aspirational qualities? A final ethnographic vignette further complicated our understanding of class distinctions within this rural English settlement.

During excavations, the archaeological team was visited by the Parkinson sisters, elderly local residents who agreed to be interviewed and filmed during their site tour. Pamela and Mary Parkinson explained that they had lived down Whitebarn Road during the 1930s, and had played with Molly Pitcher, Roy Barber and Edna Younger as children. When we showed these two ladies examples of the decorative ceramics from Area A, they also immediately linked the objects to Mrs Lena Perrin. Pamela Parkinson repeatedly used the word 'tranklements' to refer to Mrs Perrin's ceramic ornaments, which we misunderstood as 'tranquil-ments' – objects that helped her feel tranquil. Later discussions with oral history participants suggested the term was a traditional local word used to casually describe one's everyday possessions, or 'bits and pieces'.

The reference was passed on to Tony Willmott, the English Heritage Project Officer for the Alderley Sandhills Project, who discovered an alternative possible etymology of Pamela Parkinson's term. While eating a pub lunch, he suddenly realised the chutney accompaniment was embossed with the word 'Tracklement'. Of post-war origins, this term described a savoury jelly eaten with roasted meats. We realised that Miss Pamela Parkinson may not have been conjuring a nostalgic memory of Mrs Perrin's genteel tranquillity, or even her simple 'bits and pieces'. Perhaps she had referred to Mrs Perrin's ornaments as a food condiment – with subtle overtones of 'mutton dressed as lamb'. Either way, in dismissing these ornamental artefacts, she had located Mrs Perrin within the enduring and clearly hierarchical class structure of this rural English community. It was only then that we realised the implications of what had been casually described as 'living down Whitebarn Road'. The Parkinson sisters were daughters of the wealthy families who owned the nearby Villas. They had travelled up to the Hagg Cottages to play with the children of the local working households.

Did Mrs Perrin's 'tranklements' – those decorative materials that adorned both her person and household – represent a form of class aspiration? Or, as a landlady for local properties, had she actually 'achieved' a middle-class status? Her menagerie of ceramic figurines, glass ornaments, souvenirs and costume jewellery may have been purchased at auction, their seemingly garish appearance revealing a unique concept of 'taste' distinct from that displayed within the neighbouring upper middle-class Villas. Perhaps an alternative aesthetic or consumption pattern could be interpreted from this domestic collection, with issues of family composition, household status or social class guiding the acquisition, use and discard of these remarkable objects.[32] Conversely, they may have been heirlooms of the proud and long-established Barber family, a material reflection of their social standing within the local working community.

CONCLUSION

By way of conclusion, four reflections emerge from this ethno-archaeological approach to the recent past. First, the community scale of social life was of tremendous significance for the working residents of the Alderley Sandhills site (Fig. 25.6). In other words, a sense of 'social belonging' operated on a much wider scale than that of the 'nuclear family'. As a result, domestic practices served as performances of community solidarity as much as performances of prestige, class distinction or gentility.

Second, such expressions of community life did not negate individual efforts of class aspiration, as were manifest in the fine and decorative ceramics recovered during excavations. A yearning for elevated social standing and improved living conditions certainly infused the everyday lives of working people who occupied the Hagg Cottages. However, rather

RIGHT
Figure 25.6 Generations together. Roy Barber with father and grandfather (left); Edna Younger with mother, grandmother, and great-grandmother (right) (photos courtesy of M. Pitcher and E. Younger)

than a straightforward adoption of the 'etiquette and equipage of upward socio-economic standing',[33] residents of the Hagg Cottages may have clearly understood that class mobility – or the capacity to transcend one's position within the local community – ultimately remained elusive. In other words, as the British sociologist Annette Kuhn recently noted, class inequalities reside deep within people's fundamental identities:

> Class is not just about the way you talk, or dress, or furnish your home; it is not just about the job you do or how much money you make doing it; nor is it merely about whether or not you went to university, nor which university you went to. Class is something beneath your clothes, under your skin, in your psyche, at the very core of your being.[34]

Or, as Mr Roy Barber patiently explained during the last interview, 'it was always, *always*, them and us. You always knew where you stood.'[35]

Finally, by juxtaposing diverse sources of evidence, the situated, multiscalar, and frequently dissonant patterns of community life can be illuminated. As a multi-disciplinary method for understanding the recent past, such 'conversations'[36] between the artefactual, oral historic and archival sources promote a rich exchange between alternative forms of knowledge. Through this detailed interpretation, a composite portrait can be created to demonstrate the complicated dynamics of class affiliation, of kinship, and of social influence – ultimately yielding 'broader insights into the human condition at particular moments in history'.[37] It is only through this careful articulation of sources that we can use excavation of household sites to interpret the global implications of community life.

ACKNOWLEDGEMENTS

The Alderley Sandhills Project (ASP) was sponsored by English Heritage, with financial support provided through the Aggregate Levy Sustainability Fund. The ASP has been generously supported by colleagues from the Manchester Museum (John Prag, Bryan Sitch and Clare Pye), University of Manchester (Darren Griffin, Sarah Whitehead, Sarah

Croucher, Hannah Cobb), English Heritage (Jennie Stopford, Tony Willmott, Andrew Davison, and Kath Buxton), and the Derbyshire Caving Club. Valuable post-excavation analysis was undertaken by Hugh Willmott, Chris Cumberpatch and Joan Unwin of ARCUS, University of Sheffield. Paul Sorensen, landowner of the Sandhills region of Alderley Edge, provided access to the study site, and both William Harris of Whitebarn Farm and the regional office of The National Trust offered essential local assistance. Finally, Roy Barber, Molly Pitcher, Edna Younger, and Pamela and Mary Parkinson generously shared the memories and photographs of life at the Hagg Cottages. Any errors in fact or representation are naturally my own.

NOTES

1. Horning 2000; Groover 2003; Silliman 2006; Voss 2008.
2. Deagan 1983; Wall 1994; Jamieson 2005.
3. Karskens 1999; Mullins 1999; Crook 2000; Brighton 2001; Cantwell & Wall 2001.
4. Kelleher 2000.
5. Orser 1999, 281.
6. Purser 1992; Beck & Somerville 2005.
7. Dawson 1994.
8. Summerfield 1998, 17.
9. Dawson 1994, 22–3.
10. Halbwachs 1992 [1950]; Misztal 2003.
11. Hoffman 1996; Cattell & Climo 2002.
12. Summerfield 1998, 17.
13. Nuttall & Coetzee 1998, xii.
14. Casella *et al.* 2004.
15. Brunskill 1982, 70–1.
16. Casella *et al.* 2004.
17. Casella *et al.* 2004.
18. See Casella and Croucher 2009; Casella 2005.
19. Paynter 2001, 138.
20. Rule 1986, 157.
21. Mrs Edna Younger, ASP Interviews, June 2002.
22. Mrs Edna Younger, ASP interviews, July 2003.
23. Casella & Croucher 2009.
24. Coysh and Henrywood 1989.
25. Mrs Molly Pitcher, ASP Interviews, August 2003.
26. Mr Roy Barber, ASP Interviews, September 2003.
27. Mr Roy Barber & Mrs Edna Younger, ASP Interviews, September 2003.
28. Mr Roy Barber & Mrs Edna Younger, ASP Interviews, September 2003.
29. Karskens 1999, 142.
30. Cumberpatch 2004.
31. Willmott 2004.
32. Majewski & Schiffer 2001; Praetzellis & Praetzellis 2004.
33. Paynter 2001, 138.
34. Kuhn 1995, 98.
35. Mr Roy Barber, ASP Interviews, September 2003.
36. Beck & Somerville 2005.
37. Beaudry 2006, 251.

BIBLIOGRAPHY

Beaudry, M.C. 2006, 'Stories that matter: material lives in 19th-century Lowell and Boston, Massachusetts', in Green & Leech (eds), 2006, 249–68.

Beck, W. & Somerville, M. 2005, 'Conversations between disciplines: historical archaeology and oral history in Yarrawarra', *World Archaeology* **37**(3): 468–83.

Brighton, S.A. 2001, 'Prices that suit the times: shopping for ceramics at the Five Points', *Historical Archaeology* **35**(3): 16–30.

Buchli, V. & Lucas, G. 2001, *Archaeologies of the Contemporary Past*. London: Routledge.

Cantwell, A. & Wall, D. 2001, *Unearthing Gotham: The Archaeology of New York City*. New Haven: Yale University Press.

Canuto, M. & Yaeger, J. 2000, *The Archaeology of Communities*. London: Routledge.

Casella, E.C. 2005, '"Social workers": new directions in industrial archaeology', in Casella & Symonds (eds), 2005, 3–31.

Casella, E.C. & Croucher, S. 2009 (in press), *The Alderley Sandhills Project: An Archaeology of Community Life in (post-)Industrial England*. Manchester: Manchester University Press.

Casella, E.C. & Fowler, C. 2005, *The Archaeology of Plural and Changing Identities: Beyond Identification*. New York: Kluwer Academic/Plenum Publishers.

Casella, E.C. & Symonds, J. 2005, *Industrial Archaeology: Future Directions*. New York: Springer.

Cattell, M.G. & Climo, J.J. 2002, 'Introduction: Meaning in social memory and history: anthropological perspectives', in Climo & Cattell (eds), 2002, 1–36.

Climo, J.J. & Cattell, M.G. 2002, *Social Memory and History: Anthropological Perspective*. Walnut Creek, CA: AltaMira Press.

Coysh, A.W. & Henrywood, R.K. 1989, *The Dictionary of Blue and White Printed Pottery 1780–1880, Volume 2*. Woodbridge: Antique Collectors Club.

Crook, P. 2000, 'Shopping and historical archaeology: exploring the contexts of urban consumption', *Australasian Historical Archaeology* **18**: 17–28.

Dawson, G. 1994, *Soldier Heroes: British Adventure, Empire and the Imagining of Masculinities*. London: Routledge.

Deagan, K. 1983, *Spanish St Augustine: The Archaeology of a Colonial Creole Community*. New York: Academic Press.

Green, A. & Leech, R. 2006, *Cities in the World, 1500–2000*. Leeds: Maney.

Groover, M.D. 2003, *An Archaeological Study of Rural Capitalism and Material Life: The Gibbs Farmstead in Appalachia, 1790–1920*. New York: Kluwer Academic/Plenum Publishers.

Halbwachs, M. 1992 [1950], *On Collective Memory*, edited and translated by L.A. Coser. Chicago: University of Chicago Press.

Hall, M. & Silliman, S.W. 2006, *Historical Archaeology*. Oxford: Blackwell.

Hoffman, K. 1996, *Concepts of Identity: Historical and Contemporary Images and Portraits of Self and Family*. New York: HarperCollins.

Horning, A. 2000, 'Archaeological considerations of "Appalachian" identity: community-based archaeology in the Blue Ridge Mountains', in Canuto & Yaeger (eds), 2000, 210–30.

Jamieson, R.W. 2005, 'Caste in Cuenca: colonial identity in the seventeenth century Andes', in Casella & Fowler (eds), 2005, 211–32.

Karskens, G. 1999, *Inside the Rocks: The Archaeology of a Neighbourhood*. Sydney: Hale & Iremonger.

Kelleher, W. 2000, 'Making home in the Irish/British borderlands: the global and the local in a conflicted social space', *Identities* **7**(2): 139–72.

Kuhn, A. 1995, *Family Secrets: Acts of Memory and Imagination*. London: Verso.

Little, B.J. 1992, *Text-Aided Archaeology*. Boca Raton, FL: CRC Press.

Majewski, T. & Schiffer, M.B. 2001, 'Beyond consumption: towards an archaeology of consumerism', in Buchli & Lucas (eds), 2001, 26–50.

Misztal, B. 2003, *Theories of Social Remembering*. Maidenhead: Open University Press.

Mullins, P.R. 1999, *Race and Affluence: An Archaeology of African-America and Consumer Culture*. New York: Kluwer Academic/Plenum Publishers.

Nuttall, S. & Coetzee, C. 1998, *Negotiating the Past*. Cape Town: Oxford University Press.

Orser, C.E. 1999, 'Negotiating our "familiar pasts"', in Tarlow & West (eds), 1999, 273–85.

Orser, C.E. 2001, *Race and the Archaeology of Identity*. Salt Lake City: University of Utah Press.

Paynter, R. 2001, 'The cult of whiteness in western New England', in Orser (ed.), 2001, 125–42.

Praetzellis, M. & Praetzellis, A. 2004, *Putting the 'There' There: Historical Archaeologies of West Oakland: I-880 Cypress Replacement Project*. <www.sonoma.edu/asc/cypress/finalreport/> [accessed 15 August 2007].

Purser, M. 1992, 'Oral history and historical archaeology', in Little 1992, 25–38.

Rule, J. 1986, *The Labouring Classes in Early Industrial England, 1750–1850*. London: Longman.

Silliman, S.W. 2006, 'Struggling with labor, working with identities', in Hall & Silliman (eds), 2006, 147–66.

Summerfield, P. 1998, *Reconstructing Women's Wartime Lives*. Manchester: Manchester University Press.

Tarlow, S. & West, S. 1999, *The Familiar Past*. London: Routledge.

Voss, B.L. 2008 (in press), 'Gender, race, and labor in the archaeology of Spanish-Colonial Americas', *Current Anthropology* **49**(5).

Wall, D. 1994, *The Archaeology of Gender: Separating the Spheres in Urban America*. New York: Plenum.

UNPUBLISHED SOURCES

Casella, E.C., Griffin, D. and Prag, A.J.N.W. 2004, 'The Alderley Sandhills Project: Final Report', unpublished report prepared for English Heritage and the National Trust, London.

Cumberpatch, C.G. 2004, 'Ceramic report', in Casella *et al.* 2004.

Willmott, H. 2004, 'Glass report', in Casella *et al.* 2004.

Pulling the Threads Together: Issues of Theory and Practice in an Archaeology of the Modern World

By STEPHEN A. MROZOWSKI

This chapter outlines an approach to an archaeology of the modern world that seeks to identify the major streams in a seemingly disparate history of the past five hundred years. Focusing on the interrelationship of the growth of capitalism, colonisation, urbanisation and industrialisation, I argue for a unified view of the history of the modern era. Drawing on both historical and archaeological studies from a variety of geographical and temporal contexts, the discussion stresses the advantages of an approach that emphasises points of convergence and commonality among the forces that have shaped global history in the modern era. Particular emphasis is placed on the manner in which individual and group materiality interfaced with ecologies of capitalism, colonialism, urbanism and industrialisation in shaping and reshaping modernity.

INTRODUCTION

In the abstract, it would seem easy to find common ground among a group of practitioners whose intellectual focus is the archaeology of the last five hundred years. Whether your interest is industry, or colonialism or the transformation of a medieval, feudal world into something distinctly post-medieval and modern, there is no denying that these events are part of a larger historical tapestry. Yet as the three days of the *Crossing Paths or Sharing Tracks?* conference and this subsequent volume have shown, differences of tradition, educational background and point of entry have produced a somewhat fractured and eclectic intellectual landscape that makes the navigation of this complex period all the more challenging. Some of these differences are intellectual and reflect contrasting interests.[1] Some are very practical, and here I am talking about differences in funding and practice. In the United States, the division between university-based archaeologists and those employed primarily in cultural resource management (CRM) has narrowed significantly over the past twenty years due in large measure to a combination of funding realities and the growing interest in heritage and memory as topics of theoretical significance.[2] Most archaeology carried out in the United States is CRM-based research, but the character of the work has changed. Much of the work remains compliance-related, that is, normally triggered by commercial development or large federally or state-funded projects. There has also been an expansion of heritage-based research that is linked to tourism, development in national parks, or research funded by Tribal Nations who want to insure that their own development does not destroy their own archaeological legacies.

The same kinds of academic/CRM divisions that one sees in the United States exist in both Britain and Ireland, and so it comes as little surprise that issues of funding and identity would weave their way into our discussion of crossing paths. Unfortunately, I don't have much to add to this part of the discussion, except to say that as someone who was Boston's first City Archaeologist and who worked for years in CRM, I understand just how real these differences are and how frustrating they can be in trying to build a career in archaeology. Acknowledging this deficiency at the outset, I see my primary role as trying to identify some of the common threads that have contributed to an era of great historical significance and contemporary relevancy. It is, after all, the period responsible for the world we now inhabit, and for that reason alone it warrants serious interrogation.

My second purpose is to discuss some of the questions being asked, theories being employed and, perhaps most importantly, the practice of archaeology. One of the reasons I have such respect for the archaeology done in Britain and Ireland is that the practices of archaeology – field work, recording, analysis, interpretation – are all equally valued. I am, however, surprised that a particular form of archaeological practice, that of environmental archaeology, is conspicuously absent from most of the papers presented at the meeting. I know that others before me, such as Justine Bayley and David Crossley, have made this point previously with respect to the role of science in industrial archaeology.[3] Yet I would still make the point that the biological sides of large-scale processes such as colonialism, industrialisation, urbanisation, the growth of capitalism and the construction of empire are absolutely essential if we are to understand the world we have inherited.[4] Each of these processes, and they are obviously interlinked temporally, spatially and culturally, involved major movements of people and the reshaping of environments. Industry in particular has had such a dramatic effect on the earth's environment that it has imperilled human society to the point that its impact cannot be ignored by archaeologists interested in its evolution. This is one of the risks of celebrating technology without examining its transformative powers.

SCALES OF ANALYSIS: TECHNOLOGY AND THE MODERN WORLD

Technology and rapid technological change was obviously one of the driving forces of modernity, but industrial technology was just one of many forces that helped to shape the modern world. Military, logistical and transportation technologies enabled European powers to conquer North and South America, the Caribbean, parts of Asia, the eastern Arctic and Africa. Science also played a critical role, especially the celestial and geographical sciences, in shaping the modern world. Here I would point to the development of instruments of navigation. The organisation of military forces and their support is also a critical component of imperial conquest. European empires varied in their approach to conquest and colonisation, but each constructed landscapes that reinforced notions of a natural order. At the pinnacle of this order stood humans, and chief among these of course were Europeans, who had inherited their positions of power and dominance from the

Divine. Communicating this ideology through cultural practices and material form was part of a larger strategy to maintain order in an otherwise fractious moment in history.

There were also economic technologies such as writing, accounting and financial instruments such as credit and currency that also played an important role in the creation of the modern world. Some scholars view these technologies as characteristics of capitalism, and this seems undeniable, but there were pre-capitalist traditions and practices that gave form to the cultural crucible that served as both arena and engine for capitalism's mercurial rise to pre-eminence.[5] These technologies relied upon several forms of abstraction, the mathematics of commerce, or accounting most centrally, but also beneath it all was the larger process of commoditisation – the transformation of any and all forms of material reality into units that can be measured and assigned an exchange value, to use Marx's term, or a price. All empires employed some form of commodification as an instrument of imperial power, and in this sense it probably was a part of all complex societies. An institution such as slavery, which was so much a part of the ancient world, essentially involved the dehumanisation of an individual or group so that they could be exchanged.

Capitalist commoditisation is, however, different from that of the ancient world in several ways. Even if some of the institutions are similar, the scale and depth of the process under capitalism would eventually become so all-encompassing that it would alter the way many human beings perceived the world. In this sense it is the instrumentality of capitalist commoditisation that is so impressive, yet so frightening. Joined with forces such as religion and the ideologies of individualism and racism, commoditisation represents a process that in my estimation dwarfs that of industry in its impact on transforming the world from a series of interconnected environments, or natures to use Arturo Escobar's term,[6] into a laundry list of articles for disarticulation and consumption.

DEFINING DISCIPLINES: THEORY AND PRACTICE

How, then, should we set about examining the forces that have shaped the modern world in a manner that addresses their complexity and our own limitations? Well, for starters let us acknowledge some of the challenges that we face as practitioners of the study of this particular past. To begin with, does it help to establish an overarching focus, a meta-narrative that serves as a framework for all that is done in the name of Post-Medieval, Historical and Industrial Archaeologies? From a purely historical perspective the notion of the Modern World has demonstrated some utility for historical archaeology, especially those interested in global processes.[7] There is also the concept of modernity. Its appeal stems from its connections to the rise of secular nation states with liberal forms of government, global economies that penetrated virtually every corner of the globe, and the large imperial project of constructing and maintaining empires.[8] Modernity as an analytical construct is not without its problems, however, not the least of which is defining its temporal and geographical boundaries. It also suffers from being overly vague, inseparable from post-modernity, and highly contested when viewed in contrast to specific historical and cultural contexts.[9] Given the complexities and difficulties surrounding the notion of modernity and serious questions concerning its applicability outside some of the latter stages of the modern period, it seems best to leave any argument in favour of its utility for another time.

Therefore, rather than argue for an all-encompassing meta-narrative of modernity, I will instead focus on three major points: the importance of theory, the centrality of archaeological practice, and the connections between the interrelated historical processes of colonialism, industrialisation, urbanisation, the rise of capitalism and the construction of empire. Mercifully, attempting to discuss each of these processes in any detail is well beyond the scope of a chapter such as this. So instead, I will try and focus on some of the connecting threads that link these processes and some of the devices I have found useful in my own work to examine these processes. I apologise at the outset for drawing so heavily upon personal experiences and hope that it will not be too tedious for the reader. In particular, I will discuss both landscape and the broader issue of space as conceptual tools for examining some of the links between large-scale historical processes such as those noted above. I will also discuss some of the benefits and limitations of postcolonial theory, especially as it pertains to the examination of colonial and postcolonial contexts.

I will begin with theory and whether it is essential, whether it adds anything, whether it clouds things, and whether it actually aids archaeological practice. In many respects, I see many of the issues that currently occupy those who attended the conference and probably those who chose not to attend as being *practice* versus *theory* questions. Archaeology partakes of both theory and practice, and for fields of study such as historical archaeology or industrial archaeology to reach their true potential, a combination of the two is, I believe, preferred. Theory-versus-practice debates tend to polarise the issue and ultimately are not particularly productive. Archaeologists trying to understand arguably the most complex period in human history must be able to know their data – artefact types and the technologies that produced them – as well as the abstract ideas that made them possible. I don't believe you can understand industrial technology without understanding that it is abstract theory that made it possible. You must begin with abstract ideas such as production, uniformity, standardisation and profit before you can realise them as material realities.

From my perspective, you also have to place this kind of technology into an even larger picture in which social, religious and intellectual history are interwoven and linked to the growth of liberal ideas of government and, perhaps most importantly, the acceptance that commerce and the pursuit of profit were not the evils they had been one thousand years ago. That is one of the reasons I like the concept of Historical Archaeology because it liberates me to pursue the history of account practices in Italy between the 12th and 14th centuries as an important moment in the growth of capitalism.[10] I would agree with David Cranstone concerning the semantic and intellectual challenges that face attempts to construct an historical archaeology of Europe as well as those made by Adrian Green, Audrey Horning and Matthew Johnson in favour of such an enterprise.[11] A global historical archaeology that would connect the ancient world to that of our own would lay bare a deeper history and therefore should be encouraged. One obvious example is focusing on the historical growth of capitalism. Matthew Johnson has demonstrated the value of such an approach in the English context, and I would suggest at the very least we need to explore capitalism's links to early accounting practices in Italy.[12] Debit/credit accounting practices and commercial mathematics provided an abstract measure of not only accountability but of credit and credibility. The development of these technologies and their acceptance were crucial stepping stones toward the growth of notions of liberal government – that those whose lives revolved around money could be trusted as long as they demonstrated their commitment to abstract measures of their own accountability and creditability. And so I think an argument can be made for the growth of commercial and political institutions such as accounting and liberal government being inseparable from the growth of cities, industry and the modern world writ large.

Returning to the issue of practice, I would again like to draw on some personal experiences in making an argument for greater collaboration and interdisciplinary research. Few of you may know that I worked in Britain in the late 1980s with Dominic Powlesland on the West Heslerton Project.[13] During that time, I would speak often with Dominic and Christine Haughton at West Heslerton as well as with the wonderful folks at the York Environmental Archaeology Unit, in particular Harry Kenward and Alan Hall, as well as Helen Keely, then of English Heritage, and Martin Jones, then of Durham University and now at Cambridge. One of the questions that I raised was why specialists such as Martin Jones or Harry Kenward were not invited to participate in the overall planning of archaeological projects in which they were involved. To me, the fact that specialist reports were merely placed in appendices or today as CDs was to some degree understandable, but what was not to my liking was the fact that the archaeologist in charge of such projects was in most instances the sole voice in synthesising all of the information generated by the various specialists.[14]

When I was fortunate enough to start my own research centre, what is today the Andrew Fiske Memorial Center for Archaeological Research, I decided to build an interdisciplinary team such as that housed at York, and to have everyone work as a team on projects from start to finish. This meant working collaboratively and giving up some of the control over projects, but ultimately it has proven to be a very productive and exciting approach to research. Not everyone in the Center shares the same theoretical approach, but this has proven to be a healthy quality because it has meant lively debate. In terms of the actual management of the Center and Center projects, consensus rules. The Center staff bring diverse skills and approaches to the work including zooarchaeology, paleoethnobotany, remote sensing and geophysical analysis, material culture analysis, geoarchaeology and archaeological conservation. Obviously, individuals with such diverse interests bring different backgrounds to the work of the Center and the result has been a dynamic and vibrant working environment.

I would suggest to you collectively that there is more to gain from collaborating than there is from the alternative. There seems little question that many of the issues that confront the various groups working on this period are identity issues, and these are understandable. As David Landon, my colleague at the Fiske Center, said to me recently, 'industrial archaeologists don't like it when historical archaeologists who only dig up workers' housing call themselves industrial archaeologists'.[15] Well, as someone who has done just that, I fully understand the point Landon is making, and I agree with it. I have not devoted much of my career to learning about industrial technology, although I would argue that the production of industrial space, both the factory complexes and the housing complexes, are industrial technologies. Perhaps I am wrong, but I'm not sure that many historical archaeologists I know would have too much of a problem with Landon's basic statement. And knowing David, I know that he was saying this as someone who clearly has done both the industrial and domestic sides of industrial technology and considers himself to be both an industrial archaeologist and an historical archaeologist. In a 1999 publication, Landon presaged the purpose of the *Crossing Paths or Sharing Tracks?* conference by suggesting that 'thoughtful attempts to close the gap between interests in privy pottery and steam engine design will mark a major advance in the creation of a holistic archaeology of industrialisation'.[16] He too was asking whether the outcome was to be crossed paths or separate tracks.

In my estimation, taking up Landon's challenge requires that the exploration of shared paths takes precedence over following different tracks. Realising the challenge must begin with practice, and here I would offer two major recommendations. First, don't let identity get in the way of intellectual cross-fertilisation. Second, break free of your own conventions that view specialists as people who are sent samples and asked for results that are then interpreted by a single voice. Replace this with a truly interdisciplinary approach. And the key difference between interdisciplinary and multi-disciplinary approaches revolves around the issue of precisely who sets the research agenda, who asks the questions. As noted earlier, all decisions at the Fiske Center are made by consensus, and this has proven liberating. Still another advantage of the collaboration is that it generates ownership because everyone is involved in the planning from the start. Finally, and perhaps most importantly, collaboration means greater production for everyone involved. With more people involved, the workload gets spread around and allows for greater scholarly production in terms of co-authored publications.

One of the reasons I feel that interdisciplinary collaboration is so essential is because it broadens the entire field of study. For example, most of my work on industrial communities has focused on the role of industrial production and industrial workers as consumers because those are the people who interest me the most. I am not saying they are more important than the mechanics who built the machines and maintained them – I am interested in them as well – but as people and less as engineers. Why? Well, because I am not an engineer, but I do understand the importance of technology so I work with folks who have that knowledge, and as a group we draw on what they do and most importantly incorporate their questions into our work. And one of the chief reasons I have chosen to work this way is because it forces me and those whom I work with not to limit our focus to the point where we lose sight of connections between processes such as industrialisation and colonialism.

Another advantage of an interdisciplinary approach is that it provides a window on to the biological dimensions of large-scale historical processes such as colonialism, industrialism and the construction of empire. This is particularly true of colonial communities that were designed in such a manner that they communicated stability and power to both the colonised and the colonial populations themselves. In some instances, the environments in question are best described as micro-environments, such as urban backyards. Examining these has allowed me to link forces such as changes in the demographic make-up of 19th-century industrial workforces to the growth of slums and declining living conditions.[17] The same approach was useful in fostering research that has provided an answer to long-asked questions concerning the English settlement of Jamestown. Historians have asked why the

English who landed at Jamestown in 1607 were so ill prepared for what they encountered.[18] The historian who first posed this question almost forty years ago was without the key piece of information that would have allowed him to answer that question. The answer was not contained in an archive, but it was instead to be found in the annual growth rings of the trees on Jamestown Island.[19] In this instance, the information derived from the tree-ring analysis revealed that the English settlers of Jamestown landed during a period of extreme drought between 1605 and 1612 that was the worse such event in 1,200 years. Is it any wonder the English were so ill prepared? Nor is it surprising that English entreaties to the local Native populations to provide food eventually resulted in violence once the drought's impact started to lead to the failure of Native agricultural production.

LANDSCAPE AND THE CONSTRUCTION OF SPACE

Trying to examine large-scale and complex historical processes such as colonialism, industrialisation or the growth of capitalism or empire is extremely difficult without some conceptual point of entry. I have found landscape and the larger construct of space to be useful in this regard. Landscape works because it provides a vehicle for examining overlapping moments in time. It also provides a means of exploring the conjuncture of cultural and physical space into the world that we see and others saw before us. In terms of practice it facilitates the collaboration of specialists who often have to reconcile what at first appears to be conflicting data, but which ultimately results in a coherent story. It is not a case of the story being imposed on the data, but rather agreeing upon a new interpretation that resolves what had been viewed as contradictory information. Ultimately, the narrative that emerges from this kind of interdisciplinary collaboration is a richer, deeper history.

My interest in landscape archaeology also developed from working in the United Kingdom with its wonderful tradition of landscape history and archaeology.[20] More recently, I have turned to the larger concept of space in theorising landscape. All of the forces that have shaped the modern world have a spatial dimension that archaeology is perfectly suited to explore. I have worked with the theories of space formulated by Henri Lefebvre, Sharon Zukin, David Harvey, Edward Soja and Arturo Escobar.[21] In particular, I have found the concept of space as being multi-dimensional extremely useful in a variety of archaeological contexts including the cities of New England, the plantations of North-eastern North America and Barbados, and now Native American historic sites. Lefebvre's classic tripartite scheme of spatial representations, space as lived and representational spaces has proven its value to numerous archaeologists.[22] His notion of abstract space and its representation in drawings, for example, were very useful in exploring the spatial development of planned cities such as Lowell, Massachusetts or Saltaire Village in Bradford. The excitement comes when archaeology is employed to explore the evolution of the material space, the space as lived, because often it is contested and used in a manner quite opposite from that intended by those who originally conceptualised that space in the abstract as a spatial representation.[23]

The spatial scheme I am currently working with begins with the physical space in which people lived out their lives and which we explore as archaeologists. I fully recognise that these are two very different things and that what we see and what they experienced is not the same thing, yet there may be ways for us to begin transcending this metaphysical divide. My notion of physical space borrows Jim Delle's term material space and combines it with the concept of space as a biophysical reality, or what Arturo Escobar calls natures.[24] Depending upon the historical context this material space can be very different. The space that is created in colonial encounters is, after all, very different from urban industrial space, and the environments that result are different as well. As humans shape this space they are actively engaged in the creation or production of a physical reality that often becomes the focus of our intellectual gaze. Excavation, recording and interpretation are all part of the practice of exploring this space and attaching meaning to the changes that have shaped it. One of the difficulties that face archaeologists in interpreting landscape and space in general is the multiscalar character of the forces that shape its production. In some cases, the forces are very immediate and practical, linked as they are to the physical needs of the groups involved. Enclosures, yards, work areas and the like often have to meet the needs of a particular activity. Keeping animals, growing field crops or needing a space to butcher and process animals into food requires practical considerations such as defending against predators or the maintenance of ecological boundaries. It is quite another thing to construct landscapes that seek to communicate ideologies or meet the needs of more complex human endeavours such as industry.

Trying to determine the meaning of past landscapes involves imagining a second kind of space, a social space. Every material space is also simultaneously and seamlessly part of a social space, the space that you and I move through daily. There is, I would admit, a bit of Zen involved in looking at space in this manner. Unless the context is something such as Pompeii, it is difficult to imagine archaeology revealing this seamless link between past and present. Still, envisioning space in this manner does provide a vehicle for visualising the behaviour that shaped the social past that was a reality for the actors who lived it. The Zen part is how I reconcile what could be a contradiction in seeing these spaces existing simultaneously. Beyond just conceiving of space in this manner, there also comes the challenge of using techniques such as micro-stratigraphic analysis or a combination of paleoethnobotany and soil chemistry to examine its social and biophysical development. For me, there is some irony in using this kind of science to explore something seemingly as metaphysical as past social space, but in my experience that is the only way of actually doing it.[25] This assumes, of course, a rich archaeological record and in some instances such a record simply doesn't exist, and therefore it may not always be possible to succeed in exploring space in this manner.

Both material and social spaces are themselves shot through with what I call cultural historical space, that world in which people lived, the context that brought meaning to their lives. In some respects, it is this space that is the ultimate goal of all archaeology, trying to reconstruct the world of the mind and the forces swirling around it that shape that mind. Religion, ideology, notions of gender and class – these all contribute to the cultural historical space that serves as context for living. In a city such as Lowell, Massachusetts where I have worked extensively, the actual production of space involved the reification of class, gender and ethnicity in addition to meeting the core needs of industry.[26] Industrial space in cities such as Lowell as well as that of rural industry is normally conceived as serving very practical ends. Yet often these same spaces were arenas of contestation in which conflict was played out in such a manner as to accentuate the juxtaposition of planned purpose, most notably work, and its antithesis, refusing to work. An example of a contested space such as this comes from Lowell where mill yards designed to promote efficiency were used as arenas to protest working conditions or wages. In the process, the original purpose of the space was contrapuntally transformed into a representational space; a site of public protest and contestation.[27]

Other examples of these kinds of contested spaces come from colonial contexts in which the colonised seek refuge from colonial forces. In my current work, this notion of space has worked quite well in interpreting the lives of 17th- and 18th-century Native Americans who sought to carve out spaces of autonomy and resistance against the creeping forces of European colonialism. As their former world collapsed, drawing ever closer, Native peoples such as the Nipmuc of Massachusetts and Connecticut created spaces that allowed them to maintain cultural practices under the guise of religious conversion. Only through detailed analysis of material culture can such practices be discerned often as hybridised forms. These can include European material culture being used for very different purposes such as glass tumblers serving as cutting tools or, in one instance, the placement of quartz crystals – which have a long history of Native use for spiritual purposes – in the corners of a foundation of an 'English Style' meeting house of a Christianised Native community.[28] The material space in which such activities took place, and their spatial dimensions, are simultaneously and seamlessly linked to the cultural historical realities these Native peoples were experiencing while their world collapsed around them. In this sense, what might be interpreted correctly as a form of cultural mimicry – the appropriation of the cultural trappings of one's oppressors as a form of defiance – represents a form of civil disobedience.[29] The use of mimicry as a way of constructing a space of refuge and survival, what Bhabha calls 'a third space', involves the creation of something completely different from the cultural practices that contributed to its creation.[30] This third space, although new, would still be viewed by its creators as having many of the characteristics of an earlier, pre-colonial past and, as such, a space of deeper history.

I see a point of similarity between my own notions of space and the concept of home articulated by Charles Orser in chapter 1 above. This is especially true when contrasted with its opposite, knowing when you are not home. All of us understand this full well. In my work of late, I have found the concept of well-being to be useful in this way as a state that is sought when your world is under attack. Not surprisingly, the indigenous peoples of Australia and the Torres Strait have now chosen this concept of well-being as their measuring stick, what they feel they have been denied by colonialism. Trying to make sense of such a concept for archaeology has proven challenging, but it is I think possible.[31] And in this sense I want to counter one of the points made by Tadhg O'Keeffe in chapter 6 above. I fully understand his point concerning what at times can seem like an overwhelming barrage of artefacts from archaeological sites of the modern period. Yet for me, historical archaeology has always suffered from a lack of data, and I don't mean things – oh things we have enough of – I mean data, real information. Without such information, in the form of artefacts, landscapes and environmental data, it would be extremely difficult to argue for the existence of spaces of resistance or the construction of material identities of class, gender or ethnicity. There is no question that theoretical and interpretive frameworks help in the gleaning of narratives out of the artefacts, buildings and landscapes examined by archaeologists in Ireland and Britain. Yet at times, there is something as fleeting as luck involved, finding a specific artefact that helps immeasurably in constructing a narrative of industrial worker identity or the construction of Native American spaces of refuge and survival.

POSTCOLONIAL APPROACHES

Artefacts are central to what we do in that they aid our quest to understand the past as lived and just how that past is connected to the present. Theory is also obviously important, and increasingly there is a convergence between theories that serve as frameworks for interpreting the past and theory that connects that past to present. Postcolonial theory is a good example. Postcolonial approaches have proven very useful in interpreting the archaeology of Sylvester Manor, a 17th-century plantation on Shelter Island, New York that had a workforce of enslaved Africans and local Native Americans. The plantation, which was established in 1652, provided provisions for two sugar plantations on Barbados. Working both in New York and Barbados has brought me to a new understanding of what postcolonial theorists, most of whom are writing about India, Africa and the Caribbean, have to say about the experience of the colonised. This has proven useful in my collaborative research with Tribal Nations in North America as well as with descendent populations on Barbados. It has, for example, led me to appreciate the manner in which cultural mimicry may have been at work in the past. The same is true of the notion of hybridised cultural forms such as the use of European languages to serve as a vehicle in the construction and communication of anti-colonial imagery. The same is true of space and material culture. These too can serve as mediums of resistance in countering the overwhelming power of European colonisation as I have described above.

Despite its allure, postcolonial theory, like the concept of modernity, is not without its problems, not the least of which is dealing with the fact that in some instances postcolonial scholars represent a new form of colonialism. Is my own work with Native American groups, for example, just another form of exploitation? There is also the issue of defining just where colonialism ends and a postcolonial reality begins. Just because nations have gained their political independence does not mean that colonial forces have been halted. I recently heard an interview on the BBC with a woman who had interviewed Robert Mugabe, the president of Zimbabwe, and she expressed some difficulty in trying to reconcile the African Mugabe with the English Mugabe. She noted, for example, that when Mugabe first came to power and had the first meeting of his cabinet ministers he wore a blue suit. Some of his cabinet ministers wore more traditional African garb, while others wore military fatigues. Supposedly, he turned to them as a group and said we may be Africans but we are going to be setting a European-style government, so from now on we will all wear blue suits. So where, then, is the line between colonial past and postcolonial reality? It will be a long time before that colonial past and some postcolonial future are easy to discern.

Another reality that has emerged as an outgrowth of confronting the issues raised by postcolonial theory has been the importance of engaging in collaborative research. In the same manner that collaborating with my colleagues at the Fiske Center is essential in constructing a richer understanding of the past, I now find myself working with the Nipmuc Tribal Nation, since it is their history that I am pursuing. And this collaboration means working with the members of the Tribal Council to insure that the questions being pursued archaeologically are consistent with their own interests, and many of these have to do with demonstrating cultural continuity as part of legal issues surrounding Federal Tribal Recognition. For the Nipmuc, these are very serious issues, and our work is essential for them to supply scientific evidence that their people did not disappear, that in fact they participated in the same commercial and cultural arenas as their white neighbours. This kind of research also can result in having to justify your own identity as an archaeologist and trying to reconcile our own use of what I like to call Empirical Imperialism; that ability we have to abstract everything, including people, into data. Such an approach may work with the dead, although even that is not the case in North America, but when dealing with the living you must address these questions, as difficult as they may be. And this also often entails understanding the kinds of cultural baggage we each carry into our work.

Part of that cultural baggage is the baggage of empire, and here, I think, our work has a real role to play in trying to discern the connections between colonialism, industry, the growth of cities, capitalism and empire. When I worked in Britain on Anglo-Saxon sites I found myself in awe of the Romans. What impressed me the most was the manner in which they understood the connections between cities and colonial rule, industry – on a different scale, of course – and commercial integration into a larger whole that was empire. Many of the landscapes we encounter in our work are also expressions of empire. This is especially true of those that communicate order – the perfectly manicured pleasure gardens of the 17th and 18th centuries, industrial landscapes that extend from the factories to workers' housing and that of their managers, or sites of memorial to celebrate conquest. These landscapes all reinforce the notion that order is a product of nature, with Europeans at its apex.[32] As such, landscapes such as these are also vehicles for the communication of both modernism and modernity. If the concept of modernity can be extended to encompass colonialism, as Homi Bhabha and others have suggested, then it may hold promise as an interpretive framework despite its problems. According to Bhabha, modernity has its roots in early European colonialism, and if such a connection can be explored archaeologically then it might offer some conceptual utility in searching for the origins of the modern world.[33] It might also help in the pursuit of an important set of corollary questions surrounding the end of empire. In the same manner that the construction and reinforcement of empire can be read in landscapes and other material form, is it not possible to search for evidence of its demise? It may well be that the evidence would come not in some colossal collapse that might involve the large-scale replacement of one landscape with another. Instead, it might come in more subtle form, such as defective military technology[34] or evidence of slums in colonial capitals such as Jamestown, as Horning has discussed.[35] In either case, the end of empire might come in a form that could hold lessons for the neo-colonial reality of today's world.

CONCLUSION: COMING TO TERMS WITH IMPERIAL AND INDUSTRIAL LEGACIES

Celebrating empire can be a touchy business, especially when you have to confront its residue, its legacy. In Barbados, for example, the British colonial legacy is very evident in the Parish school uniforms the children still wear and which many still admire for the help they offer in maintaining discipline. And of course cricket. Here is a very good demonstration of postcolonial theory because, as you all know, the changes that Caribbean players brought to the game of cricket transformed it. Other legacies of empire are not so easy to celebrate. Many of my colleagues working in Africa or the Caribbean examine the legacies of empire, and often this involves politically sensitive issues. Yet the bounds of empire are not always so distant from the metropolitan core. Audrey Horning has discussed the use of archaeology as a way of working through political tensions, and there seems little question that this is one of the most important directions in the field's future.[36] The growth of Indigenous Archaeologies in places such as Australia, New Zealand and North America also represent attempts to confront the legacies of empire and colonialism as a whole.[37]

Industry too is difficult to celebrate unless one is willing to confront some of its social and environmental legacies. In my own work, I have tried to understand the impact of industry on the health of the workers and those who managed them. I have combined this with studies of material culture to see just how notions such as 'middle class' and 'working class' were constructed materially.[38] In Lowell, for example, I found that the material trappings of workers, overseers and mill agent's households were not so clearly defined, despite the class-laden images contained in a century of literature obsessed with class. To read that literature would leave you with an image of dire poverty and great contrasts in wealth, but in the material record the lines are not so clear. Take a practice such as drinking. Despite the temperance movement of the mid-19th century, material evidence clearly shows that virtually everyone consumed liquor, although some were more ingenious than others in the manner in which they drank. Some would literally hide their drinking, and evidence of this was found in Lowell. There was also evidence that medicines that were laden with alcohol and narcotics, especially those prescribed for women's menstrual cramps, were being widely consumed. These medicines provided cover for those who sought to conceal their consumption behaviour from either the company hierarchy or from a spouse.

Where class differences were clearly discernible was in the way the cities and companies chose to provide their workers with access to domestic technologies such as piped-in water. In Lowell, only management received these benefits despite the order of the local boards of health to rid the company housing complexes of privies. This order was given in 1880, and yet archaeology clearly demonstrates that privies were still in use until the outbreak of the influenza epidemic in 1918.

Historical archaeologists working in areas that traditionally were thought to be some of the worst slums imaginable have found evidence of a more complicated picture. This is especially true of the work done by Rebecca Yamin and her colleagues connected with the Five Points project in New York City.[39] Here once again we are confronted with mythical images that essentialise the working class in the same manner that the literature of empire portrayed the indigenous populations of much of the world.[40] Whether it is by describing their appearance, their eating practices or their sexual proclivities, the working class and indigenous populations are depicted as something 'other' than those whose ascendancy to power, in terms of either capital or empire, were somehow preordained by God. And yet, the archaeology of both the working class and indigenous communities is painting a very different picture of the past. Poverty and oppression are evident, but there is also evidence of agency and resistance, especially in the construction of hybridised realities that all too often are forgotten or silenced. Hopefully, the archaeology of the modern period can help in the realisation of a new history in which the contributions of those whose pasts have been silenced can now be celebrated. I believe that the archaeology of the last five hundred years is arguably the most important archaeology done today because it is linked directly not just to the present, but to our future. And, therefore, I would argue that the archaeology of the Modern World must be both theoretically robust and methodologically precise. If we are to use archaeology as a means of understanding the world in which we live, can we ask any less of ourselves?

NOTES

1. See Cranstone 2004; Donnelly & Horning 2002; Horning 2006a.
2. See, for example, Saitta 2007; Shackel 2000, 2001, 2003.
3. Bayley 1998; Bayley & Crossley 2004; Bell and Dark 1998.
4. See Mrozowski 2006a.
5. See Mrozowski 1999a, 2006a.
6. See Escobar 1999.
7. See, for example, Orser 1996; Green 2006; Lawrence 2006; Paynter 2000a & b; Hall 2000; Hall & Silliman 2006.
8. See Harvey 1989; Jameson 1991; Lefebvre 1995, 168–72; Parry 2004, 148–50.
9. There are a number of problems that the concept raises, not the least of which is distinguishing modernity and modernism. The latter has a long history as part of a consciousness of what is fashionable, most up to date and new (Lefebvre 1995, 1). This stands in sharp contrast to the modernity that is a programme of critical, self-reflective thought that became popular at the end of the 19th century and dominated the intellectual scene in Europe well into the 20th century (Lefebvre 1995; see also Comaroff & Comaroff 1993, xii; Harvey 1989, 2000; Jameson 1991; Parry 2004; Said 1993, 186–90).
10. See Mrozowski 1999a, 2006b, but see Cranstone 2004 for a cogent argument against the use of the term Historical Archaeology in the European context.
11. Cranstone 2004; Green 2006; Johnson 2002, 2006a; Horning 2006.
12. Johnson 1996; Mrozowski 1999a; 2006b.
13. See Powlesland 1998, 1999.
14. See Mrozowski, Bell, Beaudry, Landon & Kelso 1989.
15. David Landon, pers. comm. May 2008.
16. Landon 1999.
17. Mrozowski 2006b; see also Beaudry & Mrozowski 2001.
18. Morgan 1971.
19. Stahle *et al* 1998.
20. Johnson 2006b.
21. Escobar 1999; Harvey 1989, 2000; Lefebvre 1991, 1995; Soja 1989, 2000; Zukin 1991; see also Kofman & Lebas 1995.
22. See Delle 1998; Johnson 1996; Mrozowski 1999, 2006; Tarlow 1999.
23. Mrozowski 1999b, 2006b.
24. Delle 1998; Escobar 1999.
25. For a recent example, see Hayes & Mrozowski 2007.
26. Mrozowski 2006b.
27. Beaudry & Mrozowski 2001; Mrozowski 2006b.
28. See Law 2008; Law, Pezzarossi & Mrozowski 2008; Mrozowski, Herbster, Brown & Priddy 2005.
29. Bhabha 1985, 163; see also Ashcroft 2001, 50–5; Parry 2004, 55–72; Rutherford 1990.
30. Bhabha 1985, 1994; Rutherford 1990.
31. Mrozowski, Franklin & Hunt 2008.
32. For a good example of memorialising empire, see Petts 2006.
33. See Rutherford 1990; Jameson 1991; Parry 2004.
34. See Gould 1983.
35. Horning 2006b.
36. Horning 2006a.
37. See Atalay 2006; Echo-Hawk and Zimmerman 2006;

Silliman 2008; Smith and Jackson 2006.   39. Yamin 2000, 2001, 2006.
38. Mrozowski 2006b.   40. Parry 2004.

BIBLIOGRAPHY

Ashcroft, B. 2001, *Post-Colonial Transformation*. New York: Routledge.

Atalay, S. 2006, 'Indigenous archaeology as decolonizing practice', *American Indian Quarterly* **30**(3&4): 280–310.

Barker, D. & Cranstone, D. (eds) 2004, *The Archaeology of Industrialization*. Leeds: Maney.

Bayley, J. (ed.) 1998, *Science in Archaeology: An Agenda for the Future*. London: English Heritage.

Bayley, J. & Crossley D. 2004, 'Archaeological science as an aid to the study of post-medieval industrialization', in Barker & Cranstone (eds), 2004, 15–23.

Beaudry, M.C. & Mrozowski, S.A. 2001, 'Cultural space and work identity in the company city: nineteenth century Lowell, Massachusetts', in Mayne & Murray (eds), 2001, 118–31.

Bell, M. & Dark, P. 1998, 'Continuity and change: environmental archaeology in historic periods', in Bayley (ed.), 1998, 179–93.

Bhabha, H.K. 1985, 'Signs taken for wonders: questions of ambivalence and authority under a tree outside Dehli, May 1817', *Critical Inquiry* **12**(1): 144–65.

Bhabba, H.K. 1994, *The Location of Culture*. London: Routledge.

Campsi, J. (ed.) 2005, *Eighteenth Century Native Communities of Southern New England in the Colonial Context*, The Mashantucket Museum and Research Center Occasional Paper **1**.

Comaroff, J. & Commaroff J. 1993, *Modernity and its Malcontents: Ritual and Power In Postcolonial Africa*. Chicago: University of Chicago Press.

Cranstone, D. 2004, 'The archaeology of industrialization – new directions', in Barker & Cranstone (eds), 2004, 313–20.

Delle, J.A. 1998, *An Archaeology of Social Space: Analyzing Coffee Plantations in Jamaica's Blue Mountains*. New York: Plenum Press.

Donnelly, C.J. & Horning, A. 2002, 'Post-medieval and industrial archaeology in Ireland: an overview', *Antiquity* **76**: 557–61.

Echo-Hawk, R. & Zimmerman, L.J. 2006, 'Beyond racism: some opinions about racialism and American archaeology', *American Indian Quarterly* **30**(3&4): 461–85.

Egan, G. & Michael, R.L. (eds) 1999, *Old and New Worlds*. Oxford: Oxbow Books.

Escobar, A. 1999, 'Steps to an anti-essentialist political ecology', *Current Anthropology* **40**(1): 1–16.

Gould, R. 1983, 'The archaeology of war: wrecks of the Spanish Armada of 1588 and the Battle of Britain 1940', in Gould (ed.), 1983, 105–42.

Gould, R. (ed.) 1983, *Shipwreck Anthropology*. Albuquerque: University of New Mexico Press.

Green, Adrian 2006, 'Introduction: urban historical archaeology: challenging ambivalence', in Green & Leech (eds), 2006, 1–13.

Green, A. & Leech, R. (eds) 2006, *Cities in the World, 1500–2000*. Leeds: Maney.

Hall, M. 2000, *Archaeology and the Modern World: Colonial Transcripts in South Africa and the Chesapeake*. London: Routledge.

Hall, M. & Silliman, S.W. (eds) 2006, *Historical Archaeology*. Oxford: Blackwell.

Harvey, D. 1989, *The Condition of Postmodernity*. Oxford: Oxford University Press.

Harvey, D. 2000, *Spaces of Hope*. Berkeley: University of California Press.

Hawkes, J. & Mills, S. (eds) 1999, *Northumbria's Golden Age*. Stroud: Sutton.

Hayes, K.H. & Mrozowski, S. (eds) 2007, *The Historical Archaeology of Sylvester Manor*, special issue, *Northeast Historical Archaeology* **36**.

Horning, A. 2006a, 'Archaeology, conflict and contemporary identity in the North of Ireland. Implications for theory and practice in comparative archaeologies of colonialism', *Archaeological Dialogues* **13**(2): 183– 200.

Horning, A. 2006b, 'English towns on the periphery: 17th-century development in Ulster and the Chesapeake', in Green & Leech (eds), 2006, 61–81.

Jameson, F. 1991, *Postmodernism, or the Cultural Logic of Late Capitalism*. London: Verso.

Johnson, M. 1996, *An Archaeology of Capitalism*. Oxford: Blackwell.

Johnson, M. 2002, *Behind the Castle Gate: from Medieval to Renaissance*. London: Routledge.

Johnson, M. 2006a, 'The tide reversed: prospects and potentials for a postcolonial archaeology of Europe', in Hall & Silliman (eds), 2006, 313–31.

Johnson, M. 2006b, *Ideas of Landscape: An Introduction*. Oxford: Blackwell.

Kofman, E. & Lebas, E. 1995, *Writings on Cities, Henri Lefebvre*. Oxford: Blackwell.

Landon, D.B. 1999, 'Interpreting social organization at industrial sites: an example from the Ohio Trap Rock Mine', *Northeast Journal of Historical Archaeology* **28**: 89–103.

Law, H. 2008, 'Daily negotiations and the creation of an alternative discourse: the legacy of a colonial Nipmuc farmstead', unpublished Master's thesis, Department of Anthropology, University of Massachusetts, Boston.

Law, H., Pezzarossi, G. & Mrozowski, S.A. 2008, 'Archaeological intensive excavations: Hassanamesit Woods property, The Sarah Boston Farmstead, Grafton, Massachusetts', *Andrew Fiske Memorial Center for Archaeological Research, Cultural Resource Management Study* **24**. Boston: University of Massachusetts.

Lawrence, S. 2006, 'Overburden: the importance of the archaeology of the modern period in Britain', in Green & Leech (eds), 2006, 307–19.

Lefebvre, H. 1991, *The Production of Space*. Oxford: Blackwell.

Lefebvre, H. 1995, *Introduction to Modernity*. London: Verso.

Mayne, A. & Murray, T. (eds) 2001, *The Archaeology of Urban Landscapes: Explorations in Slumland*. Cambridge: Cambridge University Press.

Morgan, Edward S. 1971, 'The first American boom: Virginia 1618–1630', *William & Mary Quarterly*, third series **18**(2): 169–98.

Mrozowski, S.A. 1999a, 'Interdisciplinary perspectives on the production of urban industrial space', in Egan & Michael (eds), 1999, 136–46.

Mrozowski, S.A. 1999b, 'The commodification of nature', *International Journal of Historical Archaeology* **3**(3): 153–66.

Mrozowski, S.A. 2006a, 'Environments of history: biological dimensions of historical archaeology', in Hall & Silliman (eds), 2006, 23–41.

Mrozowski, S.A. 2006b, *The Archaeology of Class in Urban America*. Cambridge: Cambridge University Press.

Mrozowski, S.A., Franklin M. & Hunt, L. 2008, 'Archaeobotanical analysis and interpretations of enslaved Virginian plant use at Richneck Plantation (44WB52)', *American Antiquity* **73**(4): 699–728.

Mrozowski, S.A., Herbster, H., Brown, D. & Priddy, K.L. 2005, 'Magunkaquog: Native American conversion and cultural persistence', in Campsi (ed.), 2005, 57–71.

Mrozowski, S.A., Bell, E.L., Beaudry, M.C., Landon, D.B. & Kelso, G. 1989, 'Living on the Boott: health and well being in a boardinghouse population', *World Archaeology* **21**(2): 298–319.

Orser, C.E. 1996, *A Historical Archaeology of the Modern World*. New York: Plenum.

Parry, B. 2004, *Postcolonial Studies: A Materialist Critique*. New York: Routledge.

Paynter, R. 2000a, 'Historical archaeology and the post-Columbian world', *Journal of Archaeological Research* **8**(3): 169–217.

Paynter, R. 2000b, 'Historical and anthropological archaeology: forging alliances', *Journal of Archaeological Research* **8**(1): 1–37.

Petts, D. 2006, 'Landscapes of memory: Lucknow and Kanpur in colonial India', in Green & Leech (eds), 2006, 195–212.

Powlesland, D. 1998, 'The West Heslerton assessment', *Internet Archaeology* **5** <http://intarch.ac.uk/journal/issue5/index.html>.

Powlesland, D. 1999, 'The Anglo-Saxon settlement at West Heslerton, North Yorkshire', in Hawkes & Mills (eds), 1999, 55–65.

Rutherford, J. 1990, 'The third space: interview with Homi Bhabba', *Identity: Community Culture and Difference*. London: Lawrence & Wishart, 207–21.

Said, E.W. 1993, *Culture and Imperialism*. New York: Vintage Books.

Saitta, D.J. 2007, *The Archaeology of Collective Action*. Gainesville: University of Florida Press.

Shackel, P.A. 2000, *Archaeology and Created Memory: Public History in a National Park*. New York: Kluwer.

Shackel, P.A. 2001, 'Public memory and the search for power in American historical archaeology', *American Anthropologist* **102**(3): 1–16.

Shackel, P.A. 2003, *Memory in Black and White: Race, Commemoration, and the Post-Bellum Landscape*. Walnut Creek, CA: AltaMira Press.

Silliman, S.W. (ed.) 2008, *Collaborative Archaeology at the Trowel's Edge: Learning and Teaching in Indigenous Archaeology*. Tucson: University of Arizona Press.

Smith, C. & Jackson, G. 2006, 'Decolonizing indigenous archaeology: developments from Down Under', *American Indian Quarterly* **30**(3&4): 311–49.

Soja, E.W. 1989, *Postmodern Geographies: The Reassertion of Space in Critical Social Theory*. London: Verso.

Soja, E.W. 2000, *Postmetropolis: Critical Studies of Cities and Regions*. Oxford: Blackwell.

Stahle, D.W., Cleavland, M.K., Blanton, D.B., Therrell, M.D. & Gay, D.A. 1998, 'The Jamestown and Lost Colony droughts', *Science* **280**: 564–7.

Tarlow, S. 1999, 'Capitalism and critique', *Antiquity* **73**(280): 467–70.

Yamin, R. (ed.) 2000, *Tales of Five Points: Working Class Life in 19th-Century New York*, 6 vols. Report submitted to the General Services Administration, Region 2, Philadelphia: John Milnor Associates.

Yamin, R. 2001, 'Alternative narratives: respectability at New York's Five Points', in Mayne & Murray (eds), 2001, 154–70.

Yamin, R. 2006, 'From the mythical to the mundane: the archaeological angle on New York City's Five Points', in Green & Leech (eds), 2006, 281–97.

Zukin, S. 1991, *Landscapes of Power, From Detroit to Disney World*. Berkeley: University of California Press.

Conclusion – The Way Forward?

By MARILYN PALMER & AUDREY HORNING

INTRODUCTION

The process of conceptualising and implementing the *Crossing Paths or Sharing Tracks?* conference, and the subsequent compilation and editing of this volume, has been an interesting, mostly enjoyable, but admittedly occasionally tense experience for us as editors. To some extent, our differing backgrounds exemplify the point of the whole endeavour: we do not always agree with one another's perspective, we come from different educational, professional and cultural backgrounds, but we both believe strongly and indeed passionately that the study of the material heritage of the past five hundred years, whatever we choose to call it, is important, is valid, and has a role to play in contemporary society.

We both see archaeology as fundamentally about people rather than just about things, but equally we would argue that it is in understanding the reflexive relationship between people and things that will bring a rapprochement between the 'camps' whose perspectives have been highlighted throughout this volume. We don't pretend to have solved any of the major dilemmas facing the academic, commercial, public and avocational constituencies represented in this volume, nor to have agreed upon more unified theoretical or legislative frameworks for advancing understandings of the material legacy of the last five centuries. We do wish to promote continued dialogue and mutual respect, if not full agreement, within and beyond what Matthew Johnson referred to in his Foreword as the 'archaeological family'. With that goal in mind, the following discussion endeavours to contextualise some of the discussions raised at the conference and in this publication.

CHALLENGING CHRONOLOGY

When the Society for Post-Medieval Archaeology (SPMA) and the Association for Industrial Archaeology (AIA) were founded in the 1960s, the differences between them were perceived to be ones of chronology and approach. The Editor of the first volume of the journal *Post-Medieval Archaeology* in 1967 defined the chronological scope of the society as 'the period of the unification of states within the British Isles, the establishment of Britain upon the path of maritime colonial expansion and the initial stages of industrial growth'. At that time, then, post-medieval archaeology in Britain had a *terminus post quem* of *c.* 1750–80. Industrial archaeology was traditionally located in the period after *c.* 1750, picking up where post-medieval archaeology left off, albeit focusing on industrial sites rather than the full range of post-1750 above- and below-ground archaeology. The conference and the chapters in this book have thrown into considerable doubt these traditional chronological divisions, which the participating societies had already begun to question and discard. For its part, the Irish Post-Medieval Archaeology Group (IPMAG) has never specified any end-date for its advocacy of historical/post-medieval archaeology.

While we have framed this publication as addressing the archaeological study of post-1550 Britain and Ireland, we fully recognise that '1550' is an arbitrary date. People did not wake up and suddenly become 'post-medieval' at the turn of that year. Even with all the political, social and economic turmoil associated with the Reformation, and all the reconfigurations of the 'known' world resultant of exploration and expansion into the New World, one can easily find as much continuity as change in the archaeological and historical records of 16th-century Britain and Ireland. While a 16th-century date arguably makes greater sense as a marker for the start of historical archaeology in parts of the world penetrated by European settlers, many scholars would now argue that the break between history and prehistory, as once understood in the Americas and Australasia, has been much exaggerated. It is itself a legacy of a colonial mindset that viewed cultural change as only being driven by the forces of Western 'civilisation'. Historical archaeologists in these regions are now engaged in more sophisticated examinations of the ways in which both colonisers and indigenous peoples responded to culture contact and colonialism, a new research direction and context in which descendants of those indigenous people play a considerable part. So as our colleagues elsewhere in the world redefine their practices, we should not be constrained by our own traditional terminologies and chronologies, a point made by many of the contributors to this volume.

So if we can introduce some fuzziness to the meaning of 'post-medieval', what about the meaning of the 'industrial revolution'? In 1995, an English Heritage policy document suggested that 'it is the classic constituents of the Industrial Revolution – capital investment, organised labour, technological development, and the factory scale of production which characterise the field of industrial archaeology'.[1] By contrast, many of the contributors to the conference and this book have suggested some interesting redefinitions of the concept of the Industrial Revolution that challenge this view. These redefinitions reflect the major swings of interpretation of industrialisation in the last half-century, partly brought about by the process of massive de-industrialisation in Britain, which, arguably, has led to a crisis of identity. Whereas Peter Matthias could call his 1969 textbook on the economic history of Britain from 1700 to 1914 *The First Industrial Nation*, Britain is no longer even an industrial nation. Much of British industry has become part of the iconography of past glories – long-abandoned industrial sites have been made part of the national heritage and described by some as the 'industrial picturesque'. Paul Belford in this volume points out that industrial sites appear to be more highly valued once they are clearly post-industrial, as is the case in all the United Kingdom's industrial World Heritage Sites, including the Ironbridge Gorge in England, Blaenavon in Wales and New Lanark in Scotland.

The concept of a sudden Industrial Revolution has been replaced by emphasis on slow, continuous change rather than the dramatic break with the past that the term 'Industrial

Revolution' once conveyed, a view put forward in this volume by several contributors, including David Cranstone and Paul Belford. Furthermore, Caron Newman and Richard Newman have stressed how much industry was present in what appeared to be rural landscapes well before 1750. Cranstone then argues that this might suggest there was in fact a 'long industrial revolution' starting arguably in the 15th century, as opposed to the conventional 'short Industrial Revolution' of the 18th century.

Cranstone has also put forward an alternative hypothesis that the Industrial Revolution was in fact a two-stage process, an earlier 'extractive Industrial Revolution' whose origins could be placed at any one of several points between the mid-15th and the late 17th centuries, followed by a 'manufacturing Industrial Revolution' from *c.* 1750. This idea is well worth exploring by post-medieval and industrial archaeologists alike. Did the later 'manufacturing Industrial Revolution' bring about a greater degree of organisational change that is reflected in buildings, landscapes and settlement patterns? We would argue that more nuanced frameworks of analysis should bring out the true nature of industrialisation. For example, the roles of women – and, in fact, of children – in this later 'manufacturing Industrial Revolution' have often been hidden through the use of statistical determinants that are all based on male occupational categories. It is clear also that the new forms of industrial organisation that were deployed in a variety of industries including textile manufacture, boots and shoes and metal working included the juxtaposition of machine-based production with the continuation of outwork, something that has been the subject of considerable archaeological and architectural analysis in recent years.[2]

Undoubtedly, too, this 'manufacturing Industrial Revolution' brought about, or was brought about by, a whole series of inventions in the late 18th century and the application to industry of new kinds of mechanical power that have been of considerable interest to the avocational members of organisations such as the AIA: for example, the detailed photography by Colin Bowden of stationary steam engines in Britain and Europe, which created an invaluable archive of a vanishing artefact.[3] Finally, too, as Colin Rynne has shown in his study of the Haulbowline naval base in County Cork, British and Irish industrialisation has to be set in the framework of overseas expansion, as Britain seized the opportunity to provide the commercial and industrial needs not just of colonial territories but of many of the world's nations as they, too, industrialised. So, perhaps the term 'Industrial Revolution' still has some relevance to how society developed from the 18th century onwards, but that does not mean that the two 'industrial revolutions' that Cranstone has postulated have to be studied by two different groups of people!

It is clear, then, that the chronological divisions accepted in the 1950s are no longer valid for the study of the post-1550 archaeology of Britain. Such divisions have never really been a part of Irish archaeology, nor of English-speaking areas of the world such as Australia where industrial sites have always been treated in the same way as any other archaeological site. Ian Jack and Judy Birmingham pointed out in *Australian Pioneer Technology: Sites and Relics* (1979) that the use of the term 'industrial archaeology' in Australia was inappropriate since the time span of British industrial archaeology embraced the whole of Australian history since European settlement.

With the turn of the 21st century, archaeologists have also begun to increasingly look back at the 20th century and to consider its material manifestations from an archaeological point of view. Many of the developments in this area are directly attributable to individuals active with the Contemporary Historical Archaeology and Theory (CHAT) conferences and list-serve. Pragmatically, the growth of interest in the recent past can also be linked to the age-related criteria of much heritage legislation. However, as exemplified by the work of James Dixon and Emma Dwyer as presented in this publication, the focus on the recent past also reflects an increasing recognition that 'historic' sites and materials actively structure contemporary life and, as such, need to be understood in terms of this continuum. Somewhat paradoxically, however, the growing interest in the recent and contemporary past[4] has also led to a situation where the potential of an archaeology focusing upon non-industrial 19th-century sites and early 20th-century sites has been overshadowed. The discussions in this volume by Alasdair Brooks, Nigel Jeffries *et al.*, Craig Cessford and Eleanor Casella raise hope for greater interest in domestic sites of the 19th century.

The situation in Ireland as regards the archaeological treatment of so-called 'industrial period' sites is less settled. The cut-off date of 1700 employed in National Monuments legislation (used for defining ancient monuments) has been widely misinterpreted to mean that sites dating after that period have no archaeological value, with a review of urban archaeological practice concluding that in some developer-driven urban excavations,

virtually no post-1700 archaeology is investigated. In places this appears to be more or less a matter of policy, related to the notional cut-off date attributed to the legislation…. In other cases this trend was attributed more to a pragmatic decision that while post-medieval and industrial archaeology is sometimes important, there has usually been more than enough to do to cope with the pressures on the really important Viking and early medieval periods. [5]

It is easy to be contemptuous of what is familiar. After all, as pointed out by O'Keeffe in this volume, Irish landscapes, streetscapes and back gardens are filled with the material debris of the 19th century in particular. We hope that a growing awareness of the unique contributions of archaeologies of the 19th century in Ireland as well as in Britain will ultimately foster greater respect and interest. The expansion of interest in postgraduate research on the period, as quantified by Breen, is certainly a positive sign. However, the cautions of O'Keeffe, Cessford and Jeffries *et al.* in relation to finding creative and sensible ways to cope with the sheer volume of material culture from the period must be heeded, if we are not to collapse under the combined weight of the carefully bagged and tagged consumer products of the industrial world unearthed on excavations.

While Irish urban archaeology may still have some way to go in developing adequate criteria for addressing post-medieval and industrial deposits, it is fair to say that Ireland, north and south, has taken a more proactive and integrated approach to post-medieval maritime archaeology. In the 1990s, government agencies in the Republic and in Northern Ireland sponsored surveys geared towards identifying maritime cultural resources. Irish maritime archaeologists consciously chose to explore the Scandinavian archaeologist Christer Westerdahl's notion of the maritime cultural landscape by exploring interface zones between land and sea as well as focusing upon submerged resources. A pioneering survey of the intertidal archaeology of Northern Ireland's Strangford Lough (a 20 mile-long by 3 mile-wide sea lough in Co. Down) revealed evidence for over 680 previously unknown sites, with post-medieval remains including harbours, quays, kelp drying stations, landing places, and fish traps and weirs.[6] The success of this study has led to further survey projects on coastal landscapes throughout Ireland and has also inspired consideration of the maritime connections of inland sites situated in areas of riverine transport and economic exploitation.[7] While the establishment of IPMAG and the expansion of post-medieval/historical archaeology in Ireland is a relatively new development compared to the well-established practice and groups within Britain, the interdisciplinary approaches employed by Irish maritime archaeology in particular are worthy of the attention of the older organisations.

CHALLENGING DIVISION

So if the differences between the groups are no longer those of chronology, are they in fact characterised by differences in approaches? As noted in the Introduction, an impetus for the conference was the increasing division and seeming fragmentation of the study of the material legacy of the past five hundred years, as exemplified by the burgeoning number of societies and venues dedicated to the discipline(s). Neither of the editors believe that this 'balkanisation', to borrow a phrase employed by Matthew Johnson in his Foreword, will lead to unified development. However, it is clear that the number of individuals interested in aspects of the overall field remains small. Far from a depressing statistic, this means that in reality, the apparent different constituencies for organisations like AIA, SPMA, IPMAG and the CHAT list in fact exhibit considerable overlap. Since we are all dealing with the material heritage of the past, we are all concerned with things, be they artefacts, structures, hedgerows, machinery or buildings.

One of the problems we face is that compared with the archaeology of earlier periods, practitioners of post-1550 archaeology need to be enabled to make more use of the scientific analysis of excavated sites and of finds, including the techniques of palynology, zooarchaeological analysis and materials science, as advocated in the chapters by Justine Bayley *et al.*, Richard Thomas, Michael Berry and Stephen Mrozowski in this volume. Since most of the excavations which are undertaken on post-1550 sites are done as part of contract archaeology, funds are rarely available for such sophisticated types of analysis. The lack of funding is based upon the misperception that these analyses are 'unnecessary' for periods that enjoy a wealth of documentary evidence. It is a case of convincing those who draw up briefs for such work that post-excavation analysis of this kind is a necessity rather than a luxury. Paul Courtney's chapter draws attention to the related dilemma in which even documentary research is not always treated seriously. Similarly, Geoff Egan highlights the need for continuing finds research, particularly to cope with the welcome expansion of archaeological excavations of 19th- and 20th-century sites. It is clear that attitudes towards the excavation and post-excavation of post-1550 sites and materials still vary wildly according to geographic region and country. We hope that the discussions included in this publication will ultimately aid in improving practice.

Here we must also acknowledge the seeming lack of congruence between the academic sector and developer-funded archaeology that has been pointed out by Paul Courtney and by Craig Cessford. We are reaching the stage when the majority of archaeology is taking place outside of the academic sector, and universities, as Cessford stresses, are generally no longer supplying the trained graduates needed to work in the field. Another aim for the *Crossing Paths or Sharing Tracks?* conference was to help in some small way to bridge the gap between the academic, CRM, developer-funded and avocational sectors in post-medieval and industrial archaeology by getting representatives of all these sectors together more effectively, to listen to each other and to try to work out a way forwards. It is clear from the research presented in this volume that there is much to gain from these conversations, and from more fully integrated practice. For example, Chris Dalglish's examination of landscapes of improvement in Scotland draws from academic research in landscape history and archaeological theory; from scientific environmental analysis; and from government- and compliance-based archaeological survey. Similarly, Emma Dwyer's examination of the Grand Eastern Railway viaduct in East London took place entirely within the context of a developer-funded archaeological assessment, yet draws heavily upon contemporary archaeological theory to produce a rich and unusual study of a seemingly well-understood type of industrial monument.

While all groups engaged in the study of post-1550 archaeology share common goals in relation to the improvement of analytical and interpretative practice, each of the societies involved in the conference have historically served slightly different but complementary purposes, as is clear from the discussions by Gwyn, Courtney, Breen, O'Keeffe and Dixon in Section One. For example, AIA is by far the largest organisation that was involved in the conference, and it has long engaged with a membership drawn from a range of sectors and backgrounds, with a strong emphasis upon avocational practitioners. As Angus Buchanan said in 1972, 'the professional skills of the architect and surveyor in measuring up buildings are of tremendous value when complex industrial buildings require careful recording, and those of the engineer are similarly indispensable when it is necessary to make a drawing of a complex piece of machinery'.[8] The value of tapping the knowledge of engineers is clearly seen in Roger Holden's contribution to this book. His understanding of technology enabled him to demonstrate how, for example, increases in speeds of a weaving loom would have a significant effect on the ways in which the workforce operated.

Few would argue with the need to broaden participation and interest in the study of the material heritage of the last five hundred years. As such, the success of AIA in attracting a diverse membership should be of interest to the other societies. Results of this wide participation include the numbers of regional conferences and county societies devoted to the practice of industrial archaeology in its traditional sense of surveying, recording, researching and in some cases preserving, industrial sites and structures. This avocational group, however, has faced its own pressures because of the greater professionalisation of industrial archaeology, resulting in our national agencies undertaking much of the recording and research on a scale beyond the reach of local groups, as acknowledged in the Introduction. Volunteers who were accustomed to undertake such work in their spare time have often complained about the comparative lack of opportunities in recent years, although the annual awards made by the AIA for field recording and publication demonstrate that a great deal of work is still being done at the local and regional levels.

Industrial archaeologists have also been very much involved in the preservation and maintenance of sites and structures and with running working machinery. Sir Neil Cossons has recently suggested that

> to the extent that much of the industrial heritage taken into captivity was, and is, in the hands of locally-based voluntary organisations, it is salutary that the academic study of industrial archaeology, with its interest in priorities, standards and order, should have such little interface with, or impact upon, those who face the day-to-day task of maintaining and opening such places to the public or with their long-term sustainability.[9]

The two constituencies are not as far apart as he supposes and have some common membership, but these voluntary preservation groups do face problems such the often ageing profile of volunteers and their lack of funds for capital investment and routine maintenance. To some extent, the Heritage Lottery Fund plays a role here within the United Kingdom, as Tony Crosby has discussed, by means of its funding strand distributed through the Industrial, Maritime and Transport Group. This, though, is capital, not recurrent, funding and there is often a considerable shortfall in what is needed to keep sites open and available to the public. While Cossons sees a lack of communication between the academic and voluntary sectors, it is clear from the case studies presented in earlier chapters that the sectors are interdependent, particularly when it comes to addressing problematic and site-specific notions of 'value' and 'significance'.

This locally based work, whether carried out by volunteers or contract archaeologists, continues to be of fundamental importance. An attempt to integrate site-specific studies in England has been the production of regional research frameworks, which are discussed in this book by Shane Gould of English Heritage. The seminars that were a preliminary to the creation of these research frameworks brought together all sectors from the volunteers to the national agencies, and all those produced so far have included sections on both post-medieval and industrial archaeology, sometimes brought together as 'modern archaeology'. As Gould points out, there has yet to be a national synthesis of their content or a critical assessment of how the research agenda and strategy are helping to shape the work undertaken within the planning system, but it is a step forwards in persuading all sectors to work within a multiscalar framework of analysis.

Industrial archaeological practice has long relied upon public involvement, and issues of public engagement have now come to the forefront of archaeological practice more generally. Doubtless each contributor to this volume possesses a different understanding and different attitude towards the relationship between archaeology and that nebulous entity termed 'the public', and consequently towards the ethics of practice in relation to various 'publics'. Over the last decade, the number of publications in archaeology more broadly that trumpet the value of engaging with 'the public' have increased exponentially. The reasons for this expansion are varied. Cynically, one can attribute the desire to engage more members of the public as a survival strategy on the part of archaeologists, particularly those whose very jobs are dependent upon public funding. Central to many formulations of public archaeology is education, and the responsibility of archaeologists as keepers of information to dispense insights widely.[10] In this model, archaeologists essentially serve as gatekeepers and holders of knowledge. 'Doing' public archaeology thus can mean as little as giving a lecture and running a few site tours. At the other end of the spectrum, however, public archaeology can mean just that – archaeology done by the public. In this formulation, professional archaeologists relinquish control, allowing non-specialists to set agendas. The intellectual justification for this approach rests with the desire to move away from the elitism of the discipline and to acknowledge not only the concerns of non-archaeologists but to acknowledge the depth of knowledge they may possess. For others there is an element of political activism inherent to public, or community, archaeology.

Each of these definitions of public archaeology boils down to perceptions of the role of the archaeologist and the appropriate uses of archaeological knowledge. Arguably, the pursuit of any form of public archaeology that is focused on the relatively recent past is likely to resonate at a much more intimate level than that of other periods, given politics and personal identities. In Ireland, the development of post-medieval/historical archaeology, as discussed by Colin Breen, Tadhg O'Keeffe, Charles Orser and Colin Rynne in this volume, was clearly constrained by divisive understandings of the significance of the events of the last five hundred years marked in particular by the expansion of British control. Coping with dichotomous understandings of Ireland's colonial/non-colonial history is an integral part of the practice of archaeology on the island. Archaeology in the public realm arguably has the potential to ameliorate present-day tensions through revealing the complicated character of the past.

CHALLENGING DISCIPLINES

As Charles Orser has pointed out in this volume, archaeology is uniquely site-specific, and few archaeologists would ever wish to abandon that focus. However, he also points out that the archaeologists' connection to 'the local' has often worked against what they might accomplish on a broader scale. A number of authors in this publication raise similar concerns about the need to situate localised research into broader conceptual frameworks that acknowledge and address some of the global processes that structured everyday life in the past five hundred-plus years. These processes are explicitly tied up with the expansion of Europeans around the globe, and include colonialism, transatlantic slavery and the African Diaspora, the emergence of mercantile to industrial capitalism, and overall the development of what has been termed the 'modern' world and the global economy.

Consideration of these themes leads to another source of debate and disagreement within British and Irish post-medieval and industrial archaeology: the influence of anthropologically grounded historical archaeology as it has developed in North America and Australasia. In this volume, Paul Courtney expresses the opinions of many British practitioners when he sets out the reasons why he finds American historical archaeology to be inappropriate for European research contexts, focusing on the specifics of European nation state formation. In contrast, Tadhg O'Keeffe strongly argues that it is the anthropological and theoretical frameworks of historical archaeology that are the only way forward for Irish historical archaeology. Not surprisingly, American historical archaeologists Charles Orser and Stephen Mrozowski advocate for the incorporation of anthropological theoretical insights, while Eleanor Casella demonstrates the utility of ethnoarchaeological research in her consideration of Alderley Edge, Cheshire.

So, is anthropologically based historical archaeology truly inappropriate in European contexts, or is it more a matter of the need to construct specific, contextualised approaches that do not borrow willy-nilly from practices developed in other countries? Are American historical archaeologists imposing themselves on the rest of the world, or do they have important insights to share? For that matter, what can the rest of the world learn from the practice of post-medieval and industrial archaeology in Britain and Ireland? Steve Mrozowski provides an answer in his chapter, when he notes that one of the reasons he has such 'respect for the archaeology done in Britain and Ireland is that the practices of archaeology – field work, recording, analysis, interpretation – are all equally valued'.

Given the wide range of sources we can draw upon, it is clear that many related disciplines intersect with our study. In addition to anthropology, contributors to this volume have acknowledged the importance of materials science, environmental science, biology, geography, landscape history, economic history, engineering, art history and folklife. On the European Continent, folklife studies emerged in the late 19th century in response to the perceived erosion of tradition rural ways of life through industrialisation and urbanisation, and to a new consciousness about nationality. An expression of this movement was the creation of the first public open-air folk museum at Skansen in Stockholm in 1891, followed by others in the Baltic countries: Den Gamle By in Denmark, founded in 1909, conserved urban rather than rural buildings and made use of them to display as well as to study urban crafts and industries. St Fagans in Wales, set up in 1948, maintains a Social and Cultural History Department whose primary purpose is to illustrate and interpret the daily life and work of the people of Wales, while in Northern Ireland the Ulster Folk and Transport Museum and the Ulster American Folk Park perform a similar functions.

However, these folklife museums still rely upon the exhibition of buildings divorced from their original archaeological and landscape contexts to present essentialised rather than the contextualised understandings of rural life that would be possible through the incorporation of site-specific analysis. While the aim of the Society for Folk Life Studies is the interdisciplinary study of regional cultures and traditions, clearly of relevance to both post-medieval and industrial archaeology, there is obviously a strong need for archaeology of the post-1550 period to not only be influenced by other disciplines, but more importantly, to exert an influence upon those disciplines.

CONCLUSION: THE WAY FORWARD?

So where does the future lie for the combined study of the material legacy of post-1550 Britain and Ireland? By way of conclusion, it is worth returning to words of David Cranstone:

> While clearly there is a need at one level for a 'large tent' within which all those concerned
> with the archaeology of the later second millennium can contribute and communicate (hopefully with
> some mutual understanding and respect, despite what can be quite deep differences in background and

perception), that tent needs to contain (and actively retain) rooms within which each of its constituent groups can communicate at their own level and feel at home. Rather than aiming for too much 'muffling inclusivity' within an over-synthetic social archaeology, we need to celebrate our differences and the dialogue between them as a 'unity in diversity'.

Do the authors in this volume share any common ground to facilitate those conversations inside David Cranstone's 'tent'? Consensus arises on several points. First, there is a plea that runs through this publication that in striving to 'forge the future' for a more integrated study of the past, we must not overlook or indeed disrespect the accomplishments of those who have proceeded us in promoting industrial/historical/post-medieval archaeologies. Where would we be without the pioneering studies of landscapes, ceramics, engines, deeds, maps, pollen? Where would be without the efforts of all those volunteers as well as university scholars, finds specialists, excavation technicians, engineers, scientists and historians? Equally, where would we be without all those who sought and tested a range of interpretive frameworks in order to synthesise all of this evidence? And aren't all of these approaches, plus all those that will undoubtedly arise, worth consideration at some level? Not a single author in this volume has advocated eschewing questions of technology, questions of theory or questions of practice, while at the same time being explicit about their own interests, experiences, and contributions. Secondly, the perceived animosity between practitioners of differing perspectives that in part inspired the conference emerge as largely illusory. Finally, it is evident that the multiscalar approach advocated by Charles Orser in his opening chapter, combined with attention to interdisciplinary practice, is seen by many as one way forward in developing archaeological narratives that are well grounded in thorough analysis yet contextualised on a broad enough level to ensure that the relevancy of the work is apparent. After all, there is little value in research that does not ultimately contribute to answering the question 'why does it matter'?

NOTES

1. Industrial Archaeology, a 1995 policy statement by English Heritage, 1.
2. Barnwell, Palmer & Airs 2004.
3. e.g. Bowden 2008.
4. Best expressed through the stimulating research of many of those active with CHAT, e.g. Penrose 2007; Schofield & Johnson 2006.
5. Lambrick & Spandl 2000.
6. McErlean, McConkey & Forsythe 2002.
7. See, for example, Lyttleton & O'Sullivan 2007; Breen & O'Sullivan 2007; Horning 2007.
8. Buchanan, 1972, 30.
9. Cossons 2007.
10. See, for example, Little 2002 in contrast with Merriman 2004.

BIBLIOGRAPHY

Barnwell, P.S., Palmer, M. & Airs, M. (eds), 2004, *The Vernacular Workshop, 1400–1900*. York: Council for British Archaeology.

Bowden, C. 2008, *The End of a Revolution: The Last Days of Stationary Steam*. Ashbourne: Landmark Publishing.

Breen, C. & O'Sullivan, A. 2007, *Maritime Ireland – Coastal Archaeology of an Island People*. Stroud: Tempus Publishing

Buchanan, A. 1972, *Industrial Archaeology in Britain*. London: Allen Lane.

Cossons, N. 2007, 'Industrial archaeology; the challenge of the evidence', *Antiquaries Journal* **87**.

Hicks, D. & Beaudry, M.C. (eds) 2006, *Cambridge Companion to Historical Archaeology*. Cambridge: Cambridge University Press.

Horning, A. 2007, 'On the banks of the Bann: the riverine economy of an Ulster Plantation village', *Historical Archaeology* **41**(3): 94–114.

Horning, A., Ó Baoill, R., Donnelly, C. & Logue, P. (eds.) 2007, *The Post-Medieval Archaeology of Ireland*. Bray: Wordwell.

Lambrick, G. & Spandl, K. 2000, *Urban Archaeological Practice in Ireland*. Dublin: The Heritage Council.

Little, B. (ed.) 2002, *Public Benefits of Archaeology*. Tallahassee: University of Florida Press.

Lyttleton, J. & O'Sullivan, A. 2007, 'Post-medieval marshland reclamation in Ireland: a case-study from the Shannon estuary,' in Horning *et al.* (eds), 2007, 221–34.

McErlean, T., McConkey, R. & Forsythe, W. 2002, *Strangford Lough: An Archaeological Survey of the Maritime Cultural Landscape*, Northern Ireland Archaeological Monographs **6**. Belfast: Blackstaff.

Merriman, N. (ed.) 2004, *Public Archaeology*. London: Routledge.

Penrose, S. 2007, *Images of Change: An Archaeology of England's Contemporary Landscape*. Swindon: English Heritage.

Schofield, J. & Johnson, W.G. 2006, 'Archaeology, heritage and the recent and contemporary past', in Hicks & Beaudry (eds), 2006, 104–22.

CONTRIBUTORS

Justine Bayley leads English Heritage's Technology Team, publicising and popularising the benefits of using scientific techniques to aid the understanding and interpretation of archaeological finds, including the preparation and publication of EH Guidelines. Her publications include books as well as many papers in conference proceedings and journals. Her current research focuses on northern European metal- and glass-working of Roman and later date, including research in Ireland on Viking metalworking in Dublin. For ten years she was Secretary to the Association for the History of Glass, and has jointly edited the journal *Historical Metallurgy* since 1990.

Paul Belford has been Head of Archaeology and Monuments for the Ironbridge Gorge Museum Trust since 2000. He graduated in Archaeology from the University of Sheffield, where he also gained a MA in Historical Archaeology as well as working as a Project Officer with ARCUS. In Ironbridge, he has developed the Coalbrookdale Historical Archaeology Research and Training Programme, and since 2004 has run a field school in Bermuda with the Bermuda National Trust. He has published widely in post-medieval archaeology, particularly on the iron and steel industries, and is also the Conservation Officer for the Historical Metallurgy Society. Paul is also a Council Member for the Society for Post-Medieval Archaeology.

Michael Berry is currently a doctoral student at the University of York, working with Steve Roskams. Prior to arriving in York in 2005 he attended Wilfrid Laurier University in Waterloo Canada from 1998 to 2002, completing an Honours BA in Near Eastern Archaeology. From 2002 to 2005 he worked as an associate archaeologist and education officer with a community archaeological foundation. He currently holds a Professional Licence to Conduct Archaeological Fieldwork in the province of Ontario, Canada. Between 2004 and 2005, while continuing to work full time, he completed an MA in Archaeology and Heritage through the University of Leicester's distance learning programme.

Colin Breen is a Senior Lecturer in Archaeology at the University of Ulster, Coleraine. He was previously a Research Fellow at the Institute of Irish Studies, Queen's University Belfast and an archaeologist with the Department of the Environment in the Republic of Ireland. He has published widely in the field of maritime and historical archaeology and is currently working on a number of projects in Britain, Ireland and various parts of Africa.

Alasdair Brooks is a specialist in the analysis of post-1750 material culture. He is currently the Finds and Environmental Officer for CAM ARC, the Cambridgeshire County Council field unit, but spent most of the past six years as a post-doctoral research fellow at La

Trobe University, Melbourne, Australia. He has also worked as a freelance finds specialist in Melbourne, the post-medieval finds supervisor at the University of York's Castell Henllys excavations in Wales, the archaeology lab supervisor at Thomas Jefferson's Poplar Forest in Virginia, USA, and on smaller projects both commercial and academic, from Tasmania to Jamaica. His doctorate and MA are from the University of York, while his BA is from St Mary's College of Maryland in the US. Alasdair is also the Newsletter Editor of the Society for Historical Archaeology, and is actively seeking British, Irish and continental European contributions for the Newsletter.

Eleanor Casella is currently Senior Lecturer in Archaeology at the University of Manchester. She studied Anthropology in UC Berkeley, USA and was awarded her doctorate for a thesis entitled 'Dangerous Girls and Gentle Ladies: Archaeology and Nineteenth Century Australian Female Convicts', a theme she has pursued in her work on the Ross Female factory in Van Diemens Land, Australia. She edited, with James Symonds, *Industrial Archaeology: Future Directions* (Springer, 2005) and also contributed a chapter with him on 'Industrial Archaeology' to Dan Hicks and Mary Beaudry's edited *The Cambridge Companion to Historical Archaeology* in 2007. She is currently publishing her work on the Sandhills Project at Alderley Edge and working with Marilyn Palmer on *The Cambridge Manual of Historical Archaeology*. Eleanor is a Council Member for the Society for Post-Medieval Archaeology.

Craig Cessford has worked in archaeology since 1990, with a particular interest in urban archaeology, and he is currently a Senior Project Officer with the Cambridge Archaeological Unit. His interest in post-medieval and later archaeology came about largely through a series of accidents, which began when he worked on a clay pipe kiln overlying a Roman legionary fortress and seemed to be the only person who really cared about anything after AD 410. He has directed a number of major excavations in Cambridgeshire, including Broad Street, Ely and, most recently, the Grand Arcade site in Cambridge.

Paul Courtney is a freelance archaeologist and historian based in Leicester. After graduating in archaeology at Cardiff, he obtained an MA in Local History at Leicester before researching his doctorate on the medieval and early modern landscape of Gwent (S.E. Wales). He has since published widely on the archaeology and landscape history of Wales and Midland England as well as many synthetic and internationally orientated papers. He has a particular interest in the historiography of historical/post-medieval archaeology in both Europe and the USA, and has authored a paper on theory in European post-medieval archaeology in the forthcoming *International Handbook of Historical Archaeology* (Springer). He has been a regular contributor to SPMA conference monographs and has authored three chapters for the Gwent County History, volumes 2 and 3.

David Cranstone was originally a prehistorian, but his more recent work has centred on the archaeology of the later second millennium, and on industry and technology of any period. His interests also include the archaeologies of identity and religion, the concept of 'historical archaeology' in its broad sense, and the human and natural landscape. He is currently a freelance consultant, based on Tyneside, and a current Council Member and former Secretary of the Society for Post-Medieval Archaeology.

Tony Crosby has worked at the Heritage Lottery Fund (HLF) for over five years in the Policy and Research Department, where his work now includes a lead role on Industrial, Maritime and Transport Heritage (IM&T) – he chairs HLF's IM&T group upon which organisations such as the Association for Industrial Archaeology, English Heritage and Ironbridge Gorge Museum are represented. He has a degree in Industrial Archaeology, undertakes industrial archaeology research projects in Essex and Hertfordshire, the results of many of which he has published. He is currently Chair of the Association for Industrial Archaeology and a member of English Heritage's Industrial Archaeology Panel.

Chris Dalglish is a Lecturer with the Department of Archaeology, University of Glasgow, specialising in historical archaeology and material culture studies. He studied Archaeology at Glasgow, completing his PhD there in 2000, which dealt with post-medieval settlements and landscapes in the southern Scottish Highlands, interpreted in the context of the emergence of capitalist society. From this emerged his book *Rural Society in the Age of Reason: An Archaeology of the Emergence of Modern Life in the Southern Scottish Highlands* (Kluwer/Plenum, 2003). From 2000, Chris worked as a professional archaeologist – initially as a freelance field archaeologist, then in the Ancient Monuments Inspectorate of Historic Scotland (the Scottish Government Heritage Agency) and, from 2002 to 2007, with Glasgow University Archaeological Research Division. He took up his current post in September 2007. Chris is a Council Member for the Society for Post-Medieval Archaeology.

James R. Dixon is currently a PhD student in the UWE Faculty of Creative Arts, with a project looking archaeologically at town planning and public art in post-war Bristol. He is fully funded by a Great Western Research scholarship in Creative Arts. Prior to this, James ran the Historic Buildings and Areas Department of Pre-Construct Archaeology, with major projects in Bristol, Manchester and East London. He received an MA in Historical Archaeology from the University of Bristol in 2004 and is a committee member for Contemporary and Historical Archaeology in Theory (CHAT).

David Dungworth works for English Heritage, as a member of its Technology Team. His PhD (University of Durham, 1995) focused upon research on Iron Age and Roman copper alloy use. He is an archaeological scientist with research interests in the high-temperature industries of the past, and he and his colleagues have recently concentrated on increasing the understanding of post-medieval industries by scientific investigation of process residues. His publications include two EH Guidelines on scientific analysis, and he is a frequent contributor to both archaeological and scientific journals and conference proceedings.

Emma Dwyer is a Senior Archaeologist in the Standing Buildings Department at the Museum of London Archaeology Service, where she has worked since 2006; before that she was part of the team at Ironbridge Archaeology. Emma has led standing building recording projects across the south-east and the Channel Islands, on the site of the 2012 Olympic Games in east London, and, despite initially not knowing much about trains, the East London Line tube extension.

Geoff Egan is the President of the Society for Post-Medieval Archaeology and a specialist in medieval and post-medieval finds for the Museum of London, where he has worked since

1976. He also serves as a consultant to the Jamestown Rediscovery Project. He has written or edited many books on the archaeology of London, including *The Archaeology of Modern London* (Sutton, 2002) and *Material Culture in London in an Age of Transition* (MoLAS 2005). He also co-edited *Old and New Worlds: Papers on Historical and Post-medieval Archaeology from the Thirtieth Anniversary Conferences of the Society for Post Medieval Archaeology and the Society for Historical Archaeology* (1999).

Rupert Featherby is a Senior Archaeologist with the Museum of London Archaeology Service. His research interests include the study of household and material culture through history and archaeology, and although his primary archaeological expertise is with Roman ceramics, questions posed for the material histories for the 18th and 19th centuries can be posed for earlier periods. He is an academic contributor and co-co-ordinator of archaeological work for the Living in Victorian London project.

Shane Gould works in the Policy Department of English Heritage and convenes the English Heritage Industrial Archaeology Strategy Group. Having graduated in Archaeology at York University, he gained a Masters in Social Science in industrial archaeology at Ironbridge and a Masters in Science in historic building conservation at Oxford Brookes. He has extensive knowledge of industrial archaeology and heritage conservation, having worked in private practice and local government, and has recently authored the English Heritage policy statement on the investigation and recording of historic buildings within the English planning framework.

David Gwyn is an independent archaeological consultant with a particular interest in the industrial and modern periods and in landscape issues. A graduate of the University of Cambridge and Trinity College, Dublin, he also lectures in Heritage Management at the University of Bangor and teaches on the long-established industrial archaeology projects held under the auspices of Snowdonia National Park. He has published extensively on industrial and cultural archaeology, including *Gwynedd: Inheriting a Revolution: The Archaeology of Industrialisation in North-West Wales* (Phillimore, 2006), and is editor of *Industrial Archaeology Review*. He is also a director of both the Bala Lake and the Ffestiniog-Welsh Highland Railways, and in his spare time fires steam locomotives between Bala and Llanuwchllyn.

Dan Hicks is University Lecturer and Curator in the Archaeology of the Modern Period, based in the School of Archaeology and the Pitt Rivers Museum in Oxford as well as a Research Fellow in the Department of Archaeology, University of Boston. His work focuses on historical archaeology, the archaeology of European colonialism, the history of archaeology, archaeological approaches to cultural heritage, and theoretical and applied approaches to the study of material things in the social sciences. His publications include *The Cambridge Companion to Historical Archaeology* (Cambridge University Press, 2006), edited with Mary C. Beaudry, *The Garden of the World: An Historical Archaeology of Sugar Landscapes in the Eastern Caribbean* (BAR 2007) and *Envisioning Landscape: Situations and Standpoints in Archaeology and Heritage* (*One World Archaeology* **52**, 2007, edited with Laura McAtackney and Graham Fairclough).

Roger N. Holden is a Chartered Engineer by profession, employed by a major international company, but has had an interested in industrial archaeology for many years. After completing a doctorate in engineering he occupied his spare time by studying for the Certificate in Local History at Manchester University and then an M. Phil in History from the Open University, his thesis on Stott & Sons, the Oldham mill architects, subsequently being published as a book. He continues to be interested in the Lancashire cotton industry and has published papers in *Industrial Archaeology Review, Manchester Region History Review, Textile History* and *Journal of Industrial History*. He is currently completing a study of weaving mills in Lancashire. His interests encompass business and architectural as well as technological history, and beyond the industrial he has an interest in Christian nonconformist chapels and meeting houses.

Audrey Horning is a Senior Lecturer in the School of Archaeology and Ancient History at the University of Leicester. Her research addresses the comparative archaeology of British expansion, with particular attention to Ireland and the Chesapeake in the 16th and 17th centuries. She is a founding member and Newsletter Editor for the Irish Post-Medieval Archaeology Group; Secretary for the Society for Post-Medieval Archaeology; and is an Associate Editor for the journal *Historical Archaeology*. In 2001, she received the John Cotter Award of the Society for Historical Archaeology in recognition of her research contributions. Her books include *In the Shadow of Ragged Mountain: Historical Archaeology of Nicholson, Corbin and Weakley Hollows* (Shenandoah Natural History Association, 2004), and *The Archaeology of Post-Medieval Ireland, 1550–1850*, co-edited with R. ÓBaoill, C.J. Donnelly and Paul Logue (Bray: Wordwell, 2007).

Nigel Jeffries is a medieval and later ceramic specialist for the Museum of London Archaeology Service. His research interests are in historical archaeology, in particular household archaeologies and the associated material culture of 18th- and 19th-century London. He is also interested developing new approaches to studying 'material histories' and narratives of objects. Nigel has supervised work placement and dissertation students for the MA programme of the Institute of Archaeology, University College London (as part of the HEFCE-funded project in Archive Archaeology), and for Bristol University's MA in the Historical Archaeology of the Modern World. He has also acted as a visiting lecturer for the latter course.

Matthew Johnson is currently Professor and Head of Archaeology at Southampton University, and he has also taught at the University of Durham, University of Sheffield and St David's University College, Lampeter. His books include Ideas of Landscape (2006), Behind the Castle Gate (2002) Archaeological Theory: An Introduction (1999), An Archaeology of Capitalism (1996) and Housing Culture: Traditional Architecture in an English Landscape (1993). His research interests broadly centre upon archaeological theory and historical archaeology, with a specific focus on English architecture and landscapes of the period 1200-1900.

Stephen A. Mrozowski is Professor of Anthropology at the University of Massachusetts–Boston and Director of the Center for Cultural and Environmental History and of The

Andrew Fiske Memorial Center for Archaeological Research. His specific research interests include social theory, historical archaeology, environmental and urban archaeology, and the study of complex societies. He has directed field research throughout New England and in Virginia, and conducted fieldwork in Britain and Alaska. He has edited or authored five books, including recently *The Archaeology of Class in Urban America*, Cambridge Studies in Archaeology (2006), and published more than fifty essays dealing with topics ranging from theoretical issues in historical archaeology to the evolution of the urban landscape in New England, Virginia and Britain.

Michael Nevell read Ancient History and Archaeology at the University of Manchester and has both a master's and a doctorate from the same university for work in Roman archaeology. He has spent all his working life with the Greater Manchester and University of Manchester Archaeological Units, and is now Director of the latter. As well as continuing to publish work in Roman archaeology, he was joint editor of eight volumes on the *History and Archaeology of Tameside*, during which he developed with John Walker what is now known as the Manchester Methodology, a way of relating the first appearance of structures in the landscape to the social classes responsible for them. This was further developed in his Rolt Memorial Lecture to the Association of Industrial Archaeology, 'Industrial Archaeology or the Archaeology of the Industrial Period? Models, Methodology and the Future of Industrial Archaeology', which appeared in *Industrial Archaeology Review*, May 2006.

Caron Newman read History and Archaeology at King Alfred's College, Winchester, following by an MSc in Archaeological Computing at the University of Southampton. She has worked with a number of archaeological trusts and currently serves both as a Historic Environment Field Advisor for English Heritage and as a Consultant with Egerton Lea Consultancy. She has undertaken historical assessments of towns in Lancashire for Lancashire County Council's Extensive Urban Survey, the historic landscape characterisation of Cumbria for Cumbria County Council and worked on the industrial archaeology of Carlisle. She co-ordinated and authored the medieval chapter for the Archaeological Research Frameworks for the North-West volumes, and contributed to the Roman, early medieval, post-medieval and industrial chapters.

Richard Newman read Archaeology and History at University College Cardiff in 1979, and remained there to carry out PhD research on the post-medieval landscape of west Gloucestershire. He joined the Glamorgan–Gwent Archaeological Trust in 1983 and directed excavations on a variety of sites in south Wales. In 1991 he became Assistant Director at Wessex Archaeology, and in 1994 Director of the Lancaster University Archaeological Unit. In 2002 he was appointed County Archaeologist for Cumbria and project-managed the North West's regional archaeological research framework. Since 2007 he has been Environmental Planning Manager for Cumbria County Council. He was the principal author of the *Historical Archaeology of Britain c.1540–1900* (Sutton, 2001).

Tadgh O'Keeffe is Professor of Archaeology at University College Dublin. His research interests transgress the disciplinary boundaries between archaeology, urban and cultural geography, and landscape, art and architectural histories, and his recent publications have covered such diverse themes as ideology and historiography, the politics of heritage, landscape and memory, and Gothic parish church architecture, and have featured topics ranging from the built-environment of 13th-century pastoral care to the Carrickmines motorway controversy to Dublin's 19th-century red-light district. Recent publications include *The Gaelic Peoples and their Archaeological Identities AD 1000–1650* (Cambridge University Press, 2004) and *Archaeology and the Pan-European Romanesque* (Duckworth, 2007).

Charles Orser is Curator of Historical Archaeology at the New York State Museum, Distinguished Professor of Anthropology at Illinois State University, and Adjunct Professor of Archaeology at the National University of Ireland, Galway. His many publications include *A Historical Archaeology of the Modern World*, the *Encyclopaedia of Historical Archaeology*, the *Archaeology of Race and Racialization*, and *Unearthing Hidden Ireland*. He is the founding editor of the *International Journal of Historical Archaeology* and the series editor for *Contributions to Global Historical Archaeology* (Springer).

Alastair Owens is a Senior Lecturer in the Department of Geography, Queen Mary, University of London. He is convenor of Queen Mary's MA London Studies programme and review editor for the *London Journal*. Alastair is interested in the historical geographies of wealth, welfare and well-being in 19th- and 20th-century Britain and the material culture of everyday life in 19th-century cities. Alongside 'Living in Victorian London', he is currently working on a major collaborative ESRC-funded research project examining gender and investment practices in Britain between 1870 and 1930. This is part of a wider interest in exploring how individuals make use of markets and institutional structures to provide for themselves and others.

Marilyn Palmer is Emeritus Professor of Industrial Archaeology and was Head of the School of Archaeology and Ancient History in the University of Leicester from 2000 to 2006. She was a Commissioner with the RCHME from 1993 to 1998 and now serves on various committees concerned with archaeology and industrial archaeology for English Heritage and The National Trust. She was President of the Association for Industrial Archaeology from 1986 to 1989 and 2005 to 2008, and is also a Council Member for the Society for Post-Medieval Archaeology. She jointly edited *Industrial Archaeology Review* with the late Peter Neaverson for eighteen years, and they published many books together including *Industrial Archaeology: Principles and Practice* (Routledge, 1998) and *The Textile Industry of South-west England: A Social Archaeology* (Tempus, 2005) as well as numerous articles. She is currently working with Eleanor Casella on *The Cambridge Manual of Historical Archaeology*. She received an Award of Merit from the Society for Historical Archaeology in 2005 for her work in integrating historical and industrial archaeology into mainstream archaeology.

Sarah Paynter works for English Heritage, as a member of its Technology Team. She is an archaeological scientist with research interests in the high-temperature industries of the past. Recently she and her colleagues have focused on increasing the understanding of post-medieval industries by scientific investigation of process residues. Her publications include two EH Guidelines on scientific analysis, and she publishes frequently in both archaeological and scientific journals and conference proceedings.

Colin Rynne was Curator of the Shandon Museum, Cork, and then Director of Irish Heritage Management Studies for University College, Cork, until 2001 when he became a Lecturer in their Department of Archaeology and is now Senior Lecturer. He has written a considerable number of articles on milling in Ireland and is shortly to publish *The Archaeology of Water-power in Early Medieval Ireland, c. AD 600 – AD 1100*. In 2006 he published the comprehensive and lavishly illustrated *Industrial Ireland, 1750–1930: An Archaeology* (Collins Press), which was chosen for the first Peter Neaverson Award for outstanding scholarship in industrial archaeology by the AIA in 2008.

Richard Thomas is Lecturer in Zooarchaeology at the University of Leicester. His teaching and research interests focus on the study of animal bones as a means of understanding past human–animal relationships. He is specifically interested in the integration of zooarchaeological and historical evidence, particularly with respect to the Black Death, the Agricultural Revolution and the relationship between diet and social status. On a methodological level Richard is keen to develop the subject of animal palaeopathology – the diagnosis and interpretation of animal diseases in the past. He has published many articles in archaeological and environmental journals.

Karen Wehner is currently a Post-Doctoral Research Assistant, affiliated with the 'City Centre' in the Department of Geography, Queen Mary, University of London. Karen trained as a North American historical archaeologist, receiving her MA and a PhD in Anthropology from New York University. In addition to her current focus on Victorian London, Karen's other research includes a GIS-based reassessment of archival and material evidence for town-based craft production in 17th-century Jamestown, Virginia; the spatial and material analysis of changing social organisation in ante- and postbellum American plantation households; and archaeological surveys and fieldwork at domestic and workshop sites in Virginia and New York State.